4/1/11

Blessings on your o

Allen + Mary

HISTORICAL DICTIONARIES OF RELIGIONS, PHILOSOPHIES, AND MOVEMENTS

Jon Woronoff, Series Editor

1. *Buddhism,* by Charles S. Prebish, 1993
2. *Mormonism,* by Davis Bitton, 1994. *Out of print. See No. 32.*
3. *Ecumenical Christianity,* by Ans Joachim van der Bent, 1994
4. *Terrorism,* by Sean Anderson and Stephen Sloan, 1995. *Out of print. See No. 41.*
5. *Sikhism,* by W. H. McLeod, 1995. *Out of print. See No. 59.*
6. *Feminism,* by Janet K. Boles and Diane Long Hoeveler, 1995. *Out of print. See No. 52.*
7. *Olympic Movement,* by Ian Buchanan and Bill Mallon, 1995. *Out of print. See No. 61.*
8. *Methodism,* by Charles Yrigoyen Jr. and Susan E. Warrick, 1996. *Out of Print. See No. 57.*
9. *Orthodox Church,* by Michael Prokurat, Alexander Golitzin, and Michael D. Peterson, 1996
10. *Organized Labor,* by James C. Docherty, 1996. *Out of print. See No. 50.*
11. *Civil Rights Movement,* by Ralph E. Luker, 1997
12. *Catholicism,* by William J. Collinge, 1997
13. *Hinduism,* by Bruce M. Sullivan, 1997
14. *North American Environmentalism,* by Edward R. Wells and Alan M. Schwartz, 1997
15. *Welfare State,* by Bent Greve, 1998. *Out of print. See No. 63.*
16. *Socialism,* by James C. Docherty, 1997
17. *Bahá'í Faith,* by Hugh C. Adamson and Philip Hainsworth, 1998
18. *Taoism,* by Julian F. Pas in cooperation with Man Kam Leung, 1998
19. *Judaism,* by Norman Solomon, 1998
20. *Green Movement,* by Elim Papadakis, 1998
21. *Nietzscheanism,* by Carol Diethe, 1999
22. *Gay Liberation Movement,* by Ronald J. Hunt, 1999
23. *Islamic Fundamentalist Movements in the Arab World, Iran, and Turkey,* by Ahmad S. Moussalli, 1999
24. *Reformed Churches,* by Robert Benedetto, Darrell L. Guder, and Donald K. McKim, 1999
25. *Baptists,* by William H. Brackney, 1999
26. *Cooperative Movement,* by Jack Shaffer, 1999
27. *Reformation and Counter-Reformation,* by Hans J. Hillerbrand, 2000
28. *Shakers,* by Holley Gene Duffield, 2000

29. *United States Political Parties,* by Harold F. Bass Jr., 2000
30. *Heidegger's Philosophy,* by Alfred Denker, 2000
31. *Zionism,* by Rafael Medoff and Chaim I. Waxman, 2000
32. *Mormonism,* 2nd ed., by Davis Bitton, 2000
33. *Kierkegaard's Philosophy,* by Julia Watkin, 2001
34. *Hegelian Philosophy,* by John W. Burbidge, 2001
35. *Lutheranism,* by Günther Gassmann in cooperation with Duane H. Larson and Mark W. Oldenburg, 2001
36. *Holiness Movement,* by William Kostlevy, 2001
37. *Islam,* by Ludwig W. Adamec, 2001
38. *Shinto,* by Stuart D. B. Picken, 2002
39. *Olympic Movement,* 2nd ed., by Ian Buchanan and Bill Mallon, 2001. *Out of Print. See No. 61.*
40. *Slavery and Abolition,* by Martin A. Klein, 2002
41. *Terrorism,* 2nd ed., by Sean Anderson and Stephen Sloan, 2002
42. *New Religious Movements,* by George D. Chryssides, 2001
43. *Prophets in Islam and Judaism,* by Scott B. Noegel and Brannon M. Wheeler, 2002
44. *The Friends (Quakers),* by Margery Post Abbott, Mary Ellen Chijioke, Pink Dandelion, and John William Oliver Jr., 2003
45. *Lesbian Liberation Movement: Still the Rage,* JoAnne Myers, 2003
46. *Descartes and Cartesian Philosophy,* by Roger Ariew, Dennis Des Chene, Douglas M. Jesseph, Tad M. Schmaltz, and Theo Verbeek, 2003
47. *Witchcraft,* by Michael D. Bailey, 2003
48. *Unitarian Universalism,* by Mark W. Harris, 2004
49. *New Age Movements,* by Michael York, 2004
50. *Organized Labor,* 2nd ed., by James C. Docherty, 2004
51. *Utopianism,* by James M. Morris and Andrea L. Kross, 2004
52. *Feminism,* 2nd ed., by Janet K. Boles and Diane Long Hoeveler, 2004
53. *Jainism,* by Kristi L. Wiley, 2004
54. *Wittgenstein's Philosophy,* by Duncan Richter, 2004
55. *Schopenhauer's Philosophy,* by David E. Cartwright, 2005
56. *Seventh-day Adventists,* by Gary Land, 2005
57. *Methodism,* 2nd ed., by Charles Yrigoyen Jr. and Susan Warrick, 2005
58. *Sufism,* by John Renard, 2005
59. *Sikhism,* 2nd ed., by W. H. McLeod, 2005
60. *Kant and Kantianism,* by Helmut Holzhey and Vilem Mudroch, 2005
61. *Olympic Movement,* 3rd ed., by Bill Mallon with Ian Buchanan, 2006
62. *Anglicanism,* by Colin Buchanan, 2006
63. *Welfare State,* 2nd ed., by Bent Greve, 2006

Historical Dictionary of Anglicanism

Colin Buchanan

Historical Dictionaries of Religions, Philosophies, and Movements, No. 62

The Scarecrow Press, Inc.
Lanham, Maryland • Toronto • Oxford
2006

SCARECROW PRESS, INC.

Published in the United States of America
by Scarecrow Press, Inc.
A wholly owned subsidiary of
The Rowman & Littlefield Publishing Group, Inc.
4501 Forbes Boulevard, Suite 200, Lanham, Maryland 20706
www.scarecrowpress.com

PO Box 317
Oxford
OX2 9RU, UK

British Library Cataloguing in Publication Information Available

Library of Congress Cataloging-in-Publication Data

Buchanan, Colin Ogilvie.
Historical dictionary of Anglicanism / Colin Buchanan.
p. cm. — (Historical dictionaries of religions, philosophies, and movements ; no. 62)
Includes bibliographical references.
ISBN-13: 978-0-8108-5327-0 (hardcover : alk. paper)
ISBN-10: 0-8108-5327-2 (hardcover : alk. paper)
1. Anglican Communion—Dictionaries. 2. Anglican Communion —History. I. Title. II. Series.

BX5007.B83 2006
283'.09—dc22

2005018798

The paper used in this publication meets the minimum requirements of American National Standard for Information Sciences—Permanence of Paper for Printed Library Materials, ANSI/NISO Z39.48-1992.
Manufactured in the United States of America.

Contents

Editor's Foreword *Jon Woronoff* vii

Preface ix

Acknowledgments xiii

Reader's Note xv

Acronyms and Abbreviations xvii

Chronology xxi

Introduction xxxix

THE DICTIONARY 1

Appendixes

A Bishops and Archbishops of Canterbury 489

B The Thirty-Nine Articles of Religion 493

Bibliography 509

About the Author 551

Editor's Foreword

Perhaps due to its location and strong native traditions, Christianity in England has often moved in somewhat different directions—different from Rome in the early centuries, and then different from the churches arising out of the Reformation. The result was a Church of England that resisted some of the continental Protestantizing tendencies from the 16th century on but also distanced itself from Roman Catholicism or tendencies in that direction. Anglicanism was the compromise, which was doubtlessly easier to understand when the choices were simpler. For this is now only one of the major religions of England and more so the United Kingdom, while itself becoming one of the major religions of numerous African, Asian, and American countries that were once part of the British empire, including the Episcopal Church in the United States. Thus, to understand Anglicanism, it is necessary to shift the emphasis from the clearer and more familiar formative period to the intriguing and less-known developments of the past half-century.

The *Historical Dictionary of Anglicanism* is particularly helpful in this respect. It situates the crucial events in the reigns of Henry VIII and Elizabeth I in their historical context and follows the many high and low church movements over succeeding centuries. But history did not just end some time back, so important figures of the recent past and present are also included, archbishops of Canterbury, bishops, theologians, and others. England, while receiving its due, does not overshadow the broader Anglican Communion and places such as Australia, Kenya, and Papua New Guinea. Further entries deal with the essential beliefs, doctrines, institutions, and other aspects of Anglicanism and the burning issues with which it is still grappling. This dictionary section is flanked by an informative introduction and a helpful chronology. Additional knowledge about the Anglicanism of yesterday, today, and maybe tomorrow can be sought in the many works listed in the bibliography.

It would be hard to find anyone who knows Anglicanism better than the author of this volume, Colin Buchanan. Ordained a deacon in 1961, he has spent various periods in various significant positions and has also ministered in a visiting capacity in many of the provinces of the Communion. His final appointment, until 2004, was as bishop of Woolwich in the diocese of Southwark in South London. For around 40 years, he participated in Anglican and ecumenical commissions and conferences, and from 1990 he was a member of the House of Bishops of the Church of England. Since retirement, he has moved to Leeds, where he continues ministering as an assistant bishop in the Bradford diocese. Within this full career, he himself would give high value to his 21 years as a liturgist on the staff of a major theological college of the Church of England, the last six of them as principal. He has lectured widely and also written or edited a fair number of books, the former on such topics as infant baptism and disestablishment, the latter a series on liturgies. It is thus gratifying that, on top of his numerous duties, he could find the time to write such an insightful and also readable reference work. As series editor, I am pleased about this and I am certain that readers in the general and more specialized public will also appreciate it.

Jon Woronoff
Series Editor

Preface

The Scarecrow Press has a well-proven record of publishing historical dictionaries of worldwide Christian denominations. I therefore counted it as a great privilege when the series editor, Jon Woronoff, approached me about editing—or conceivably writing myself as sole author—the volume that would do historical justice to Anglicanism. It is a tall order, and it might be viewed as overconfidence on my part that led me not only to accept the commission but to prefer the latter option of writing the entire dictionary myself. I was perhaps better placed than many (both in geographical location and in personal experience) to undertake such a task, and I reckoned that time that would have been spent on administration, were I to have been editor, would be better spent enlarging my own knowledge, were I to be author. So, in broad terms, it has proved to be; but I know my own timetable as a working bishop has brought the project some years into arrears, and I can only apologize to a patient press and series editor for that.

Readers will recognize that, even if I were not limited in time, I have nevertheless been limited in space. In a dictionary handling 470 years of church history, with virtually the whole globe coming into its purview, yet of less than 200,000 words in length, there is bound to be a selectivity in the contents. The omissions are legion. And in the selectivity both of the entries themselves and of the scale and presentation of each chosen entry, there lies an inevitable subjectivity. I know myself as a man with a particular—and, I trust, coherent—view of Anglican history. So that view always affects the task. I have made what I think are due allowances (and have sought help) where issues are known to be controversial, but the reader must reckon that, like all historians of a living organic institution, I cannot help but have an angle. In this discipline—as in all other historical disciplines—there is in fact no possibility of a wholly dispassionate history.

Not all the angles that affect me are theological ones. I write in England, and from my own context I emphasize the obvious importance of the Reformation in England not only for the Church of England but also for the formation of worldwide Anglicanism; it may also well be that the English, who are deeply bred in Anglocentricity, take for granted an obvious centrality of the see of Canterbury for the structure of the resultant worldwide Communion, although elsewhere that may well be questionable. Equally, I suspect that I cannot help but be more enthusiastic about some historical movements in Anglicanism than about others, and I certainly cannot help but know some parts of the Communion better than others. Furthermore I cannot be fully informed about what I do not know (vast though it may be), and my only excuse is that I am to some extent aware of these limitations and have tried to compensate for them. I have much experience of various sorts of Anglicans being convinced that they are the only (or at least the standard) exemplars of the genus *Anglican*, only to be astonished when they meet others of a totally different set of practices and understandings who have the same beliefs about *their* position. There is always more to discover.

One relevant illustration of the problem of possible subjectivity of treatment concerns the issue of how far the Communion should be viewed as "confessional." There is a part of Anglicanism that points to the Thirty-Nine Articles of Religion of 1571 and insists that, though the Articles are less comprehensive than, say, the decrees of the Council of Trent, yet they provide a doctrinal confession that is definitive of Anglicanism. There is alongside this an alternative Anglicanism which believes not only that the ethos of the Elizabethan Settlement was intended to be broad and comprehensive but also that the continuing character of worldwide Anglicanism owes more to organic relationships and corporate development in the faith than to a dated and limited set of Articles from 16th-century England. I cannot necessarily claim to have picked my way aright through this minefield, but I am well aware of it and have endeavored to be clear-eyed in finding the way. I cite this instance of disagreement simply as an illustration, in order that readers may be warned of the likelihood of multifaceted interpretation across all the historical phenomena of Anglicanism. But I would add that one of the advantages of engaging in single authorship (as opposed to a vast farming out of the entries to a multiplicity of contributors) is that, at least in theory, there should be a much greater consistency of presentation throughout the entries than a multiplicity would afford.

The disadvantages of a one-man dictionary cannot be denied, even though I have done my utmost to limit them. One drawback that would have been difficult to foresee at the outset is the sheer length of time the task has taken—virtually the whole of my seven and a half years as bishop of Woolwich and some months into my retirement. Entries have been written in spare moments over this time, checks with libraries and individuals have often been done after great intervals of time from the original drafting, and new entries have presented themselves as necessary to the integrity of the project, even when they were inconvenient to the desired timetable for it. Meanwhile, the Anglican Communion itself has not stood still. I accepted the task well before the 1998 Lambeth Conference, and I am finishing it when the 2008 Conference is coming into view and a new archbishop of Canterbury is at the helm. During the last 18 months, prior to this preface taking its final form, the Communion has been riven over the consecration as a bishop in America of a practicing homosexual; irrespective of the outcome of that rift, it has been hard to keep the entries, many of them first drafted some years ago, up to date and consistent with each other during such fast changes in the Communion. The goal of consistency I have sought in the latter stages is that information should be accurate up to 31 December 2004, although some entries are necessarily updated into 2005.

Acknowledgments

While I have done all the drafting of this dictionary, I have not done so without advice. I have, of course, been dependent upon the series editor, Jon Woronoff, who has been both patient and encouraging. I have also been regularly in touch with the Anglican Communion Office in London, where I have been not only supported but also trusted in the task by the Rev. Canon John Peterson, the secretary-general of the Communion until the end of 2004; by Canon James Rosenthal, the press officer; by the Rev. Canon Gregory Cameron, who was appointed as ecumenical officer in 2003 and became deputy secretary-general in late 2004; and by the Rev. Terrie Robinson. Scores of other people have answered particular queries as I have approached them (and a few have not). One area where I have known myself to be not only ignorant (which is curable) but also incompetent (which is less so) is that of music, and I acknowledge with gratitude the help I have received in the relevant entries from Mrs. Anne Harrison of Durham, who has gone nearer to holding my hand as I drafted the relevant entries than has anyone else. With those acknowledgments, and subject to the limitations, which are inevitable, I take sole responsibility for the whole dictionary and every word in it. I should be glad to receive corrections. Most of the photos are copyright Canon James Rosenthal of the Anglican Communion Office and are reprinted by his kind permission. A few are my own.

Reader's Note

In preparing this dictionary, it was necessary to adopt a few conventions, which the reader should bear in mind. First, all dating here, as far as it can be traced, follows the Gregorian calendar, which was not adopted in England until 1752. The previous (Julian) calendar began the New Year on 25 March, so that today's dating of an event as being in, say, February 1645 (by Gregorian dating) will have appeared in documents of the time as being in February 1644.

Second, in most cases Tudor and Stuart spelling has been updated from original documents. The occasional exceptions—retained for effect—are obvious at sight.

Third, virtually all translations from Latin and Greek (including the Septuagint and the New Testament) are my own and not necessarily traceable to copyright or other historic texts, even if they broadly coincide with them through relative faithfulness in translation.

Fourth, Roman numerals have been used solely for the enumeration of the Forty-Two Articles of Religion of 1553 and the Thirty-Nine Articles of Religion of 1571. The numbers of other subdivided documents (such as the canons of 1604 or decrees of the Council of Trent) are rendered in Arabic numerals, whatever variant uses may have been employed at different points in history.

Finally, with reference to Church of England Prayer Books, the text consistently uses the form "1549 Book of Common Prayer"—or the equivalent with the further Books of Common Prayer of 1552, 1559, 1604, 1637 [the Scottish Book], and 1662—at its first occurrence in any entry. Thereafter in that entry it may appear as simply "1549."

Acronyms and Abbreviations

AAALC	All-Africa Anglican–Lutheran Commission
AABC	African Anglican Bishops Conference
ABIC	Anglican-Baptist International Conversations
ABM	Australian Board of Missions
ACC	Anglican Consultative Council
ACK	Anglican Church of Kenya
ACNS	Anglican Communion News Service
ACO	Anglican Communion Office
ALIC	Anglican–Lutheran International Commission
ALIWG	Anglican–Lutheran International Working Party
AMIC	Anglican–Methodist International Commission
ANITEPAM	African Network of Institutions of Theological Education Preparing Anglicans for Ministry
APCK	Association for Promoting Christian Knowledge
ARCIC	Anglican–Roman Catholic International Commission
BCMS	Bible Churchmen's Missionary Society
BCP	Book of Common Prayer
BFBS	British and Foreign Bible Society
CAPA	Council of Anglican Provinces of Africa
CESA	Church of England in South Africa
CIBC	Church of India, Burma, and Ceylon
CIPBC	Church of India, Pakistan, Burma, and Ceylon
CLAD	Canadian Lutheran–Anglican Dialogue
CMJ	Church Mission to Jews
CMS	Church Mission Society (until 1994 Church Missionary Society)
CNI	Church of North India
CPK	Church of the Province of Kenya

CPSA	Church of the Province of Southern (formerly South) Africa
CR	Community of the Resurrection
CSI	Church of South India
ECUSA	Episcopal Church (United States of America)
EFAC	Evangelical Fellowship of the Anglican Communion
EKD	Evangelische Kirche in Deutschland
ELLC	English Language Liturgical Consultation
FCE	Free Church of England
FD	*Fidei Defensor*
GROW	Group for Renewal of Worship
IAFN	International Anglican Family Consultation
IALC	International Anglican Liturgical Consultation
IARCA	Iglesia Anglicana de la Region Central de America
IARCCUM	International Anglican–Roman Catholic Commission for Unity and Mission
IASCER	International Anglican Standing Commission on Ecumenical Relations
IASCOME	International Anglican Standing Commission on Mission and Evangelism
IATDC	International Anglican Theological and Doctrinal Commission
ICAOTD	International Commission of the Anglican–Orthodox Theological Dialogue
ICEL	International Committee on English in the Liturgy
ICET	International Consultation on English Texts
ICS	Intercontinental Church Society
IMC	International Missionary Conference
ISPCK	Indian Society for Promoting Christian Knowledge
KJV	King James Version
LMS	London Missionary Society (Congregationalist)
MISAG	Mission Issues Strategy Advisory Group
MRI	Mutual Responsibility and Interdependence
MU	Mothers' Union
NIV	New International Version
NRSV	New Revised Standard Version
PECUSA	Protestant Episcopal Church in the United States of America

PEV	Provincial Episcopal Visitor
PiM	Partners in Mission
RC	Roman Catholic
RCE	Reformed Church of England
RCIA	Rite for the Christian Initiation of Adults
RCL	Revised Common Lectionary
REC	Reformed Episcopal Church
RSCM	Royal School of Church Music
SACC	South African Council of Churches
SAMS	South American Missionary Society
SCM	Student Christian Movement
SEC	Scottish Episcopal Church
SOMA	Sharing of Ministries Abroad
SPCK	Society for Promoting Christian Knowledge
SPG	Society for the Propagation of the Gospel
SSF	Society of Saint Francis
SSJE	Society of Saint John the Evangelist
SSM	Society of the Sacred Mission
TEAC	Theological Education in the Anglican Communion
UMCA	Universities Mission to Central Africa
URC	United Reformed Church
USPG	United Society for the Propagation of the Gospel
WCC	World Council of Churches
WMC	World Methodist Council
YMCA	Young Men's Christian Association

Chronology

Note: New dioceses of the Anglican Communion are noted only until 1850, and not all dioceses, for example, in the United States, are listed at inauguration prior to that.

A.D. 30 Probable year of the crucifixion and resurrection of Christ.

43 Emperor Claudius invades Britain.

3rd Century Martyrdom of St. Alban.

313 Decree of Constantine.

314 Council of Arles, with three British bishops present.

410 Sack of Rome and the end of the Roman empire in Britain.

444 Foundation of Armagh, claimed as the oldest see in the Anglican Communion today.

447 Foundation of the see of Man (or Sodor and Man), claimed as the oldest see in the Church of England today.

563 Columba lands from Ireland at Iona.

597 Augustine lands in Kent and founds the see of Canterbury. Columba dies.

627 Paulinus, coming from Rochester, baptizes in York and founds the see of York.

635 Aidan, coming from Iona, establishes the see of Lindisfarne on Holy Island, beginning Celtic Christianity in northern England.

664 Council of Whitby, with Hilda facilitating, agrees to follow Roman uses throughout England.

687 Death of Cuthbert on Farne Islands.

735 Death of Bede, the first historian of the English Church.

995 Final interment of Cuthbert's body in Durham Cathedral.

1012 Martyrdom of Alphege, archbishop of Canterbury, by the Danes at Greenwich.

1054 "Great Schism" separates the Eastern and Western churches.

1066 Battle of Hastings leads to the Norman Conquest of England.

1109 Death of Anselm, theologian and archbishop of Canterbury.

1170 Martyrdom of Thomas à Becket, archbishop of Canterbury.

1215 Fourth Lateran Council defines transubstantiation, leading to withdrawal of the cup from the laity.

1384 Death of John Wycliff, translator of the Bible into English.

1401 Law *De Haeretico Comburendo* passed by Parliament.

1415 John Hus, Bohemian reformer, is burned at the Council of Florence.

1477 Caxton sets up the first printing press in England.

1485 Henry Tudor wins the battle of Bosworth, becoming King Henry VII.

1487 Birth of Prince Arthur.

1491 Birth of Prince Henry, later King Henry VIII.

1502 Death of Prince Arthur, leaving as his widow Catherine of Aragon.

1509 King Henry VIII inherits the throne of England and marries Catherine.

1516 Birth of Princess Mary, later Queen Mary I, the only child of Catherine to survive infancy. Erasmus publishes his edition of the Greek New Testament.

1517 Martin Luther nails his 95 theses to the castle church door in Wittenberg.

1521 Henry VIII publishes *Assertio de Septem Sacramentis* against Luther; in response, Pope Leo X confers title *Fidei Defensor* upon Henry VIII.

1526 First printed copies of Tyndale's New Testament in English arrive.

1527 Henry VIII begins his quest for a judgment of nullity on his marriage.

1530 Thomas Cranmer undertakes the quest regarding nullity around European universities and marries Osiander's niece.

1532 Death of William Warham, archbishop of Canterbury since 1503. Submission of the clergy.

1533 Nomination of Cranmer as archbishop of Canterbury; the pope approves and sends his pallium. Restraint of Appeals Act. Henry VIII's marriage to Catherine of Aragon is declared null and his marriage to Anne Boleyn is publicized. Coronation of Anne Boleyn as queen. Birth of Princess Elizabeth, later Queen Elizabeth I.

1534 Acts of Forbidding Papal Dispensations, of Supremacy, and of Ecclesiastical Appointments complete the severance from Rome.

1536 Execution of Anne Boleyn. Henry VIII marries Jane Seymour. Ten Articles of Religion are promulgated by the Convocation. William Tyndale is burned in the Low Countries. Beginning of the dissolution of the monasteries.

1537 Birth of Prince Edward, later King Edward VI. Death of Jane Seymour. *Institute of a Christian Man* is published.

1538 Royal injunctions require an English Bible to be set up in every church.

1539 Six Articles Act. Completion of the dissolution of the monasteries. Publication of the Great English Bible.

1543 *The King's Book* is published.

1544 Publication of the first English litany.

1547 Death of Henry VIII, succeeded by nine-year-old King Edward VI. Monarchical powers are assumed and exercised by a council with a

Protestant weighting, chaired by Edward Seymour, Duke of Somerset and the king's uncle, during the king's minority. Mary, the king's half-sister, is next in line to the throne, but retains her allegiance to Roman Catholicism. Royal *Injunctions* order the reading of biblical passages in English at the mass, along with the destruction of images and the provision of a "poor men's box" for alms. Publication of the First Book of Homilies. Parliament passes an Act against the abuse of sacrament and for receiving Communion in both kinds.

1548 *The Order of the Communion* is published. Compilation of the First Prayer Book at Chertsey. Act of Uniformity debated in the House of Lords.

1549 Act of Uniformity enacted. Book of Common Prayer is published and enforced from Whitsunday. Fall of Somerset, who is succeeded by the Duke of Northumberland. Nicholas Ridley is appointed bishop of London.

1550 Ridley's action in London leads to an order-in-council for the destruction of images and the replacement of stone altars with wooden tables. Publication by royal warrant of ordination services in English. Bucer is appointed Regius Professor at Oxford.

1551 Publication of Cranmer's *Defence of Answer*. Nomination of John Hooper as bishop of Gloucester. Peter Martyr is appointed professor of theology at Cambridge.

1552 Second Act of Uniformity is enacted. Revised Book of Common Prayer is published and enforced from All Saints' Day. John Knox preaches before the king, objecting to the requirement of kneeling for Communion.

1553 Publication of the Forty-Two Articles of Religion. Death of King Edward VI. Cranmer is involved in the unsuccessful plot to make Lady Jane Grey monarch. Mary rides triumphantly into London, succeeds as queen, and drops title of "Supreme Head of the Church of England." Parliament repeals church legislation of Edward VI's reign, including the Acts of Uniformity.

1554 Cranmer, Latimer, and Ridley are charged with heresy and treason. Mary marries Philip of Spain. Parliament repeals all church legislation of Henry VIII's reign passed since 1528 (save the dissolution of the monasteries). Cardinal Reginald Pole, the pope's legate, reconciles the monarch, Parliament, and nation to the Roman Catholic Church.

1555 Hooper and Ferrar are burned in their own sees. Latimer and Ridley are burned at Oxford.

1556 Cranmer is burned at Oxford after first recanting and then disavowing his recantation. Pole is appointed archbishop of Canterbury. Philip of Spain leaves England for Spain and does not return.

1558 Mary dies in November; Elizabeth I succeeds. Cardinal Pole dies in same night as Mary, leaving the archbishopric of Canterbury vacant.

1559 New Act of Uniformity. The 1552 Prayer Book is reimposed with small variants. Elizabeth issues her *Injunctions*, covering, among other things, clergy vesture. Matthew Parker is nominated and consecrated as archbishop of Canterbury.

1560 Ireland and Scotland accept the Reformation.

1566 Archbishop Parker's "Advertisements" are published. Mary, Queen of Scots, gives birth to son James.

1567 Mary, Queen of Scots, resigns throne in favor of her son (James VI), seeks refuge in England, and is imprisoned.

1570 Pope excommunicates Elizabeth.

1571 Thirty-Nine Articles are confirmed and authorized. New proposed canons are not authorized.

1575 Archbishop Parker dies. Grindal becomes archbishop of Canterbury.

1576 Grindal is sidelined by the queen.

1579 First Prayer Book celebration of Communion in America.

1583 Grindal dies. Whitgift becomes archbishop of Canterbury.

1587 Judicial death sentence is executed on Mary, Queen of Scots.

1588 Spanish Armada is defeated.

1595 Lambeth Articles.

1603 Elizabeth dies and is succeeded by James VI of Scotland, son of Mary, Queen of Scots, as James I of England. Coming south from Scotland, James is met by the Millenary Petition and promises to convene a conference.

1604 Hampton Court Conference. New code of canons is adopted. Slightly revised Prayer Book is issued by royal warrant. Archbishop Whitgift dies and is succeeded by Richard Bancroft.

1605 Gunpowder Plot fails.

1610 Bishops are consecrated for Scotland.

1611 King James Bible (the "authorized version") is published. Bancroft dies, and George Abbott becomes archbishop of Canterbury.

1615 Irish Articles are adopted by the Irish Convocations.

1621 Archbishop Abbott accidentally shoots his gamekeeper and is sidelined by the king.

1625 Death of James I. His son, Charles I, inherits.

1629 Charles dissolves Parliament.

1633 Archbishop Abbott dies; William Laud becomes archbishop of Canterbury. *Book of Sports* is reissued. Privy Council charters the bishops of London to exercise jurisdiction over British subjects overseas.

1637 Publication by royal warrant of the 1637 Scottish Book of Common Prayer. Rioting greets its introduction into worship at St. Giles, Edinburgh.

1640 Parliament is convened after a break of 11 years. Convocation continues to sit after the dissolution of Parliament and passes canons that are later agreed to have no standing.

1642 Civil war breaks out.

1643 Parliament summons the Westminster Assembly.

1645 Westminster Assembly produces the Westminster Confession of Faith and *A Directory for the Public Worship of God in the Three Kingdoms.* Parliament prohibits use of Book of Common Prayer. Laud is executed.

1646 Final defeat of King Charles I and victory of Parliament.

1649 Execution of King Charles I. Beginning of Commonwealth, led by Oliver Cromwell the Protector.

1658 Cromwell dies.

1660 Declaration of Breda. Restoration of King Charles II. Worcester House Declaration. William Juxon becomes archbishop of Canterbury.

1661 Savoy Conference. Reimposition of the episcopacy in Scotland. Revision of the Prayer Book in Convocation.

1662 **24 August:** Act of Uniformity imposes the 1662 Prayer Book. More than 1,000 ministers leave the Church of England rather than conform.

1663 Juxon dies, and Gilbert Sheldon, bishop of London, succeeds as archbishop of Canterbury.

1665 Plague strikes England.

1666 The Fire of London destroys much of the city, including Old St. Paul's Cathedral.

1670 James, Duke of York and heir presumptive to the throne, becomes a Roman Catholic.

1678 Archbishop Sheldon dies. William Sancroft becomes archbishop of Canterbury.

1685 Charles II dies and his Roman Catholic brother succeeds as James II. Revocation of the Edict of Nantes brings French Huguenots to England in flight from persecution by the Roman Catholic hierarchy.

1688 James II issues the Declaration of Indulgence. Seven bishops, including Archbishop Sancroft, refuse to read or require it and are put on trial for treason, but are found not guilty. An infant son and heir is born to James II. William, the Protestant prince of Orange and the son-in-law of James, responds to invitations and lands in the West Country. James flees.

1689 Parliament, after negotiation with William, declares the throne vacant and invites William and Mary to occupy it jointly. New oaths of allegiance are required, thus driving some, who in conscience do not believe the throne to be vacant, to decline the oath and become "nonjurors." All Scottish bishops and nine English ones, including the archbishop of Canterbury, William Sancroft, become nonjurors. Bill of Rights brings toleration for nonconformists.

1690 Bishops who declined the oath are deprived of their sees. Battle of the Boyne finally secures the reign of William and Mary in Ireland.

1694 Queen Mary II dies. William III continues to rule as sole sovereign. Consecration of George Hickes by nonjuring bishops begins the continuation of nonjuring succession.

1698 Foundation of the Society for the Propagation of the Gospel.

1700 Act of Settlement.

1701 Foundation of the Society for Promoting Christian Knowledge.

1702 King William III dies; Queen Anne inherits.

1703 Birth of John Wesley.

1707 Act of Union unites England and Wales with Scotland under one Parliament—though with two differing church establishments.

1710 Will of General Codrington provides for founding of Codrington College in Barbados.

1714 Death of Queen Anne and succession of George I, beginning the Hanoverian dynasty.

1715 Jacobite rising in Scotland in support of the Old Pretender.

1717 Suspension of the Convocation.

1738 Conversion (or heart-warming) experience of Charles and John Wesley.

1745 Bonnie Prince Charlie leads a Jacobite rising in Scotland in support of the Old Pretender. He defeats the English at Prestonpans, near Edinburgh, and marches south to Derby, but goes back in December.

1746 Defeat of the Jacobite army at Culloden Moor, near Inverness. Reinforcement of penal laws and subjugation of the Scottish Highlands.

1764 Last recension of the Scottish (Episcopal) Communion rite becomes the definitive one.

1776 American Declaration of Independence.

1783 Election of Seabury as bishop of Connecticut. He departs to England for consecration, but the archbishop of Canterbury is unable to perform the ceremony.

1784 Seabury is finally consecrated by Scottish bishops in Aberdeen.

1785 The Protestant Episcopal Church in the United States of America (PECUSA) holds its first General Convention, in Philadelphia, without Seabury's participation.

1787 Consecration of White and Provoost for PECUSA in London. Consecration of Charles Inglis for Nova Scotia in London.

1788 Bonnie Prince Charlie dies without an heir (save his Roman Catholic cardinal brother, who lived until 1807), ending Jacobite hopes.

1789 Second General Convention of PECUSA is held in Philadelphia, with participation of all three bishops, and adopts the PECUSA Book of Common Prayer.

1791 Death of John Wesley.

1792 Lifting of penal laws against Jacobites in Scotland.

1799 Foundation of Church Missionary Society (CMS).

1800 Act of Union unites the Dublin Parliament with Westminster from 1 January 1801, thus creating the United Church of England and Ireland.

1801 Birth of John Henry Newman.

1807 Abolition of the slave trade in the British Empire.

1811 First Synod of the Episcopal Church of Scotland.

1814 First bishop of Calcutta is consecrated.

1815 Battle of Waterloo.

1824 First bishops of Jamaica and Barbados are consecrated.

1832 Election of the Reform Parliament.

1833 John Keble's Assize Sermon inaugurates the Oxford Movement, which begins its *Tracts for the Times*. Abolition of slavery throughout the British Empire.

1836 Foundation of the diocese of Australia. Creation of the diocese of Ripon, the first new diocese of the Church of England since the Reformation.

1841 Foundation of the dioceses of New Zealand and Jerusalem. Tract 90 is published.

1842 Foundation of the dioceses of Antigua, Gibraltar, Guiana, and Tasmania.

1844 Foundation of the diocese of Shanghai.

1845 Foundation of the diocese of Colombo. John Henry Newman becomes a Roman Catholic.

1847 Foundation of the dioceses of Cape Town, Newcastle (New South Wales), Melbourne, and Adelaide.

1848 Creation of the diocese of Manchester, England. Archbishop Howley dies, succeeded by John Bird Sumner.

1849 Foundation of the diocese of Victoria (Hong Kong).

1850 Judicial Committee of the Privy Council renders the Gorham Judgment.

1851 Religious census in Great Britain. Allen Gardiner, seeking to establish a South American mission, dies of hunger on Tierra del Fuego.

1852 Restoration of the Convocation in Canterbury Province.

1854 Pope Pius IX defines and imposes the doctrine of the Immaculate Conception of the Blessed Virgin Mary.

1857 Inauguration of the province of New Zealand.

1860 Publication of *Essays and Reviews*.

1861 Charles MacKenzie is consecrated in Cape Town to be bishop on the Zambezi. John Coleridge Patteson is consecrated in Auckland to be bishop in Melanesia. Inauguration of the province of Canada. Civil War begins in the United States.

1862 MacKenzie dies of fever. Death of Archbishop Sumner; Charles Thomas Longley succeeds him.

1863 Robert Gray, archbishop of Cape Town, deposes William Colenso, bishop of Natal, on grounds of heresy. Colenso appeals to the Judicial Committee of the Privy Council.

1864 Samuel Crowther is consecrated as bishop on the Niger—the first African to become an Anglican bishop.

1865 American Civil War ends. Colenso is upheld in his bishopric by the Judicial Committee of the Privy Council in London. Canadians ask Archbishop Longley to convene a worldwide conference to address the issue.

1867 First Lambeth Conference is held, led by Charles Longley as archbishop of Canterbury.

1868 Death of Archbishop Longley. Archibald Campbell Tait succeeds.

1869 Vatican I convenes in Rome.

1870 Vatican I promulgates a decree on papal infallibility and ends prematurely. Archbishop Gray of Cape Town summons a provincial synod and separates legally from the Church of England to found a province of South Africa.

1871 Church of Ireland is disestablished and forms a General Synod. Martyrdom of Bishop Patteson.

1873 Cumminsite Schism begins in the United States.

1874 Public Worship Regulation Act is enacted by the Westminster Parliament.

1878 Second Lambeth Conference, led by Archibald Campbell Tait as archbishop of Canterbury. Church of Ireland Book of Common Prayer authorized.

1882 Death of Archbishop Tait.

1883 Edward White Benson becomes archbishop of Canterbury. Inauguration of the province of the West Indies.

1884 James Hannington is consecrated as bishop of Eastern Equatorial Africa.

1885 Bishop Hannington is killed at eastern frontier of Uganda.

1886 Page boys are burned to death by King Mwanga and become known as the Martyrs of Uganda.

1887 Inauguration of the province of Japan (Nippon Sei Ko Kai).

1888 Third Lambeth Conference, led by Edward White Benson as archbishop of Canterbury.

1890 Bishop of Lincoln is tried before the archbishop's court for ceremonial irregularities; The "Lincoln Judgment" goes largely in his favor. Cardinal Newman dies.

1892 Revision of PECUSA Book of Common Prayer.

1896 Leo XIII issues encyclical, *Apostolicae Curae*, condemning Anglican ordinations. Archbishop Benson dies, succeeded by Frederick Temple. Bernard Mizeki, a lay evangelist, is martyred in Mashonaland, Central Africa.

1897 Archbishops of Canterbury and York issue a reply to papal encyclical, entitled *Saepius Officio*. Fourth Lambeth Conference, led by Frederick Temple as archbishop of Canterbury.

1901 Queen Victoria dies.

1903 Archbishop Temple dies. Randall Davidson succeeds as archbishop of Canterbury.

1904 Royal Commission on Ecclesiastical Discipline is established in England.

1906 Royal Commission on Ecclesiastical Discipline reports.

1908 First pan-Anglican Congress. Fifth Lambeth Conference, led by Randall Davidson as archbishop of Canterbury. Frank Weston is consecrated as bishop of Zanzibar.

1910 Edinburgh Missionary Conference. King Edward VII dies.

1912 Episcopal Church of Scotland authorizes its own Book of Common Prayer.

1913 Kikuyu missionary conference in Kenya leads to accusations of heresy by Bishop Frank Weston.

1914 Beginning of World War I.

1917 Overthrow of Czarist rule in Russia. William Temple's Life and Liberty Movement grows in England.

1918 End of World War I.

1919 Enabling Act in England confers powers on the Church Assembly. First conference in South India to seek union of the main denominations.

1920 Sixth Lambeth Conference—famous for its "Appeal to All Christian People"—is held, led by Randall Davidson as archbishop of Canterbury. Church in Wales separates from the Church of England and is disestablished. Church Assembly meets with powers to create legislation and addresses Prayer Book revision.

1921 Beginning of the Malines Conversations.

1922 Ireland is partitioned.

1926 End of the Malines Conversations.

1927 First defeat of the new Church of England Prayer Book in the House of Commons.

1928 Second defeat of the new Church of England Prayer Book in the House of Commons. Davidson resigns as archbishop of Canterbury; Cosmo Gordon Lang succeeds him. New Prayer Book is authorized by the General Convention of PECUSA.

1929 New Prayer Book is authorized by the Episcopal Church of Scotland.

1930 Seventh Lambeth Conference, led by Cosmo Gordon Lang as archbishop of Canterbury. Constitution for Church of India, Burma, and Ceylon comes into force. Provincial status of the Holy Catholic Church in China is recognized.

1931 Bonn Agreement with Old Catholic Churches.

1933 Adolf Hitler comes to power in Germany.

1936 King George V dies. Edward VIII succeeds him, but soon abdicates. George VI becomes king. Spanish Civil War begins.

1937 Life and Work Conference at Oxford. Faith and Order Conference in Edinburgh.

1938 Conference at Utrecht initiates moves toward a World Council of Churches and appoints a provisional committee.

1939 Spanish Civil War ends with Franco's victory. World War II begins.

1941 Pearl Harbor leads to the United States joining Britain and to Japan joining Germany in World War II.

1942 Lang resigns as archbishop of Canterbury. William Temple succeeds him.

1944 Archbishop Temple dies in office; George Bell is passed over to succeed him. Bishop R. O. Hall of Hong Kong and Macao ordains Florence Li Tim Oi as a presbyter during the Japanese occupation.

1945 Geoffrey Fisher becomes archbishop of Canterbury. Germany surrenders in the European war. Atomic bombs end the Pacific War.

1947 Indian independence is achieved with division of the country; the Anglican Church becomes the Church of India, Pakistan, Burma, and Ceylon (CIPBC). (United) Church of South India is inaugurated, leaving CIPBC.

1948 Eighth Lambeth Conference, led by Geoffrey Fisher as archbishop of Canterbury. World Council of Churches is formed in Amsterdam.

1949 Communist state is proclaimed in China; exodus of expatriates begins.

1950 Pope Pius XII defines and imposes on Roman Catholics a doctrine of the Bodily Assumption of the Blessed Virgin Mary into heaven. Church of South India liturgy is authorized by its General Synod.

1951 Inauguration of the province of West Africa.

1952 King George VI dies. Queen Elizabeth II succeeds him.

1954 Anglican Congress is held in Minneapolis.

1955 Inauguration of the province of Central Africa.

1957 Jerusalem archbishopric is inaugurated.

1958 Ninth Lambeth Conference, led by Geoffrey Fisher as archbishop of Canterbury. Pope Pius XII dies; Pope John XXIII succeeds at 77 years of age.

1959 Pope John announces the convening of a General Council.

1960 Inauguration of the province of East Africa.

1961 Archbishop Fisher retires; Michael Ramsey succeeds as archbishop of Canterbury. Inauguration of the province of Uganda, Rwanda, and Burundi.

1962 Formation of the General Synod and constitution of the Church of England in Australia (retitled the Anglican Church in Australia in 1971). First session of Vatican II.

1963 Anglican Congress is held in Toronto. Pope John XXIII dies and is succeeded by Pope Paul VI. Second session of Vatican II promulges Constitution on Sacred Liturgy.

1964 Third session of Vatican II.

1965 Fourth session of Vatican II. Inauguration of the province of Brazil.

1966 Archbishop Ramsey visits Rome and agrees with the pope on a procedure for joint Anglican–Roman Catholic theological consultation. Beginning of period of liturgical experiment in the Church of England.

1968 Tenth Lambeth Conference, led by Michael Ramsey as archbishop of Canterbury.

1969 Appointment of the first Anglican–Roman Catholic International Commission (ARCIC-1).

1970 Provinces of Tanzania and Kenya are formed from the province of East Africa. United churches, including Anglicans, are inaugurated in Pakistan and in North India. Inauguration of the province of Myanmar (Burma). Beginning of General Synod in the Church of England.

1971 Gen. Idi Amin stages a coup in Uganda and seizes power. United Church of Bangladesh is formed in the wake of political conflict. First meeting of Anglican Consultative Council (ACC-1) at Limuru votes narrowly in favor of a request from Hong Kong for goodwill regarding the ordination of women as presbyters. First women (apart from Florence Li Tim Oi) are ordained as presbyters in Hong Kong. ARCIC-1's agreed statement on the eucharist is published.

1972 Final defeat of Anglican-Methodist Scheme in England.

1973 ACC-2 meets in Dublin. Inauguration of the province of the Indian Ocean. ARCIC-1's agreed statement on ministry and ordination is published.

1974 Archbishop Ramsey retires. Donald Coggan succeeds as archbishop of Canterbury.

1975 Inauguration of the province of Melanesia.

1976 ACC-3 meets in Trinidad, West Indies. Jerusalem archbishopric, formed in 1957, is discontinued as the new province of Jerusalem and the Middle East is inaugurated. Inauguration of the province of Sudan. ARCIC-1's first statement on authority is published. Canada ordains its first women as presbyters.

1977 Women are ordained as presbyters in the United States and New Zealand. Inauguration of the province of Papua New Guinea. Janani Luwum, archbishop of Uganda, is martyred by Amin.

1978 Eleventh Lambeth Conference, led by Donald Coggan as archbishop of Canterbury. Year of the three popes; John Paul II begins his papacy.

1979 ACC-4 meets in London, Ontario, Canada. Province of Nigeria is inaugurated by separation from the province of West Africa.

1980 Archbishop Coggan retires; Robert Runcie succeeds him. Formation of the diocese of Gibraltar in Europe. Spanish Reformed Episcopal Church and the Lusitanian Church of Portugal affiliate with the Anglican Communion.

1981 ACC-5 meets in Newcastle upon Tyne, England.

1982 ARCIC-1 publishes its second Statement on Authority and brings all its work together in *The Final Report* before disbanding. Publication of the "Lima document," *Baptism, Eucharist and Ministry*.

1983 Appointment of ARCIC-2. Inauguration of the province of the Southern Cone of South America.

1984 ACC-6 meets in Lagos, Nigeria.

1987 ACC-7 meets in Singapore.

1988 Twelfth Lambeth Conference, led by Robert Runcie as archbishop of Canterbury. Launch of the Decade of Evangelism.

1989 Consecration of the first woman bishop, Barbara Harris, coadjutor bishop of Massachusetts.

1990 ACC-8 meets in Wales. Consecration of first woman diocesan bishop, Penelope Jamieson Bishop of Dunedin, in the province of New Zealand. Inauguration of the province of the Episcopal Church in the Philippines.

1991 Archbishop Runcie retires. George Carey succeeds as archbishop of Canterbury.

1992 Inauguration of the provinces of Korea, Burundi, Rwanda, and Zaire (name changed to Congo in 1997). New Zealand's province retitles itself "Aotearoa, New Zealand, and Polynesia," reflecting a constitution incorporating three ethnic and cultural *tikanga*. Church of England General Synod approves ordination of women as presbyters.

1993 ACC-9 is held jointly with the Primates Meeting in Cape Town, South Africa.

1994 Inauguration of the province of Mexico.

1995 Inauguration of the province of Southeast Asia.

1996 Porvoo Declaration agreed. ACC-10 meets in Panama City.

1998 Thirteenth Lambeth Conference, led by George Carey as archbishop of Canterbury. Inauguration of the provinces of the Central Region of America and of Hong Kong and Macao.

1999 ARCIC-2 publishes the agreed statement *The Gift of Authority*. ACC-11 meets in Dundee, Scotland.

2000 Primates Meeting is held in Porto, Portugal.

2002 ACC-12 meets in Hong Kong. Archbishop Carey retires; Rowan Williams succeeds as archbishop of Canterbury.

2003 Primates Meeting is held in South Brazil. Consecration of Gene Robinson as bishop of New Hampshire. Emergency meeting of primates at Lambeth and establishment of the Lambeth Commission.

2004 Lambeth Commission publishes the Windsor Report.

2005 Primates Meeting in Belfast, Northern Ireland, calls on ECUSA and the Anglican Church in Canada to withdraw from the ACC. ARCIC-2 publishes its agreed statement *Mary: Grace and Hope in Christ*. ACC-13 meets in Nottingham.

Introduction

HOW IT STARTED

There are arguably three views of how Anglicanism as seen today in the third millennium got its start. The first view is that Christianity in what is now England began in Roman times (A.D. 43–410)—probably through the witness of Roman soldiers posted to Britain from other parts of the empire—and, though the continuity of that witness is hard to trace, lies behind later English Christianity in a way that is not separable from it. There is considerable archaeological evidence of Roman Christianity. The first British martyr is usually reckoned to be St. Alban, who may well have lived and died in the early third century, and three British bishops are listed at the Council of Arles in 314. Furthermore, even if the faith was nearly extinguished in the parts of Britain where—in the wake of the Roman departure around 410—the Angles formed England, yet St. Patrick preached and founded churches in Ireland in the first half of the fifth century, and the Isle of Man runs Ireland close for the earliest foundation of a see. In Wales, there is evidence of named sees of British Christianity from the sixth century (with the probability that Christian discipleship there was longstanding from rather earlier times, in addition to the Christian refugees from the invasions of the pagan Angles and Saxons in eastern regions of Britain in the fifth and sixth centuries). One does not have to believe that Joseph of Arimathea planted his staff in Glastonbury in the first century A.D. to believe that English Christianity with a visible historical line down to the present day took its roots in the Roman occupation, possibly as early as the first century.

The second view takes the relative obliteration of the faith by the Angles and Saxons seriously. It traces the origins of today's English Christianity instead to the new evangelization of the land that began in Iona in the Western Isles of Scotland. There, Columba, coming from Ireland, established a monastery in 563 and in due course sent missionaries to southern Scotland and Northumbria. Aidan is generally reckoned to have been the first bishop of Lindisfarne in 635, and Celtic Christianity then took root in the northeast. However, the more widely acclaimed refounder of Christianity in England is Augustine, who landed in Kent from Rome in 597 and became the first bishop of Canterbury later that same year—from which point an unbroken continuity of the Christian church to the present day can be traced. At the Council of Whitby in 664 the Roman ways of the area of Canterbury's influence gained the ascendancy over the Celtic ways of the northeast, and Canterbury itself has a historic centrality in all developments since. Wonderfully, the parish church of St. Martin's stands there as it did in the late sixth century when Augustine first preached in the city (and possibly even baptized converts in St. Martin's). The majestic Canterbury Cathedral of the 12th–14th centuries flourishes in all its grandeur still today, and the 104th archbishop of Canterbury, Rowan Douglas Williams, resides in the Old Palace at Canterbury as well as the medieval Lambeth Palace in London. If the Anglican Communion is to be defined as provinces of the universal church in Communion with the see of Canterbury, then this second view of the origins of Anglicanism has a strong claim to credibility in the very story and continuity of Canterbury itself.

THE 16TH CENTURY

The third account of the origins of Anglicanism looks to the 16th-century Protestant Reformation as the key formative factor in the distinctive culture, ethos, doctrine, and organization of the Anglican Communion we know today. This approach, which provides the basic rationale for Anglicanism in this dictionary, begins with King Henry VIII of England. His severance of the church in England from all relationship to the bishop of Rome set the Church of England on a path of independent development.

Admittedly, the immediate visible effect was small. To almost all outward appearance, the Church of England was the same church after 1534 that it had been before 1532. Yet, within that external continuity, it had undergone a profound internal change. If all the power and authority over the church were now to spring solely from the whims and directives of its visible head on Earth—that is, the monarch of England, and not the pope—then in fact it was in position to change very thoroughly. And when Henry VIII died, the change of monarch did indeed lead to enormous changes in the church, simply because the powers were now located with the Crown. King Edward VI, the sole surviving son of Henry VIII, inherited at the age of nine and died before reaching 16. During the whole of his reign (1547–1553), the powers that belonged to the monarch were in fact exercised by a Council Regent. Here the dominant voices sought a doctrinal reformation and a practical reformation, and Thomas Cranmer, archbishop of Canterbury, was the penman who gave vent to their desires.

The reform was put through by a fast-moving program, at the core of which was a series of enforced liturgical changes. Liturgy was in fact integral to many of the primary concerns of the reformers, whether it was the restoration of the cup to the laity, the use of the vernacular in worship, the excision of the intercession of the saints, or the positive assertion of biblical truths. Therefore, to carry the country with them, the liturgy had to express and teach the biblical principles they were identifying, inculcating them deep into people's devotions. At the same time, they determined to make the changes in a staged way and at a controlled speed, though it is reasonable to conclude that Cranmer knew from the start the point he wished to reach.

The stages of the reform can be set out on a year-by-year basis:

1547 King Edward VI inherits on 29 January. Royal *Injunctions* in July provide for the Epistle and Gospel to be read in English and forbid a large measure of the ceremonial previously used at the mass. In August, the First Book of Homilies is published, furthering reformed principles. An Act of Parliament in November orders the provision of Communion with both bread and wine; it urges, and attempts to facilitate, more frequent lay Communion.

1548 In March, *The Order of the Communion* is published to implement the Act of Parliament. This is a short liturgical insert in English to be added to the Latin mass to give a devotional approach to Communion and to provide for the distribution of both bread and wine. In September, a conference at Chertsey prepares a complete new Prayer Book, which is taken to Parliament soon after. In December, there is the great debate in the House of Lords in relation to the projected Act of Uniformity to implement this complete English-language Book of Common Prayer. In this debate, Cranmer declares himself for the first time to be on the reformed side of the fence with regard to eucharistic presence.

1549 In January, the Act of Uniformity is approved in both the Lords and the Commons; it requires the use of the new Book exclusively from Pentecost (9 June). In May and June, copies of the Book are printed and made available, ready for the inaugurating date. In September, there is a revolt against the new Book of Common Prayer in Devon and Cornwall.

1550 In January, an Act of Parliament empowers the monarch to appoint a small group to provide ordination services. In March, the new rites are published and ordered by royal command. In November, an order-in-council requires the breaking down of stone altars and their replacement with movable wooden tables.

1552 In April, the new Act of Uniformity is passed in Parliament, imposing the second Book of Common Prayer from All Saints' Day (1 November). In September, while the Books are being printed, John Knox preaches before the king, inveighing against the requirement to kneel at Communion—and the Council slips the "Black Rubric" into the closing rubrics of the Communion service.

1553 In May, the Forty-Two Articles of Religion are published. In July, the king dies.

Queen Mary I succeeded to the throne and, as the daughter of Catherine of Aragon, returned the country to Roman Catholicism, restoring the mass, submitting to the pope, burning reforming bishops (including Cranmer) at the stake, and marrying Philip of Spain. When she died childless in November 1558, however, and her archbishop of Canterbury, Cardinal Reginald Pole, died in the same night, the new queen, Elizabeth I, found the country ready to return to a Protestant form of religion. The 1552 Book of Common Prayer was restored by a 1559 Act of Uniformity, a Protestant archbishop of Canterbury, Matthew Parker, was very correctly consecrated by four Edwardine bishops, and in due course the Forty-Two Articles of religion were retouched to become Thirty-Nine. When the pope excommunicated Elizabeth in 1570 and encouraged his followers to kill her, these Articles were imposed as the test of belief from 1571.

Elizabeth, childless, was concerned lest the throne revert to a Roman Catholic, as her cousin—Mary, Queen of Scots, a Roman Catholic—would inherit on her death. So Elizabeth first imprisoned her cousin and ultimately signed her death warrant, ensuring that Mary's Protestant son, King James VI of Scotland, would become heir to the throne of England. Another threat from Spanish Catholicism was posed by the Armada in 1588, but it was defeated.

THE RISE OF PURITANISM

Elizabeth was typical of all the Tudor monarchs in allowing no dissent. "Uniformity" meant what it said. However, the Puritan movement viewed the Reformers as having been checked midcourse, and leading Puritans not only pressed for further reforming moves but also showed themselves ready to act unilaterally, for example, dispensing with the surplice, which had been retained as mandatory clerical vesture for officiating in liturgy. The Puritans' fundamental principle was that the church could order no practice as mandatory unless it could be shown to be required by scripture.

The tensions became ever sharper in the period from the beginning of Elizabeth's reign right through to the outbreak of the Civil War in 1642; they were attributable in part to the intransigence of the Puritans, but the division was made deeper and wider by provocations from the churchmen. These included a rising emphasis upon the absolute necessity of bishops in the economy of God and insistence upon the wearing of the surplice and the other "excepted ceremonies."

One key stage in this process came in 1603, when King James VI of Scotland inherited Elizabeth's throne as King James I of England. On coming south, he was met by the Puritans and their Millenary Petition, and he agreed to convene the Hampton Court Conference (1604) to hear the complaints. When he chaired the conference, though, he allowed only the tiniest trimming of changes in the liturgy and mocked the Puritans from the chair. Nevertheless, his name passed into history by his accession to their request for a new translation of the Bible to replace the Great English Bible and the Geneva Bible, the main existing texts. This led to the King James Version (as it is now known)—the Authorized Version, as it has been traditionally dubbed.

Both kings James I (1603–1625) and Charles I (1625–1649) proved totally insensitive to Puritan *desiderata*. Under Charles I, William Laud, archbishop of Canterbury (1633–1645), required Communion tables be placed altar-wise against the east wall of chancels (in defiance of the rubric in the Prayer Book Communion service). At the same time, the provisions of the *Book of Sports* (reissued in 1633) ordered that part of Sundays be given to archery practice (in defiance of the sabbatarianism of the 17th-century Puritans). The Civil War came in 1642, and Parliament completed victory over the Royalist armies by 1645 and attempted to coerce the captured monarch into agreeing to the abolition of episcopacy and a kind of submission to their sovereignty. But Charles I steadfastly refused all such negotiations, and so he was finally put on trial for high treason and, though he rejected any validity in the process, he was found guilty and was executed in Whitehall on 30 January 1649.

Parliament had meanwhile taken action with respect to the Church of England and, with the participation of the Scottish Parliament, had summoned in 1643 an "Assembly of Divines" in Westminster. The Puritans were themselves divided into two groups—the Presbyterians, who would accept the principle of a set liturgy, and the Independents (or Congregationalists), who would not. For a minister to retain his position, he had to subscribe to the Solemn League and Covenant. The upshot of the Westminster Assembly was therefore in 1645 a compromise worship book, *The Directory for the Public Worship of God in the Three Kingdoms* (popularly known as the "Westminster Directory"), which provided guidelines for those officiating in worship, but virtually no *verbatim* liturgical text. The assembly also produced the Westminster *Confession of Faith*, a strongly Calvinist document that became a point of reference for Presbyterians for centuries thereafter, though it was without long-term influence on Anglicans.

The first half of the 17th century also saw certain developments of longer-term significance for Anglicanism worldwide. The union of the crowns in the Stuart kings in 1603 brought the Church of Scotland to march more closely in line with the Church of England. Although it was bracketed on equal terms with the Churches of England and Ireland in the 1604 canons, when it was still Presbyterian in its polity, it became Episcopal in 1610. Thereafter steps were taken to make it also liturgical, culminating in the ill-fated 1637 Scottish Book of Common Prayer, imposed (as the 1604 Book had been in England) solely by royal authority. The rejection of the Book was in Scotland a precipitating cause of the Civil War.

In North America, meanwhile, settlements with Anglican chaplains had started to appear with the foundation of Jamestown in 1607 onward. The first missionary to the indigenous people of the land was John Eliot, who began his labors in 1646. For reasons more to do with the continent of Europe than with North America, by order-in-council in 1633 the bishop of London was entrusted with jurisdiction over all chaplains of overseas clergy serving Anglican congregations. Anglicanism was ceasing to be coterminous with the lands of England and Ireland.

THE RESTORATION AND GLORIOUS REVOLUTION

When Oliver Cromwell died in 1658, the Commonwealth Parliament soon ran out of self-confidence, and by early 1660 it was negotiating with Charles I's older son, Charles, who was living in exile in Holland, about his possible restoration to the throne. This came to pass in May of that year, and King Charles II returned to England, having first promised liberty of conscience in religion. The new king followed this up in October with the Worcester House Declaration, in which he undertook to convene a conference to address the revision of the Book of Common Prayer.

As promised, the king summoned delegates to the Savoy Conference, held from April to July 1661. The two sides were represented by 12 bishops and 12 Puritans. These latter were usually called Presbyterians as, by definition, the Independents could not, on their own principles, participate in the revision of liturgy; however, the actual men participating (including one, Edward Reynolds, who was already a bishop) described themselves as moderate Episcopalians. The conference proved to be a disappointment to the Presbyterians, and in 1662 the Book of Common Prayer, only marginally retouched, was imposed by a new Act of Uniformity. In response, more than 1,000 clergy, led by Richard Baxter, refused to conform and went into secession.

In the lax style of the Restoration modes of behavior, standards of holiness and discipleship fell in the Church of England. The situation was not helped when Charles's brother James, the Duke of York and—as Charles lacked legitimate offspring—heir to the throne, became a Roman Catholic in 1670 and ultimately inherited the throne in 1685. King James II was suspected of promoting Roman Catholics to positions of influence and undermining the Church of England by these transparently clumsy moves. In 1688, the king ordered the bishops to have his "Declaration of Indulgence" read from all the pulpits in their dioceses. When they declined, on the grounds that he was claiming a dispensing power that circumvented the role of Parliament, the seven London-based bishops who had delivered their refusals personally to the king were charged with seditious libel and were confined to the Tower of London. However, when their case came to trial, a jury found them not guilty—an act of such defiance, and yet such a cause of celebration in the capital, that the king got the message that he had lost the people's loyalty.

Thus when Prince William of Orange (who was married to Princess Mary, King James's Protestant daughter) was invited over from the Netherlands and landed in the West Country in November 1688, James II fled to the Continent. After much negotiation, the throne was declared vacant by Parliament, and the crown was offered to William and Mary jointly. This "Glorious Revolution" was accomplished without bloodshed, but was nevertheless a true revolution, as the declaration that the throne was vacant and that Parliament had the power to invite a new monarch to occupy it was strictly unprecedented, an act of constitutional violence. In fact, it was seen as illegal by many citizens, not least by some 400 clergymen, led by the archbishop of Canterbury, who, however unwelcome they had found King James II to be, also believed their oaths of loyalty to him to be sacred as long as he lived and therefore would not swear allegiance to King William III and Queen Mary II. They thus became "nonjurors" (or nonswearers). This was the position of the whole Scottish episcopate as well. When the original nonjuring bishops later consecrated further bishops, they prolonged their schism. Meanwhile the Bill of Rights (1689) and the Act of Settlement (1700) ensured that no Roman Catholic could thereafter succeed to the throne.

A seminal move for the future of what became the Anglican Communion, perhaps somewhat countercultural for the times, was the formation of two missionary societies: the Society for Promoting Christian Knowledge (SPCK) in 1698, and the Society for the Propagation of the Gospel (SPG) in 1701.

THE 18TH CENTURY

The Church of England entered upon the 18th century (and soon after, the Hanoverian era) in a condition of declining fervor and a low state of religious devotion. Zeal was to be found initially among the nonjurors, who kept their separate Jacobite line going as long as a credible Stuart claimant to the throne was alive on the Continent. But they were a tiny number, losing hope steadily as the century went on, and they finally lost all credibility on the death of Bonnie Prince Charlie in 1788. The established church meanwhile benefited from the Evangelical Revival, traceable back to the conversion or "heart-warming" of John and Charles Wesley in 1738. From their preaching and that of George Whitefield arose not only the Methodist Connection but also new life in many Church of England parishes. In the second generation, the Clapham Sect, the ministry of Charles Simeon in Cambridge, and a great spread of Evangelical clergy across the land led to a new spiritual thrust, an evangelistic concern, and worldwide horizons for mission. A further set of voluntary missionary societies was established, including the Church Missionary Society (CMS) in 1799, the British and Foreign Bible Society in 1804, and the Church Mission to Jews in 1808. Evangelicals founded orphanages and schools and, led by William Wilberforce, fought a 50-year-long battle for the abolition of slavery that was successful in 1833.

Anglicanism spread well beyond England in the 18th century. Chaplains in the American colonies, Canada, the West Indies, India, and (from 1788) even Australia were technically under the oversight of the bishop of London, though they were in fact virtually independent. In Scotland, tiny numbers belonged to the Episcopal Church of Scotland, a church greatly harassed by the government and whose bishops at one point abandoned any diocesan jurisdiction and simply became a college. This small church did its own liturgical revision, independently of any influences from England, and with a keen eye to primitive Eastern sources. It also provided a formative moment in history when, in November 1784, three Scottish bishops consecrated the first Anglican bishop for a diocese outside the British Isles. Following the American Declaration of Independence in 1776, the clergy ministering in the United States had to renounce their allegiance to the Crown. In 1783 the clergy of Connecticut elected Samuel Seabury as their bishop and sent him to England to seek consecration. However, the archbishop of Canterbury was legally barred from consecrating him without a royal mandate and an oath of allegiance to the monarch, so Seabury went to Scotland and received Episcopal ordination there.

In the United States, a new province of the Communion was coming to birth. Representatives of the Episcopal Church from various states (though not from Connecticut) met at a General Convention in 1785. The name "Protestant Episcopal Church in the United States of America" (PECUSA) was adopted. By the time the next two American bishops had been elected, the law in England had been changed so that the archbishop of Canterbury was able to consecrate them in London. The next General Convention of PECUSA in 1789 was correspondingly more representative, and it authorized its own Book of Common Prayer, in which the eucharist drew heavily upon the Scottish model.

An Anglican church still loyal to the English monarchy was also developing in Canada, and its first bishop was consecrated in London in 1787. Elsewhere the SPCK and SPG were employing Lutheran pastors in an Anglican role in India, and in the last years of the century the overtures that led to the formation of the CMS gave strong further hints of great developments to come.

THE 19TH CENTURY

The Church of England in the 19th century was the fountainhead of a worldwide mission, largely conducted through the missionary societies existing at the turn of the century but also seeing new ones formed as opportunities and incentives arose. However, the story did not run on a straight path from the Evangelical Revival, enormous though its influence was. The picture was complicated by the rise in England itself of the Anglo-Catholic movement, the beginnings of which are usually traced to 1833. This not only changed the face of the Church of England, not least by the foundation of theological colleges, but also led to the inauguration of religious communities that worked in many countries and to the formation of the Universities Mission to Central Africa (UMCA) and a number of smaller societies.

A significant modest step in giving shape to the Anglican Communion came in 1814, when the first bishop of Calcutta was appointed—the first Anglican bishop for Asia, with a remit that included not only India but, in a more shadowy way, Africa and Australasia also. Barbados and Jamaica received bishops in 1824, and the first bishop for Australia was appointed to Sydney in 1836. Thereafter sees were divided and new ones created at an ever-increasing rate, milestones being reached with the first bishop in New Zealand in 1841, the first in Africa (Cape Town) in 1847, the first in eastern Asia (Shanghai) in 1849, the first actual African (Samuel Crowther, bishop of the Niger) in 1864, and the first in East Africa in 1884. Independent provinces slowly took shape as further dioceses were created in each region.

A major force in international Anglicanism, the Lambeth Conferences, took shape almost by accident in the 19th century. In 1863, Robert Gray, the archbishop of Cape Town, accused one of his comprovincial bishops, William Colenso of Natal, of heresy. He tried him in a provincial court, found him guilty (Colenso was, by today's standards, merely somewhat liberal), and deposed him. Colenso then appealed to the Judicial Committee of the Privy Council in London, and in 1865 the sentence was quashed on the grounds that Gray's court had no such legal jurisdiction. The bishops of the province of Canada (which covered only part of the present nation of Canada) then appealed to the archbishop of Canterbury to summons a meeting of Anglican bishops from around the world to take counsel together to solve what was viewed as a crisis in Natal. Archbishop Charles Longley agreed to invite the bishops, but made it clear that it would only be a conference, not an authoritative council, and that Natal must not be on the agenda. Seventy-six bishops attended that first 1867 Lambeth Conference, and despite Longley's preconditions, they did manage to get Natal onto the table and they encouraged the archbishop of Cape Town to provide a new bishop for the diocese. However, the first of Longley's conditions—that the gathering should be a conference, not a council—has governed the convening of further Lambeth Conferences, usually at 10-year intervals, since then. The bishops come simply by invitation of the archbishop of Canterbury to a consultative gathering that has power neither to determine its own membership nor to act in any way that has binding authority.

During the 19th century, independent provinces were formed not only in South Africa but also through a negotiated process in Australia and Canada (in each of which there would in time be several provinces forming a nationwide church), in New Zealand, in the West Indies, and in Japan. Four dioceses have usually been requisite as a minimum number for forming a province. In other parts of the world, single dioceses, still under the care of the archbishop of Canterbury, were the usual form of Anglican presence. However, missionary districts of PECUSA that became dioceses in, for example, Shanghai, Liberia, and Haiti were incorporated into the framework of PECUSA and took part in its General Conventions.

Although the term "Anglican Communion" was coming into currency during the 19th century, it was not until the Westminster Parliament passed the Colonial Clergy Act 1874 that clergy ordained by overseas bishops could minister in the Church of England. To that extent, the inter-Communion of the Communion was strictly limited. A notable step in both giving unity to the Communion and in setting out terms for reunion with others came in the "Chicago-Lambeth Quadrilateral." The four sides of the quadrilateral were the scriptures as the final authority for faith, the Apostles' and Nicene Creeds as accurate summaries of the faith, the holding to the two "sacraments of the gospel" (i.e., baptism and the eucharist), and the retention of the "historic episcopate." This quadrilateral was adopted at the 1888 Lambeth Conference and was then reiterated regularly during the 20th century.

THE 20TH CENTURY

The 20th century saw a great burgeoning of the Communion from its 18th and 19th century origins. Lambeth Conferences were held every decade (though hindered by two world wars), and some reinforcing of relationships within the Communion was assisted by Anglican (or Pan-Anglican) Congresses (in 1908, 1954, and 1963), by the appointment of an executive officer in 1959, and by the formation of the Anglican Consultative Council (ACC) in 1971. New provinces were formed, though slowly at first—only Wales (1920), China (1930), and India, Burma, and Ceylon (1930) before World War II. After the war, the Church of South India (CSI) came into being in 1947, through four dioceses leaving the Anglican province to become an ecumenical church. Then the process quickened, with independent provinces being formed, then subdividing, until by 2000 there were 12 African provinces (including the Indian Ocean), seven in the Americas, one in the Middle East, and 10 in eastern Asia and the Pacific. There were also four in Britain and Ireland by the turn of the 21st century, and by then the united churches of South India, North India, Pakistan, and Bangladesh had also rejoined the Communion. A few single dioceses continued under the metropolitical care of the archbishop of Canterbury, and their number was increased by the accession of the Lusitanian Church of Portugal and Reformed Episcopal Church of Spain in 1980. Around 750 bishops attended the 1998 Lambeth Conference.

The Communion has not been without its internal tensions, arising not only from historic theological differences but also from new questions, such as to imperil its unity. Some of these related to ecumenical relationships—where the 1920 Lambeth Conference made brave noises in its "Appeal to All Christian People." There were various conversations with other Churches following this appeal, but the most promising negotiations were those which, by the early 1930s, clarified terms upon which Anglicans, Methodists, and an existing union of Presbyterians and Congregationalists were ready to unite with each other as the Church of South India. This finally came to pass on 27 September 1947, a month after Indian independence, but the 1948 and 1958 Lambeth Conferences were hostile to the actual terms on which the churches in southern India had united to form CSI. By contrast, the united churches in Pakistan (1970), North India (1970), and Bangladesh (1971) got a warmer welcome because they had had an (ambiguous) Episcopal laying on of hands upon every presbyter at the point of union. A different, but highly significant, change on the ecumenical front came to pass through the Roman Catholic Council known as Vatican II (1962–1965). Following this assembly, serious theological questions were tackled beginning in 1969 by a joint commission (the Anglican–Roman Catholic International Commission), and agreed statements were published starting in 1971.

Soon afterward, the issue of the ordination of women arose—with little problem about having female deacons, but vast polarization over their ordination as presbyters. By 1980 the diocese of Hong Kong, the Anglican Church in Canada, the Episcopal Church (United States of America)

(ECUSA), and the province of New Zealand had ordained women as presbyters, and, as other provinces would not necessarily recognize them as presbyters, there had been a resultant loss of full Communion among provinces. By the time of the 1988 Lambeth Conference, it was clear that very soon there would even be women bishops—in ECUSA and elsewhere—and that the Communion had to take steps to evaluate this process and, if possible, to regulate its consequences. The first woman bishop was consecrated in ECUSA in early 1989. At the 1998 Lambeth Conference, there were 11 women bishops—from the United States, New Zealand, and Canada—and there were signs of division within provinces as well as between provinces over this extension of the historic threefold order.

At the 1998 Lambeth Conference a different issue, which had been in the background at the 1988 Conference, came to the fore. Although previous conferences had wrestled with issues of polygamy, divorce and remarriage, and birth control, there had never been an approving voice for homosexual relationships. But 1988 had given warning, and the 1998 Conference was dominated by the defensive deployment of bishops from all around the world to reassert "traditional" sexual morality. The famous resolution I.10, passed by 526 votes to 70, resulted from this. However, because Lambeth Conference resolutions have no legislative force, this resolution has been studiously ignored in parts of the world that have chosen to do so.

Archbishops of Canterbury have not only continued to have the sole responsibility of inviting bishops to Lambeth Conferences but have also become *ex officio* presidents of the Anglican Consultative Council and conveners of annual meetings of primates of the Communion. When Archbishop George Carey retired in October 2002, he was succeeded by Archbishop Rowan Williams, who was already primate in Wales. Within weeks of his coming into office, issues of homosexual relationships rent not simply the Church of England but (through events in Canada and the United States) the whole Anglican Communion. Through his appointing of the Lambeth Commission in November 2003, and through its unanimous "Windsor Report" in October 2004, there has been a realistic grappling with the problems of holding the Communion together. Nevertheless, in 2005 both official meetings (such as those of the primates in February and of the ACC in June) and unofficial groupings around the

Communion revealed strongly polarizing tendencies also, and the unity of the Communion remained at risk.

Any point at which a dictionary of this sort is to be published may well justify a caution attached—that the Anglican Communion, with a great and fascinating history, is also very clearly engaged in unfinished business.

The Dictionary

– A –

ABBEY. The term "abbey" originates from the French *abbaye* and was used in the Middle Ages as a name for the whole **monastic** community over which an abbot presided. The title was also used for the main chapel or church building that served the community, and it thus survived as the title of those buildings when they remained in use after the time of the dissolution of the monasteries—hence, "Westminster Abbey." With the revival of monastic life within Anglicanism in the 19th century, the title of "abbey" has come back into use to identify a **religious community**; and in such cases the church building of the community is often called the "abbey church."

ABSOLUTION. The Latin *absolvere* means "to set free" and corresponds fairly closely to the Greek *luo* (cf. Rev. 1.5) and *aphiemi* (John 20.23). Like *luo* (from which it itself derives), it has a person rather than a sin as the normal object of the verb. In the Middle Ages, absolution was given by the **priest** in the context of the "**sacrament** of **penance**," and the conveying of the **authority** to give absolution was articulated in the **ordination rites** by means of a secondary laying on of hands upon the candidates after **Communion**, in which the text of our Lord's commissioning of his first disciples from John 20.23 was used.

The Reformers eliminated penance from the list of sacraments (*see* appendix B, Article XXV), although a residual place remained for the text of an "indicative" absolution ("by his authority committed to me I absolve thee from all thy sins") provided in the Visitation of the Sick for use with those in danger of **death**. In the 1549 **Book of Common Prayer**, this was accompanied by the instruction, "The same form of absolution shall be used in all private confessions"—a provision that related to the retention in 1549 of the (voluntary) "auricular and secret confession to the Priest" (1549, "Warning Exhortation to the receiving of communion"). In 1552 the **rubric** in the Visitation of the Sick was removed (leaving the form of absolution as related solely to the dying), and the warning exhortation in the Communion rite was changed so that the would-be communicant with an uneasy conscience was now to resort "to me, or to some other learned minister of God's word, and open his grief . . . that by the ministry of God's word he may receive comfort and the benefit of absolution"—a form of words that implies not a sacramental formula but the particular and targeted application of "God's word," which was to bring absolution.

The provision for those in danger of death remained in 1662, though now the form was only to be used "if he humbly and heartily desire it." The indicative absolution was entirely omitted from the Prayer Books of the **Protestant Episcopal Church in the United States of America** of 1789, 1892, and 1928, though interestingly the first two of those Books had a separate provision for visits to prisoners and a rubric urging, when they were under sentence of death, their special confession and the use of the absolution from the Communion service. In 1928, in the Visitation of the Sick, there was no absolution but only the requirement that the **minister** was to "assure him of God's mercy and forgiveness." This would appear to be in conformity with **Thomas Cranmer**'s 1552 provision in **Morning and Evening Prayer** that the minister was to "declare and pronounce . . . the absolution and remission of sins," as well as the **collect** of the 24th Sunday after **Trinity Sunday**, which began ". . . absolve thy people from their offences."

From 1833 on, the sacramental revival of the **Oxford Movement** led quickly to the restoration of auricular confession, in which the indicative form of absolution was regularly used. In **England** an attempt in modern **liturgical** revision to give this a wider official currency came in a text entitled "The Reconciliation of a Penitent," which was defeated in **General Synod** in 1983. Then in 1986, the House of Bishops "commended," in the context of **Lenten** services, a text that read, "I declare that you are absolved from your sins"—and by its "commendation" gave weight to the idea that private **ministry** does not need to rely solely upon official texts that have to be authorized as part of public worship. The provisions in relation to **Common Worship** (the liturgical texts that were authorized or commended in the Church of England to be used beginning in 2000) include a range of absolutions in the form of a prayer, and one in the "Ministry at the Time of Death" section in the imperative: "By the ministry of reconciliation . . . receive his pardon and peace."

Modern ordination rites have generally removed the John 20.23 reference, which Cranmer had made part of the main text at the laying on of hands, but make reference to the ministry of absolution within the exhortations or prayers. The use of the precatory form of absolution ("May God forgive you") in the **eucharistic** and other rites is commonly thought to be confined to **bishops** and **presbyters**, whereas others, such as **readers**, regularly say "forgive *us*"; in fact, the **canons** of some **provinces** require such a substitution. But it is impossible to say what difference this makes as to how and upon what conditions God actually forgives, and (in parallel with **Roman Catholic** uses) in many places bishops and presbyters say "us" rather than "you" in liturgical absolutions in any case.

ACTS OF UNIFORMITY. The **Books of Common Prayer** of 1549, 1552, 1559, and 1662 were enforced as the sole (and therefore "**uniform**") texts for use in public worship in the Church of **England** by parliamentary Acts of Uniformity. In each case except 1559, the Book concerned was annexed to the relevant Act; in 1559, the Act revived the 1552 Book with certain stated changes (and a complexity in relation to the "**ornaments** of the **ministers**"). Each Act named a date from which the use of the Book was enforced and prescribed penalties for noncompliance. The 1604 Book and the 1637 **Scottish** Book were ordered by royal proclamation or warrant without the respective Parliament or an Act of Parliament being involved.

The 1559 Act was printed as the first of the contents of the Book enforced under the 1662 Act and ought still to be present in lawful printings of that Book. In 1661–1662, the major work of revision of the Book was undertaken in **Convocation**, though Parliament retained the right to amend the text (but did not exercise that right). In this case also, in the wake of the **Commonwealth** period and the **Restoration** of the monarchy, the provisions of the Act went beyond the text of the Prayer Book and included the requirement on ministers to renounce the Solemn League and Covenant and to obtain Episcopal **ordination** by the prescribed date—24 August 1662.

While the 1662 Act of Uniformity was enforceable only in England and **Wales**, the 1662 Book of Common Prayer went around the world in Anglican congregations and its **authority** in due course had to be established on nonparliamentary grounds. In England itself the Act was amended by the Act of Uniformity Amendment Act 1872, was drastically curtailed by the Prayer Book (Alternative and Other Services) Measure 1965, and was finally replaced by the Church of England (Worship and Doctrine) Measure 1974, although this last still required that the 1662 Book should remain "available" and entrenched it as the norm of Church of England usage and **doctrine**.

ADVENT. The four Sundays prior to **Christmas** have, since the sixth century in the West, marked out weeks of preparation for Christmas, and they have come to begin the Christian year. While the "advent" to which the church looks forward is primarily the celebration of the **Incarnation** (and hence the regular Sunday themes in the four weeks include John the Baptist and **Mary**), the theme of the second advent of **Jesus Christ** (and thus of "the four last things") has also marked the season. **Thomas Cranmer** provided a **collect** of Advent 1, which brought both advents into relationship to each other, and in 1662 a new **rubric** required this to be read throughout Advent, in addition to the collect of each particular following Sunday. However, the Gospel of Advent Sunday in 1662 still recorded Jesus' triumphal entry into **Jerusalem**. Following **Roman Catholic** usage, there has been a tendency in recent centuries to omit the Gloria in Excelsis and to wear purple in Advent, indicating a penitential season somewhat on the **Lenten** pattern. This purism has, however, been considerably disrupted by a popular culture that tends to observe Christmas, with readings and carols in particular, long before Advent is finished and the Christmas festive season truly begun.

In the 1662 **Book of Common Prayer**, Advent began the church year but had little impact upon the end of it (there being merely provision for an invariable "last Sunday after **Trinity**"—that is, "Stir Up Sunday"). Modern **calendars**, however, tend to make more of a season of approach to Advent prior to Advent Sunday. In the Church of

England's **Alternative Service** Book of 1980, there was a nine-week period of preparation for Christmas that swallowed up the traditional Advent and even gave a new starting place to the church year. That has been overtaken by a pattern that started from Roman Catholic revisions and is linked to the three-year Sunday **lectionary**, that is, a pre-Advent pattern of four weeks of a "Kingdom Season" culminating in the **Feast** of Christ the King on the Sunday next before Advent. Any season prior to Advent is, however, firmly located at the end of the previous church year, and its place in the calendar thus leaves Advent Sunday unchallenged as the beginning of the church year.

AFFUSION. *Affusion* is the technical term for "pouring" water on a **baptismal** candidate. It has usually been the second of two alternative uses in Anglican baptismal **rubrics**, the first being "dipping" or **submersion** of the candidate. For affusion to be distinguishable from **sprinkling**, a continuous flow of water should be sustained, however briefly.

AFRICA, AFRICAN. *See* ANGOLA; BURUNDI; CAMEROON; CENTRAL AFRICA; CONGO; COUNCIL OF ANGLICAN PROVINCES OF AFRICA (CAPA); EAST AFRICA, PROVINCE OF; EASTERN EQUATORIAL AFRICA; KENYA; MOMBASA; NIGERIA; RWANDA; SIERRA LEONE; SOUTHERN AFRICA; SUDAN; TANZANIA; UGANDA; WEST AFRICA; ZAMBIA; ZANZIBAR; ZIMBABWE.

AGAPE. *Agape*, the Greek word usually translated in the New Testament as "love" (cf. 1 Cor. 13), is a term which, from the first century onward, came more specifically to mean "love-feast" (cf. Jude 12). As the **Lord's Supper** appears to have been observed within the context of a larger meal (cf. 1 Cor. 11.17–31), it is perhaps not surprising that "agape" and "**eucharist**" were on occasion among the very early **Fathers** used interchangeably (cf. Ignatius of Antioch, *Smyrnaeans* 8). While the meal and the **sacrament** became detached from each other at a comparatively early stage, it was only the sacrament that survived in Western usage until the **Reformation**. The idea and indeed the experimental use of an agape have been found in some Anglican churches in their new **Books of Common Prayer** of recent decades—not least, through the advocacy of Trevor Lloyd, in the Church of **England**'s explicit reuniting of the agape and eucharist in the *Lent, Holy Week, Easter* provision of 1986.

AGNUS DEI. The Agnus Dei chant, while its scriptural basis is in John 1.29, appears to have forked off from the canticle Gloria in Excelsis (which juxtaposes "Lamb of God, who takes away the sins of the world" with "have mercy upon us") in the seventh or eighth century and to have become associated with the **eucharistic fraction** thereafter. In **Roman Catholic** uses at requiem **masses**, the end of the third line was "rest eternal grant them." In the 1549 **Book of Common Prayer**, **Thomas Cranmer** kept the shape of the **mass**, though without an explicit fraction, and Agnus Dei became a **Communion** anthem. In 1552, all such singing disappeared, and the Agnus went also (although an extra "Thou that takest away the sins of the world, have mercy upon us" appeared, possibly as a compensation, within the Gloria in Excelsis).

As sung Communions reappeared among Anglicans in the 19th century, so unchartered usage of the chant began, and its inclusion in the Communion rite in **England** was allowed by the Lincoln Judgment (1890). In the 20th century, most revisions of the eucharistic text, following an earlier shape, have reintroduced a separated fraction and have frequently followed it with Agnus Dei. As such texts have come into modern English, so a free translation by Geoffrey Cuming, adopted and recommended by the **International Consultation on English Texts** and by its successor, the **English Language Liturgical Consultation**, has come into widespread use:

> Jesus, Lamb of God, have mercy on us;
> Jesus, bearer of our sins, have mercy on us;
> Jesus, redeemer of the world, give us your [or grant us] peace.

See also HYMNODY; MUSIC.

AIDAN (d. 651). Aidan was the archetypal Celtic **missionary** to **England**, coming from Iona at the invitation of King Oswald of Northumbria, who earlier had himself been converted by the monks of Iona when in exile in **Scotland**. Aidan was **consecrated** as a **bishop** in 635 and established his see at Lindisfarne on what is now

Holy Island. He preached the **gospel** and established churches throughout the northeast of England. Aidan is widely commemorated through the **Anglican Communion**, not least in church **dedications**. His day in church **calendars** is 31 August.

ALB. *See* VESTMENTS.

ALBAN, SAINT (fl. c. 3rd century). Alban is generally reckoned as the first British **martyr**. He was a Roman soldier, probably of the third century, who, according to **Bede**, gave hospitality in his house in Verulamium to a Christian **priest** during a time of persecution and was converted through his witness. When soldiers came to arrest the priest, Alban presented himself to them in the priest's clothes and was taken off in the priest's place and executed. In the course of time, the site of his martyrdom was marked by a Christian church and **monastic** community and became known as St. Albans. The story is subject to dispute at most points, not least as to the period of persecution concerned, for Bede located this in the Diocletian persecution of the early fourth century, but recent scholars prefer the time of Septimius Severus a hundred years earlier. Bede records the date of Alban's death as 22 June, which is the date generally observed by modern Anglicans, though in the **Books of Common Prayer** of the 16th and 17th centuries, Alban is listed on 17 June.

ALCUIN CLUB. The Alcuin Club is an Anglican society named after the English liturgical scholar, Alcuin of **York** (c. 735–804), who became a religious adviser to Charlemagne. The club was formed in 1897 to promote detailed and historical study of Anglican **liturgy** and its context and accoutrements. For more than a hundred years, the club has published series of tracts and pamphlets; in some periods (including the years from 1992 to the present), an annual collection (or monograph); and since 1987, jointly with the Group for Renewal of Worship (GROW), a series of Joint Liturgical Studies.

ALL SAINTS. Anglicans keep 1 November as All Saints' Day, in continuity with Western practice since the eighth century. It usually ranks as of prime importance among **saints**' days, and its "octave day" (8 November) has in the 20th century been kept in **England** as a remembrance of the "Saints, Martyrs and Doctors of England." Its alternative title (with the same meaning) is "All Hallows," and this is preserved both in occasional church **dedications** and in the name of its eve (31 October), known as "Hallowe'en" (and in popular culture is often associated with witches and **demons**, though its title and origins are distinctly Christian).

ALL SOULS. All Souls' Day, observed on 2 November, derives from Benedictine practice in the 10th century, from which it became universal in the Western medieval church. It was dependent upon a distinction among the dead between "**saints**," who were assumed to have gone straight to **heaven** and were commemorated on 1 November, and "souls," who were in process of going through **purgatory** and could be assisted in the process by **masses** on their behalf. Both the observance of the date and the **liturgical** (and financial) obligations that went with it were abolished by the **Reformers**, in the interests of an assurance of heaven equally promised to all the **justified**. Under the influence of the **Anglo-Catholic** movement, the observance was revived in the 19th century in some parts of the **Anglican Communion**, and in the 20th century the date has in some **provinces** lodged itself, usually in an optional and minor role, in official **calendars**. In the process it has often been renamed so as neither to imply a **doctrine** of purgatory nor to distinguish too strongly between "saints" and "souls"—a typical modern title being "Commemoration of All Faithful Departed" (**Episcopal Church [United States of America] Book of Common Prayer**, 1979).

ALLEN, ROLAND (1868–1947). Roland Allen was a **missionary** theologian of great foresight. He was an Englishman, the son of a clergyman, and from an early age of an **Anglo-Catholic** persuasion. Allen was **ordained** as a **deacon** in 1892 and as a **presbyter** in 1893 and volunteered to the **Society for the Propagation of the Gospel** in 1895. He was sent to the Society's North **China** Mission in Peking, where he trained men "for a native **ministry**" and suffered through the siege of the British Legation during the Boxer Rebellion of 1900. After a spell in England during which he married, Allen returned to China in 1902, but his health broke down and he came back to England the following year, becoming vicar of Chalfont St. Peter. In

1907, he resigned this office, on the grounds that at infant **baptisms** he was inevitably conniving at widespread hypocrisy by encouraging parents and **godparents** to pretend to a Christian commitment that they did not otherwise exhibit.

For the next 40 years, Allen was a freelancing missionary theologian. His chief thesis was the absolute necessity of indigenizing the leadership and responsibility of newly evangelized converts and of growing the ordained **ministry**—of a "voluntary" or nonstipendiary sort—from the new Christians rather than shipping in professional expatriate missionaries from abroad. Allen traveled in Asia, Africa, and North America (and lived his last 15 years in **Kenya**), and he lectured, corresponded, and argued about his principles throughout these years; the results are contained in his books, the most notable of which are *Missionary Methods: St Paul's or Ours?* (1912), *Pentecost and the World: Educational Principles and Missionary Methods* (1917), *Spontaneous Expansion of the Church and the Causes Which Hinder It* (1927), and *The Case for Voluntary Clergy* (1930). His own prediction that his thinking would come into its own 50 years after his time is generally reckoned to have been proved exactly true.

ALTAR. In the Old Testament, the "altar" is the place of sacrifice and of offering to **God**, and there is a distinction between the place of sacrifice and the place of eating (the "**table**") from the sacrifice (as can be seen in 1 Cor. 10.18–22). However, from soon after the apostolic age, the **eucharistic** table became known as the "altar," and this shift of terminology interrelated with two other growing **sacramental** ideas in the West: first, that the eucharist was itself a sacrifice (which by the Middle Ages was identified with the sacrifice of **Jesus Christ** and was called "propitiatory"); and, second, that the officiating or "**presiding**" **presbyter** is actually a sacrificing **priest** who offers the **mass** sacrifice upon the altar. Thus in the **liturgical** transition of 1549, **Thomas Cranmer** used "altar," "table," and "God's board" interchangeably in the **rubrics**, whereas in the 1552 **Prayer Book** he used "table" alone. Stone fixed altars were destroyed by order-in-council in 1550 and were replaced by movable tables. Popular usage has retained the use of the word "altar" (as in a bride and groom "going to the altar"!), and it has been regularly used in **coronation** services, although it has been the text of the 1662 rite of **Communion**

that has been used in most other respects in those services. The **Anglo-Catholic** movement has promoted the use of "altar." In the **Episcopal Church (United States of America)**, "altar" has reappeared in the rubrics since 1979, and in different **languages** in other parts of the world, various words are used with differing nuances.

ALTERNATIVE SERVICES. In the Church of **England**, the 1662 **Book of Common Prayer** is still entrenched by parliamentary statute as the legal norm for public worship. In the 1927–1928 proposed Prayer Books, the 1662 and the newly drafted services would in fact have been "alternative" to each other. But the word "alternative" got actual legal force with the passing of the Prayer Book (Alternative and Other Services) Measure 1965, which provided for the 1662 Prayer Book services to remain as the entrenched normal services of the Church of England and as the **doctrinal** standard to which assent was given by the **clergy**, but also provided for short-term "alternative" services to be authorized by the **Convocations** and House of Laity of the Church Assembly (from 1970 of the **General Synod**) without need to go to Parliament (and only to be used with the agreement of the Parochial Church Council). This provision was taken further by the Church of England (Worship and Doctrine) Measure 1974, which removed any time limit on the use of such services. Services that are authorized under the **canons** that gave expression to the **measure**, if they correspond with services already present in the 1662 Book, are "alternative" services; the Book of such services authorized from 1980 to 2000 was entitled the "Alternative Service Book." The **Common Worship** services that succeeded those in the Alternative Service Book are also "alternative services."

Similarly in **Ireland**, the 1926 Book (which is very close to the 1662) remained the norm, and the 1984 Book was entitled *The Alternative Prayer Book 1984*. In 2004, however, both were superseded by a new Church of Ireland Prayer Book. In the **United States**, the services for "trial use" in 1967, 1970, and 1973 were "alternatives" to those in the 1928 Book of Common Prayer, but they were all superseded by the 1979 Book of Common Prayer. In **Canada**, the 1962 Book remains the official norm and the 1985 one is the *Book of Alternative Services*.

AMERICA. *See* BRAZIL; CANADA; CENTRAL REGION OF AMERICA; MEXICO; SOUTHERN CONE OF SOUTH AMERICA; UNITED STATES.

AMICE. *See* VESTMENTS.

ANAMNESIS. The paragraph in classic **eucharistic prayers** that follows the **narrative** of institution begins by echoing the dominical command from 1 Cor. 11.24–25, "Do this in remembrance [*eis ten emen anamnesin*] of me," and has therefore been widely called the "anamnesis." Its grammatical form relates to the institution narrative in this way: "**Jesus Christ** said, 'Do this in remembrance of me.' Therefore, in remembrance of him, we do this." The form has, however, provided a great range of content, as the pre-**Reformation** texts known to us did not simply repeat "we do this," but instead gave a more specific description in the anamnesis of *what* we are doing in obedience to Jesus' command. Thus in the pre-Reformation missal, the anamnesis included the statement that, in obedience to the command, "we offer the pure victim, the holy victim, the unspotted victim."

Thomas Cranmer, persuaded that the Lord's command to eat and drink did not include or imply any such offering to him, removed the central wording in 1549 and replaced it with "we . . . do celebrate and make . . . the memorial which thy Son hath willed us to make." In 1552 he struck off the end of the eucharistic prayer and made the very act of eating and drinking the response to the dominical command (with anamnesis-type words used at the distribution: "Take and eat this in remembrance that Christ died for thee"). The **Scottish** 1637 rite restored the second half of the 1549 prayer and thus brought back the anamnesis quoted above, and so it passed into 18th-century Scottish usage, where a specific offering of the **elements** to **God** was added into the anamnesis. Thus in 1789 it came into the rite of the **Protestant Episcopal Church in the United States of America**.

As the 1662 shape has been abandoned in almost all modern Anglican revisions of the **eucharist**, so a more traditional shape to the eucharistic prayer has brought the classic anamnesis into more regular usage. Controversies as to whether such a paragraph should include oblationary features have remained, and the arising in the 20th century of interest in the third-century text of Hippolytus of Rome sharpened such controversy, for here was a truly ancient author whose anamnesis read, "Remembering therefore his death and resurrection, we offer the **bread** and cup." Yet such a text not only raises **doctrinal** questions about the nature and propriety of eucharistic "offering" but also touches on the question of simple logic as to whether Jesus' command to "do this" *was* a command to offer bread and wine to God.

In most **provinces** where these difficulties have been experienced, the drafting of the anamnesis paragraph has been done cautiously and less explicitly than a straight following of Hippolytus or later Roman prayers would have indicated. Instead, the question has often been asked, "What are we clear that Jesus intended us to do when he gave his command?" The official answers in **liturgical** texts vary greatly, including phrases like "we do this as he commanded" and "we celebrate the memorial which he has willed us to keep."

It is possible that, with hindsight, we may reckon that the tight logical following from the institution narrative was weakened when acclamations were inserted between the two, a practice that began in the Church of **South India** (drawing on the ancient Syrian Liturgy of St. James) in 1950. This break was further widened when a cue word for the acclamations was introduced, following Rome's new texts of 1966. So it has been a small step for new texts to take ever greater liberties with the tight logical form taken for granted in the discussion above, and since around 1990, any sense that an anamnesis *must* have a particular shape or wording has been greatly diminished.

ANAPHORA. *See* EUCHARISTIC PRAYER.

ANDREWES, LANCELOT (1555–1626). Lancelot Andrewes was bishop of successively Chichester (1605), Ely (1609), and Winchester (1619) under King **James I**. He was one of the translators of the **King James Version** of the **Bible** and was noted in his lifetime as an outstanding preacher, but he has been valued in later generations for the distinctive self-understanding he brought to Anglicanism—royalist, Episcopalian, learned, godly, and non-Calvinist. His writings, not least his *Preces Privatae,* have been prized accordingly, and he is almost the earliest of writers whose works were published in the Library of **Anglo-Catholic** Theology. He is commemorated in various provincial **calendars** on 26 September, the anniversary of his death. His tomb is in Southwark **Cathedral** in **London**, which was the **parish** church of his Episcopal palace on the South Bank (and in those days within Winchester **diocese**) at the time he died.

ANGELS. While there is nothing distinctively Anglican about angels or the study of them, the **saint**'s day of St. Michael and All Angels (29 September), often called Michaelmas, was retained at the **Reformation**, as an **ordination** season with its related **ember** days. The traditional form of the **collect** refers to the angels "defending" us on Earth. They have always figured in the lead-in to the Sanctus in the **eucharistic prayer**, the basic form of this text being—"Therefore with angels and **archangels** . . . we praise your name . . . saying, 'Holy, holy, holy.'"

ANGLICAN CENTRE, ROME. *See* ROME, ANGLICAN CENTRE IN.

ANGLICAN COMMUNION. The 1930 **Lambeth Conference** described the Anglican Communion as "a fellowship, within the one holy catholic and apostolic **church**, of those duly constituted **dioceses**, **provinces** or regional churches in **communion** with the see of **Canterbury**." It stated that the provinces are "particular or national churches and, as such, promote within each of their territories a national expression of Christian faith, life and worship." The overall title "Anglican" refers in principle not to anything cultural or specifically English, save that the Communion's existence is traceable historically to the **Reformation** in **England** and is sustained internationally today by the concept of "communion with the see of Canterbury." In some parts of the world, the respective provinces have preferred to call themselves the "Episcopal" Church, rather than to appear to give the misleading impression of being in some way directed or influenced from England.

The parliamentarily led Reformation in England was paralleled in **Ireland**. In **Scotland**, the **bishops** and many others in 1689 went underground (as "**nonjurors**") rather than swear loyalty to King **William III** and Queen **Mary II** while King **James II** was still alive. They thus kept a tiny Jacobite Church alive.

When the Anglican (or Episcopalian) chaplains and congregations in the former American colonies were inevitably severed by political events from the royalist Church of England in the years after the creation of the **United States** in 1776, it was from the Episcopal Church of Scotland in 1784 that **Samuel Seabury** gained Episcopal **consecration** to become the first bishop in the independent **Protestant Episcopal Church in the United States of America** (PECUSA). The first **General Convention** of PECUSA in 1785 then constituted the separate structure, government, polity, and worship of this independent province.

Colonial churches and chaplaincies were thereafter heard more favorably in England when they requested the consecration of bishops, and the parliamentary law was changed to allow the consecration in England of bishops for distant parts—the first two being for PECUSA (**William White** and **Samuel Provoost** in February 1787) and the next (**Charles Inglis**) for Nova Scotia in what is today **Canada** (August 1787).

Colonists, however, were not the only English people to spread their church life across the globe. The voluntary **missionary societies**, originating with the **Society for Promoting Christian Knowledge** in 1698 and the **Society for the Propagation of the Gospel** in 1701, were also building a spread of more or less Anglican congregations (e.g., in **India**) among many people not particularly of English descent. The **Evangelical Revival**, coinciding with new exploration and annexation of territories across the world, led to a renewed impetus for world **evangelization** and to the formation of the **Church Missionary Society** in 1799 to further it.

The provision of bishops and diocesan organization lagged well behind this impetus, but after 1787 there were further bishops consecrated for **Calcutta** (1814), Barbados (1824), Jamaica (1824), Madras (1835), **Australia** (1836), New Zealand (1841), **Jerusalem** (1841), and Cape Town (1847). Further consecrations for each area followed on these first ones, although the relationship was hardly one of "**full communion**," as those **ordain**ed outside of Britain (including those ordained within PECUSA) were unable, until the Colonial Clergy Act 1874, to be licensed to **minister** in England or Ireland.

During the 1840s and 1850s, the issue arose as to what extent such overseas dioceses were part of the Church of England or were self-governing and therefore able to form a provincial organization in their own areas. **Synods** were forbidden by English statute law, but overseas bishops did not know whether they were subject to this law or free of it. The first synod was held in 1857 by **George Augustus Selwyn**, bishop of New Zealand (1841–1868), but the real trial of strength came in South Africa.

In 1863, Robert Gray, the bishop of Cape Town and **metropolitan**, held a provincial court and deposed **William Colenso**, the bishop of Natal, for **heresy**—but Colenso then appealed to the Judicial Committee of the Privy Council in **London** and was reinstated in 1865. This overruling of metropolitical **authority** caused anxiety across the Anglican world and led the synod of the ecclesiastical province of Canada to call on the **archbishop** of Canterbury to summon a common conference "of the members of our Anglican Communion" to take counsel together. Archbishop Charles Thomas Longley did indeed call such a conference (though warning that it should not address the question of Natal), and 76 bishops attended this first **Lambeth Conference** in 1867. Many English bishops, including the archbishop of **York**, declined to attend, however, fearing that, despite the archbishop's warning, Colenso would be condemned by the conference. In fact, the bishops present did overthrow the agenda, asking a committee to report on Natal and ultimately, after the conference was over, receiving a report recommending that the see be deemed vacant, and thus favoring the consecration by Gray of a new bishop for Natal.

Gray, anticipating further legal tangles in England, in 1870 formed a new Church of the Province of South Africa, convened and constituted by voluntary participation, and thus "separated root and branch" from the Church of England. This left Colenso and many individual congregations not participating, and Gray's new province gained its internal cohesion and identity at the expense of a kind of localized schism. In other parts of the world, fortunately, the transition from chaplaincies or **mission** stations to first dioceses and then independent provinces has been accomplished more smoothly and has often marched with the emergence of erstwhile British colonies into political self-government and then independence.

Lambeth Conferences have been convened on the same basis as the first, roughly every 10 years, ever since then. The membership of such conferences has been determined solely by the invitation of the archbishop of Canterbury of the time, and that determination by the same token for almost a century also defined the membership of the Anglican Communion. From 1867 until 1958, while all Anglican provinces and churches had historical origins in the English (or Irish) Reformation and all shared a common (though not identical) **liturgical** inheritance, it was the office of the archbishop of Canterbury alone that gave the Communion contemporary structural relationships. The Lambeth Conferences have been true to Longley's originally stated intention that they should neither have, nor claim to have, any statutory, constitutional, or legislative force.

In the years since 1958, further developments have ensued and, while respecting provincial autonomy, have provided closer bonds of Communion in a period of shrinking distances and fast-changing information technology. They may be summarized as follows:

- The appointment of an **executive officer of the Anglican Communion** with a London office following the 1958 Lambeth Conference. This led to the development of the **Anglican Consultative Council** (ACC) following the 1968 conference, at which point the executive officer became the **secretary-general** of the ACC. The council in due course became the **Anglican Communion Office** (ACO).
- The establishment of **ecumenical** commissions with an international Anglican membership, such as the **Anglican–Roman Catholic International Commission** (ARCIC), first appointed in 1969.
- The convening by the archbishop of Canterbury of **Primates Meetings**. The 1998 Lambeth Conference requested that the primates should also become the representative bishops of each province. This has not been implemented, but in 2005, ACC-13 voted that primates should belong to ACC *ex officio*.
- The development of the role of the archbishop of Canterbury himself, with a primacy of respect, a pivotal role in the definition of the Anglican Communion and in the convening of Lambeth Conferences, a built-in presidency of the ACC and of Primates Meetings, and an undefined moral duty to intervene (in an

advisory, not a constitutional, way) when any province has clearly gotten into difficulties.

- The Communion has also been strengthened by the adherence (as extraprovincial dioceses) in 1980 of the **Lusitanian Church** of Portugal and the **Spanish Reformed Episcopal Church**. It has also more recently included as full members the four united churches in which Anglicans were participants at union, namely the churches of **South India**, **North India**, **Pakistan**, and **Bangladesh**.

Nevertheless, despite all such bonds, provincial autonomy remains, and individual provinces may make policy decisions with which others do not at the time agree, such as the admission of unconfirmed children to Communion (begun synodically in New Zealand in 1970), the **ordination** of **women** as **presbyters** (begun in **Hong Kong** in 1971) or as bishops (begun in the **United States** in 1989), or provincial decisions on **divorce** and remarriage, **polygamy**, or **homosexual** relationships. Where such a division exists within the Communion, the archbishop of Canterbury, the primates, the ACC, or a Lambeth Conference may advise or warn, but they cannot require or command. Divisions have indeed arisen. Some are formal, in that not all provinces recognize the ordination of women in other provinces, and provinces that do not ordain women as bishops often do not accept ordinations performed by women bishops. Other divisions, mostly dating from 2002 on, relate to the approval or otherwise of homosexual relationships, particularly among presbyters and bishops; these divisions are less constitutional, but are very far reaching, and their implications are the subject of the **Windsor Report**. A feature of this report is the exploration of the interdependence implicit and theologically necessary within a Communion of constitutionally independent provinces.

At the time of writing, there are within the Communion 38 autonomous churches (or provinces) including the four united churches. There are, in addition, six other extraprovincial churches: the dioceses of Spain and Portugal mentioned above, the dioceses of Bermuda and **Cuba**, the Anglican Church of **Sri Lanka** (itself two dioceses), and the **cathedral** parish of the Falkland Islands. The archbishop of Canterbury is the metropolitan for each of these except Cuba. Around

750 bishops attended the 1998 Lambeth Conference. Lay membership is hard to measure or define (and this is particularly true in England, where an "**establishment**" count yields up to 30 million members, while a "worshipping" count goes little beyond a million). But the total number of known adherents throughout the world is probably somewhere between 50 million and 100 million persons. *See also* COMPASS ROSE.

ANGLICAN COMMUNION OFFICE (ACO). The **Anglican Consultative Council** (ACC) has a permanent secretariat based in **London** known as the Anglican Communion Office. Originally, in 1978, the office was located on the premises of the **United Society for the Propagation of the Gospel** (USPG) at 15 Tufton Street, London SW1, and when the USPG moved to the premises of the **Church Missionary Society** at 157 Waterloo Road, London SE1, in 1988, the ACO moved with it. In 2003 the ACO moved to new premises in West London at St. Andrew's House, 16 Tavistock Crescent, London W11 1AP, the former home of the **Deaconess** Community of St. Andrew. The secretariat, led by the **secretary-general** of the ACC, is responsible for staffing and servicing directly or indirectly the ACC itself, the various commissions and **networks** of the **Anglican Communion**, and the other corporate instruments of unity: the **Lambeth Conferences** and the **Primates Meetings**. It sustains the Anglican Communion News Service (ACNS) and publishes the Anglican Cycle of Prayer. It also publishes and distributes a journal, which originated as a newssheet entitled *Anglican Information* from 1971 until 1992 and became *Compassrose* in 1992 and subsequently *Anglican Episcopal World*.

ANGLICAN CONGRESS. A **Pan-Anglican Congress** was held in London in 1908. There have been two other "Anglican Congresses," one in Minneapolis in 1954 and the other in Toronto in 1963. In each case the participants included **bishops**, **clergy**, and **laity** from across the **Anglican Communion**. The Minneapolis Congress was initiated by a suggestion at the 1948 **Lambeth Conference**, and the Toronto one by reflections on Minneapolis at the 1958 Lambeth Conference and Resolution 68 there. The Toronto conference's theme was "The World-Wide Mission of the Church," and the actual work there led to the adoption of a principle of "**mutual responsibility and interdependence**" (MRI), which outlined a concept of provinces helping one another in a way that has in fact grown considerably since that date.

There has been no Anglican Congress since 1963, but there is an adumbration of such a congress in an appendix to *The* ***Virginia Report***, published in the 1998 Lambeth Conference report. This was followed up by recommendations of the 11th **Anglican Consultative Council** meeting (ACC-11) in **Scotland** in 1999, though by 2005 this had had to be canceled for logistical and other reasons.

ANGLICAN CONSULTATIVE COUNCIL (ACC). Following the 1968 **Lambeth Conference**, and on its recommendation, the Anglican Consultative Council was formed in 1969 as an agency of the **Anglican Communion**. The ACC's constitution initially provided for each autonomous **province** to be represented by up to three members, the number depending upon the size of the province but always including one **layperson**, with **presbyters** or **bishops** as the second and third representatives as applicable. The **archbishop** of **Canterbury** is the *ex officio* president, and the council is served by an office in **London**, now known as the **Anglican Communion Office** (ACO), under the **secretary-general**, the chief executive officer of the council.

The ACC has met every two or three years since its formation, though the holding of a Lambeth Conference every 10 years has affected the rhythm. The actual years of meeting have been: 1971, 1973, 1976, 1979, 1981, 1984, 1987, 1990, 1993, 1996, 1999, 2002, and 2005. Each meeting has been followed by a published report, and these have at intervals touched on issues affecting the Communion deeply, not least at the very first meeting in 1971, when, by a tiny majority (24–22), ACC-1 passed a motion expressing goodwill toward the projected **ordination** of **women** to the **presbyterate** in **Hong Kong**.

In a matter of similar importance, prior to the ACC meeting in June 2005 in Nottingham, England, the **Primates Meeting** in February asked the Anglican Church of **Canada** and the **Episcopal Church (United States of America)** not to take part in the ACC "for the period leading up to the next Lambeth Conference" until they could take requisite actions consequent upon the **Windsor Report**. In June, representatives of these two Churches did attend, but only to make statements of their Churches' positions, not otherwise to participate in the business. At the meeting, the ACC endorsed the **primates**' request that both Churches withdraw, by a vote of 30–28 with four recorded abstentions.

The ACC office and other overheads (such as the servicing of commissions) are supported by graded financial contributions to the Inter-Anglican Finance and Administration Committee from the member provinces, and the finances are always tightly stretched. While some provinces have desired more officers and more international commissions, the constraints of available resources have always imposed strict limits. There are some areas where the international responsibilities of the archbishop of Canterbury's personal staff overlap with the roles of ACC personnel, and that structural problem remains to be resolved.

In addition to (funded) commissions, the ACC has also various international Anglican **networks** linked to it, usually originating from an initiative of the ACC (or of a Lambeth Conference or a Primates Meeting) and officially recognized, though without official funding. The networks typically report to ACC meetings, keep in touch with the ACO, and are accordingly reported in the journal *Anglican World*. As networks, however, they have no institutionalized accountability, official work program, predictable membership, frequency of meetings, or scale of output. The ACC also recognizes and supports, in a slightly different category, the **International Anglican Liturgical Consultations**, and via the ACO it services the primates' working party on "Theological Education for the Anglican Communion" (TEAC).

In 1988 and 1998 the respective archbishops of Canterbury invited the ACC members to take part in the Lambeth Conferences of those years. In 1993 for the first time the ACC met jointly with the primates; and at the 1998 Lambeth Conference a resolution was passed calling for the primates themselves to participate as the bishops representing their provinces within the ACC. This could in the course of time assimilate the ACC and the Primates Meeting into a single structure, though thus far there remains a limit upon the length of time individual members may serve on the ACC. Instead, ACC-13 at Nottingham in 2005 proposed that primates should belong to ACC *ex officio*, in addition to Episcopal members. But the separate meetings of primates have continued and been intensified in the years following Lambeth 1998.

ANGLICAN EXECUTIVE OFFICER. *See* EXECUTIVE OFFICER OF THE ANGLICAN COMMUNION.

ANGLICAN URBAN NETWORK. In the light of worldwide trends in globalization and urbanization, the 1998 **Lambeth Conference** in resolution II.7 asked "the **Anglican Consultative Council** [ACC] to give support to the formation of an Anglican Urban **Network** to share information and experience on urbanization and urban mission." This was underlined at the next meeting of the ACC (ACC-11 in **Scotland** in 1999), as a result of which a steering group was established in 2001, and the members of it took part in the **United Nations** Special Sessions on Human Settlement in June that year. A first international consultation was held in **London** in 2003 with participants from many places, and an annual newsletter has been started. The steering group has identified four foci for future work: training for leadership, empowerment of the poor, interchange between regions, and theological and sociological reflection.

ANGLICAN–BAPTIST RELATIONSHIPS. *See* BAPTIST CHURCHES.

ANGLICAN–LUTHERAN RELATIONSHIPS. *See* LUTHERAN CHURCHES; MEISSEN; PORVOO.

ANGLICAN–METHODIST RELATIONSHIPS. *See* METHODIST CHURCHES.

ANGLICAN–MORAVIAN RELATIONSHIPS. See MORAVIAN CHURCH.

ANGLICAN–ORTHODOX RELATIONSHIPS. *See* ORTHODOX CHURCHES.

ANGLICAN–REFORMED RELATIONSHIPS. *See* REFORMED CHURCHES.

ANGLICAN–ROMAN CATHOLIC INTERNATIONAL COMMISSION (ARCIC). Official talks between the **Roman Catholic Church** and the **Anglican Communion** would usually have been unthinkable in the years before **Vatican II**, despite the short period of the semiofficial **Malines Conversations** in 1921–1926. However, in late 1960, shortly before the opening of the Roman Catholic General Council, Archbishop **Geoffrey Fisher** paid a brief, semiprivate visit to **Pope** John XXIII; later, at the Council, some brief kind words about Anglicans were included in the decree on **ecumenism**. At the end of the Council's last session in November 1965, the Anglican observers at the council were received by Pope Paul VI prior to their departure. There was a forward-looking conversation, in which the possibilities of a change in relationships that might spring from the projected official visit to Rome of Archbishop **Michael Ramsey** were explored.

The archbishop duly came in March 1966 and made with Pope Paul a "Common Declaration," at the heart of which was a stated intention of setting up a serious dialogue ("*Colloquia*" in the Latin text) between the two Communions, a dialogue to include scripture, **tradition**, **liturgy**, and practical difficulties. This dialogue came to pass in two stages.

In autumn 1966, a Joint Preparatory Commission was established. It first met in January 1967 and then held four sessions at different places, ending with the "Malta Report" in January 1968. This report recommended the establishment of a more definitive international commission between the two Communions, and it gained encouraging responses from both the Vatican and the 1968 **Lambeth Conference**. As a result, the longer-term "permanent" Anglican–Roman Catholic International Commission was established in 1969, holding its first meeting in Windsor in January 1970. Its joint chairmen were Bishop Alan Clark (RC) and Archbishop Henry McAdoo (Anglican). At its third meeting (also in Windsor) in September 1971, the commission agreed on a joint statement entitled **"Eucharistic Doctrine**," which was published on 31 December 1971.

That commission (now known as ARCIC-1) went on to publish the statements "**Ministry** and **Ordination**" (1973), "**Authority** in the Church I" (1976), and "Authority in the Church II" (1981). After the statements were published, a vast amount of comment was received, and the commission issued further explanatory statements on each subject. These were described as "elucidations" and were published as "Eucharistic Doctrine: Elucidation" (1979), "Ministry and Ordination: Elucidation" (1979) and "Authority in the Church: Elucidation" (1981). The statements and elucidations were all agreed upon by the whole commission, although certain features of the Authority statements (largely touching on the role of the pope and of universal primacy) simply set out the incompatible viewpoints side by side. Before ARCIC-1 disbanded in 1982, the whole set of documents was published together as *The Final Report*, and official responses of the two Communions were sought.

The Anglican Communion generally welcomed the "substantial agreement" demonstrated in the statements on Eucharist and on Ministry and Ordination, but was more cautious in relation to those on Authority; these differing evaluations were expressed in resolutions of the 1988 Lambeth Conference. The Vatican response in 1991, however, was so qualified as to put the second commission, ARCIC-2, in the position of attempting to "clarify" the two statements of ARCIC-1 to which Anglicans had already given a warm response in their original form.

After 1982, a new commission, ARCIC-2, had been formed under cochairmen Bishop Cormac Murphy-O'Connor (RC) and Bishop Mark Santer (Anglican) to follow up the work of ARCIC-1. It published various further documents, including *Salvation and the Church* (1987), *Church as Communion* (1991), *Life in Christ: Morals, Communion and the Church* (1994), and ***Clarifications*** (1994). The first three of these were welcomed at the 1998 Lambeth Conference—which never mentioned the existence of the fourth at all.

A further statement came in 1999: *The Gift of Authority*, which claimed to conclude with agreement on the issues left unresolved in the two Authority statements of ARCIC-1. The agreement included the acceptance of a "universal **primate**" who, in certain defined circumstances, would be "preserved from error." This was presented to the 11th **Anglican Consultative Council** (ACC-11), which met in **Scotland** later that year, but was not seriously debated or evaluated there. There was virtually no official response to this statement from either Communion until the Church of England **General Synod** debated it in early 2004 and gave it a very cautiously phrased provisional welcome, qualified by requests for greater clarity at some points.

Bishop Santer resigned the cochairmanship in 2000 and was replaced by Frank Griswold, the presiding bishop of the **Episcopal Church (United States of America)**. In November 2003, after Bishop Griswold had officiated at the **consecration** of an actively **homosexual presbyter** to be bishop of New Hampshire, he resigned from the cochairmanship and was replaced by Peter Carnley, the archbishop of Perth and primate of the Anglican Church in **Australia**, shortly before he himself retired from his see.

One of the major points not covered in *The Gift of Authority* was the relationship between papal authority and the two papal decrees about the **Immaculate Conception** and the Bodily **Assumption** of the Blessed Virgin **Mary**. Mary was the next theme for ARCIC-2 to address, and at its meeting in 2003 the commission made it clear that it hoped to publish an agreed statement on Mary in 2004. *Mary: Grace and Hope in Christ* was agreed upon in 2004 but was not published until May 2005. This completed the agenda of ARCIC-2, and the two Communions will review the needs of future theological dialogue. *See also* INTERNATIONAL ANGLICAN–ROMAN CATHOLIC COMMISSION FOR UNITY AND MISSION.

ANGLICAN–ROMAN CATHOLIC RELATIONSHIPS. *See* ANGLICAN–ROMAN CATHOLIC INTERNATIONAL COMMISSION; INTERNATIONAL ANGLICAN–ROMAN CATHOLIC COMMISSION FOR UNITY AND MISSION; MALINES CONVERSATIONS; REFORMATION; ROMAN CATHOLIC CHURCH; VATICAN I; VATICAN II.

ANGLO-CATHOLICISM. While all the Anglican Reformers and 17th-century divines would have asserted that the Church of **England** was "catholic" and part of the worldwide catholic church, the term "catholic" acquired a new significance through a movement that arose in the 19th century and dubbed itself "Anglo-Catholic." The origins of the movement are conventionally traced to **John Keble**'s Assize Sermon at Oxford on 14 July 1833; in this sermon, entitled "National Apostasy," he protested against the action of the Reform Parliament in abolishing Irish bishoprics without any reference to the

United Church of England and Ireland and insisted that the foundations of that Church should be identified as located not in the state establishment but in the "apostolical descent" of the **bishops** and clergy.

Within a matter of days, a number of Oxford **clergy** met at the vicarage of Rose of Hadleigh, and on 9 September 1833 the ***Tracts for the Times*** series was launched. These publications appear to have been inspired primarily by **John Henry Newman**, vicar of St. Mary the Virgin, Oxford, and fellow of Oriel College. The tracts ran from 1833 to 1841 and varied in length between pamphlets of a few hundred words and monographs of several thousand words. The main authors were Newman himself, Keble (a professor of poetry), **Edward Pusey** (a professor of Hebrew), and Hurrell Froude, who died in 1836. The Anglo-Catholic movement they began was also called the "**Oxford Movement**."

The "**Tractarians**" and their tracts provoked widespread opposition (for their teaching was seen as contrary to the formularies of the Church of England and disloyal to the **Reformation**), but the whole idea of "Anglo-Catholicism" propounded by this group of Oxford dons caught the imagination of an ever-growing army of adherents. The central theme was "**apostolic succession**" and the **authority** and divine commission of the threefold **orders** retained by the Church of England at the Reformation, thus providing for a secure pattern of **sacraments**.

As each year passed, so the "catholic" claims of the Church of England were pressed the harder by the tracts and their authors. Their advocacy was flanked and supported by great scholarly enterprises: The Library of the **Fathers** was begun in 1837; the Library of Anglo-Catholic Theology, reprinting "high" Anglican authors mostly from the 17th century (and giving them a label they had not given themselves), followed from 1841.

The end of the movement's initiating period was reached with the massive and manipulative Tract 90 (1841), in which Newman reinterpreted the Thirty-Nine **Articles** so as to be compatible (through vagueness or ambiguity that he alleged to be visible in their teachings) with **Roman Catholic** doctrine. In his own words, he was "proving the cannon"—that is, seeing how heavy a charge of gunpowder, beyond anything tried before, the existing framework (of the

Church of England) would bear. Tract 90 was condemned by Oxford University and opposed by various bishops. The movement was now sufficiently overt, and teaching a Christianity sufficiently unlike the normally understood position of the Church of England, as to attract charges of **heresy** and disloyalty.

Newman himself went to Rome in 1845, and other secessions accompanied or followed his. These secessions highlighted the precarious theological position the Anglo-Catholics were building. They claimed to have the full **doctrine** and inheritance of the catholic church, but in separation from Rome. Yet without Rome, it was difficult on the one hand to measure what was truly "catholic" and on the other hand to detach the single great agreed mark of catholicity—that is, the state of being visibly "one"—from that measure of catholicity and to say it did not matter being in separation from Rome. The more romantic followers (and the whole movement was imbued with romanticism) might simply cite the pre-Reformation church of the English and desire to restore that church, without reference to the worldwide character of the contemporary Roman Church, but the great majority had to both look toward Rome for models of catholicism and also distinguish what in Rome was true catholicism and what was corruption—and at the same time retain a sufficient critique of the corruptions of Rome as to justify remaining in separation from her. The criteria for such judgments were not easy to establish objectively.

Nevertheless, the result was a growing and dynamic force within the life of the Church of England (and soon after in the **United States** and in many other parts of the world to which Anglo-Catholics went as chaplains or **missionaries**). It was a force with a constant seepage toward Rome, and it was seen by the growing Roman Catholic forces as an agency working unknowingly on their behalf—as the seepage itself constantly confirmed. One of those who joined the Roman Catholic Church in 1850, after the **Gorham** Judgment, was Henry Manning, who went on to become cardinal archbishop of Westminster.

The dynamism within the movement was electrifying. The proponents built **theological colleges**, founded **religious communities**, revolutionized church **architecture** with the **Gothic** Revival, reintroduced Roman **ceremonial** into **liturgy** from 1850 on, advanced the use of **music** including **hymnody** and chant, started journals, promoted **retreats**, organized overseas missionary efforts, built public schools, inaugurated Keble College and Pusey House at Oxford, and dramatically changed the face of the **parish** church in almost the whole of the Church of England. They turned an almost nonsacramental church into a highly sacramental one, entrenching a weekly **eucharist** in moderate parishes and a daily one in more specialist parishes, and reintroducing the Roman "sacrament" of **penance** as a desirable, if not absolutely requisite, precondition for receiving **Communion**. They altered liturgy almost beyond recognition, even though the 1662 **Book of Common Prayer** remained the only official text—by the 1860s the more advanced **priests** went to **eastward** position, wore Roman **vestments**, used candles and wafers, genuflected and rang bells at the **consecration**, engaged freely in crossing themselves, insisted on **fasting** Communion, debarred the unconfirmed from Communion, invoked the intercession of the **saints**, prayed for and offered masses for the departed, and began to introduce incense and the use of Latin texts.

Throughout the period from 1850 to 1890 in England, these second-generation Anglo-Catholics faced court cases and not infrequently got off on technicalities. But, when they were found in breach of the law of the Church of England, they both denounced the "state" courts as unlawful in relation to the Church and ignored their injunctions—and a few went to jail for contempt of court, and "the blood of the **martyrs** was the seed of the Church." In effect, within their own sphere, they changed the final authority in matters of doctrine from the clear teaching of scripture to "the teachings of the church," but by their very refusal to accept the plain teaching of the Church of England's formularies, they also left open the issue as to *where* the authority called "the church" was located, let alone as to *what* it might then authoritatively teach. While they had an enormously high doctrine of **episcopacy** and of **ordination** and orders, they often had to battle against the hostility of the actual bishops of their own time, so that their understanding and practice of their own catholicism was inevitably weighted toward parochial independence and unaccountability. Their parish practice coupled this independence with an enormous priestly prestige and power for the incumbent, as compared with a more corporate understanding of the life and authority of the living Church of England. Their independence was protected legally by the freehold, but morally by the willingness of **celibate** priests to live lives of enormous self-sacrifice in the growing slum areas of the towns of England.

There is little doubt that Anglo-Catholicism must be traced back in its origins to those Oxford years, 1833–1841. But it was by no means confined to the Church of England, and in the years following 1850 it found fires laid ready for the spark to be applied in the **United States**, **Scotland**, **New Zealand**, and **South Africa**. Through the particular agency of the **Universities Mission to Central Africa**, but also through the ready backing of the preexisting **Society for the Propagation of the Gospel** and other smaller societies, it provided the pioneer **evangelism** undertaken by Anglicans in many parts of the Earth, and thus in those parts started to produce monochrome "catholic" dioceses. That which had been a disloyal faction in the 1830s was by the 1870s becoming *de facto* accepted as one of differing valid ways of being Anglican. Bishops of this persuasion started to appear—in England, Edward King (bishop of Lincoln, 1885–1910) was the first—and the teachings of Anglo-Catholicism, giving such a high place to episcopacy, have had their own appeal for bishops. Pre-Reformation Episcopal vesture followed, and the miter, unknown since the Reformation—save on diocesan coats of arms—started to reappear also. The first **archbishop** of **Canterbury** since the Reformation to wear a miter was **Cosmo Lang** in 1929!

Anglo-Catholicism, once accepted, continued expanding in England (and in other provinces) until, for the first half of the 20th century, the movement became the dominant force in Anglicanism. There was a notable phalanx of theologians and scholars resourcing this expansion, and an intellectual self-confidence assisted that dominance. It was Anglo-Catholics who pressed for liturgical revision and who insisted that the **historic episcopate** was of the *esse* of the church—and for this reason resisted the formation of the Church of **South India**. It is, however, arguable that increasingly during the 20th century the movement was slowly penetrated by **liberalism** and then, more suddenly, by changes in Rome from the 1950s on—changes that **Vatican II** (1962–1965) multiplied beyond all expectation. In more recent years, this movement, despite a division between its members, has taken the lead in resisting the ordination of **women** in Anglicanism. But its years of worldwide dominance in the **Anglican Communion** were fading from the time of the 1968 **Lambeth Conference**.

ANGOLA. Angola lies on the west coast of Africa, south of **Congo**, and was until 1974 a Portuguese colony. No Anglican **missionary society** ever officially sent expatriate missionaries to the land, and virtually no reports of an Anglican presence ever came from the country until 1985. Nevertheless, an Anglican layman named Archibald Patterson had been moved to go the Portuguese territory on a one-man unofficial basis after the 1910 **Edinburgh Missionary Conference**, and between the two world wars he taught among the Bakongo tribe in the north of the country and saw thousands converted. He himself **baptized** them and taught them both to **evangelize** and to worship with the Church of **England**'s **Book of Common Prayer**.

After World War II, in extraordinary needy circumstances, Patterson himself in 1947 "**ordained**" six Angolans as **presbyters**. But then, as demands for independence arose in African colonies, the Portuguese expelled foreign missionaries and persecuted **Protestant** Angolans. As Patterson was put on board a ship in 1961, he was handed a list of the names of leading Anglicans who had been executed, including two whom he had ordained. Others fled into the bush, and many crossed to the almost equally dangerous Zaire.

Church life continued under the harassment, and Patterson in his old age visited the exiles in Zaire in 1973, and, in the extraordinary circumstances, "ordained" Alexander Domingos, the senior itinerant lay pastor of the scattered people. When the Portuguese left Angola in 1974, the exiles in Zaire returned, but they also split, many becoming the United Evangelical Reformed Church, linked to Switzerland. Patterson too returned in 1974, as civil war broke out, and ordained three more men that year, and more the following year, before he departed to England, where he died soon after. It appears that Patterson had hoped to undergird the Anglicanism of the church by linking it with the **Lusitanian Church**, but this proved impossible.

Domingos came to Selly Oak in Birmingham in 1985, stating that he was from the then unknown "Anglican Church in Angola." He was put in touch with the **United Society for the Propagation of the Gospel**, and they linked him with Dinis Sengulane, **bishop** of Lebombo in Mozambique—also an ex-Portuguese colony—who had a common language with the Angolans. On Sengulane's first visit to Angola in 1990, he was widely welcomed, and he ordained Domingos as a presbyter and other leaders as **deacons**, to be presbyters in

1991. Domingos died in 1993 and was succeeded as leader by Andre Soares. A new civil war raged until 2002, but in that year Angola was constituted a missionary **diocese** of the **province** of **Southern Africa**, led by Soares, appointed as **archdeacon**, still under the Episcopal care of Bishop Sengulane. There were reckoned at the time to be around 10,000 Anglican Christians in the diocese, mostly living in conditions of extreme poverty and without funding for stipends or development. On 13 September 2003, Soares was **consecrated** as the first bishop of Angola.

ANNEXED BOOK. The manuscript standard text of the 1662 **Book of Common Prayer** was written by hand to show the outcome of the revision in the **Convocations** in November and December 1661, was then sent to the Privy Council (where the "**Black Rubric**" was added, as can be seen in the different hand that wrote it), and finally was annexed to the 1662 **Act of Uniformity**, which enforced the use of the Book. The Annexed Book thus became the standard of judgment of textual accuracy, from which the "sealed copies" deposited in each **cathedral**, and all printed copies thereafter, were supposed to derive.

ANNUNCIATION. The annunciation of the **angel** Gabriel to **Mary**, recorded in Luke 1.26–38, became part of the **calendar** of the Western Church possibly as early as the fourth century, when a schema developed to unite the summer and winter solstices and the autumn and spring equinoxes, which had been important celebrations since pre-Christian days. As the annunciation to Elizabeth came six months before the annunciation to Mary, and the pregnancy of each took nine months, the annual sequence of observances thus began with the annunciation to Mary on 25 March ("Lady Day"), followed by the birth of John the Baptist (24 June), the annunciation to Elizabeth (around 21 September), and **Christmas**, the birth of **Jesus Christ** (25 December). The starting point may have been the adoption of a date for the nativity of Jesus and a working back from that, but a theory that the annunciation began the schema also has credibility. The annunciation to Mary at intervals falls in **Holy Week**, and then has to be transferred. Under the Julian calendar, followed in Britain until 1752, the calendar year began on Lady Day, and documents before 1752 are dated accordingly.

ANOINTING. In the Old Testament, anointing is a special sign of **God**'s favor and commissioning—as, for example, in the appointment of **priests** or the **coronation** of kings. In the New Testament, the expected "Christ" is a translation of the "Messiah," where both words mean "the anointed one." Physical anointing is reported at one point in the **Gospels** as being used by the disciples of **Jesus Christ** for **healing** (Mark 6.13), and it is similarly commended for a healing ministry in the apostolic church in James 5.14. Other New Testament references (particularly to the anointing of the **Holy Spirit**, as in Acts 10.38 or 1 John 2.27) are clearly metaphorical. In the early church, anointing was used in connection with **baptism**. By the Middle Ages, it had also developed for those in danger of **death** (and was known as *extrema unctio*, extreme unction, literally the last anointing).

In the 1549 **Book of Common Prayer**, anointing was restored to the Visitation of the Sick (in conformity to the James 5.14 injunction), but in 1552, when it was eliminated from the ceremonies in other services, such as baptism, it was dropped again from the Visitation of the Sick. In the 20th century, there was a widespread reversion to the use of anointing, not only for the sick but also in connection with baptisms and **confirmations**, and, in some places, at **ordination** also. There is some imprecision as to whether anointing (or unction) should invariably be ministered by a **bishop** or **presbyter** or can be properly delegated to **laypeople**.

The provision of a **Maundy Thursday** diocesan rite for the "blessing of oils" has also been inaugurated in recent years in some parts of the **Anglican Communion**, though in **England** in 1982 actual texts proposed for such a rite were defeated in **General Synod**, which leaves the provision of such services at the discretion of individual bishops. The oils thus provided are usually for three different purposes: for anointing the sick, for anointing baptismal candidates, and for anointing confirmation candidates. In the case of confirmations, olive oil is often mingled with balsam to provide a scented oil known as "**chrism**."

Anointing of kings and priests in the Old Testament has also found its equivalent in Anglican practice, as, whether the precedents are valid or not, anointing is used at coronations and, as noted, in some **provinces** at ordination.

ANSELM (c. 1033–1109). Anselm was born in Italy in 1033 and was domiciled in France. In adult life, he became a monk at Bec, where he succeeded the prior, Lanfranc, in 1063. Anselm succeeded Lanfranc again in 1093, this time as **archbishop** of **Canterbury**, when, after a four-year delay inflicted by William Rufus, he was nominated to that office. Anselm proved to be of rare intellectual stature, and his writings on the faith from his time as archbishop, particularly his *Cur Deus Homo?* concerning **Jesus Christ**'s **Incarnation** and redemption, have been landmarks in the development of Western historical theology. He also finally settled the priority of Canterbury over **York** in ecclesiastical **authority** and secured clerical **celibacy**. After his death, he was growingly recognized as a **saint** in the centuries that followed (though never formally declared as such by papal process), and his commemoration is kept on 21 April.

ANTHROPOLOGY. Anglicans have generally held to the classic formulations of the **doctrine** of the human race—that humankind is created in the image of **God**, is fallen and caught in the entail of **original sin**, and is redeemed by **Jesus Christ**. The status of human beings as created and the universality of sin as stemming from the entail are reflected in the forms of prayer and confession in use in the various **provinces**. These doctrines are set out with some Calvinist rigor in **Articles** IX–XVII and are reflected in the forms of general confession provided in **Morning and Evening Prayer** and in **Holy Communion** in the 1552 and 1662 **Books of Common Prayer**.

AOTEAROA. "Aotearoa" is the Maori term for New Zealand, meaning "The long white cloud," and since 1992 the **province** of New Zealand has been named the "Anglican Church in Aotearoa, New Zealand, and Polynesia." The change in title reflects a change in internal structure explained below.

The first white settlers came to New Zealand in the early years of the 19th century, and the first **eucharist** was celebrated on New Zealand soil by Samuel Marsden in 1812. In 1840 the Treaty of Waitangi secured the future of the land as British territory, and organized immigration began. The first **bishop**, **George Augustus Selwyn**, came in 1841 and remained bishop until 1868. He purchased land (the Selwyn Trust is a major financial asset to this day), built St.

John's **Theological College** in Auckland (almost before there were colleges in **England**), established **mission** stations, divided the **diocese**, created **synods**, and provided for a mission to **Melanesia**, to which in 1861 he **consecrated John Coleridge Patteson** as the first bishop. The province of New Zealand was formed in 1857, taking its place in the **Anglican Communion**. It in turn duly set the diocese of Melanesia free to become an autonomous province in 1975.

In 1989 New Zealand had eight dioceses (seven in New Zealand, plus Polynesia, with an additional "Maori jurisdiction"—which, although it covered the whole country, was then technically a **suffragan** see in the diocese of Waiapu). The **archbishopric** of the province arises from election by the House of Bishops, and the appointment is not tied to any one see. Diocesan synods meet annually and **General Synod** every other year.

The province is numerically small, scattered, and rural in its population, for New Zealand itself, which is comparable to England and **Scotland** together in size, has less than four million people. But the province has in recent decades had a notable history of ecclesiastical pioneering. In 1966 it provided the first authorized **liturgical** text in modern English; in 1970 it gave the first official permission for unconfirmed children to receive **Communion** on the basis of their **baptism**; in 1977 it was one of the first provinces to ordain **women** as **presbyters**; and in 1990 it provided the first woman diocesan bishop in the Anglican Communion, Penelope Jamieson, bishop of Dunedin.

In addition, New Zealand created a unique internal structure at its 1989 General Synod, and this came into effect in 1992. It was recognized that the people and congregations were separated from each other not just spatially but also ethnically. The province included Maori, European (or "*Pakeha*"), and Polynesian strands, and the church then acknowledged each of these as a distinct and distinctive *tikanga* or culture. Each has its own bishops, who—although they might overlap with each other geographically, and subject to the ultimate **authority** of General Synod (where the three tikangas meet and unite)—have relative independence as tikangas. The province of New Zealand was consequently renamed the Anglican Church in Aotearoa, New Zealand, and Polynesia (thus taking it to the top of the alphabetical list of Anglican provinces). The **primate** is now called not the "archbishop" but the "presiding bishop."

APOCRYPHA. The Apocrypha is the title usually given to certain books from the end of the Old Testament period that are found in the Greek version of the Hebrew scriptures, the Septuagint. The books concerned are missing from the Massoretic, or standard Hebrew, manuscripts and are not quoted as scripture by the New Testament authors (in distinction from the Old Testament books, almost all of which are quoted in the New Testament and cited as scripture). The books of the Apocrypha were given a semidefinitive place within the **canon** of scripture by Jerome, when he translated the Hebrew and Greek scriptures into Latin and published the "Vulgate," or standard Latin text, in the fifth century of the Christian era. He himself, however, acknowledged in his preface that the Apocryphal books did not have the same standing as the canonical books.

In Article VI of the Thirty-Nine **Articles** of 1571, the Apocryphal books are listed, and the Church of **England**, with a reservation to be noted below, confirmed that selected Apocryphal passages could be read in church in place of the canonical books, but "the Church doth not look to them to establish any **doctrine** thereby" but "readeth them for instruction in life and manners"—and quoted Jerome's own preface as the basis for this distinction. It appears that the Reformers were keen to dislodge the Apocrypha from canonical status, at least in part because in 2 Macc. 12.39–45 there is apparently explicit encouragement to engage in **petitions for the departed**. For exactly the same reason, the **Roman Catholic** authorities kept the Apocrypha within the canon and insisted that the Reformers were bowdlerizing the **Bible** in excising it.

It is worth noting, in order to understand the division of opinion, that, in the 15 centuries of the Christian church prior to the Reformation, there had been no definition of the canon and of its limits by a General Council. It was, in formal terms, an open question awaiting resolution, but Jerome's preface to the Vulgate was highly germane evidence. The historical process until that point had been that the canonical books of the Bible had, as it were, chosen themselves. The definition of the canon in Article VI has always underlain the question to **deacons** at **ordination** as to whether they "unfeignedly believe the canonical scriptures of the Old and New Testaments."

Historically, the Apocrypha was regularly printed between the two Testaments in the "Authorized Version" (**King James Version**) until the beginning of the 19th century. Select passages from it (in theory only such as were useful "for instruction in life and manners") were designated for reading in public worship in the Prayer Book **lectionary**. After the **Puritans** complained about Apocryphal passages at the **Savoy Conference** in 1661, the revision that followed contained Apocryphal additions (e.g., of Bel and the Dragon) that arguably went beyond the utilitarian provision and seem to have been introduced specifically to annoy the Puritans.

When the British and Foreign Bible Society was formed in 1804, at an early stage a policy decision was made to print the Bible in the various **languages** of countries where overseas **missionaries** were working—but without the Apocrypha. In the years since then, it has become normal, outside of Roman Catholic circles, to print Bibles without the Apocrypha. As a result, binding Old and New Testaments together without the Apocrypha is now thought to be normal and the addition of the Apocrypha is a relatively rare exception. Many **provinces**, however, still include Apocryphal readings (sometimes with a canonical alternative) in their lectionaries. Roman Catholic Bibles, in conformity to the Council of **Trent**, invariably include the Apocrypha.

APOLO KIVEBULAYA (c. 1864–1933). Apolo (as he is known—"Kivebulaya" is more like a nickname) was a Baganda from the west part of what is now **Uganda**. While nominally a Moslem, he met **Alexander Mackay** and other **Church Missionary Society** (CMS) **missionaries** around 1884 and was deeply impressed. When the "Christian Revolution" occurred in 1890, he was forced to join the Moslem army, but, sickened by the cruelty he encountered, deserted and joined the **Protestant** Christians in Ankole. He decided to "read" the Protestant literature, primarily the **Bible**, which was in effect to prepare for **baptism**. In 1893 he was part of a British-led, largely Sudanese, army of pacification to Toro and was there further influenced by missionary George Pilkington. When he returned in 1894, Apolo asked for baptism, and after he was baptized on 27 January 1895, immediately asked to become a teacher. He quickly became an itinerant lay **evangelist**, and in 1896 became the first to preach the **gospel** across the border to the west in Mboga (later called Boga), in what is now **Congo** but was then disputed territory. This led to the first baptisms in the area. Sometime around 1898, possibly when he was briefly imprisoned on a mistaken charge, he had a vision of Christ that deepened his spiritual life and empowered his preaching and teaching. He was **ordained** as a **deacon** by Bishop Tucker in 1900 and as a **presbyter** in 1903. From then until his death, he conducted an itinerant **ministry**, visiting and revisiting converts and congregations, at intervals crossing back to Mboga, where the church seems to have regularly declined between his visits. From 1921 on, he added a ministry to the pygmy people whose forests came close to Mboga. On his death, Apolo left extensive diaries, but he also left a profound impression of Christianity lived to the full, and this is marked by the title of his biography, *African Saint*.

APOSTLES' CREED. The Apostles' Creed is a brief summary of apostolic teaching, though it is not traceable as a formula to the first century. It derives from the **baptismal** confession that developed from the second century onward. It became used also by **monastic** communities within the daily offices; and in this role, as well as in its baptismal one, it passed into the 1549 **Book of Common Prayer** in **Morning and Evening Prayer**. It has also since 1549 been one of the formulas expounded in the **catechism**, and for several centuries it could be found with the **Ten Commandments** and the **Lord's Prayer** displayed on the walls of church buildings. It stands with the **Nicene Creed** as the second of the four sides of the **Lambeth Quadrilateral**.

APOSTOLIC SUCCESSION. The phrase "apostolic succession" was in use in some Anglican circles as early as 1800. It refers to the unbroken lineage of **bishops** (carrying the apostolic **authority**) from the time of the apostles, evidenced by a continuous succession of the laying on of hands during **ordination** of bishops. This process has conveyed to the Church of **England** bishops a linear tactual descent, as by a pedigree, from the original apostles themselves. It was, of course, a claim to continuity from the apostles that was also maintained by **Roman Catholics**, but care about the succession of bishops was a hallmark of the separated autonomous Church of England from King **Henry VIII**'s reign onward—most notably seen in the **consecration** of **Matthew Parker** to be **archbishop** of **Canterbury**

at **Lambeth Palace** in December 1559 near the beginning of Queen **Elizabeth I**'s reign. At a time when most bishops were opposed to the new severance from Rome and were unwilling to participate in the Elizabethan settlement, four reforming bishops were sought out to consecrate Parker as the new archbishop before he could take office. Similar care was exercised in the conveying of **episcopacy** to **Scotland** in 1610 and 1661 and in the reestablishing of the English **episcopate** itself in 1660–1661 and, to a lesser extent, in 1690–1691. The importance of succession clearly passed also into the bloodstream of the **nonjurors** and was seen in their Episcopal consecrations. The efforts to get **Samuel Seabury** consecrated by three undoubted bishops in 1783–1784 reflect the same concern.

Until 1833, this idea—"apostolic succession"—was present in the wings of theological discussion (**John Henry Newman** claimed to have learned it as a **doctrine** from William James in 1823). But the **Tractarians** brought it from the wings into a center-stage position, and the great single thrust of the *Tracts for the Times* is the importance of "our apostolical descent." The requirements of the preface to the **Ordinal** in 1550, 1552, and 1662 that the existing **orders** of **ministry** should be "continued" by the use of the forms of Episcopal ordination contained in the respective ordinals were invoked as the charter for the claim to such descent—a descent, it was argued, which had been guarded by the Reformers, rather than appearing as a mere accident of history. In an "**Augustinian**" theory of orders, unbroken "descent" is the only criterion to be fulfilled for **validity**, just as Augustine of Hippo had urged the recognition of Donatist **baptisms** and ordinations as valid acts even though he was writing roughly a hundred years after the catholic and Donatist strands of North African Christianity had split apart.

The **Anglo-Catholic** part of the **Anglican Communion** has continued to lay enormous emphasis upon the apostolic succession as guaranteeing the authenticity of the Anglican churches, the good standing of their ordinations, and thus the validity of their **sacraments**. Such emphasis upon the issue of orders links the Anglican Churches with the **Roman Catholic Church** as being similar, and closely related, historic churches. It has also been a foundational issue in the recognition by the Anglican churches of the **Old Catholic Churches**, and in the 1996 **Porvoo** Declaration of mutual recognition and interchangeability of **ministers** between the Scandinavian and Baltic Episcopal **Lutheran Churches** and the Anglican Churches of Britain and **Ireland**. That very emphasis, however, has made reunion with non-Episcopal churches difficult. The **Lambeth Quadrilateral** (1888) included as the last of its four sides "an agreed form of ministry" as a necessary condition of reunion. It then forecast that this would prove in practice to mean that uniting Churches would have to be episcopally ordered (it did not employ the term "apostolic succession," preferring "**historic episcopate**"). This particular insistence has been determinative of most moves by Anglican **provinces** toward reunion with non-Episcopal churches in the 20th century. As the Anglican provinces have asserted the true historicity and Christian standing of their episcopate **vis-à-vis** Rome (where **Pope** Leo XIII in ***Apostolicae Curae*** in 1896 called Anglican orders invalid), so it has seemed important to many Anglicans not to compromise the succession in dealings with non-Episcopal churches.

However, as severe doubts have arisen about whether the original Tractarian claims for the apostolic succession are sustainable, the names have changed slightly. There has been a widespread view that, if "apostolic succession" has relevant meaning at all, it is the whole church—bishops, **presbyters**, **deacons**, and **laity** together—who are in that succession, even if an unbroken line of bishops may be adduced as a visible sign or symbol of it and may be valued as such. It is this wider concept that has led to a labeling of the Episcopal part in the succession as the "historic episcopate." Whether the "historic" features of that episcopate can actually be traced back historically to the first-century apostles has also been called into question, as has whether demonstrating an unbroken succession is even actually of great theological or ecclesiological significance.

APOSTOLICAE CURAE. In 1896 **Pope** Leo XIII issued an encyclical concerning Anglican **orders**, of which the first two words in the Latin text (and thus the title) were *Apostolicae curae* ("[It belongs] to our apostolic care"). It has appeared to Anglicans that the pope, under some pressure from the **Roman Catholic** hierarchy in England, wished to condemn Anglican orders as invalid, and thus was seeking a theological basis for that particular conclusion. But, because the

Roman Catholic theory of orders has always been strictly **Augustinian**, the pope could not simply reach his conclusion by saying, "Because these supposed orders were conferred outside the framework of the true Church, they are, by that sheer fact, invalid." To conform with Roman Catholic historical theology, which allows the possibility that true orders can be conferred in schism, there had to be another basis.

Along with some lightweight flanking points (such as that, in the 1552 **Book of Common Prayer**, **Thomas Cranmer** omitted any mention at the laying on of hands as to *which* order it was that was being conferred—a lack which was corrected in 1662), the central thrust of the encyclical was that, at the **Reformation**, the Church of **England** abandoned all **doctrine** of **mass** sacrifice (a point that brought **eucharistic** rites under scrutiny as well as **ordination** ones). The argument ran that, if there were no sacrifice of the mass, there could be no ecclesial "intention" of ordaining true **priests** to offer this sacrifice, and Anglican orders are thus "absolutely null and utterly void" through this defect of intention. While the encyclical is not an *ex cathedra* **infallible** judgment, its own conclusion says that it is not open to revision, and the Roman Catholic Church has always treated newcomers who had previously received Anglican orders as in fact **laypeople**.

The **archbishops** of **Canterbury** and **York** made a joint reply in 1897, entitled ***Saepius Officio***. This rejects most of the grounds alleged, though claiming that in some sense the Anglican churches do believe in the **eucharistic sacrifice**. *See* APOSTOLIC SUCCESSION.

ARCHANGELS. In the scriptures there is but one archangel, Michael (Jude 9, cf. Rev. 12.7 and 1 Thess. 4.16); this evidence of there being but one would appear to be marginally supported by the title of the festival "St. Michael and All **Angels**." On the other hand, the lead-in to the Sanctus in the **eucharistic prayer** has from earliest times included "with angels and archangels," both categories being in the plural. "Saint Gabriel" and "Saint Raphael" have also been conventionally described as archangels, which in Gabriel's case goes beyond the text of scripture (Dan. 8.15, 9.21; Luke 1.19, 1.26) and in Raphael's is dependent upon **Apocryphal** texts (Tobit 12.12, 12.15).

ARCHBISHOP. An archbishop is the chief **bishop** in a **province**—"arch-" means "chief"—also called the "**metropolitan**." The powers held by a metropolitan in the **Anglican Communion** vary from province to province according to the **canons** or constitution of each. In some churches, for example in the **Episcopal Church (United States of America)** (ECUSA) and the **Scottish** Episcopal church, the metropolitan is not called "archbishop" but has a different title. In some Anglican churches, such as those of **Canada**, **Australia**, and **Nigeria**—not to mention **England** and **Ireland**—there are several ecclesiastical provinces, each with an archbishop and together comprising a single church. In Canada, where (as in ECUSA) the **primate** does not have a particular **diocese** or province of which he is bishop or archbishop, the primate nevertheless carries the title "archbishop."

"Archbishop" is a title that relates not to **orders**, but to a specific **ministerial** office, and the title is properly dropped in favor of "bishop" when the bearer of the title relinquishes the office. Archbishops are conventionally identified in protocol as "The Most Reverend," and the traditional style of address in formal circles, still found in some places (though the bishops at the 1968 **Lambeth Conference** disavowed any such titles), has been "Your Grace." *See also* ARMAGH; CANTERBURY; DUBLIN; YORK.

ARCHBISHOP OF CANTERBURY. *See* CANTERBURY.

ARCHDEACON. While in origin archdeacons were simply chief **deacons**, the title in Anglicanism today usually refers to a **presbyter** who is next in **authority** to the **bishop** in the administration of a **diocese**, covering a territorial subdivision of the diocese known as an archdeaconry. It is an appointment, not an **order**, and it may be held by, for example, a **suffragan** bishop, in combination with his or her Episcopal role. A diocese may have one or more archdeaconries within it, and the responsibilities of an archdeacon will be partly statutory or canonical (and consequently vary according to the constitution of the **province** or diocese and the policy of the diocesan bishop). Anglican **ordination** rites traditionally assume that an archdeacon has prepared and examined the candidates before ordination, and for that reason the archdeacon presents them to the bishop within the rite. The formal identification of an archdeacon is as "The Venerable."

ARCHIEPISCOPAL. *See* ARCHBISHOP.

ARCHITECTURE. While in the New Testament there are no identifiable buildings for Christian worship and Christians tended to keep a very low profile during times of persecution, once Constantine had issued his decree, buildings of every sort flourished, much of it of a scale and opulence far beyond the actual local needs for worship and sometimes in distinct competition with other grand buildings. Christendom has thus bequeathed an architectural inheritance still often in use, of which a major phenomenon in England is some thousands of medieval church buildings (frequently in a "**Gothic**" style) that provide one great continuity of the Church of **England** through the **Reformation** period. The **Books of Common Prayer** of King **Edward VI** (that is, in 1549 and 1552) tended to assume a two-room building, of **nave** and **chancel**, and their **rubrics** reflected the new **liturgical** use to which the rooms were being put.

There have been subsequent fashions of architecture for new church buildings—broadly speaking, of a classical style in the 18th century; of "Gothic Revival" in the 19th century, subsequent to the **Oxford Movement**; and a somewhat freer approach often with a one-room worship chamber of a more obviously functional sort in the 20th. These various fashions have spread around the world, and the celebration of the liturgy is vitally affected, sometimes adversely, by the particular building within which it is celebrated. Because of these differing architectural fashions inherited from the past, rubrics in modern services rarely refer to nave or chancel or any architectural feature that assumes a particularity of architectural style.

Anglicanism inherited from its historical origins the particular concept of a "**cathedral**" as a large central church in each **diocese**, where the **bishop** would keep his "seat" or *cathedra*. *See also* BASILICAN.

AREA BISHOP. In some parts of the **Anglican Communion**, **suffragan** or assistant **bishops** each take special responsibility for one part, or "area," of the territory of the diocesan bishop, and exercise some of the **ministry** of the diocesan bishop within their own areas by formal delegation of powers. In the Church of **England**, the formal bestowing of powers on area bishops comes through incorporating the case for the division of any **diocese** into areas into an "area scheme."

ARMAGH. Armagh is a small town in Northern Ireland, the senior archiepiscopal seat of both the Church of **Ireland** and the **Roman Catholic Church** in Ireland, both of which trace their origins and formation to **St. Patrick** (c. 390–460). While the date of the foundation of the **diocese** by Patrick cannot be exactly traced, the likelihood that it occurred before 450 and possibly as early as 444 gives Armagh a strong claim to be the oldest see in the **Anglican Communion**.

ARTICLES OF RELIGION. After the split from Rome in 1534, the way chosen, by King **Henry VIII** and by those who came after him, to ensure continuity of the Church in the faith was to provide "Articles of Belief." In 1536 there were the Ten Articles, marginally distanced from **Roman Catholic** belief; these were followed in 1539 by the Six Articles, of a highly reactionary and unreformed sort. **Thomas Cranmer** obviously thought that the provision of **doctrinal** articles of belief was integral to the **Reformation**, and in 1553, just before the death of King **Edward VI**, he produced the Forty-Two Articles, thoroughly on the reformed side. Finally, these were slightly altered and were enforced during Queen **Elizabeth I**'s reign as the Thirty-Nine Articles of 1571. They were issued in both English and Latin, and the two languages of the text are equally authoritative and were intended to interpret each other. They have remained the basic confession of faith of the Church of **England** since then, although in the Church of **Ireland**, from 1615 to 1634, they were replaced by a more detailed code of 104 Articles of a more strongly Calvinistic character.

In the Church of England, under the Clerical Subscription Act 1865 and the related **canons**, the Thirty-Nine Articles were subscribed in total by the candidate at **ordination** and by the ordained person on being instituted or licensed thereafter (and they were to be read in full from the pulpit by the newly instituted incumbent on the Sunday following his institution). The **Declaration of Assent** used since 1975 presents the Articles more as a historic witness to the doctrine of the Church and less as a dogmatic foundation of it.

In the **Protestant Episcopal Church in the United States of America**, the Articles were authorized by the **General Convention** of 1801 in a form that prints the whole text but imposes a revised and reduced form, not least by the excision of references to monarchs and royalty. Other **provinces** have dealt with the Articles in different ways.

In essence the doctrinal character of the Thirty-Nine Articles is that of a mild Calvinism. They assert the supreme **authority** of scripture, **justification** through faith alone, and a reformed doctrine of the **sacraments**, including the reduction in the number of sacraments from the medieval seven to the reformed two—**baptism** and the **Lord's Supper**. They are strongly antipapal and acknowledge also that General **Councils** not only may err but have erred. They also guard against the errors of Anabaptists and other fanatics. They assert the royal supremacy very strongly.

Because of their reformed character, the Articles were generally viewed by the original **Tractarians** as an obstacle to their own growth and progress as a movement. It was this factor that led **John Henry Newman** in 1841 to devote Tract 90 to a lengthy (and, by general consent, casuistical) restatement of the meaning of the Articles to demonstrate that the text of the Articles was, despite appearances, totally compatible with full Roman Catholic doctrine. This has been generally deemed unsuccessful in actually changing the **Protestant** meaning of the Articles, and it has been more usual for **Anglo-Catholics** to deny the authority of the Articles than to attempt to distort their meaning to that extent.

The text of the Thirty-Nine Articles of 1571 appears in appendix B. *See also* IRISH ARTICLES; LAMBETH ARTICLES.

ASCENSION. The ascension of **Jesus Christ**, recounted in Acts 1.1–11, is an article of the **Creed**; it is foundational to the Anglican approach to the Father through Christ, and it is also specifically celebrated every year on the Thursday of the week of the fifth Sunday after **Easter** (or of the sixth Sunday *in* Easter), which is 40 days from the **Resurrection** (cf. Acts 1.3). It passed in the fourth century into the celebrations in **Jerusalem** in which the believers attempted to follow the footsteps of the Lord, and thus in turn it became a general Christian celebration. It has been retained in all Anglican **calendars**, and it ranks as a principal holy day. The theme of the Lord's ascension is usually sustained on the following Sunday, the sixth after

Easter (or seventh in Easter). Many **parish** churches have a dedication as "Church of the Ascension."

ASH WEDNESDAY. The first day of **Lent** is called "Ash Wednesday." It originated in the enrollment of **catechumens** for the period of preparation leading to **baptism** at **Easter**, from which Lent itself is derived. Thus the day is also traditionally the beginning of Lenten **fasting** for the whole church. The use of ashes within the **liturgy**, traceable in the West to before the 10th century, stems from the Jewish background of using ashes to express sorrow and self-humiliation (cf. Matt. 11.21), though there has usually been a secondary theme of a reminder of mortality (cf. Gen. 3.19). The **imposition of ashes** was prohibited by the 1549 **Book of Common Prayer**, which inaugurated instead the **commination** service. In **Thomas Cranmer**'s Prayer Books, the day was entitled "the First Day of Lent, commonly called Ash Wednesday"—a clear indication that the old title was now viewed as misleading. The use of ashes has slowly reappeared in some Anglican **provinces** over the last 100 years under the influence of the **Anglo-Catholic** movement, and consequently official provision is now made within modern Prayer Books, as in the Church of **England**'s *Lent, **Holy Week**, Easter*. There is a widespread custom of burning palm crosses distributed on the previous year's Palm Sunday in order to provide the ashes for use on Ash Wednesday.

ASSEMBLY, CHURCH. *See* ENABLING ACT; ESTABLISHMENT.

ASSUMPTION. There is a devotional tradition, covering many centuries in the **Roman Catholic Church**, that **Mary**, the Mother of the Lord, being without sin, did not suffer the corruption of her body in, through, or after death, but instead was "assumed" (bodily) directly into **heaven**. The date of the commemoration of this event was 15 August, but in the Church of **England** that was struck from the **calendar** when the 1549 **Book of Common Prayer** was compiled.

Until 1950 in the Roman Catholic Church the belief was a widespread pious conviction, without being **doctrinally** entrenched, and had had distinguished persons oppose it at intervals in history. However, in 1950 **Pope** Pius XII declared it, *ex cathedra*, to be part of the revealed Christian faith, to be believed as *de fide*. The form of the decree left open whether she was "assumed" while still alive or her body was assumed shortly after her death.

Anglicans in general have been unconvinced about the Assumption, not only because of the lateness in history of the papal decree but more because there is no mention of this event in scripture; neither have Anglicans found the underlying doctrine of the **Immaculate Conception** (and of Mary's sinlessness) in scripture, and they have thus not reached in large numbers the deductive conclusion from it. However, in various ways, the observance of the date of 15 August has been reintroduced into Anglican calendars, sometimes, as in the **Episcopal Church (United States of America)** (ECUSA), as simply the Feast Day of the Blessed Virgin Mary. Nevertheless, ECUSA, in its 1979 Book of Common Prayer, has a **collect** drafted to be open to differing interpretations: "Lord, you have taken to yourself the Blessed Virgin Mary." But the simple dedication, without further qualification, would strongly suggest that it is the day when, as with the days commemorating apostles and **martyrs**, the commemoration is specifically of her death (and may even have originated from a belief that she died on that date).

The doctrine of the Assumption is one of those clear points where Anglicans have regularly told Roman Catholics that they have created a credal requirement out of an unscriptural and highly arguable speculation. It remained initially as a barrier between the two Churches in the **Anglican–Roman Catholic International Commission** (ARCIC) agreements. ARCIC-1's **Authority** statements in 1976 and 1981 treated it as disputed by Anglicans and in need of serious treatment in future statements, but the doctrine was completely evaded in 1999 in the ARCIC-2 agreed report *The Gift of Authority*. Instead, ARCIC-2 delayed treatment of the subject until its agreed statement *Mary: Grace and Hope in Christ* in 2005.

ATHANASIAN CREED. The lengthy confession of faith known as the Athanasian Creed almost certainly dates from the fifth century and, unlike the **Apostles'** and **Nicene Creeds**, defends **Chalcedonian** orthodoxy about the **Trinity** and Christology with anathemas. Its **doctrinal** detail and choice of language make it virtually certain that Athanasius was not the author. It was retained by the **Reformers** and was entrenched in principle in **Article** VIII of the Thirty-Nine Articles, and in the **Book of Common Prayer** provision to use it at **Morning Prayer** on 13 occasions in the year in place of the Apostles' Creed. It was printed in the 1549, 1552, and 1662 Books under the title *Quicunque Vult*, the first two words of the Latin text, at the end of Morning Prayer. In the 19th century, doubts arose as to its suitability to be used **liturgically** as a creed, and in the **Lambeth Quadrilateral** of 1888 it was specifically omitted from the second clause, which concerned only two creeds, the Apostles' and the Nicene. It has been almost wholly omitted from 20th-century revisions of Morning and Evening Prayer, though its text is often retained, for instance, in the **Canadian** Books of Common Prayer of 1918 and 1959, in an appendix to the **Episcopal Church (United States of America)** Book of Common Prayer of 1979, or in a similar appendix to *A Prayer Book for* ***Australia****, 1995*. The heart of it has been retouched as a canticle in the Church of **England**'s *Patterns for Worship*.

AUGUSTINE OF CANTERBURY (543?–604). Augustine, the prior of St. Andrew's **monastery** in Rome, in 596 was commissioned by **Pope** Gregory the Great to take the **gospel** to the "Angles"—the Anglii, a pagan tribe in southeast Britain from which the pope had encountered some youths in the slave-market—better known to us today as "Anglo-Saxons." Augustine set out, then turned back from the task, and then very reluctantly reaccepted it. He landed with a band of followers at Ebbsfleet (a sandbar off the east coast of Kent) in 597 and led them to **Canterbury**, the seat of Ethelbert, the king of Kent. There he was welcomed at the court, as the queen, Bertha, was already Christian. He preached and administered his first **baptisms** there (quite possibly in the **parish** church of St. Martin's, which is still standing and in use). After crossing the Channel again to be **consecrated** as a **bishop** in Arles, Augustine used Canterbury as his base for spreading the gospel over the land. He founded the next see at Rochester in 604, the year of his death.

Today the **archbishopric** of Canterbury is often identified as "St. Augustine's chair." He was recognized by Rome as a **saint** from early times, and his Feast Day is 26 May.

AUGUSTINIANISM. Augustine of Hippo (354–430) clashed with the British heretic **Pelagius** over the fallen nature of the human race.

Pelagius emphasized free will and the power of the human will to achieve good results by sheer effort, while Augustine emphasized **original sin**, the bondage of the will, and the necessity for **God**'s love to be sovereign if people are to receive it—and this in turn introduced predestination. The emphasis of the Middle Ages lay much closer to Pelagius, but at the **Reformation**, Augustinianism was revived, particularly by Martin Luther and John Calvin but also with a strong impact in **England**. The doctrine of predestination duly passed into the Thirty-Nine **Articles** (*see* appendix B, Articles XV–XVII), but in a slightly restrained form of expression.

Augustine's teaching has also had a great effect upon the ministering of **baptism**—especially in emergency—as Augustine taught, along with his doctrine of original sin, the absolute necessity of baptism if an infant were to be delivered from God's judgment. This created a framework of belief in which, right through the Middle Ages, infants were frequently baptized by midwives straight after birth. To this day, sufficient relics of folk memory remain for there to be a constant call for "clinical" baptism of infants in danger of death. *See also* APOSTOLIC SUCCESSION.

AUMBRY. A lockable cupboard, usually inset into the wall near the east end of a church building, or sometimes in a side chapel, where consecrated **eucharistic elements** (usually **bread** only, in the form of wafers) may be **reserved** for later use. *See also* PYX; TABERNACLE.

AURICULAR CONFESSION. *See* ABSOLUTION.

AUSTRALIA. The first Anglican presence in Australia arose from and with the first convict ships establishing New South Wales as a colony in 1788, for they carried a chaplain, Richard Johnson, who was one of the associated emigrants. In 1824, when the second **bishop** of **Calcutta** was appointed, far distant Australia and New Zealand were specifically included in his **diocese**. In 1836 William Grant Broughton was **consecrated** as the first bishop of Australia. Bishops of New Zealand and Tasmania were added in 1841 and 1842, respectively. Then, with the appointment in 1847 of bishops of Adelaide, Melbourne, and Newcastle (New South Wales), Broughton became the bishop specifically of **Sydney** and also the **province**'s **metropolitan**. At that stage, there was little national unity across the enormous distances, though distances were somewhat reduced in 1857 when New Zealand became a separate province. One instance of a commonality of purpose was the formation at a public meeting in 1850 of an Australian **Board of Missions** (ABM). A consultative, though fully constituted, **General Synod** began in 1872, and at its first meeting gave formal standing to the ABM. This led to pioneer **evangelism** among aboriginal people and Torres Straits Islanders.

Over the next 90 years, the dioceses divided and groups of dioceses became provinces generally corresponding to the states—New South Wales, Victoria, Queensland, and western Australia, with Tasmania as an extraprovincial diocese. South Australia did not become a separate ecclesiastical province until 1973. Churches in the Northern Territory belong to Queensland province; **Papua New Guinea** was also a diocese within the province of Queensland until 1977, when it too became a separate province.

Although the nation of Australia became a self-governing federal commonwealth on 1 January 1901, even in the 20th century the Anglican dioceses were, on legal advice, deemed to be still part of the Church of **England**, bound by English laws. In 1962 a new constitution was adopted for the Anglican church of the whole country—though, under strong pressure from the Sydney bishops, it initially retained the title "Church of England in Australia." The constitution left great diocesan autonomy; with such vast distances to bridge, the General Synod was to meet only once every four years (though extraordinary meetings have been held at times, and the ordinary period was reduced in the 1990s to three years instead of four). A need for high diocesan autonomy has also arisen from the somewhat polarizing or centrifugal theological forces in differing dioceses, of which the evangelicalism of the diocese of Sydney has been the most prominent. The **primate** is chosen from among all the diocesan bishops by a specially convened Board of Electors, without the primacy attaching to any one metropolitical see. In 1981 the name of the church was changed to the Anglican Church of Australia.

AUTHORITY. "Authority" in the church has two wholly separate meanings. First, there is *authority for belief*, which was the great principle at stake at the **Reformation**; the issue was whether the authority of scripture in mediating the knowledge of **God** and his truth was both supreme and transparent. While the assertion that the findings of scripture could not be overthrown by the **pope** started King **Henry VIII** on the path to nullifying his marriage to Catharine, and thus led to independence from Rome, the Church of **England** that emerged from the later Tudor reigns had greatly reinforced this principle.

To take one instance, the Church of England adhered to the **Creeds** only "for they may be proved by most certain warrants of holy Scripture" (**Article** VIII). This was in contradistinction to the teachings of the **Council** of **Trent** (1546–1563) that authority for belief comes from twin sources (both of which are the word of God): the written word of the scriptures, and the unwritten word handed down from the apostles in the **tradition** of the church and only discerned in written form as it historically finds expression in later writers or Council formulations. The Reformers made the distinction very clear in their insistence that nothing was to be taught as integral to salvation save what could be proved or demonstrated from the scriptures themselves.

The **Anglo-Catholic** movement in effect enthroned tradition over scripture, producing the slogan "the church to teach and the **Bible** to prove," and it has been normal for Anglicans to treat tradition as a source of **doctrine**. The issue is actually whether it is an *autonomous* source, which is what it becomes if all scriptural teaching is filtered through tradition and tradition is not itself open to reform by the direct teaching of scripture. But it is not only in the Thirty-Nine Articles and **Thomas Cranmer**'s **ordination rites** that the supremacy of scripture itself is asserted; the same is to be found in the **Lambeth Quadrilateral**, affirmed and reaffirmed at the **Lambeth Conferences** of 1888, 1920, and 1958, where the first "side" listed is the scriptures as "being the rule and ultimate standard of faith."

Tradition is an inevitable feature of the handing on of the faith and the conveying of God's word from generation to generation, and Anglican churches accept this and make much of tradition in this sense, but subject to the supreme authority of scripture. Some modern statements also treat "reason" as a source of truth—indeed they may speak of scripture, tradition, and reason as a "three-legged stool"—but reason is more a tool than a source and is employed in the seeking and applying of truth contained in scripture and conveyed in tradition.

Second, there is *authority of office*. Thus Anglicans have located responsibility for governing and sustaining the church with different authorities, that is, persons or institutions with constitutional or conventional legislative and overseeing roles in relation to the church. These have included (in times and places of the Anglican church being **established**) the monarch in Parliament, and almost everywhere the **episcopate**, the local **clergy**, and various forms of **synodical** association of **bishops**, clergy, and **laity** together. There have been three **Anglican–Roman Catholic International Commission** (ARCIC) statements on "authority"; the third, entitled *The Gift of Authority*, was published by ARCIC-2 in 1999. These have wrestled with ways the **Anglican Communion** could recognize the authority of the pope as "universal **primate**," but their findings have been controversial among Anglicans.

Because neither of these forms of authority appears to be simple, single, and clearly defined, Anglicans have often used the phrase "dispersed authority." This was first used by the 1948 Lambeth Conference with reference to authorities for belief, but in that case the phrase was located there only after an assertion of the primary place of scripture in revelation, and thus it referred solely to a distribution of secondary authorities. The phrase is neither a self-evident nor an univocal description of the working of authority within the Anglican Communion.

AZARIAH, SAMUEL (1874–1945). Azariah (as he was always known) was born to Christian parents, his father having been brought up as a Hindu, converted as an adult, and **ordained** in 1869. Azariah grew up as a strong Christian, spending his early adult years as secretary to the YMCA of South **India**; there he learned Christian leadership and gained such a **missionary** vision that in 1905 he joined with other Indian Christian leaders to found at Serampore the interdenominational National Missionary Society of India, of which he was appointed as the first secretary. The task was to stir Indian Christians into taking responsibility for the **evangelizing** of their own country, and this became a driving motive in Azariah's life. He met Henry Whitehead, the **bishop** of Madras (1899–1922), and was ordained as a **deacon** and **presbyter** in 1908. He addressed the 1910 **Edinburgh Mis-**

sionary Conference on cooperation between expatriate missionaries and native Christians in the younger Churches. Then in 1912 he was **consecrated** bishop of Dornakal (in Hyderabad), as the first Indian national to become an Anglican bishop. In the next 33 years he became known as an evangelist, teacher, organizer, and prophet. He drew a firm line between Christianity and Hinduism. Within the Christian churches, he was a prime mover of the events that led to the formation after his death of the Church of **South India**.

– B –

BANGLADESH. The state of Bangladesh arose as the name of the Bengali territory that between 1947 and 1970 constituted East **Pakistan**, a largely Muslim area. During these years, it was linked constitutionally and by its religion (which had separated it from **India**) to West Pakistan, but it was ravaged at the end of 1970 by the Pakistani army. When India intervened militarily because of the vast numbers of refugees crossing its borders, the separate state of Bangladesh was formed.

The united Church of Pakistan, which included the Church in East Pakistan, had just come into existence on 1 November 1970, but because of the political situation, the two **dioceses** in the new nation of Bangladesh formed themselves into the autonomous Church of Bangladesh in 1971. Their **bishops** were invited as guests to the **Lambeth Conferences** in 1978 and 1988, and the Church of Bangladesh became a full member of the **Anglican Communion** in 1990.

BAPTISM. Baptism is one of the two **sacraments** recognized by Anglicans as ordained by **Jesus Christ** himself, and having an outward and visible sign (the application of water) and an inward and spiritual "grace" (rebirth or regeneration). The **Reformers** inherited a pattern of infant baptism, a pattern deeply reliant upon the **Augustinian doctrine** of **original sin** and its remission. The English Reformers retained the practice of universal infant baptism, but still made provision for private (or "clinical") baptism. **Thomas Cranmer**'s baptismal rites of 1549 and 1552 used Mark 10.13–16 as a **Gospel**

reading and as a basis for an exhortation giving a brief and thin explanation as to why infant baptism was retained. So universal was infant baptism in **England** in those days that there was no need for a rite for the baptism of adolescents or adults, and none was provided.

The **Book of Common Prayer** baptismal rite was an insertion to come after the second lesson at **Morning** or **Evening Prayer**. The formula of baptism was "*N*., I baptize thee in the name of the Father and of the Son and of the Holy Ghost." In 1549 triple dipping was ordered, but in 1552 the requirement was reduced to a single dipping—in each case with pouring as a fallback alternative if the **godparents** certified the child could not withstand the shock of **submersion**. All secondary ceremonies were dropped through the two stages, except that in 1552 a signing with the **sign of the cross** was retained after baptism, the sole place where the sign of the cross remained in Anglican rites. As a mandatory ceremony, it attracted **Puritan** opposition for over 100 years, on the grounds that it was not commanded in scripture.

Article XXVII concerned baptism and stated that only in those who received baptism "rightly" (the Latin text says "*recte*") did it have a beneficial effect. In 1604 a section on sacraments was added to the Prayer Book **catechism**, which stated that baptism and the **Lord's Supper** were "generally necessary to salvation," a phrase that goes a little beyond the wording of Article XXV.

In 1662 a service for those "of riper years" was added, as many of those born since 1645 had escaped infant baptism during the **Commonwealth** period. The rite could not use Mark 10 as a reading, for obvious reasons, and instead it set out John 3.1–8 and a much more robust exhortation based on it. It appears likely that the **Restoration** leaders who brought in the 1662 Book did not expect the rite to be much needed in England after the initial catching up with those born during the Commonwealth period (1649–1660) had been completed, though the preface added that it might also be useful for "natives in our plantations and others converted to the faith." The **rubric** before the actual baptism still provided for dipping as the first mode of baptism, with pouring as an alternative. One rubric ordered the **clergyman** to inform the **bishop** of such baptisms, and another required the newly baptized to come before the bishop and be **confirmed** as quickly as possible.

A major adjudication on the meaning of the baptismal rite occurred in England in the **diocese** of Exeter in 1847–1850, when **Charles Gorham** was accused of **heresy** by his bishop, Henry Philpotts, on the grounds that he did not believe that all infants were invariably regenerated in baptism. Gorham was first found to be a heretic by the Court of Arches, the ecclesiastical court of the **province** of **Canterbury**, but, on appeal to the Judicial Committee of the Privy Council, his teachings were declared fully compatible with the Church of England's formularies.

In the years since 1950 there has been a widespread move to revise the baptismal rites around the **Anglican Communion**. Modern rites tend to locate baptism within a **eucharistic** context, and there have been moves to unite infant and adult baptism in a single celebration, often with confirmation also included. A much greater variety of readings is to be found, as is a fuller prayer over the water (or "blessing of the **font**"). Submersion has reappeared, particularly as there has been a growth in the incorporation of baptismal tanks into the fabric in new church buildings. Lesser ceremonies (such as the giving of a candle, **anointing**, or clothing in a white robe) have also been welcomed. In the case of infants, there have been various attempts in **liturgical** revision to nudge parents to confess their own faith as well as taking proxy vows on behalf of the infants. At the same time there has been a growing concern within the church that infant baptism should not be administered without real care being taken to build the parent or parents into the worshipping life of the church.

Because baptism is a once-for-life ceremony, the Anglican churches have never been able to accept applications for baptism from those who, having been baptized as infants, at a later stage of life deny that they have been truly baptized and so instead seek a "second" baptism. A renewal or reaffirmation of baptismal undertakings is as far as Anglican churches are able to go to meet this pastoral need, though in some places such renewal has been so arranged as to include submersion. *See also* BAPTISM IN THE SPIRIT; BAPTISTERY; GODPARENTS.

BAPTISM IN THE SPIRIT. The Anglican Reformers, citing John 3.1–8, identified the outward and the inward in Christian **initiation** as "**baptism** in water and the Spirit," though, as the **Gorham** controversy in the 19th century disclosed, they were careful to make the distinction that the outward did not automatically and invariably convey the inward (cf. **Article** XXVII of 1571). Many second-generation **Anglo-Catholics** in the late 19th century placed so much emphasis upon the gift of the Spirit in **confirmation** that they developed a two-stage **doctrine** of **sacramental** initiation, in which baptism in water was the first stage and confirmation, conferring baptism in the Spirit, was the second. This school of thought, sometimes dubbed the "Mason-**Dix** Line" (after two of its proponents) ran strongly in the **Anglican Communion** from around 1890 to around 1970. At the very point where it was losing its momentum, the term "baptism in the Spirit" was adopted by the **Charismatic Movement**, taking the term from its use in classic **Pentecostalism**. This detaches it from any sacramental ministration and identifies it with an experience of being swamped or extraordinarily overcome by the **Holy Spirit**, often (but not invariably) betokened by "speaking in **tongues**." In such usage it is not initiatory but a new step in discipleship. It relies upon the same (relatively few) texts of scripture as the confirmation school, though, because it is highly experiential, it is commended on experiential rather than exegetical grounds.

BAPTIST CHURCHES. The Baptist churches through the world are the heirs of a radical **Protestantism** arising within the **Reformation** era in Europe, often labeled as "Anabaptist" (as *ana-* means "again" as a Greek prefix). The churches are generally characterized by their distinguishing features of a nonrecognition of infant **baptism** and a congregational independence and autonomy. They thus appear well distanced from traditional Anglicanism, though in many cases they are **ecumenically** oriented. Observers from the Baptist World Alliance have attended **Lambeth Conferences**, and at the 1988 conference, Resolution 10 requested the **Anglican Consultative Council** to initiate conversations with the Alliance to begin a dialogue. This did not occur and so became the subject of Resolution IV.15 at the 1998 Lambeth Conference. In 2000 formal Anglican–Baptist International Conversations (ABIC) were begun, and the dialogue was remitted to regional conversations, though these are serviced and coordinated by the participation of the central Continuation Group members in the regional meetings. The intention was that a five-year program would lead to a single major report in 2005. Within 12 months of beginning, conversations had been held in the regions of Europe (the Church of

England and the Baptist Union were in conversations from 1992 through 2005), Asia/Oceania, and Africa; Latin America, North America, and the Caribbean followed soon after.

BAPTISTERY. Technically, "baptistery" has traditionally meant the space (such as a room or chapel or area) in which **baptisms** take place and where the **font** is accordingly located. There has been a derived (though unhelpful) use of the term among other denominations, and sometimes among Anglicans, to denote a bath or tank sufficiently large for **submersion** of the candidates. This is, however, simply a variant form of font, and it muddles counsel to call it a "baptistery"; it may better be described as a "baptismal pool."

BASILICAN. The original shape of Christian church buildings, derived from Roman public buildings and larger private houses, was oblong, with a line of sight directed along the long axis to the east end. Set into the east wall there might well be an *apse* (sometimes entered through an arch), where the **eucharistic table** stood. At each side of the central aisle or seating would be a line of pillars, also following the long axis, supporting both the roof and the clerestory and giving a distinctive center aisle and side aisles to the interior. This shape and style, often entitled "Basilican" (from the Greek for a "palace"), was imitated quite widely in 18th-century church **architecture** in England, and **dissenting** chapels have used the pattern also. Many such buildings survive as places of worship to the present day.

BECKET, THOMAS À (1118–1170). Thomas à Becket was born in France. As a young man, he joined the household of **Archbishop** Theobald in **Canterbury** and was **ordained** as a **deacon** by him. In 1154 he became **archdeacon** of Canterbury, and in 1155 chancellor of King Henry II. His royal patron secured his election in 1162 as archbishop of Canterbury, and Becket then resigned as chancellor and gave himself to the promotion of the interests of the Church, even if this were to bring him into conflict with the king.

After Henry published the Constitutions of Clarendon in 1164, Becket opposed the transfer of the trial of **clergy** to secular courts and had to flee from Henry to France. A reconciliation with Henry was negotiated in 1170, and Becket returned to **England**, but then refused to absolve two **bishops** who had sided with Henry. Henry was furious and sent four knights to "rid me of that turbulent priest." They found Becket in his **cathedral** on 29 December 1170 and slew him there.

There was an outcry at this deed, and Becket was recognized immediately as a **martyr**. He was **canonized** by the **pope** in 1173 and was the subject of Henry's public **penance** the following year. His shrine in Canterbury Cathedral became a famous place of **pilgrimage**, until it was destroyed by King **Henry VIII** in 1538. This Henry had no wish for an archbishop who had been martyred through resisting a monarch to continue to be commemorated and known as a **saint**.

A shrine **altar** in Canterbury Cathedral today marks the place of his martyrdom. He is commemorated on 29 December in many Anglican **calendars**.

BEDE, SAINT (c. 673–735). Bede is sometimes called the "Father of English History," and certainly he comes to us as the earliest author of English Christian writings. He was a monk of Jarrow from a very early age and was **ordained** as a **deacon** around the age of 19 and as a **presbyter** at 30. He lived and died as a member of his community, devoting himself to study, to teaching, and to prolific writing. His crowning work was *A History of the English Church and People*. This provides our earliest consistent account of Celtic Christianity in the northeast, as well as recording the **Synod** of **Whitby** and the transition to Roman ways. Bede has been generally dignified as "The Venerable," though he has also been generally recognized since soon after his death as a **saint**, and there are many churches **dedicated** to his memory. His bones are buried in Durham **Cathedral**, and his **feast** day is 27 May.

BENEDICTION. While the Latinate word "benediction" simply means "blessing" and is in most uses interchangeable with "blessing" (e.g., in the phrase "grace and heavenly benediction" in **Thomas Cranmer**'s **Books of Common Prayer**), the word has also acquired a particular meaning as shorthand for "Benediction of the Blessed **Sacrament**." This is a quasi-liturgical short office that has come into use in the **Roman Catholic Church** since the Counter-**Reformation**, in which a reserved **consecrated** wafer is withdrawn from its place of **reservation**, placed in a monstrance, and then used for blessing the people. Its origins appear to lie in the medieval requirement that the **mass** must not be celebrated later than noon, and "Benediction" came in as an evening devotion. **Anglo-Catholics** borrowed its use from Rome from around the end of the 19th century onward, though, of course, this was an option only open to bold spirits who had already secured permanent reservation in their church buildings. In Rome itself, the permission to have evening masses, which was given in the 1950s by **Pope** Pius XII, undermined the need for Benediction, while the reforms of **Vatican II** and the emphasis upon **liturgical** integrity further undermined it, and it is clearly now on the decline. That is probably also mirrored in Anglicanism.

BENEDICTUS. The song attributed to Zechariah upon the birth of John the Baptist in Luke 1.68–79 passed into Christian worship at an early stage. It was retained (as scriptural) by **Thomas Cranmer** at the **Reformation**. The Benedictus is usually associated with morning "office" worship.

BENEDICTUS QUI VENIT. The short anthem "Blessed is he who comes in the name of the Lord; hosanna in the highest" derives from Psalm 118, and its application to the Messiah was prophesied by **Jesus Christ** (Luke 13.35) and was fulfilled on his triumphal entry into **Jerusalem** at the beginning of the passion week (Luke 19.38). From early times it was used in the **eucharist** after the Sanctus within the **canon**, and it still immediately followed the Sanctus within the Sarum canon from which **Thomas Cranmer** crafted the 1549 text. Cranmer retained the Benedictus Qui Venit in 1549, when the shape of the canon was similar to Sarum, but in 1552, when the order was radically changed, the Benedictus Qui Venit disappeared. The Sanctus now came after the opening dialogue and a short preface, but was followed by the Prayer of Humble Access.

While it has often been alleged that Cranmer thought that the words of the anthem pointed to a "physical" coming of Jesus (as in the original triumphal entry to Jerusalem) and that it was for this reason that he omitted it from the eucharist, it is far more likely that his reconstruction of the canon depended upon the logical and neat transition from "Holy, holy, holy" (the **angels**' song in the temple in the vision of Isaiah in Isa. 6) to the admission of sin and inadequacy in the Prayer of Humble Access (the equivalent of "I am undone; for I am a man of unclean lips, and I dwell in the midst of a people of unclean lips"—words which follow the angels' song in Isa. 6). The logic of this transition would have squeezed out the Benedictus Qui Venit from between Sanctus and Humble Access, irrespective of any question about **doctrinal** orthodoxy or about eucharistic overtones.

From the 19th century on, the anthem has been slipped in again in general Anglican usage, to follow the Sanctus as in the Roman rite. In modern revisions, where the Prayer of Humble Access has invariably been removed from the 1552 position immediately after the Sanctus, the tendency for the Benedictus Qui Venit to return and round up the Sanctus has been very strong, though it has sometimes been left optional and has also occasionally been left as a movable anthem, which may come at a different point in the rite.

In the Syrian tradition, which is followed by the Church of **South India**, the text runs "Blessed is he who has come and is to come in the name of the Lord."

BENSON, EDWARD WHITE (1829–1896). Benson became the first **bishop** of Truro in 1877 when it was formed by a dividing of the **diocese** of Exeter. He was translated to become **archbishop** of **Canterbury** in 1883, possibly because of a letter that **Randall Davidson**, who had been chaplain to Archbishop Tait when Tait died, wrote to Queen Victoria, expressing Davidson's understanding of Tait's preferences for the succession. In 1890, with only doubtful precedent to guide him, he formed an archbishop's court to try Edward King, the bishop of Lincoln, on charges of ritual misdemeanor. In 1896 **Pope** Leo XIII issued his encyclical ***Apostolicae Curae***, condemning Anglican **orders**, and Benson, before he died in autumn of that year, commissioned the drafting of the reply that was issued in the name of the two archbishops the following year as ***Saepius Officio***. His own life's study was realized in the posthumous publication of his massive *Cyprian: His Life, His Times, His Work*.

BERKELEY STATEMENT. The **International Anglican Liturgical Consultation** held its sixth gathering (IALC-6) at Berkeley, California, in August 2001. Earlier IALCs had previously made statements on **baptism** (the **Toronto Statement**, 1991) and on the **eucharist** (the **Dublin Statement**, 1995), and the sequence of topics in the **Lima** Statement led next to a consideration of **ordination**. IALC-6 was originally convened for Kerala in **South India** in 1999, but difficulties in getting full representation there delayed the consultation until 2001. The Berkeley Statement is entitled "To Equip the Saints" and sets out principles for ordination rites around the **Anglican Communion**.

BIBLE. The Bible is the book, itself a collection of books, which for Christians constitutes the unique and authoritative revelation of **God** and is therefore read centrally within public worship. It is the prime source for private reading, study, and meditation in the Christian faith, is taught in all places of Christian education, and is enshrined at the heart of articles of belief or statements of **doctrine**.

At the **Reformation**, the Church of **England** in its **Articles of Religion** and **Ordinal** defined the supremacy and sufficiency of the Bible for all matters of salvation in contradiction to the **Roman Catholic Church**'s claims. The assertion of the supremacy of the Bible was repeated in a different context by the **bishops** of the whole **Anglican Communion** in the **Lambeth Quadrilateral** (affirmed in 1888, 1920, 1958, and 1998), of which the first principle is "the Holy Scriptures as the ultimate standard and unique test of faith." The limits of the **canon** of scripture were defined in Article VI of 1571. The provision of **vernacular** Bibles was encouraged by state and church officials from 1537 until King **James I** at the **Hampton Court Conference** in 1604 ordered the new translation that in due course became the "Authorized" or **King James Version**.

It is part of the principle of the supremacy of the Holy Scriptures that the Bible is open for all believers to understand it. Preaching and teaching rely upon an open text freely available to hearers, learners, and worshippers. Anglicans have accordingly worked from the beginning of the **missionary** movements to provide vernacular Bibles in every country and **language** group. English translations have been regularly updated also, and care has been taken to provide liturgical **lectionaries**, scriptural teaching and preaching, and aids to personal Bible study as well.

BIBLE CHURCHMEN'S MISSIONARY SOCIETY (BCMS). A major **Evangelical** overseas **missionary society** of the Church of **England**, the Bible Churchmen's Missionary Society was founded through a split in the **Church Missionary Society** (CMS) in 1922. Criticism of CMS had arisen both within its supporters in England

and at times from senior missionaries overseas, who were receiving junior partners recently sent out to join them by the society. The criticisms related to a perceived tendency toward a more **liberal** theology being embraced by the officers and new recruits of the society than had been expected until World War I. The reaction led to a growing confrontation, and at the annual general meeting of CMS in 1922, the more conservative supporters made their protest and left to form the new society. They undertook that they would not work anywhere in the world where they would impede or rival the task of CMS, but would instead go to areas where no Anglican **evangelism** was in operation. BCMS founded a college for men in Bristol in 1925, the Bible Missionary Training College (this became a recognized **theological college** of the Church of England in 1927 and was renamed Tyndale Hall after World War II). A women's college (Dalton House) was founded by BCMS soon after this college, and these two united with a third (Clifton Theological College) to form Trinity College, Bristol, in 1971. The society itself achieved parity with the other major Anglican missionary societies in England in the 1960s, and in 1994 changed its name to Crosslinks.

BIRTH CONTROL. Although the Anglican churches have no entrenched position on birth control, it is worth noting that, while the 1930 **Lambeth Conference** condemned artificial means of birth control, the 1958 Conference by contrast commended responsible "family planning," which is widely secured through the use of artificial means. Such a commendation precludes recourse to "natural theology," as invoked by the **Roman Catholic Church**. In the final analysis, the attitude involved is deeply theological, insisting that the union of man and woman in **marriage** (Gen. 2.24) is deeper and more profound than would be implied by a statement that the primary and indefeasible purpose in sexual union is procreation. In the Genesis passage, the union does not particularly have children in view, but only the belonging of the two partners to each other. In line with this understanding, there has been a tendency in modern marriage rites to change the 1662 **Book of Common Prayer**'s order of "purposes for which matrimony was ordained"; thus the procreation of children, which headed the list in 1662, now usually comes third. Anglicans generally have a clear critique of the Roman Catholic position on the use of artificial birth control.

BISHOP. The Greek word *episkopos* (overseer) both means "bishop" in the New Testament and, by corruption in Anglo-Saxon times, itself became the English word "bishop," as can be seen in other cognate derivatives "Episcopal," "**episcopacy**," and so forth. The use of the word in the New Testament is virtually interchangeable with "**presbyter**" (cf. the Greek text of Acts 20.17 and 20.28 and of Titus 1.5–7 and the implications of 1 Peter 5.1).

In Phil. 1.1 and 1 Tim. 3.2, 3.8, there seem to be two kinds of **ministers** only, bishops and **deacons**. This twofold pattern is found in 1 Clement and in the Didache in the immediately postapostolic period, but in the same period the letters of Ignatius of Antioch very clearly demarcate a structure where there is one bishop with both presbyters and deacons assisting him. This does, however, appear to indicate a very local **episcopate**, where the bishop was simply chief pastor in what might be a single congregation in one town. **Diocesan** episcopacy developed from the end of the second century, and it is in that context—of an oversight of a region and of a plurality of congregations—that the role of a bishop has been generally conceived since then.

The English **Reformation**, being "top-down" in its implementation, was inspired and led by reforming bishops, maximizing on the position they held in the land through their appointments. Thus the diocesan organization of Anglicanism survived intact through the Reformation, and that pattern of episcopacy has become so basic to the spread of Anglican churches through the world that "Episcopal church" has become the normal alternative title to "Anglican church," being preferred in any place where the suggestion of special English associations (such as the word "Anglican" might imply) would be unhelpful.

The role of a bishop varies enormously according to the constitution of a particular **province** and to the size and resourcing of the diocese. It is common to Anglicanism that only bishops can **ordain** or **consecrate** further bishops, and that only a bishop can ordain presbyters and deacons or minister **confirmation**. The restriction of ordination to bishops is common to all Episcopal churches (with very minor exceptions in some Episcopal **Lutheran Churches**), but the Anglican unqualified restriction of ministering confirmation to bishops is unique among Episcopal churches. A diocesan bishop will usually preside over a diocesan **synod** and belong to a House of Bishops of the province. The powers and roles of the varying forms of assistant bishops—**area bishops**, **coadjutor bishops**, **suffragan** bishops—vary greatly from one diocese to another and in principle depend upon the delegation of the particular diocesan bishop.

Since **women** were first ordained as presbyters in the **Anglican Communion** in the 1970s, the Anglican churches concerned have one by one also addressed the question of women being consecrated as bishops. The first was Barbara Harris, consecrated to be assistant bishop in the diocese of Massachusetts in the **Episcopal Church (United States of America)** in 1989; and the first woman diocesan was Penelope Jamieson, consecrated to be bishop of Dunedin in the province of **Aotearoa**, New Zealand, and Polynesia in 1990. At the 1998 **Lambeth Conference**, there were 11 women bishops present from **Canada**, the **United States**, and Aotearoa, New Zealand and Polynesia.

BLACK RUBRIC. The 1552 **Book of Common Prayer** contained among the closing **rubrics** in the **Communion** service a "Declaration on Kneeling," which was not part of the Book imposed by the 1552 **Act of Uniformity** but was inserted into the text at the last minute before publication by order-in-council. This followed a sermon by John Knox before King **Edward VI** in September 1552 in which he denounced the requirement in the Book for the communicants to kneel to receive Communion (a posture which, curiously, had not been overtly required in the 1549 Book and was therefore, it could be argued, being newly imposed in 1552). Knox asserted that the required posture implied a worshipping of the **sacramental elements**, and the declaration was drafted to deflect the objection and to insist that kneeling is a good and godly posture but does not imply any worshipping of the elements. The declaration included the blunt assertion that the true body of **Jesus Christ** "is in heaven, *and not here*" (emphasis added).

It is often stated that the presses were stopped and the declaration was then inserted after the other rubrics, but that does not entirely describe the case—some printed copies lack it altogether, while others have it in the middle of the rubrics and a few do have it at the end. It appears that there may have been efforts in successive printings to move it higher up in the printed order of rubrics, so as to conceal its manner of being added.

The 1559 Act of Uniformity revived the Book attached to the 1552 Act, which therefore meant that the declaration, not having been in that original Book, was equally omitted when the Book was revived. At the **Savoy Conference** in 1661, the **Puritans**, to whom kneeling at Communion remained a central "excepted ceremony," asked for the rubric to be restored. This was not done in **Convocation**, but the declaration was restored by the Privy Council in February 1662 prior to the progress of the Book through Parliament—and it thus came in the **Annexed Book** in a different hand and was this time inevitably placed last. It was changed in one detail, now denying any "corporal" presence of Christ in the rite, rather than any "real and essential" presence. But the import was still very **Protestant**, and it was thus disliked by the **Anglo-Catholic** movement of the 19th century, which dubbed it the "Black Rubric" (though that title may have derived from the then popular two-color printings of the rite, in which the rubrics generally came in red, but the declaration was published in black).

In modern rites all over the world, the posture for receiving Communion has been left optional, the vogue of receiving standing has grown greatly, and any residual need for the Black Rubric has therefore disappeared, and it has taken its place in history.

BLESSED VIRGIN MARY. *See* MARY, MOTHER OF JESUS CHRIST.

BOARD OF MISSIONS. In the **Protestant Episcopal Church in the United States of America**, a Board of Missions replaced the **Domestic and Foreign Missionary Society** in 1835 and thus represented the whole church as an official arm instead of being a voluntary society. The board acted as a kind of "standing committee" for the **General Convention** until 1919, when it was itself replaced by the National Council, renamed the Executive Council in 1964.

In the Church of **England**, a Board of Missions was proposed in early days of the revival of the **Canterbury Convocation** in 1852. Uncertainty about what its role would be in relation to the existing societies and to the burgeoning overseas **dioceses** led to delays, and the Convocation Committees did not hurry the process. It thus took until 1887 before the board actually met, and 1892 before those appointed by the **York** Convocation officially met jointly with the Canterbury members—though they were even then entitled the Joint Boards of Mission before becoming in 1895 the "United Boards . . . of Canterbury and York." While the weight of responsibility for Anglican overseas **missions** always remained with the voluntary **missionary societies**, the Boards of Missions apparently took a part in organizing the Anglican Missionary Conference in 1894 and in convening the **Pan-Anglican Congress** that preceded the **Lambeth Conference** of 1908. With the coming of the **Church Assembly** in 1920, the existing boards were swallowed into subordinate bodies of the Assembly.

An Australasian Board of Missions was formed by the six **bishops** of **Australia**, Tasmania, and New Zealand in 1850, and when New Zealand detached to become its own **province** in 1857, it continued as the Australian Board of Missions. Despite its title, it was technically a voluntary society. It professed responsibility for taking the **gospel** to the aboriginal inhabitants of Australia as well as to places overseas, but appears to have done little initially to further that object. Unlike the Church of England's boards, it did expect to send and fund missionaries to fulfill its task, but it was flanked by other voluntary societies also, often with more commitment and energy.

In other provinces and in many individual dioceses, Boards of Mission, or their equivalent, have been formed to give missionary outreach official standing and promotion within the life of the province or diocese.

BOGA-ZAIRE. *See* CONGO.

BONN AGREEMENT. When, in the years following 1870, the **Old Catholics** who left the **Roman Catholic Church** after **Vatican I** had received **episcopacy** from the earlier Dutch Old Catholics of Utrecht, they quickly invited Anglicans to share in conference with them. Two conferences of theologians from across several denominations were held in Bonn in 1874 and 1875, and interaction with Anglicans began then and continued thereafter, including inter-Communion. The organization of the Old Catholics themselves took time to settle down, but the 1908 and 1920 **Lambeth Conferences** made reference to them. However, it was not until 1925 that the Dutch Old Catholics came to recognize the **validity** of Anglican **orders**, which cleared the way for real convergence. An Old Catholic contingent visited the

1930 Lambeth Conference as guests, and from that visit, a conference at Bonn in 1931 was planned. On 2 July 1931 Church of **England** and Old Catholic representatives, without attempting to get full **doctrinal** accord, signed the Bonn Agreement, to this effect:

1. Each communion recognizes the catholicity and independence of the other and maintains its own.
2. Each communion agrees to admit members of the other communion to participate in the **sacraments**.
3. Intercommunion does not require from either communion the acceptance of all **doctrinal** opinion, sacramental devotion, or **liturgical** practice characteristic of the other, but implies that each believes the other to hold all the essentials of the Christian Faith.

In the following years, Old Catholic Churches and Anglican **provinces** endorsed this form of words, and it has become the normal foundation for all relationships between the two Communions.

BOOK OF COMMON PRAYER. The first Book of Common Prayer was the 1549 Book authorized and imposed in the Church of **England** from Whitsunday (9 June) 1549, under the terms of the **Act of Uniformity** of January that year. Printed copies were on sale from early March. The Book was designed to supersede all the service books in **parish** use, and its overall design revealed the way in which the compilers (of whom Archbishop **Thomas Cranmer** was undoubtedly chief) dealt with the different previous books in turn. Thus the order of contents in the 1549 Book was:

- The **Calendar** (from the Calendarium)
- **Morning and Evening Prayer** (from the Breviary)
- **Collects**, psalms, epistles, and **Gospels** for the **Eucharist** (from the Missal)
- The ordinary and **canon** of the Eucharist (from the Missal)
- The **Litany** (from the Processional)
- The occasional offices (from the Manual)
- The Psalter

There was no English version of the Pontifical provided in 1549, and when the **Ordinal** came the following year, it was not legally part of the Book of Common Prayer.

The word "Common" in the title reflects the nationally imposed "**uniformity**"—after the small variants that existed in different places due to the texts being copied by hand, there was now to be, through printing, only one use everywhere, and all that was needed was to be found within the one Book (along with the **Bible**).

The second Book of Common Prayer was that authorized under the 1552 Act of Uniformity and imposed from 1 November 1552. The Act was repealed and the Book banned during the reign of Queen **Mary I**. When Queen **Elizabeth I** succeeded in 1558, a new Act of Uniformity in 1559 brought back the 1552 Book with very tiny changes. The 1559 Book of Common Prayer was in turn very slightly revised (though by royal warrant, rather than parliamentary act) in 1604.

The Book of Common Prayer was banned during the **Commonwealth** period (1649–1660). After the **Restoration**, details of a possible revision were debated at the **Savoy Conference** between April and July 1661. It was minimally revised in **Convocation** in late 1661, and in its revised form was authorized by the 1662 Act of Uniformity, which imposed it exclusively from 24 August 1662. In England that 1662 Book remains *the* Book of Common Prayer.

As other countries or separate Anglican **provinces** developed **liturgical** lives distinct from that of the Church of England, so each tended to provide for itself a distinct "Book of Common Prayer." The first such separate one was the ill-fated Scottish Book of 1637. The next full Book was that of the **Protestant Episcopal Church in the United States of America** (PECUSA) in 1789. In the 19th century, the Church of **Ireland**, having become disestablished and independent in 1871, authorized its own Book of Common Prayer in 1878. PECUSA revised its Book and authorized the new Book of Common Prayer from 1892. Other countries or provinces continued to use the 1662 Book, though often in a **vernacular** translation.

In the early 20th century a new complete Book of Common Prayer was authorized in **Scotland** (1912) and in **Canada** (1921), and a further revision of the American Book came in 1928. In the same year, the second and final rejection of the attempted revision in the Church of England was effected in Parliament. A series of further such Books of Common Prayer has followed in other provinces in the second half of the 20th century. It is characteristic of the term "Book of Common Prayer" that, when a Book with this title exists in a province, it is the foundational liturgical book of that province, superseding any that came before and setting a **doctrinal** standard for the province. Books that are subsidiary or contain **alternative services** are never called by the simple title "The Book."

BOSTON STATEMENT. The first **International Anglican Liturgical Consultation** (IALC-1) met in Boston, Massachusetts, in July 1985 and addressed the issue of children and their admission to **Communion**. The subject was determined by a combination of scholarly concerns and clearly discerned pastoral need. The 13 participants, from six Anglican **provinces**, issued an agreed "Boston Statement" in which they affirmed that children are in principle admissible to Communion on the basis of their **baptism**—even from infancy—and should not have to wait upon age or educational attainments or upon the rite of **confirmation**. The Boston Statement provided a starting point for the later **Toronto Statement** (1991) of IALC-4 which, by treating the whole of Christian **initiation**, expanded the Boston material, integrated it into a fuller context, and gave the topic greater publicity throughout the **Anglican Communion**.

BRAZIL. Brazil, as part of South America, was generally reckoned by Anglicans until the 19th century to be a **Roman Catholic** country, and therefore, in the view of many, was not appropriate for Anglican **missions** or church planting. Nevertheless, an initiative from the **Protestant Episcopal Church in the United States of America** (PECUSA) in 1887 led to James Watson Morris and Lucien Lee Kinsolving sailing for Brazil as missionaries in August 1889. Their foundation of the Anglican church in the south of Brazil is usually dated to 1890. In 1898 Kinsolving became the first **bishop** for Brazil, and in 1907 the **General Convention** fixed the title of the "Missionary District of Southern Brazil." In 1950 this became three **dioceses** of PECUSA, and on 25 April 1965 they became a separate **province** of the **Anglican Communion**. Brazil is Portuguese speaking, and the province has developed its own constitution, created new dioceses, invested in theological training, and established its own indigenous **liturgy** and **music**. Its official title (in English) is the Episcopal Anglican Church of Brazil. In 1999 there were seven dioceses, mostly of enormous size geographically, though with a concentration of Anglicans in the southernmost parts. In 2004–2005 a kind of internal schism occurred in the province. After the consecration of Gene

Robinson in New Hampshire in 2003, the bishop of Recife, Robinson Cavalcanti, had in 2004 ministered confirmation in an ECUSA parish that had objected to the consecration and had done so without the invitation of their bishop. He was then deposed by his **metropolitan**, the **primate** of Brazil. Then 32 clergy, two-thirds of the clergy of his diocese, expressing support for him, were themselves deposed by his **suffragan**, and at that point the primate of the **Southern Cone of South America** offered them "a special status of extra-provincial recognition" and took them under his episcopal care.

BREAD. The medieval use of the wafer in the Western Church was changed at the **Reformation**. In the 1549 **Book of Common Prayer**, a thicker, larger wafer was ordered, each one to be broken between two or more communicants. In 1552 the provision of the **rubric** was changed to "bread . . . such, as is usual to be eaten . . . but the best and purest wheat bread that conveniently may be gotten." This fitted well with other 1552 features, notably the end of all provision for an objective **consecration** and thus of **reservation**, and so any bread left at the end of the service could be taken home by the **curate** for his own use. When in later revisions an objective consecration was fitted back onto the 1552 text by stages, the **rubric** about the kind of bread to be used remained through to, and including, 1662. Here, however, a difference had now to be made between consecrated and unconsecrated bread remaining at the end of the service—and the consecrated had to be consumed, and only the unconsecrated could be taken home for the curate's use.

Wafers reappeared in the 19th century under the influence of the **Anglo-Catholic** movement, and in many places replaced leavened bread. After tussles in the courts in **England**, wafers then became viewed as normal Anglican use, despite the 1662 rubric. This in turn prepared the way for the practice of permanent reservation, which cannot well be done with leavened bread. On the other hand, the **Liturgical Movement** in the 20th century has led to a return by some to the use of leavened bread, while among others there has been a growth in the use of sheets of wafers or of very large wafers, such that they are no longer atomized in origin but can be visibly broken and shared as from a "common loaf" (1 Cor. 10.17). *See also* BREAKING OF THE BREAD; COMMUNION, HOLY.

BREAKING OF THE BREAD. The biblical phrase "the breaking of the **bread**" (Acts 2.42) has usually been understood to mean the **sacrament** of Holy **Communion** observed as **Jesus Christ** commanded at the Last Supper (cf. Acts 20.7; 1 Cor. 10.16). It has recurred as a title at times in history among various Christian groups. The words are also used to describe the actual act of breaking the bread within the **liturgical** rite. *See also* FRACTION.

BRENT, CHARLES HENRY (1862–1929). Brent was a Canadian, who, after **ordination** in 1887, moved the following year to Boston, Massachusetts, and thus joined the **Protestant Episcopal Church in the United States of America** (PECUSA). In 1901 he became the first **bishop** of the **Philippines**, then a **missionary** district of PECUSA. In 1917 he was elected bishop of Western New York, and in 1926 of the American congregations in **Europe**. He was famed, however, for his part in the development of the **ecumenical** movement. He participated in the 1910 **Edinburgh Missionary Conference**, and from then on was fired by a vision of a "world conference on faith and order." A large part of his energies thereafter were invested in the promotion of ecumenical activity, and his vision came to pass in the first world conference on Faith and Order at Lausanne in 1927. He himself was president of the conference, a symbolic role to crown his life's endeavors.

BROOKS, PHILLIPS (1835–1893). Phillips Brooks is celebrated as an outstanding American Episcopalian preacher of the 19th century. He was **ordained** as a **deacon** in 1859 and a **presbyter** in 1860. The greatest part of his American reputation arises from his 22 years as rector of Holy Trinity Church, Philadelphia (1869–1891); from his actual preaching and his lectures on preaching while there; and from the publication of those lectures and sermons. He is, however, better remembered through the rest of the English-speaking world for his authorship of the **Christmas** carol "O Little Town of Bethlehem," first published in 1868 but compiled, it is said, when he was actually looking at Bethlehem near Christmastime two or three years earlier. It was not published in **England** until the *Treasury of Hymns* in 1896. In 1891 Brooks became **bishop** of Massachusetts, but his **episcopate** was cut short by early death.

BUCHANAN, CLAUDIUS (1766–1815). Claudius Buchanan was born in Scotland and, as a young man, left his studies at Glasgow University to stroll through the continent of Europe with a violin. When in poor straits, he was led to faith in **Jesus Christ** by John Newton and was sent to Cambridge at the expense of Henry Thornton. There he came under the influence of **Charles Simeon**, and he was **ordained** as a **presbyter** in 1796. Buchanan became a chaplain to the East India Company through Simeon's good offices and went out to **Calcutta** in 1797, where he wrote strongly on behalf of the need for Christian **missionaries** in **India**. His visit to Travancore (now Kerala) around 1806 led, through his subsequent advocacy, to the beginning of **Church Missionary Society** work in that part of India 10 years later. Part of Buchanan's task had been to review the condition of the ancient Syrian Orthodox Church of that region, and part of his advocacy was to urge that the **Bible** should be translated into the local **language**, Malayalam, and that missionaries should work alongside and with the Syrian Church. In 1808 Buchanan returned to **England** and gave himself to pamphleteering and preaching on behalf of missions to India. His keynote writing in this cause was a sermon published as "The Star in the East" (1809). His labors, along with those of others, led to an Act to open India to Christian missions (including education) in 1813, and the appointment of the first **bishop** of Calcutta in 1814. *See also* MAR THOMA SYRIAN CHURCH OF MALABAR

BURIAL. Burial is the traditional way of disposing of the bodies of the Christian dead, inherited from Judaism and canonized for Christians by the burial of not only **Jesus Christ** himself but also of others in the New Testament. It appears to have been almost universally practiced by Christians until the late 19th century, although it was also known that those who, for example, died in fires or were drowned at sea would be no less partakers of the resurrection of the body than those who were buried.

In the 16th- and 17th-century **Books of Common Prayer**, burial was the only form of disposal of the corpse that was allowed (of which burial at sea was a special case). During the **Commonwealth** period (1649–1660), the **Westminster Directory** forbade all services or rites surrounding interment. Until the late 18th century in **England**, for all except the nobility, burial would occur in a churchyard without the place being marked by marble or stone curbs or permanent memorial. But permanent marking of the location of dead bodies spread from the nobility to other classes during the 18th century in England and grew greatly in Victorian times, as the population increased and the rate of death with it. This led to a difference in funeral rites, as the "service in church" would take place at a distance from a cemetery, rather than in close juxtaposition to a churchyard, which became more and more characteristic of rural churches only. Furthermore, in time, the sheer quantity of burials induced a rethinking of the necessity of interment and led to the rise of **cremation**.

English customs tended to predominate initially as Anglicanism spread around the world, but local **inculturation** has also widely affected burial practices. The **Anglo-Catholic** movement in the 19th century brought features of **Roman Catholic** uses into the rites also, not least in respect of **petitions for the departed** and "requiem **masses**." In the 20th century, services that had previously been called "burial of the dead" became known more often as "**funeral**" services, as a broader title was needed in order to include cremation, and "funerals" did not necessarily imply literal burial.

BURMA. *See* MYANMAR.

BURUNDI. Burundi was a Belgian colony in the 19th century and is a Francophone nation as an outcome of that. It achieved independence in 1962. **Roman Catholic missions** there date back to 1898, but the first Anglican missionaries entered the country in 1935, sent by the Ruanda Mission (often known as "CMS Ruanda," though it was a separate society from the **Church Missionary Society** [CMS]). The first missionaries and their converts were participants in the **East Africa** Revival Movement and keenly **evangelistic**. The first **ordinations** of Burundians as **presbyters** came in 1954. The **diocese** of Buye was formed in 1960 to become part of the new **province** of **Uganda**, Burundi, **Rwanda**, and Boga-Zaire in 1961, and the first Burundian national became **bishop** in 1965. Uganda became a wholly separate province in 1980, and the resultant province of Rwanda, Burundi, and Zaire itself split into three separate national provinces in 1992; in Burundi its title became the Episcopal Church of the Province of Burundi.

The Church has five dioceses, but it was deeply damaged by the civil war of 1994, when, following the murder of two successive presidents in October 1993 and April 1994, intertribal animosity led to widespread bloodshed and the flight of refugees. Christians had grave difficulty in holding to each other across the great rift that opened up.

– C –

CALCUTTA. At the end of the 18th century, Calcutta was the seat of the British governor-general in **India**, and a great center of the East India Company. It had a British garrison, and Anglican chaplains came out to it. Through the influence of two chaplains, David Brown and **Claudius Buchanan**, in the early 19th century and the work of **William Wilberforce** and the **Clapham Sect** in **England**, a new East India Company Act (known as the Charter Act) was passed in Parliament in 1813. This provided, among other legislation, for the Crown to appoint a **bishop** and **archdeacons** for a see of Calcutta. Steps were then taken for the appointment and **consecration** in 1814 of Thomas Middleton as the first bishop of Calcutta, with unspecified limits to his bishopric (though it probably included the whole of Asia). He was bound at every point by English law and believed himself thereby inhibited from **ordaining** Indians, while unclear how to relate to **clergy** sent from England by **missionary societies**. He died in 1822.

Middleton's successor, Reginald Heber (1823–1826), had **Australia** and **New Zealand** explicitly added to his jurisdiction, but found ways to unite chaplaincy and missionary forces. After two further short **episcopates**, both also terminated by early deaths, the fifth bishop, Daniel Wilson (1832–1858), became **metropolitan** in 1833 as provision was made for other **dioceses** to be formed (and Australia and New Zealand to be detached). He built St. Paul's **Cathedral** in Calcutta, the first Anglican cathedral in Asia, which was consecrated in 1847. He is also credited with having prompted the beginning of the P&O steamship travel between Britain and India.

Calcutta remained the metropolitical see through to the severance of the Church of India, **Burma**, and **Ceylon** (CIBC) from the Church of England in 1930. In the Indian Church Measure 1927 and the Indian Church Act 1927, which together provided for this severance, the bishop of Calcutta is treated as metropolitan, although wording is provided to allow the reconstituted church to make different arrangements for the office of metropolitan. But in fact the position of Calcutta remained unchanged until all parts of India (and **Pakistan**) ceased to be Anglican when united churches were formed in 1970. The bishop of Calcutta was the only metropolitan there has been among Anglicans to be known simply as "the metropolitan" and not to have another title, such as **archbishop**.

CALENDAR. The origins of a church calendar are to be found in the two great Jewish festivals that marked the great events of the **gospel** of **Jesus Christ**—**Passover**, the time of the crucifixion and resurrection of Jesus Christ, and **Pentecost**, the time of the coming of the **Holy Spirit**. There is evidence in the Acts of the Apostles of Paul observing these **feasts**, and he may well have done so for Christian purposes (see Acts 20.6 and 20.17; cf. 1 Cor. 16.8). By the early second century, the annual observance of Passover was entrenched in the Christian churches, and by the end of the century there was a period of 50 days thereafter that was known as a season of Pentecost. **Christmas**, the other great focus of the Christian calendar, is traceable to the early fourth century.

By the time of the **Reformation**, the "temporale"—that is, the great festivals like Christmas and **Easter**, the associated seasons such as **Advent** and **Lent**, and the Sundays counted from those seasons—were being overlaid and cramped by the "sanctorale"—that is, the fixed **saints**' days, usually derived from the supposed date of death of each saint, which came on the same day of the month each year, without regard to the movements of Easter Day and its associated seasons or to the days of the week on which the anniversaries fell. The sanctorale increased in number and complexity throughout the Middle Ages.

The Reformers retained the temporale virtually untouched, but pruned the sanctorale so that only biblical ("red-letter") saints had any **propers** provided. However, some other ("black-letter") saints, after being initially purged from the calendars in the **Prayer Books** of King **Edward VI**, returned in the calendar listings in Queen **Elizabeth I**'s reign.

The secular Julian calendar was used in England through the Reformation period and the 17th century, while on the Continent, in 1582 **Pope** Gregory VII reformed the calendar to correct the inexactitudes that had arisen. The Gregorian calendar, adopted by one nation after another, took the continent 11 days out of line with Britain (which was reluctant to follow the papal lead). In 1752, the English Parliament finally ordered the use of the Gregorian calendar (and unsurprisingly required it in the colonies also), requiring the omission of 11 days from September that year. The new pattern of leap years has since then not only has provided a common pattern worldwide but has also ensured a sustained correspondence of the month of the year with the climatic season. New Year's Day was moved from 25 March (the Feast of the **Annunciation** or "Lady Day") to 1 January—an important point to be understood by those handling English documents or events with contemporary dating prior to 1752.

No coherent **lectionary** can be produced except on the basis of a calendar, so the revisions of lectionaries in recent years have been done through prior amending of the ecclesiastical calendar. The Revised Common Lectionary (RCL), which, deriving from **Roman Catholic** origins, offers a common lectionary to the world's churches, operates on a calendar close to the traditional Western one. Anglican churches have liberty to add names (with or without proper provision) to the sanctorale, and, although there is no process of **canonization** in Anglicanism, such additional listing has been done in various and often imaginative ways. The Church year generally begins with Advent, four Sundays before the calendrically fixed point of Christmas (25 December).

CAMEROON. Cameroon is a **missionary diocese** of the **province** of **West Africa**.

CANADA. The first Europeans to land in what is now Canada were Norsemen in the 11th century, who did not establish a long-term presence. The next were the ship's company of John Cabot, setting foot in Newfoundland in 1497. During the 16th century, both France and **England** established footholds there.

The first recorded Anglican services were held in Queen **Elizabeth I**'s reign during Martin Frobisher's exploration for the Northwest

Passage—and possibly not long after by Francis Drake's company, if his exploration of the west coast in fact took him as far north as what is now Canada. The first resident chaplain went to Newfoundland in 1612. It may be that the labors of John Eliot (the "apostle to the Indians," as he was called) from the 1640s onward led to the reference in the preface to the 1662 **Book of Common Prayer** to the prospective usefulness of the rite for the **baptism** of those "of riper years" for "the baptizing of Natives in our plantations *and others converted to the Faith*" (emphasis added).

The history of Canada from the mid-17th to the mid-18th centuries is one of settlements in some parts by the French and in others by the English, and of conflict between the two. The English often provided for a resident Anglican **clergyman**, and the territories were technically under the Episcopal jurisdiction of the bishop of **London**, though no such prelate ever crossed the Atlantic to exercise his **episcopate** there. When Quebec was captured in 1759, French political rule was ended, and Anglican clergy, assisted partly by the **Society for the Propagation of the Gospel** and the **Society for Promoting Christian Knowledge**, were to be found scattered through the various colonies. The concept of a coherent British Canada was reinforced by the migration of "loyalists" from the former American colonies to the south, after those colonies had declared their independence as the **United States** and thrown off the British yoke, while the Canadian colonies remained "loyal" to King George III.

In the same year that the clergy of Connecticut elected **Samuel Seabury** as their **bishop** (1783), a group of Canadian clergy were seeking from the Church of England the appointment of a bishop of Nova Scotia. Following the debacle in London around the **consecration** of Seabury, legislation was passed in the Westminster Parliament to allow the **archbishop** of **Canterbury** (with due governmental authority) to consecrate bishops for overseas territories. This was first used in early 1787 for the provision of two U.S. bishops, **William White** and **Samuel Provoost**, but on 12 August that year **Charles Inglis** was consecrated to be bishop of Nova Scotia, and the Canadian episcopate was started.

Inglis's labors led to the consecration of Jacob Mountain as bishop of Quebec in 1793, and Quebec **cathedral**, consecrated on 28 August 1804, was the first purpose-built Anglican cathedral outside the

British Isles. The next sees to be formed were Toronto and Newfoundland, both in 1839, and there were five more before 1860. In 1861, all of the eastern sees except Nova Scotia were formed into the ecclesiastical **province** of Canada, with a **metropolitan** and an independent constitution. This led to the first consecration of a bishop on Canadian soil, Terry Lewis becoming the first bishop of Ontario on 25 March 1862.

It was the **synod** of the Anglican province of Canada that in 1865 called upon the archbishop of Canterbury to summon an international Episcopal conference to deal with the matter of the bishop of **Natal**, and thus led to the first **Lambeth Conference** in 1867. The Dominion of Canada was created in 1867, but the Anglican province also included Newfoundland, which remained a separate dominion until 1948. Nova Scotia joined the province only in 1874.

The province of Rupert's Land, with **dioceses** to the west of Ontario but not including British Columbia, was formed in 1875. It included the whole northern area that is now the diocese of the Arctic. Its formation led in due course to the creation of a **General Synod**, which first met in 1891, and, by taking authority over the existing two provinces, provided a basis for a scheme of four ecclesiastical provinces. This latter came to pass with the creation of the provinces of Ontario (taken from the province of Canada) in 1912 and of British Columbia (subdivided from the extraprovincial diocese of British Columbia) in 1914. A first Canadian Book of Common Prayer was authorized in 1918.

In the years between the wars, the role of the General Synod was greatly strengthened, and the office of a separated **primate**, who was permitted to have a diocese but in fact never did, was created. The last new diocese to be formed was the diocese of the Arctic, created in 1933. The Anglican Church of Canada was in the forefront of the **ordination** of **women** as **presbyters** (beginning from 1976) and as bishops (beginning from 1994). In 2001 the Anglican church entered into a concordat of **full Communion** with the Evangelical **Lutheran Church** in Canada on the basis of the **Waterloo Declaration**.

In 2000–2002, court claims for damages caused to individuals years earlier in church-run children's homes for indigenous people deeply affected many dioceses, and in 2001 the diocese of Cariboo went into bankruptcy and ceased to exist. A settlement involving the federal government brought this pressure to a close in 2002. A different issue, in relation to "same-sex blessings," began to split the diocese of New Westminster (which contains Vancouver) in 2002, and the authorization of such rites led not only to involvement of the General Synod but also to effects of that division that are felt all around the **Anglican Communion**. *See also* ANGLICAN CONSULTATIVE COUNCIL; HOMOSEXUALITY; LAMBETH COMMISSION; WINDSOR REPORT.

CANON. *Canon* is a Greek word meaning a "rule," with a great variety of consequent church use. Thus the *canon of scripture* (cf. the "canonical books" of scripture) implies the rule as to which books are to be treated *as* scripture. There is a clear statement for Anglicans of the limits of the canon in **Article** VI, where the **Apocryphal** books are listed as uncanonical. In the **ordination** of **deacons**, the candidates are asked if they "unfeignedly believe all the canonical scriptures of the Old and New Testament." The *Canon of the* ***Mass*** was the pre-**Reformation** (and Counter-Reformation) single unvarying **eucharistic prayer**, and the title has in part faded from use as alternative eucharistic prayers have come into use in recent years in the **Roman Catholic Church**. The *canons of a* ***cathedral*** are the officers who are jointly trustees and governors of it, traditionally ordained and resident and forming a **chapter**. This has been varied since the 1830s, first by the additional appointment of honorary canons (who, together with the residential canons, formed the "greater chapter"); and second, through the creation of "lay canons," who in **England** since 2000 have, with the greater chapter, formed the "college of canons." The *canons ecclesiastical* are the disciplinary rules that govern an institutional church and give rise to the term "**canon law**."

CANON LAW. In the **Roman Catholic Church**, **canon** law is highly developed, severely legal in its application, and an academic discipline in its own right. The Church of **England**, inheriting this corpus of ecclesiastical law from its Roman Catholic background at the **Reformation**, retained it on a provisional basis, though, as the separation from Rome was achieved by parliamentary statute, the claims of statute law outstripped those of canon law from that first point of separation onward. **Thomas Cranmer** prepared a new body of canon law during King **Edward VI**'s reign to accompany the reform of the

liturgy that was being implemented and thus to promote discipline and good order in the work of the **ordained ministry** and in the use of the liturgy within its context in both the building and the **parish**. This corpus, entitled *Reformatio Legum Ecclesiasticarum*, was published in 1553, just before Edward VI died. Thus it was shelved and never adopted.

When Queen **Elizabeth I** succeeded to the throne in 1558, a new project for canon law was initiated and a code of canons was approved by the **Convocations** in 1571. This code, however, never gained the queen's assent and lapsed. Finally, a further new attempt made at the beginning of King **James I**'s reign succeeded and became the code known as the 1604 Canons (sometimes, incorrectly, dated "1603"). Additions to these (largely relating to Church courts) were approved by the Convocations in 1640, but after the **Commonwealth** period it was agreed that they were without force, as the Convocations had illegally, or at least improperly, continued sitting when Parliament had been dissolved.

The 1604 Canons, while substantial, were not fully comprehensive, and case law in succeeding centuries has at intervals drawn upon a disputable hypothesis that medieval canon law still governs the life of the Church of England except at the points where statute law (which is sovereign) or the actual canons of 1604 have overridden that code.

In other parts of the **Anglican Communion**, **synods** have drawn up their own codes of canon law as their **provinces** have become independent and self-governing. The canons are then, insofar as they are rules, part of the constitutional structuring of those provinces. In England, following the 1947 report of the Canon Law Commission, a large part of the postwar synodical energies concentrated on the revision of the 1604 canons. The new canons were then authorized, often by a two-stage process: first, by an enabling **measure** through Parliament; and second, by the Convocations then enacting the canons and sending them for the monarch's assent. Since 1970, canons have been enacted not by the Convocations alone but by the whole Synod together. In the overall process, many powers (e.g., in relation to authorizing liturgical forms) have been devolved from Parliament to the General Synod. There remain some areas (e.g., in relation to the appointment of **bishops**) where powers remain with the state, and in those areas, Parliament has not devolved to the Synod powers to make canons.

There also remain some unresolved questions about the application of canon law. On the one hand, how far can it be viewed as binding upon **laypeople**? On the other hand, how far can it be viewed as being actually law rather than guidelines? There is at times a gap between the way these questions are answered by those who wish to apply the canons and by those who wish to evade their force.

CANONIZATION. In the **Roman Catholic Church**, there is an official process whereby distinguished (but now deceased) Christians are recognized as **saints**. At the **Reformation**, the Church of **England** retained the results of this process in principle, though in King **Edward VI**'s reign only for biblical ("red-letter") persons. During Queen **Elizabeth**'s reign, the names of a variety of postapostolic saints down to St. Richard of Chichester (who died in 1253 and was the latest one included) were restored to the **calendar**. Others (notably **Thomas à Becket**) were not restored. The Church of England never took over or produced a process for canonization, so no later names have ever been added with the confident prefix "Saint" attached. This has at times been experienced as a grave deficiency in the **Anglican Communion**, and on occasion **Lambeth Conferences** have given time and space to considering the need and how it might be met. The mind of the Communion would currently appear to be that individuals might be commemorated for their sanctity or courage (especially those who are **martyred**), but that no process for their recognition as "saints" either does or should exist. Some undergirding of this mindset was provided by detailed guidelines accepted by the ninth **Anglican Consultative Council** (ACC-9) in Cape Town in 1993. The retention of saints' names down to the 13th century has about it an element of assertion of Anglican continuity with the church from the time of the apostles onward, while other forms of commemoration now take up the witness, mutely attesting to the break in continuity that qualifies the continuity itself.

CANTERBURY. Canterbury is the city in Kent where **Augustine** first preached and **baptized** in England in 597. When he was made a **bishop**, he established his see there, and the office of bishop—later

archbishop—of Canterbury has retained the leading role in the Church of **England** ever since. The provision of a northern **metropolitan** at **York** led to minor tussles about seniority, but this was resolved by the 14th century, with the archbishop of York as "**primate** of England" and the archbishop of Canterbury as "primate of all England."

Augustine is said to have adopted an existing building as his **cathedral**, but this burned down in 1067, and the first stages of the medieval cathedral were begun. It was completed and **consecrated** in 1130, and it was there that **Thomas à Becket** was **martyred** in 1170. The cathedral again suffered from fire in 1174 and was largely rebuilt over the next two centuries. During this period, the shrine of Becket became a focus and central attraction for **pilgrimages** (as in Chaucer's *Canterbury Tales*). The cathedral and its shrine confirmed the leading place the archbishop held in both church and society. Canterbury in the Middle Ages held a position honored throughout Europe as of eminence second only to that of the bishop of Rome.

At the **Reformation**, the archbishops of Canterbury broke free from the **pope** and, while subject to the arbitrary power of the Tudor and Stuart monarchs, gained a striking independence as Christian leaders of a Christian nation. Two more were put to death—**Thomas Cranmer** by papists, **William Laud** by **Puritans**—and a third, **William Sancroft**, was deprived of his see because in 1689 he would not switch his **oath** of loyalty to the monarch from King **James II** to King **William III** and Queen **Mary II**.

Canterbury Cathedral continues to exercise a fascination and to draw pilgrims from all around the world. Both in England and elsewhere, Anglicans look to it as the place associated with the archbishops of Canterbury from **Communion** with whom they assert their identity as Anglicans. But the drawing power of the cathedral goes far beyond that particular symbolic role. Its scale is enormous, its **architecture** breathtaking, and its historical associations highly evocative. The **Lambeth Conferences** of 1978, 1988, and 1998 were held at the University of Kent, neighboring the city of Canterbury, because the city and cathedral of Canterbury are valued so highly by the bishops from all over the world. *See also* COMPASS ROSE.

CAREY, GEORGE LEONARD (1935–). George Carey, **archbishop** of **Canterbury** from 1991 to 2002, was **ordained** in 1962, and in the next 25 years he taught in three **theological colleges** and was for seven years vicar of St. Nicholas, Durham. In 1987 he was nominated to be **bishop** of Bath and Wells; he was **consecrated** in December 1987 and enthroned in February 1988. Then in July 1990 he was nominated as 103rd archbishop of Canterbury to succeed **Robert Runcie**. He was confirmed as archbishop in March 1991 and enthroned in April 1991.

Archbishop Carey's time in office was deeply affected in **England** by the demanding processes of getting the **ordination** of **women** as **presbyters** through the **General Synod** in 1992 and of following this up with the Episcopal Ministry Act of Synod in 1993, an Act that provided for the concept of "extended Episcopal care" for **clergy** who claimed in conscience their **Communion** with their diocesan bishops had been "impaired" by the ordination of women. Archbishop Carey was generally known as an **Evangelical**, and he held **mission** to be of top priority, taking various initiatives to promote the church's mission. He traveled more internationally than any previous archbishop of Canterbury, and he strengthened the **Anglican Communion** at a time when it was under great pressures. Carey convened the 1998 **Lambeth Conference**, the first such conference to include women bishops and the one that reaffirmed a conservative conviction about sexual—especially **homosexual**—relationships.

Carey was in office for the millennium year and retained his office in order to see through the Golden Jubilee of Queen Elizabeth II in 2002. He then retired in the autumn of that year in order to give his successor, **Rowan Williams**, time to address questions related to the projected next Lambeth Conference.

CAROLINE DIVINES. The Caroline period in England is, strictly speaking, the length of the reigns of King **Charles I** (1625–1649) and his son, **Charles II** (whose dates as king were 1649–1685, though he reigned in fact only from his **Restoration** in 1660). During this period, there arose a body of theologians, writers, preachers, and church leaders of a "high church" persuasion, such as **Lancelot Andrewes** (who died in 1626), Jeremy Taylor, and John Cosin. It was their principles (especially when tactlessly implemented by such as **Archbishop William Laud**) that created the polarization from the **Puritans** which led to the English Civil War and was evidenced in the continued polarization at the **Savoy Conference** in 1661. The spiritual and theological writings of the "Caroline Divines" have often been prized as rising far above their contemporary conflicts, and they were accorded a compliment, which they themselves might have disavowed, when they were treated by the early **Tractarians** as being the forerunners of the **Anglo-Catholic** movement of the 19th century.

CASSOCK. *See* VESTMENTS.

CATECHISM. The origins of the word "catechism" lie in the Greek *katecheo*, with overtones of *echo*, or sounding back. In the early church, those being prepared for **baptism** were known as "**catechumens**," and the process itself was called *catechisma*. It appears that in the early 16th century, "catechism" then shifted its meaning slightly to imply the *content* of the teaching and not simply the *method*, though the teaching was in fact done by scripted questions and answers. The Continental **Reformation** was marked by a plethora of catechisms, often hundreds of questions long, by which the young were to learn the reformed faith. The English Reformation gave birth to similar ones, such as those by Alexander Nowell, Thomas Becon, and John Ponet, the first of which was officially approved for teaching purposes by the **Convocation** in 1563.

However, the **Book of Common Prayer** catechisms were of a different order. In 1549, 1552, and 1559, the catechism consisted of a brief set of questions and answers on the **Apostles' Creed**, the **Lord's Prayer**, and the **Ten Commandments**, and it was contained within the **confirmation** service as, in effect, the candidates' ratification of their baptismal obligations. The **minister** was to teach the catechism before **Evening Prayer** to prepare young people for confirmation, and, in effect, the **bishop** himself was being required to test the children's knowledge before confirming them. In 1604 a section on the **sacraments** was added to the catechism, and this is usually attributed to Bishop John Overall, though its wording closely follows Nowell's "short" catechism. Then in 1662, the catechism was removed from the confirmation service and made a separate item in the Prayer Book on its own, and the instruction in it had to come after the second lesson at Evening Prayer. At the confirmation itself, instead of the use of the catechism, the bishop asked a new, single, comprehensive, question: "Do ye here . . . renew the solemn promise and vow that was made in your name at your Baptism . . . ?"

Until the 1950s, attempted revisions of the Prayer Book usually left the catechism virtually unchanged. Since then, however, there has been a tendency to remove from the **liturgical** books what has been seen more as a teaching aid than as a form of service. There has also been a growing decline in teaching by rote on the one hand and of viewing the contents of the Prayer Book catechism as sufficient instruction in the faith on the other. In **England**, a "Revised Catechism" was issued by the **Convocations** in 1962 and has been commended for use by the **General Synod** since. In the **Episcopal Church (United States of America)**, the 1979 Prayer Book contains at the back "An Outline of the Faith, Commonly Called the Catechism"—and it is 18 pages long. In **Australia**, *A Prayer Book for Australia 1995* has, in the "Supplementary Material" section, a somewhat shorter compilation, much closer to the 1662 structure and text, entitled "A Catechism: Questions and Answers on Christian Faith and Conduct." *See also* CATECHIST.

CATECHIST. A catechist is, in modern Anglicanism, a **layperson** authorized to teach the faith to inquirers and **catechumens**. The office was brought into use in countries where the Christian faith was newly planted and an indigenous **ministry** had not yet developed. It continues as a lay office alongside **ordained** ministry in many **provinces**, especially in Africa, to this day.

CATECHUMENATE. The term "catechumenate," while technically the term for both the time and the content of a course preparatory to **baptism**, has not been in widespread use in the **Anglican Communion**. However, in many places there has been an impact on Anglican practice from the **Roman Catholic** RCIA ("Rite for the Christian **Initiation** of Adults"), which proceeds by a combination of instruction, assimilation into the believing community, and liturgical rites marking the successive stages. Anglicans have shown a wide, if far from universal, interest in such a process, and, even for those who have been previously baptized, it is often referred to as a "catechumenate." The use of the terms "catechumen" and "catechumenate" do not now necessarily imply a rigorous learning and responding by rote to a set **catechism**. *See also* CATECHIST.

CATHEDRAL. A **bishop**, from long tradition, has a throne (Greek *thronos*) or seat (Greek *kathedra*; cf. Matt. 23.2) that marks the place of his bishopric and represents his teaching office. The cathedra is placed in a church building, which then becomes his "cathedral." In large **dioceses** (as in **England**), a complex organization grew up in medieval England to run each cathedral. In some of the cathedrals, the **chapter** (or ruling body of **clergy**) was a monastic body, though in others it was constituted by secular clergy. Enormous buildings were created, many of which last to the present day, and great resources were developed, often in such separation from the bishop and his household as to establish a nearly independent financial and intellectual power base. The cathedrals remained through the **Reformation** period, though the **monasteries** were destroyed by King **Henry VIII** and the monastic cathedrals were thereafter all run by secular clergy.

The English tradition is that a cathedral is managed by the **dean** and chapter, which legally comprise a single corporate entity. Some **parish** churches that have become cathedrals remain as "parish church cathedrals," and until 2000 the incumbent was then usually called not a dean but a **provost**. Since the 1830s the number of "residentiary **canons**" (i.e., those who belong to the legal entity, with stipends and governing powers) has been strictly limited, while a new category of "honorary canons"—distinguished clergy of the **diocese** who are not in residence—has arisen to create a much wider "greater chapter," or, as it has been titled since 2000, the "college of canons." It is this latter body that, when in England a see is vacant, traditionally receives the monarch's ***congé d'élire***, commanding them to hold an election—and to vote for the Crown's nominee as the next bishop.

While it is usual in the Anglican Communion, when a new see is founded, for an existing building to become the cathedral or for a wholly new cathedral church to be planned, it is not crucial to the existence of a see that there should be a cathedral, and other models for a bishop placing his cathedra are available. In each **province**, there are different provincial rules, and sometimes individual sets of cathedral statutes, determining the composition and powers of cathedral government and its relationship to the diocesan structures.

CELEBRATE. To "celebrate" appears at the time of the **Reformation** to have meant little more than to observe or perform, though with undertones of the occasion being one of joy and of worship; it may have particularly meant to hold a **eucharist**. It is used with a plural subject (or collective noun) three times in the 1549 **eucharistic prayer** ("this congregation which is here assembled . . . to celebrate the commemoration" [in the intercessory section], "did institute, and in his holy Gospel command us, to celebrate a perpetual memory" [in the section concerning the cross], "we . . . do celebrate and make here . . . the memorial which thy Son hath willed us to make" [in the **anamnesis** section]). In the 1552 **Book of Common Prayer**, the verb disappeared from the text of the rite, although a closing **rubric**, based on 1549, still stated, "And there shall be no celebration of the **Lord's Supper**, except there be a good number . . . ." **Canon** 13 of 1604 contains the phrase "All manner of persons . . . shall henceforth celebrate and keep the **Lord's Day** . . . and other Holy-days," and the means stated included both participation in public worship and performing of private good deeds, with merely incidental mention of receiving **Communion**. It is only in 1662 that the use of the first person singular for the **minister** of Communion alone is found, in the exhortation to the negligent: "On _____ I intend, by God's grace, to celebrate the **Lord's Supper**." The whole **liturgy** of the **sacrament** is called a "celebration." The **Scottish** 1637 and 1764 rites, and the derivative American tradition, revived the 1549 anamnesis text, "We do celebrate and make here . . . the memorial."

By derivation from the first person singular use, the minister has in recent years been identified in rubrics in some rites as the "celebrant," for example, in the **Episcopal Church (United States of America)** 1979 Book of Common Prayer. This has itself allowed in some places the importation of the **Roman Catholic** terminology of "**concelebration**," by which is meant a eucharist with more than one officiant. But a countertendency, which is probably stronger and has been growing around the world, has been to view the whole congregation as together "celebrating" the eucharist (or, indeed, celebrating **baptism**, or a festival, or any worship occasion or event); it has thus become more usual to name the primary officiant not the celebrant but the "**president**."

In the Church of **England** the idea of "celebrating" Jesus Christ's saving work led to the direct transitive use in the anamnesis of the first **eucharistic prayer** in Rite A in the **Alternative Service** Book 1980: "We celebrate with this bread and this cup his one perfect sacrifice." This text was changed in 2000 when **Common Worship** came in, but now Prayer D includes "We celebrate the cross on which he [Christ] died."

CELIBACY. While the Latin *caelebs* means simply "single," the English derivative "celibate" usually means "committed by **vow** to lifelong singleness and continence." When the separation from Rome was effected in King **Henry VIII**'s time, the **clergy** were still bound by those vows, although **Archbishop Thomas Cranmer** himself took a wife even before he was made archbishop in 1533, and others, more or less secretly, followed him. When the monks were evicted from the **monasteries** in 1536–1537, they were still treated as bound by their vows, and in 1539 Henry VIII reinforced general clerical celibacy in the reactionary Six **Articles**. During King **Edward VI**'s reign and from Queen **Elizabeth I**'s reign onward, there has been no requirement of clerical celibacy, and there was no resurgence of the monastic movement in the Anglican churches until the 19th century. *See also* RELIGIOUS COMMUNITIES.

CENTRAL AFRICA. The **Province** of Central Africa was formed in 1955 putting together the **dioceses** of Mashonaland and Matabeleland, which had belonged to the Church of the Province of **South Africa**, with the dioceses of Northern Rhodesia and Nyasaland, as they were then called, which were separate dioceses of the **Canterbury** jurisdiction with a history of being supported by the **Universities Mission to Central Africa**. The formation of the province matched the political creation of the (ill-fated) Central African Federation, which had come two years earlier. The province has run on beyond independence for Botswana, **Zambia**, and Malawi and through the years of the Smith regime in Rhodesia, until **Zimbabwe** became independent also in 1980. There is no fixed see for the **archbishop** and virtually no provincial structure or resources. It has tended to use the **Book of Common Prayer** of the Church of the Province of South Africa, originally authorized in South Africa in 1954 but then translated in the Central African countries into differing **languages**. English-language rites have often drawn upon Church of **England** uses.

CENTRAL AMERICAN REGION. *See* CENTRAL REGION OF AMERICA.

CENTRAL REGION OF AMERICA. The **Protestant Episcopal Church in the United States of America** from the 19th century organized chaplaincies and other **ministries** in the countries of Latin America, including the Canal Zone, administered as an American territory within Panama. This led to the formation of a Missionary Diocese of the Canal Zone in 1919. Other chaplaincies were grouped first into a Missionary District of the Episcopal Church in Central America in 1957, which included representation from former British chaplaincies in the region. In the following years, a transition was made from a chaplaincy to an indigenous and "national" set of Churches. Five countries of Central America came to constitute the "Central Region," comprising the dioceses of Costa Rica, El Salvador, Guatemala, Nicaragua, and Panama. These remained as Province IX within the renamed **Episcopal Church (United States of America)** (ECUSA) until they became a separate Spanish-speaking **province**, La Iglesia Anglicana de la Region Central de America (IARCA), on 18 April 1998. On leaving the framework of ECUSA, the new province was promised continued financial and other support from the parent Church for a 40-year period, during which it would move toward self-sufficiency.

CEREMONIAL. The medieval growth of the ceremonial accompaniments of the **liturgy**, and particularly of the **eucharist**, provoked a strong reaction by the **Protestant Reformers**, who took the view that excessive ceremonial in worship in principle returned the church of **God** to a kind of bondage that, like the levitical ceremonial of the Old Covenant, obscured the light of the **gospel**. It was therefore the aim of the Church of **England**'s Reformers to purge the rites of such excesses, though they recognized that some ceremonial is necessary to good order, that such ceremonial may help underline and enforce the word of God, and that **sacraments** in particular inevitably involve some physical action, including the use of a sacramental **element** and actual physical movements in using it.

Much of the existing Sarum ceremonial was reduced or eliminated by the royal *Injunctions* of 1547, and **Thomas Cranmer**, in the preface to the 1549 **Book of Common Prayer**, made it clear that the level of ceremonial was much reduced, though a note at the end of the Book allowed that "touching, kneeling, crossing, holding up of hands, knocking upon the breast, and other gestures . . . may be used or left as every man's devotion serveth, without blame." The 1552 Book made further excisions, and a second preface to the Book was included, drawing upon the note at the end of the 1549 Book and now entitled "Of Ceremonies, why some be abolished and some retained." This remained in 1662, and apparently in its original context meant that ceremonies that were not specifically *allowed* in the **rubrics** were by implication *abolished*.

The somewhat innovative use made of the 1662 rite in the Church of England in the 19th and 20th centuries pushed out the previous ceremonial boundaries, leading to a permissive (but widespread) reintroduction of a plethora of **Roman Catholic** ceremonial practices that the 1549 and 1552 Books had been specifically seeking to remove. This trend has often been based on the view that ceremonies not mentioned in the rubrics of the rites may be freely reintroduced. The **Oxford Movement**, from 1850 on, was often called the "Ritualist Movement," but, despite the title, it was in fact a "ceremonialist" movement, to which objections were strongly registered. Despite such objections, the ceremonial revival prevailed in many parts of the **Anglican Communion**, and that which was controversial and unlawful (e.g., genuflecting or the use of wafer **bread** for **Communion**) in the second half of the 19th century was being treated as a normal pattern of Anglicanism across the world in the 20th. The modern style of writing **liturgy** provides rubrics not in order to inhibit or straitjacket **parish** practice but rather to offer coaching and facilitation, and this has itself both enlarged and deepened the understanding and use of ceremonial. *See also* ANGLO-CATHOLICISM; EASTWARD POSITION; SIGN OF THE CROSS; TRACTARIANS; VESTMENTS.

CEYLON. *See* SRI LANKA.

CHALCEDON, COUNCIL OF. The Council of Chalcedon in 451 completed the four "Great **Councils**" that defined the orthodox ways of stating the **doctrines** of the **Trinity** and **Incarnation**. Chalcedon placed the coping stone on the doctrines by insisting that there were two natures in **Jesus Christ**, the human and the divine—thus condemning Monophysitism. The Chalcedonian formula is expressed in detail in the history of Anglicanism in the **Athanasian Creed**.

CHANCEL. The typical pattern of **Gothic architecture** in the **parish** church buildings of the 16th century had a wide **nave**, and then a narrow chancel forming a second chamber beyond a screen at the east end of the building. In some **Reformed Churches** on the Continent, the chancels were pulled down to make a single chamber for worship, but the 1549 **Book of Common Prayer** ordered the **Communion** to be ministered within the "quire" to those who had come there from the nave to put their money in the poor men's box and had then remained there to receive Communion. In 1552, however, a radical change was that for the first time there was to be a single-chamber use of the **Lord's Supper**; the fourth **rubric** before the Communion service read, "The **Table** . . . shall stand in the body of the Church, or in the chancel, where **Morning Prayer** and **Evening Prayer** be appointed to be said." In other words, **Thomas Cranmer** was now keeping two separate chambers, but choosing one or other to use, almost certainly in accordance with the size of the congregation, rather than letting services occur through the screen. The first rubric before Morning Prayer similarly ordered the **minister** to use the best place for the people to hear him, whether "Church, Chapel, or Chancel." The same rubric finished, "And the Chancels shall remain, as they have done in times past"—in other words, there was to be no destruction of chancels, but a retention of them as providing a second and smaller room.

By the time 1662 came, the **Laudian** requirement of putting Communion tables back permanently against the east wall and railing them in had greatly changed the Edwardian and Elizabethan use, and Communion services were now more usually conducted through the screen. Curiously, the fourth rubric before Communion was retained unchanged as quoted above, though a table standing anywhere but against the east wall was rare. Whether by accident or not, the rubric before Morning Prayer (later dubbed the "**Ornaments Rubric**") minutely changed the 1552 text, and the last sentence now read, "And the Chancels shall remain as they have done in times past." There would appear to be great import in that elimination or loss of the comma after "remain," whether its loss was deliberate or accidental.

Chancels have had a checkered history since 1662. The classical galleried auditory chambers of 18th-century church building provided but an apse for the Communion table, but the Gothic Revival from 1840 on restored both medieval architecture and the accompanying mystique of the screened-off chancel and even more remote "**sanctuary**," where only chosen people ministered. Robed choirs were introduced in collegial-style choir stalls in imitation of **cathedral** choirs, and mystical expositions taught that the nave symbolized the church on Earth, and the chancel the church in **heaven**. The prevalence of the design entrenched in many minds that this was how a church building "ought to look."

In the 20th century the **Liturgical Movement** has often led back to single-room architecture, or in existing medieval or Gothic Revival buildings, to a full separation of the chancel to provide a single-room nave and a distinct separate chapel. Ministering through or across a screen in two chambers at once has become less and less popular, so that chancels have become less and less indicative of how a building should "look like a church."

CHANT. *See* HYMNODY; MUSIC.

CHAPTER. The English word "chapter" is derived from the Latin *capitulum* (from which more obviously is derived the adjectival form "capitular"). It has traditionally been used as a collective noun to describe a constituted meeting of **clergy**. Thus the **canons** of a **cathedral** have been known as a chapter (and their meeting place a chapter house); the clergy of a **deanery** (and sometimes of a nonterritorial grouping) are often known as a chapter also.

CHARISMATIC MOVEMENT. On the world church scene, **Pentecostalism** was born in 1906 in the **United States**. For 50 years it attracted away from the historic denominations those who had "spoken in **tongues**" or had entered into a moving and direct experience of the **Holy Spirit**, often known as "**baptism in the Spirit**." However, in the late 1950s, on the U.S. west coast a form of "neo-Pentecostalism" appeared within the **Protestant Episcopal Church in the United States of America** (PECUSA) and was contained there without mass secessions into Pentecostalism. This originally required a combining of a high church and **ceremonialist Anglo-Catholicism** with the powerful new experiential Christianity of the Spirit. This has grown and been found also in **Roman Catholicism** and across the **Protestant** denominations.

Within worldwide Anglicanism, partly from the direct impact of the new movement in PECUSA and partly from a spontaneous stirring not causally linked to the American phenomena, from 1962 onward a similar neo-Pentecostalism, now dubbed the "Charismatic Movement," flared up within the Church of **England**. In England it was led by ministers from an **Evangelical** background and never affected the Anglo-Catholic side of the Church as it had done in America. A great center of its life has emerged in Holy Trinity Church, Brompton, in **London** and from there the Alpha Course in discipleship has spread around the world.

The rest of the **Anglican Communion** has experienced the Charismatic Movement in many unpredictable and often surprising ways. In **Australia** and New Zealand, it was largely a high church movement, which in New Zealand in time discovered the existing Evangelicals and made some common cause with them; however, the **Sydney** diocese in Australia, a bastion of worldwide Anglican evangelicalism, has always looked askance at such a theologically untethered movement. In **Southern Africa**, an old-fashioned catholicism suddenly in the 1970s and early 1980s melted into a strongly charismatic stance—though one which, in the person of **Archbishop** Bill Burnet and others, did not abandon its forthright opposition to apartheid. In other parts of Africa, there were some convergences with the prewar Holiness Movement or the **East African** Revival. In the **Southern Cone of South America**, English charismatic **missionaries** found great allies in the Latin American temperament, while in Singapore and other parts of Malaysia, the Chinese of the diaspora not only have experienced the charismatic revival and made it their own but also have combined it with something not always seen elsewhere, a vibrant **evangelism**.

Following a pre-Lambeth celebration at **Canterbury** in 1978, at which charismatics (not least **bishops** en route for the **Lambeth Conference**) from all around the **Anglican Communion** joined together in conference and worship, an international Anglican organization entitled SOMA was formed on the initiative of Michael Harper. SOMA, while it has its own New Testament Greek meaning, was an acronym for "Sharing of Ministries Abroad." It has been led from England and has been characterized by the interchange between nations of teams for witness, evangelism, and renewal.

From an observer's point of view, the movement has seen fashions: in the 1960s, baptism in the Spirit, "tongues," and **prophesying**; in the 1970s, **healing** and "spiritual warfare"; in the 1980s, "words of knowledge" and "the gift of discernment"; and in the 1990s the "**Toronto Blessing**." It has spawned a vast new repertoire of songs and choruses, less concerned with credal proclamation than with loving God, and it has liberated concerns for "every-member ministry" and for the experiential side of Christian spirituality and worship. There have been criticisms, many of them well based, relating to the **doctrinal** flimsiness, superficial culture, primitive exegesis, and tendency to spiritual smugness that have at times characterized the practitioners.

In some **provinces**, as in the Church of England, there have been official reports on the development and progress of the movement. However, in its second and third generations, it has continued a witness to the almost luminous close presence of a God of blessing, love, and power, where lay standards of sacrificial living tend to outrun previous Anglican norms and where life and growth in the Spirit outweigh any residual Anglican instincts toward fear, shyness, and anonymity.

CHARLES I, KING (1600–1649). Charles I, son of King **James I**, inherited the throne in 1625. His religious policy was characterized by his backing of **William Laud**, whom he made **archbishop** of **Canterbury** in 1633, and of Laud's provocative swing from the reformed faith of the Tudor divines to the stiffer churchmanship of the **Caroline Divines**. The **Puritan** suspicion of the direction in which even small changes were taking the Church of **England** was heightened by the **Roman Catholicism** of Charles's queen-consort, Henrietta Maria, but it was his personal unwisdom that was determinative.

In **Scotland** in 1637 the king endeavored—by sheer weight of his personal **authority**—to impose a Laudian **Book of Common Prayer** upon a church resistant to all **liturgical** forms, and in the process he set the country into revolt. In England the actual policy of Laud, and the draft, supposedly "high church," **canons** of 1640 brought on the Civil War in 1642. Charles lost the war, was taken captive, and declined to negotiate about the Church of England, particularly about **episcopacy**, with his captors. He even declined to recognize the jurisdiction of a court convened to try him. The king was condemned to death for treason and was executed in Whitehall on 30 January 1649. The *eikon basilike*, lauding his "solitudes and suffering," was published immediately and affected the later view of him.

On the **Restoration** in 1660, when his son, **Charles II**, took possession of the throne, a service to commemorate "King Charles the **Martyr**" was instituted for 30 January; it was included in the 1662 Book of Common Prayer and remained in use until 1859. This treatment of Charles as a martyr has sometimes been said to provide the first post-**Reformation** Anglican precedent for the principle of recognizing new **saints** and martyrs. There are in England a few church buildings **dedicated** to his memory (e.g., in Tunbridge Wells and Falmouth), and his name appears in various **calendars**, as "Charles I, King and Martyr," on 30 January.

CHARLES II, KING (1630–1685). Charles II was the son of King **Charles I** and nominally inherited the throne when his father was executed in 1649. He lived in exile until 1660, when emissaries from the **Puritan** Parliament came to him in Breda in the Low Countries to negotiate his return. Charles issued the Declaration of Breda, which promised "A Liberty to tender Consciences, and that no man should be disquieted or called in question for differences of Opinion in Matters of Religion, which do not disturb the Peace of the Kingdom," and on that basis was welcomed back to **London**. His "**Restoration**" on 29 May 1660 was thereafter celebrated annually on the anniversary with a special service of thanksgiving appended to the 1662 **Book of Common Prayer**.

Charles took the possibility of a true reconciliation a stage further with his Worcester House Declaration on 25 October 1660. In this, he promised to convene a conference of the different parties in order to find agreement on the **liturgy** of the Church of **England**. He duly named the participants of the **Savoy Conference** and ordered them to meet at the Savoy chapel in London from the end of March to the end of July 1661. However, a "cavalier" House of Commons was elected in place of the Puritan one in March and April 1661, so that at the Savoy Conference the **bishops** knew that they needed to make few concessions to the Puritans' "exceptions" and thus did not reach agreement with them. The previous Book was marginally revised in the **Convocation** meetings of November and December 1661 and was then enforced by the draconian **Act of Uniformity** of 1662.

There is reason to think that, rather than passing further Acts of Parliament that oppressed **dissenters**, Charles II himself would have preferred a toleration that would have conciliated them. However, the general stance of Anglican authority from 1662 on was discriminatory to the point of persecution, and Charles was inevitably involved in it.

Charles's wife, Catherine of Braganza, was barren, and thus his younger brother James, the Duke of York, was his heir presumptive. James, however, following the wishes of their mother, Henrietta Maria of France, became a **Roman Catholic** in 1670. Attempts were then made to get Charles to bequeath the Crown to a **Protestant**, but Charles, relying heavily upon dynastic right as interrelated with the divine right of kings, refused to vary the succession. Some hopes of others gravitated to his most senior illegitimate son, the Duke of Monmouth, but Charles distanced himself totally from this. He is reliably reported to have been received into the Roman Catholic Church himself on his deathbed and was duly succeeded by his brother, who ruled as King **James II**.

CHASUBLE. *See* VESTMENTS.

CHICAGO-LAMBETH QUADRILATERAL. *See* LAMBETH QUADRILATERAL.

CHIMERE. *See* VESTMENTS.

CHINA. The origins of Anglican church life in China derive from both American and British sources. The British took possession of **Hong Kong** Island in 1841, and chaplaincy work began there. On the mainland, the **Protestant Episcopal Church in the United States of America** took immediate advantage of the opening of ports for access to commerce by foreigners in 1844, beginning a **mission** headed by Bishop Boone in Shanghai. A **diocese** originating from the Church of **England**, with the title of "Victoria," was created for Hong Kong in 1849. The early English and Americans were followed by missionaries from the Anglican Church in **Canada**, the **Society for the Propagation of the Gospel**, the **Church Missionary Society**, and the interdenominational China Inland Mission. New dioceses were created, broadly representing these different spheres of missionary impact.

A conference of representatives from the different dioceses was held in 1912, and a common identity was asserted as Chung Hua Sheng Kung Hui (the Holy Catholic Church of China). From 1918 on, Chinese nationals were **consecrated** as **bishops**, initially as assistants in expatriate-led dioceses but in time as diocesan bishops. A central **theological college** was created in Shanghai as well. The 1920 **Lambeth Conference** treated the church as on the way to recognition as a fully self-governing **province** of the **Anglican Communion**, and the 1930 Lambeth Conference gave it that recognition. No **archbishopric** was created, but there was an elected chairman of the House of Bishops. The first **General Synod** was held in 1931.

The Communist Revolution in 1949 led to a one-party oppressive state in mainland China. Expatriate missionaries withdrew or were expelled. The diocese of Hong Kong and Macao was detached from the province and pursued a separate path, first within the Council for the Church of **Southeast Asia** and since 1998 as the separate province of Hong Kong and Macao. Nevertheless the life of Chung Hua Sheng Kung Hui continued after 1949, though under great pressure. A feature of later as well as contemporary interest was the consecration of Kwang-Hsun Ting as a bishop in 1955. In 1956 Bishop Ting attended the Consultative Committee of the **Lambeth Conference**. That same year, Archbishop **Howard Mowll** of **Sydney** was invited to make a return visit to the Church for which he had first become a bishop in 1922. But no Chinese bishop attended the Lambeth

Conference itself, and the isolation continued until church buildings were closed in 1966 in the wake of the Cultural Revolution. When these were reopened in 1979, Chinese Christians were pressed into a "postdenominational church," and Anglicanism ceased to have a recognizable identity.

Christianity, with certain limitations upon it, has been widely practiced on the postdenominational basis since, with apparent vigorous growth in numbers. It has been officially tolerated, and believers are no longer portrayed as essentially disloyal to the state. **Bibles** are printed and distributed, and links with the rest of the world have been reopened. The same Bishop K. H. Ting, now chairman of the postdenominational China Christian Council, was present as a guest at the 1988 Lambeth Conference. In 1994 he in turn hosted a visit to China of the **archbishop** of **Canterbury**, **George Carey**. However, the story has since the 1960s largely ceased to have any specific Anglican relatedness.

CHRISM. The word "chrism" literally means the action of **anointing**, but in modern speech the verbal sense has been confined to the hybrid compound "chrismation," and the noun "chrism" has come to refer to an actual oil. One of the three oils specifically distinguished in **Roman Catholic** use, chrism includes balsam mixed with olive oil, thus giving it a special aroma. This augmented oil is used in **confirmation** (the other two, unaugmented, are for **healing** and for **baptisms**). The use of all three oils has become normal in many parts of the **Anglican Communion**.

CHRIST. *See* JESUS CHRIST.

CHRISTMAS. The **Feast** of the Nativity of **Jesus Christ** has been observed on 25 December at least since the fourth century and possibly since earlier. It quickly became a pivotal point in the Church **calendar**, with the **Advent** season running for the four Sundays before it, and **Epiphany** and the weeks following Epiphany being calculated from the "12 days of Christmas" which terminate on 6 January. Christmas kept its pivotal role at the **Reformation**, and the **Book of Common Prayer** called it "The Nativity of the Lord, commonly called Christmas Day." Oliver Cromwell tried to abolish it by law because both the actual date and the annual commemoration lack overt scriptural **authority**, but the instinct for celebration in midwinter, quite apart from religious motivation, made his effort unsuccessful. When the **Puritans** objected at the **Savoy Conference** in 1661 that the dating was not warranted, the scruple was met in part when the 1662 Prayer Book altered a phrase in the **collect** to read "as at this time."

Christmas retains its focal place in the **liturgical** year in the Revised Common **Lectionary**, which has evolved from **Roman Catholic** sources and is widely followed among Anglicans. It is frequently celebrated with an opening **eucharist** of the day, which in fact begins late in the evening on Christmas Eve, though it may be dubbed the "midnight **celebration**." It echoes the widespread belief that Jesus was born during the night (for the shepherds had been watching their flocks "by night" [Luke 2.8]). However, in some parts of the world—especially those where public holidays follow Christmas—there has been an ever-growing tendency for a **liturgical** celebration of Christmas to precede the actual day and come during Advent. The famed "Nine Lessons and Carols" is the most notable instance of this.

CHURCH. Articles XIX and XX of the Thirty-Nine **Articles** show a continued belief in the visible church, although Article XXXIV, referring to "particular or national churches," allows for a series of differing autonomous churches spread through the nations. The Anglican **provinces**, in their adherence to the **Nicene Creed**, express belief in the one holy catholic and apostolic church, and each province claims to belong to it. Roman Catholics who become Anglicans are usually required to acknowledge that the Anglican church they are joining is part of the one holy catholic and apostolic church. The **Lambeth Quadrilateral** expresses some basic features of ecclesiality valued by Anglicans, though there is no wide consensus about the "notes" of the true church. Because of the distinct position that Anglicanism has come to occupy upon the world ecclesial scene, the definition and assertion of an Anglican **ecclesiology** has been a major topic of theological concern since the days of **John Jewel** and **Richard Hooker**. It is clear that the general run of **doctrinal** teaching has asserted the reality of a visible church—a church that is in some sense one throughout the world—along with refusing to identify it solely with the **Anglican Communion** or any one Communion or tradition. Thus the claim at **baptism** is that the candidate is baptized into the church catholic, and the claim at **ordination** is that the candidate is ordained as a **deacon**, **presbyter**, or **bishop** "in the church of **God**" rather than in a particular denomination, region, or **diocese**. *See also* ANGLO-CATHOLICISM; APOSTOLIC SUCCESSION; AUTHORITY; EVANGELICAL MOVEMENT; LAMBETH CONFERENCE.

CHURCH ASSEMBLY. *See* ENABLING ACT; ESTABLISHMENT.

CHURCH MISSION SOCIETY (CMS). *See* CHURCH MISSIONARY SOCIETY.

CHURCH MISSIONARY SOCIETY (CMS). In the second generation of the **Evangelical Revival** in **England**, a widespread concern arose among leading Evangelicals of the Church of England as to the means by which they might proclaim the **gospel** throughout a world that was being fast explored and colonized and opened for trade by the European powers. Eugene Stock, the historian of CMS, locates the origins of the society in simultaneous concerns that grew from 1786 onward. These included William Carey's famous challenge to **Baptist** congregations to consider ways to convert the heathen, **William Wilberforce**'s political campaigns to abolish slavery, the beginnings of the transportation of convicts to **Australia**, and the increasing provision of Evangelical chaplains to **minister** to the English expatriate populations in the distant corners of the Earth.

The question of "foreign **missions**" began to concern the **Clapham Sect** and the Eclectics, an Evangelical clerical society, and it was strongly pressed by **Charles Simeon**, vicar of Holy Trinity, Cambridge, from 1783. The Church Missionary Society was founded on 12 April 1799, with John Venn, the rector of Clapham, in the chair and Thomas Scott (the famous commentator on the **Bible**) as secretary. Wilberforce was vice president. It was formed (in Venn's words) on "the Church-principle, but not the high-Church principle." The **archbishop** of **Canterbury**, when consulted, gave very qualified approval ("He would look on the proceedings with candour, and . . . it would give him pleasure to find them such as he could approve").

The society was marked from the start by great vigor and a worldwide vision, but had few actual missionaries to send abroad—in the first 15 years, almost all who were sent were German **Lutherans**. However, as the society got into its stride, its **missionaries** began to plant indigenous churches in every land to which they were admitted. Many died (especially on the west coast of Africa), but more came. In the 31 years that the younger Henry Venn (the son of the rector of Clapham) was general secretary of CMS (1841–1872), it was said that he had more power in the Anglican churches than the archbishop of Canterbury. On occasion in the 19th century, the work chartered by CMS came into collision with the **authority** of **bishops** sent overseas from England by royal letters patent. CMS adhered without hesitation to the "voluntary principle"—that Christian effort could be better furthered by volunteers bonding into a society than by "official" action by bishops or **synods**. It was this voluntary principle that both led to occasional tensions with bishops in different parts of the world and secured the continuance of overseas **missionary societies** to the present day.

CMS turned broader in its theology in the 20th century, and this led to a split, from which a new society, the **Bible Churchmen's Missionary Society** (BCMS), was formed in 1922. But CMS continued to serve many evangelical **dioceses** around the **Anglican Communion**. It parented CMS Ruanda (that is, of the land that is now **Rwanda**) in England and formed alliances with sister societies, the Church Missionary Societies of **Australia** and New Zealand. In the latter part of the 20th century, its influence was enhanced by a series of notable general secretaries: Max Warren (1942–1962), John V. Taylor (1962–1975), and Simon Barrington-Ward (1975–1985).

In 1992, when Michael Nazir Ali was general secretary, the name was changed to Church Mission Society—still contractible to CMS—in order to supersede the word "missionary," which had lost its original adjectival connotation.

CHURCH OF . . . . For a treatment of individual churches of the **Anglican Communion** (e.g., the Church of the **Province** of Southern Africa or the Church of Uganda), see the name of the country or region concerned (in these examples, **Southern Africa** or **Uganda**).

CHURCH OF ENGLAND. *See* ENGLAND.

CIRCUMCISION. The circumcision of **Jesus Christ** has traditionally been observed on 1 January, the "eighth day" from the feast of his birth (as in Luke 2.21), and it appears, usually in a minor role, in most Anglican **calendars**. The title of the day has in recent years sometimes been superseded by the "Naming of Jesus." Literal circumcision in the flesh has not been required of Christians from the first days of the Christian mission to Gentiles, and for any Church or church leader to make such a requirement is denounced as contrary to the **gospel** in St. Paul's letters. Male circumcision is nevertheless permitted to Christian believers (cf. Acts 16.1–3), so long as it is not made compulsory or a prerequisite of receiving **Communion** (cf. Gal. 2.1–3). However, so-called female circumcision (which is claimed as a tribal or inherited cultural practice in some parts of Africa and the Middle East) has been generally deemed a deviant and abusive practice; it was condemned at the first Anglican Consultation on **liturgical inculturation** in Africa at Kanamai, **Mombasa**, in 1993 and was similarly denounced in the Church of **England**'s **General Synod** in 2002.

CLAPHAM SECT. The so-called Clapham Sect comprised a number of eminent **Evangelical** Anglicans who lived in or near Clapham in South **London** in the latter decades of the 18th century and the first decades of the 19th. John Venn, from a famous Evangelical family, was rector of Holy Trinity, Clapham, from 1792 to 1813, and his **parish** and **ministry** provided a focus for the "sect," the members of which were largely **lay**. They exhibited enormous reforming and creative energies, including a large influence in the formation of the **Church Missionary Society** in 1799 and the British and Foreign Bible Society in 1804. They pressed for the provision of a **bishop** in **India** and for the formation of Sunday Schools at home. Foremost among the members of the Clapham Sect was **William Wilberforce** (1759–1833), who represented two successive Yorkshire constituencies in the House of Commons but lived in Clapham from 1797 on. He devoted his central energies to the abolition of slavery, securing the banning of the slave trade in 1807 and (just before his death) the emancipation of all slaves in the British Empire in 1833. The

Clapham Sect was also concerned for the welfare of freed slaves (and was influential in the creation of Freetown in **Sierra Leone**) and assisted in the formation of charitable societies in England.

CLARIFICATIONS. In 1994 the second **Anglican–Roman Catholic International Commission** (ARCIC-2) published a report entitled *Clarifications*. This was an attempt to restate more clearly the agreed statements of ARCIC-1 on **Eucharist** and on **Ministry** and **Ordination**—which had already been the subject of "elucidations," as ARCIC-1 called the supplementary statements it issued, in the light of public comment, to clear up points where the original statements might have been ambiguous or confusing.

The original statements, with their respective elucidations, had received broadly positive evaluations from the Anglican **provinces** and the 1988 **Lambeth Conference**. However, the response of the **pope** in 1991 to the ARCIC-1 documents was less enthusiastic than that of the Anglican **bishops** and called into question whether "substantial agreement" had really been reached at all. He stated that specific issues had been raised that "would need greater clarification from the Catholic point of view." By this time ARCIC-1 had long been superseded by ARCIC-2, so it was this second commission that, in a further statement submitted to the Vatican in 1993, attempted to provide "clarifications" in answer to the issues raised by the pope. This statement was then published as *Clarifications on Eucharist and Ministry* in 1994, which included a letter of welcome from Cardinal Cassidy, the president of the Pontifical Council for Promoting Christian Unity, expressing almost total acceptance of the "clarifications" offered and saying that "no further study would seem to be required at this stage."

The upshot of this procedure has been concealed confusion. The Vatican had asked for greater clarification, including, among other points, that the eucharist is a "propitiatory sacrifice," that there is agreement on "the adoration of Christ in the **reserved** sacrament," and that there is acceptance of various Roman concepts of the **priesthood** of the **ordained ministry**. ARCIC-2 went a long way in *Clarifications* toward giving the assurances desired by the pope, but in the process raised a yawning contradiction between the two Communions. All Anglican acceptance of the ARCIC-1 statements had been based on discussion of the statements themselves (about which the Vatican had reservations), while Roman Catholic acceptance was based on the clarifications, which were no part of ARCIC-1's own thinking and had never been referred to the **Anglican Communion** (and have unofficially proved highly controversial when studied by Anglicans). At the 1998 **Lambeth Conference** all the then existing statements from ARCIC-2 came under review—except *Clarifications*; in the section report, it was simply omitted from the list of ARCIC-2 materials as though it did not exist.

CLERGY. In the English language, the term "clergy" (derived originally from the Greek *kleros*) is a broad collective noun to include all the **ordained**. It covers **bishops**, **presbyters**, and **deacons** and is sufficiently informal to cover non-Episcopal **ministers**. However, it also has a slightly more formal use, in that **synods** tend to be constituted of distinct Houses of Bishops, Clergy, and **Laity**. In such usage, "clergy" means presbyters and deacons together but not bishops. In an old-fashioned use, retained in some of the language attaching to the **Convocations**, the presbyters and deacons were sometimes described as the "inferior clergy."

COADJUTOR BISHOP. A **bishop** elected as a coadjutor is a **suffragan** or assistant bishop with right of succession as diocesan bishop in that **diocese** when the existing diocesan departs by death, retirement, or translation. It has been a particular feature of **episcopacy** in the **Episcopal Church (United States of America)** and is rare or nonexistent in other parts of the **Anglican Communion**.

COGGAN, FREDERICK DONALD (1910–2000). Donald Coggan had a brilliant academic record in theology as an undergraduate and went from Cambridge in 1931 to teach the New Testament at Manchester University. He was known thereafter as an **Evangelical** and a lover of the **Bible**. Coggan was **ordained** to a **curacy** at St. Mary's, Islington, **London**, in 1934 and went from there in 1937 to teach the New Testament at Wycliffe College, Toronto, **Canada**. In 1944 he returned from Canada to take up an appointment as principal of St. John's Hall, Highbury, only to find the buildings bombed and two students and a porter sharing the premises at Oak Hill. He quickly reestablished the identity of the College (as the London College of Divinity) and purchased premises at Northwood, where, after years of temporary accommodation in first Harrow and then Lingfield, the college took up residence in 1957. By then, Coggan had gone to be **bishop** of Bradford in 1956. From there, he went on to become **archbishop** of **York** in 1961 and archbishop of **Canterbury** in 1974. His years at **Lambeth** were marked by a call for an increase in **ordination** candidates and some recovery of confidence in the Church of **England**. He presided over the 1978 **Lambeth Conference**. Archbishop Coggan retired in 1980, after which he continued an active **ministry** of writing and preaching until near the time of his death.

COLENSO, JOHN WILLIAM (1814–1893). William Colenso was ordained in **England** in 1837. In 1853, under letters patent from Queen Victoria, he was appointed bishop of Natal in **Southern Africa**, and he was **consecrated** for the task by the **archbishop** of **Canterbury**, John Sumner, in **London**.

In 1863 Robert Gray, the archbishop of Cape Town and **metropolitan**, accused Colenso of **heresy**, on the grounds that he taught that the Pentateuch could not be taken literally and that substitutionary **doctrines** of the atonement were incredible and immoral. Colenso declined to recognize Gray's **authority** to try him, and, when sentence of deposition had been pronounced against him, he appealed to the Judicial Committee of the Privy Council in London. In 1865 the Privy Council upheld the appeal, confirmed him in office, and secured his stipend from the Colonial Bishoprics Fund. Archbishop Gray was indignant, but saw no redress.

However, the **bishops** of the ecclesiastical **province** of **Canada** called for a pan-Anglican gathering of bishops to debate and resolve the question. Archbishop Charles Longley cautiously ventured to invite the bishops to what became in 1867 the first **Lambeth Conference**, although stating that Natal could not be on the agenda and, significantly, not inviting Colenso. The bishops nevertheless found a way to state (by a narrow majority) that they would support the archbishop of Cape Town if he were to consecrate another bishop for Natal.

Gray in 1869 consecrated W. K. Macrorie as bishop of Maritzburg and Natal, and then in 1870 summoned a **General Synod**, which, by voluntary compact, would determine who were of the province of

South Africa—and who, by ignoring the summons and evading the compact, were not. The courts later ruled that he had, by this unilateral declaration of independence, separated "root and branch" from the Church of England. Colenso was not summoned to the **synod**, and so he remained a bishop remotely of the Church of England, exercising oversight of the congregations that remained with him in Natal, though in a territory that now had two Anglican bishops and overlapping jurisdictions. When Colenso died, the nonprovincial parishes (both in Natal and elsewhere) stayed in touch with each other until forming in 1938 the Church of England in South Africa (CESA), a separate body still describing itself as Anglican and still in existence today.

COLLECT. A collect is a short prayer, with a slightly stylized form, which **Thomas Cranmer** inherited from the Latin rites and incorporated into the English-language **liturgies** he was creating. In a few cases, he wrote collects afresh, often rather fuller than the Latin forms had been. In general, there is a collect "of" (or pertaining to) each Sunday of the year and every other occasion that has a distinct **proper** provision, as, for example, **Christmas** Day, **saints**' days, and "votive" occasions. Cranmer also wrote general collects, for example, those that come at the end of his **Communion** service, to be used when there is no Communion.

The distinctive "proper" collect of a Sunday or festival is usually read at the end of the introductory section of the **eucharist**, before the ministry of the word, and is marked as a collect by its position in the rite as well as by its length and formal shape. Once so demarcated, it may be used in other rites, such as daily offices, as the "collect of the week [*or* season]," irrespective of where it comes in the order.

It is uncertain whether the Latin term, *collecta*, refers at root to a gathering up of the people (i.e., a prayer that joins them into a congregation) or a gathering up of themes (i.e., a succinct highlighting of a general petition, which includes much else). The classic collect form is best seen when five components are visible:

- The address
- The acknowledgment (or attribution of God's character to him)
- The petition itself

- The aspiration
- The pleading of **Jesus Christ**'s mediation

However, many collects lack one or even two of these features, yet fulfill the classic role. The convention at the eucharist has been to have but one seasonal collect, though the 1549 **Book of Common Prayer** ordered the collect of the first day of **Lent** (**Ash Wednesday**) to be used throughout Lent after the collect of the day, and the 1662 Book ordered the same use throughout **Advent** of the collect of Advent Sunday.

COLONIAL AND CONTINENTAL CHURCH SOCIETY. *See* INTERCONTINENTAL CHURCH SOCIETY.

COLORS. Liturgical colors were abolished at the **Reformation** with the cessation of eucharistic **vestments** and cottas, dalmatics, burses, and frontals. The **presbyters** were from 1559 on to wear a surplice with scarf and hood, vesture that does not provide for seasonal variation. When the **Anglo-Catholic** movement reintroduced pre-Reformation vestments in the mid-19th century, **liturgical** colors reappeared as part of that reintroduction. White or gold is used for **Christmas**, **Easter**, **baptisms**, **ordinations**, and special occasions of thanksgiving; red is used for **martyrs** and for the **Holy Spirit**; violet or black is used in **Advent**, **Lent**, and **burial** rites, with a "Lenten array" (of unbleached linen) as an alternative in Lent; and the rest of the year is in green.

COLUMBA (c. 521–597). Columba has traditionally been known as the **evangelist** of **Scotland**. He was a monk in **Ireland** who in 563 sailed to Iona, a small island off the coast of Mull itself, a larger island off northwest Scotland. There he founded with his 12 companions a **monastery** of which he was abbot. From Iona, Celtic Christianity spread into Scotland generally, and, in the next generation, **Aidan** from Iona became a **missionary** to Northumbria and thus was instrumental in bringing Celtic Christianity into England. Columba himself retained influence in Ireland, but is commemorated for his seminal work in Scotland. In the 20th century, Iona itself has been restored, largely through the vision of Scottish **Presbyterians**, as a place of spiritual **pilgrimage**. Columba is **celebrated** on 9 June.

COMMANDMENTS. *See* TEN COMMANDMENTS.

COMMINATION. The commination is a form of service denouncing sin. In the 1549 **Book of Common Prayer**, there was a service labeled "The First Day of **Lent**, commonly called **Ash Wednesday**," and the content of it (though without the other title) later became "A Commination." In the 1552 Prayer Book, it is called "A Commination against Sinners with certain prayers to be used divers times in the year." So, the title dates from then—though the occasion of the first day of Lent seems to have been lost. In the 1662 Prayer Book, both "Commination" and the identifying of the first day of Lent are present in the title. It is unclear how consistently such a service has been used around the **Anglican Communion**, and modern Prayer Books tend to make a different kind of provision for the beginning of Lent.

COMMON WORSHIP. "Common Worship" is the overall title given to the most recent rites of the Church of **England**, authorized as **alternative services** beginning in 1997. The **calendar** and **lectionary** began in **Advent** 1997, the **initiation services** at **Easter** 1998, and the bulk of the main services from Advent 2000, so that the date "2000" is often attached to the use of the title. Other materials under this title added after 2000 have been Daily Prayer (an interim text in 2002, a definitive one in 2005) and **ordination** services (2005).

COMMONWEALTH. The "Commonwealth" is the title usually given to the polity of **England** after the execution of King **Charles I** in January 1649. Until that point, even his **Puritan** opponents recognized the nation as a kingdom (so that, for example, the ***Directory for the Public Worship of God*** of 1645 included "*in the Three Kingdoms*" in its title). After Charles I's death, male citizens had to subscribe (under the "Engagement") to be "true and faithful to the commonwealth of England, as it is now established, without a king or House of Lords." Thus the Commonwealth period is strictly from 1649 to 1660. This usage has little bearing upon later uses of the term in different political contexts.

COMMONWEALTH AND CONTINENTAL CHURCH SOCIETY. *See* INTERCONTINENTAL CHURCH SOCIETY.

COMMUNION. The Latinate term "communion" usually translates the Greek *koinonia* and has varied meanings in English theological and **ecclesiological** usage. Its basic reference is to a relationship or fellowship, and it is thus used of the relationship between churches. It has also become the collective title of the Anglican churches worldwide, the **Anglican Communion**. Through its use by the Apostle Paul in 1 Cor. 10.16, "Communion" has become the normal title for the **Lord's Supper**. The **Apostles' Creed** includes an apparently different reference, the "**Communion of saints**." *See also* COMMUNION, HOLY; EUCHARIST; FULL COMMUNION.

COMMUNION, HOLY. The **sacrament** instituted by the Lord at the Last Supper has had many names down through history, but "**Communion**," deriving from 1 Cor. 10.16, has had a central place in Anglicanism. The name has at times been used to refer narrowly to the action of distribution of the **elements** (cf. the Communion rite in the **Roman Catholic Church** and *The Order of the Communion* in 1548), but from the 1549 **Book of Common Prayer** onward, it has been prominent as meaning the whole **celebration**. Thus 1549 has as its title "The **Supper of the Lord** and the Holy Communion commonly called the **Mass**"; 1552 goes on to "The Order for the Administration of the **Lord's Supper** or Holy Communion," and this is retained in 1662. The alternative of the "Supper of the Lord" is also drawn from scripture, from 1 Cor. 11.20, and this seems to be the key to the promotion of these titles, and the excision of pre-**Reformation** titles such as the "Mass" or the "Sacrament of the **Altar**" or even the "**eucharist**."

Changes of title indicated changes of both **doctrine** and **liturgical** emphasis. The medieval mass had little or no expectation of the people receiving Communion, save on **Easter Day**; and the purpose of the celebration was the transubstantiation of the elements, followed by elevation and adoration and the offering of the **eucharistic sacrifice** of the mass to the Father. The initial principle at the time of the Reformation was the need to restore regular lay Communion, and this was intended to be implemented by the 1548 *Order*. Yet, though in theory such an addendum to the text of the mass might involve no other change in liturgical texts, it actually presaged a vast shift in the focus and purpose of the rite.

In the further successive steps of the 1549 and 1552 Books of Common Prayer, **Archbishop Thomas Cranmer** not only put the rite into English but also put through a revolution in its meaning. He did not believe in transubstantiation or any other concept of the presence of Christ "in" the sacramental elements, but transferred the weight of the liturgy to a dynamic understanding of reception, most characteristically expressed in the changes to the "petition for consecration" (or ***epiclesis***) that preceded the **narrative** of institution in three successive rites, as seen in table 1.

The doctrine of Communion was carefully defined in the Reformation formularies (including **Articles** XXV, XXVIII, XXIX, and XXXI in 1571) so as both to express the "**receptionist**" position and also to protect the doctrine from any assimilation to the Roman Catholic position. In furtherance of this concern, **rubrical** provision was made beginning in 1552 to require the **bread** to be such "as is usual to be eaten" (i.e., not to be unleavened wafer bread). However, the trend between 1559 and 1662 was also to recreate the concept of **consecration** of the elements and to identify the dominical words ("This is my body," and so on) in the narrative of institution as the point where consecration occurred. Such change in the liturgical provision does not imply any necessary doctrinal shift, though it has facilitated the determination of one section of the **Anglican Com-**

Table 1. Epiclesis Preceding the Narrative of Institution in Three Successive Rites

Roman Rite	*1549*	*1552*
Which oblation we beseech thee, O Almighty God, in all things to make blessed, + appointed, + ratified, reasonable and acceptable; that it may be the + body and + blood of thy most dearly beloved Son our Lord Jesus Christ.	Hear us (o merciful Father) we beseech thee; and with thy Holy Spirit and Word, vouchsafe to bl+ess and sanc+tify these thy gifts and creatures of bread and wine, that they may be unto us the body and blood of thy most dearly beloved Son Jesus Christ.	Hear us, o merciful Father, we beseech thee; and grant that we, receiving these thy creatures of bread and wine, according to thy Son our Saviour Jesus Christ's holy institution, in remembrance of his death and passion, may be partakers of his most blessed body and blood.

munion to read semi–Roman Catholic doctrines into the rite. It has been further complicated in the **Scottish** and **American** liturgical traditions, where the "consecratory" epiclesis comes after the narrative of institution and the **anamnesis**, and it is therefore difficult to allocate consecration to the dominical words in the narrative (and corresponding care has to be observed in respect of accompanying **ceremonial**).

Liturgies compiled in the second half of the 20th century tend to lay less emphasis upon a "moment" of consecration but rather invite the understanding that consecration is effected by the total thanksgiving of the whole prayer. The 1958 **Lambeth Conference** section report on revising liturgy stated: "We desire to draw attention to a conception of consecration which is scriptural and primitive and goes behind subsequent controversies . . . and may be called consecration through thanksgiving."

The rise of the 19th-century **Anglo-Catholic** movement has had tremendous effects upon Anglican sacramental practice. The more partisan effects were seen in **fasting** Communion, noncommunicating masses, Latin texts, requiem masses, Communion in one kind, **reservation**, exposition of the reserved wafer, and devotions before reserved elements. The more widespread sacramental effects have been of a different order, for, as a far-reaching outcome of the movement, a very large proportion of Anglicans now expect the main Sunday worship of the church to be Holy Communion and view themselves as weekly communicants. Baptized guests from other denominations are welcomed. Communion is also celebrated midweek, and in many places even daily. **Baptisms** are celebrated within Communion rites, unlike the 1662 Prayer Book provision. The admission of young children to Communion on the basis of their baptism, rather than their age or their **confirmation**, has also flourished in many **provinces**. Informal house and group Communions have grown, **agapes** are used in some places, and local adaptation of rites has become normal. Communion of the sick is often done by extended distribution, whether by clergy or **laypeople**, of elements from a main celebration and sometimes by **intinction**. In some **provinces**, **deacons** or laypeople may officiate at rites where a service of the word leads on to a distribution of Communion from reserved elements. *See also* DUBLIN STATEMENT; YORK STATEMENT.

COMMUNION OF SAINTS. The phrase "communion of saints" appears as part of the articles of faith in the latter part of the **Apostles' Creed**. Its Latin origin is the phrase *communio sanctorum*, which might mean a sharing with holy people ("**saints**") or might mean a sharing in holy things, probably the **sacrament** of Holy **Communion**. It has generally been taken in modern Anglicanism to refer to an invisible unity in **Jesus Christ** that binds the living and **dead** together.

COMPASS ROSE. The Compass Rose *motif* (see the illustration in the photospread) is a symbol or logo of the **Anglican Communion**. It was originally designed, probably in the early 1950s, by Edward West, **canon** of New York **Cathedral**, and was apparently first used publicly on the front cover of the report of 1954 Minneapolis **Anglican Congress**. It became the regular symbol for the Anglican Communion thereafter, invariably being found on the covers of reports of **Lambeth Conferences**, of the 1963 Toronto Anglican Congress, and of the **Anglican Consultative Council** meetings, which began in 1971. The motif was slightly redesigned in the 1980s by Giles Bloomfield and gained official approval and definitive form through the reproduction of that design in the floor of the **nave** of **Canterbury** Cathedral, where it was dedicated by **Archbishop Robert Runcie** at the farewell **eucharist** of the 1988 Lambeth Conference.

From the start, it has contained at the center of the design the cross of St. George, surrounded by the inscription in Greek "The truth will set you free" and by the points of the compass, indicating the worldwide spread of the Anglican Communion. "The Truth Will Set You Free" also became the title of the 1988 Lambeth Conference report. The design has been taken up and used in many places of the Communion. There is also a Compass Rose Society, founded in 1998, composed of persons voluntarily uniting across the world to express Christ's compassion, particularly by providing resources in needy parts of the Communion.

CONCELEBRATION. In the **Roman Catholic Church** at the **ordination** of **presbyters**, it has been customary for centuries for the newly **ordained**, having just received the paten and chalice within the rite, then to shadow the words and actions of the officiating **bishop** who "**celebrates**" **Communion**, thus "concelebrating" with him. The Roman Catholic Church expanded this use greatly in the wake of **Vatican II** and provided that on any occasion when two or more presbyters are present at a celebration of the eucharist, they may "concelebrate"—and should do so in preference to celebrating two separate "private" **masses**. Some Anglicans have taken up this practice in imitation of Rome, and in some **provinces**, the **rubrics**, **canons**, or customs allow it. However, contemporary thinking—which conceives of the whole congregation as "celebrating" the eucharist—militates against the concept of clerical "concelebration" and so expounds **presidency** as facilitating the celebration of the whole congregation (rather than the placarding and demonstrating of the presbyteral **orders** of those present who are in those orders) as to leave little scope for what would be better described as "copresidency."

CONCEPTION OF THE BLESSED VIRGIN MARY. The nativity of **Mary** has traditionally been observed on 8 September, so it is not surprising that her conception has been dated to 8 December. Her mother has in tradition been named as St. Anne. In 1854 **Pope** Pius IX defined and imposed for the **Roman Catholic Church** the **doctrine** of the **Immaculate Conception** as being *de fide*. The doctrine states that, in the economy of **God**, Mary was miraculously exempted at the point of conception from the entail of **original sin** and was thus able to bestow a sinless human nature upon **Jesus Christ** when he in turn was conceived in her womb. The vision of St. Bernadette at Lourdes in 1858 (when the Virgin Mary is said to have appeared to her and declared, "I am the Immaculate Conception") and the retrospective decree of **Vatican I** in 1870 that papal definitions *ex cathedra* are **infallible**, greatly strengthened the cult of the Immaculate Conception in the Roman Catholic Church. Anglicans, on the other hand, although they have a natural readiness to take note of the conception of Mary in the womb of her mother, recognize anything beyond that mere fact as speculation. Not only does the papal doctrine lack scriptural warrant, but the scriptures reveal no information or interest whatsoever in respect of the conception and birth of Mary. The papal **authority** to define such a doctrine is thus in turn thrown deeply into question. *See also* ANGLICAN–ROMAN CATHOLIC INTERNATIONAL COMMISSION.

CONFESSION. *See* ABSOLUTION.

CONFIRMATION. Confirmation is one of the five rites labeled by **Article** XXV as those "commonly called **sacraments**" which the Church of **England** inherited from the **Roman Catholic Church** at the **Reformation** that are no longer viewed as sacraments. The Reformers viewed **baptism** alone as sacramental **initiation** and thus restructured the place of confirmation. They made it not an *ex opere operato* rite for giving the **Holy Spirit** but rather an "approval" by the church of those who, having been baptized in infancy, were now coming to the age of discretion and were able to answer for themselves. Admission to **Communion** was to be by means of confirmation, in order to ensure that children were properly instructed before receiving Communion, and the **catechism** was included within the confirmation rite to demonstrate this rationale and make it effective.

In the revision of the confirmation service by two stages through the 1549 and 1552 **Books of Common Prayer**, the laying on of hands was restored as the only outward ceremony in the rite, and the postconfirmation prayer claimed that the **bishop** was using the ceremony "after the example of thy holy apostles." The formula at the laying of hands ceased to have a sacramental ring to it and became a simple prayer ("Defend, O Lord, thy servant . . .")—one that could be used on any occasion, sacramental or nonsacramental, without any oddity. Whereas in 1549, 1552, 1559, and 1604 the catechism was included within the confirmation rite, in 1662 it was made a separate item within the Prayer Book, and at the confirmation the candidates were instead asked whether they renewed the promises made for them by their **godparents** at their baptism, to which they in reply simply stated "I do."

A question arose in 1662 as to whether those baptized in "riper years" (a new category for which the need of baptism had newly arisen) then also needed to be confirmed, but the ruling of the **rubrics** was that such people, although they had recently answered for themselves in baptism, should still "renew" their baptismal vows in confirmation and be admitted by this route to Communion. There would appear to have been a political rather than a theological impulse behind this requirement, as the newly restored bishops would thus ensure that the children of Anabaptist families—families whose children had escaped being baptized during the **Commonwealth** period—should now kneel before a bishop as part of the royalist and Anglican **Restoration** and should thus accept that settlement. "Riper years" has as its first point of reference those between 12 and 17 years of age who had been born since 1645 (when confirmation had ceased) but were of age to answer for themselves.

Despite the apparent insistence on the necessity of confirmation, it appears that from the mid-17th to the mid-19th centuries there was much neglect in its administration. In **England**, **dioceses** were large, suffragan bishops did not exist, bishops could not retire (and hence there were always some infirm and fairly static ones in office), and travel was difficult. Abroad, no bishop of **London** ever visited the American colonies to give confirmation, and—although an overseas **episcopate** began in the late 18th century in North America, followed in the first half of the 19th by pioneering bishops in **India**, the **West Indies**, **Australia**, **New Zealand**, and **South Africa**—the enormous size of the overseas bishops' jurisdictions still left the availability of confirmation in most local churches somewhat unpredictable. However, in the second half of the 19th century, dioceses were divided in every part of the world; suffragan, assistant, and **coadjutor bishops** were appointed; provision was made even in England for bishops to retire—and the railways came. It then became credible to expect a bishop to confirm annually in large towns and cities, and bishops in turn came to expect to travel and confirm in this way.

A change of **doctrine** began in the late 19th century, led by the second generation of the **Anglo-Catholic** movement. It began in the 1870s with an unprecedented appeal to the "confirmation rubric" to exclude all the unconfirmed (particularly non-Episcopalians) from Communion. F. W. Puller in 1880 and Arthur James Mason in 1891 taught that confirmation is the coming of the Spirit to the candidate, that is, that sacramental initiation is in principle in "two stages": baptism for rebirth and confirmation for the gift of the Spirit. This teaching was very shakily based in the New Testament, but when Anglican Prayer Books were revised in different **provinces** in the years down to 1950, the reading from Acts 8.14–17—a text that stands almost alone in the New Testament as giving warrant to the "two-staging" view—was usually incorporated into the rites. The teaching was reinforced by **Gregory Dix** and J. D. C. Fisher in the 1930s and 1940s and became known jocularly, from its major exponents, as the "Mason-Dix Line." The proponents urged that, despite the polarizing of theologies between water and the laying on of the hand, in fact if the two were administered within the same rite, then the initiation would be "complete." This had a profound effect in the structuring of new rites of initiation in the last three decades of the 20th century.

Since 1970, despite this impact on the shape of rites, the theological pendulum has swung back. Baptism in water has been seen again as the sole and complete sacrament of initiation; unconfirmed non-Episcopalians have been welcomed to Communion; children below the age for confirmation have been admitted to Communion on the basis of their baptism; and in various ways, rites of confirmation have been moved away from "initiation" and are instead located among "pastoral rites" or "Episcopal services." The admission of unconfirmed children to Communion was strongly recommended in the 1985 **Boston Statement** of the First **International Anglican Liturgical Consultation** (IALC) and was reinforced by the 1991 **Toronto Statement** of the fourth IALC. That sacramental initiation is complete in water baptism was also affirmed by the section report at the 1988 **Lambeth Conference**.

In modern rites, the Acts 8 passage has disappeared again from the authorized readings, and other passages about continuance in the life of the Spirit have come in its place. Various provinces have added, alongside confirmation, similar rites for reception into the Anglican church (particularly for ex–**Roman Catholics**, who may have already been confirmed) and for reaffirmation of baptismal vows (for those who are already confirmed but have lapsed and are being restored). The restored theological significance given to baptism has tended, particularly for those baptized as adults, to diminish the importance of confirmation, and the Toronto Statement recommended ending the requirement for confirmation to follow adult baptism.

CONGÉ D'ÉLIRE. When a see is vacant in the Church of **England**, under the provisions of King **Henry VIII**'s Act of 1534, the monarch issues an instruction to the **dean** (or **provost**) and **chapter** of the **cathedral** of the vacant **diocese** to hold an election to fill the vacancy. The instruction is named a *congé d'élire* (French for "holiday to hold an election"). It is accompanied by a further instruction containing the name of the one nominee whom the chapter is to elect—whose name has been published weeks before. Although the penalties once prescribed for failure to elect were abolished in 1969, no election has yet led to the defeat of the monarch's nominee. Since 2000 the instruction has been issued to "the college of **canons**," rather than the "dean and chapter." *See also* ESTABLISHMENT.

CONGO. The first known Anglican **missionary** work in the Congo came through a **Ugandan** evangelist, **Apolo Kivebulaya**, preaching in what was then the Belgian Congo in 1896. However, there was little established Anglican presence until the 1970s, when the **dioceses** of Boga-Zaire and Bukavu—within the then **province** of Uganda, **Burundi**, **Rwanda**, and Boga-Zaire—were formed. Burundi, Rwanda, and Boga-Zaire became a French-speaking province separate from Uganda in 1980, and the Zairean dioceses were subdivided during the 1980s until the province of Zaire was formed in 1992. By 1997 there were six dioceses. In the wake of political change, as Zaire became the Democratic Republic of Congo, the church's name was changed to the Anglican Church of Congo, which enables congregations in the Republic of Congo (a separate nation to the north) to be part of the province. There is a provincial **synod** as well as diocesan ones, and the **archbishop** is chosen by the six diocesans and can only be elected when there are no vacancies among them. He is elected to serve for five years only, but the appointment is renewable.

CONGREGATIONALISTS. Congregationalism dates back to the strand of **Puritans** in the 16th and 17th centuries known as "Independents." Their church polity was such as to make each congregation wholly autonomous and responsible for its own life, and for each congregation to make its decisions by full participation of all members. In **South India**, the Congregationalists joined with the **Presbyterians** in 1908 to form the South India United Church, and it was that church that united with the Anglicans and Methodists in 1947. In **England** a similar union with Presbyterians in 1972 produced the United Reformed Church (URC), and that church voted in favor of a "covenant" for unity in 1982. These instances illustrate how Anglicans and Congregationalists may come into discussions of unity at one remove from pure Congregationalism. In **South Africa**, Congregationalists have been part of the Concordat of 1996 for interchangeability of **ministers**. But in any one country, the only central body is a federal association of individual congregations, and each has to make its own separate decision in relation to any unity proposals.

CONSECRATION. "Consecration" is the term used before the **Reformation** for the action by which the **eucharistic elements** are deemed to be changed in their substance into the body and blood of **Jesus Christ**. The term was retained in the 1549 **Book of Common Prayer**, though **Thomas Cranmer**, in his writings in opposition to Stephen Gardiner, expounded the 1549 usage as meaning not the elements' change in substance but a change in use—a setting apart for a divine use. He went on in 1552 to remove all possible reference to consecration, such that the term "consecration" and its cognates do not appear, there is no mention of handling the **bread** and wine before the distribution, there is no provision for "supplementary consecration" if the supply runs out, and there is no provision for consuming "consecrated remains" after the rite (instead the **curate** can take home any remaining bread or wine for his own personal use, without any distinction between "consecrated" and "unconsecrated" elements). The text lays all the emphasis upon the giving and receiving of the bread and wine, and none upon what has been effected "out there" independently of reception.

In Queen **Elizabeth I**'s reign, **John Jewel**, in his *Apologia pro Ecclesia Anglicana*, insisted that, in the use of the **narrative** of institution in the 1559 **eucharistic** rite (a rite that was verbally identical to that of 1552 save in an expansion of the words of distribution), the Church of **England** did have a consecration. A **Puritan**, Robert Johnson, was jailed soon after for not repeating the words of institution when he took additional supplies of the elements after his original stock ran out—though there were no written requirements to do so. These came when the **canons** of 1604 required the repetition of the narrative for such occasions.

The 1637 **Scottish** rite entitled the (1549-like) **eucharistic prayer** the "Prayer of Consecration." Finally the **Puritans** at the **Savoy Conference** themselves wanted the consecration made "more explicit," and in the 1662 rite there were added the title ("Prayer of Consecration"), five **manual acts** ordered by **indented rubrics** to be used during the narrative of institution, provision for supplementary consecration (as in the 1604 canons), and the requirement for the consumption of any consecrated remains immediately after the service (while any unconsecrated remains could still be taken home by the curate). Thus a concept of consecration of the elements had been fastened onto the rite.

For nearly three centuries after 1662, all Anglican **liturgies** provided indented rubrics prescribing manual acts during the narrative of institution, some method of supplementary consecration, and a clear distinction after the rite was over between consecrated and unconsecrated remains. The only exception was the use of an Eastern-type **epiclesis**, invoking the sending of the **Holy Spirit**, in the Scottish/American tradition. While such an epiclesis came before the narrative in the Scottish 1637 rite, it was changed to come in the eastern position after the narrative and following the **anamnesis** in the Scottish rites of 1755 and 1764 and was part of the Scottish inheritance that passed into the 1789 Book of Common Prayer of the **Protestant Episcopal Church in the United States of America**.

An epiclesis coming after the narrative of institution strongly suggests that consecration has *not* been effected by the use of the narrative, and this has been unwelcome to a strand of rigorously "Western" **Anglo-Catholics**. It was included in the abortive 1927–1928 proposals in the Church of England and was a factor contributory to their defeat. It should be noted that insistence that there is an objective consecration of the elements, and even a debate about how that is effected liturgically, do not entail any specific belief about what has thereby happened to or in the consecrated elements. This is summarized further below.

At the 1958 **Lambeth Conference**, the view was propounded in the conference report that consecration is effected by the total thanksgiving and that we should not be seeking or advertising a single special "moment" of consecration. This view would leave the narrative of institution as a "warrant text" (in an adjectival dependent clause), but without unique or special consecratory force. Such a **doctrine** would seem to exclude much of the **ceremonial** that, in Anglo-Catholic usage, has clustered around the narrative of institution. Most modern eucharistic rites (though not the American) do indeed remove the indented rubrics that provided for manipulation of the elements in the 1662 rite—and a use has also arisen whereby assisting distributants stand around the eucharistic **table** during the eucharistic prayer, each holding a vessel and then moving to distribute the particular element at the appropriate point in the rite, when that element has neither been touched by the **ordained president** nor even been placed on the eucharistic table.

It would appear important therefore to distinguish in relation to the eucharist two separate questions: on the one hand, what effects consecration, and on the other, what consecration effects.

The term "consecration" is not confined to the eucharistic elements. People also are consecrated. "Consecration" was the term used in the Reformation **Ordinals** for the conferring of the **episcopate** upon a **presbyter**, possibly in order to avoid saying that **bishops** are "ordained," about which at the time there appeared to be some doubt. In distinction from this, in 1662 the term "ordination" was deliberately introduced to emphasize that the episcopate is an "**order**" (as had in fact been very strongly suggested by the **preface** to the Ordinal in 1550 and 1552), though the term "consecration" also continued.

Buildings also are consecrated—usually **parish** churches or **cathedrals**—as is furniture within church buildings, notably **altars** or Communion tables.

All three uses would appear to have in common that it is not anticipated that consecration can be reversed. If the latter two uses (for bishops and buildings) are viewed as determinative, then it is clear that consecration is done with a view to a change of use and not of nature. But if the consecration of eucharistic elements is deemed to be *sui generis*, then any doctrine of "change" in the elements through consecration can be asserted. *See also* RECEPTIONISM.

CONSULTATIVE BODY. *See* LAMBETH CONSULTATIVE BODY.

CONTINUING ANGLICANS. Schisms from the Anglican churches have occurred at least since the **nonjurors** split in 1690. There are also 19th-century precedents in the **Reformed Episcopal Church** in the **United States** and the **Free Church of England**. However, the term "Continuing Anglicans" has been generically used for the various breakaways that have occurred in the latter part of the 20th century in several parts of the world precipitated by the provision for the **ordination** of **women**. There are many such Churches in existence, mostly of tiny numbers, but the single term "Continuing Anglicans" comprehends the whole genre. Such bodies are not recognized as Anglican churches by the **Anglican Consultative Council** (ACC) and cannot be counted as members of the **Anglican Communion**. At the beginning of the 21st century, further tensions over open acceptance of **homosexually** active **clergy** have threatened to precipitate further breakaways of a similar, though not identical, sort. *See also* COLENSO, JOHN WILLIAM; CUMMINS, GEORGE DAVID; *EPISCOPUS VAGANS*; WINDSOR REPORT.

CONVENT. *See* MONASTERY; NUN.

CONVOCATION. At the time of the **Reformation**, the Convocations were representative bodies of the **clergy** of the two **provinces** of **Canterbury** and **York** and were responsible for raising taxes from the clergy. They consisted of Upper Houses (of which the diocesan **bishops** were the members) and Lower Houses, which contained the "inferior" clergy and a high proportion of *ex officio* members. The independence of the Church of **England** from Rome was originally secured by the submission of the clergy in Convocation to the supreme **authority** of King **Henry VIII** over the Church of England in 1534 and their disavowal of the **pope**.

The Convocations have remained in existence in England since the Reformation, sometimes preparing legislation for Parliament (as with the 1661 revision of the **Book of Common Prayer**), sometimes debating issues of current concern. Traditionally, the Houses convened only by royal command and were dissolved with Parliament. They transacted only such business as the monarch allowed—and from 1717 to 1852 the monarch remitted no business to them at all, and their meetings were merely formal.

Their reemergence into a significant role in the life of the Church of England came through agitation, largely by **Anglo-Catholics**. Convocations met for business in Canterbury from 1852 and York from 1861. After that point, they were assumed to be taking responsibility for the welfare and progress of the Church of England and were helping give it an identity separate from the organs of state. Thus the alteration of subscription and assent ordered by Parliament in the Clerical Subscription Act 1865 was the outcome of moves made in the Convocations. However, the parliamentary passage of the Public Worship Regulation Act 1874 and the establishment of the Royal Commission on Ecclesiastical Discipline (1904) were carried through without reference to the Convocations, indicating that true power over the life of the Church of England still rested with the state.

In 1919, in anticipation of the "**Enabling Act**," the Convocations adopted a constitution for a "National Assembly of the Church of England." The two Upper Houses became for this purpose a single House of Bishops, and the two Lower Houses a single House of Clergy. They were joined to a single House of **Laity** to form the Assembly. However, the provincial Convocations on their own retained many distinct roles, particularly in relation to **doctrinal** matters and the passing of **canons**. The last occasion for the dissolving and election of Convocations at the same time as Parliament came in October 1964. The Lower Houses then elected were to stay in office until 1970. Then the **General Synod** came into being, with Convocations and the House of **Laity** being elected at the same time as each other once every five years. But with the integration of the Houses into a single General Synod, separate meetings of the two provincial Convocations fairly quickly ran into the sand, except for the rare occasions (such as voting on the **ordination** of **women** as **presbyters**) when the constitution of Synod itself provided for a "separate reference" to the Convocations and the House of Laity.

Anglicans in other provinces do not, as far as can be ascertained, run representative Convocations of the clergy, and (apart from a period in the history of the Church of **Ireland**) the title, history, and role of the Convocations in England appear to be unique in the **Anglican Communion**.

CONVOCATION ROBES. *See* VESTMENTS.

CORONATION. Since Saxon times, the monarchy of **England** (with other varied territories added to the kingdom at different times) has been viewed as a divinely established institution, to which a Christian coronation (or crowning) rite has both witnessed and added credibility. While each coronation of a monarch is devised afresh, the general pattern has been that the crowning has been done by the **archbishop** of **Canterbury** of the time, in the context of a **Communion** service in Westminster **Abbey**, with the monarch seated on the Coronation Chair. A great range of **ceremonial** has been employed, of which the **anointing** of the monarch is probably the central and most significant one, though the actual crowning is the most visible feature and is that which gives the title to the whole service.

Since the **Reformation**, the rite has been based on the authorized Communion service of the time, except in the case of the **Roman Catholic** king **James II** (1685–1688), whose coronation, for obvious reasons, had no Communion rite at all. After his flight from the throne, the text of the rite since then has included specific promises by the monarch to uphold the Church of England. Most of the rite, however, stems from the work of the archbishop of Canterbury of the time, to whom the task of compilation is given by the Privy Council.

When the present monarch, Queen Elizabeth II, was crowned in 1953, the moderator of the Church of **Scotland** (which is **Presbyterian** in its polity) exercised a minimal role in presenting the monarch with a **Bible** ("the most valuable gift that this world affords"), while also raising the question of how far beyond both England and the Church of England the monarch's reign is being recognized in the rite. The consort of the monarch, when female and being known as queen, has also been crowned alongside her husband. It is recognized that future coronations may have to handle new questions about the relation of Church and State, about the relationship of the Church of England to other Churches, and about what role (if any) other faith communities in Britain may exercise in the rite. *See also* ESTABLISHMENT.

COUNCIL OF ANGLICAN PROVINCES OF AFRICA (CAPA). As new African **provinces** of the **Anglican Communion** came into being in the 1960s and 1970s, so steps were taken to enable matters of common concern to be handled jointly. The **archbishops** of the provinces met in Malawi in 1979 and formed the Council of Anglican Provinces of Africa. A subsequent meeting in **Kenya** outlined these aims and objectives:

a) [to] help the Anglican churches in Africa develop beneficial relationships between themselves and the entire Anglican Communion;

b) [to] provide a forum for the Church in Africa to share experiences, consult and support each other;
c) [to] confer about common responsibilities on the African continent;
d) [to] establish opportunities for collaboration and joint activities and render assistance whenever necessary. (Council of Anglican Provinces of Africa, 2005)

A secretariat, based in Nairobi in Kenya, was formed and is accountable to a management group of members drawn from different provinces. Its initial tasks have been the training of **bishops**, for which a pan-African residential course is held every two years; coordinating programs to combat HIV/AIDS; and developing communications.

In 1992 CAPA backed a project to link Anglican theological training institutions in Africa, and from this in 1993 sponsored the launch of the African Network of Institutions of Theological Education Preparing Anglicans for Ministry (ANITEPAM). ANITEPAM has continued from its beginnings with both occasional conferences and a regular newsletter, and it sponsored a consultation of Anglican contextual theologians in 2004. CAPA sponsored consultations on **liturgical inculturation** in Africa in 1993 and 1996, with participation from around the provinces. Furthermore, it was as chairman of CAPA that Archbishop Peter Akinola, **primate** of **Nigeria**, convened at Lagos at the end of October 2004 the first African Anglican Bishops Conference (AABC) to respond to the publication of the **Windsor Report**. The conference's communiqué emphasized its continued opposition to same-sex unions and looked for African theological training to be both contextualized in Africa and administered and delivered from African resources.

The member provinces in 2004 were Nigeria, **West Africa**, **Sudan**, Kenya, **Uganda**, **Tanzania**, **Congo**, **Rwanda**, **Burundi**, **Central Africa**, **Southern Africa**, and **Indian Ocean**. The **diocese** of **Egypt**, which belongs to the province of **Jerusalem and the Middle East** but has its own borders solely within Africa, is also a member.

COUNCILS. The **Anglican Communion** holds in respect those first four Councils that helped define orthodox belief with regard to the **Trinity** and to the **Incarnation** of **Jesus Christ**: **Nicea** (325), Constantinople (381), Ephesus (431), and **Chalcedon** (451). The basis of their original **authority** lay in their composition—that is, that they brought together all the **bishops** of the worldwide **church** (and were entitled **Ecumenical** Councils because of their worldwide character, "worldwide" being the root meaning of "ecumenical"). The decrees of these Councils, incorporated into the ecumenical **creeds**, are deemed to be accurate summaries of the faith. However, the creeds were received at the **Reformation** not because they derived from General Councils but because they might "be proved by most certain warrants of holy Scripture" (**Article** VIII). The overall stance of Anglicans has been to say that "General Councils . . . may err, and sometimes have erred, even in things pertaining unto God" (Article XXI).

There were some efforts made at intervals during the Reformation period to get an international and representative **Protestant** Council to meet and agree upon **doctrinal** statements in contrast to those of the Council of **Trent**, but it is clear that any hypothetical statement coming out of such a body would have had authority only if adopted by the particular participating Churches individually—and even if adopted, such a statement would always have had a provisionality subject to further reform in the light of scripture. In the event, there has been no opportunity for a General Council outside of the **Roman Catholic Church** since the Reformation, and the Roman Catholic councils have qualified as "general" only by the exclusion of all other Churches.

Other bodies that include the word "council" in their titles (e.g., the **World Council of Churches**, the **Anglican Consultative Council**, and so on) do not thereby claim to be "General Councils" nor expect to define the Christian faith for all times ahead in an irreformable way. The meetings of the Anglican bishops every 10 years are called **Lambeth Conferences**, and this title was chosen deliberately to avoid making any claim to be a Council that would exercise worldwide powers. *See also* VATICAN I; VATICAN II.

COUNTER-REFORMATION. *See* TRENT, COUNCIL OF.

CRANMER, THOMAS (1489–1556). Thomas Cranmer, the **archbishop** of **Canterbury** from 1533 to 1556, had a unique role in the **Reformation** of the Church of **England**. While it has become commonplace to say that Anglicans are not based upon a one-man creative work at the time of the Reformation (as, say, the **Lutheran Churches** are), if there *is* one man to whom the carrying through of the English Reformation can be attributed, then it is Thomas Cranmer.

Cranmer married young, and his first wife died around 1515. He was then **ordained** and became a Cambridge don. From 1527 on, he was known as a supporter of King **Henry VIII** in the monarch's quest for an annulment of his **marriage**, and in 1529 he came into prominence for the suggestion that, in the logjam the king had reached with the **pope**, an appeal to the universities of the Continent might provide a surer and swifter answer. Henry delighted in the solution and sent Cranmer himself on a quest around the universities of Europe. He returned with a verdict favorable to Henry—and also with a new wife for himself, the niece of Osiander, the Lutheran Reformer of Nuremburg.

In late 1532 Cranmer was nominated by Henry to be archbishop of Canterbury, and in early 1533, at the very point when Henry's marriage to Anne Boleyn in defiance of the pope was being made public, his nomination was accepted by the pope, who duly dispatched the **metropolitical** pallium. Cranmer was consecrated on 30 March 1533, and thereafter he denounced the pope and became the leading ecclesiastical exponent of the supreme headship of the monarch.

Cranmer remained archbishop of Canterbury until the end of Henry's reign, surviving various changes of those years. It appears that he was reflecting on his knowledge of scripture and unobtrusively revising his **doctrine** of the **eucharist**. He is held responsible for the text of the Ten **Articles** of 1536, which showed slight reforming tendencies, and for the setting up of **vernacular Bibles** in every Church in 1537. On the other hand, he opposed the reactionary Six Articles of 1539. Cranmer commissioned the First Book of **Homilies** in 1542, and he compiled the first English-language official **liturgy** in 1544, which took the form of a vernacular **litany**.

But the greatest work associated with Cranmer was yet to come, during the reign of King **Edward VI**. When Henry died in January 1547, his son Edward inherited at nine years of age. Cranmer was a powerful figure on the Council that governed the land during the king's youth, and he had not only the political power but also both reformed convictions and a brilliant touch for writing English liturgical texts. These all came together in the provision of, first, *The Order for* *the Communion* in 1548, followed by the first full **Book of Common Prayer** in 1549, the first English **Ordinal** in 1550, and the second Book of Common Prayer (with a revised Ordinal) in 1552. Alongside this magisterial liturgiography, Cranmer was fulfilling a great range of other tasks: changing the interiors of church buildings, writing at vast length on the eucharist in dispute with Stephen Gardiner, engaging in an intensive correspondence with Continental Reformers, composing a complete draft of new ecclesiastical laws, and drafting a set of Articles of Faith (the Forty-Two Articles of 1553). Despite other interpretations offered, the 1552 Communion service not only was the climax of his liturgical program but almost certainly had been in view from before the time the 1549 Book was published.

When Edward VI died in July 1553, Cranmer briefly supported the claims to the throne of Lady Jane Grey, but then accepted Queen **Mary I**. The acceptance was not mutual, however, and although charges of treason were not pressed, charges of **heresy** (especially in relation to the eucharist) were. He was imprisoned in Oxford and examined as to whether he believed in transubstantiation; he was also pressed closely as to whether, in the light of his own advocacy of the divine right of kings in previous reigns, he would not now obey Queen Mary and yield to Rome. After **Hugh Latimer** and **Nicholas Ridley** were burned at the stake in October 1555, Cranmer reached a point where he formally, in a signed statement, recanted his beliefs about the **Lord's Supper**. On 21 March 1556 he was brought before the tribunal that was to sentence him at St. Mary the Virgin Church, Oxford, when, without warning, he abjured his own recantation and reaffirmed his reformed position. He was hurried to the stake, and there put his right hand ("this hand hath offended") first into the flames. His memory is kept on 21 March in many Anglican **calendars**.

CREEDS. Three creeds were received by tradition and sustained within the life of the Church of **England** at the **Reformation**: the **Apostles' Creed**, the **Nicene Creed**, and the **Athanasian Creed**. Their retention is clearly stated in **Article** VIII as dependent upon the rationale that "they may be proved by most certain warrants of holy Scripture." **Thomas Cranmer** incorporated each of them in the **Book of Common Prayer**—the Apostles' Creed in **Morning Prayer**, **Evening**

Prayer, **baptism**, and **catechism**; the Nicene Creed in **Communion**; and the Athanasian Creed on 13 specified days in the year in place of the Apostles' Creed at Morning Prayer. The Apostles' and Nicene creeds are cited as the second side of the **Lambeth Quadrilateral**. *See also* COUNCILS.

CREMATION. The burial of the **dead** has a Jewish background in the New Testament and is attested in a variety of ways—including the burial of **Jesus Christ**—as the normal procedure. The whole later history of Christian **funeral** rites was, until the late 19th century, bound up with **burial** as the method of both respecting the corpse and relinquishing it. In English society, the churchyard developed as the place of burial alongside the church building. In the Church of **England**'s 1662 **Book of Common Prayer** and in the **Protestant Episcopal Church in the United States of America**'s 1789 Book of Common Prayer, the only funeral services are entitled "The Burial of the Dead." However, the practice of cremating dead bodies grew through various civic pressures in the 19th century, particularly in Western urban contexts, and the Churches had to come to terms with it. Theologically, a conservative Christian spirit (still to be found in some parts of the **Anglican Communion**) reacted against cremation as insufficiently honoring of the body and improperly ignoring the **doctrine** of the **resurrection** of the body. Nevertheless, these scruples have been widely overcome and the funeral **liturgies** adapted accordingly. Cremation may be viewed as final a leave-taking of the dead person's mortal remains as is interment; but it is sometimes followed by a further burial, or scattering, of the ashes (with a further liturgical rite), sometimes at a distance in time or space from the cremation service.

CROSS. The **sign of the cross** in **liturgy** has a distinct Anglican history. In the 1549 **Book of Common Prayer**, the provision of a printed + within the text of the liturgy was retained in five places, but all of these disappeared in 1552 except the use of the sign of the cross in **baptism**—and even that single use became one of the four chief "excepted ceremonies" that the **Puritans** fought against.

From the beginning of the **Anglo-Catholic** movement, there has been a wide resurgence of the use of the sign of the cross by **lay** Anglicans and also a vast growth of actual crosses (and sometimes crucifixes)—on the walls and steeples of church buildings; on **Communion tables**, or on ledges behind them; and hung around people's necks (not least the **bishops**' pectoral crosses). Wafers, stoles, service books, service cards, letterheads, and almost anything else in church buildings or church circles have equally been marked without controversy with what is now a universal Christian sign, much beloved of most Anglicans. In recent years, the **Roman Catholic** practice has in some places been adopted whereby bishops signing their names precede them with the sign of the cross, for example, as "+ Noel St. Helena."

CROSSLINKS. *See* BIBLE CHURCHMEN'S MISSIONARY SOCIETY.

CROWN APPOINTMENTS COMMISSION. *See* CROWN NOMINATIONS COMMISSION.

CROWN NOMINATIONS COMMISSION. In the Church of **England**, diocesan **bishops** are nominated by the Crown, and the College of **Canons** of the **cathedral** of the vacant **diocese** is required by King **Henry VIII**'s legislation of 1534 to elect the person named to them by the monarch. In the 19th century, much of the power of choice passed from the monarch to the constitutional adviser to the monarch, the prime minister. In the 1960s, vacancy-in-see committees were formed to write a profile of the vacant diocese for the prime minister, and in 1974 the **General Synod** went on to ask for "the decisive voice" for the Church in the appointment of diocesan bishops. While the political party leaders in the House of Commons would not agree to this, they did accept that a Crown Appointments Commission should submit two names to the prime minister for him or her to choose one of those two—or to ask for more names.

From its inception in 1977, the commission was composed of the two **archbishops** of **Canterbury** and **York**, three **clergy** elected from the House of Clergy of the General Synod, three **laypersons** elected from the House of **Laity** of the General Synod, and four persons elected from the vacant diocese (with slight variations for a vacancy in an archbishopric). A major review of the operating of the system was put in train in 1998. Two changes made in the wake of this review in 2003 were to alter the name of the commission to the Crown Nominations Commission and to increase the diocesan representation to six persons. Other changes involved improving the information on prospective appointees, but in principle the whole procedure continues to be surrounded by the utmost confidentiality.

CROWTHER, SAMUEL (c. 1807–1891). Samuel Crowther was a slave from the Yoruba people of what is now Western **Nigeria**. When still not yet 20 years of age, while being transported across the Atlantic by Portuguese slavers, he was released by the British Navy and taken to **Sierra Leone**. There he became Christian and took an Englishman's surname at his **baptism**. Crowther was one of the first students of the **Church Missionary Society** (CMS) training college, Fourah Bay College, around 1827. In 1841 he went as CMS representative on T. F. Buxton's expedition up the Niger River. After **ordination** studies in **England**, he returned to Yorubaland and **ministered** there from 1843 (close to his own blood relatives), as the first native African to be **ordained** as an Anglican **presbyter**. A major enterprise Crowther undertook was the production of a high-quality Yoruba Bible.

After a visit to England in 1851, Crowther was asked to lead a new CMS **mission** on the Niger. His work was so exemplary that in 1864 he was consecrated **bishop** of "the Countries of Western Africa beyond the Queen's Dominions"—thus becoming the first-ever native African bishop in the **Anglican Communion**. He took part in two **Lambeth Conferences**. In his **episcopate** Crowther led pioneer missionary work with energy and vision. However, the times moved against him; it seems that European missionaries doubted the capacity of his staff, and he was slowly marginalized in his own sphere of work. He died of a stroke in 1891—thought to be due to a broken heart. From 1971 to 2005, the CMS training college in Selly Oak, Birmingham, was named "Crowther Hall" in memory of him.

CUBA. The Caribbean island of Cuba was a (largely **Roman Catholic**) colony of Spain until its fight for independence in 1895. In the 20th century, Episcopalians from the **United States** imported their own pattern of Anglican church life, and the island became in 1901 a **mis-**

sionary district within the **Protestant Episcopal Church in the United States of America** (PECUSA). The first Cuban **bishop** was consecrated in 1904.

After Fidel Castro came to power by revolution in 1959 (and the United States sponsored the unsuccessful Bay of Pigs invasion and other anti-Castro activities), the relationship with PECUSA became politically compromising for the Cuban Episcopalians and difficult to sustain. In 1966 the district was constituted a **diocese** and was formally separated from PECUSA, becoming an extraprovincial diocese with **metropolitical authority** being exercised by a specially appointed Metropolitan Council consisting of the **primates** of the Anglican Church in **Canada** and of the **province** of the **West Indies**, along with the **president** of Province IX of the renamed **Episcopal Church (United States of America)** (ECUSA). When Province IX became the Anglican Church of the Central Region of America in 1998, its primate took over the role previously occupied by the president of Province IX. In 2002, when the political tension between the United States and Cuba had lessened slightly, the diocese sought briefly to return to ECUSA, but it was thought inappropriate to proceed.

CUMMINS, GEORGE DAVID (1822–1876). George Cummins was born in December 1822 in Delaware. He graduated from Dickinson College in Carlisle, Pennsylvania, in 1841 and became a **Methodist** preacher. Cummins left Methodism in 1845 and became a candidate for **ordination** in the Delaware **diocese** of the **Protestant Episcopal Church in the United States of America** (PECUSA); he was **confirmed** and then **ordained** as a **deacon** the same year. Ordained as a **presbyter** in 1847, Cummins became rector of Christ Church in Norfolk, Virginia. In 1853 he moved on to become rector of St. James's in Richmond, Virginia, and in 1863 he moved again to be rector of Trinity Church in Chicago.

In 1865, immediately following the end of the American Civil War, Cummins moved a resolution at the **General Convention** to welcome the deputies from the Southern states, and to interpret their presence as a token and pledge of the reunion of PECUSA after the rending through war. He was duly noted and in 1866 was nominated as assistant **bishop** in the **diocese** of Kentucky.

Cummins was a convinced **Evangelical** and lived by his principles. In 1873 he was invited to participate in an assembly convened in New York by the Evangelical Alliance (to which the **dean** of **Canterbury** was sent as emissary by **Archbishop** Campbell Tait), and he was glad to be identified with this interdenominational occasion. However, the dean of Canterbury was denounced to Horatio Potter, the bishop of New York, by William Tozer, the retired bishop of **Zanzibar**, for participating in the **Communion** service of the assembly. Cummins insisted he must take responsibility with the dean for their participation. Potter publicly backed Tozer in a letter to the press, and both humiliated Cummins and showed him that the future was closing against his theological stance.

Cummins resigned from the Episcopal Church on 14 November and advertised that he would hold a public meeting on 2 December to form a **Reformed Episcopal Church**. The new Church was established, with Cummins elected as its bishop and Charles Edward Cheney as "**missionary** bishop." Cummins went to Chicago and **consecrated** Cheney a few days later, thus ensuring the Episcopal succession in the Reformed Episcopal Church (from which, in due course, the **Free Church of England** and the Reformed Episcopal Church of England received Episcopal consecration of bishops also).

A statement of the **presiding** bishop of PECUSA, endorsed by all the American bishops present at the 1888 **Lambeth Conference**, concluded that the Episcopal consecrations of Cheney and W. R. Nicholson by Cummins were "**null** and void." While this conclusion was not made the subject of a general resolution, the conference committee report "Mutual Relations" stated that the view of the American episcopate "may be taken as a sufficient guide to all Bishops of the Anglican Communion." It is, however, open to question theologically and was, in effect, set aside in conversations held with the Reformed Episcopal Church in 1938.

Cummins died in 1876. The "Cumminsite Schism" almost totally depleted the already declining forces of evangelicalism in the Episcopal Church, which only marginally revived a century after his death. The Reformed Episcopal Church continues as a small Evangelical Episcopal body. *See also* CONTINUING ANGLICANS.

CURATE. The original term "curate" denotes one who has the "cure" (or "care") of a **parish**—that is, the chief pastor—who is now usually designated "rector" or "vicar" or (in clumsy English) "incumbent." **Ordained** assistant **clergy** are technically "assistant curates," but the simple term "curate," in contradiction to its own etymology, has come to be attached to the assistant rather than to the incumbent.

CUTHBERT (634–687). Cuthbert was a Celtic Christian who became a monk in 651 at Melrose in **Scotland**. Soon afterward, he moved with the abbot of Melrose to Ripon in **England**, but he returned to Melrose in 661 and became prior soon after that. In 664 Cuthbert moved with his abbot to Lindisfarne on what is now Holy Island, and in 676 he became a hermit on neighboring Farne Island. Finally in 685 Cuthbert became **bishop** of Lindisfarne and then **evangelized** with energy in Northumbria for two years before dying on Farne. He was buried at Lindisfarne.

Cuthbert was famed for his self-discipline and holiness of life. In later centuries, when the Danes began to raid and invade the northeast coast, the monks of Lindisfarne took his body and, after a circuitous journey, finally interred it behind the high **altar** in Durham **Cathedral**. The tomb was opened at the **Reformation**, and legend has it that the body was found uncorrupted, but then quickly decayed when exposed to the atmosphere—or, following a more supernaturalist view, to the desecrators. There have been other exhumations since, and the bones are there to this day. Cuthbert died on 20 March, and his **feast** day is observed then in many **provinces** of the **Anglican Communion**.

– D –

DALMATIC. *See* VESTMENTS.

DANCE. Dance in the context of worship has little official provision in Anglican **liturgical** rites, but, like drama and varieties of **music**, it is used in many parts of the world to embellish and enliven patterns of worship, usually by a process of local **inculturation**.

DAVIDSON, RANDALL THOMAS (1848–1930). Randall Davidson, a Scot by birth, was **ordained** in 1874 and became domestic chaplain to **Archbishop** A. Campbell Tait in 1877; a year later, he married

Tait's second daughter, Edith. When Tait died in 1882, Davidson corresponded with Queen Victoria about Tait's hopes regarding his successor and apparently thus influenced the appointment of Edward Benson, the **bishop** of Truro, as the next archbishop of **Canterbury**. From then on, Davidson became the queen's confidante. He became in quick succession dean of Windsor, bishop of Rochester, and bishop of Winchester, before succeeding Frederick Temple in 1903 as the 96th archbishop of Canterbury.

Davidson's long archiepiscopate (1903–1928) was marked by the Royal Commission on Ecclesiastical Discipline (1904–1906), the **coronation** of King George V (1911), the **Kikuyu Controversy** (1913–1914), World War I (1914–1918), two **Lambeth Conferences** (1908 and 1920), the "**Enabling Act**" (1919) and the beginning of the National Assembly of the Church of **England** (1920), the **Malines Conversations** (1921–1926), the last creation of new **dioceses** in England (1927), the abortive **Book of Common Prayer** Revision (1927–1928), and the consequent church–state crisis. Finally, at the age of 80, in 1928 he became the first archbishop of Canterbury ever to retire voluntarily from office, not because of the defeat of the revised Prayer Book but in order to allow a younger successor to convene the 1930 Lambeth Conference. He was made a baron, as Lord Davidson of Lambeth—a precedent for retiring archbishops that has been followed ever since.

DEACON. Deacons constitute the most junior of the three "historic" **orders** that were continued by the Church of **England** at the **Reformation**, tracing their origins back to the late first or early second century. Partly because of the "serving" role that is propounded as the key to their function in the church, there has been a tendency to see their **ministry** as rooted, or at least adumbrated, in the appointment of the seven assistants to the apostles in Acts 6. Certainly the apostles distinguished between their own role ("prayer and the ministry of the word") and that which they were delegating to the seven because they themselves were administratively overstretched ("the serving of tables"). The passage also provides the earliest example in the apostolic church of the laying on of hands with prayer. But there are difficulties in reading the origins of the later diaconate in the Acts 6 passage, in that the only two of the seven of whom we read more—that is,

Stephen and Philip—do not appear to have done what they were "**ordained**" to do but rather to have acted as **ministers** of "the word"! Furthermore, the word *diakonia*, from which "deacon" and "diaconate" derive, is a very general term for "serving" or "ministering," and the apostles themselves are recorded as *defending* their own *diakonia* (i.e., their "ministry" of the word; Acts 6.4) as much as *conferring* a *diakonia* (i.e., a "ministry" of tables) uniquely on the seven!

Others in the New Testament are called "deacons," including a woman, Phoebe, in Rom. 16.1 and identifiable ministers of the Philippian church in Phil. 1.1. There are various details of their qualifications and right conduct in the Pastoral Epistles, though little about their distinctive functions or how they relate to other ministers. The word appears to be used somewhat elastically, or at least unreflectively, not so much to identify an "order" (a concept that is hard to find in an explicit form in the New Testament) as simply to indicate a serving or "ministering" person, who might sometimes be in an officially recognized church role, sometimes not.

The "threefold" order becomes fairly clear from the time of Ignatius of Antioch onward, and a distinctive role for deacons starts to emerge, at least in broad outline. They appear to have been assistants to the **bishop**, in both administrative and **liturgical** roles. In Justin (d. 160), they are found taking the **eucharistic elements** from the **celebration** to those who are absent from it. In Hippolytus's *Apostolic Tradition* (c. 215), there are the earliest known **ordination rites** for deacons, and they are described as having a special service of individual support to render to the bishop, partly but not exclusively of a liturgical nature. In later years deacons were gradually absorbed into a linking of the various orders into a *cursus*, in which the lowest "major order" was not that of deacon but of subdeacon, and the highest was not that of bishop but of **presbyter**. In this linking of the orders, being a deacon was thus the final step toward being a presbyter, and by the time of Thomas Aquinas (d. 1274), being a presbyter was the final goal of the *cursus*, for it was the presbyter who **consecrated** the eucharist. The three major orders were distinguished from the minor orders by the requirement of **celibacy**. In this cursus, there might be distinctive roles for the deacon (one notable one was the reading of the **Gospel** at the eucharist), but it was a transitory function in which the crucial feature of being a deacon was that the time of "priesting" would soon come, and the fullness of ministerial potential would be worked out in that climactic order.

This was the pattern inherited by the Reformers in England, and, while they established the three orders as bishops, presbyters (or **priests**), and deacons, they retained the expectation that those made deacon would go on to be ordained as presbyters after a probationary period. That expectation is explicit in the Reformation rites for ordaining deacons. The requirement of celibacy was abolished also. In the ordination rites, the distinction was retained between the orders, in that the bishop alone laid hands on those being made deacons, whereas several assisting presbyters joined the bishop to lay hands on those being made presbyters. For the *porrectio instrumentorum* at the ordination of deacons, the Gospel Book of the pre-Reformation rites was replaced with a New Testament.

Until the 19th century there was little provision for **laypeople** to exercise any official ministry or to hold responsibility within Anglicanism, and so at times men were ordained as deacons to fulfill roles requiring a "clerk" but without expecting to go on to become presbyters. Thus **Nicholas Ferrar** was made deacon in 1625 simply in order to read **Morning and Evening Prayer** in the Little Gidding community. There is also evidence of men being made deacon in order to hold fellowships at Oxford and Cambridge, for which ordination was required. This was, however, rare, and the ordination rite for deacons still anticipated that they would continue toward becoming presbyters.

The question of **women** becoming deacons was heavily debated among Anglicans around the world in the second half of the 20th century, sometimes as an issue in its own right (it is acknowledged that women were deacons at intervals in different places in the early church) but more often as the first step to be taken toward their being ordained as presbyters. When the diaconate was opened to women, in one or two places (for instance, in **Wales**), those who were already **deaconesses** were deemed to be deacons already, but in most **provinces** they were ordained *ab initio*.

Alongside the issue of ordaining women, some **provinces** (or at least some **dioceses** in some provinces) have taken steps in the latter years of the 20th century to reestablish a "permanent diaconate"—an identifiable order to which people would be selected and called, and for which they would be trained. This has been elaborated at times into a rationale for the order, sometimes weighted toward the liturgical, sometimes toward more mission-oriented roles. There has also been related pressure in some quarters to eliminate the ordaining of "transitional deacons" (i.e., those expecting to be presbyters in a year's time or less), and instead to engage in "direct ordination" to the presbyterate for those selected and called to be presbyters, thus clarifying the true standing of the diaconate through the ordination of deacons providing only those who actually believe themselves called to be deacons.

DEACONESS. The "office" of deaconess was invented in several **provinces** of the **Anglican Communion** in the 19th century to provide an official framework for a licensed **ministry** of **women**. The first recorded instance of such an appointment is that of Elizabeth Ferrard, who in 1861 formed a small community of women in King's Cross in **London** and was made deaconess by the bishop of London, A. Campbell Tait, in 1862. It remained an "office," not an **order**, so as not to breach the **tradition** that only men would be admitted to holy orders; the holders of the office were therefore categorized as "**lay**" for the purposes of electing **synodical** representatives and in similar ways. The 1969 **canons** of the Church of **England** stated that deaconesses were in an "order" but not in "holy orders."

Deaconesses have not usually been subject to the same canonical requirements as those in holy orders; for example, in **England**, where until 1990 no one who had been divorced and remarried (or whose marriage partner had been) could be **ordained**, women in that position could nevertheless be made deaconesses. However, the actual rites for making women deaconesses tended to be assimilated to those for making men **deacons**, and the two **liturgical** functions would often be performed in succession to each other within the same rite and with very little to actually distinguish one from the other. As around the world moves have occurred to allow women to be ordained as deacons, so the office of deaconess has in many places fallen into desuetude. In some provinces, for example, in the Church in **Wales**, deaconesses were recognized as being already ordained deacons prior to being ordained as **presbyters**.

DEAF. In the scriptures, as in life today, the profoundly deaf are also frequently dumb—for they never learn the category of sound nor how to communicate by sound. In recent years, skills at converting sound **language** to sign language have helped the deaf to participate fully, so that in many places worship is conducted "bilingually" and in others by sign language alone.

DEAN. The word "dean" derives from the Latin *decanus*, with its implications, now obscured by history, of being a 10th person or in charge of 10 units of some sort. Its etymology runs on in the (very English) adjective "decanal." While in secular usage heads of academic houses (or occasionally other officers) are sometimes known as "deans," in ecclesiastical usage a dean is the chief pastor of a **cathedral** or, as "rural dean" (sometimes "area dean" or "borough dean"), is the leading **presbyter** in a series or group of **parishes** in a specified area. The conventional honorific for the dean of a cathedral is "The Very Reverend." *See also* DEANERY; PROVOST.

DEANERY. A deanery is either the official dwelling place of the **dean** of a **cathedral** or the area of responsibility of an area or rural dean.

DEATH. The only guaranteed future event in an earthly life is death. In **Jesus Christ** and his **resurrection** from the dead, however, there is a promise of eternal life; in Jesus' words, "Whoever lives and believes in me shall never die." So the Christian church has the task of proclaiming the fact of death to those in full life on Earth as well as to the dying, and thus to bring people to face the reality of death and the promise of eternal life. This perspective affects prayers with those who are dying and with those who are facing or experiencing bereavement. The classic Anglican **funeral** service, as reformed by **Thomas Cranmer** in the 1552 **Book of Common Prayer**, brought the bodies of believers to their graves "in sure and certain hope of resurrection to eternal life through our Lord Jesus Christ."

One feature of the pre-**Reformation** church that the 1552 service excluded was **petitions for the departed**. The excision of all reference to **purgatory** (see appendix B, **Article** XXII) and the removal of all **liturgical** material that depended upon belief in purgatory led to the confident **gospel** proclamation of "sure and certain hope." But the **Anglo-Catholic** Revival within Anglicanism in the 19th century and the sheer convention that has led many to seek a Christian funeral when the deceased had shown little sign of Christian faith up until death have together brought many to seek appropriate forms of commendation of the departed into the hands of a merciful **God**. But such revision of texts has usually been accompanied by a denial that a door is being opened to a belief in **purgatory**.

DECLARATION OF ASSENT. Each **province** of the **Anglican Communion** has its own form of subscription, intended to ensure that the teachers of the faith hold the faith in the form that that province expresses it. Provinces also vary as to the occasions on which **clergy** (and sometimes authorized lay **ministers**) are required to subscribe to their declaration. In the Church of **England**, the form of subscription and assent required of clergy at the point of **ordination** or licensing—a form that had stood from 1865 under the Clerical Subscription Act—was changed (under the terms of the Church of England [Worship and Doctrine] **Measure** 1974) from 1 September 1975. A preamble sets out the **doctrinal** stance of the Church, and a question of the candidate leads to the response:

> I . . . do so affirm, and accordingly declare my belief in the faith which is revealed in the Holy Scriptures and set forth in the catholic **creeds** and to which the historic formularies of the Church of England bear witness; and in public prayer and administration of the **sacraments**, I will use only the forms of service which are authorized or allowed by **Canon**.

DECLARATION ON KNEELING. *See* BLACK RUBRIC.

DEDICATION. In the Church of **England**, **parish** church buildings are usually "**consecrated**," which gives them an almost inalienable status in law as church buildings. Other buildings (e.g., church halls, "daughter" churches, dual-purpose buildings, parish worship centers, or chapels belonging to institutions) are usually "dedicated"—a purely religious procedure that has no standing in law. Similar distinctions are to be found in some other parts of the **Anglican Communion**.

Despite this, the term "dedication" is used in relation to anniversaries and other commemorations for all worship buildings, whether originally consecrated or not, so that "**feast** of dedication" usually means the anniversary of the date when the building was inaugurated, with an implication that it was "dedicated" in the name of a particular **saint** (whose own commemoration, probably on a different date, will be a "**patronal festival**"). Some **provincial calendars** and **lectionaries** make "**proper**" provision for such a festival.

DEFENDER OF THE FAITH. The **pope** conferred upon King **Henry VIII** (apparently at Henry's request) the title of "Defender of the Faith" in honor of his book attempting to refute Martin Luther—*De Septem Sacramentis* (1521). When, after the break with Rome, Henry nevertheless continued to use the title, such use was validated in 1544 by Parliament, and it remains a hereditary title for the monarch of England to this day. It is abbreviated to "Fid Def" (*Fidei Defensor*) or "FD" on coins of the realm.

DEMON. Demons in the New Testament appear to be evil spirits, under the aegis of the **devil**, or chief demon. In various Churches, there exist rites of more or less official standing for "**exorcizing**" such infesting spirits from places or people.

DEVIL. The devil appears in the New Testament as the archopponent of God—and thus of **Jesus Christ**—in the sphere of the spirit. The name *diabolos* (from which our "diabolic" comes directly and "devil" indirectly) initially meant "accuser" (cf. Rev. 12.10, 12.12). He is also entitled the "Evil One" (cf. Matt. 13.19), and it is likely that the 10th line of the **Lord's Prayer** should actually be read as "Deliver us from the Evil One" (Matt. 6.13). At intervals, theologians have denied the existence of a "personal devil" (as reflecting a medieval dualism), and belief in such a being is neither **credally** expressed nor asserted as *de fide*. Nevertheless, references to the devil continue in Anglican **liturgy**—usually in **baptism** rites (where renunciation of the devil, however phrased, has a continuous Christian history since the second century, and exhortations to resist the devil have reinforced that renunciation), but often also in traditional **litanies**. *See also* DEMON.

DIACONATE. *See* DEACON.

DIOCESE. The area, region, territory, or people within the care of a **bishop**. In early church theory, a bishop was the chief pastor of all the Christians of a defined territory, and the word "diocese" has thus come to imply the whole machinery of ecclesiastical administration for the people as well as the physical territory within which they are found. The diocese is commonly regarded by Anglican theorists as the basic organizational unit of which the worldwide church is comprised, such that it is sometimes called "the local church"—but in some cases a diocese can be more than 1,000 miles across, and a true "local church" will be much more local than that.

DIRECTORY FOR THE PUBLIC WORSHIP OF GOD IN THE THREE KINGDOMS, A. When Parliament gained the ascendancy in the Civil War in **England**, the members commissioned an assembly of divines to meet at Westminster, inviting the **Scottish** Parliament to send representatives to it also. The upshot was an Act of Parliament in January 1645 entitled "An Ordinance of Parliament for the taking away of the Book of Common Prayer and for the establishing and putting in execution of the Directory for the public worship of God." The directory itself was annexed to the ordinance and has been regularly, if not quite accurately, known ever since as the "Westminster Directory." The directory contained outline instructions for the gathering of the congregation, for the prayers, and for the preaching; it then provided for **baptism**, **Communion**, and occasional offices (though **burial** had to be conducted without prayer, ceremony, or preaching). It contained no texts, only broad "directions." The directory was a compromise, being insufficiently **liturgical** for those who wanted a set order but overrestrictive for those who wanted complete freedom from any book. It remained current, though often ignored, during the **Commonwealth** period and was finally discarded after the **Restoration** by the **Act of Uniformity** of 1662. It had a shadowy continued life in Scotland, but for Anglicans has become almost entirely of historical interest.

DISESTABLISHMENT. *See* ESTABLISHMENT.

DISSENT. The principle of "**uniformity**" of religion, as enshrined in the **Act of Uniformity** of 1662 and enforced the more strongly by the

Clarendon Code, produced terminology which stated that those loyal to that **Restoration** Settlement "conformed" to the Church of **England**, the state religion. Those who did not conform (i.e., the nonconformists) were "dissenting" or "dissenters." English nonconformity has often been known corporately as "Dissent" and the meeting places of nonconformists as "dissenting houses." Paradoxically, in **Scotland** it was the Episcopalians who in 1689 would not "conform" to the **Glorious Revolution** and thus, arguably, went into "dissent." But, in general, "nonconformity" and "dissent" have been used interchangeably in England to denote the non-Episcopal ("free") churches. In countries that never had an **established** church with which to conform, the concept of "dissent" is almost meaningless.

DIVORCE. Divorce is the legal or formal dissolution of an existing **marriage**, without prejudice to its previous **validity**, propriety, or legitimacy. In this, it is in contrast with an annulment, which in effect states that no marriage between the two parties ever occurred or subsisted in the first place. It was annulment, not divorce, that King **Henry VIII** was seeking with respect to his marriage to Catherine of Aragon.

Provision for "civil divorce" was not authorized in the laws of **England** until 1857, when a procedure for civil divorce was made lawful. The Act protected **clergy** who chose not to officiate at "second marriages"; over the course of time, when the grounds for divorce were widened, the **Convocations** of the clergy passed resolutions in 1938 calling upon the clergy not to officiate at such ceremonies, and thus the Church of England established a discipline different from that of the state. In recent years, this has been somewhat eroded. There was also a restriction whereby those who had married again after a divorce, or those who had married someone who had a previous marriage partner still living, were debarred from **ordination**; this restriction was lifted in 1990.

In some places, notably in the **province** of **Southern Africa**, where marriage in church is permitted under defined circumstances for those who have been previously divorced, a different preface is provided for the marriage service in such cases. Elsewhere, couples are required or desired to seek a civil registration of their marriage, but prayers and other features of the marriage service may be used for a service of prayers and blessing in church after the civil ceremony. *See also* NULLITY.

DIX, GREGORY (1901–1952). Gregory Dix, born George Eglington Alston Dix, read history at Oxford, went to Wells **Theological College**, and was **ordained** in 1924 to be a tutor at Keble College, Oxford. In 1926 he became a professed monk of the Anglican Benedictines and moved from Pershore to Nashdom soon after he joined. Dix quickly made a lasting impact upon the Church of **England** and the world of theological scholarship, writing with great learning that he could always turn to his own purposes with persuasion, humor, and mischief. Dix loved to mock the **episcopate** of his time. His most obvious fields for such labors were those particularly distinctive of the extreme **Anglo-Catholicism** he professed—church, **ministry**, and **sacraments**. His patristic studies are epitomized in his edition of Hippolytus. On **baptism**, he reemphasized the "two-staging" or "**confirmationist**" advocacy of Arthur James Mason (which thus became known as the "Mason-Dix Line"). On **orders**, he both defended Anglican orders against Rome and also contributed a major essay (on the concept of the *shaliach*) to Kenneth Kirk's book *The Apostolic Ministry* (1946), which was intended to defy the prospective formation of the Church of **South India**.

But it was for his work on the **eucharist** that Dix is most remembered. *The Shape of the Liturgy* ("my fat green book") was published in 1945 and for both its scholarship and its raciness has become one of the great theological books on **liturgy** of the 20th century. The memorable heart of his writing was that the eucharist has a "four-action" *shape*, and its shape is prior to its wording. His first impact on actual liturgical revision was (ironically) on the Church of South India where a uniting rite was devised in 1949–1950, but his fame was soon widespread in Anglicanism, while his principles were also acknowledged in the **Roman Catholic Church**. In the course of time, a measured critique of his work has arisen (not least in respect of "**offertory**"), but his stature remains.

Dix succumbed to cancer when barely 50, when the era of serious Anglican liturgical revision had not begun. Had he lived, Dix would surely even more greatly have affected liturgical revision worldwide.

DOCTRINE. While Anglicanism generally has declared the scriptures to be supremely authoritative for matters of doctrine and has broadly subscribed to the **Apostles'** and **Nicene creeds**, the different **provinces** have varied greatly as to the status given to the Thirty-Nine **Articles** and other secondary statements of faith (including the 1662 **Book of Common Prayer**). They have also varied considerably as to the limits of orthodoxy and the appropriate sanctions (if any) for breaching those limits. A very brief summary of a worldwide common Anglican stance is to be found in the **Lambeth Quadrilateral**, and individual provinces have established doctrine commissions or doctrine and worship committees to advise the House of **Bishops** and the **General Synod** or comparable body on doctrinal issues. The House of Bishops in each province is generally held to have a special responsibility for guarding the faith and its formulation in each generation. The 1978 **Lambeth Conference** called for the creation of an **Inter-Anglican Theological and Doctrinal Commission**, and this commission in 1986 produced a report, *For the Sake of the Kingdom*. The 1988 Lambeth Conference called for a "common declaration" that would assist a coherent doctrinal identity for the Communion. This, however, has not been agreed or adopted. There are some echoes of this call in the 2004 proposal of the **Windsor Report** that provinces should bind themselves to each other by an inter-Anglican "covenant."

DOMESTIC AND FOREIGN MISSIONARY SOCIETY. The **General Convention** of the **Protestant Episcopal Church in the United States of America** founded the voluntary Domestic and Foreign Missionary Society in 1821. It was entrenched into the constitution of the General Convention itself in 1835, and from 1919 became identical with the Executive Committee of the General Convention.

DUBLIN. Dublin has traditionally been the civic capital of **Ireland**. It was the seat of the Irish Parliament prior to the Act of Union that united the Westminster and Irish parliaments from the beginning of 1801, and it was the place of British administration thereafter. After partition in 1922, Dublin was the capital of the Irish Free State (which became the Republic of Ireland in 1948). While the senior

Irish see has always been in **Armagh**, Northern Ireland, where **St. Patrick** is reputed to have planted the church in the fifth century, Dublin has been a **diocese** from the 11th century and an **archbishopric** from the 12th. Since the suppression of two other Irish archbishoprics (Tuam and Cashel) in the years following the Irish Church Temporalities Act of 1833, the **province** of Dublin has covered roughly half the geographical territory of Ireland, with the province of Armagh covering the rest. Dublin has had its own Church of Ireland ecclesiastical identity, including Trinity College (founded as a **Protestant** place of learning in 1592), the provision of two **cathedrals** (one, Christ Church, being a "diocesan" cathedral, the other, St. Patrick's, a "national" one), the location of the Church of Ireland **Theological College** (once the "Divinity Hostel"), and the place of the **General Synod** office.

DUBLIN AGREED STATEMENT. *See* ORTHODOX CHURCHES.

DUBLIN STATEMENT. The "Dublin Statement" is the shorthand title for the international Anglican **liturgical** statement "The Renewal of the Anglican **Eucharist**," produced by the fifth meeting of the **International Anglican Liturgical Consultation** (IALC-5) in Dublin in 1995. This should not be confused with the 1984 "Dublin Agreed Statement" between the **Anglican Communion** and the **Orthodox Churches**.

– E –

EAMES COMMISSION. Robert ("Robin") Eames became **archbishop** of **Armagh** and **primate** of all **Ireland** in 1986. At the 1988 **Lambeth Conference**, when there was a clear likelihood that a **woman** would soon be consecrated as the first female **bishop** in the **Anglican Communion**, **Robert Runcie**, the archbishop of **Canterbury**, was asked to appoint a commission to investigate the implications of **consecrating** women anywhere in the Anglican Communion to the **episcopate**. Runcie asked Eames to chair the commission to fulfill the brief, and it became known as the "Eames Commission."

Its nine members first met in November 1988. After the first woman bishop, Barbara Harris, had been consecrated to be assistant bishop in Massachusetts in March 1989, it provided its first report. A second report came in 1990 after two more meetings. **George Carey** then became archbishop of Canterbury and asked the Eames Commission to reconvene. Thus a third report came after a meeting in December 1993. After that, a smaller Eames Monitoring Group was created, and this reported to the 1998 Lambeth Conference. By then there were 11 women bishops (in **Canada**, the **United States**, and **Aotearoa**, New Zealand, and Polynesia), and the major issues concerned relationships between **provinces** with different disciplines, which became the subject of a resolution of the Lambeth Conference. All the reports were published in *Women in the Anglican Episcopate: Theology, Guidelines, and Practice* (1998).

Eames later also chaired the **Lambeth Commission** appointed in 2003, but its agenda were completely different, and it has not been known as an "Eames Commission."

EAST AFRICA, PROVINCE OF. The **dioceses** in the British colony of **Kenya** and in the Tanganyika and **Zanzibar** protectorates were until 1960 extraprovincial dioceses under the **metropolitical** care of the **archbishop** of **Canterbury**. In that year, the Kenyan diocese of **Mombasa** was divided into new dioceses. These were then joined with the Tanganyika and Zanzibar dioceses into a single **province** of East Africa. During 1963–1965, the province was involved with **Lutheran**, **Methodist**, **Presbyterian**, and **Moravian** Churches in the two nations (Tanganyika and Zanzibar were by this time the single nation of **Tanzania**) in an East African Church Union Consultation, seeking a union of the five denominations. This was followed in 1966 by a Swahili-**language** "Union **Liturgy**," which in turn became a parent to the Anglican Tanzanian liturgy. However, the projected union was never implemented. In 1970, the province of East Africa was dissolved, becoming the two separate provinces of Kenya and Tanzania. *See also* KIKUYU CONTROVERSY.

EAST ASIA, COUNCIL OF CHURCHES OF. *See* SOUTHEAST ASIA, COUNCIL OF CHURCHES OF.

EASTER. **Jesus Christ** rose from the dead on the first day of the week within the days of unleavened bread, the Jewish *Pascha* or **Passover**. In some **languages**, the "pascha" stem has remained (as in the English adjective "paschal"), but in English the Christian term for the day of **resurrection** is "Easter."

The annual celebration of Easter is one of the earliest features of the Christian **tradition** that has lasted unbroken to the present day. Whereas the Jewish Passover was an annual event, Jesus' own command to "do this in remembrance of me" seems from the earliest times to have been understood as inaugurating a weekly cycle of **celebration**; it would be difficult to demonstrate from the New Testament that the apostolic church kept any annual observance *as Christians* at all. The most that is visible is that Luke, the historian author of the Acts of the Apostles, himself a Gentile, records carefully the incidence of Jewish **feasts** (as in Acts 20.6 for the Passover), and it is a possible inference that Christians were celebrating their own distinctive "passover" (cf. 1 Cor. 5.7) at that time.

From the second century onward, there is clear evidence, first, that the church was determined (after a struggle) to abandon the Jewish basis of a set date and instead to commemorate the Lord's resurrection on a **Sunday**, however movable that made the date, and second, that it became the centerpiece of the church's year, marked especially by **baptisms** and the welcoming of newcomers into the life of the church. It thus became determinative of the dating of more than half of the **liturgical** year, for from it were derived the anticipatory seasons of **Lent** and **Holy Week** and the 50 days of the resurrection season (sometimes called **Pentecost**); in time, this led to the identification of **Ascension** Day, of an actual day of Pentecost, and derivatively of other occasions, such as the (Anglican) **Trinity Sunday** and the (very **Roman Catholic**) feast of Corpus Christi. At least three Sundays before Lent and all the Sundays after Trinity (or, in some cases, after Pentecost), with the possible exception of the last one, in turn took their dating from the date of Easter.

While the **Reformers** kept the framework of the same Christian year, they diminished the emphasis on any particular feast. Easter emerged as one of the few occasions for which a **proper** preface was provided, and as the only specified occasion when the **laity** were required to receive **Communion** (they had to do so thrice in the year, "of which Easter to be one"). However, most moves in liturgical revision in Anglicanism in the 20th century have reemphasized the distinctive themes of the Sundays in Lent, of the days of Holy Week, and of the Easter Vigil, thus heightening the impact and importance of the core role given to Easter in the church's year.

Some Eastern Churches determine a date for Easter that differs from the Western practice followed and shared by the Anglican churches. The Anglican churches have joined with other member churches of the **World Council of Churches** in the quest for a common date for Easter, which is a slightly different issue from that which the British Parliament has approved—which is that, once the churches have agreed in principle (which, of course, they have not and are not likely to), there should be a *fixed* date for Easter. *See also* CALENDAR; EASTER ANTHEMS.

EASTER ANTHEMS. In the 1549 **Book of Common Prayer**, the **propers** of **Easter** Day began with "these anthems" (as the **rubric** called them): Rom. 8.9–11 and 1 Cor. 15.20–22. They were to be said or sung before Matins began. In 1552 this was changed so that the anthems now replaced Venite within **Morning Prayer** on Easter Day. In 1662, 1 Cor. 5.7b–8 was added at the beginning. These anthems provided continuing precedent for turning New Testament text into canticles, and the actual Easter anthems themselves have been deployed within Morning and Evening Prayer on a weekly or seasonal basis in various **provinces**' modern **liturgical** books.

EASTERN EQUATORIAL AFRICA. James Hannington was **consecrated** as the first **bishop** of Eastern Equatorial Africa in 1884. Though based in **Mombasa**, at that date this see included all of what is now **Kenya** and **Uganda** and part of what is now **Tanzania**. A separate diocese of Uganda was not formed until 1897, at which point the parent diocese was renamed "Mombasa."

EASTERN ORTHODOX. The Church of Western Europe was sundered from Eastern Orthodoxy through the mutual **excommunications** of 1054 and was further sundered in practice by the Crusades (1095–1291), by the Western papacy and its claims, and by the developing patterns of Western theology (e.g., in relation to the **eucharist**) between the 11th and 16th centuries. Some attempts were made (as at the **Council** of Florence in 1435) to bring about reconciliation, but on such Western terms as to make reunion impossible for the Greeks. The capture of Constantinople by the Turks in 1453 led to both more movement toward the West by Orthodox Christians and more concern for their plight in the face of Islam by Western Christians.

Anglicans since the 17th century have valued links with the Eastern Orthodox Churches, often seeing them as modeling a non-Roman, nonpapalist **Episcopal** church system of a relatively unchanging character, drawing upon a deep historical **tradition**. Eastern Orthodoxy, however, has not discerned in Anglicanism sufficient agreement in the faith for there to be **Communion** between them. An official dialogue has existed between the **Anglican Communion** and the **Orthodox Churches** since 1973, and these conversations have led to the Moscow Statement (1976), in which the Anglicans agreed that the ***Filioque*** ought to be dropped from the **Nicene Creed**; the Athens Report (1978), which first took note of the **ordination** of **women** in the Anglican Communion; the Dublin Agreed Statement (1984), which handled large questions of **ecclesiology**; and further interim agreed statements (1998). The task of narrowing the ground between the two Communions has been made easier in these years through a slowly growing practice among Anglicans of omitting the *Filioque* clause from the Nicene Creed, along with interest in the invoking of the **Holy Spirit** in a more or less Eastern way in the **epiclesis** in the **eucharistic prayer**. On the other hand, the Eastern Churches have reacted very negatively to the ordination of women in the Anglican Communion. *See also* ORIENTAL ORTHODOX CHURCHES.

EASTWARD POSITION. In the later Middle Ages, it became almost universal in the Western Church that the **Communion table** should take the form of a stone **altar** and that the main high altar should be fixed to the east wall of the **chancel** (with a similar arrangement in the side chapels also). Thus the celebrant stood with his back to the congregation, facing east.

At the **Reformation**, this was changed. In the 1549 **Book of Common Prayer**, the **priest** was directed to stand "humbly afore the altar." But in 1550 by an order-in-council, the altars were torn down and replaced by movable wooden tables, and in the 1552 Book the opening

rubrics of the rite both required that the table should stand "where morning and evening prayer are appointed to be said" and ordered that the priest should stand "at the **North side**" of the table. It is likely that the table was thereafter in the 16th century usually turned through 90° compared with the 1549 provision, so that "North side" actually meant in the middle of the longer side of an oblong table.

However, when **Archbishop William Laud** in the 17th century got the tables moved back against the east walls, the rubric was still followed literally, so that the priest was now facing south standing at the short end of the oblong. The opening rubrics of the 1662 Book remained virtually unchanged from 1552, but rubrics later in the rite allowed for the priest to move in relation to the table in order to prepare the **elements** and, by implication, move them from the center to the north side. The main position under these rubrics has normally been dubbed (not "southward," but) "north side."

One branch of **nonjurors** in the early 18th century made a return to eastward position, but there is little or no evidence of use of that position in the mainstream of the Church of **England** before 1850. After the **Methodist** separation in the 18th century, it appears to have been a folk memory of the Church of England's norm of north side that prevailed when the Methodist preachers began to officiate at Communion. Church building in the 18th and early 19th centuries continued to assume that the Communion table would be placed against the east wall, quite often in a shallow apse or recess, and the officiant would expect to take north side, not least in order to be heard. Many churches, of course, having been built in the Middle Ages, still had a **Gothic** ground-plan with a long narrow chancel and often a heavy screen—but north side at a table along the east wall was still the normal pattern for the celebration of Communion.

It was the coming of the **Anglo-Catholic** movement in 1833 that precipitated a change. In its second generation, roughly from 1850 on, the more pioneering spirits of this movement introduced **Roman Catholic ceremonial** into their Communion celebration, and a reversion to eastward position was one of their keynotes. **Protestant**-minded parishioners frequently objected, and this on occasion led to court cases. Eastward position was declared illegal in the Purchas Judgment (1872), but when a case was brought in 1889–1890 against

Edward King, the **bishop** of Lincoln, the Archbishop's Court, summoned by Archbishop Edward Benson, found in favor of the bishop and permitted eastward position, provided that, in accordance with the rubric, he broke the **bread** "in the sight of the people."

There was a large theological background to these controversies, as Protestants saw (probably rightly) a linkage of teachings, in that the Anglo-Catholic **doctrines** of **eucharistic** presence and **eucharistic sacrifice** were bound up with the return of stone altars, wafer bread, ceremonial ringing of bells at the **consecration**, reverencing of consecrated elements, eucharistic **vestments**, and eastward position. However, the rapid progress of eastward position into the 20th century outstripped the doctrinal concerns and simply became "normal" Anglicanism in England, the **United States**, and the Anglo-Catholic **provinces** generally. North side remained a distinctive use of the Church of **Ireland** and of **Evangelical** provinces, **dioceses**, and **parishes** around the **Anglican Communion** until the 1960s, and in some cases beyond.

"**Westward position**," which developed through a variety of influences in the second half of the 20th century (including changes in Rome itself), largely replaced both eastward position and north side during the last 50 years and has proved a reconciling force within Anglican usage.

ECCLESIOLOGY. Ecclesiology is the study of the nature, structure, and dynamics of the church. The pre-**Reformation Roman Catholic Church** was clear that the church of God is a single visible society, confessing one credal faith, bound together by common **sacraments** and a single **hierarchy**, and with all its members in **Communion** with each other. But the Reformers inevitably found themselves out of Communion with Rome and yet still seeking to confess (in the words of the **Nicene Creed**) "one holy catholic and apostolic church." In part, their answer was that "every particular or national Church" (*see* appendix B, **Article** XXXIV) has some autonomy; thus it may differ in rites and ceremonies from its neighbor, and, by implication, may even be out of favor with its neighbor, but without thereby automatically unchurching such a neighbor.

In broad terms, Anglicans have attempted to arrange their own polity on a territorial basis, where an area has a single chief pastor, a

bishop; the **parishes** and congregations of that area (or **diocese)** are bonded to each other through a common belongingness to the bishop; and the **ministers** have received their mission and authority from the bishop. Three or more dioceses may then become a **province**, very often forming a "particular or national Church" thereby.

This ecclesiology has many echoes of the **doctrine** of Cyprian (200–258), but it comes under strain and is in danger of incoherence under certain pressures: It cannot well take account of other Episcopal churches (especially the Roman and **Orthodox** Communions) that overlap its territory; it cannot easily resolve its own points where two jurisdictions overlap (as happens in **Europe**); and it has no power to hold together two separate provinces that are polarizing from each other or even invading each other's territory with "**missionary**" bishops or **presbyters**. It is open to the charge of putting organizational unity above doctrinal consensus, but is in grave danger of disintegration if differing notions of doctrinal orthodoxy are viewed as of higher priority than retaining the territorial integrity. This has proved to be particularly the case where questions have arisen in the late 20th century for which no precedent appears to exist—whether of the **ordination** of **women** or of the approval of same-sex unions and the ordination of persons within such unions.

The **Anglican Communion** has certain internal bonds between provinces—some by federal provisions; some by material, spiritual, and personal linkings; some by a kind of organic empathy—but they have rarely been tested to the limit, and it is uncertain what pressures they could ultimately stand. *See also* EAMES COMMISSION; ECUMENISM; EPISCOPACY; HOMOSEXUALITY; LAMBETH COMMISSION; LAMBETH QUADRILATERAL; WINDSOR REPORT.

ECUMENICAL MOVEMENT. *See* ECUMENISM.

ECUMENISM. The etymology of "ecumenism" is that it derives directly from the Greek word *oikoumene*, itself a passive participle used to mean "the inhabited [earth]" (cf. Luke 2.1; Acts 17.6; Rev. 3.10). Thus when, beginning in the fourth century, **councils** of **bishops** were gathered together from all places where the church existed, these meetings were known as "ecumenical councils" and their findings as "ecumenical **creeds**." The same sense of worldwide coverage is implied in the term for the leading bishop of the **Eastern Orthodox** Churches to this day—the "ecumenical patriarch."

This ancient use of the word in accordance with its own etymology has become rare and specialized. In the 20th century, "ecumenical" came to mean "joining different denominations together." The century itself has sometimes been called "the ecumenical century," that is, the time when the various denominational bodies across the Earth were discovering each other and seeking new relationships, sometimes even a convergence or union. The etymology has so far disappeared that it is perfect sense now to speak of "local ecumenism."

For Anglicans, major milestones in the century came with the interdenominational **Edinburgh Missionary Conference** in 1910, the "Appeal to All Christian People" at the **Lambeth Conference** of 1920, the not-really-official **Malines Conversations** with **Roman Catholics** in the 1920s, the years of approach to union with non-Episcopalians in **South India** from 1919 to 1947 (when the union occurred), and the various steps from the "Faith and Order" and the "Life and Work" Conferences between the world wars to the inauguration of the **World Council of Churches** (WCC) at Amsterdam in 1948. Relationships of **Communion** and the interchangeability of **ministers** have been negotiated with Episcopal churches such as the **Old Catholic** Churches and the **Mar Thoma Syrian Church** in South India. Further actual unions have followed in **Pakistan** and **North India** in 1970 (with the consequent creation of the Church of **Bangladesh** in 1971); and relations with other world denominations have been addressed by the work of successive **Anglican–Roman Catholic International Commissions** (ARCIC) from 1969 on, by worldwide bilateral conversations with other confessional families, and by the coming in the 1990s of the **Porvoo** agreement with **Lutherans** in Northern Europe and of concordats in 1996 with non-Episcopalians in South Africa, and in 2000 and 2001 with Lutherans in the **United States** and **Canada**, respectively.

Anglican **provinces** have joined in councils of Churches in their own countries and have been members of the WCC. They have often invited ecumenical observers to their own **synods**. The **Lambeth Quadrilateral** was originally adopted at the 1888 Lambeth Conference as a minimal basis upon which Anglicans could approach reunion with other denominations, and successive Lambeth Conferences have given more and more weight to relationships with other Christian bodies. **Archbishops** of **Canterbury** have invited a whole range of ecumenical guests to these conferences. In 1978, 1988, and 1998, major statements on ecumenical relations were made by the respective conferences, usually with the help of these guests.

Several meetings of the **Anglican Consultative Council** (ACC) have similarly handled ecumenical issues, and until 1998 the ACC received advice from a (pan-Anglican) Ecumenical Advisory Group. However, ACC-10, meeting in Panama City in 1996, recommended the formation of a weightier commission. This recommendation was accepted by the 1998 Lambeth Conference, and Resolution IV.3 of the conference brought into existence the **Inter-Anglican Standing Commission on Ecumenical Relations** (IASCER) and gave it specific terms of reference. Among other watching briefs, it was charged to "ensure theological consistency" in all ecumenical conversations of Anglicans. *See also* BONN AGREEMENT; EMMAUS REPORT.

EDINBURGH MISSIONARY CONFERENCE (1910). A large number of main, non–**Roman Catholic** denominations sponsored a seminal conference on world mission at Edinburgh in 1910. Anglicans took part with varying degrees of enthusiasm, and, in particular, many Anglicans were fearful of moves to **evangelize** in predominantly Roman Catholic or **Eastern Orthodox** areas. This fear was met in part by the exclusion of **South America** from consideration, on the grounds that it was already an evangelized **Roman Catholic** continent, but that very exclusion was viewed by many **Protestants** as defective in both analysis and theology. The Anglican involvement was considerable: **J. H. Oldham**, an Anglican layman, was secretary of the conference, **Azariah** of Dornakal gave a paper, and **William Temple** was an usher. The conference gave birth more or less directly to the International Missionary Council and somewhat indirectly to the other two great spheres of ecumenical encounter and sharing between the wars: Life and Work, on the one hand, and Faith and Order, on the other. These in turn led to the formation of the **World Council of Churches** in 1948.

EDWARD VI, KING (1537–1553). Edward VI was king of **England** from January 1547 to July 1553. He was the only son of King **Henry**

VIII to survive from infancy, being born in September 1537 to Jane Seymour, Henry's third wife, who herself died in giving birth to Edward. Her family was **Protestant**, and, by the provision of Henry when he died, her brother, Edward Seymour, Duke of Somerset, became Lord Protector, leading the council that was to conduct affairs of state in the name of the nine-year-old king, his nephew. The council had a majority of convinced Protestants, among whom **Archbishop Thomas Cranmer** was a very significant emergent champion of reformed theology. Thus, under the freedom given by the independence from Rome that Henry had seized, and employing the consequent supreme headship of the monarch over the church bequeathed by Henry, the council, in the name of the king, set about attempting to implement a swift, thorough, top-down, and irreversible **Reformation**. While the program had to be handled in successive stages, it was in fact a revolution that the council planned—and it was enacted at speed because, as long as the king was too young to marry and breed, the succession to the throne lay with his older half-sister **Mary I**, who was a dyed-in-the-wool papist.

The march of the English Reformation then came with royal *Injunctions* in summer 1547; the First Book of **Homilies** the same summer; an Act to restore **Communion** in both kinds in autumn 1547; *The Order of the Communion*, a **liturgical** text in English to be inserted into the **mass** to enable people to receive both **bread** and wine, in March 1548; the first **Act of Uniformity**, passed in January 1549; the publication of the full English-language **Book of Common Prayer** to be used from **Pentecost** 1549; the publication of the English-language **Ordinal** in summer 1550; the order-in-council for the breaking down of **altars** in November 1550; the second Act of Uniformity in April 1552; the publication of the revised Book of Common Prayer from summer 1552, to take effect on **All Saints'** Day 1552; and then the preparation and publication of the Forty-Two **Articles** of Religion, published in May 1553, just before Edward died. Forms of daily prayer and a complete reform of **canon law** were also prepared but were cut short by his death.

Edward's own part in these revolutionary moves is difficult to trace. Cranmer calls him "our young Josiah"—a reference to the seventh-century B.C. king of Judah who, from the age of eight onward, brought about a reformation in the land of Judah (2 Kings 22 and 23; 2 Chron. 34.1–7). Edward is reported to have personally struck out the **oath** "by the holy **saints** and the evangelist" in the 1550 service for the **consecration** of **bishops**, when **John Hooper** objected to it. But at this distance, distinguishing between the actions of the council in the name of the king and the real beliefs and initiatives of the child (and then teenage) king himself is not easy to do with accuracy. His name has passed into history by association with Cranmer's Prayer Books. They are called by later generations "The First and Second Prayer Books of Edward VI."

ELDER. The Greek word *presbuteros* occurs frequently in the New Testament, and, where it refers to a Christian pastor or leader, it clearly lies behind the development of the **order** of **presbyters** from the second century on. In the English-language translations of the **Bible** at the time of the **Reformation**, *presbuteros* was rendered as "elder." On the other hand, where the Latin *presbyterus* occurred in, for instance, the Latin text of the Thirty-Nine **Articles**, then the English translation was sometimes "priest." "Priest" was used throughout the 1549 and later **Books of Common Prayer**, and thus an uncertainty was brought into English usage. The Church of **England** had no office or order of which the members were called "elders," and the word "presbyter" has lurked almost out of sight among Anglicans for more than four centuries (save in the **Scottish** Episcopal Church, where it was always used in the Prayer Book **rubrics**). It was used famously by **John Henry Newman** at the beginning of Tract 1 of ***Tracts for the Times*** in September 1833: "I am but one of yourselves—a presbyter." Partly through its adoption in the Church of **South India** and partly through growing dissatisfaction with the use of the ambiguous word "priest" in its place, "presbyter" showed signs in the latter part of the 20th century of undergoing a slow revival. "Elder" has never become part of English-language Anglican usage

ELEMENTS. This is a term used for convenience (often as "**eucharistic** elements") when a single term is needed for the **bread** and wine of **Communion** together. It is thus possible to refer to "**consecrated** elements" or "**reserved** elements." More rarely, they have been called "species."

Anglicans have always had a question as to how narrowly the character of the elements is or should be defined in **canon law** or conventional understanding of the **sacrament**—and **provinces** with problems about wheat bread or grape wine have pressed the question, while central bodies of the **Anglican Communion** have tended to discourage variations from these norms. One major instance of this was when the sixth **International Anglican Liturgical Consultation** (IALC-6), meeting in Berkeley, California, in 2001, discussed the possibilities of more thorough **inculturation** in the use of sacramental elements. Then, at a December 2001 meeting of the **Inter-Anglican Standing Commission on Ecumenical Relations** (IASCER), the IASCER members, mindful of their **ecumenical** task, drew up and circulated a memorandum solidly defending the inherited **tradition**. This did not close the question.

ELIZABETH I, QUEEN (1533–1603). Elizabeth I reigned as queen from 1558 to 1603. She was the daughter of Anne Boleyn, King **Henry VIII**'s second wife, who was executed for adultery. When Henry died, Elizabeth stood third in the royal succession, but she inherited the throne when first King **Edward VI** died young and later Queen **Mary I** also died childless.

Elizabeth's education had been strongly antipapist, so that she was recognized as a threat to the restored **Roman Catholicism** during Mary's reign, and her own life was under threat as a result. She came to the throne on Mary's death and made it clear from the start that her faith—and that of the country—was to be **biblical** and reformed. Elizabeth secured an **Act of Uniformity** that restored the 1552 **Book of Common Prayer** from Edward's reign. However, she left herself liberty to have a crucifix in her chapel and may well have been personally responsible for uniting the separate words of distribution at **Communion** from the 1549 and 1552 Prayer Books into a single formula in her 1559 Book.

A very considerable threat to Elizabeth derived from the hostility of Rome, and in 1570 she was **excommunicated** by a papal bull that declared that whoever put her to death would do God service. This meant that every loyal Roman Catholic in the land became a potential traitor, confirming Elizabeth in her antipapal stance and leading to ruthless punishment of "recusants" as traitors. King Philip of Spain unsuccessfully sent his Armada against England to wrest the throne from her, and she in turn had Mary, Queen of Scots, put to death lest Roman Catholics rally to her as the next in line to inherit.

On the other hand, Elizabeth was also ruthless in dealing with those **Puritans** who took the view that the Reformation had not proceeded far enough. She insisted on the **ceremonies** that they opposed (the use of the surplice, kneeling for Communion, the **sign of the cross** in **baptism**, and the ring in **marriage**); she put a stop to their "**prophesyings**" (or meetings for mutual encouragement from the scriptures); and she marginalized Edmund Grindal, the **archbishop** of **Canterbury** from 1575 to 1583, for being too soft in controlling the Puritans. Grindal's successor, **John Whitgift** (archbishop from 1583 to 1604), was entirely to her taste and, although strongly Calvinist in his own theology, harried the Puritans relentlessly.

The forms of Anglicanism that Elizabeth passed on after her 45-year reign are generally known as the "Elizabethan Settlement." These include not only the concept of **uniformity** but also the Thirty-Nine **Articles** of Religion (authorized in 1571 [see appendix B]), church and state relationships, and the Book of Common Prayer. A project for providing a new code of **canon law** proved abortive in 1571, and no provision was made until 1604.

EMBER. In the **Books of Common Prayer** of the 16th and 17th centuries, four seasons of the year were earmarked for **ordinations**—the last Sunday in **Advent**, the second Sunday in **Lent**, **Trinity Sunday**, and the **Feast** of St. Michael and All **Angels** (29 September). The Wednesday, Friday, and Saturday prior to these dates were known as the "ember days"—days of prayer for those about to be **ordained**—and "**proper**" prayers were provided for those days. The origin of the term "ember" is uncertain, though it is possibly a corruption of *quattuor tempora*—the "four seasons" (and is so understood in **canon** 31 of the 1604 canons). The **provinces** of the **Anglican Communion** have in the 20th and 21st centuries varied from these seasons for all sorts of local reasons, not least the shape of the academic year (in which the Southern Hemisphere differs from the Northern), the pattern of public holidays, and the need to have dates that are relatively fixed within the **calendar** year and do not move by up to a month as a consequence of a movable **Easter**.

EMMAUS REPORT. At the end of January 1987, a consultation was held at the Emmaus Centre at West Wickham, Kent, in order to prepare a document on the **ecumenical** relationships of the **Anglican Communion**. This was to be available initially to the **Anglican Consultative Council**, meeting soon afterward in Singapore (ACC-7), but more especially to the 1988 **Lambeth Conference**. It was led by the chair and vice-chair designates of the Ecumenical Relations section of the conference, and the outcome was *The Emmaus Report: A Report of the Anglican Ecumenical Consultation, 1987* (London: Church House Publishing, 1987). Its scope covered a review of existing relationships with world Communions and some categories of other Churches. It was deemed to need supplementing as a preparatory document for the Lambeth Conference, and, although the relevant section of the conference covered the same ground, it does not appear to have been particularly dependent upon this report, turning instead to the primary sources.

ENABLING ACT. The Church of **England** Assembly (Powers) Act 1919 is informally known as the "Enabling Act." It arose in part from the Life and Liberty Movement, launched only two years earlier by **William Temple** and advertising a readiness for even disestablishment, if that were needed in order to gain liberty from the state. The Act referred to "The National Assembly of the Church of England (hereinafter called 'the Church Assembly')," as constituted by prior action in 1919 by the **Convocations**, to join their Houses together and add a House of **Laity** and thus provide an "Assembly" with separate Houses of **Bishops**, Clergy, and Laity. Parliament by the act devolved powers of creating Church legislation to the Assembly. In other words, Parliament was careful not to create the Assembly, but simply to empower it. Church legislation was from then on to be decided in the Assembly and to go in fixed form, via the Ecclesiastical Committee of Parliament, to the Lords and Commons, each of which would have a single yea-or-nay vote. Such church legislation has been known as a "**Measure**." The powers of veto in the Lords and Commons have been used on occasion, most notably in the Commons when the members twice (in 1927 and 1928) rejected a new **Prayer Book** supported by large majorities in the Assembly. The Church Assembly itself gave way to the **General Synod** in 1970, and the legislative powers of the Assembly were then transferred by measure to the Synod. *See also* ESTABLISHMENT.

ENGLAND. The Church of England is the mother church of the **Anglican Communion**, a relationship honored by the other churches and **provinces** of the Communion as they define themselves as being "in Communion with the See of **Canterbury**." The very word "Anglican" in the title of the Communion attests the point of historical origin, though it must not be understood to suggest any current subordination of one province to another, nor any necessary cultural or other dependence of one province upon another. The historical origin does, however, make an overview of the Church of England's own history the key to understanding and interpreting the history and character of the whole Communion.

That history of the Christian church in the land of England begins in the early years of the Christian era, and it provides the background to the distinctive Church of England that emerged from the 16th-century **Reformation** in separation (**doctrinal**, **ecclesiological**, and **sacramental**) from Rome and in the following four and a half centuries gave birth to a worldwide Communion. The major steps in the formation of the pre-Reformation Church of England may be summarized as follows.

43–410: Christianity was first brought to Britain via the occupying Roman army from A.D. 43 onward, but it was treated as a *Religio illicita* until Constantine's decree of 313 gave it recognition and lawful standing. The first recorded **martyr** was **Alban**, himself a Roman soldier, who died where the city of St. Albans now stands, possibly during the Diocletian persecution (c. 303), but more probably up to 100 years earlier. The first identifiable **bishop** was Restitutus, bishop of **London**, who was recorded as being present at the **Synod** of Arles in 314.

410–597: Christianity was overrun by the massive invasions of eastern, central, and southern Britain by Angles (hence "England"—and "Anglican") and Saxons, but believers found refuge in **Wales** and **Ireland** and on the Isle of **Man**.

597–664: Missionaries from Celtic churches began to **evangelize** in Northumbria, at about the same time that **Augustine** began his **mission** in Kent (where the queen was already Christian) in 597 and founded there the see of Canterbury. The Synod of **Whitby** in 664 reached a reconciliation of the two separate cultures, resolving issues largely in favor of the Roman view.

664–1066: English Christianity started to shape the nation of England, exercising considerable national autonomy, while acknowledging the primacy of the bishop of Rome. During this period, Canterbury and **York** emerged as the two **archbishoprics** of England, with a southern and northern jurisdiction, respectively, but with a clear seniority belonging to Canterbury.

1066–1532: The Norman Conquest began a period of much closer association with the papacy, a period also of growing claims and burgeoning power on the part of the papacy. During this period, Wales was conquered and its sees were incorporated into the province of Canterbury. During this period also, the medieval doctrines of the **Roman Catholic Church** were developed and systematized, and the English Church was as committed to this system as any other part of the Western Church. Initiatives such as those of **John Wycliffe** (c. 1330–1384) to challenge the system or to translate the scriptures into the **vernacular** were severely repressed.

1532–1534: Motivated by his matrimonial aims, King **Henry VIII**, through a series of far-reaching Parliamentary laws, severed the nation of England, and thus the Church of England, from all dependence upon, or submission to, the papacy. From 1534 onward, there was constitutionally a distinct "Church of England," exhibiting very many features of the earlier papal Church in England, but governed now by the monarch in Parliament, as simply the religious aspect of the life of the king's subjects in his realm of England and Wales (and sometimes parts of France). The Reformation in England had begun, and it had begun with the expropriation of the **pope**.

1534–1547: During the remainder of Henry VIII's reign, while the supreme **authority** over the Church of England had changed, the character of worship in the local **parish** church remained virtually as it had been before 1532. Nevertheless, some intermittent changes occurred. The **Bible** in an English translation was ordered to be set up in each parish church in 1537, the **monasteries** were dissolved, and one of the first indications of change was the provision in 1544 of a **litany** in English, a sign of the events to come.

1547–1553: Reign of **Edward VI**. When Henry VIII died, he left a broadly **Protestant** Council to rule the country during his son's minority. Through this pattern of government, with full parliamentary support, the six years of Edward's reign were the period of the doctrinal Reformation. The vast changes included a radical reorganization of the interiors of church buildings, the restoration of the cup to the **laity**, two complete new **Books of Common Prayer** in English, a thorough remodeling of the nature and role of the threefold **ministry**, and, in Edward's last days, the provision of Forty-Two **Articles** of Religion of a reformed character.

1553–1558: Reign of **Mary I**. Queen Mary restored the country to the pope and to the whole Roman Catholic system of life and worship. On the grounds of **heresy**, she burned at the stake five Protestant bishops, including Archbishop **Thomas Cranmer**, and hundreds of other members of the **clergy** and laity. But she died childless without a Roman Catholic heir.

1558–1603: Reign of **Elizabeth I**. Queen Elizabeth's long reign saw Protestantism reestablished, though from 1570 onward she was constantly under threat from Roman Catholics, which led her to put to death her cousin, Mary, Queen of Scots, who was next in succession to the throne of England. The Prayer Book was restored in 1559, the Thirty-Nine Articles imposed in 1571, and a running battle with **Puritans** was conducted with great severity.

1603–1625: Reign of **James I**. James was the son of Mary, Queen of Scots, and when she abdicated during his infancy, he had succeeded her as King James VI of **Scotland**. When he then succeeded Elizabeth I, he became King James I of England. He embraced the Church of England keenly and ordered an Episcopal government for Scotland from 1610, and further pressed the need of liturgical services upon Scotland. The **Hampton Court Conference** in 1604 led to minute changes in the Prayer Book and to a new translation of the Bible, known as the **King James Version**. **Canon law** was codified for England in 1604. Puritan dissent ran on, curbed and driven semiunderground by law.

1625–1649: Reign of **Charles I**. The son of James I, Charles I further antagonized the Puritans and finally provoked the Civil War. This lasted from 1642 to 1645, when Charles finally surrendered to Parliament. When he refused the constitutional and ecclesiastical reforms demanded by his opponents, he was tried for treason and executed. Meanwhile, Parliament had abolished

episcopacy and the Prayer Book, the ***Directory for the Public Worship of God*** had been imposed, and the parish clergymen were often replaced by **Presbyterian** or Independent **ministers**.

1649–1660: **Commonwealth** period. Oliver Cromwell became "protector" and ruled first with parliamentary support and later without it. He died in 1658, and Parliament soon lost confidence in itself and approached Charles I's son, **Charles II**, the "king in exile," to invite him to assume his throne in England.

1649–1685: Reign of Charles II. The Restoration of Charles II took place in May 1660. He brought back episcopacy, and by stages also reimposed the Prayer Book, which (with tiny changes from the texts of 1552 and 1604) was required for use in every parish by **Act of Uniformity** from 1662. More than 1,000 Puritan clergy left the parish **ministry** and went into nonconformity. They were harried by law thereafter. Charles himself was without legitimate heir, and he not only defended the propriety of his Roman Catholic brother, James, the Duke of York, being heir to the throne, but also joined the Roman Catholic Church himself on his deathbed.

1685–1688: Reign of **James II**. The younger brother of Charles II, James had become a Roman Catholic during Charles's reign. By both his position and his disposition, he then became a threat to the identity and continuance of the distinctive Church of England. He duly inherited on his brother's death, but, when he overreached himself and had to flee the land, all pretense of "the divine right of kings" slid away and a more pragmatic and less doctrinaire relationship between monarch and nation developed.

1689–1702: Reign of **William III** and **Mary II**. After James II fled England, Parliament declared the throne vacant and offered the monarchy to William and Mary in what came to be known as the **Glorious Revolution**. But hundreds of clergy who had sworn loyalty to James, led by **William Sancroft**, the archbishop of Canterbury, judged that they could not in good conscience swear loyalty to the new joint monarchs while James was still alive. They thus became "**nonjurors**," and the resultant schism lasted for nearly 100 years. (In Scotland, all the bishops refused to swear and became nonjurors there.) But nonconformists gained toleration and entered into a new legal liberty. By the Bill of Rights (1689), reinforced by the Act of Settlement (1700), no

Roman Catholic nor anyone married to a Roman Catholic could thereafter succeed to the throne.

1702–1714: Reign of Anne. Queen Anne was a pious sympathizer with the Church of England and was the last monarch for a long time to take a close interest in it.

After Queen Anne's death, under the Hanoverian dynasty, changes in the Church of England were no longer closely related to any change of monarchs. Soon after her death, in 1717, the **Convocations** were prorogued and did not meet for business again until 1852. The Church of England thus lacked any means of its own to initiate structural or other change.

At the end of the 17th century, in 1699, the first overseas **missionary society** of the Church of England, the **Society for Promoting Christian Knowledge** was formed, followed in 1702 by the **Society for the Propagation of the Gospel**. In the 18th century, the **Evangelical Revival**, coinciding with the opening of world trade, discovery, and colonization, led not only to the breakaway of **Methodism** and some smaller bodies but also, within Anglicanism, to the forming of vast, new, and energetic "voluntary" societies for mission, both in England and overseas. The first bishops were **consecrated** for the **United States** in 1784 and for British overseas possessions in 1787.

In the 19th century, the **Anglo-Catholic** movement began in England in 1833, **theological colleges** were founded, and resources from the early and medieval churches were tapped and brought into use in a host of fields. The religious census of 1851 showed that only one-third of the population worshipped with the Church of England, and church and nation were no longer coterminous. The Convocations were reestablished, and an identity was sought for a Church of England that would be more specific, creedal, and worshipping than simply a count of the citizens of England would suggest. Overseas troubles in **South Africa** paradoxically laid foundations for the **Lambeth Conferences**. The Church of **Ireland**, which had been united with the Church of England in 1801 by the Act of Union that created a single government in Westminster, was sundered from it again in 1870 and became by disestablishment a "voluntary" body. In the Church of England itself, complaints about "ritualism" ran on and led to pressure in Parliament for "clergy discipline."

In the early 20th century, the Royal Commission on Ecclesiastical Discipline (1904–1906) investigated the complaints about **liturgical** irregularities, and its report recommended a broadening of the **rubrical** permissions about **ceremonial**. This led, by an extraordinary set of steps, to the proposals a quarter of a century later for a completely new Prayer Book for the Church of England. Meantime, Parliament had, through the "**Enabling Act**," established legislative powers for the Church Assembly beginning in 1920—but had correspondingly weakened the powers of Parliament in respect of church legislation. In 1920 also, the four **dioceses** of the province of Canterbury in **Wales** were separated from Canterbury and were disestablished by parliamentary action; they then formed themselves, by voluntary compact, into the "Church in Wales." The new delegation of legislative powers meant that, when the new Prayer Book came for parliamentary sanction in 1927 and 1928, the members of the House of Commons had no power to amend it where they disliked it (mostly in relation to permanent **reservation** of the **consecrated elements**), and so they vetoed it two years running, thus precipitating a church–state crisis.

The second half of the 20th century saw vast changes. These included a serious loss of numbers of worshippers, new canon law that allowed the Church of England to devise and authorize new forms of worship without sending them to Parliament for approval, a resurgence of the evangelicalism that had been so eclipsed by Anglo-Catholicism since the 1870s, the formation of a **General Synod** in 1970, and various initiatives for reunion, which were largely frustrated, although a restored practice of "open Communion" allowed unconfirmed nonconformists from 1972 onwards to receive Communion. The **Porvoo** Declaration, inaugurating **full Communion** with the **Lutheran** Nordic and Baltic Churches, came into force in 1996. The **ordination** of **women** as **deacons** began in 1987 and as **presbyters** in 1994.

ENGLISH LANGUAGE LITURGICAL CONSULTATION (ELLC). The first **ecumenical**, internationally agreed English **liturgical** texts came from the **International Consultation on English Texts** (ICET) between 1969 and 1974. ICET then went into abeyance, but it was succeeded in 1985 by the English-Language Liturgical Consultation. ELLC followed up the work of ICET and, meeting every two years, agreed upon new texts (many of them hardly altered from 1974) in

1987 and then added an introduction and commentaries; the full result was published as *Praying Together* in 1988. The texts largely comprise material that is shared among Christian denominations: the **Lord's Prayer**, Gloria in Excelsis, **Creeds**, Sursum Corda, Sanctus, and **Agnus Dei**. The most notable changes from the ICET texts of 1974 have been in the **Nicene Creed**, particularly in the lines now translated as ". . . was born of the **Holy Spirit** and the Virgin **Mary** / and was made fully human." The recommendations did not include a definitive direction in respect of the ***Filioque***.

It remains a matter for individual Churches—and, in the case of **Anglicans**, for autonomous **provinces**—as to whether they adopt the changes recommended by ELLC. Most liturgical revision using the English language in the **Anglican Communion** has in fact followed closely upon the ELLC recommendations, the main variant being in the ninth line of the Lord's Prayer (where "Lead us not into temptation" has survived in some provinces, despite ELLC's recommendation of "Save us from the time of trial").

A major force in the original formation of ICET, and in the continuing work of ELLC, has been the **Roman Catholic** International Commission on English in the Liturgy (ICEL). By the constitution of ELLC, ICEL provided half of the membership of ELLC and a cochairman, with national interdenominational commissions providing the other half of membership and the other cochairman. However, in 2001 ICEL was required by the (Roman Catholic) Congregation for Divine Worship to withdraw from ELLC at its meeting in August that year, as the Congregation had ruled (in the "Fifth Instruction") that it was incorrect for ICEL to do other than translate into English the texts supplied from Rome in Latin. This has had a weakening effect on ELLC.

EPICLESIS. The Greek word *epiklesis* literally means "calling upon" or "invocation." It has been used specifically as the name of a particular form of prayer within a **eucharistic prayer**, denoting in the first instance a form in which the Father is asked to send the **Holy Spirit** upon the elements or upon the action. In the historic Eastern rites the epiclesis came in a sequence after the **narrative** of institution and the **anamnesis**. The medieval Roman Catholic mass had a prayer for **consecration** (*Quam oblationem*) before the narrative, but this had no reference to the Holy Spirit. In the **1549 Book of Common Prayer**

this prayer was rewritten, and an invoking of "thy Holy Spirit and word" was included, which has meant that the formulation has often been called an epiclesis. In 1552 this was changed again, and the reference to the Spirit was omitted. However, the 1549 form recurred in the **Scottish** 1637 rite, and this became in the 18th century the basis for the text which was used in the "wee bookies" produced by the Episcopal Church of Scotland. During the 18th century the epiclesis was transferred to the historic eastern position after the anamnesis, and this was the position in the definitive 1764 rite, which itself became the basis for the new American rite authorized by the **General Convention** of the **Protestant Episcopal Church in the United States of America** in 1789. In the 20th century various new Anglican rites adopted this position for the epiclesis, and, whether or not this position was adopted, the petition for consecration has in new rites regularly included reference to the Holy Spirit. When the 1549/1552 (or "Western") position is retained, the later petition for fruitful reception is sometimes called the "second epiclesis."

EPIPHANY. The Greek word *epiphaneia* means "shining out" or "demonstration." From early times in the West, 6 January has been kept as a **feast** separable from **Christmas**, marking the end of the "12 days of Christmas" and itself becoming the departure point for counting the Sundays that follow. All these features were retained by the Church of **England** at the **Reformation**. The festival is marked in **liturgy** by the stories of the coming of the Magi, of the **baptism** of Jesus Christ by John, and of the miracle at the marriage at Cana, each of which has an element of the revelation of Jesus to the world. In some **provinces**, its baptismal theme has been taken up as providing an occasion for the renewal of baptismal vows. It is sometimes observed on the nearest Sunday to 6 January.

The Epiphany has also developed as not simply a single feast but also a season that runs from the traditional day of the Epiphany, 6 January, to the Presentation of Christ in the Temple, which is kept on 2 February, 40 days from Christmas.

EPISCOPACY. This word is derived more directly than is its cognate term, "**bishop**," from their common etymological origins in the Greek word *episkopos*. It is an abstract noun used to denote the institutional structuring of bishops into the life and government of a church.

EPISCOPAL CHURCH (UNITED STATES OF AMERICA) (ECUSA). In 1967, the **Protestant Episcopal Church in the United States of America (PECUSA)** changed its official title to the Episcopal Church (United States of America). The two titles are used in this dictionary to be accurate for the point in time to which reference is being made, whether before or after 1967. It appears that the change was made not only in order to get away from the maligned word "**Protestant**" but also to play down the location of the Church as being *in* the United States, when in fact many of the overseas and Central American dioceses were in the Episcopal Church but were not in the United States. The change was made definitive at the 1979 **General Convention**.

EPISCOPATE. This word is used as a common noun to describe the total number of **bishops** in a particular Church (e.g., "the American episcopate"). It is also used, as an alternative to "bishopric," as an abstract noun to denote the particular exercise of the role of a bishop by a stated individual (e.g., "during the episcopate of George Bell").

EPISCOPUS VAGANS. The churches of the **Anglican Communion**, both because of their Western background and because of the circumstances in which the **Episcopal** succession was conveyed at the beginning of Queen **Elizabeth I**'s reign, have generally held an "**Augustinian**" view of **orders**. By this theory, the **validity** of Episcopal **ordinations** (to whichever order) is based solely upon the historic succession in which the ordaining **bishops** stand, irrespective of their contemporary ecclesial context. This is the starting point for **Roman Catholic** decisions on validity, and it acknowledges that schismatic and **excommunicated** bishops can confer true orders. Thus, part of the Anglican debate with the Roman Catholic Church about the validity of Anglican orders involves a "worst case" presentation—that is, even if, from a strictly Roman standpoint, the bishops who **consecrated Matthew Parker** in 1559 were schismatic and excommunicate, nevertheless they ordained him validly and he became a true "bishop in the Church of God," and, in the ordinations he conducted, he himself conferred true orders, which have thus been preserved in Anglicanism. Similarly Roman Catholic objections to Anglican orders, such as are found in depth in ***Apostolicae Curae*** (1896), have focused on issues of intention, rather than any allegations of breaks in the historical succession.

After 1689, the **nonjuring** and **Scottish** Episcopal Church Episcopal successions had, from the Church of England's point of view, some of the same characteristics of separation, but the English nonjuring line in time died out, and the Scottish bishops ultimately accepted the Hanoverian regime and ceased to be underground rebels. So the real rise of the problem came later, in the wake of the **Anglo-Catholic** movement in the 19th century. Then, through the mischievous activities of a tiny number of independently acting bishops—Eastern, Western, and in one case **Old Catholic**—whole lines of "succession" arose, through which some hundreds of "validly ordained" bishops exist around the world, mostly without congregations or church life, and many in different stages of delusion and fantasy, not least in the Episcopal styles they confer on themselves. The title *episcopus vagans* specifically identifies the lack of a true see or the lack of real church life to oversee as the distinguishing mark of such bishops. By that criterion, the bishops of most forms of "**continuing Anglicans**" (a category that has arisen around the world largely through the ordination of **women**) are not necessarily to be classified as *vagantes*, but they are always in danger of becoming such.

A further pattern of bishops possibly describable as *vagantes* has arisen since the 1998 **Lambeth Conference**, as Anglican **archbishops** in good standing in their own **provinces** have consecrated bishops to work (in a "**missionary**" or proselytizing mode) in other Anglican provinces, on the grounds that these latter have so lapsed from the faith and morals proper to the Christian church that their congregations need to be rescued from their own bishops and **synods**. Here again, if actual congregations accept the Episcopal oversight of such bishops, then—though questions of schism, or at least of overlapping "jurisdictions," may arise—the term *vagantes* may be inappropriate. *See also* APOSTOLIC SUCCESSION; HISTORIC EPISCOPATE.

ESCHATOLOGY. Anglican churches are orthodox in their general affirmation of the Second Coming of **Jesus Christ**, highlighted in their **calendars** by the season of **Advent**. At the time of the **Reformation**, there was little difference between **Roman Catholics** and Anglicans about the Final Resurrection and the fact of the Last Judgment (though a classic distinction existed in relation to their respective **doctrines** of **justification**). The difference that stood out was one about the "intermediate state," in particular, whether this was a real **purgatory** and whether those in purgatory could be assisted by the prayers (and **masses**) of the living. **Thomas Cranmer** made little of the Second Coming in the reform of the **liturgy**, save the completely new **collect** of Advent 1 and a reference from 1 Cor. 11.26 inserted into the **epiclesis** (actually a petition for fruitful reception of the **sacrament**) in 1552.

There was, however, a conflict on another front with the "millenarii," or extreme Anabaptists, whose eschatological expectations were thought to make them less dutiful toward state or church **authority**. Articles XXXIX–XLII of the Forty-Two **Articles** of 1553 were directed against them, and, though these were excised in **Elizabeth I**'s reign, Articles XXXVII–XXXIX of the Thirty-Nine Articles leave a caution standing.

In latter days, Anglicans have differed about their expectations of the nature of the Second Coming of Christ, although provision of **propers** for Advent 1 has looked more consistently toward that Second Coming than did the 1662 **Book of Common Prayer**. **Eucharistic prayers** now regularly include acclamations of which the third is "Christ will come again," and a variant addresses Christ himself, "Lord Jesus, come in glory." On the one hand, there has been a diminution of secular optimism and of the hope that the human race would simply evolve into a better and better society, in which by moral improvement all would live in peace and righteousness; on the other hand, the outcropping of virulent premillennialism, often leading to political unwisdom in giving a favored place in God's economy to today's political state of Israel, has reinforced the natural caution in Anglican circles about overexact **prophesying** about the nature of the Lord's Return.

ESTABLISHMENT. At the **Reformation**, the Churches of **England** and **Ireland** (and particularly their **clergy**) were torn from their allegiance to the **pope** and became by legal decree a department of state under the control of the monarch in Parliament. This subordination of the Church to the state is known as "establishment." Apart from the **Commonwealth** period (1649–1660), Parliament's theory of establishment until 1689 was that the Church of England enjoyed a state monopoly of religion; after 1689 and the advent of "toleration," this changed from a monopoly to a position of high privilege.

In 1832 the Westminster Parliament, which legally governed the **United Church of England and Ireland**, itself ceased to be composed exclusively of Anglicans. At this point, the **Anglo-Catholic** movement began in 1833 with **John Keble**'s attack on parliamentary rule over the church in his sermon on "National Apostasy." The leaders of the movement opposed state roles in relation to the Church of England and in time sought the restoration of real functions and powers for the **Convocations**. This led to a revival of the Convocations, which therefore provided a church voice that was clearly distinct from the parliamentary voice. This, however, did not wholly prevent Parliament taking action in ecclesiastical matters without consulting the Convocations.

In 1870 the Church of Ireland was separated from the Church of England and disestablished, and a similar move followed for the Welsh **dioceses** of the Church of England in 1920, when they became the (disestablished) Church in **Wales**. In England further steps have followed to devolve powers from Parliament to Church organs of government (powers which, since 1970, have been transferred to the **General Synod**), but the Church of England remains formally established.

From 1689 onward, the **Scottish** Episcopal Church was not only not a state Church, but was actually a Jacobite rebellion. Thus it existed solely by free association of its members, and this became characteristic also of Episcopalians in the independent American states after they had thrown off their colonial status. The first **General Convention** in 1785 saw the Anglicans of the various states affiliating voluntarily to each other. The federal government of the **United States** by its constitution does not permit the establishment of any particular brand of Christianity or other religion, either federally or in any individual state.

However, a different situation arose in the 19th century in many territories that were still in different ways subject to the British Crown. Initially chaplaincies and **mission** stations would view themselves as part of the Church of England, and the first **bishops** were usually appointed under letters patent of the monarch and were **consecrated** in **London**, confirming this view. However, step by step and territory by territory, the overseas churches discovered the problems of being part (and a relatively undefined part) of the established Church of England. In **South Africa**, Robert Gray simply announced in 1870 a unilateral declaration of independence, while in other lands constitutions were produced that moved the Anglicans in each country or region into being a separate new independent **province**. The last such territory to retain a relationship with the state was the island of Barbados, where disestablishment came in 1961.

The English establishment is marked by five main distinctive features:

1. The monarch is the "supreme governor" of the Church of England, and the **coronation** rites have up to the present time included a special vow of upholding the Church of England.
2. The diocesan bishops (and the **suffragan** bishops and most **cathedral deans**) are appointed by the monarch on the nomination of the prime minister of the day.
3. Twenty-six senior diocesan bishops sit in the House of Lords as "Lords Spiritual" (though the membership, character, and powers of the House and its possible reform, not excluding the role of the bishops, came under close examination in a series of largely abortive attempts at the reform of the membership beginning in 1997).
4. Church legislation has to go on from the General Synod to gain the approval of both Houses of Parliament before it becomes the law of the Church.
5. In certain respects, the boundaries of **parishes** have an existence in law, and parishioners, whether Christian or not, are entitled to be married (for the first time, at least) in their parish church. They are also entitled to burial in the churchyard (where one exists).

It is an open question as to how long this establishment can last. There are several contemporary defenses of it, but they fall far short of being compelling. And the problem of being the officially recognized and entrenched religious stance of the nation, when all the signs are that Anglicanism has, in terms of numbers of worshippers, the adherence of only a small minority of the nation, looms very large. Reunion with other denominations is also impossible to achieve while the Church of England is established.

EUCHARIST. The Greek word for "thanksgiving" is *eucharistia*, and the participle from the stem, *eucharistesas*, is used of **Jesus**' prayer over each of the **elements** at the Last Supper prior to his distribution of them. The **Lord's Supper** itself is called "*eucharistia*" in the Letters of Ignatius of Antioch at the beginning of the second century, and widely and uncontentiously thereafter. However, the Reformers carefully excised the title, preferring only those they believed to be warranted by scripture: "**communion**" (1 Cor. 10.16) and the "Lord's Supper" (1 Cor. 11.20). "Eucharist" was sometimes used as a term for the service in the 17th century, and it crept back into widespread (though far from universal) use in Anglicanism in the 19th and 20th centuries, originally through the deliberate archaizing and borrowing from Rome of the **Anglo-Catholics**, but more recently as being somewhat nearer to an ecumenical common term (cf. the **Lima** Statement, *Baptism, Eucharist, and Ministry*). Its common use is also probably related to the easy provision of a simple adjective ("eucharistic"), which the other titles of the Supper do not provide at all. *See also* EUCHARISTIC PRAYER; EUCHARISTIC SACRIFICE.

EUCHARISTIC PRAYER. The central prayer over the **elements** in the **Communion liturgy** was known in the Middle Ages in the West as the "**canon** of the **mass**" and in the Eastern Churches as the "anaphora." In Anglicanism, at least from the 17th century onward, the most usual term was "the prayer of **consecration**," and this continued until the middle of the 20th century, sometimes varied by the informal term "the long prayer." **Gregory Dix**'s assertion of the four-action "shape" of the **eucharistic** liturgy in 1945 denominated the second action as "he gave thanks," which led to the use as a title of the prayer of first "the thanksgiving" or "the great thanksgiving," and later "the eucharistic prayer."

In the 1662 **Book of Common Prayer**, the prayer of consecration ended somewhat abruptly with the **narrative** of institution. Most liturgical revision in the **Anglican Communion** since that date has, in one way or another, been seeking to provide a fuller eucharistic prayer. Typically, a modern eucharistic prayer will contain an **anamnesis** after the narrative, and some form of petition for fruitful reception (whether or not that is dubbed an "**epiclesis**") will also be found, leading into a weighty doxology. Most modern eucharistic prayers also provide congregational responses over and above the traditional opening dialogue and Sanctus after the **preface**. The 1958 **Lambeth Conference** expressed a view that "consecration is by thanksgiving," and that concern has lain behind much textual revision. There has been a lightening of the concept that consecration is effected solely by recitation of the dominical words within the narrative—and in prayers where, as in Eastern rites, a consecratory epiclesis comes subsequent to the narrative of institution, it is very difficult to hold to the "moment of consecration" theory.

EUCHARISTIC SACRIFICE. In the New Testament, the **eucharist** is a **feast** with strong reference to the sacrifice of **Jesus Christ**, but of itself is neither called a sacrifice nor presented as operating as a sacrifice. Nevertheless, in the course of church history from the first century to the 16th, the idea grew that the rite itself is in some sense a sacrifice and was appropriately offered by a **priest** on an **altar**. In the latter part of that era, each separate offering of the sacrifice could be reckoned to have specific value with **God**, so that a stated number of **masses** would be said for the repose of the soul of someone who had died, the success of the king in war, and so forth.

The Reformers reverted to the scriptural view, holding not only to the positive **doctrine** that the purpose of **sacraments** was that we should receive them but also to the implications of reading from the New Testament that Christ made upon the **cross** the "full, perfect and sufficient, sacrifice, oblation and satisfaction" for sins forever, thus precluding any possibility of a substantial sacrifice being offered in or at the eucharist. **Archbishop Thomas Cranmer** changed all such language of oblation of the **elements** in the medieval mass into offering of prayers, and he distinguished carefully between the propitiatory sacrifice offered ("there") on the cross by Christ and the purely responsive sacrifice of "ourselves, our souls and bodies" offered ("here") by the communicants. "Altar" was excised from the service books and replaced by "**table**."

In the 17th century there were some Anglican divines who wished to blur or abolish the distinction between Christ's sacrifice and ours, though the **Laudian** draft **canons** of 1640 still asserted that distinction, and the view was without any impact on the 1662 revision of the **Book of Common Prayer**. The line of thinking became stronger among the **nonjurors** and **Scottish** Episcopalians of the 18th century. The Scottish **Communion** rite of 1764 added, in the reference to the **bread** and wine in the **anamnesis**, the adjectival clause "which here we offer unto thee." This addition would seem to import a Godward offering of the elements into the text with at least some symbolic significance. The same clause then came into the American rite of 1789 from the Scottish. In **England**, the **Anglo-Catholic** movement of the 19th century drew upon **Roman Catholic** ideas, and the movement's **hymnody**, **catechisms**, and **ceremonial** attempted to fasten such ideas upon the 1662 rite.

When **Pope** Leo XIII condemned Anglican **orders** in ***Apostolicae Curae*** in 1896, a crucial part of the judgment was based upon the papal assertion of a lack of any doctrine of eucharistic sacrifice in Cranmer's Communion rite—in other words, any **bishop ordaining** a **presbyter** with the reformed **Ordinal** would on this view not be ordaining a true catholic priest, because a defect of intention was built into the ordination process. The charge was that the nature of the 1559 eucharistic rite of the Church of England made it fully clear that the ordination of a priest to preside over such a eucharistic rite could not have been "intended" to make the man a priest "to offer sacrifice for the living and the dead" (as the Roman ordinal put it).

The reply of the two English archbishops, ***Saepius Officio*** (1897), while generally challenging the initial assumptions of the pope's encyclical, also stated that in the Church of England's rite (i.e., the Communion service in the 1662 Book of Common Prayer), there is a true eucharistic sacrifice, in which we "set [the elements] before God," and do in fact thus meet the pope's criteria. Not all Anglicans agreed that the pope's criteria should have been accepted (though it was arguable that it would be helpful for the pope to accord recognition on the basis of his own criteria); but even on his criteria it remained doubtful both whether the archbishops' argument was a fair exposition of the text of Cranmer's rite, and, even if it was, whether it met the pope's criteria.

In the first half of the 20th century, most liturgical revision originated in the more Anglo-Catholic **provinces** of the **Anglican Communion**. There thus tended to be a return to some form of explicit oblation of the elements expressed in the anamnesis. **Gregory Dix** expounded the word "anamnesis" itself as a synonym for offering sacrifice. However, when revision started in provinces where **Evangelicals** and Anglo-Catholics were both involved in textual revision, such explicit departures from Cranmer's doctrinal weighting, even with changes in his actual form of words, were less easily implemented.

EUROPE. On 1 October 1633 an order of the Privy Council gave to the **bishop** of **London** responsibility for the oversight of Anglican chaplains and their congregations in foreign countries in Europe and in other colonial territories further afield. Embassy churches were the predominant category covered by this order in Europe, and the responsibility in any particular area remained with the bishop of London until a separate diocesan bishop was appointed. Thus in 1842 the extraprovincial **diocese** of **Gibraltar** was formed, covering southern Europe and some of North Africa, but northern Europe remained the responsibility of the bishop of London.

Chaplaincies developed in the 19th and 20th centuries not solely where there were British embassies but also in cities with numbers of businesspeople and other expatriates, as well as in tourist centers (sometimes on a seasonal basis). In 1926 the **suffragan** see of Fulham was formed, enabling the bishop of London to delegate most of his responsibilities to the bishop of Fulham. In the 1970s a need was expressed for the European chaplains to be fully within the life of the Church of **England**, at the very least in order that **clergy** from England should retain their participation in the noncontributory pensions scheme then operating.

A **measure** passed through the **General Synod** and Parliament to create a new diocese "in Europe," which would be part of the **province** of **Canterbury** and thus of the structures of the Church of England itself. The new diocese, with its **cathedral** in Gibraltar, came into existence in 1980, the first and only new diocese of the Church of England since Leicester, Guildford, Portsmouth, and Blackburn were formed in 1926–1927. Its territory stretches from the Azores in the west to Vladivostok in the east. It has representation on the General Synod of the Church of England, but its own synodical structures are unlike those of any English diocese. As the monarch and Parliament have no Continental jurisdiction, the diocese is wholly disestablished. Accordingly the appointment of the bishop follows a process like that of other dioceses as far as consideration by the **Crown Nominations Commission**, but at the latter stages the choice between the two nominated persons is made jointly by the **archbishop** of Canterbury, the bishop of London, and a representative of the **Anglican Communion**, rather than by the prime minister.

The Church of England diocese does not, however, provide the whole picture of Anglicans and Anglican-related Churches in Europe. The following further elements are also part of the picture:

- The American Congregations in Europe, fully part of the **Episcopal Church (United States of America)**, occur in eight major centers and have a bishop exercising oversight of them. The American and English bishops appoint each other as assistant bishops in their own jurisdictions.
- The **Lusitanian Church** in Portugal and the **Spanish Reformed Episcopal Church** each form a separate extraprovincial Anglican diocese. Their origins lay in the departure of numbers of **Roman Catholics** from their own Roman Catholic Church in the years following **Vatican I**. Both dioceses have received Episcopal ministrations, including the **consecration** of bishops, from the Church of **Ireland**, the **Protestant Episcopal Church in the United States of America**, and more recently, the Church of England. Until 1980 they were independent dioceses, but in that year both were admitted, at their own request, into the Anglican Communion with the archbishop of Canterbury as their **metropolitan**. Their numbers are small, but they are nationals of Portugal and Spain, respectively, and worship in their own **languages** and with their own rites.
- The **Old Catholics**, while not part of the Anglican Communion, are in Communion with the Anglican churches. They are found in Holland, Germany, Switzerland, Austria, Poland, the Czech Republic, and elsewhere.
- The **Lutheran churches** of Sweden, Norway, Finland, Latvia, Estonia, and Lithuania (but not the Church of Denmark) share with the Anglican Churches of Britain and Ireland in the **Porvoo** Common Statement and are developing new forms of interchange and sharing at the local level.

Some consultations have been sustained between the Church of England diocese in Europe and these other bodies listed above, and a joint statement in May 1999 adumbrated the possibility, admittedly somewhat distant, of an Anglican province of Europe.

EVANGELICAL MOVEMENT. The roots of evangelicalism lie in the **Reformation** controversies of the Church of **England**, and in the resultant formularies, particularly as they set out the supreme **authority** of the **Bible**. However, the title “Evangelical” was not consistently used in the 16th and 17th centuries to denominate a particular strand of church life, and the divisions, for example, between **Laudians** and **Puritans**, did not usually involve any labeling of one group as "Evangelical."

The term came in strongly in the 18th century, when the jibes of opponents led to the **gospel** movement associated with the **Wesleys** and George Whitefield being described as the "**Evangelical Revival**." Springing from the Evangelical Revival, there has been an Evangelical Movement in the Church of England and in many parts of the **Anglican Communion** ever since. In England it has been characterized and sustained in being by a great **network** of voluntary societies and independent institutions. Among these have been the overseas and home **missionary societies**, youth and children's organizations, church press, **theological colleges**, patronage boards, conference centers, and a vast number of single-issue pressure groups. Some of these have been paralleled in other parts of the Communion, but in some **provinces** evangelicalism has been so much the norm of Anglican church life as to undercut any rationale of such independent action, while in others evangelicalism has scarcely been known at all.

Evangelicalism was squeezed in the second half of the 19th century by the growing forces of **Anglo-Catholicism** and **liberalism**. After being the strongest and most vigorous feature of Anglicanism in England in the mid-19th century, it was seriously in decline by the beginning of the 20th. While numbers were sustained in places newly evangelized (e.g., in East and West Africa), Evangelical scholarship was eclipsed in the first half of the 20th century, and Evangelical leaders around the Anglican Communion were almost without influence.

After World War II, this trend was reversed, however, and evangelicalism both reappeared in provinces from which it had been absent and also strengthened greatly in provinces (e.g., in the Church of England and the province of **Southern Africa**) where it had been previously weakened. It was also strong in the younger churches of the Communion, where new **dioceses** and provinces were springing up in the second half of the 20th century.

A new and confident scholarship led to Evangelicals taking a leading place (not least among the **bishops** and theologians) in the Communion. Creative new ways of worshipping emerged, some of them at odds with traditional Anglican styles. A strong ally, with overlapping influence and agendas, was found in the **Charismatic Move-**

ment, and a dynamism for **evangelism** was rediscovered. However, the participation of Evangelicals with other Anglicans has frequently been in tension, partly because of some basic incompatibilities with blinkered forms of Anglo-Catholicism, partly because of liberal inroads threatening to undermine credal Christianity, and partly because of new threats to the stability of the Communion through the acceptance by liberals of **homosexual** practices. In England, a turning point came with the Keele Congress of 1967, at which 1,000 Evangelicals pledged themselves to full participation in the life of the Church of England, but many of the tensions—not least that relating to homosexuality—have arisen since then. Evangelicals around the Communion have been linked since the 1960s in an Evangelical Fellowship of the Anglican Communion (EFAC), which has held international conferences on occasion and has provided bursaries for **clergy** from developing nations to do further studies in England.

EVANGELICAL REVIVAL. The Evangelical Revival was a great spiritual movement that originated in **England** in the 18th century. The central figure in this movement was **John Wesley** (1703–1791), whose **evangelistic ministry** dated from his heart being "strangely warmed" on 24 May 1738. The chief outcome of his ministry and that of his associates is usually celebrated as the birth of **Methodism**. Nevertheless, he and several other leaders were members of the Anglican **clergy**, and where they were welcomed in Anglican **parishes**, the revival was often contained within Anglicanism. Those Evangelical parish clergy saw their **doctrinal** position as entirely in accord with the Thirty-Nine **Articles** and traced their origins to the **Reformation** formularies and principles. It is arguable that in the 18th century they were distinguished in their position not by having different doctrines from others but by *profoundly* believing that which others nominally believed—and this fervor was characterized by opponents as "enthusiasm."

The face of the Church of England was altered by this, as a great stream of Evangelical clergy arose within the second half of the 18th century, and their **gospel** reached the highest and the lowest in the land. In those 50 years, the so-called **Clapham Sect** led to the formation of the **Church Missionary Society** (CMS) in 1799; **Charles Simeon** began his greatly influential ministry at Holy Trinity, Cambridge (1783–1836); **William Wilberforce** started his parliamentary campaign to end the slave trade and free the slaves; and the spiritual impact of the movement was found in the **Protestant Episcopal Church in the United States of America**, the Church of **Ireland**, and many of the places of incipient Anglicanism throughout the world. During the 19th century, this grew to become a massive **missionary** movement, which established evangelicalism as normal Anglicanism in many parts of what is now the **Anglican Communion**.

EVANGELISM. The historic sociological context from which Anglicanism emerged was a Christendom that took it for granted that all infants were **baptized**, all growing children were **catechized**, and all adults attended worship and heard sermons. Within such a context, the main spiritual thrust, as in 17th-century **England**, was to spell out the personal and social implications of the faith that all were assumed to possess. The 17th century saw the first mention of persons "converted to the faith" in the preface to the 1662 **Book of Common Prayer**. However, in the 18th century, the alienation from the church of much of the nation meant that the preaching of the **Evangelicals** and their call to repentance and faith stood nearer to true basic evangelism than any normal practice of the previous centuries. The rise of the overseas **missionary** movement took the need for such evangelism for granted and promoted it strongly throughout the known world.

Anglicanism in the 19th and 20th centuries presents a curious tension between evangelism and complacency. It has been said that the basic model set up by the English **parish** system is in essence pastoral, and that the patterns of **ministry** exercised where that model has been established are likewise pastoral. Yet in every **province** of the **Anglican Communion**, there has also been passionate evangelism practiced, and much church growth resulting from it. The 1988 **Lambeth Conference**, in its Resolution 43, called for the 1990s to be a "Decade of Evangelism." The results of this decade appear to have been disappointing in the provinces of Britain, Ireland, North America, and Australasia, but very encouraging in many African and other provinces.

The **Anglican Consultative Council** included in its staff in the 1990s a director of **mission** and evangelism, Cyril Okorocha of **Nigeria**. Although his post was closed before the 1998 Lambeth Conference, Resolution II.2 at that conference called for a reassessment of budgetary priorities to provide staff for "mission and evangelism." This was achieved with the appointment of Marjorie Murphy as director of mission and evangelism Anglican Communion in the years following.

The 1998 Lambeth Conference, in its five "marks of mission," listed the first two as "to proclaim the Good News of the Kingdom" and "to teach, **baptize** and nurture new believers (incorporating them into the body of Christ)." This formulation places evangelism at the forefront of mission. *See also* INTER-ANGLICAN STANDING COMMISSION ON MISSION AND EVANGELISM; MISSIO.

EXCOMMUNICATION. The 16th-century **Books of Common Prayer** and 1604 **canons** of the Church of **England** confidently provided for the excommunication of individuals in a variety of ways. The opening **rubrics** of the **Communion** service provided for the **presbyter** to restrain certain categories of offenders from receiving Communion until they had been reconciled to others or had repented of open and notorious sins. The first 12 of the 1604 **canons** enforced their positive teachings by requiring the excommunication of those who might transgress against their **doctrines** or precepts. The 1662 Book of Common Prayer added a rubric to the Communion service (in fact within the ante-Communion, so that it would occur each Sunday) to have excommunications read aloud in church.

In theory such disciplines have run on into the 21st century, and many **provinces** sustain canons or rules that have excommunication as their sanction, to encourage conformity to the rules. But there has also arisen a distrust of adversarial confrontation to deal with minor pastoral matters, and the comprehensiveness of widely accepted Anglican **ecclesiology** has clearly promoted a culture of relative permissiveness.

In the 19th century, in the wake of the **Anglo-Catholic** movement, a serious move was made in many provinces to excommunicate the unconfirmed (in line with the literal wording of the "**confirmation** rubric" of 1662, but out of line with its conventional interpretation). This line of action was generally abandoned in the second half of the 20th century, and rubrics and canons affirming that the **baptized** are to be received at Communion on the basis of their baptism alone have sometimes given expression to this.

At intervals, the **Anglican Communion** has faced issues of one **diocese** or province excommunicating another. The most notable occasion in history was when **Frank Weston**, **bishop** of **Zanzibar** from 1908 to 1924, formally excommunicated the bishops of **Mombasa** and **Uganda** for sharing Communion with **Methodists** and **Presbyterians** at the **Kikuyu** conference in 1913. Lesser occasions included when, after the formation of the Church of **South India** in 1947, Anglo-Catholic parishes in England stated that they would not give Communion to members of the united church.

A concept of "impaired communion," which has arisen since the **ordination** of **women** as presbyters and then as bishops, has led to a polarization, where those who do not accept the **sacramental** ministrations of a woman presbyter, or the Episcopal acts of a woman bishop, have declined to receive Communion from such women or from male bishops or other clergy too closely associated with them. There are signs that a comparable polarizing is occurring as between supporters and opponents of **homosexual** unions, particularly insofar as **clergy** are involved in such unions.

EXECUTIVE OFFICER OF THE ANGLICAN COMMUNION. The 1958 **Lambeth Conference** recommended the widening of the terms of reference of the existing "Consultative Body" for the **Anglican Communion**, which it now called "a Continuation Committee of the Lambeth Conference." The task of coordination of the **provinces** and advising on the formation of new provinces was moving beyond the powers of an **archbishop** of **Canterbury** and his staff to sustain. This led to the appointment of Stephen Bayne, **bishop** of Olympia in the **Protestant Episcopal Church in the United States of America**, as first executive officer of the Communion in 1959. He was followed in 1964 by Ralph Dean, bishop of Cariboo in the Anglican Church of **Canada**. The 1968 Lambeth Conference proposed the formation of the **Anglican Consultative Council** (ACC). Bishop Dean's appointment ended in April 1969, and John Howe, bishop of St. Andrews in **Scotland**, was appointed executive officer from May 1969 to prepare for the establishment of the ACC. When this formally came about later that year (though its first meeting as a Council did not come until 1971), his post was changed from executive officer of the Anglican Communion to **secretary-general** of the ACC.

EXORCISM. In the **Gospel** accounts, **Jesus** and his disciples "cast out" **demons** from those who were possessed or invaded by them. Interestingly, in the New Testament the term "exorcist" is found used only of Jewish practitioners (Acts 19.13–14). However, the term passed into regular Christian use, and exorcism (now meaning "casting out demons") was used in the early church with respect to not only persons visibly troubled but also, as a matter of routine, candidates for **baptism** whether they had shown signs of being possessed or not. This baptismal exorcism ran on through the Middle Ages, though used specifically for infants, and it was retained in the rite in the 1549 **Book of Common Prayer**, though it was then omitted in 1552. While it has not recurred since, there has nevertheless been a conscious drafting of prebaptismal prayers for protection from attacks of the Evil One—prayers usually called "apotropaic" (or "warding off"). A pastoral use of various degrees of exorcism has also recurred during the 20th century, and some **dioceses** have advisers on what is often called "deliverance **ministry**." There are also spiritual exercises and **liturgical** texts and **ceremonial** used in relation to places or buildings that seem to be affected by evil influences—whether through some element of their previous history or some more contemporary animistic phenomenon. The theological undergirding of such ministry is not yet resolved by consensus. *See also* DEVIL.

– F –

FALKLAND ISLANDS. *See* SOUTHERN CONE OF SOUTH AMERICA.

FASTING. Fasting in the Old Testament is an outward symbol of grief or mourning, just as **feasting** is a symbol of joy and celebration (cf. Job 1.4). These *motifs* recur in the New Testament, not least with the penetrating commentary **Jesus** offers on both practices (cf. Matt. 6.16–18; Mark 2.18–20). Fasting is found from early times in preparation for **baptism** (Didache 7; Justin *First Apology* 1.65), but is also to be on a twice-weekly regular basis in Didache 8. It then passed into regular use as a **Lenten** discipline and a feature of the rules of **monastic** communities. In medieval times each Friday was deemed a fast day, in commemoration of the death of Jesus, and was marked by the eating of fish in place of meat.

The **Reformers** kept Lent as in principle a time of self-denial, but they gave little encouragement to specific guidance about fasting. In the **homilies** of Queen **Elizabeth I**'s reign, there is insistence on fish-eating (the **traditional** substitute for meat on fast days), but on inspection it seems that the purpose was to keep the fishing industry in a healthy state, as it was the fishermen who were recruited for the navy when the Spanish fleet was threatening an attack. The **Puritans** of the 16th and 17th centuries wanted fasting to be proclaimed and observed not on a weekly or annual cycle but rather for special occasions of prayer, intercession, or repentance as national or local affairs determined. Some of this tradition lives on among **Evangelical** Anglicans. In the 1662 **Book of Common Prayer**, there is a list of "Days of Fasting, or Abstinence," consisting of the 40 days of Lent, the **ember** days, the three rogation days (the Monday to Wednesday following the Sunday after **Ascension** Day), and all Fridays in the year (except **Christmas**, if it falls on a Friday). There is no hint as to the kinds of fasting or abstinence that will make for appropriate observance of the days.

The 19th-century **Anglo-Catholics**, drawing upon **Roman Catholic** models, not only revived the use of Fridays for fasting (or at least for eating fish rather than meat) and taught a much more rigorous pattern for keeping Lent but also insisted on fasting from midnight at all times of the year prior to receiving **Communion** (both for **ministers** and **laypeople**). This of itself meant that people, if they were to receive Communion, would have to come early in the day, and thus in those circles this reinforced a division between an "early service" for receiving Communion and a later noncommunicating "high mass." The same Roman Catholic precedent meant that Anglo-Catholics denounced the **celebration** of Communion after midday, but Evangelicals did not view themselves as bound in the same way.

The **parish Communion** pattern of Sundays, which started between the world wars of the 20th century, initially observed the principle of communicants fasting by keeping the service relatively early in the morning, and often provided a parish breakfast after the rite. However, in the 1950s **Pope** Pius XII relaxed the "fasting from midnight" rule for Roman Catholics, and Anglo-Catholics duly followed suit. Evening celebrations of the **eucharist** followed, and the tradition of fasting before receiving Communion has virtually ceased in most parts of the **Anglican Communion**, except possibly as a personal and private feature of the spirituality of individuals.

FATHERS. The category of "Fathers" was well known and accepted among the leaders of the **Reformation** in **England**. There are three references to the ways of the "ancient fathers" or "old fathers" in the preface by **Archbishop Thomas Cranmer** to the 1549 **Book of Common Prayer**, reprinted in the 1662 Book as "Concerning the Service of the Church." All the controversies between Reformers and **Roman Catholics** were conducted with constant citation of the Fathers by both sides. However, in the last analysis, the Reformers drew their **doctrine** not from a consensus of the Fathers but from the text of scripture, and they viewed scripture as having the supreme **authority** (as is demonstrated in their treatment of the **Creeds** in Article VIII of the Thirty-Nine **Articles**).

To what purpose then did the Reformers draw upon the Fathers? There are two most obvious answers: first, to confute the Roman Catholic apologists and, second, to add confirmatory witness to their own teachings when a useful quotation could be adduced. The former of these two purposes is well illustrated in **John Jewel**'s famous "Sermon at Paul's Cross" in 1559 (repeated in 1560) in which he set out a long list of contemporary Roman beliefs and practices and challenged any opponent to show that such were current in the first six centuries of the Christian era. The latter purpose is illustrated in the controversial writings of almost all the Reformers and is further evidenced in, for example, the debate on the doctrine of the **eucharist** in the House of Lords in connection with the **Act of Uniformity** of 1549. The reformed Church of England had a high doctrine of **tradition** and great respect for the teachings of the Fathers, but it did not view them as having a consensus that was autonomous or *a priori* determinative for matters of faith. If, in the controversies of the **Elizabethan** and Stuart periods, the churchmen were more fond of quoting the Fathers than were the **Puritans**, this was only a difference with respect to secondary authorities and did not touch on the supremacy of scripture.

With the 19th-century **Anglo-Catholics**, there was a shift toward recognition (albeit a romantic one) of the patristic era as the golden age in which the Christian faith came to its fully revealed fruition. The early ***Tracts for the Times*** included reprints of particular works of the Fathers, and the earliest academic project of the **Tractarian** leaders was a Library of the Fathers, which had a symbolic as well as a substantial purpose. Furthermore, the mood set up by Anglo-Catholicism passed into the bloodstream of many Anglicans and has in many **provinces** led to an atmosphere (if not actual formularies) in which it has been assumed that the patristic era had a unique authority in the life of the church. It is to be noted that no such assumption is found in the **Lambeth Quadrilateral**.

In the Church of England **canon** A5 (promulgated in 1969) reads:

> The doctrine of the Church of England is grounded in the Holy Scriptures, and in such teachings of the ancient Fathers and Councils of the Church as are agreeable to the said Scriptures.
>
> In particular such doctrine is to be found in the Thirty-Nine Articles of Religion, *The Book of Common Prayer,* and the **Ordinal**.

This formulation gives a secondary authority to the catholic **creeds**, but makes all patristic teaching itself subject to scrutiny in the light of scripture.

FEASTS. From the time of the **Reformation**, the concept of "feast" days has been retained in the Anglican churches. The 1549 **Book of Common Prayer** referred, in its heading to "The Introits, **Collects**, Epistles, and **Gospels**," to "**Proper** Psalms, and Lessons for divers Feasts and Days." It thereby marked as "feasts" the Sundays, **Christmas** Day, **Ascension** Day, and **saints**' days for which provision was made. The concept was slightly more fully contained in the 1552 Book, and in 1662, after the **calendar**, there is introductory material headed "Tables and Rules for the Moveable and Immoveable Feasts," including a list called "A Table of all the Feasts that are to be observed." The list begins with "All Sundays in the Year" and then lists the saints' days and others for which **liturgical** propers are provided (with the exception of **fasting** days, such as Good Friday). No other indication of how a feast should be observed is included. It appears that "All Sundays" includes those in **Lent**, so that they are still feast days, and the "Forty days of Lent" that are listed as fasts clearly (on a straight count) exclude the Sundays.

There is no mention in the 16th- and 17th-century formularies of **patronal festivals** or festivals of **dedication**. These **celebrations** have arisen largely in the wake of **Anglo-Catholic** efforts to enrich the Christian year, and in many **provinces** special liturgical provision is made for them. Patronal festivals come on the feast day of the saint (or other Christian) in whose name the church building is dedicated (usually the death day); festivals of dedication come on the anniversary of the dedication or **consecration** (or first use) of the church building.

FEMINISM. God is portrayed in scripture and in virtually all longstanding Christian **tradition** as "Father" and all nouns and pronouns referring to the godhead are masculine, but since the 19th century there has been a slowly growing reaction against this practice. **Women** have been at the forefront of this move, and it has run through all Christian denominations, making inroads into the tradition in varying ways—not least in the quest initially for the opening of both lay offices and **ordained ministry** to women. This in turn has led to **rubrical** styles that have ceased to distinguish leaders of worship or liturgical **presidents** as being normally male.

Feminism in its more radical forms has gone on to challenge even the wording in which the **doctrine** of the **Trinity** is expressed ("Father, Son, and Holy Spirit"), as well as seeking to expunge masculine pronouns from references to God in **liturgy** and **hymnody**. An examination of the modern liturgies and hymns of the different Anglican provinces illustrates how far these efforts have succeeded. While such particular points of conflict have been highlighted, they are symptoms of a much larger underlying body of doctrine and of policy concern, and feminist theology has become a respectable theological discipline in many parts of the world.

It has been always open to traditionalist opponents of feminism to insist that feminism's origins lie in secular trends toward sexual and gender equality that not only do not honor the differentiation of nature and role between the sexes given in creation, and reinforced in the New Testament revelation, but actually obliterate it. To the charge of following secular trends, feminist theologians reply that the historical oppression of women, whether in Western Christendom or in pagan tribal practices in non-Christian parts of the world, has also had a secular (and even sinful) component to it, from which true Christianity should deliver it.

FERRAR, NICHOLAS (1592–1637). Nicholas Ferrar was the son of a **London** merchant, and a devout Anglican from his earliest days. Of the keenest intellect, he entered Cambridge University at the age of 13, but his health was poor, and after graduating he had spells abroad for his health. His fame derives from his founding of a Christian community at Little Gidding in Huntingdonshire in 1625. This was to be centered around his own family—chiefly his mother, brother, and sister and their respective marriage partners, and a growing number of children and grandchildren belonging to them. The community was to be shaped by a pattern of daily offices; in 1626 he was **ordained** as a **deacon** in order to lead this worship. The community lived under a unique rule of life, adapted to the varied states of life of its members, but came under growing suspicion from the **Puritans** in the 1630s. Ferrar himself lived by a stricter rule of life than the rest of the community, with great devotion to prayer, **fasting**, and the reading of the psalms, to which the larger part of the night was given. He died on 4 December 1637, and the community was brought to an end soon after by the English Civil War. He is commemorated on 4 December in many Anglican **calendars**, and Little Gidding has become a place of **pilgrimage**.

FESTIVAL. *See* FEASTS; PATRONAL FESTIVAL.

FILIOQUE. The compound Latin word *Filioque* occurs in the Latin version of the **Nicene Creed** and is translated "and [from] the Son" in the line that says that the **Holy Spirit** proceeds "from the Father and the Son." The word constitutes an **ecumenical** and **doctrinal** problem, for, irrespective of whether it is defensible as a feature of the eternal nature of the Holy **Trinity**, it is very clear that it was no part of the text of the original Nicene-Constantinople confession of faith. It was added in the West by stealth or accident in the years from the late sixth century onward, and it reached the Church of **England** through the Western text of the Creed at the **Reformation**. The statement that the Spirit proceeds "from the Father and the Son" is contained in Article V of the Thirty-Nine **Articles**, and the *Filioque* itself passed from the Church of England's **Books of Common Prayer** into those of almost every part of the **Anglican Communion**.

In the second half of the 20th century, dialogue with the **Eastern Orthodox** Churches has raised questions about whether the *Filioque* should not be dropped from the creed, and this was listed as an option in the **English Language Liturgical Consultation** texts in 1989. The omission, whether mandatory or optional, has been adopted in a few **provinces** in the course of their **liturgy** revisions. The last three **archbishops** of **Canterbury** to be enthroned (**Robert Runcie**, **George Carey**, and **Rowan Williams**) have each included the Nicene Creed without the *Filioque* in their enthronement services, which has been reckoned to be a gesture of friendship toward Orthodox guests and their Communions.

FISHER, GEOFFREY (1887–1972). Geoffrey Fisher was **ordained** as a **deacon** in 1912 and joined the staff of Marlborough College that year; he was ordained as a **presbyter** in 1913. In 1914, at the age of 27, he became headmaster of Repton College in succession to **William Temple**. Fisher was made **bishop** of Chester in 1932, bishop of **London** in 1939, and the 99th **archbishop** of **Canterbury** in 1945. In **England** he made a main task of his archiepiscopate the revision of **canon law**, but overseas he had the task in many places of appointing and **consecrating** nationals as bishops in lands where English bishops had been the normal Anglican leaders up to that point. In so doing he was pursuing an aim of creating separate independent Anglican **provinces** in all parts of the world that were ready for it. He weathered the formation of the Church of **South India** in 1947 and the **Anglo-Catholic** attacks on it both before and after its formation. His own "Cambridge Sermon" in November 1946, inviting the Free Churches in England to "take **episcopacy** into their own systems," stemmed in part from the South India experience. Archbishop Fisher presided over two **Lambeth Conferences**, those of 1948 and 1958. He made a private visit to **Pope** John XXIII in autumn 1960, the first archbishop of Canterbury to do so since before the **Reformation**. Fisher retired in 1961, and he then publicly attacked the Anglican-**Methodist** Scheme that was under discussion in

England from 1963 to 1972. He was the last archbishop of Canterbury to officiate at a **coronation**, when he crowned Queen Elizabeth II in June 1953.

FONT. A font is the receptacle used in church buildings to hold water for use in **baptisms**. At the time of the **Reformation**, in most cases fonts were made of stone and stood just inside the west (or side) door of the church building. In the 1549 **Book of Common Prayer**, the service started outside the door and led to the admission within it, to where the font stood and the baptism would take place. The font thus portrayed by its very location the entry into the people of **God**, which baptism itself signified dynamically. In 1549 the water in the font was "blessed" at least once a month, but, once blessed, was then left in place in the font until the next time it was changed. In 1552 the whole service was moved into the church, and the only "blessing" of the water was done, on a "**receptionist**" basis, within the rite. **Canon** 81 of the 1604 canons ordered that every church should have one (but only one) stone font "the same to be set in the ancient usual places." This latter provision was "excepted" against by the **Puritans** at the **Savoy Conference**, but without result.

In the development of the **Anglican Communion**, the first provision in most **rubrics** governing baptism (whether for infants or adults) has been that the officiant shall dip the candidate; pouring is only a second option. Where dipping is used for an adult, traditional fonts will not usually serve the purpose, and then baptisms are done in rivers, swimming pools, the sea, or specially provided tanks. Fonts themselves are not necessarily nowadays located at a west door; they may be portable, be in a separate side chapel, be related to an ambo or **Communion table**, or otherwise depart from the pre-Reformation provisions.

In the last decades of the 20th century, there was a growth in the use of fonts for the **sprinkling** of **confirmation** candidates, or others renewing their baptismal vows, as a reminder of their baptism. Alternatively such people may dip their hands in baptismal water and make the **sign of the cross** with it. *See also* BAPTISTERY.

FOOT WASHING. In John 13.1–17, **Jesus** washed his disciples' feet at the Last Supper and told the disciples that he had set them an example that they should do likewise. While this has been generally interpreted as a command to Christians to be ready to give even menial service to one another, it has also been understood at intervals as a command to engage in a literal (if somewhat ritualized) foot washing. It was not inherited as a necessary or desirable part of the observance of **Maundy Thursday** by the Reformers and did not figure in their limited **liturgical** provision for that day. The tradition of English monarchs washing the feet of the poor had been commuted for cash in the Middle Ages, so hardly touched the liturgical provision of the **Reformation**.

In the latter decades of the 20th century, a restoration of foot washing within Maundy Thursday rites has been slowly occurring in Anglicanism. There is distinct reference to it in various **Books of Common Prayer**, including that of the **Episcopal Church (United States of America)** in 1979; the ***Lent, Holy Week, Easter*** services of the Church of **England** of 1986; the **Southern Africa** Prayer Book of 1989; and others. In the Church of **North India** *Book of Worship* of 1995, foot washing is included in the "Covenant Service," which the united church received from **Methodism**. Other specific uses have also been found, such as the unofficial experiments made at **ordination rites** in both England and Peru with the **bishop**'s washing of the feet of the newly ordained **deacons**. In England this became an official option with the authorization of the **Common Worship** Ordinal in 2005. At the 1998 **Lambeth Conference**, the formal part of an extended quiet day was marked by the whole company of around 700 bishops each washing the feet of their neighbor.

FOXE, JOHN (1516–1587). John Foxe was a convinced **Protestant** whose views matured at the end of the reign of King **Henry VIII** and found full expression in the **Reformation** that was implemented during the reign of King **Edward VI**. He fled to the continent when Queen **Mary I** succeeded to the throne in 1553, and he there began writing his history of the persecution of true Christian believers, a first edition of which was published in Latin in 1554 in Strasbourg, France. Foxe returned to **England** when Queen **Elizabeth I** came to the throne and was **ordained** by Edmund Grindal, then **bishop** of **London**. He produced an expanded version of his book, in English, in 1563, under the title *Acts and Monuments of matters happening in* *the Church*. The title is usually shortened for formal purposes to *Acts and Monuments*, although in the requirement of the 1571 (draft) **canons** that all **archbishops**, bishops, **deans**, and **archdeacons** should possess both the **Bible** and Foxe's book (the only book named apart from the Bible), it is called *The Monuments of* ***Martyrs***. Since those days it has in fact been more frequently known informally as *Foxe's Book of Martyrs*. While the book treats all of Christian history, its main purpose is to glorify the memory and magnify the martyrdom of those Protestants who had been burned under Queen Mary. In this it succeeded well, and its readable, if sometimes somewhat loaded, description of the trials and deaths of men and women, many of whom he had himself known, imprinted itself deeply in the minds of English people and helped confirm the nation in Elizabeth's reign in its distrust of Rome.

FRACTION. The **breaking of the bread** in the **eucharist** is often known by its Latinate title as the "fraction." Its medieval position followed the **Lord's Prayer** after the **canon** of the **mass**. In the 1549 **Book of Common Prayer**, **Thomas Cranmer** removed the provision for a ritual fraction at that point in the rite, but instead required the **bread** of **Communion** to be "something more larger and thicker than it was, so that it may be aptly divided in divers pieces: and every one shall be divided in two pieces, at the least"—so the bread was all to be broken during the distribution of Communion, though without any particular display or highlighting of such breaking. In 1552 the bread was to be leavened "such as is usual to be eaten," and there was no mention of breaking it, though that was built into the choice of leavened bread and presumably occurred during the distribution. There was still no mention of breaking the bread in the 1604 canons or the **rubrics** of the 1637 **Scottish** Book.

At the **Savoy Conference** in 1661, one of the **Puritans**' requests was that the breaking of the bread "be made more explicit." They appear to have wanted the breaking of the bread (accompanied by a pouring of the wine) to be a visible sign of the crucifixion. In the revision of the rite, the **Convocation** added a rubric before the "prayer of **consecration**" (itself a new title from the Scottish 1637 rite), directing the officiant so to order the bread and wine "that he may with the more readiness and decency break the Bread before the people."

The 1662 rite then followed the logic of treating our Lord's words, as recited during the **narrative** of institution, as the equivalent of rubrics to be followed by the officiant in the rite; one of the three new "**indented rubrics**" added at the point where the officiant says, "He brake it," directs "and here [the officiant] shall break the bread." Clearly this was to illustrate publicly that the bread was indeed broken, though equally clearly ordinary bread could hardly be broken into large numbers of small pieces during the simple words "he brake it" and a functional further breaking necessarily continued before or during the distribution.

Despite encouragement from the corrupt *textus receptus* (the Greek text underlying the **King James Version** of the **Bible**), the narrative of institution in Anglican **liturgy** has never been written as "this is my body which is broken for you"—and thus the text of the liturgy has never required Anglicans to believe on poor evidence that the breaking of the bread is somehow a dramatized portrayal of Calvary; the simpler notion that it ushers in a true sharing (as **Jesus**' own breaking of bread did) provides a more transparent and biblical understanding. This in no way severs the theological connection between the atonement and the **Lord's Supper**, but it does remove any incentive to give the fraction a visual significance of doubtful origin.

The fraction remained within the narrative of institution in all the revisions of the 18th and 19th centuries. The introduction of atomized wafer-breads in the latter part of the 19th century meant that the fraction now had no hint of being related to the distribution of the loaf to the many people. In the next stage, the imitation of **Roman Catholic** practice separated it out from the narrative in some more daring early 20th-century rites, and it became in them its own separate action within the overall sacramental **celebration**. **Gregory Dix**'s book *The Shape of the Liturgy* (1945), with its emphasis upon the fourfold action (of which the fraction was the third), gave a new impetus to excising the fraction from within the second action (the thanksgiving, or **eucharistic prayer**) and relocating it as its own separate liturgical item, the third action. This has in turn in modern rites given rise to various uses of 1 Cor. 10.16–17 to supply a liturgical text to accompany the action. The slow return to either leavened bread or at least sheets of wafers has brought the separated fraction into prominence as the time for real breaking in preparation for sharing. The actual breaking then often continues during the **Agnus Dei** (or similar anthem).

FREE CHURCH OF ENGLAND (FCE). As the **Tractarian** movement grew in **England** in the 1840s, so a polarization arose between **Evangelicals** and the new **Anglo-Catholics**. An actual separation occurred when in 1844 the "high" (and arbitrary) **bishop** of Exeter, Henry Philpotts, withdrew the license of one James Shore, the Evangelical **minister** of a "chapel-of-ease" (i.e., an Anglican place of worship without a territorial **parish** attached to it) on the estate of the Duke of Somerset in Bridgetown. After six months, the duke reopened the chapel, now registered as a non-Anglican (i.e., **dissenting**) place of worship. Two other similar places of worship were also opened in the Exeter **diocese** soon after. Shore was, however, still regarded by the bishop as an Anglican **clergyman** acting illegally within an Anglican parish, and in 1849 he was prosecuted for this, had an injunction made against him, and was made liable for the costs of the action—which he refused to pay and therefore went to jail.

A large public meeting of protest in **London** led a quest for a nationwide "Free Church of England" that would provide a spiritual home for Evangelical Anglicans who viewed their established church as being subverted by Anglo-Catholicism. Much of the befriending and legal help came from the Countess of Huntingdon's Connexion, a small Evangelical denomination that had begun in a similar way nearly a century earlier, first by the Evangelical countess using Anglican ministers in her private chapels and then, as the "Connexion" took on its own life and outgrew the legal limits of her unique patronage, by her licensing them as dissenting chapels.

The Free Church of England was ultimately constituted in February 1863, and for five years it shared in a federal way (not least through an annual conference) with the Countess of Huntingdon's Connexion. The FCE was in theory an Episcopal church adhering to the **doctrine** and **liturgy** of the Church of England, though in fact it had no bishop. In doctrine, a focal point was the desire (provoked by the **Gorham** controversy) to omit from the **baptismal** services the words "Seeing, therefore . . . that this child is regenerate," and the FCE use of the **Book of Common Prayer** allowed this omission.

In 1868, the FCE severed its relationship with the Connexion, and Benjamin Price was appointed by the annual Convocation (the title of its **synod**, including clergy and **laity**) as its first bishop, though without **consecration** being available. When news reached the FCE of the formation in 1873 of the **Reformed Episcopal Church** (REC) in the **United States** under the leadership of Bishop **George Cummins**, steps were taken to enter into a "federative union" with that organization in 1874. This led to Bishop Cridge of the REC visiting England in 1876 and consecrating first Price and then two more bishops.

The situation in England became more complicated when, the following year in America, the REC bishops consecrated an Englishman, Huband Gregg, who was to be a bishop not of FCE but of a separate "Reformed Episcopal Church," organically part of the REC in the United States. This latter body subsequently had an internal division of its own when Gregg himself separated from the Americans, leading some congregations into the "**Reformed Church** of England" (RCE) while others continued as the REC. Gregg became mentally incapable around 1891, and the RCE and REC reunited in 1894, and thereafter continued as a single separate denomination, though apparently living by exactly the same principles as the FCE. Years of negotiation led to a full union in 1927, with the legal title becoming the "Free Church of England, otherwise called the Reformed Episcopal Church in the United Kingdom of Great Britain and Ireland."

Lambeth Conferences have at long intervals addressed the existence and rationale of the REC and the RCE. At the 1888 conference, a Statement by the American bishops present declared the consecrations by Cummins invalid, thus making all subsequent **ordinations** and consecrations equally void. In 1920, when the "Appeal to All Christian People" was at the forefront of the conference agenda, Resolution 31 dealt with an approach from the (English) RCE for reunion; with "regrets" as the key verb, it declined the approach and recommended conditional ordination where individual clergy asked to join Anglican churches.

The FCE itself did not figure in Lambeth Conference discussions or resolutions until 1998. By then, informal discussions with Anglicans in the late 1980s had led to a formal request in 1992 by the FCE Convocation for official talks with the Church of England about reunion. This led by two stages to a joint report outlining very modest possible next steps in convergence. It was presented to the **General Synod** and **Convocation** in 1997. However, a change of leading vocal characters in the FCE, including one new bishop, meant that an anti-Anglican stance developed between 1992 and 1997, and the Convocation rejected it. The 1998 Lambeth Conference comment (in the report of Section IV, p. 228) was that the separation was a cause of sadness, but the very occurrence of talks gives hope.

FULL COMMUNION. "Full Communion" is a technical term, regularly used among Anglicans, to describe a particular relationship between two Christian churches. It has been normally understood to entail a complete interchangeability in principle between the two churches in question of **ordained ministers** and of communicants in their respective roles. It is the ideal of the relationship of the churches and **provinces** of the **Anglican Communion**, though it has been subject to various limitations. Until 1874 (a period that includes the first **Lambeth Conference** in 1867) no one ordained outside of **England** and **Ireland** could minister within the Church of England itself. In the 20th century the controversy over the **ordination** of **women** meant that women ordained in one province would not necessarily have their ordination recognized and accepted in another—and those opposed to the ordination of women have reckoned themselves excluded by the very fact of women presiding at the **eucharist**. Further complications have ensued where issues of **homosexual** relationships have affected the necessary mutual recognition.

Full Communion with other churches has come slowly for Anglicans, largely through the insistence, set out in the **Lambeth Quadrilateral**, on ordination through the **historic episcopate** as a *sine qua non*. There have been agreements with the **Old Catholic** Churches, the **Mar Thoma Syrian Church**, and the Baltic and Nordic **Lutheran Churches** (under the **Porvoo** Declaration). The united churches of **South India**, **North India**, **Pakistan**, and **Bangladesh** have been brought first into full communion and then into membership of the Anglican Communion. There have also been exceptions since 1996 to the asserted need of Episcopal ordination in local agreements in **Southern Africa** with non-Episcopal churches, and in the **United States** and **Canada** with Evangelical Lutheran churches.

FUNDAMENTALISM. The rise of theological **liberalism** in the Western world in the 19th century led to a vigorous reaction in conservative circles. Around the turn of the 20th century, this led to a listing of central beliefs in which "the fundamentals" of the Christian faith were deemed to consist. A series of substantial tracts was published in America from 1909 under the title *The Fundamentals*, and this led to the adherents of the position being labeled "fundamentalists." The label has remained in use to the present day, even when its origins have been forgotten, and "fundamentalism" has passed into use as a pejorative term, usually fixed upon anyone who holds strongly to his or her theological foundations, even though few Anglicans would be happy to apply the term to themselves and its exact connotations are elusive. The term has in recent years also been applied to the strictest adherents of other religions.

FUNERAL. In virtually all faith communities, the **burial** of the **dead** has **traditionally** been conducted with religious observances. The Anglican **Reformers** inherited practices that they viewed as highly superstitious, and they set out, in the two stages of reform in King **Edward VI**'s reign, to deliver the rites from any suggestion of **purgatory** and from any belief that the actions or prayers of the living can bring deliverance from purgatory to the departed. The Puritans who compiled the **Westminster Directory** went further, and the Directory orders that no ceremony, forms of worship, or sermon should accompany the interment of a corpse. The provision in the 1662 **Book of Common Prayer** was therefore restoring the whole concept of holding funeral services at all, and the text, under the title "The Burial of the Dead," assumed that a service occurred in church and was followed by a burial in the churchyard.

In recent years funeral rites have been revised in many countries, but they usually continue to assume the Christian faith of the deceased and affirm the limited length of life on Earth, the necessity of parting, the reverent disposal of the body, the **resurrection** of **Jesus Christ**, and the consequent hope of eternal life. Prayers include thankful remembrance of the dead person (and in some places petitions on their behalf) and intercessions for the bereaved. Nevertheless, in many parts of the world, Christian rites are often used for those who have shown little or no sign of being Christian during their lifetimes, and this practice at times involves some adaptation of the rites. The coming of **cremation** has also affected the content of the rites, and the traditional title of "burial" has ever increasingly given way to the more general "funeral," as "burial" has become less apt in societies where thousands are cremated each year.

– G –

GARDINER, ALLEN (1794–1851). Allen Gardiner was an Anglican **layman** who, after service in the Royal Navy during which he had an **Evangelical** conversion, spent the rest of his life in frontier exploration around the world to open routes for Christian **missions**. In the mid-1830s he was in **South Africa** urging the **Church Missionary Society** to establish a Zulu mission. When this venture was aborted by warfare, he toured the world, starting in **Brazil** and visiting Argentina, Chile, **Australia**, the Dutch East Indies, Cape Town, and Rio de Janeiro. In 1841 he landed at Tierra del Fuego at the extreme southern tip of **South America** and sought to preach the **gospel** to the local inhabitants, who had not been drawn into the fabric of any South American nation or society. He received sufficient encouragement to found in **England** the "Patagonia Mission" and himself accompanied the first missionary to the territory—but it proved impossible to settle there and the missionary was withdrawn the following year. After a short spell in Bolivia, Gardiner again reconnoitered around Tierra del Fuego, and from this he concluded that a mission could be conducted using a ship as base. So in 1850 he returned with a small party, but with insufficient provisions, and the whole party died in early 1851. From the publicity arising from this tragedy, the Patagonia Mission flourished and in time became the **South American Missionary Society** (SAMS). Gardiner is commemorated in the Church of England **calendar** on 6 September.

GENERAL CONVENTION. The General Convention is the chief **synod** of the **Episcopal Church (United States of America)**. It was first convened in 1785 and thus was formed under what was then the **Protestant Episcopal Church in the United States of America**. It provided the unifying instrument for the scattered Episcopalians who were loyal to the **United States** after the Revolutionary War. The initial Convention adopted a constitution, including provision for a House of **Bishops**, although no bishops were then present (the only American bishop of the time, **Samuel Seabury** of Connecticut, stood aloof with his **diocese** from the formation of the Convention). The next General Convention was held in 1789. This time, Connecticut was represented, and further bishops had meanwhile been consecrated for New York (**Samuel Provoost**) and Pennsylvania (**William White**); in accordance with the constitution, Seabury chaired the House of Bishops. It was this 1789 General Convention that authorized the first American **Book of Common Prayer**.

The General Convention meets every three years, though a majority of bishops may call for a Special General Convention at an earlier point. The composition of its Houses is unique in the **Anglican Communion**: There is a House of Bishops, in which not only all serving but also all retired bishops are seated, and the only other house combines the **clergy** and **laity** in a single House of Deputies. This "lower" house has four elected clergy and four elected **laypersons** from each diocese (irrespective of its size). For some formal voting, the house votes by dioceses, each diocese's eight deputies taking an internal vote among themselves and then recording a single vote "for" or "against" the motion or legislation. The two houses regularly meet and handle legislation separately from each other, but they have to concur for legislation to be passed. The Convention elects half the members of the Executive Council under the chairmanship of the presiding bishop, and this council conducts the General Convention's business between the triennial meetings.

GENERAL SYNOD. In many **provinces** (and in some Churches with more than one province), the **synod** that represents the whole Church and has the highest **authority** is called the "General Synod."

GIBRALTAR. The extraprovincial **diocese** of Gibraltar was formed in 1842 to provide Episcopal oversight for Anglican chaplaincies in southern Europe, Malta, and elsewhere in the Mediterranean. It was originally intended that Malta should provide the see city, and the Anglican Church in Valetta was duly dubbed the "**cathedral**"; but objections from **Anglo-Catholics** that this would appear to rival the **Roman Catholic** see located there (and would thus be "uncatholic") led to the locating of the diocesan cathedral in Gibraltar, which was British in its population (and therefore appropriately Anglican) territory. After the diocese of North Africa ceased to function in 1943, some of the chaplaincies of that coast also came under the diocese of Gibraltar.

In 1980 a new diocese of "Gibraltar in **Europe**" was formed, uniting the "Fulham jurisdiction" of northern Europe ("Fulham" because the **bishop** of Fulham, a **suffragan** of the bishop of **London**, usually acted on behalf of the bishop of London) with the previous diocese of Gibraltar and constituting the resultant diocese as formally and synodically a part of the Church of **England**. It is counted as a diocese of the **province** of Canterbury, but it has its own constitution distinguishing it from the **established** Church of England, which is governed by the Westminster Parliament in 42 of its other 43 dioceses. It retains the cathedral in Gibraltar, with "pro-cathedrals" in Malta and Brussels.

GLORIOUS REVOLUTION. When King **James II** inherited the thrones of **England** and **Scotland** in 1685 as a **Roman Catholic**, it was clear that his reign would encounter difficulties. The beginning of the end came in spring 1688 when he ordered the **bishops** in England to have his Declaration of Indulgence read from the pulpits of the **parish** churches and they refused. The king then had seven bishops who were in **London** and leading this noncompliant resistance arrested on a charge of seditious libel and imprisoned in the Tower of London. But when they were tried before a jury, they were found not guilty—and became the toast of London.

The groundswell against James II was increased by the birth that same summer of a son, also named James, who necessarily overtook the claims to succession of his two older half-sisters, Princesses Mary and Anne. The two princesses had been brought up as **Protestants** and had married Protestant husbands, but the new heir to the throne would certainly be brought up as a Roman Catholic. This prompted some members of Parliament to start negotiations with William, the Protestant prince of Orange in the Netherlands and husband to James II's daughter, Mary. As a result, William landed in Ilfracombe on 5 November 1688 with clearly hostile intent (which is part of the reason the events were accounted a "revolution"), but James fled without attempting to resist.

Parliament then officially negotiated with William about the throne, with members very conscious of existing **oaths** of allegiance to James and aware that many might not be willing to break their oaths. They thus looked for James to remain lawfully king, even if in exile, and for William to be appointed regent in his place. William, however, was not content to be regent and insisted he must either be king or return to the Netherlands.

In February 1689 Parliament voted on a motion to declare the throne vacant through James's flight and to offer the throne to William and Mary jointly. This passed in the House of Lords by a slender majority of three—in the absence of the six or more of the bishops who believed it impossible to switch allegiance to another king while James was still alive. **William III** and **Mary II** thereby became joint monarchs.

The general verdict of history has been that, under the terms of the monarchy that then existed, Parliament acted beyond any powers it possessed, and thus the transfer of the monarchy, for all that it was done by the votes of the members of both Houses of Parliament, was an act of force rather than of law, a *coup d'état* rather than a legislative change. For this reason, too, it is described as a "revolution," albeit without force of arms. It is characterized as "glorious" because it was generally viewed as the deliverance of the nation—and particularly the Church of England—from an arbitrary captivity into a liberty illustrated by the Bill of Rights of 1689. Parliament amended the service of thanksgiving from **James I**'s reign, which had been incorporated into the 1662 **Book of Common Prayer** to be used each year on 5 November for deliverance in 1605 from the (papist) Gunpowder Plot, now adding thanks also for the landing of the Prince of Orange in this country on that same date in 1688.

A **Scottish** "convention of estates" followed suit in declaring the throne vacant and offering it to William and Mary jointly. In Scotland, however, the whole **episcopate** declined to swear a new oath of loyal allegiance, in effect leading the Episcopalians into a century of semi-underground Jacobite activity. The parish structures and national church polity reverted to **Presbyterianism**. *See also* KEN, THOMAS; NONJURORS; SANCROFT, WILLIAM.

GLOSSOLALIA. *See* TONGUES.

GOD. There is no peculiarly Anglican **doctrine** of God. Anglican **provinces** adhere to the **Creeds**, which embody the conciliar definitions of the **Trinity** and **Incarnation**. The revelation of God is supremely and authoritatively known through the written word of scripture. Prayers are directed to the Father through the Son in the **Holy Spirit**, **baptisms** are conducted into the same threefold name, and a starting point in respect of God's relations with this world is the understanding that he is almighty, all-knowing, all-powerful, and all-loving. Such affirmations open considerable problems in areas of sin, suffering, human will, and providence, but it is normal in Anglicanism to acknowledge these areas as problems, and to wrestle with them as problems, rather than to deny the starting affirmations about God upon which the Christian faith depends.

GODPARENTS. Godparents have no standing in the **Bible**, but are mentioned by postapostolic writers from the second century onward. In Tertullian, they appear to bear the whole moral weight of being answerable for the response of the growing child to **God** and his ways—and Tertullian urges on these grounds that infants should not be **baptized**. In Hippolytus, godparents appear simply as voices to articulate the baptismal confession on behalf of those too young to utter it themselves. Christian history thereafter has hovered between these two extremes.

In the Middle Ages in the West, the godparent relationship was decreed to be a substantial quasi-family connection, such as to bring the two persons concerned within the prohibited decrees of **marriage**. At the **Reformation**, the godparents, rather than the natural parents, were still expected to present the child for baptism. **Canon** 29 of 1604 required people appointed as godparents to have received **Communion**, a protection at that time against both children under the age of discretion and schismatics being allowed to take the role. In the 1662 **Book of Common Prayer** a minimum number of godparents was ordered: two godparents of the same sex as the child and one of the opposite sex. In the 19th century in **England**, the law was changed to allow parents themselves to be godparents to their children, and in the **Episcopal Church (United States of America)**

1979 Book of Common Prayer, the notes "Concerning the Service" say that "it is fitting that parents be included among the godparents." In some **provinces** the canons require godparents to be confirmed. Those presenting adults for baptism or confirmation are usually called "sponsors."

GORE, CHARLES (1853–1932). Charles Gore was of an **Anglo-Catholic** persuasion from his Harrow schooldays onward. A scholar of Balliol and a first-class graduate, he was **ordained** as a **deacon** in 1876 and **presbyter** in 1878. He served two short periods as assistant **curate** in Liverpool and visited **Calcutta** before, in 1884, becoming the first principal of Pusey House in Oxford. Gore edited *Lux Mundi* in 1889 and gave the Bampton Lectures in 1891, and in these two publications opened a "kenotic" **doctrine** of the **Incarnation**. He initiated the foundation of the Community of the Resurrection (CR) at Pusey House in 1892 and became its first superior. In 1894 Gore left for a country incumbency, and the following year became a **canon** residentiary at Westminster **Abbey**. In 1902 he became **bishop** of Worcester, and in 1905 when, at his own instigation, the **diocese** was divided, he became the first bishop of Birmingham. In 1912 Gore was translated to Oxford, and from there resigned and retired in 1919, a decision precipitated by the decision of the Representative Church Council that the franchise for election to the impending Parochial Church Councils should be based on a **baptismal** qualification and not a **confirmation** one. He then devoted his old age to further writings on scripture, the church, and the claims of the Church of **England**. He was also nominated by **Archbishop Randall Davidson** to participate in the **Malines Conversations**. Among Anglican **theologians**, Gore had a formative part in establishing an "incarnational theology," and his original work mentioned above has generally been viewed as foundational to that. Incarnational theology became, largely through Gore, a characteristic feature of 20th-century Anglo-Catholicism.

GORHAM, GEORGE CORNELIUS (1787–1857). George Gorham was a learned **Evangelical** vicar of St. Just in Penwith, Cornwall, who, on being nominated to the living of Brampford Speke near Exeter in 1847, was summoned by the **bishop** of Exeter, Henry

Philpotts, to account for his **doctrine** of **baptism**. The bishop interrogated Gorham for a total of eight days and in March 1848 declared him to hold doctrines contrary to the Christian faith and on that basis declined to institute him to the incumbency of the **parish**. Gorham held and taught that not all infants are necessarily born again by virtue of being baptized and argued his case with scholarly attention to detail, but it was on this doctrine that the bishop declared him unfit.

Gorham then appealed to the provincial Court of Arches seeking an injunction exculpating him from the charge of **heresy** and thus requiring the bishop to institute him. This process made the bishop the defendant. The court found in the bishop's favor in March 1849, but then Gorham appealed to the Judicial Committee of the Privy Council, the only court of appeal from ecclesiastical cases at the time. The summer of 1849 saw the publication of Dean Goode's *Effects of Infant Baptism*, a massive book which demonstrated that Gorham's doctrine was consistent with most leading Anglican divines from the **Reformation** onward and that Bishop Philpotts's doctrine had had widespread credence only from earlier in the 19th century. The Judicial Committee, including the **archbishops** of **Canterbury** and **York** and the bishop of **London**, in March 1850 upheld the appeal, cleared Gorham's doctrine of formal heresy, and required the bishop to institute him (which he still refused to do, and it was done by the archbishop of Canterbury's deputy instead). The bishop of London dissented from the judgment, which did not insist that Gorham alone was right and Philpotts wrong but rather declared that the Church of **England**'s formularies allowed room for both doctrinal opinions.

The Gorham Judgment led to the secession to the **Roman Catholic Church** of Henry Manning and Robert Wilberforce, but preserved evangelicalism within the Church of England. J. B. Mosley, one of the original **Tractarians**, wrote a discerning account of the whole affair, *The Baptismal Controversy* (1862), in which he concluded that a belief in the invariable regeneration of infants in baptism was not *de fide* and was not imposed by the Church of England's formularies.

GOSPEL. The Greek word *euangelion*, which is translated "gospel," means "good news." One use of the word refers to the actual spoken word of good news in **Jesus Christ**. A second is as the title of the first four books of the New Testament, the "Gospels" (Mark 1.1). In a related usage, it denotes the climax of the three **liturgical** readings from scripture at the **eucharist**, a passage from one of the four Gospels, which is almost invariably marked in Anglican celebrations by the people standing for the reading and sometimes by other **ceremonies**. In some, but not all, **provinces**, in imitation of the **Roman Catholic Church**, there is a requirement that the "Gospeller" should be in holy **orders**, and the reading of the Gospel is viewed as central to the **deacon's** role. In the three-year Sunday **lectionary** that has passed into widespread use in Anglican provinces, each year is known by the Gospel book from which the vast majority of its liturgical Gospel passages are taken—the years of Matthew, of Mark, and of Luke (John's Gospel being represented in a more occasional way, spread across all three years).

GOTHIC. The Gothic style of **architecture** prevailed in church building in the Middle Ages in **Europe**. Its characteristic features were the pointed arch and soaring roof, in a building with a **chancel** narrower than the **nave** and usually raised above it by one or more steps, often separated from it by a screen. The Reformers varied in their approach to such inherited buildings, which by their very nature and shape militated against reformed worship; in some countries, chancels were pulled down and single-room chambers resulted. In **England**, however, chancels were retained, and the worship was adapted to them.

Church building in England and America in the 18th century was conducted on a very different model, reflecting the needs of a **reformed church**—with a strong tendency toward a single chamber, often with square galleries around three sides of the building and a **Communion table** tucked behind the triple-deck pulpit that dominated the fourth side. This "classical" style was itself superseded by "Gothic Revival," stemming in large part from the Cambridge-based Camden Society and its journal, *The Ecclesiologist*. These, by the late 1830s, had close links with the **Tractarians**. From then on, for over a century, virtually all Anglican church building was deeply affected by the basic concepts of the Gothic Revival, a trend as visible in Africa as in England. The **Anglo-Catholic** imitation of **cathedral** worship in **parish** churches meant that chancels asserted their own necessity, now being not only symbolic but also, because of their symbolism, the location of choirs.

The **Liturgical Movement** started to replace the taste for Gothic with the building of one-room worship chambers in the second half of the 20th century. Alongside this developed a worldwide "reordering" of the interiors of existing Gothic buildings, usually to turn the nave back into a one-room **eucharistic** chamber, accompanied by an adoption of "**westward position**" for the **president** of the eucharist.

– H –

HAMPTON COURT CONFERENCE. In 1603 the English **Puritans** presented their "Millenary Petition," containing objections to the Elizabethan **Book of Common Prayer**, to King James VI of **Scotland** as he was on his way to **London** to take the throne as King **James I** of England. He promised that he would convene a conference and did so the following year at Hampton Court (previously the London home of Cardinal Wolsey). **Archbishop John Whitgift**, now very elderly, took a small part in the conference, but the main Episcopal spokesman was Richard Bancroft, then **bishop** of London.

The Puritans, led by John Rainolds, **dean** of Lincoln, presented their complaints, particularly against the requiring of the "excepted ceremonies": the surplice, the **sign of the cross** in **baptism**, the ring in **marriage**, and kneeling for **Communion**. They had perhaps hoped that the king, raised in **Presbyterian** Scotland, would be sympathetic, but it soon was clear that he was looking forward to being monarch over an Episcopal church and had little sympathy with either the Puritans or Presbyterians. Indeed, he mocked the Puritans slightly for making such a to-do about such small items.

In the end, the surplice was enforced in the 1604 **canons**, and the others remained mandatory in the **rubrics**; the only concession was an explanation in canon 30 of the sign of the cross. The Prayer Book was marginally altered at the king's command by royal warrant (i.e., without going to Parliament), the most notable change in its text being the addition to the **catechism** of the section on the **sacraments**, usually attributed in its drafting to John Overall, then dean of St. Paul's. However, the major outcome of the conference was not any alteration of the Prayer Book, but the king's ordering of a new translation of the **Bible**. The New Testament was ready in 1608, and the whole Bible in 1611, and, although it has been regularly called the "Authorized Version" it is now known throughout the world as the "**King James Version**." *See also* SAVOY CONFERENCE.

HANNINGTON, JAMES (1847–1885). James Hannington was **ordained** in 1876, and in 1882 had one short-lived period of **missionary** service in **Central Africa** with the **Church Missionary Society** (CMS) before returning sick to **England**. After his recovery, he was **consecrated** in 1884 to be first **bishop** of **Eastern Equatorial Africa**. In 1885 he led an expedition into what is now **Uganda**, following up earlier **evangelistic** work by CMS missionaries. In October, Bishop Hannington fell into the hands of Chief Mwanga, and he and his whole group were put to death on 29 October 1885. He is commemorated on this date in various **provinces**, and there are churches in **England dedicated** to his memory, as well as a Hannington Chapel in Namirembe Cathedral in Uganda. *See also* MACKAY, ALEXANDER MURDOCH; MOMBASA.

HEALING. Clearly, a practice of healing the sick—and even of raising the dead—was a feature of **Jesus**' public **ministry** on Earth, and to a less prominent degree was also practiced by the apostles in the first Christian generation. **Anointing** for healing is mentioned in Mark 6.13 and is enjoined in James 5.13–16. While accounts of miraculous healings are found at intervals in church history (not least, in the medieval church, in connection with relics of **saints** and **pilgrimages** to shrines), the practice of anointing was reduced to an administration solely to those *in extremis*. This rite was found among the seven **sacraments** of the medieval church as "extreme unction," an anointing of the dying person, accompanying confession and the *viaticum* (or final administration of **Communion**) as a complex of rites in preparation for **death**. The 1549 **Book of Common Prayer** translated this extreme unction into an anointing with prayer for healing and located it in the Visitation of the Sick; the anointing was, however, omitted in 1552, and the dominant expectation of the rite was that the patient was going to die and had to be prepared for death.

Physical healing through ordinary medical treatment and care has sprung up in the West from Christian conviction, and overseas **missions** from Britain and the **United States** have regularly included a strong emphasis on medical missionary work, a caring for people's physical condition that has marched with a proclamation of the **gospel**. To this day, many parts of the **Anglican Communion** have **diocesan** hospitals and clinics. Prayer for healing has remained part of that witness to **God**'s love. Furthermore, an awareness of the possibility of anointing in accordance with the James 5.13–16 passage remained in Anglican consciousness, but with very little official backing until the 20th century.

Within the 20th century, from many different beginnings and in many different parts of the world, there arose among Anglicans a new concern for a ministry of holistic healing that includes the healing of bodily ailments. This led to the inclusion of provision for anointing of the sick within the **Protestant Episcopal Church in the United States of America**'s 1928 Book of Common Prayer, and a growth in other **provinces** of official forms for anointing thereafter. A ministry of laying on of hands with prayer, frequently by **laypeople**, whether within a **liturgical** context or in a much more informal one, has also developed throughout the world. The **Charismatic Movement** has laid enormous emphasis upon physical healing and has looked for miracles of healing to be granted by God much more consistently than previous generations had dreamed possible. By the end of the 20th century a range of practices had been established in many provinces, and official liturgy in various places gave witness to it.

HEAVEN. Heaven, in the New Testament, is always conveyed by the Greek word *ouranos*, a word as wide in its meaning as "heaven" is in English, ranging from mere "sky" (as seen above us with physical eyes) to wholly **eschatological** glory. It is the dwelling place of **God** (though "place" itself is a metaphor when applied to God's presence), as stated in "Our Father in heaven." In Matthew's **Gospel**, the kingdom of God is called the "kingdom of heaven." In this sense, it contrasts with "Earth" (e.g., in 1 Cor. 15.47–49 or in the balancing of "heaven" and "Earth" in the **Lord's Prayer**). An interesting double sense of "heaven" is found at **Jesus**' **ascension** (Acts 1.11, where *ouranos* comes three times in the Greek).

Anglicanism has no distinct or emphasized **doctrine** of heaven, save to underline **justification** through faith and, in its classic formularies, to exclude any doctrine of **purgatory** or any expectation that petitions or oblations (let alone individual or corporate merits) of those on Earth would serve to provide benefits for those who have died.

HELL. The English word "hell" is used to translate both *Hades* (the place of the departed; cf. Acts 2.27) and *Gehenna* (the place of final condemnation; cf. Matt. 10.28). This confusion is eased by the modern translations of the **Apostles' Creed**, whereby the line "he descended into hell" (which in the medieval Latin was *descendit ad inferos*) is now rendered in the **English Language Liturgical Consultation** (ELLC) **ecumenical** text as "he descended to the dead." The other sense of "hell" thus holds the field, as a place of ultimate destiny separated from **God**—but it also is subject to a wide range of interpretations. At one extreme, **biblical** terminology about flames and eternal torment are presented as literally awaiting all unbelievers; at the other, a kind of godless eternity that is not necessarily unpleasant provides a kinder-sounding picture. A different school of thought would look for a merciful extinction as the implication of the biblical pictures. In any view, whatever hell there may be is final—the fourth of the "four last things." None of the interpretations, conservative or radical, carries necessary implications as to who or how many the likely occupants would be. **Liberal** theology has generally asserted concepts of hell to be incompatible with the love of God, and in **England** the **heresy** trials of two contributors to *Essays and Reviews* (1861–1862) led to a condemnation of H. B. Wilson for his essay dispensing with hell, but this was reversed on appeal to the Judicial Committee of the Privy Council. The essay was nevertheless condemned in the **Canterbury Convocation** in 1864. More recently, C. S. Lewis in various writings has given an element of popular credibility to a concept of hell, not least in the reassertion that **Jesus Christ**'s redemption is a substantial deliverance. His hell however, unlike any teaching in the Bible, allowed the occupants a second chance.

HENRY VIII, KING (1491–1547). King Henry VIII's older brother Arthur died before their father, King Henry VII, so Henry as the younger son inherited the throne at the age of 18 and had to consolidate the unity of the kingdom that his father had established by conquest. Henry quickly married Catherine of Aragon, his deceased brother's widow, after gaining a dispensation from the **pope** to do so, as such a **marriage** was understood to be forbidden in the **Bible**. Henry also fancied himself as a theologian from his youngest days and came to religious prominence when (at the age of 29) he wrote a book, *De Septem Sacramentis*, attacking Martin Luther's teachings. For this, the pope accorded him the honorific title of *Fidei Defensor*, "**Defender of the Faith**."

No male offspring of his marriage to Catherine lived beyond a short time, and by the mid-1520s Mary Tudor (later Queen **Mary I**) was his only living child. Henry supposedly thought that he was being punished by God for marrying Catherine, and he therefore sought to have his marriage to her set aside as incestuous. However, when Henry approached him in 1527, Pope Clement VII was unable to rule the marriage invalid (as popes in other generations might well have done), as he was himself captive to Catherine's nephew, Charles V of Spain. After much vacillation, it became clear in 1529 that no decree of **nullity** would be granted by the pope. Henry, prompted by a Cambridge don, **Thomas Cranmer**, sought the opinion of the universities of Europe as to whether the pope could dispense from what was thought to be God's law. Having gathered sufficient weight of scholarly opinion behind him, he viewed himself as unmarried, and thereupon took Anne Boleyn as his wife in late 1532, publicizing it in spring 1553. In the same period, when the see of **Canterbury** fell vacant, the king nominated Cranmer to be the next **archbishop** of Canterbury.

Anne Boleyn was crowned queen, and in September 1533 she gave birth to a daughter, Elizabeth (later Queen **Elizabeth I**). Henry then set in train a series of legislation that completely removed the nation of **England**, and particularly the **clergy**, from any obedience to the pope; he vested in the monarchy the powers in the realm previously held by the pope, including that of nominating **diocesan bishops**—a power still exercised by the Crown under Henry's legislation to the present day. By the end of 1534 these steps were complete, making Henry "the only Supreme Head in Earth of the Church of England," and leading to the pope's **excommunication** of him. In the process,

Henry put to death the **layman** Thomas More and the bishop of Rochester, John Fisher, for refusing to subscribe to the new legislation. Parliament bestowed on Henry the title *Fidei Defensor* when the pope withdrew it.

From the end of 1534 until his death in January 1547, Henry VIII personally prescribed the religion of which he was the "defender." In the words of one commentator, "He made it up as he went along." The prescription, though basically unreformed, varied somewhat from one year to another. In broad terms, Henry remained deeply opposed to the Continental **Reformation**. He retained all the Latin unreformed **liturgical** rites of papal times, but he dissolved the **monasteries**, annexed the chantry trust funds, allowed the publication of the very slightly reformed Ten **Articles** of 1536, ordered the Bible to be available in English in 1537, defended Cranmer in his archbishopric, and allowed his own son (Edward, later King **Edward VI**, born of his third wife, Jane Seymour) to be brought up as a **Protestant**. Yet in the Act of Six Articles in 1539, he reinforced transubstantiation and clerical **celibacy**, while at other times he appeared somewhat more tolerant; he both allowed the publication of the slightly reforming *Bishops' Book* in 1537 and also republished it with his own, admittedly slightly more reactionary, corrections as *The King's Book* in 1543. In 1544 he approved the publication of an English-language **litany** and ordered its use. Henry died with the separation from Rome complete and leaving his son, then nine years of age, in the care of a council led by convinced Protestants, which led with great speed to the reform of the Church of England.

HERESY. The Greek word *hairesis*, found in the New Testament in various places (cf. Acts 5.17, 26.5; 1 Cor. 11.19), means by etymology "choice," and in general use "party" or "sect." However, as Christian truth became more and more exactly defined in the early centuries, so the concept of false belief also took defined shape and was labeled "heresy." The word seems to be first used in that sense in the letter of Ignatius of Antioch to the Trallians in the early second century, and the concern to avoid and eliminate heresy was a major preoccupation of the church of succeeding centuries, a factor that led directly to the great Ecumenical **Councils** of the fourth and fifth centuries.

In **England**, Parliament in 1401 passed *De Haeretico Comburendo* ("Concerning the Need to burn Heretics"), an Act aimed specifically at the Lollards. This showed the fanatical concern of the authorities to preserve Christian truth, as they saw it, in a dogmatic and unassailable form. It was repealed within the batch of legislation by which King **Henry VIII** separated from Rome, but it was restored by Queen **Mary I** on her accession in 1553 and was employed by her in the burning to death of hundreds of Protestants, including **Archbishop Thomas Cranmer** and four other **bishops**. The Act was finally repealed at the beginning of Queen **Elizabeth I**'s reign.

While the **doctrinal** position of Anglicanism has usually been reasonably clearly defined, the means of arraigning a teacher of the faith on charges of heresy has always proved elusive. Certainly, in South Africa, Robert Gray convicted **William Colenso** of heresy in his absence, but he was unable to sustain the judgment in law. Attempts in England to convict George Denison of false teaching on the **eucharist** (1853–1857), **Charles Gorham** of heresy in relation to **baptismal** regeneration (1849–1850), or H. B. Wilson, a contributor to *Essays and Reviews*, of heresy in relation to eternal punishment (1862–1863) were all, for differing reasons, unsuccessful.

Throughout the **Anglican Communion**, there has generally been a wide toleration of **Roman Catholic**, **liberal**, and **modernist** opinions, even where the authorities of a particular **diocese** or **province** have deeply regretted the expression of those opinions. Generally any doctrinal discipline has been exercised in nonforensic ways, though this has left **clergy** who have simply held a license but have enjoyed no other security in their appointment in a much more vulnerable position than those with security. On the whole, the variety of belief permitted or even encouraged within the Communion has often made even the idea of doctrinal discipline difficult to embrace.

HERMENEUTICS. Hermeneutics is the science of interpreting scripture. In the early church and the Middle Ages, as a body of belief developed that was accepted as "**tradition**," so the scripture was usually raided in arrears to provide support for faith, often with an explanation of a mystical or analogical character. The Reformers took the radical approach that scripture was clear in its meaning and authoritative in its revelation, though in fact their understanding of it and of its application in their lives and in the life of society was enormously affected by their own outlooks, by their political situation, and by their memories of papal times and their fears of impending papal aggression. The principle of the perspicuity of scripture was enshrined in the question in the **Ordinals** of 1550 and 1552 to those being **ordained** as **presbyters**:

> Are you persuaded that the holy scriptures contain sufficiently all **doctrine** required of necessity for eternal salvation through faith in **Jesus Christ**? And are you determined out of the said scriptures to instruct the people committed to your charge, and to teach nothing (as required of necessity to eternal salvation) but that which you shall be persuaded may be concluded and proved by the Scripture?

A question of this sort presupposes that the scripture is a single unity with a consistent and coherent message; it also presupposes sufficient transparency in that meaning for the **clergy** at least to understand and communicate the meaning of scripture aright.

The field of scholarship has in the 20th century expressed various cautionary principles that might modify this *prima facie* transparency. At root, each such principle stems from a reckoning that the human authorship of the books receives insufficient weighting in any simple statement that this is God's book in its truth, **authority**, unity, and perspicuity. The scholars divide roughly into two groups: those who emphasize the human authorship over the divine (and thus may call in question the unity and authority of the books), and those who recognize the human authorship without diminishing the divine (and thus call for deeper entry into the circumstances and disposition of each author for a clearer understanding of the nature of each book). Both sets would also emphasize that which was little recognized in the 16th and 17th centuries: that the present contemporary circumstances and disposition of the reader or hearer of the scriptures affects the understanding of them. In varying degrees, scholars would also build in a sensitivity to **tradition**, that is, as to how the passage, book, or doctrine has been understood and received in the past by the church at large or by a particular denomination. Anglicans generally have been content to assert the supreme authority of scripture—as in the first "side" of the **Lambeth Quadrilateral** where the Old and New Testaments are "the rule and ultimate standard of faith" (1888 text)—and then to leave issues of hermeneutics to the scholars without trying to inject particular principles of hermeneutics further into the formularies of the faith.

HIERARCHY. In its etymology, "hierarchy" means "government by the **priests**." In view of the ambiguity attaching to the word "priest" (or other derivatives from the "hier-" stem) its strict meaning is unhelpful. However, it has come to refer to the **orders** of **ministers** with the greatest part in church government—very usually, therefore, but not exclusively or necessarily, the **episcopate**. Even in this meaning, it does at times retain overtones of an overdictatorial "top-down" style of church government.

HISTORIC EPISCOPATE. The phrase "historic episcopate" came into public Anglican terminology through its inclusion in the **Lambeth Quadrilateral**, adopted at the 1888 **Lambeth Conference**. It makes a claim that the **episcopate**, as the **Anglican Communion** has received it and continues it, is "historic" in the sense that the **consecration** of Anglican **bishops** lies within a continuity of the consecration of bishops that can be traced back historically to the earliest evidence available to us from the first centuries of the Christian church. The claim to historical succession is nevertheless arguably less strong than the high claims for "**apostolic succession**," as the claim goes no further than simply saying, "It has been thus," while apostolic succession would seem to be claiming, "It has been thus, and had to be thus in the economy of God to be the channel of God's grace." The term has been particularly used by Anglicans in **ecumenical** dialogue (in line with the original purpose of the Lambeth Quadrilateral) and has figured strongly in conversations with non-Episcopal churches. The term is also found in the **World Council of Churches** (WCC) **Lima** document *Baptism, Eucharist, and Ministry*.

HOBART, JOHN HENRY (1775–1830). John Henry Hobart represents the second stage of the independent development of the **Protestant Episcopal Church in the United States of America** (PECUSA) subsequent to the end of British colonial rule. **Ordained** in 1798, he was secretary to the House of **Bishops** at the 1799 **General Convention** and to the House of Deputies at the 1804 and 1808 conventions. While a rector in New York, he was **consecrated** as assistant bishop of New York in 1811 (at the age of 35) and went on in 1816 to become both rector of **Trinity Church, Wall Street**, in New York and **diocesan** bishop. His (pre-**Tractarian**) high-church views, his part in the foundation in 1817 of the General Theological Seminary, and his relationship to it thereafter helped establish that high-church position within the life of PECUSA. Hobart became known also for his **architectural** ideals, which, in the context of the Hanoverian auditory churches, centered on placing the pulpit against the east wall and putting the **table** and **font** in front of it, all three items being enclosed by rails. This arrangement was, paradoxically, known as a "Hobart Chancel"! He died still in office in 1830 and is commemorated in the 1979 **Book of Common Prayer** on 12 September.

HOLY COMMUNION. *See* COMMUNION, HOLY; EUCHARIST.

HOLY SPIRIT. Anglicans throughout the world are fully **Trinitarian**, as affirmed not only in scripture and the **creeds** but also in their **baptismal** formula, their **liturgical** benedictions, their basic euchological principles, and their **hymnody**. Thus Anglicans confess that the Holy Spirit is **God**, one of the three "persons" of the one God. **Pentecost**, the feast of the coming of the Spirit 50 days after **Easter**, is celebrated on a par with **Christmas** and Easter. There has been an issue in relation to the propriety of including the "***Filioque***" clause in the **Nicene Creed**, but there has been little questioning of its theology. Anglicans generally have approached questions about the Holy Spirit coolly and rationally rather than experientially, but that approach has been deeply challenged worldwide by neo-**Pentecostalism** in the **Charismatic Movement**. The role of the Spirit in the action of the **eucharist** has been an issue in liturgical revision, and this affects both the form of an **epiclesis** and the exact location of it within a **eucharistic prayer**.

HOLY WEEK. The New Testament provides a pattern whereby a large part of each **Gospel** is devoted to **Jesus**' actions and movements from the time of his triumphal entry into **Jerusalem** to his death at Passover time. This pattern initially had little **calendrical** impact, and for two centuries or more, the only issue among Christians was to identify the anniversary of Jesus' death and **resurrection** and to keep that festival as the focus of the church year. However, when the Spanish nun Egeria visited Jerusalem in the late fourth century, she found and recorded an existing scheme of devotions, whereby in the days prior to the major anniversary of **Easter**, Christians went on a kind of **pilgrimage** around the sites associated with the particular Gospel stories, keeping what were later known as "stations" at them. From this, there developed a sense of a "week" that begins with Palm Sunday (and the triumphal entry), is marked by the reading of the passion narratives, and moves toward a kind of interim climax with a **Maundy Thursday** evening **liturgy** commemorating the institution of the **Lord's Supper** (and often today including **foot washing**). The rite is often followed by a "watch," during which the people keep a time of (often extensive) meditation in quiet semidarkness; in many places, a **consecrated** wafer remaining from the **celebration** of **Communion** is escorted to an "**altar** of repose" to remain overnight (with or without those who keep the watch) and is used on Good Friday for a distribution of Communion without a new full celebration. Following this come the distinctive celebrations of Good Friday, Holy Saturday, and Easter Sunday (with or without a vigil). The keeping of the Holy Week was reduced in its **ceremonial** and **proper** provision by the Reformers, but by various stages it has been built up again to provide an eight-day centerpiece to the church's year.

HOMILY. While in ordinary usage and **rubrical** direction, "homily" is a term interchangeable with "sermon" (and "homilist" with "preacher"), there is also a distinct history of "homilies" within the Church of **England**. In 1542 in the **Convocation** of **Canterbury**, **Archbishop Thomas Cranmer** proposed that a book of homilies be compiled and published with **authority**, although it does not seem that this actually reached a vote. Then in July 1547, soon after King **Edward VI**'s accession, a *Book of Homilies* was published, from which a homily is enjoined to be read each Sunday in the royal *Injunctions* issued on the last day of that month (and making reference to further future homilies). The Book contained 12 homilies, of which five are credited to Cranmer, and generally represented the reformed position. One of these, on "salvation," received special commendation (as the "Homily of **Justification**") in an amendment added in Queen **Elizabeth I**'s reign to Article XI of the Thirty-Nine **Articles**. The Book as a whole was commended in Article XXXIV of the Forty-Two Articles of 1553, and the **rubric** about the sermon in the 1549 **Book of Common Prayer** said, ". . . shall follow the Sermon or Homily, or some portion of one of the Homilies, as they shall be hereafter divided." In 1552 the rubric read, ". . . if there be no sermon, shall follow one of the homilies already set forth, or hereafter to be set forth by common authority."

In 1562 a second *Book of Homilies* was duly issued, and Article XXXV of the Thirty-Nine Articles in 1571 commended the first *Book of Homilies* and listed the contents of the second. They received further commendation in **canon** 46 of the 1604 canons, which prescribed their use by any beneficed **clergy** who were not allowed to preach—an interesting category of **ministers**. Finally, they reappeared in a form close to that of 1552 in the rubric about the sermon in the **Communion** service in the 1637 **Scottish** Prayer Book and the 1662 English one. After that, they disappeared from all revisions of **eucharistic** rites.

In the revision of the Thirty-Nine Articles in the **Protestant Episcopal Church in the United States of America** in 1801, the reference in Article XI to the "Homily of Justification" survived, while Article XXXV (entitled "Of the Homilies") was printed with a bracketed footnote:

> [This Article is received in this Church, so far as it declares the Books of Homilies to be an explication of Christian doctrine, and instructive in piety and morals. But all references to the constitution and laws of England are considered as inapplicable to the circumstances of this Church; which also suspends the order for the reading of said Homilies in churches, until a revision of them may be conveniently made, for the clearing of them, as well from obsolete words and phrases, as from the local references.]

This can still be found in the 1979 Book of Common Prayer of the **Episcopal Church (United States of America)** on page 875.

HOMOSEXUALITY. The word "homosexuality" generally refers to a condition or orientation by which people of either gender are sexually attracted to people of the same gender (from *homoios*—Greek for "same"). The issue of such attraction is morally neutral, but the Old and New Testaments are strongly opposed to homosexual practices, and that opposition has been the stance of all Christian churches until the second half of the 20th century. It has often in the past also been reflected in the criminal laws of countries with a Christian or Islamic basis. However, in the **United States** and in other Western nations, homosexual pairing and sexual union slowly became socially respectable in the years after World War II, and the impact on the Christian churches became profound.

In the United States, the **Episcopal Church (United States of America)** (ECUSA) has by various stages approved such unions, has **ordained** men and **women** engaged in such practices, and has allowed, at least on a local basis, **liturgical** rites for the blessing of such unions. Attempts were made by American **bishops** in particular to get the 1988 **Lambeth Conference** to recognize and approve such unions. These attempts were unsuccessful, but they alerted bishops from around the world as to the direction in which some of the Western **provinces** were heading. During the 1990s the preparations for the next Lambeth Conference indicated that there would be a powerful reaction from more conservative quarters.

At the 1998 Lambeth Conference, there was a major section report entitled "Called to Full Humanity," which included a relatively brief treatment of "human sexuality." In it, the members of the section acknowledged that they were of different minds, but they were overtaken by a powerful groundswell in the conference that wished to oppose homosexual unions. The plenary meeting of the conference carried by 526 votes to 70 (with 45 recorded abstentions) Resolution I.10:

> This Conference:
>
> (a) commends to the Church the subsection report on human sexuality;
> (b) in view of the teaching of Scripture, upholds faithfulness in **marriage** between a man and a woman in lifelong union, and believes that abstinence is right for those not called to marriage;
> (c) recognises that there are among us persons who experience themselves as having a homosexual orientation. Many of these are members of the Church and are seeking pastoral care, moral direction of the Church, and God's transforming power for the

living of their lives and the ordering of relationships. We commit ourselves to listen to the experience of homosexual persons and we wish to assure them that they are loved by God and that all baptised, believing and faithful persons, regardless of sexual orientation, are full members of the Body of Christ;

(d) while rejecting homosexual practice as incompatible with Scripture, calls on all our people to minister pastorally and sensitively to all irrespective of sexual orientation and to condemn irrational fear of homosexuals, violence within marriage and any trivialisation and commercialisation of sex;

(e) cannot advise the legitimising or blessing of same sex unions nor ordaining those involved in same gender unions;

(f) requests the **Primates** and the ACC [**Anglican Consultative Council**] to establish a means of monitoring the work done on the subject of human sexuality in the Communion and to share the statements and resources among us;

(g) notes the significance of the Kuala Lumpur Statement on Human Sexuality and the concerns expressed in resolutions IV.26, V.1, V.10, V.23 and V.35 on the authority of Scripture in matters of marriage and sexuality and asks the Primates and the ACC to include them in their monitoring.

The voting on this resolution suggests that even the ECUSA bishops, of whom there were around 130 present, may have had a majority voting in favor of the motion. But the overwhelming number of those in favor came from Africa, Asia, and South America. The passing of a Lambeth Conference resolution is purely advisory—it has no legislative force and is not binding upon **provinces**. In conformity with paragraph (f), the **archbishop** of **Canterbury**, **George Carey**, asked a cross-section of 12 bishops from different parts of the **Anglican Communion** to participate in a series of "conversations" about issues in human sexuality. They met three times over the following years, under the chairmanship of Frank Griswold, the presiding bishop of ECUSA. Their report in 2002, while it indicated some narrowing of gaps between them, also measured the remaining sharp-edged differences. And the polarization between the two groupings continued in those post-Lambeth years.

In 2003 the stage was reached in ECUSA where a man in an openly homosexual union, Gene Robinson, was elected bishop of New Hampshire, and the election was confirmed by the **General**

Convention that year, overwhelmingly in the House of Deputies and by 62 votes to 45 in the House of Bishops. Previous activities in ECUSA had already led to a very strong reaction in other parts of the world, including the **consecration** of bishops elsewhere specifically to lead a "**mission**" to the United States to draw **parishes** away from allegiance to ECUSA.

The international situation was also complicated over the 2002–2003 period by the action in **Canada** of Michael Ingham, the bishop of New Westminster (the **diocese** centered on Vancouver). During this time, he won sufficient support from his diocesan **synod** for him to go ahead with authorizing official forms of worship for the solemnizing of same-sex unions. This action led to the attempted secession from the diocese of eight parishes opposed to such provision, and their seeking Episcopal oversight from the bishop of the Yukon, the neighboring diocese. The Canadian position changed from a diocesan issue to a national one when the biennial **General Synod** passed a motion in June 2004 that affirmed "the integrity and sanctity of committed adult same-sex relationships."

Archbishop Carey's successor as archbishop of Canterbury, **Rowan Williams**, faced further complexities in **England** itself, when in May 2003 theologian Jeffrey John was nominated by the bishop of Oxford to be one of his **suffragan** bishops, the **area bishop** of Reading. John had publicly stated that he had previously been in a committed sexual relationship with another man and had written publications commending "faithful, stable, permanent" same-sex physical relationships, though he also stated that he and his friend no longer had any such relationship and that he was now technically **celibate** and abstinent. Nevertheless, there was an outcry against his appointment, precipitated in England by an open letter of opposition from nine diocesan bishops, and strengthened by the overseas voices that were already expressing distress about the American practices. This opposition led in July 2003, prior to the scheduled date for his consecration, to John's withdrawal from the appointment. The following year, he was appointed **dean** of St. Albans with rather less public outcry.

Archbishop Williams summoned an emergency meeting of the primates of the Communion in October 2003, just before Robinson was consecrated on 2 November, and they issued a public warning of the serious implications of his consecration going ahead. As an outcome of their discussions, once the consecration had happened, Williams appointed the **Lambeth Commission** to examine how the Communion could retain an organic unity under such pressure, to report by September 2004. The commission, under the chairmanship of Archbishop Robin Eames, produced the **Windsor Report** by the required date. Provinces were asked to address its recommendations, and that task began. Further action was taken by the primates in February 2005 and by the **Anglican Consultative Council** in June 2005. The situation remains unresolved within the Communion, but has proved deeply divisive between provinces and, up to a point, within particular provinces.

HONG KONG. Hong Kong became a British colony in 1841 and thereafter had expatriate Anglican congregations. The first chaplain, Vincent Stanton, arrived in 1843, and the first **bishop**, entitled bishop of Victoria, came in 1849. Other **dioceses** were formed on the **Chinese** mainland as **missionary** work there spread, and a **province** (Ching Hua Heng Kung Hui—the Holy Catholic Church in China) was formed in 1912. The diocese then became the diocese of Hong Kong and South China. Under the exigencies of Japanese occupation during World War II, Bishop R. O. Hall **ordained** a **woman**, Florence Li Tim Oi, as **priest** or **presbyter**, the first occasion on which a woman was so ordained in the **Anglican Communion**.

When the Communist Revolution succeeded in China in 1950, the province was in effect dissolved, and the diocese—now solely Hong Kong again, but soon to add "and Macao" to its title—passed back to the **metropolitical** care of **Canterbury**. It became a member of the Council of Churches of **Southeast Asia** when it was formed in 1960. Its diocesan **synod** asked the first meeting of the **Anglican Consultative Council** (ACC-1) at Limuru, **Kenya**, in 1971 to approve the ordination of women as priests or presbyters, and when this was granted by a narrow majority, the first such ordinations were conducted at **Advent** 1971.

When in 1997 Hong Kong was being transferred from British colonial rule to become a Special Administrative Region of China, steps were being taken to create two new dioceses within Hong Kong and form a province. This came to pass, as the 38th province of the

Communion, on 25 October 1998. It includes a **missionary** district in Macao, which was a Portuguese colony until 1999 and is now also incorporated in the Chinese Special Administrative Region.

HOOKER, RICHARD (1554–1600). Richard Hooker was the second-generation apologist for the **Elizabethan** Settlement, more profoundly theological in his task than any who went before him. After a short period as a reader in Hebrew at Oxford, Hooker left his fellowship in order to marry and then was **ordained** in 1582. He was appointed master of the Temple in **London** in 1585 and there contended with Walter Travers, a leading **Puritan** who was also a lecturer at the Temple (it was said "the pulpit spake pure **Canterbury** in the morning and Geneva in the afternoon until Travers was silenced"). Hooker himself resigned from the Temple in 1591 and held two country incumbencies before his death. It was during those years that his major works, the eight volumes of *The Laws of Ecclesiastical Polity*, were written and five of them published, though they drew upon his close encounters with unyielding Puritanism in his London days. The task he set himself was **ecclesiological**, and in particular he defended the Elizabethan union of church and state, and established basic principles of Anglicanism. The remaining three volumes were published some 60 years later.

Because he distinguished the Church of **England** from both the **Roman Catholic Church** and Puritanism, Hooker is often hailed as the purveyor of the "*via media*," which to some is the glory of Anglicanism. But his beliefs on the supreme **authority** of scripture, on **justification**, on the **eucharist**, and on the **ordained ministry** locate him firmly in the reformed camp, a successor to **John Jewel** and an ally of **John Whitgift**. His task differed from previous apologists, in that both **Thomas Cranmer** and Jewel were defining the Church of **England** vis-à-vis Rome, whereas Hooker was making the first major theological statement against Puritanism. He thus defends the continuity of the church, the church's right to make laws in secondary matters not covered explicitly in scripture, and the need for the whole church (or at least the whole national church) to move as a unity and not break into factions. In the process he gives a high place to **tradition** and to reason, but not such as to make him the founder of the notion of a three-legged stool of scripture, tradition, and reason—for

Hooker, the supreme revelation of God is in scripture. He is commemorated in various Anglican **calendars** on 3 November.

HOOPER, JOHN (1495–1555). John Hooper's early life is relatively unknown, but he must have been **ordained** at some point in the 1520s or 1530s, and during that same period became a convinced **Protestant**. He was at Oxford when the Act of Six **Articles** was passed in 1539, and he then left and became chaplain to Sir Thomas Arundel. Soon after he departed to the Continent, where his convictions were reinforced in Strasbourg, Basel, and Zurich. He returned to **England** in 1549 and was chaplain for a while to the protector, the Duke of Somerset, and started to make his name as a fearless **Evangelical** preacher.

In mid-1550 Hooper was nominated to be **bishop** of Gloucester, but he declined to wear the traditional Episcopal **vestments** and refused to take the **oath** of allegiance to the monarch on the grounds that he had to invoke not only God but also "all **Saints** and the holy evangelist." These refusals at length provoked the Privy Council to send him to prison to concentrate his mind! Finally, a mediating way was found, as the king himself struck out the offending words in the oath, and Hooper brought himself to wear the vestments on rare occasions. He was **consecrated** in March 1551 and devoted himself to proclaiming the **gospel** throughout his **diocese**. The following year Worcester was added to his see.

When Queen **Mary I** inherited the throne, Hooper was one of the first indicted for **heresy** and, remaining absolutely steadfast, was by judicious process burned to death outside his own **cathedral** on 9 February 1555. His **martyrdom** is recorded by **John Foxe**. Hooper's name does not appear in **provincial calendars**, but he is frequently viewed as the forerunner of the **Puritans** of Queen **Elizabeth I**'s and the Stuart reigns.

HUDDLESTON, ERNEST URBAN TREVOR (1913–1998). Trevor Huddleston was **ordained** as a **deacon** in 1936 and **presbyter** in 1937. After a **curacy** in **England**, he joined the Community of the Resurrection (CR) and was sent to South Africa in 1943. He ministered largely in Sophiatown, an African location on the edge of Johannesburg and is recorded in the biography of **Desmond Tutu** as having been, in the early 1940s, the first white man ever seen to raise his hat to Tutu's mother. He became a South African citizen.

In 1949 Huddleston became the CR's superior in South Africa. He exercised a **ministry** that ignored or opposed the apartheid laws of the country, and in the mid-1950s wrote his famous book, *Naught for Your Comfort*, first published in 1956. Yet, despite his every provocation of the regime, it was his own Community, conscious both of the political situation and of the strain on his own person, that finally withdrew him from South Africa in 1956. He was then in England with the CR for four years, bending his every effort to bring a peaceful end to the South African regime. In 1960 he became **bishop** of Masasi in Tanganyika (soon after to become **Tanzania**). He wrote there the distinctive prayer for Africa:

> God bless Africa;
> Guard her people;
> Guide her rulers;
> and give her peace.

He returned to England in 1968 and became suffragan bishop of Stepney in the **London diocese**. On retiring from that **episcopate** in 1978, he was promptly appointed bishop of Mauritius and **archbishop** of the **Indian Ocean**, from where he finally retired in 1983. He continued a life of campaigning against injustice, notably as president of the Anti-Apartheid Movement. He lived to see the political transition in South Africa and make a final return visit there, some 40 years after his enforced recall.

HUGH OF LINCOLN, SAINT (c. 1140–1200). Hugh was born in Burgundy and became a Carthusian monk in 1160; he then came to **England** in 1175 at King Henry II's invitation to be prior of the first Carthusian House in England, at Witham in Somerset. There his reputation grew until he was nominated in 1186 to be **bishop** of Lincoln; it is said he insisted on an open election before he would exercise the **episcopate**. In Lincoln, a **diocese** that stretched from the Humber to the Thames, he traveled widely in visitations and to encourage the faithful. He also founded schools and started the rebuilding of his **cathedral** after an earthquake. Hugh apparently remained on good terms with three successive monarchs, though he would never himself compromise. He was remembered for tending lepers. On his death in 1200, a cult arose in honor of him. His bones are reputed to lie under his cathedral (which was finished to his own instructions), but searches have failed to locate them. He was **canonized** by **Pope** Honorius III in 1220, and the cult spread much more widely. Many **parish** churches in England and elsewhere are **dedicated** in his name. His **feast** day is kept on 17 November, and he is listed in the **calendars** of several Anglican **provinces**.

HUNTINGTON, WILLIAM REED (1838–1909). William Huntington was a leading thinker and innovator of the **Protestant Episcopal Church in the United States of America** (PECUSA) in the last third of the 19th century. His pioneering book, *The Church-Idea: An Essay towards Unity* (1870), contained the first sketch of the "quadrilateral" he put forward for **ecumenical** purposes as providing the minimal basis for reunion of other Churches with PECUSA. This quadrilateral was adopted for exactly that purpose by the House of **Bishops** when the **General Convention** met in Chicago in 1886, and it was broadly the same quadrilateral that was in turn adopted by the 1888 **Lambeth Conference**. This has led to it being called the "Chicago-**Lambeth Quadrilateral**." Huntington also instigated the process that led to the revision of the **Book of Common Prayer** of PECUSA in 1892 and was himself the author of new material, chiefly **collects**, in it. He never had any other appointment than being rector for more than 20 years in each of two **parishes**, the second of them Grace Church, New York. Nevertheless he became popularly known as "First **Presbyter** of the Church." In the 1979 American Prayer Book, he is commemorated on 27 July.

HYMNODY. Hymnody almost disappeared during the English **Reformation**. At one stage, it appears that **Thomas Cranmer** planned to retain some of the office hymns at daily prayer, but they were omitted from his 1549 **Book of Common Prayer** and did not appear in subsequent Prayer Books. In the 1552 Book almost the only provision for singing (apart from psalms) was, as an option, for the Gloria in Excelsis at the end of the **Communion** service (it is thought that Cranmer may have retained that provision for singing and located it at the end of the rite as a way of following out the scriptural pattern of the Last

Supper—that "when they had sung a hymn, they went out . . ." [Mark 14.26]). In addition, from the publication of the first **ordination** services in 1550 on, there was permission in those rites to sing Cranmer's ponderous translation of the hymn "Veni, Creator Spiritus."

After 1559 the Psalter, though principally used by recitation in the nonmetrical version of Miles Coverdale, was often sung from Sternhold and Hopkins's metrical version (a collection compiled in various stages, the first complete set being published in 1562). Congregational singing of metrical psalms in English, completely unknown before the Reformation, was to become a popular form of active participation in public worship. Furthermore, Queen **Elizabeth I**'s *Injunctions* in 1559 gave a slightly grudging-sounding, but actually positive, encouragement to singing, whether by trained singers or by the people:

> A modest and distinct song . . . as plainly understood as if it were read without singing; and yet nevertheless, for the comforting of such as delight in **music**, it may be permitted, that in the beginning, or in the end of common prayers, either at morning or at evening, there may be sung an hymn, or suchlike praise to Almighty God.

Thereafter, there was a very slow regrowth of singing within the Church of England, particularly in the use of metrical psalms before or after **Morning** or **Evening Prayer**, and in the 1662 Book, a **rubric** at Morning and Evening Prayer now said, "In quires and places where they sing, here followeth the anthem." In other rubrics, such as those before the **Apostles' Creed** and introducing the **Litany**, the alternatives of "said or sung" appeared. And John Cosin's new (and more memorable) version of the "Veni, Creator Spiritus" was put as an alternative to Cranmer's text in the ordination rites.

The Sternhold and Hopkins Psalter (known as the "Old Version," from which the "Old Hundredth"—"All People That on Earth Do Dwell"—is still sung today) remained popular for more than two centuries. However, it was officially succeeded in 1696 by Tate and Brady's "New Version," which sought to improve the literary merits of the verse while remaining faithful to the psalm texts. In **Scotland**, a collection of "Psalms of David in meeter" (1650) was adopted and remains the official psalter of the Church of Scotland today. Other Christian verse of the 17th century (e.g., the compositions of George

Herbert and **Thomas Ken**) was initially conceived as poetry and sung only at a later date.

Hymnody as known today was to burst on the Christian churches in the 18th century, with the poetry and power of Isaac Watts and **Charles Wesley**. These were the songwriters whose hymns rang out with and from the **Evangelical Revival** beginning in the 1730s. From then on, congregational hymn singing, while lacking official sanction in the Church of England, became an ever-growing feature of English **parish** worship. John Newton, William Cowper, and Augustus Toplady added to the creative range. Catherine Winkworth was one of a number of women who translated German hymn texts. Collections of hymns started to be published, **John Wesley**'s *Collection of Hymns for the People called Methodists* in 1780 being the most famous.

Some bishops muttered that hymns were illegal because they added to the services in the Book of Common Prayer, which, it was argued, rigidly excluded that for which no provision was made. However, a judgment by the **archbishop** of **York** in 1820 in favor of a parish printing of a locally compiled hymnbook may have been a watershed, after which complaints about legality ceased.

The field was thus clear for 19th-century hymnody to have its own part in promoting the devotion and doctrine of the **Anglo-Catholic** movement. **John Keble**'s verse in *The Christian Year* (1827) was a forerunner of a vast flow of books and collections that flourished not least through *Hymns Ancient and Modern* (1861), originally dubbed (by opponents who recognized its contents and its purpose) "*Hymns Popish and Protestant*." It in fact provided a model of a hymnbook arranged on the basis of both **doctrinal** categories and also the church **calendar**. It is a model that has been widely followed in the succeeding century and a half.

In the **Protestant Episcopal Church in the United States of America**, a small selection of hymns to accompany the Prayer Book was authorized at the second **General Convention** in 1789. It was later expanded into the first version of *The Hymnal*, which has been regularly revised and updated since. In due course in **Ireland** and **Canada**, too, the **General Synods** have authorized official hymnbooks of this style for their Churches, but in most **provinces** the use of hymnody remains strictly a matter for local provision, without any national or provincial check upon the contents of the actual books chosen.

In the second half of the 20th century, liturgical revision has led to specific places for hymns in the **liturgy** being rubrically advertised. In the same period, Anglicanism worldwide has moved away from a musically monochrome style of hymnody, which had previously been found in a dominant role even when translated (with the same organ music) into **vernacular languages** all over the Earth. Lately, hymnody has come to provide a great expression of linguistic and cultural diversity, as each ethnic or language group more and more provides that which springs from its indigenous culture and is distinctive to it. *See also* INCULTURATION.

– I –

ICON. Literally, "icon" (*eikon* in Greek) means a "likeness" or "image." In the course of time, it became a technical term for a two-dimensional symbolic picture (often created by marquetry or inlaying), as opposed to a three-dimensional statue or "graven image." The **iconoclastic** controversy (as it is called) of the eighth century was an Eastern dispute as to whether such representations were legitimate or not (not least in face of the rise of Islam). In the process, the second **Council** of Nicea (787), partly influenced by the West, defined a positive use of icons. In the West itself, a practice of devotions related to three-dimensional images seems to have grown slowly through the first millennium, and then to have become at the Great Schism a focus of a difference of culture as between the Eastern Churches, which rejected three-dimensional representations and used only icons, and the Western Church, which valued images and thus created statues of the Madonna and Child, with roods and crucifixes and many images of **saints**.

At the time of the **Reformation** in **England**, the inherited statues and images were ruthlessly eliminated, and Article XXII of the Thirty-Nine **Articles** reads: "The Romish doctrine concerning purgatory, pardons, worshipping and adoration as well of images as of relics, and also invocation of the Saints, is a fond thing, vainly invented, and grounded upon no warranty of Scripture, but rather repugnant to the word of God."

It has always been possible, however, either to ignore the thrust of this Article or to interpret it as strictly referring only to "worshipping and adoration" or even to deflect its force by treating "Romish" as meaning only some supposed popular distortion of true "Roman" **doctrine**. Certainly, in the 19th and 20th centuries there was very little inhibition about the provision of pictures, statues, and representations among Anglicans. A growing interest in the Eastern Churches in the 20th century has also brought a widespread introduction of what are strictly Eastern two-dimensional icons. *See also* ORTHODOX CHURCHES.

ICONOCLASM. Iconoclasm, as its Greek roots in *eikon* and *klasma* demonstrate, is the breaking up of **icons** or images and has had a literal significance in the approach of the **Reformers** and **Puritans** to actual images either in church or elsewhere associated with worship. Considerable destruction of images occurred both at the Reformation itself and again during the Puritan hegemony of the **Commonwealth** period (1649–1660) 100 years later. The word is more widely used in its metaphorical sense to refer to the overthrow of inherited customs, conventions, or outlooks.

IGLESIA ANGLICANA de la REGION CENTRAL de AMERICA (IARCA). *See* CENTRAL REGION OF AMERICA.

IMAGES. *See* ICONS.

IMMACULATE CONCEPTION. In 1854 **Pope** Pius IX declared *ex cathedra* that the Virgin **Mary** had herself been immaculately conceived. The pronouncement of her Immaculate Conception was a statement that Mary had been preserved from the inherited taint of **original sin** at her conception in the womb of her own mother. This miracle at the origin of her life both secured her own sinlessness and qualified her in due course to bear the Son of **God**. However, the **doctrine** was actually formulated by historical development in the opposite direction viz—(1) Mary gave birth to **Jesus Christ**, who was without sin and without the entail of original sin; (2) she must therefore have been sinless herself to have conceived him thus; and (3) she must therefore have been preserved from sin at her own conception.

Anglicans have never given authoritative credence to the second and third of these propositions, and they remain at most pious speculations.

The **Roman Catholic** Church, however, had a further stage of underlining the doctrine yet to come. At **Vatican I** in 1870, the General **Council** declared that doctrinal formulations made by the pope *ex cathedra* were **infallible**. It is obvious that the 1854 statement on the Immaculate Conception was particularly in view in this decree, and thus itself became the first test case of papal infallibility. This is recognized in the statements on **Authority** of the first **Anglican–Roman Catholic International Commission** (ARCIC-1) as a problem between Roman Catholics and Anglicans that was in need of resolution, but it became a curious feature of the documents of ARCIC-2 that the agreed statement on papal authority, *The Gift of Authority* (1999), attributed protection from error (i.e., infallibility) to the papal office but failed even to mention, let alone to discuss, those two Marian decrees—on the Immaculate Conception and on the Bodily **Assumption**—which provide the test cases of the principle. They are instead the subject of ARCIC-2's final report, *Mary: Grace and Hope in Christ*, published in May 2005. *See also* CONCEPTION OF THE BLESSED VIRGIN MARY.

IMPOSITION OF ASHES. In the medieval church, ashes were "imposed" (i.e., smeared) onto the foreheads of worshippers on the first day of **Lent**, which, as the 1552 **Book of Common Prayer** declared, was "commonly called **Ash Wednesday**." The rationale for the title "Ash Wednesday" was removed in the Reformers' deletion of any use of ashes on that day, but with the **Anglo-Catholic** revival in the 19th century, borrowings from **Rome** brought back the use of ashes in many parts of the **Anglican Communion**. There is a long-standing **tradition** that the palm branches (often in the form of palm **crosses**) kept from the previous year's Palm Sunday should be burned to provide the ashes on Ash Wednesday.

INCARNATION. Incarnation is a technical term (from the Latin *carnis*, i.e. "flesh") for the Son of God becoming human in the womb of the **Virgin Mary** and being born as an infant (cf. John 1.14). Anglican theology from the **Reformation** on has generally confessed the incarnation of the Son of **God** in terms identical to those of the universal church in the preceding millennium (cf. Article II of the Thirty-Nine **Articles**). However, theologians have at intervals insisted that the incarnation is *the* central Christological dogma, which has earned this school of thought the label of "incarnational theology." Although this emphasis has roots in the **Laudian** school of the 17th century, it has flourished most notably among **Anglo-Catholic** theologians of the 20th century, taking its origins from **Charles Gore**. Incarnational theology emphasizes the significance and efficacy of the Creator's identifying with his creatures, and the emphasis may then be carried to the point where critics submit that there is a diminishing of the reconciliation effected by the **cross**.

INCLUSIVE LANGUAGE. In the English language, widely used in the **Anglican Communion**, the words "man" and "men" were traditionally used as inclusive of the human race in all documents, whether **liturgy** or **canons** or other ecclesiastical texts, until the second half of the 20th century. This corresponded to the use of *anthropos* in the Greek, a word that, while grammatically masculine, had no specific overtones of referring only to males.

But in the latter part of the 20th century, starting in the **Episcopal Church (United States of America)** and the preparatory books for its 1979 **Book of Common Prayer**, the whole English-speaking world has conformed to a change in the understanding of "man" and "men" (and compounds, such as "mankind"), as being gender-specific and referring only to males. This has led to changes in the texts of well-known **liturgical** texts, such as the move in the **Nicene Creed** from the 1974 **International Consultation on English Texts** (ICET) version, "For us men and our salvation," to the 1989 **English Language Liturgical Consultation** (ELLC) one, "For us and for our salvation." It also meant that new texts (whether **rubric** or spoken **liturgy**) would be written so as not to transgress on this point. It is reflected in the updating in English-language **Bibles** from the New International Version (NIV) in the 1970s to the New Revised Standard Version (NRSV) in 1989.

At the time of writing, there is a worldwide women's lobby opposing all theological references to God, whether in prayer, **hymnody**, or simply conversation, that involve use of masculine pronouns and possessive adjectives. This, however, is resisted by **traditionalists** on the grounds that it tends to eliminate the language of "Father" and "Son" and not only does less than justice to New Testament terminology, but also damages the classic **credal** formulations of the **doctrine** of the **Trinity**. The lack of masculine pronouns touches upon the internal relation of the Son to the Father within the Godhead, not only as incarnate under the limitations of time and space, but also as "begotten" from all eternity. A widely used exemplar of these principles has been an alternative Trinitarian formula in baptisms and blessings in the form of "God, creator, redeemer and sustainer," but it is doubtful whether Nicene orthodoxy can be safeguarded once the classic formula has disappeared from view.

In languages other than English, a similar category of problems presents itself in differing ways in differing languages. *See also* FEMINISM.

INCULTURATION. The culture of a people, tribe, region, or nation is a complex pattern of repeated social conventions, usually including a shared **language**, that characterizes the particular grouping concerned. Such conventions may be without religious significance or may be deeply imbued with the local religious beliefs. The process of inculturation, whereby Christianity is clothed in a local, pre-Christian culture, is a function of Christian **mission**, partly theological, partly practical.

Theologically, the impulse to inculturation is the **Incarnation**. As the Son of **God** became incarnate in a particular culture at a particular point in history and in many ways conformed to that culture, so Christianity has to present itself in and for the culture of its each local context. Practically, it has made sense not to present cultural obstacles to conversion (unless absolutely required to do so by the **gospel**), and thus **missionary** activity has sought to reduce the cultural gap to be crossed in conversion, a practice for which there is strong New Testament precedent in the mission (led by Jewish Christians such as St. Paul) to the Gentiles. This inevitably means that mission is prosecuted transculturally, but it leaves open the question, current in New Testament days as well as in the nearly 500 years of Anglicanism, of how far Christianity itself should seek to wear and promote a common culture with common *mores* across the whole globe. This latter question is particularly focused in the issue of whether **Communion** should everywhere be celebrated with wheat bread and grape wine or the everyday food and drink of individual regions or localities should be, or could be, employed. But the major incarnational principle also raises a question about how far local culture is so entwined with non-Christian religion or un-Christian morality as to necessitate its rejection rather than its adoption at **baptism**.

Anglicanism has a very mixed history in respect of the principle of inculturation. **Pope** Gregory instructed **Augustine** of **Canterbury** to make selection of the customs in the Roman, Gallic, and other churches and to use what was most appropriate. It is not self-evident that this principle surfaced well at the **Synod** of **Whitby**. But the assertion in Article XXXIV of the Thirty-Nine **Articles** that "Every particular or national Church hath **authority** to **ordain** . . . ceremonies . . . ordained only by man's authority" does restate Pope Gregory's principle. In practice, Anglicanism has on the one hand had a distinguished history in respect of the use of **vernacular** languages in every place where it has gone. Learning the local language and translating **Bible** and worship book into that language have had high priority. On the other hand, the march of **Gothic** Revival **architecture**, Western church **music**, medieval **vesture** of **ministers** (and choirboys), and a host of secondary and even trivial other matters have looked in many places like a cultural imperialism—and in many places are, paradoxically, highly valued by local Anglicans as enabling them to belong to a recognizable world family, which is thus valued more highly than a true local inculturation would be.

Issues about inculturation often only arise in a second generation of Christians, as first-generation converts may in reaction disavow strongly even neutral features of their culture of domicile. The issues have been debated in various ways at the **Lambeth Conferences** almost from the first conference in 1867. Resolutions 22 and 47 of the 1988 conference strongly affirmed the principles of inculturation, and these were reaffirmed in Resolution III.14 of the 1998 conference. Inculturation was the theme of the third **International Anglican Liturgical Consultation** (IALC-3) at **York** in 1989, when the "York **Statement**" "Down-to-Earth Worship" was adopted. It was also the theme of the first **Council of Anglican Provinces in Africa** (CAPA) **liturgical** consultation at Kanamai, **Kenya**, in 1993, when the very comprehensive Kanamai Statement was adopted. Liturgical revision around the **Anglican Communion** since the latter part of the 20th century has shown the first, if cautious, signs of each country taking its indigenous culture seriously.

INDENTED RUBRICS. In the 1662 **Communion** service, five **rubrics** are placed beside the **narrative** of institution in the "prayer of **consecration**," directing five "**manual acts**." These rubrics are usually printed by indentation into the main text, so that the rubrics have become known as the "indented rubrics." In the original two such rubrics in the 1549 **Book of Common Prayer**, they were actually placed in the margin of the printed text and were therefore not technically "indented."

INDIA. Christianity in India is traced traditionally to the reported coming of St. Thomas in the first century A.D. to the Malabar Coast in what is today Kerala, though the actual historical accuracy of the report is difficult to verify. The Syrian Orthodox Church under the jurisdiction of the patriarchs of Antioch was already there when the Portuguese arrived in 1499. A complex history that bears upon the character of the **Mar Thoma Syrian Church**, but is largely confined to the development and division of the **Orthodox Churches** within Kerala, ensued. Other parts of the subcontinent received Christianity through European colonization and trade, and Anglicanism was planted in India initially through trade. The East India Company, which had been incorporated at the end of 1600, withdrew from the East Indies themselves in 1622 and instead concentrated on trade with India. The company's ships often had chaplains aboard, and when the first ambassador was appointed to the Moghul court in Surat in 1615, a resident chaplain accompanied him. By the end of that century, there were chaplains at trading stations as well, although always on the supposition that they were there for the sake of spiritual ministrations to the expatriate English, because, for the sake of commerce and political stability, the company was opposed to **missionary** work among Hindus or Moslems.

In the 18th century, **Lutheran** missionaries from Denmark, based in the Danish territory of Tranquebar, south of Madras, began to evangelize the native population. In due course they spread into the sphere of the East India Company's jurisdiction and gained financial support from the **Society for Promoting Christian Knowledge** (SPCK) in **London**. Three changes can then be discerned in the last years of that century:

- When the **Baptist** Missionary Society was newly formed, its instigator, William Carey, came as its first missionary to Bengal in 1793, and he was joined by others in 1800. They settled in Serampore, also Dutch territory, and concentrated on **Bible** translation, founding schools, and opposing infanticide and suttee.
- The members of the "**Clapham Sect**," notably **William Wilberforce**, worked for an insertion into the charter of the East India Company (when it was to be renewed in Parliament in 1793) committing it to sending "schoolmasters and missionaries." This was passed in Parliament but then deleted through pressure from the company. It remained a very live issue for those who had originated it, and the desire to **evangelize** the Indian population at large grew ever stronger in England over the next two decades, during which time the task was focused by the formation of the **Church Missionary Society** in 1799.
- The **Evangelical Revival** in England did have an opening in the appointment of chaplains to the company. From the arrival of David Brown in **Calcutta** in 1787, the pattern was set, and in 1800 the governor-general brought Christianity out of the private circle of European expatriates and encouraged its planting in society generally. Brown and **Claudius Buchanan** became instructors for the young civil servants, the Baptists from Serampore were welcomed within the British sphere of influence, and spreading the **gospel** to Indians became an accepted pattern of behavior. This was furthered in the immediately following years by the coming of Henry Martyn, Daniel Corrie, and Thomas Thomason.

In 1813 a new Act opened the way officially for missionaries and also provided for the **consecration** of a **bishop**. The first bishop of Calcutta, Thomas Middleton, arrived in 1814, technically with the Episcopal care of Anglicans in the whole of Asia, Australasia, and the Pacific. He died in 1822 and was succeeded by the Evangelical hymn writer, Reginald Heber; it was he who first conducted Anglican

ordinations of Indians. The **diocese** was divided by the creation of the see of Madras in 1835, and then of **Australia** in 1836 and of Bombay in 1837.

A milestone was reached in 1912, when **Samuel Azariah** was consecrated bishop of Dornakal, the first native-born Indian to be so consecrated. He remained in office for more than 30 years and modeled a truly indigenous **ordained ministry** for those years of transition.

A further milestone came in 1930 when the separate dioceses of India, **Burma**, and **Ceylon** came together in a single constitution to form an independent **province** of the Church of India, Burma, and Ceylon (CIBC), with the bishop of Calcutta as the **metropolitan**. After World War II, India was divided at independence on 15 August 1947, and the largely Islamic areas of the northwest and northeast became **Pakistan**, and the Church accordingly became the Church of India, Pakistan, Burma, and Ceylon (CIPBC).

On 27 September 1947, after conversations and negotiations lasting 28 years, and in the teeth of **Anglo-Catholic** opposition throughout the **Anglican Communion**, the four southern dioceses of CIPBC left the Anglican church and joined with South Indian **Methodists** and the South India United Church (itself the result of an earlier union of **Presbyterians** and **Congregationalists**) to become the Church of **South India**.

The CIPBC **synod** authorized its own **Book of Common Prayer** (fairly closely related to the 1662 Book) in 1960. Negotiations continued toward united churches, and they came to fruition with the formation of the Church of Pakistan on 1 November 1970 and the Church of **North India** on 29 November 1970. There then remained no specifically Anglican dioceses or other presence in India. *See also* BANGLADESH.

INDIAN OCEAN. The **province** of the Indian Ocean grew from very separate origins, though each island had French involvement and the official **language** of the province is French. The island of Mauritius was a colony of France until the British captured it in 1810. An Anglican **bishopric** was established (largely for expatriates) in 1854, and there has been a continuity of a single **diocese** there ever since. The Seychelles were from the start part of that diocese.

In Madagascar there was **evangelistic** work done by **missionaries** from the (Independent) London Missionary Society (LMS) between 1818 and 1833. The missionaries were expelled in 1833, but Christianity flourished through the churches they had planted. From 1861 on, the island reopened to Western trade, and the bishop of Mauritius visited there and arranged for **Church Missionary Society** (CMS) missionaries to be invited into the coastal areas under his supervision, while LMS missionaries would have the capital, Antananarivo, as their sphere of responsibility. However, a campaign arose in England (with the involvement of the **Society for the Propagation of the Gospel**) for the consecration of a bishop for Madagascar. This was resisted by LMS and also by their friends at CMS, and, when **Archbishop** A. Campbell Tait asked for a royal license to **consecrate** a bishop for Madagascar, Lord Shaftesbury got it defeated. However, Tait suggested that the bishops of the Episcopal Church of **Scotland** might act instead, and the first bishop of Madagascar was consecrated in 1874.

The two dioceses were each divided in 1969, Seychelles being separated from Mauritius, and Madagascar being divided into three. These all remained under the **metropolitical** care of the archbishop of **Canterbury** until 1973, when the five dioceses were joined together into the province of the Indian Ocean; a further diocese was created in Madagascar in 1996. In 1978, Bishop **Trevor Huddleston** became the second archbishop of the province. The archbishop is elected from among the diocesan bishops without there being a fixed metropolitical see. The province belongs to the **Council of Anglican Provinces of Africa** (CAPA), although it has no territory on the African mainland.

INFALLIBILITY. The question of infallibility lurked on the sidelines of the **Reformation** disputes and surfaced probably most clearly in the statements in Article XIX of the XXXIX **Articles** that "the Church of Rome hath erred . . . in matters of faith" and in Article XXI that "General Councils . . . may err and sometimes have erred." At that point in time, and until 1870, the claim of the **Roman Catholic Church** that was being resisted by Anglicans was simply a claim that, in its **Councils**, it spoke for the totality of the "catholic church" with the voice of **Holy Spirit**. Indeed, it was claimed that such statements were not only compatible with scripture but, even if not traceable directly to the text of scripture, were nevertheless to be received as apostolic truths that had been retained by **tradition** within the fabric of the Church without coming within the **canon** of scripture. In practice, this was a claim to infallible interpretation of scripture, and a refusal to let the scriptures speak for themselves.

It was against such a straitjacket that the concept of the (much misunderstood) "private judgment" was erected at the Reformation. This is exemplified among Anglicans in the question to the candidates to be **priests** (or **presbyters**) in the 1552 **Ordinal**, a question that has largely continued in revised ordinals throughout the **Anglican Communion**: "Are you persuaded that the Holy Scriptures contain all things necessary to salvation, and are you prepared to teach nothing (as requisite for eternal salvation) but *such as you may be persuaded* are contained within the said Scriptures?" (emphasis added).

The question, however, took a new turn when **Vatican I** in 1870 declared the **pope** to be infallible in his own person, even without the convening of a Council, when he speaks *ex cathedra* to define **doctrine**. This papal infallibility had often been denied by Roman Catholic apologists of earlier centuries and of the first part of the 19th century, and its adoption by the Council not only led to a widespread defection from Rome but also necessitated a new kind of Anglican *apologia* regarding Rome. Although since 1870 this infallibility has been invoked only once by Rome—in the papal definition in 1950 of the Bodily **Assumption** of **Mary**—yet that very definition of 1950 raises a double problem for other Christians. There appears no warrant (apart from Vatican I) for so defining doctrine irrevocably on papal **authority** alone on the one hand, and there has been enormous doubt about the actual content of what was defined on the other.

The first **Anglican–Roman Catholic International Commission** (ARCIC-1) nudged toward these problems in their two statements on **Authority** in 1976 and 1981, and they identified the "Marian decrees" as focusing the issues of authority concerned, but these two statements of ARCIC-1 did not claim to have reached a common mind between Roman Catholics and Anglicans, stating instead that the issues awaited resolution. Nevertheless, the more recent agreed statement on the subject from ARCIC-2, *The Gift of Authority* (1999), both accepted the concept of a universal **primate**, located in Rome, who under certain conditions, would be "preserved from error," and yet at the same time completely omitted any discussion of the Marian decrees that are the standing test case of the credibility of the teaching. The ARCIC-2 statement on Mary, *Mary: Grace and Hope in Christ* (2005), in turn omits discussion of infallibility.

INGLIS, CHARLES (1734–1816). Charles Inglis was born in **Ireland** and graduated from Trinity College, Dublin. He was a **missionary** of the **Society for the Propagation of the Gospel** in America from 1757 on. He was initially rector of Christ Church, Dover, Delaware, and from 1775 was rector of **Trinity Church, Wall Street**, in New York. He was a loyalist and returned to **England** some time after the American colonies won their independence. In 1786 (after the **Samuel Seabury** episode), legislation was passed in the Westminster Parliament to allow the **archbishop** of **Canterbury** (with due governmental authority) to consecrate **bishops** for overseas territories. After **William White** and **Samuel Provoost** had been **consecrated** for American **dioceses** in February 1787, on 12 August that year Charles Inglis was consecrated to be bishop of Nova Scotia in what is now **Canada**, the first overseas Anglican bishop for a British territory. Appointed by the Crown, he was initially salaried by the Westminster Parliament. Inglis's energies over his 29 years as bishop led to a developed diocesan organization and **episcopate** in Canada. In the 1959 Canadian **Book of Common Prayer**, Inglis is commemorated on 12 August, the date of his consecration. Curiously, he is omitted from the listings in the 1985 *Book of Alternative Services*, although Seabury and a small number of later Canadians are included.

INITIATION. "Christian initiation" is a 20th-century turn of phrase. Its origins lie in the school of thought that, arising in the late 19th century, asserted that **baptism** and **confirmation** were in essence one **sacrament** of admission into the church and into life in **Jesus Christ**. This usage necessitated a new term to describe baptism and confirmation under a single head, and it was from that need that "initiation" was adopted. So it was that in 1948 the Church of **England** had an official report entitled *The Theology of Christian Initiation*; the title recurred in the "Ely" report in 1971, *Christian Initiation: Birth and*

Growth in the Christian Society. The Church of England continued this usage when, in its 1980 and 1998 revised baptismal **liturgies**, it put baptism and confirmation together under the heading "Initiation Services."

Meanwhile, scholarship moved on, particularly in the years since 1970, and in the **Episcopal Church (United States of America)**'s 1979 **Book of Common Prayer**, baptism alone is presented as "initiation," and confirmation is among "Episcopal services." Similarly in the **Canadian** *Book of Alternative Services* (1985) and in the New Zealand Prayer Book (1989) confirmation is listed among "pastoral services." The section report on liturgy of the 1988 **Lambeth Conference** stated that sacramental initiation is complete in water baptism. The 1991 **Toronto Statement** of the fourth **International Anglican Liturgical Consultation** (IALC-4) made it very clear that water baptism alone is full sacramental initiation, and confirmation cannot claim an initiatory role. Thus the term "initiation" runs on, though the original rationale for its introduction has largely collapsed.

INSPIRATION. The **Anglican Communion** has received as part of the New Testament St. Paul's assertion that "all scripture is inspired of God" (2 Tim. 3.16). This is well illustrated in **Thomas Cranmer**'s **collect** of the second Sunday in **Advent**: "Blessed Lord, who hast caused all holy scriptures to be written for our learning." This collect itself drew upon Rom. 15.4, part of the set epistle of that Sunday. The emphasis is upon the outcome, that is, the text of the scriptures, as being the word of God, rather than upon either the credentials or skills of particular authors or the processes by which they wrote. While the implications of different understandings of inspiration may be of importance between conservative and **liberal** or **modernist** views of the scriptures, such issues did not arise in such a way as to elicit close definition in the 16th and 17th centuries when the classic Anglican formularies were being constructed. *See also* AUTHORITY; CANON.

INTER-ANGLICAN STANDING COMMISSION ON ECUMENICAL RELATIONS (IASCER). The IASCER was set up for the **Anglican Communion** in response to resolution IV.3 of the 1998 **Lam-**

beth Conference. It monitors progress in bilateral and multilateral conversations with other denominations in the different parts of the world and endeavors to ensure a consistent approach by Anglican **provinces** involved in them. It first met as a full commission in 2000 and 2001 and established three smaller working groups to study general issues that touch upon different dialogues in which Anglicans are involved: **Communion** with and within the Anglican Communion; Holy **Orders**, **Ecclesiology**, and Communion; and Anglican identity and coherence in dialogue.

INTER-ANGLICAN STANDING COMMISSION ON MISSION AND EVANGELISM (IASCOME). The **Anglican Consultative Council** (ACC) at its 11th meeting (ACC-11), which took place in **Scotland** in late 1999, called in resolution 11 for the formation of a new standing commission on **mission**—IASCOME—for the **Anglican Communion**. Its task ran in continuity with that of **MISSIO**, which ceased as IASCOME began. The commission was duly formed from around the Communion, and it presented a substantial "interim" report to ACC-12, which met in **Hong Kong** in October 2002. This covered the promotion of companionship links between different **dioceses**, the facilitation of sharing of resources, the networking of **provincial** coordinators of mission, **ecumenical** cooperation in mission, relationships with Islam, justice and peace issues, and many others. The report also included a report of an Anglican Communion Consultation of the provincial coordinators held in April that year in **Kenya**, a statement from the All-Africa Anglican HIV/AIDS Planning Framework held in Johannesburg in August 2001, and a series of short summaries giving the "mission focus" of 21 of the different provinces. IASCOME then hosted at Cyprus in February 2003 an Anglican Communion Mission Organizations Conference on "Transformation and **Tradition** in Global Mission," which was attended by 110 mission practitioners and advocates from 40 countries and was expected to be repeated within five years.

INTER-ANGLICAN TELECOMMUNICATIONS COMMISSION. The **Anglican Consultative Council** (ACC) at its 2002 meeting (ACC-12) endorsed a recommendation from the Joint Standing Committee of the ACC and the **Primates Meeting** that there should be an "Inter-Anglican Standing Commission on Telecommunications" and welcomed a grant from **Trinity Church, Wall Street**, to bring the commission into formation and initial operation. Its inaugural meeting (which slightly changed the commission's title) was held in **Canterbury** in February 2004 and was attended by members from nine Anglican **provinces**. They adopted a mission statement and resolved to conduct a comprehensive survey across the **Anglican Communion** to discover the ways telecommunications are being used or planned. Amid dramatic portrayals of the benefits of good technological communications, the meeting also addressed the needs of places that do not yet enjoy them.

INTER-ANGLICAN THEOLOGICAL AND DOCTRINAL COMMISSION (IATDC). The original IATDC arose from an idea conceived at the third meeting of the **Anglican Consultative Council** (ACC-3) in 1976. The proposal was endorsed by the 1978 **Lambeth Conference**, and a commission of 15 members was appointed, with terms of reference (to study "Church and Kingdom in Creation and Redemption") provided by the ACC. The commission met, under the chairmanship of **Archbishop** Keith Rayner from **Australia**, in 1981, 1983, and 1985 and then produced its report, *For the Sake of the Kingdom* (1986).

At the 1988 Lambeth Conference, the commission, to be newly constituted, was to address issues of **Communion** arising from the **ordination** of **women** as **presbyters** and their prospective ordination as **bishops**. The task of this commission became that of the **Eames Commission**, which produced the **Virginia Report**.

After the 1998 Lambeth Conference, the commission was again reconstituted, and Bishop Stephen Sykes of **England** was appointed chairman. The new commission met for the first time in September 2001—meeting in England through force of circumstances, as transatlantic flights were totally disrupted in the days following 11 September that year. Its terms of reference were to take further the nature and basis of Communion, a study to undergird strains upon the structure of the **Anglican Communion** itself. It began by issuing four questions for public response, and thus, when it met again in September 2002, it followed up the responses by similarly issuing "Six Propositions" for further response. It met again in September 2003 in Virginia.

INTERCONTINENTAL CHURCH SOCIETY (ICS). The Intercontinental Church Society is a **missionary society** of the Church of **England** formed in 1824, originally as the Colonial and Continental Church Society, to provide an Anglican **Evangelical** ministry to English-speaking people abroad. While at intervals it has provided chaplaincies or other **ministries** in most continents of the world, the largest part of its energies has in the years since World War II been directed to providing chaplaincies on the continent of **Europe**. Many of these are permanent appointments where the society acts as though exercising patronage, but others have been short-term holiday-period appointments. The original name was changed at the end of the colonial era to the Commonwealth and Continental Church Society, and the current name was adopted in 1994.

INTERNATIONAL ANGLICAN FAMILY NETWORK (IAFN). The IAFN originated in **Australia** in 1987 and provided resource papers for the 1988 **Lambeth Conference**. Its headquarters then moved to **England** where, under the umbrella of the Children's Society, it has since the early 1990s put those working in family **ministries** across the world in touch with each other. Financial help from the **Scottish** Episcopal Church then enabled a part-time coordinator to be appointed. Until 2003 the communication was focused largely through a constant flow of news from different provinces in the form of a newsletter. This was published regularly in its own right and also consistently formed the center pages of the **Anglican Consultative Council**'s journal *Anglican World.* However, in 2003 a residential consultation of IAFN representatives from African countries was held in **Kenya**, and from the consultation a series of agreed recommendations was given wider circulation. The needs of those with HIV/AIDS and the sufferings of women through domestic violence figured prominently.

INTERNATIONAL ANGLICAN LITURGICAL CONSULTATIONS (IALC). While the spread of Anglicanism across the world in the 18th and 19th centuries was usually represented **liturgically** by the 1662 **Book of Common Prayer** or by the **Scottish** or American minor variants on that Book, in the 20th century a considerable variety of liturgical uses emerged. In the first half of the century, these were not viewed as taking any particular **province** out of the general Prayer Book stream, and the expectation was that they would vary only in minor ways from that general ethos.

In the second half of the 20th century, from the time of the first Church of **South India** liturgy in 1950, fears arose lest the liturgical unity of the **Anglican Communion** be impaired by particular provincial revisions. Various initiatives were taken to keep provinces in touch with each other. These included a positive and extensive statement on principles of liturgical revision at the 1958 **Lambeth Conference**; two separate occasions when an international document (entitled "pan-Anglican") on the "Structure of a **Eucharistic** Liturgy" was produced (1965 and 1969); a period in which a (relatively abortive) "Liturgy for Africa" was drafted by correspondence among African **metropolitans** (1961–1964); a consultation of **bishops** in conjunction with the 1968 Lambeth Conference; the compiling by first the **executive officer** of the Anglican Communion and then the **Anglican Consultative Council** (ACC) of a list of liturgical correspondents in each province; and the provision of reports on liturgy around the Communion in the ACC reports of 1973, 1984, and 1996.

In 1989 the Anglican Church of **Canada** seconded its liturgical officer to become the Communion's part-time coordinator for liturgy, and he reported to each ACC meeting thereafter. There were also statements of policy on liturgy at the 1988 Lambeth Conference and in some ACC reports. On two occasions proposals were made for a pan-Anglican Liturgical Commission, and at the 1988 Lambeth Conference an ill-judged resolution was carried to provide a kind of **doctrine** commission to monitor and correct the potential errors of each province's liturgists. In addition, each province had to respond to the **World Council of Churches** "Faith and Order" **Lima** text, *Baptism, Eucharist, and Ministry* (1982).

None of these different moves amounted to an actual **networking** of the Communion's liturgists. But many Anglican liturgists did meet each other under the aegis of the biennial congress of the (**ecumenical** and worldwide) Societas Liturgica, which was founded in 1961. An informal conversation at the end of the 1983 congress led to a (purely voluntary) Anglican Consultation being convened in tandem with the next congress, due at Boston, Massachusetts, in 1985. Thirteen people attended this embryonic consultation, where they decided on its title (i.e., "International Anglican Liturgical Consultation"), agreed on the **Boston Statement** on "Children and Communion," and arranged to meet again when the next Societas congress was due in 1987.

In 1987, a larger number, meeting in northern Italy, made a submission to the ACC asking for some official linkage. At the third consultation (IALC-3), held in **York**, **England**, in 1989, a constitution entrenching that linkage was adopted, and it was then accepted by the ACC, making the IALCs an official network of the Communion. IALC-3 produced the **York Statement** on **inculturation** of the liturgy, IALC-4 in 1991 produced the **Toronto Statement** on Christian **initiation**, IALC-5 in 1995 produced the **Dublin Statement** on the eucharist, and IALC-6 in 2001 produced the **Berkeley Statement** on **orders** and **ordination**. Volumes of essays have also been published in connection with most of these statements. The Steering Group has also arranged interim "conferences" between these main consultations, and some of the work of these has also been published.

Meanwhile in 1993 the joint meeting of **primates** of the Communion together with the ACC in Cape Town had allocated to the IALCs the "monitoring" task requested in the 1988 Lambeth resolution mentioned above. The 1998 Lambeth Conference, in resolution III.16, commended the work of IALCs to the provinces, asking for their scholarly, practical, and financial support.

INTERNATIONAL ANGLICAN–ROMAN CATHOLIC COMMISSION FOR UNITY AND MISSION (IARCCUM). IARCCUM arose as a joint initiative from the international meeting of Anglican and **Roman Catholic bishops** at Mississauga, near **Toronto**, **Canada**, in 2000. It was recognized that more than 30 years had passed since the first **Anglican–Roman Catholic International Commission** (ARCIC) had been inaugurated, and there was a need for a more focused task of applying and implementing the progress made by ARCIC. The intention was that the commission could provide a practical outworking in cooperation and **mission** of the actual convergence of the two Communions. Its first meeting was held in November 2001, and issues of interfaith relationships came onto the agenda then. It met in November 2002 and again in June 2003. However, in the wake of the **consecration** of Gene Robinson as bishop of

New Hampshire in the **Episcopal Church (United States of America)** in November 2003, the Roman Catholic Church suspended its participation in IARCCUM. Its resumption of participation was announced in early 2005. *See also* HOMOSEXUALITY.

INTERNATIONAL CONSULTATION ON ENGLISH TEXTS (ICET). After **Vatican II** provided for **Roman Catholic liturgy** to be conducted in the **vernacular**, the English-speaking **provinces** of that Church set up a body to coordinate translations (and deal with the Vatican), the International Committee on English in the Liturgy (ICEL). By 1969 ICEL was meeting with representative liturgists of other Christian denominations on an **ecumenical** and worldwide basis, with a view to finding agreed English-language texts of well-known and shared liturgical material—such as Gloria in Excelsis, Sanctus, and the **Lord's Prayer**. This body took the title of International Consultation on English Texts, and it came into existence at exactly the point where English-speaking worshippers (and liturgiographers) were beginning to address God as "you" rather than "thou," thus requiring a totally new set of texts. This need of new texts itself threatened to create a centrifugal pattern if each church body around the world worked independently of others in translating historic texts. Thus in 1969 ICET sent preliminary drafts around the world for comment, and then, in the light of these responses, in 1970, 1971, and 1974 produced a series of more and more definitive proposals in publications entitled *Prayers We Have in Common*. Virtually all English-language writing of new liturgical texts in all denominations drew deeply upon these proposals, though at intervals individual churches varied them slightly—and in many places a traditional form of the Lord's Prayer proved too deeply entrenched to give way to a modern version. After 1974, ICET soon ceased to meet, and it was replaced in the 1980s by the **English Language Liturgical Consultation** (ELLC).

INTINCTION. Intinction is the practice of dipping **bread** into wine or floating bread within the cup in order to provide bread that has been touched (or "intincted") by wine to the recipient. Anglicans have generally regarded it as far less satisfactory than the separate distribution of the separate **elements**, but as preferable to giving Communion "in one kind only" (i.e., bread on its own). It is used in a variety of situations, such as where there is fear communicants might drink too freely of wine (particularly in parts of the world where grape wine is very expensive), where there is (rightly or wrongly) fear of infection from the cup, or where there is reason to think the wine might be spilled if the communicant seeks to drink from the cup (as can happen when the recipient is lying flat in a hospital bed). Words of distribution are usually then combined to provide a joint formula, beginning, for example, "The body and blood of Christ." In some places, individual communicants themselves take responsibility for holding their portion of bread until the cup is offered, and then intincting the bread themselves before receiving both kinds together.

IRAN. Anglicans in Iran in the 19th century were almost entirely expatriates from the United Kingdom or North America. A **diocese** was formed in 1912. It was supported by Western **missionary societies** and ran schools and hospitals, and by the 1950s had around 1,000 Iranian Christians baptized and in membership. In 1957 it was incorporated into the "Jerusalem **Archbishopric**" and remained in that **province** when it was reconstituted as the Episcopal Church in **Jerusalem and the Middle East** in 1976. In 1979, when the Ayatollah's Islamic revolution occurred in Iran, the **bishop**, Hassan Deqhani-Tafti, himself an Iranian, was forced into exile, and the diocese has only continued since then under very great political constraints. He continued in office until retirement, and his successor, Bishop Iraj Mottahedeh, also an Iranian, lives in the diocese and **ministers** to the small number of congregations.

IRELAND. Ireland has the oldest sees in the **Anglican Communion**, as **St. Patrick** is credited with founding **Armagh** in 444, although all datings of his life and **mission** have a measure of uncertainty attaching to them. Claims to have been founded in the fifth century are also made by Ardagh (now in Kilmore) and Clogher. **Dublin** has only a shadowy history before the 11th century.

The **Reformation** was experienced as an alien and imperialistic imposed religious program by the great majority of the native Irish, who neither spoke English nor enjoyed their subjection to English rule and English landlords. Thus, when the **bishops**, **cathedrals**, endowments,

parishes, and **liturgy** were reformed, first under King **Edward VI** and again under Queen **Elizabeth I**, this top-down effort at detaching the Church of Ireland from Rome had no effect on the masses. The great majority decamped from the Churches to become distinctly **Roman Catholics**, meeting in "chapels" and resenting English rule in all its aspects.

The reformed Church of Ireland emerged from the Reformation with four **archbishoprics** and a related structure of **dioceses** and cathedrals, parishes and endowments, far outstripping the need for oversight and **ministry** commensurate with attendance at the parish churches. For a period between 1615 and 1634, the **clergy** subscribed an expanded confession, the 104 **Irish Articles**, of a more determinedly Calvinist character than the English Thirty-Nine Articles on which they were based.

In 1801 the Dublin Parliament was united with the Westminster Parliament, and the Church of Ireland was by the same Act united with the Church of **England**, the resultant Church becoming the "**United Church of England and Ireland**." Then the Reform Parliament in 1833 exercised these Westminster powers in order to rationalize the structure of the Church of Ireland, by sheer legislative enactment reducing its four archbishoprics to two and uniting dioceses in areas with few Anglican worshippers, with the stated intention to divert their revenues to the more populous northern dioceses. It was this action, beneficial and sensible in its intention, that provoked the cry of Erastianism, led to **John Keble's** "Assize Sermon" on 14 July that year, and launched the **Oxford Movement**.

But in 1868 a general election for the Westminster Parliament, held across both countries virtually on a single-issue basis, gave a clear majority for W. E. Gladstone's manifesto of disestablishing the Church of Ireland. The program was put in hand immediately and on 1 January 1871 the Church of Ireland was again severed from the Church of England, this time losing its relationship to the state and a high percentage of its endowments. Every encouragement was given to it to regroup as a voluntary body, and it did so, forming a **General Synod** with a strong **lay** emphasis and providing by **canons** for a distinct Irish Church. In 1878 a new **Book of Common Prayer** (very slightly retouched from the 1662 Church of England Prayer Book) was authorized, and the canons and the Book reflected the strongly anti–Roman Catholic character of the Church of Ireland, and the fear of the creeping **Anglo-Catholicism** of which they were aware in England. Thus no **crosses** or candles could be placed on **Communion tables**, **north side** for the officiant at Communion was requisite, and the form of **absolution** in the Visitation of the Sick in the 1662 Prayer Book was changed into a precatory form. From the 1870s until 1958 it provided Episcopal ministrations for the **Lusitanian Church** and the **Spanish Reformed Episcopal Church**.

From 1909 on, steps were taken toward a slight revision of the Prayer Book. The printing plates of the large-size volumes of the 1878 Book of Common Prayer were destroyed during the Easter uprising in Dublin in 1916, which furthered the case for revision. Then in 1922, when the territory of Ireland was partitioned, the Church of Ireland (like all other Irish Churches) declined to be split and remained a single ecclesial body, straddling the border (which runs through dioceses and even through parishes). The opportunity was used to provide in 1926 a new Prayer Book, a feature of which was that the state prayers provided for prayers north of the Border for the British monarch, but south of the Border for the leaders in the Irish Free State (which in 1948 became the Republic of Ireland). Further liturgical revision followed over the decades, leading to a modern-language *Alternative Prayer Book* (APB) in 1984, and a definitive replacement for the existing books in *The Book of Common Prayer* in 2004.

Because of its distinctiveness as a **Protestant** Church as opposed to the dominant Roman Catholicism of the Republic, the Church of Ireland has been slow to follow any catholicizing trends from elsewhere. It is, however, by no means monochrome, and much of the worldwide breadth of Anglicanism is represented in it. In particular it has had many, bishops and others, who have held a high **doctrine** of **episcopacy**. There are two archbishoprics—Armagh and Dublin—and the archbishop of Armagh is senior through the seniority of his see. In the General Synod there are but two houses, as the elected clergy and elected laity (who comprise twice the number of the elected clergy) sit and vote in a single House of Representatives. The **theological college**, the General Synod office, and a "National Cathedral" (additional to the diocesan one) are located in Dublin. The Church of Ireland was the first of the Anglican Churches of Britain and Ireland to **ordain women** as **presbyters**. It participates in the **Porvoo** Common Statement and the relationship of inter-Communion with the Baltic and Nordic **Lutheran** Churches.

IRISH ARTICLES. In 1615 an Irish **Convocation** held in **Dublin** agreed on a body of 104 Articles, and they were imposed on the **clergy** of the Church of **Ireland** in the sense that all were forbidden to teach contrary to them. The character of the Articles, possibly under the influence of James Ussher, was highly Calvinist, and the text reproduced parts of the **Lambeth Articles** of 1595 *verbatim*. In 1634 the Irish Convocation adopted a **canon** that approved and accepted the Church of **England**'s Thirty-Nine Articles, and this has generally been viewed as replacing the Irish Articles with the English. Some voices, however, with some warrant from the text of the canon, have urged that the English Articles were then merely added to the Irish, whose currency ran on.

– J –

JACOBITES. *See* NONJURORS.

JAMES I, KING (1566–1625). James was the son of Mary, Queen of Scots, who was herself descended from King Henry VII of **England** and thereby became next in line to the English throne when Queen **Elizabeth I** succeeded in 1558 and, like King **Edward VI** and Queen **Mary I** before her, had no offspring. Mary abdicated from the Scottish throne in 1567 and James at one year old thus became James VI of **Scotland**. After her execution in 1587, James became heir presumptive to the English throne, and on Elizabeth's death in 1603, he inherited as James I of England.

On his way to his **coronation**, James was met by **Puritans** bearing the Millenary Petition, which sought a shift in the Elizabethan Settlement toward a more Puritan position. He placated them by summoning the **Hampton Court Conference** in 1604, but there gave little ground to the Puritans, except for ordering a new translation of the **Bible**. Completed in 1611, this translation has been generally known since as the "Authorized Version," due to the note on its title page, "Appointed to be read in Churches" (which probably reflects the later provision in the 1662 **Book of Common Prayer** that the Epistles and **Gospels** at Holy **Communion** should be taken from that version). In countries outside England, it has often been known as the **King James Version**, a title that has been adopted more and more in recent years in England also.

Following the Hampton Court Conference, the Prayer Book was marginally amended and republished on James's own **authority**, a new code of **canons** was passed by **Canterbury Convocation**, and Richard Bancroft was appointed **archbishop** of **Canterbury** in **John Whitgift**'s place. Each of these changes indicated James I's preference for English **episcopacy** and **liturgy** over the more Puritan pattern of the Church of Scotland. From 1610 on, he took steps to introduce first episcopacy, then **liturgy**, into Scotland. In 1618 the Five Articles (enforcing ceremonies such as kneeling for Communion) were accepted by the Church of Scotland at Perth, and these were later enforced by the Scottish Parliament. James (dubbed by lampooners "the wisest fool in Christendom") in both countries prepared the way for his son, King **Charles I**, to drive the countries to civil war.

JAMES II, KING (1633–1701). James II was the second son of **Charles I** and, through the barrenness of the wife of his older brother, **Charles II**, was heir to the throne throughout his brother's reign. Son of a **Roman Catholic** mother, he himself became a Roman Catholic in 1670 and thereafter worked for a return of both **England** and **Scotland** to Roman Catholic obedience. When he succeeded his brother in 1685, he declined to have **Communion** at his **coronation** service, and he took such steps to promote Roman Catholics in the realm as to entrench suspicion that both the nation and the Church of England would again be brought under the aegis of the **pope**. This anxiety led to an unsuccessful revolt led by the Duke of Monmouth, an illegitimate son of Charles II. The fear was greatly strengthened by the outcome of the revocation of the Edict of Nantes in France late in 1685, after which the persecution of French **Protestants** led many to flee for refuge to England and evoked much sympathy there.

When James directed the **bishops** to order their **clergy** to publish his second "Declaration of Indulgence" in 1688, he provoked the outright noncompliance of the seven bishops who were in **London** at the time, and this spurred him to order their arrest and trial on the charge of seditious libel. The jury found them not guilty, however, and they paraded through London to ecstatic acclaim—and James knew his time was up. The opposition to James was increased by the fact that his second wife had recently given birth to a son, who was bound to be raised as a Roman Catholic, whereas until then the next two in line for the throne had been his daughters Mary and Anne, both of whom, born of his first wife before he became a Roman Catholic, were Protestants.

James fled and was replaced by his daughter Mary and her husband, William of Orange, in the **Glorious Revolution**. Many of the clergy, though, including some of the English bishops who had resisted James II, as well as all the bishops in Scotland, viewed their **oaths** of allegiance to James as unbreakable, and thus refused to swear new oaths to the new monarchs, **William III** and **Mary II**. This group became known as "Jacobites" (that is, loyal to James, "James" being the anglicized form of the Greek "Jacob") or "**nonjurors**" (not swearing) and thus began a schism in Anglicanism that lasted for 100 years. Such nonjuring churchpeople were associated—whether in actual fact or merely in the suspicion of others—with the two armed rebellions against the Hanoverian monarchy in 1715 and 1745.

James himself died in 1701 and was succeeded in the eyes of the Jacobites by his son, known to them as "James III" (1688–1766) but labeled by those loyal to the Protestant succession as "The Pretender" (a title which in turn became "The Old Pretender" when his son, Bonnie Prince Charlie, led the 1745 rebellion and was called "The Young Pretender").

JAPAN. Christianity first came to Japan with Francis Xavier in 1549. However from the 17th century to the 19th, foreigners were completely excluded from the country, and Christianity was suppressed. When the country was reopened to immigration in 1858, the first Anglican to enter was the American Episcopalian John Liggins in 1859. The first **diocese** (South Tokyo) was formed in 1883. The Church was renamed Nippon Sei Ko Kai ("Holy Catholic Church in Japan") in 1887 at its first **synod**. It grew slowly, but the dioceses of Kyushu (1894), Hokkaido (1896), and Kobe (1896) were formed before the

Archbishops Runcie and Ramsey. Courtesy of James Rosenthal

Archbishops Williams and Eames. Courtesy of James Rosenthal

Extract from Lambeth Conference Photo 1988 (Showing Runcie). Courtesy of James Rosenthal

Archbishop Runcie and Pope John Paul II. Courtesy of James Rosenthal

Exterior View of Canterbury Cathedral. Courtesy of James Rosenthal

Interior View of Canterbury Cathedral, Showing the Compass Rose Motif. Courtesy of James Rosenthal

All Saints Cathedral in Cairo, Egypt. Courtesy of the Author

Washington National Cathedral in Washington, D.C. Courtesy of James Rosenthal

Bishop of Colombo, Sri Lanka, and His Clergy Outside His Cathedral. Author Pictured Sixth from Left. Courtesy of the Author

The Maramon Convention of the Mar Thoma Church in South India in 1989 at an Early Morning Bible Study. Courtesy of the Author

Worship in the Church of South India in Kerala. Courtesy of the Author

Worship Outdoors in the Solomons Islands, Melanesia. Courtesy of the Author

Baptism in Seattle Cathedral. Courtesy of James Rosenthal

The Author Giving the Bible to a Newly Ordained Presbyter in St. Laurence Church in Catford, South London. Courtesy of the Author

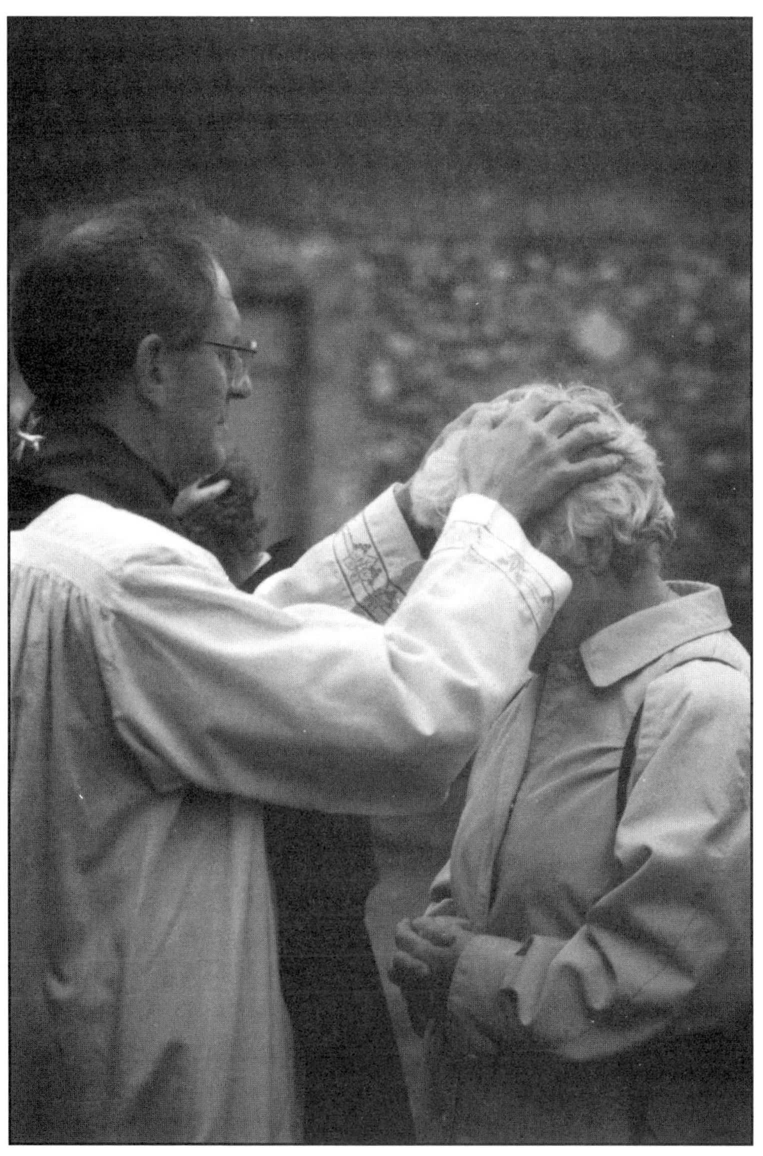

Healing. Courtesy of James Rosenthal

Mizeki (Anglican Martyr) Annual Commemoration in Marondera, Zimbabwe. Courtesy of the Author

turn of the century. The first Japanese **bishops** were **consecrated** in 1923. The regime viewed the Church as unpatriotic during World War II because it would not join the government-ordered united church, and so it went semiunderground. Its own **Book of Common Prayer**, with a heavy dependence on forms from the **Protestant Episcopal Church in the United States of America**'s 1928 Prayer Book, came in 1959.

The bishops of its 11 dioceses have had an honored place in **Lambeth Conferences**, where in 1988 and 1998 they presided at the **eucharist** on the **Feast** of the Transfiguration, 6 August, because that is also the anniversary of the dropping of the first atomic bomb on Hiroshima in 1945. At the 1998 conference they presented a synodical statement of repentance for their Church's collusion with Japanese cruelties during World War II (though Christians in Japan had themselves suffered persecution during the war), and they invited as their preacher on the feast the Reverend Susan Cole-King, daughter of Bishop Leonard Wilson, who had been **bishop** of Singapore when the island was overrun by the Japanese in 1942 and was himself imprisoned and tortured. Her sermon is printed within the 1998 Lambeth Conference report.

JERUSALEM. Jerusalem is the central place of **God**'s dealings with the human race in both Old and New Testaments. In the Old Testament, Jerusalem is visible from the story of Melchisedek in Genesis 14, through the foundation of the Temple in 1 Kings 6, to the return from Exile recorded in the book of Ezra and the rebuilding of the Temple described by the prophet Haggai. In the New Testament, Jerusalem has a high profile in the significance given to **Jesus**' triumphal entry into the city, his last week there, and his death and **resurrection** there. At the same time, he warned about giving a specially "holy" status to any one place on Earth once he had gone and the **Holy Spirit** had come (cf. Matt. 18.20; John 4.23). Christians have never had a charter in the scriptures to focus in any generation on the present-day city of Jerusalem and have almost been warned not to make too much of it in Paul's contrast in Gal. 4.25–26 between "the present city of Jerusalem" and "Jerusalem that is above." This contrast is sustained in the Book of Revelation, where the "New Jerusalem" is the **heavenly** city, the dwelling place of the redeemed, and is specifically entitled "the holy city" in Rev. 21.2. The New Testament gives no indication that Paul wished to visit sites associated with Jesus when he went to Jerusalem. Nevertheless, since his day Christians have often looked to Jerusalem as the place of their foundation, both in the crucifixion and resurrection of Christ and in the coming of the Spirit and the forming of the Church.

Historically, the earthly Jerusalem has been a center for Christian aspirations and **pilgrimage**, as well as a place of tension between Jewish and Islamic ambitions. The importance attached to the earthly Jerusalem by Christians lay at the heart of the Crusades (around 1090–1290), and the city has been at the center of both ideological and physical conflict in the 20th and early 21st centuries. In Christian terms, it not only is an original Eastern patriarchal see, associated with the name of St. James, but also has been a center for other **Oriental Orthodox** Communions and for **Roman Catholics** also.

Anglicans first became officially concerned when a Prussian **Lutheran** plan to found a see jointly with Anglicans led to a **bishop** being **consecrated** for Jerusalem in 1841. (This was a precipitating factor in **John Henry Newman**'s secession to Rome, as, quite apart from the Lutheran participation, the creation of an Anglican bishopric in what he saw as an **Orthodox Church** region appeared to him as straightforward schism, revealing the Church of **England** as uncatholic.) Between 1957 and 1976, the see became a **metropolitan** diocese, as the four individual **dioceses** of the Middle East were grouped into an **archbishopric** with the "archbishop in Jerusalem" at its heart. After 1976, the titles "archbishop" and "archbishopric" were dropped, as a full **province** with slightly different constituent dioceses was formed (entitled the Episcopal Church in **Jerusalem and the Middle East**), and the **primacy** ceased to be attached to the single see. The reorganization included the uniting of the diocese of Jordan, Lebanon, and Syria with the see of Jerusalem; the formation of a diocese of Cyprus and the Gulf; and the recreation of an earlier diocese of **Egypt** (the diocese of the **Sudan** had already separated in 1974 in preparation for its being divided into four dioceses to become a separate province).

Jerusalem enjoys a special affection from Anglicans, and St. George's **Cathedral** and St. George's College in Jerusalem provide foci for pilgrims, scholars, and other visitors from the **Anglican Communion**.

JERUSALEM AND THE MIDDLE EAST. The Anglican **province** of the Holy Land, technically the "Episcopal Church in Jerusalem and the Middle East," includes the four **dioceses** of Cyprus and the Gulf, **Egypt**, **Iran**, and **Jerusalem**. It was formed from the previous "Jerusalem **Archbishopric**" in 1976 and differs from it not only in geography (for **Sudan** became a separate province at that time), but also in having a provincial structure and a **metropolitan** who may be **bishop** of any one of the four dioceses and is not now titled "archbishop."

JESUS CHRIST. Anglicans adhere to the credal **doctrines** of the **Trinity** and **Incarnation** and therefore confess both that Jesus is the eternal Son of **God**, the second of the three persons of the Trinity, and that he was born from the **Holy Spirit** and the Virgin **Mary**, being both God and human, without confusion of the natures or division of the person. These doctrines are set out in the **Creeds** and in Articles II–V of the Thirty-Nine **Articles**. The assertion that he is the sole mediator between God and the human race is set out in many prayers (in which the phrase "our only mediator and advocate" is typical), partly in protest against the pre-**Reformation** tendencies to rely on both the merits and the mediation of the **saints**.

Because he is God, it is appropriate not only to pray "through" him but on occasion to pray "to" him—as is indicated by the historic "Jesus Prayer": "Lord, Jesus Christ, Son of the Living God, have mercy upon us." **Traditional** Anglican examples of this are in the **litany** of the **Book of Common Prayer** (e.g., "By thy baptism, fasting and temptation / Good Lord, deliver us"), in the "Prayer of St. **John** Chrysostom" ("and hast promised that when two or three are gathered together in thy name, thou art there in the midst of them"), and in the **Agnus Dei** ("Jesus, Lamb of God, have mercy on us"). A more modern example is a widely used acclamation within the **eucharistic prayer** (which is otherwise addressed to the Father):

> Dying, you destroyed our death;
> Rising, you restored our life;
> Lord Jesus, come in glory.

JEWEL, JOHN (1522–1571). John Jewel was a fellow of Corpus College, Oxford, when King **Edward VI** came to the throne in 1547. He showed himself a convinced Reformer and able theologian, and therefore in Queen **Mary I**'s reign spent time in exile on the Continent. He returned after Queen **Elizabeth I**'s accession and quickly became **bishop** of Salisbury (1560). Jewel published his major and enduring work, *Apologia Ecclesiae Anglicanae*, in 1562. This was orientated against the claims of the **Roman Catholic Church** and asserted both the freedom of the Church of **England** to reform itself and the actual contrast between the church of the first six centuries and the contemporary realities and claims of the Church of Rome. He was answered by the Romanizing Thomas Harding, and further controversy ensued. Richard Bancroft, **archbishop** of **Canterbury** (1604–1610), later ordered that the *Apologia* be placed in every **parish** church.

JOSEPH OF ARIMATHEA, SAINT. Joseph came from the Judean town of Arimathea (Luke 23.50–51) and was a "prominent member of the sanhedrin" (Mark 15.43). It was he, a secret disciple (John 19.38), who asked for the body of **Jesus** from Pilate (Matt. 27.57–58) and placed it in his own newly constructed tomb. His fame has been enhanced by the late legends in **England** that he came in subsequent years to Glastonbury, bringing with him the Holy Grail, and that he planted at Glastonbury the thorn that bears roses at Christmas. Joseph is commemorated in the **Episcopal Church (United States of America)**'s 1979 **Book of Common Prayer** on 31 July.

JULIAN OF NORWICH (c. 1342–c. 1417). Julian was an anchoress, an English mystic writer whose fame, derived from her *Revelations of Divine Love*, has run on into modern Anglicanism. The *Revelations* were all given to her in May 1373 and were written down soon after. A "Long Text" written perhaps 20 years later includes her own reflections on the *Revelations*. Their interest for modern Anglicans has been heightened because of her readiness to use imagery of motherhood to apply to **Jesus Christ**. She was never **canonized** as a **saint** by the **Roman Catholic Church** and is commonly known as "Mother Julian." There is a shrine to her in Norwich, and she is commemorated on 8 May in the modern **calendars** of the Church of **England** and of some other Anglican **provinces**.

JUSTIFICATION. The Reformers, both on the Continent and in **England**, made much of the cardinal **doctrine** of justification through faith alone—*articulus stantis aut cadentis ecclesiae*, as Martin Luther called it. Its heart was the imputing by **God** of the righteousness of **Jesus Christ** to the sinner who, repenting of his sinfulness, put his trust in Christ. It was the reading of this doctrine in the scriptures that precipitated the 16th-century polarization from **Roman Catholicism**, for the doctrine undercut all doctrines of human merit (whether earned by oneself or transferred from a pool of the merits of **saints**) and all doctrines of mediation by the saints or of **purgatory** and the associated chantry **masses** and payment for indulgences. The Forty-Two **Articles** of 1553 were composed to give central expression to this doctrine, and it is to be found in identical wording deeply enshrined in Articles IX–XVIII of the Thirty-Nine Articles of 1571. Article XI makes reference to the "**Homily** of Justification," which almost certainly means the homily on "Salvation" in the First Book of Homilies, where justification through faith alone is taught with great clarity.

Although the **Council** of **Trent** provided an alternative doctrine of "imparted" righteousness (with the consequence of the possibility of a growth in justification), the Tridentine text and contemporary writings suggest that "justification" was not a usual theological concept among Roman Catholic leaders, and they found themselves having to respond on ground they would not naturally have chosen. The doctrine of imputed righteousness became the great test of belonging to a Church of the Reformation, but Anglicans, although very clearly on the side of the Reformers in the reign of Queen **Elizabeth I**, have at intervals been muted in their affirmation of the doctrine. **Evangelicals** in particular have reveled in the doctrine and have based their **gospel** preaching upon it.

– K –

KEBLE, JOHN (1792–1866). John Keble, the son of a clergyman, became a fellow of Oriel College, Oxford, in 1811 and was **ordained** in 1815. He then did a short **curacy** with his father at Coln St. Aldwyn's near Fairford, but returned to a tutorship at Oriel in 1818. Keble resigned the tutorship in 1823 and went back to the countryside at Southrop. There in 1827 he published his poems, *The Christian Year*, a book that, in its care for the **liturgical** seasons, adumbrated many of the ideals of the **Oxford Movement** and had a part in bringing the movement to birth. Its influence runs on in "Blest Are the Pure in Heart" and other **hymns** that are still sung.

In 1832 Keble was elected professor of poetry at Oxford (a part-time, five-year, appointment), and on 14 July 1833 he preached the Assize sermon "National Apostasy," which is usually treated as having actually given birth to the Oxford Movement. As a mentor also of Isaac Williams and Hurrell Froude, Keble imparted much indirectly as well as directly to the thrust of the movement over the subsequent years. He was a close friend of **John Henry Newman** and was the author of seven of the ***Tracts for the Times***, but as Newman moved toward Rome between the years 1839 and 1845, so Keble buried himself the more in his country **parish** of Hursley, of which he was vicar from 1836 to his death.

Keble's memory is preserved through the foundation in 1870 of Keble College, Oxford, and his name is found on his death day, 29 March, in the **calendars** of some **provinces** of the **Anglican Communion** (but in the Church of **England**, although he was commemorated on that date in the 1980 **Alternative Service** Book calendar, in the **Common Worship** 2000 Book he is listed on 14 July).

KEN, THOMAS (1637–1711). Thomas Ken was **ordained** after the **Restoration** in 1662 and in the next 10 years held three livings and a fellowship of Winchester College. In 1679 he was appointed chaplain to Princess (later Queen) Mary at The Hague. His holiness of life famously came to the notice of King **Charles II** in 1683, when, as a royal chaplain, he declined to offer a room to Nell Gwyn, the king's mistress. Charles then made him in 1684 **bishop** of Bath and Wells, and Ken attended Charles on his deathbed, though the king when dying became a **Roman Catholic**. The **hymns** for which he is famous—notably "Awake, My Soul, and with the Sun" and "Glory to Thee, My God, This Night"—were written prior to his becoming bishop.

Ken was one of the seven bishops who refused the command of King **James II** in 1688 to read the "Declaration of Indulgence," and thus he stood trial with the others for seditious libel—and was duly acquitted by the jury. Nevertheless, like **Archbishop William Sancroft**, he found himself unable in conscience to take the **oath** of allegiance to King **William III** and Queen **Mary II** while James II still lived, and thus became technically a **nonjuror**, for which he was deposed from his see and replaced by Richard Kidder in 1691.

Ken lived for another 20 years in exemplary holiness of life, declining any part in creating a nonjuring Episcopal succession. He is commemorated on 20 March (his death day) in the Church of **England** 1980 **Alternative Service Book**, but on 21 March in the **Episcopal Church (United States of America)**'s 1979 **Book of Common Prayer** and on 8 June in the Church of England **Common Worship calendar** (which commemorates **Cuthbert** on 20 March and **Thomas Cranmer** on 21 March).

KENYA. Johann Ludwig Krapf, sent by the **Church Missionary Society** (CMS) in **London**, was the first Anglican **missionary** to **East Africa**, landing at **Mombasa** in 1844. He provided the first Swahili translations of the New Testament and the **Book of Common Prayer**. CMS sent further missionaries at intervals, though much of their efforts was directed toward the interior, especially **Uganda**. A bishopric of **Eastern Equatorial Africa** was established at Mombasa in 1884, and the first African was **ordained** immediately after. A **diocese** was formed from within it for Uganda in 1897, so it then became the diocese of Mombasa, and it came briefly onto a world stage just before World War I through the **Kikuyu Controversy**. The diocese of Central Tanganyika was formed from it in 1927. The diocese remained the lone diocese for Kenya, under the **Canterbury** jurisdiction, until 1960; at that point it still had a European, Leonard Beecher, as its diocesan bishop, but African assistant bishops had been consecrated in 1955. Anglican Christians were torn by the Mau Mau Uprising that led to independence in 1960, but for the most part resisted the calls for "oathing" in support of the Mau Mau, while looking forward to the end of colonization.

In 1960, new dioceses were created, and these were joined with Tanganyikan dioceses and **Zanzibar** to form the **province** of East Africa, with Beecher as its first **archbishop**. In 1970 Kenya and **Tanzania** separated and a separate Church of the Province of Kenya (CPK) was formed, with Festo Olang as the first archbishop. The province was renamed the Anglican Church of Kenya (ACK) in 1998. By 2002 it had 28 dioceses. Kenyan bishops have been ready to oppose the government of the day, even at risk to themselves. The ACK has also led the way in **liturgical** revision among the African provinces outside of **Southern Africa**; its 1989 **eucharistic** liturgy was used at the inaugural service of the 1998 **Lambeth Conference**, and its full hardback Prayer Book, *Our Modern Services: Anglican Church of Kenya*, was published and authorized in 2002 on the very day that its chief architect, Archbishop David Gitari, retired.

KIKUYU CONTROVERSY. Kikuyu is the name of both a major tribe in the center of **Kenya** and a village within the tribal area. In 1913 a **missionary** conference with an **ecumenical** purpose was held at Kikuyu. It was chaired by J. J. Willis, the Anglican **bishop** of **Uganda**, and W. G. Peel, the bishop of **Mombasa** (i.e., of Kenya), also took part. They, with some of their **clergy**, were constructing, along with **Presbyterians**, **Lutherans**, and other non-Episcopalians, a scheme for federating the different missionary bodies of **East Africa** together to provide a mutual acceptance, a common policy, and even a united structure. At the end of the conference, a **Communion** service was held for all the participants. Though held in a Presbyterian church building, it was a **Book of Common Prayer** service, and Bishop Peel presided at it; all present, except some Quakers, received Communion. These proceedings incurred the wrath of the bishop of **Zanzibar**, **Frank Weston**, whose **Anglo-Catholic** principles were deeply offended by them. He denounced the two Anglican bishops to the **archbishop** of **Canterbury**, **Randall Davidson** (who was **metropolitan** of all three dioceses, as no independent **province** had yet been formed in East Africa). Davidson was clear that no judicial hearing such as might lead to penal action or rebuke was needed, and he personally had little sympathy for Weston's charge that to give any credence or support to non-Episcopal bodies was "propagating **heresy** and committing schism." He declined to convene an Episcopal tribunal, but referred the matter to the **Consultative Body** of the **Lambeth Conference**.

The Consultative Body met in July 1914, and the question of publishing its findings was overtaken by the outbreak of World War I. Finally, Davidson published the findings, along with a lengthy memorandum of his own, in spring 1915. Both the Consultative Body and the archbishop approved the quest for reunion, though indicating that overlooking some features of Anglican identity might have occurred. They also declined to disapprove of the "open" Communion service (for which they were aware there was ample precedent), but thought it best for Anglicans to refrain in the future. The findings of the Consultative Body were pithily summarized by a wit as, "The event at Kikuyu was eminently pleasing to God, and must on no account be repeated."

KINGS. *See* CHARLES I; CHARLES II; EDWARD VI; ENGLAND; HENRY VIII; JAMES I; JAMES II; WILLIAM III. *See also* ELIZABETH I; MARY I; MARY II.

KING JAMES VERSION (KJV). At the **Hampton Court Conference** in 1604, King **James I** yielded to the **Puritans**' request for a new and definitive English version of the **Bible**. Translators' panels were set up, and the New Testament was completed in 1608; the Old Testament (and **Apocrypha**) were published in 1611, the date usually attributed to the complete Bible. It was never actually authorized in any systematic way, but it clearly drove out its predecessors on sheer merit, and within a few years became *the* English Bible. At the **Savoy Conference** in 1661, the Puritans again asked for this version to be made official, and as a result, the Epistles and **Gospels** printed in the 1662 **Book of Common Prayer** were changed to that version, and soon after the wording on the title page of the Bible became "Appointed to be read in Churches." It was regularly known (though without apparent basis) as the "Authorized Version" until the second half of the 20th century. This latter period saw a gradual transition in its popular name, particularly outside Britain, to "King James Version."

KOREA. The first recorded **missionary** work of Anglicans in Korea is that of **Bishop** Charles Corfe, who was **consecrated** in **England** on **All Saints**' Day 1889 and arrived at Inchon, Korea, in 1890 with a medical doctor who opened a hospital. The **Society for the Propagation of the Gospel** made a small grant, and other missionaries followed, including members of **religious communities**. The earliest converts were **Japanese**, as Japanese literature was available, and the first Koreans were **baptized** in 1897. After Corfe's death in 1904, a succession of expatriate bishops followed. The first Korean to be **ordained** was Mark Kim, ordained as **presbyter** in 1915. A **cathedral** was under construction at Seoul from the 1920s until 1962. The **diocese** was torn and weakened by both World War II and the Korean War of 1950–1953. However, in 1965 it was divided into two, Seoul and Taejon, and the first Korean bishop, Paul Lee, became bishop of Seoul. The last English bishop, Richard Rutt, became bishop of Taejon in 1967 and remained until the diocese was divided into Pusan and Taejon in 1974; Korean bishops were consecrated for each of these two resultant dioceses. The three dioceses were formed into a **province**, the Anglican Church in Korea, in April 1992.

– L –

LAITY. While a point often made by purists is that the whole church, without exception, is the *laos*—the people of **God**—for most practical and **canonical** purposes, the laity are all the people of God *except* those **ordained**. Because the independence of the Church of **England** from Rome and its doctrinal **Reformation** were both effected by the monarch in Parliament, it was possible for 300 years to claim that the laity exercised in the houses of Lords and Commons a strong national control of the Church. The role of the **Convocations** of **clergy** was in fact much less substantial, not least because the Convocations were suspended for long periods, and they were in any case subject to Parliament. Nevertheless, the traditions of the Church of England were for hundreds of years to give no place in local church government to the laity, save only the longstanding office of **wardens**. But step by step in the 19th and 20th centuries, there came church councils of clergy and lay representatives at **parish** levels, and these were matched in the coming of **diocesan** and **provincial** **synods**. The development of these synods around the world has seen the constitution of a "chamber" (or "house") of lay representatives to sit in synods alongside **bishops** and other **clergy**. In two notable cases, namely the **Episcopal Church (United States of America)** and the Church of **Ireland**, the lay representatives do not form a third house but sit jointly with the clergy in a single House of Deputies or

Representatives (though the pattern of joint membership differs greatly as between the two Churches). Similarly, since the 19th century there has come into being a whole series of authorized "lay **ministries**," varying from one province to another, such as **readers**, **catechists**, **evangelists**, parish workers, and **deaconesses**. *See also* LAY PRESIDENCY.

LAMBETH. *See* LAMBETH PALACE.

LAMBETH ARTICLES. In 1595 **Archbishop John Whitgift** held a small conference at **Lambeth Palace** and then issued nine **Articles** relating to **justification** and, particularly, to "double predestination"—the assertion that the elect are predestined to **heaven** and the nonelect are predestined to damnation. The purpose of these Articles was not that they should become confessional, but rather that they should end a dispute raging in the University of Cambridge where an avowedly Arminian preacher had attacked the predominant Calvinism on the grounds that it was wholly incompatible with Anglicanism. Whitgift's Articles were intended as an assertion of the allowability of Calvinist teaching in the Church of **England**, and his covering letter to the heads of the colleges stated that they were to be taken as "propositions . . . not as laws and decrees." They were treasured thereafter by the **Puritans** and were cited at the **Hampton Court Conference** in 1604. They may also have had an effect on the **Irish Articles** of 1615.

LAMBETH COMMISSION. In October 2003 the **archbishop** of **Canterbury**, **Rowan Williams**, who had been in office 10 months, convened an emergency meeting of the **primates** to consider the impending **consecration** of Gene Robinson, a man in an openly **homosexual** relationship, as **bishop** of New Hampshire in the **Episcopal Church (United States of America)**. Robinson's election by the **diocese** and the confirmation of that election by the **General Convention** in August 2003 posed a vast problem for the **Anglican Communion**. Were the provinces now by mere silence to connive at an Episcopal lifestyle that directly undercut the principles expressed so strongly in Resolution I.10 of the 1998 **Lambeth Conference**? The New Hampshire election raised not only first-order questions about sexual morality and the exemplary character of the **episcopate**

but also major consequential questions about how a Communion of 38 autonomous **provinces** can hold together when so divided about a first-order question.

At the emergency meeting, the primates concluded that at least one further effort should be made to find a unitive way forward. Thus, at the request of the meeting, the archbishop of Canterbury established an international Lambeth Commission under the chairmanship of Robin Eames, archbishop of **Armagh**, to consider issues of holding the Communion together (rather than to rule directly on issues of sexual morality). The consecration of Robinson as bishop of New Hampshire duly occurred on 2 November 2003, so the task of the commission became urgent.

The commission included 17 members from 14 provinces, plus staff members and assistants. It met in February, June, and September 2004 and then reported in October 2004 to a further meeting of the primates. After its first meeting, it asked for all members of the Communion to avoid strident language until they had reported. The report was published by the **Anglican Consultative Council** as *The* ***Windsor Report*** *2004* on 18 October 2004.

LAMBETH CONFERENCE. A Lambeth Conference is a meeting of **bishops** of the **Anglican Communion**, invited by the **archbishop** of **Canterbury** to meet together in conference. Such meetings originated in the request of the bishops of the ecclesiastical **province** of **Canada** to Archbishop Charles Longley in 1865 to convene an authoritative meeting of bishops of the Communion mainly in order to pass judgment on the bishop of Natal, **William Colenso**, who had earlier been declared to be deprived of his see for teaching **heresy**, by a sentence passed on him by Archbishop Robert Gray of Cape Town. Colenso had been restored to his see on appeal to the Judicial Committee of the Privy Council in **London**, which had ruled that, for technical reasons, Gray had no jurisdiction to deprive Colenso. This created a worldwide outcry, leading to the Canadian request for stronger ecclesiastical pressure upon Colenso and consequent relief for Gray, who, if the see of Natal were declared vacant, would be in position to **consecrate** a successor.

Longley hesitated, but ultimately agreed—but with the proviso that the bishops must not discuss Natal nor pretend to be able to give rulings about it! This first conference then met at **Lambeth Palace** in August 1867, although it was boycotted by several English bishops who feared it would in fact discuss and condemn Colenso—a fear wholly justified by events. The Lambeth Conference took its name from its venue, and all such gatherings have been called "Lambeth Conferences" ever since, even when they have met in Canterbury, as has been the practice since 1978.

Archbishop Longley was clear from the start that this was not a legislative or **synodical** body, but a personal gathering of bishops for interchange of ideas and experience and for mutual support. Thus, while it has become the practice for Lambeth Conferences to issue statements and pass resolutions, such findings have no binding power on any province unless or until the particular province adopts them itself by synodical or comparable process.

Because the membership of the conference is formed by personal invitation from the archbishop, each succeeding archbishop has had discretion as to whom he should invite. In the first 100 years of such conferences, the archbishop's invitation was the chief indicator as to which church bodies around the world were or were not considered member churches of the Anglican Communion. The archbishop's discretion has also meant that, until 1998, **suffragan** and assistant bishops were not all invited, but only a proportion of them. In 1978 Archbishop **Donald Coggan** invited bishops to bring their wives (who then and in the following conferences formed a separate conference of their own alongside the men). In 1988 Archbishop **Robert Runcie** invited the members of the **Anglican Consultative Council** (ACC) to join the conference. In 1998 Archbishop **George Carey** invited all serving bishops of the whole Communion to come, which had never happened before. By then there were 11 **women bishops**, and so a few husbands came too, to join what was now the "spouses' conference." It has been regular practice, at least since 1968, to have theological and ecumenical guests participate also.

The general rhythm has been to hold a Lambeth Conference every 10 years, though this pattern was disturbed in the 20th century by both world wars. This disturbing led to the sequence: 1908, 1920, 1930, 1948, and every ten years thereafter. At intervals, especially notable statements or decisions have been registered at the conferences, such as the **Lambeth Quadrilateral** (first articulated in 1888), the "Call to All Christian People" in 1920, and the call for a Decade of **Evangelism** in 1988. It is not known at the time of one Lambeth Conference whether or when there will be another—there is no standing rule about meeting every 10 years, and the holding of each conference stems from a separate new decision, usually made by the archbishop of Canterbury of the time after taking wide soundings across the Communion. The next Lambeth Conference is being planned for 2008, and a great departure from precedent lay in the original hope that it would be held in Cape Town, **South Africa**. As the conference was intended to be accompanied by a great **Pan-Anglican Congress**, it became hard to see how to hold it in South Africa, and it will be in England as previously.

LAMBETH CONSULTATIVE BODY. The **Lambeth Conference** of 1897 in its resolution 5 initiated a Consultative Body of **bishops** from around the **Anglican Communion**, to advise the **archbishops** of **Canterbury** on the agenda and character of further Lambeth Conferences. The role was to be purely advisory. The body was consolidated at the 1908 Lambeth Conference, and it was to that body that Archbishop **Randall Davidson** referred the **Kikuyu Controversy** in 1913. Its composition and role were affirmed and further regulated at the 1920 and 1930 Lambeth Conferences. However, it appears to have had no further role in later conferences. These have since World War II been organized by *ad hoc* planning groups, appointed separately for each conference and since 1968 serviced first by the **executive officer** of the Anglican Communion and then (after 1978) by the **secretary-general** of the **Anglican Consultative Council**.

LAMBETH PALACE. The **London** residence of the **archbishops** of **Canterbury** has since medieval times been Lambeth Palace, an imposing building at the south end of Lambeth Bridge. The building itself began as Lambeth Manor, which was acquired (by an exchange for the Convent of Rochester) by Archbishop Hubert Walter in 1197. The crypt may still contain 12th-century work, and the Great Hall and the Chapel have remains from the extension undertaken by the archbishops in the 13th century. The name gradually changed over the centuries, being first Lambeth House and then Lambeth Palace.

This latter title was regularized from the time of Archbishop William Howley's major renovations and extension in the 1830s.

The sheer accident of being the place of residence of archbishops has rendered the name "Lambeth" into a code name for the activities or policies of archbishops of Canterbury—so that it is possible to speak, for example, of the "views of Lambeth." That identification led by association to the name "**Lambeth Conference**" for the major **bishops**' conferences convened by the archbishops (a term used even when a Lambeth Conference is held in Canterbury), and this in turn has transferred the shorthand title "Lambeth" for the corporate activities or mind of the bishops assembled such a conference (e.g., a "Lambeth Resolution" or "Lambeth report"). While archbishops of Canterbury had a string of residences at the time of the **Reformation**, now they have only the Old Palace at Canterbury and Lambeth Palace in London.

LAMBETH QUADRILATERAL. The Lambeth Quadrilateral is a text that is sometimes called the "Chicago-Lambeth Quadrilateral," a title that betrays its origins. The **General Convention** of the **Protestant Episcopal Church in the United States of America**, meeting in Chicago in 1886, set out four points that it viewed as the basic requirements to be met by any other denominations desiring to enter into union with Anglicans:

1. the holy scriptures of the Old and New Testament as the revealed word of **God**
2. the **Nicene Creed** as the sufficient statement of the Christian faith
3. the two **sacraments**—**baptism** and the **supper of the Lord**—ministered with unfailing use of Christ's words of institution and of the **elements** ordained by him
4. the **historic episcopate** locally adapted

This text was then introduced to the 1888 **Lambeth Conference**, and, with tiny amendments—such as the clarification in (1) that the Holy Scriptures are "the rule and ultimate standard of faith" and the addition of the **Apostles' Creed** to (2)—was there reaffirmed for worldwide Anglicanism. It thus became known as the "Lambeth Quadrilateral." It was later reaffirmed at the Lambeth Conferences of 1920, 1948, 1958, and 1998.

The only significant change in that time has been that later versions phrased (4) as "a **ministry** acknowledged by every part of the church as possessing not only the inward call of the Spirit but also the commission of Christ and the **authority** of the whole body"—but then immediately claimed that only the historic episcopate would be found to satisfy this condition. The 1998 conference, however, reaffirmed 1888 "as a basis on which Anglicans seek the full, visible unity of the Church and also recognizes it as a statement of Anglican unity and identity." The actual church unions in **North India**, **South India**, **Pakistan**, and **Bangladesh**; the **Porvoo** Common Statement; and the concordats with **Lutherans** in the **United States** and **Canada** have kept the quadrilateral steadily in view, though in each case provision (4) has been expounded and implemented in slightly varying ways. *See also* HUNTINGTON, WILLIAM REED.

LANG, COSMO GORDON (1864–1945). Cosmo Lang was the son of a Scottish manse. He read for the Bar, but was **confirmed** at the age of 25 and then **ordained** in 1890. He became vicar of Portsea in 1896, **suffragan bishop** of Stepney in 1901, and **archbishop** of **York** in 1909. In 1928 he was translated to be archbishop of **Canterbury**, where his **ministry** was marked by the problems in the wake of the defeat of the 1927–1928 **Book of Common Prayer** revisions in Parliament, by the **Lambeth Conference** of 1930, by the abdication crisis of 1936 (in which he was reckoned to have played a decisive role), by the **coronation** of King George VI and Queen Elizabeth in 1937, and by the coming of World War II in 1939. He resigned in 1942 after 34 years as an archbishop. He was the first archbishop of Canterbury since the **Reformation** to wear a miter.

LANGUAGES. It was a starting principle of the reformed Church of **England** that it is contrary to the word of **God** to address people or lead them in prayer in a language they do not understand (see the preface to 1552 **Book of Common Prayer**, reproduced as "Concerning the Service of the Church" at the beginning of the 1662 Book of Common Prayer—and cf. Article XXIV of the Thirty-Nine **Articles**). Hence from the earliest stages of providing new **liturgical** forms, the English language was in use for these forms, and the 1549 Prayer Book, which was entirely in English, virtually spelled the end of the

Latin language in **parish** churches. Parliament was slower to address minority needs (and the West Country rebellion against the 1549 Book included among its alleged grievances the complaint that Cornish people did not understand English), but in 1662 the **Act of Uniformity** required that the Book be translated into **Welsh**, for the benefit of the four Welsh **dioceses** in the **province** of **Canterbury**. The Prayer Books of 1559 and 1662 were also both translated into Latin at an early stage (for use at the universities and other places of learning), and the Thirty-Nine Articles of 1571 (which were not part of public worship) were issued in English and Latin together, with the two languages being equally authoritative. Translations of successive Prayer Books into French, for the Channel Islands, also followed, but translating into Irish appears to have been totally neglected.

As the **Anglican Communion** spread around the world, so translation of first the **Bible** and then the Prayer Book (and sometimes English hymnbooks) into local **vernacular** languages had a high priority in the program of **evangelizing** and might well be presented as the chief Anglican concession to the principle of **inculturation**. In some parts of the world, a province may contain several language groups, and then the work of its **synod** and provincial committees may well be conducted in English; thus the liturgy of the Church of **South India** was first compiled in English in 1948–1950, and the 2002 **Kenya** Prayer Book was available only in English for a substantial period after publication. However, in **Tanzania** the **eucharistic** liturgy was compiled in Swahili from the start, and an English-language text had to follow later. In **Wales** and other provinces, liturgy is published in two languages facing each other on left and right pages of books or booklets; in the province of **Aotearoa**, New Zealand, and Polynesia, all English texts are sprinkled with Maori interjections and responses (so as to assist worshippers to become bilingual); in the **Episcopal Church (United States of America)**, the 1979 Book is officially published in three separate editions—English, French, and Spanish; and in **Southern Africa**, the 1989 Book was published from the start in six languages, and others followed soon after.

There is a word, *glossai,* in the Greek of the New Testament that may be translated equally as "languages" or "**tongues**." The exercise of "the gift of tongues" in Anglican worship has been a feature of the **Charismatic Movement**.

LATIMER, HUGH (c. 1485–1555). Hugh Latimer was **ordained** as a **priest** around 1515 and held for years to an unreformed theology as a fellow of Clare Hall, Cambridge. He himself stated that he was then brought to a biblical faith around 1524 through Thomas Bilney making his confession to him and telling him his own story. His support of King **Henry VIII**'s case for putting away Catherine of Aragon won him favor with the king, and after the split from Rome he was made **bishop** of Worcester in 1535. Latimer's unashamedly **Protestant** stance brought him into opposition to the Act of the Six **Articles** in 1539, and he resigned his see, after which he was held in such suspicion that in 1546 he was imprisoned. Latimer was released on King **Edward VI**'s succession and became a famous reformed preacher. When Queen **Mary I** succeeded in 1553, he was again arrested and imprisoned; and in due course, having consistently denied the **doctrines** of the **mass**, he was condemned to death for **heresy** and was burned at the stake outside the north wall of the city of Oxford on 16 October 1555. **Nicholas Ridley** was burned beside him, and Latimer's last words were "Fear not, Master Ridley, and play the man, and we shall by God's grace light such a beacon this day in England as I trust shall never be put out." He is commemorated jointly with Ridley in many **calendars** on 16 October.

LAUD, WILLIAM (1573–1645). William Laud was **ordained** as a **deacon** in 1600 and a **presbyter** in 1601, gained his doctorate of divinity in 1608 for a thesis on the divine right of **episcopacy**, and became president of St. John's College, Oxford, in 1611 and (in plurality) **dean** of Gloucester in 1616. In this latter appointment he moved the main **Communion table** back against the east wall, a hint of future actions to come. His theological and monarchist position matched the concerns of first King **James I** and then King **Charles I**, and he became in turn **bishop** of St. David's (1621), Bath and Wells (1626), and **London** (1628). In his London post, he exercised in effect the role of the **archbishop** of **Canterbury**, while the actual holder of the office, George Abbot, was under a cloud through inadvertently shooting his gamekeeper (Abbot was also a **Puritan** by conviction, which was unwelcome to the Stuart kings). When Abbot died in 1633, Laud succeeded him and immediately began a two-year **metropolitical** visitation of his **province**, the main purpose of which was to bring good order to the **parishes** and to reform the lax ways of many **cathedrals**. His requirement to bring Communion tables back against the east wall was characteristic of the visitation and increased Puritan suspicion of him.

One of Laud's last initiatives was to attempt to get the **Convocation** in 1640 to revise the existing **canons**, mostly in the direction of strictness and orderliness. When the English Civil War supervened, he was imprisoned in the Tower of London and subjected to a long trial for treason. As it appeared that the charges might not stick, he was instead attainted by Parliament and condemned to death by Act of Parliament. Laud was executed in January 1645. His style of churchmanship and theology has passed into history as that of the "Laudian" school.

LAY. *See* LAITY; LAY PRESIDENCY.

LAY PRESIDENCY. It was axiomatic at the time of the **Reformation** that the officiant at the **eucharist** would be an **ordained presbyter**. Although the understanding of the eucharist itself was drastically changed, so that the presbyter was no longer to be viewed as a **priest** offering the sacrifice of the **mass**, yet the discipline was unchanged, and **ordination** conferred the power and duty to officiate. As all discipline in the reigns of King **Edward VI** and Queen **Elizabeth I** was tight, covering matters of great and small importance alike, it is difficult to discern whether matters of substantial theological weight or of relative indifference underlay the individual requirements or prohibitions of the Elizabethan Settlement. If the Reformers were not driven by medieval mass theology, they were nevertheless confident that the **clergy** held responsibility for "word and **sacraments**." The particular discipline was reinforced by the **Act of Uniformity** of 1662, which was enforcing Episcopal ordination for those who had been ordained by other (e.g., presbyteral) methods during the **Commonwealth** period. The Act imposed a penalty of £100 upon any who, without Episcopal ordination, presumed to **consecrate** the **elements** of **bread** and wine for **Communion**. In the process, the Act made very clear that no **layperson** could **preside** at the eucharist. As the **Presbyterians** also had a high **doctrine** of ministerial **authority** (though without a requirement of Episcopal ordination), it appears that the ministerial presidency of the eucharist was common ground between them and Anglicans. This was certainly consistent with the Puritan opposition to lay **baptism**, which had been considered at the **Hampton Court Conference** and had been met by a change in the **rubrics** for private (or emergency) baptism of infants in the 1604 **Book of Common Prayer**.

This position is further confirmed by the practice of **John Wesley** in the mid-18th century. When he gave responsibilities to laypeople in his societies far beyond anything for which there was precedent in Anglicanism (including being preachers and class leaders), he was very clear that, despite all pressures from them, he gave them no authority to preside at the eucharist. It was only after his death that the conference gave them such authority, and it did so by treating them as **ministers**.

Within the Church of **England**, there is no evidence of any groundswell in favor of lay presidency in the 18th and 19th centuries. The **Evangelicals** were not usually seeking frequent Communion; in England Anglicanism, high or low, was generally clericalist; and in overseas church planting, it was generally assumed that the provision of regular Communion would be a feature of a fully developed church life, which was neither urged on converts quickly nor expected to occur in the first few decades of **missionary** work in most areas. Part of the task of pioneer **bishops** was to assess both the possibilities of importing more expatriate clergy from England and the propriety and timetable for ordaining local Christians. Lay presidency was never part of such planning. The rise of the **Anglo-Catholic** movement after 1833 simply confirmed the existing pattern—lay presidency was not so much rejected as never considered.

The second half of the 20th century saw the issue very slowly emerge and be identified. Anglicanism had seen a rise in sacramental expectations at the same time as, in many places, both a fall in readily available clergy and a rise in responsible lay leadership. The resurgence of evangelicalism slowly allowed the question to be reopened. A first public engagement with it was in the **General Synod** of the **province** of the **Southern Cone of South America** in 1986, when a request from the **dioceses** of Chile and of Peru with Bolivia that would have allowed them to authorize lay presidency of the eucharist in certain defined circumstances was defeated by eight votes to seven. It was not allowed into the report of the 1988 **Lambeth Conference**, which listed local ordained clergy and "communion by extension" as the ways to meet a need of providing Communion in areas short of clergy.

Lay presidency was vigorously debated in principle by the diocesan **synod** of the **Sydney** diocese in the Anglican Church in **Australia** in 1983 and 1994, and it was accepted in principle in 1999, but was then vetoed by the **archbishop** of Sydney, on behalf of retaining relationships with the rest of Australia and with other churches of the **Anglican Communion**. The process was broadly repeated in 2003 and 2004, with a new archbishop, and the issue was restated in a formulation that no action would be taken against any presbyter who provided for lay presidency in his parish. There was, however, a determination by an appellate tribunal that the Sydney diocese had no legal basis for taking such action independently of the General Synod and of the national constitution of the Anglican Church in Australia.

In the province of **Southern Africa**, a diocesan working party in the Cape Town diocese in the late 1990s recommended carefully controlled lay presidency for areas without sufficient clergy, but neither the diocese nor the province has acted on it.

In the Church of England, a private member's motion in the General Synod in 1994 asked the House of Bishops to state the theological reasons why eucharistic presidency was limited to bishops and presbyters. The House of Bishops got this amended to a request for a general statement on eucharistic presidency, and they then commissioned a theological investigation. The results of the study were published as *Eucharistic Presidency* in 1997, but it was not made the subject of resolutions in the General Synod. The report states that the restriction of eucharistic presidency to bishops and presbyters is entirely appropriate and also unitive, but it does not go as far as to say it is theologically revealed or absolutely necessary.

LAY READER. *See* READER.

LAYPERSON. A member of the **laity**, as distinct from the **clergy**. *See also* READER.

LECTERN. A lectern is the stand upon which a **Bible** is placed for reading in public in church. It has no prescribed shape, but is often in the form of a brass eagle with the Bible on its spread wings.

LECTIONARY. A lectionary is the provision for an ordered reading of the scriptures through the year, often with a course of psalmody included as a separate provision. It presupposes an ordered ecclesiastical **calendar** into which the appropriate (or "**proper**") readings are fitted. **Thomas Cranmer** was determined that the church should read through whole books of the Bible in sequence, and from the 1549 **Book of Common Prayer** onward, he provided at **Morning and Evening Prayer** for this to be done on a daily basis through the calendar year, without distinction of Sundays. For **Communion**, he retained the somewhat arbitrary and excerptive pre-**Reformation** pattern of unconnected Epistle and **Gospel** readings. In the 20th century, lectionaries were produced that distinguished between Sunday courses of readings and midweek ones and, by relating to the church year rather than the civil year, enabled high seasons to be properly **celebrated**. The centrality of the **eucharist** in weekly worship was more emphasized as the century moved on, and this led to a desire both for the inclusion of readings from the Old Testament in the eucharistic lectionary and for a more coherent rationale for the overall pattern of readings. Many Anglican **provinces** now use for Sunday eucharistic provision the three-year "Revised Common Lectionary," itself adapted from the post–**Vatican II** usage of the **Roman Catholic Church**. *See also* COLLECT.

LENT. Lent takes its origin in ancient preparation periods leading to **Easter baptisms**, but the discipline by which all the people of God **fasted**, prayed, and studied along with the candidates led to the period being institutionalized as a basic in the church's year. The 40 days of **Jesus**' temptation came to provide the model from the fourth century on, although initially the Sundays were not counted as fast days (for, *qua* Sundays, they *had* to be **feast** days) and the 40 days were thus six weeks of six weekdays each and four more at the beginning, meaning that Lent started on a Wednesday—**Ash Wednesday**. Lent has been popularly associated with fasting, self-discipline, and self-examination, though Anglican **provinces** have tended to affirm those principles only generally, leaving the outworkings of them to the individual. The development of **liturgical** themes through the season has begun with the temptations of Jesus, but has then tended more to follow his footsteps on the way to **Jerusalem** rather than to continue on themes of temptation. Thus the Sunday before Easter is Palm Sunday, highlighting Jesus' triumphal entry into Jerusalem prior to the events leading to his arrest, trial, and crucifixion.

Other features of the liturgical observance of Lent do emphasize its penitential character, especially in more **Anglo-Catholic** parts of the **Anglican Communion**. Ash Wednesday, the first day of Lent, has traditionally been associated with penitence and self-humiliation (portrayed in the **imposition of ashes**). The liturgical **color** of the season has been purple, though an alternative "Lenten array" is made up of unbleached linen. The widespread veiling of the **cross** in church buildings has typified the manner of observing the major penitential season of the church year. *See also* COMMINATION.

LIBERALISM. Anglicanism has at most periods of its existence, at least since 1689, incorporated an element of enabling and encouraging individuals to think for themselves. Such freedom has not infrequently taken people right up to the edge of orthodoxy and over it, but the general run of Anglican life has tended to unite an interest in fairly closely defined **doctrinal** formulations with a sustained distaste for closely executed discipline, let alone for **heresy** trials. So the Latitudinarians of the late 17th century were the forebears of the liberal theologians of the 19th century. It was the liberalism the **Tractarians** thought they detected being imported from Germany in the 1820s and 1830s, and found exemplified in the writings of Thomas Arnold, that led to the very conservative backlash of their own **Oxford Movement**. The challenge was greatly increased by the publication and impact of Charles Darwin's *On the Origin of Species* (1859). This was followed by the court cases in England in relation to *Essays and Reviews* (1860) and to the famous **William Colenso** controversy in **South Africa** (1863–1865). The polarization was increased over the following years—a trend that in time led to the flurries of the Scopes "monkey" trial in Tennessee in 1928 and the reaction into "creationism." Liberalism is also associated with universalism, a "social gospel," a relativist or situationist view of ethics, and a determined undogmaticism.

LIBERATION THEOLOGY. Liberation theology is a fruit of **Roman Catholic** theologians, chiefly in South America, theologizing from the position of the poor and oppressed and expounding the scriptures from the position of such commitment. It is experiential, not scholastic, concerned with praxis not theory. And it is socialistic, egalitarian, and in principle revolutionary. While Anglicans in South America have been strong neither numerically nor in popularist theology, many of the ideas of the liberation theologians have helped sustain Anglicans in struggles elsewhere—as, for instance, against apartheid in **South Africa** and against racism, colonialism, xenophobia, and *laissez-faire* theologies in other places.

LIMA. Lima is the capital of Peru and was the venue in 1981 for the **World Council of Churches** (WCC) "Faith and Order" Conference, which issued the definitive **ecumenical** text, *Baptism, Eucharist, and Ministry* (1982). This was the culmination of a lengthy international ecumenical process, and the statement was sent to every member Church of the WCC with a request to respond as to whether each particular Church could identify its own **doctrinal** stance within the agreed text. The text is often denoted by the simple title "Lima" without qualification. In the years subsequent to its publication, it passed into regular ecumenical usage, both because the requirement to respond to the text stirred discussion in the participant churches and also because the actual themes treated in the text ran close to the contents of much ecumenical dialogue and became a clear point of reference for such dialogues. Resolution IV.12 of the 1998 **Lambeth Conference** urged that liturgical revision around the **Anglican Communion** should be consonant with ecumenical texts such as Lima.

Associated with the same conference is the "Lima **Liturgy**," an ecumenical **eucharistic** liturgy, composed for the Conference, which deliberately develops the themes of **baptism**, eucharist, and **ministry** as the core themes within its text. This has been used since that time at specific ecumenical occasions, including assemblies of the WCC.

LITANY. A litany is a form of responsive prayer, structured so that a developing series of main petitions spoken or chanted by a leader or a series of leaders is punctuated by a repeated response by the congregation. The three-line lead-in to worship, "Lord, have mercy," "Christ, have mercy," "Lord, have mercy," is often known as the "Lesser Litany," while the full litany of the 16th- and 17th-century **Books of Common Prayer** can be traced back to medieval forms and to the first-ever English-language **liturgical** text, the Litany of 1544, composed by **Thomas Cranmer** and issued in the latter years of King **Henry VIII**'s reign (on the occasion of his undertaking war in France). In this latter text, the lengthy catalog of **saints** and **martyrs**, who in the previous Latin "Litany of the Saints" had been asked one by one to pray for us, was reduced to three petitions only. By the time of the 1549 **Book of Common Prayer**, they had been wholly elided. A notable feature of the 1544 text, which was preserved in 1549 and 1552 but dropped in 1559, was the petition "From the tyranny of the Bishop of Rome, and all his detestable enormities, Good Lord, deliver us." In modern Anglican worship books, a litany in direct descent from Cranmer's 1549–1552 one is often still in use, its tradition being both penitential and petitionary. The older Prayer Books provided for its use on **Sundays**, Wednesdays, and Fridays, and it formed and usually still forms a main feature of the intercessions at **ordinations**. Variant forms of litany are also to be found within the options for the intercessions in the **eucharist** and in other places of liturgical prayer.

LITURGICAL MOVEMENT. "Liturgical Movement" is a title used first in **Roman Catholicism** to denote a growing tide of concern to make the **liturgy** intelligible, participatory, and authentic, with a view to the nurturing of the people of **God** and the building up of each congregation as an actual community of love. The movement had roots in the post-Napoleonic recovery of Catholicism in France, in particular the restoration of Gregorian chant at Solemnes by Dom Guéranger in the 1830s. However, its clear continuity as a "movement" can best be traced to the encyclicals of **Pope** Pius X, namely one in 1903 (his first year in office) in which he called for "praying the liturgy" rather than "praying at the liturgy," and another in 1905 in which he called for more frequent reception of **Communion**. Another pivotal point in the early emergence of the movement has been identified as the Church Congress at Malines in 1909, when a young monk, Lambert Beauduin, read a paper on the renewal of the church through the liturgy and followed it up in 1914 with his book *La Piété de l'Eglise* (which included a call for the liturgy to be made available in **vernacular** languages—although this should not be misunderstood, as it was not at that point a call for **celebrating** in any vernacular but only for the provision of translations that the people could follow alongside the Latin in the public texts).

It appears that during and after World War I, the momentum for such change was generated and sustained centrally through the **monasteries** at Maria Laach in the Rhineland of Germany and at Mont Cesar in Louvain, Belgium. The persons whose names are associated with these centers, Odo Casel and Beauduin, respectively, communicated with the **parishes** rather at the level of ideas through academic journals than through actual changes in the liturgy as celebrated. By the 1930s and 1940s, however, the movement was affecting actual worship in several parts of Europe—here with new styles of **architecture**, there with "dialogue masses," elsewhere with "**Bible** services." Pope Pius XII (1939–1958) began reforms of **Holy Week** and relaxed the rules on **fasting** Communion, and then Pope John XXIII (1958–1963) convened **Vatican II**, and vast reforms sprang from that, fostered by the 60 years of preparation that had preceded it. The Constitution on the Sacred Liturgy was the first and the most far-reaching of the documents of Vatican II.

In various ways in various parts of the world, Anglicans have borrowed and benefited from the Roman Catholic groundwork. The desire to bring word and **sacrament** together (and to bring parents and children together also) probably generated the Anglican Parish Communion (traceable to St. John's, Newcastle upon Tyne, in December 1927), and did so as a purely Anglican and largely practical move. But Gabriel Hebert's book *Liturgy and Society* (1935) is usually viewed as having brought the thinking of the Continental Roman Catholic pioneers into the bloodstream of Anglicans, not least through its being written in English. The upshot, perhaps better known as the "Parish Communion Movement," has still had a lower intellectual profile than the Roman Catholic Liturgical Movement, but it has had greater freedom to act first and theologize later. It was reinforced in its early stages by the comprehensive symposium edited by Hebert, *The Parish Communion* (1937).

The latter half of the 20th century saw enormous changes in the worshipping face of Anglicanism, as a central rite of Holy Communion became basic to the Sunday morning worship in a high proportion of Anglican parishes that had a **presbyter** available to **preside**.

The collapse of the (Rome-inspired) fasting Communion enabled whole congregations to receive Communion at a more reasonable hour; Communion **tables** were pulled forward, while presiding **ministers** took up "**westward position**"; **laypeople** began to read the scripture passages, lead the intercessions, and distribute the **elements**. Ritual become simpler, and architecture (including the reordering of church interiors) tended to look for congregational worship to be "in the round" or somewhat nearer to it. This patterning was also assisted by the sharing of the **Peace**, which became more and more popular from the late 1960s on. New **eucharistic** texts both reflected and prompted such changes, with ever less emphasis upon the necessity of reading through the service from the authorized book and more emphasis on so using varied resources as to construct rites that would be pastorally helpful, in the local context, and would be so used as to develop the people both in spirituality and in their sense of **mission**.

LITURGY. "Liturgy" is a word of Greek roots (*leitourgia*, meaning "service") and exhibiting some of the ambiguity of the English word "service." In the New Testament, it is used, in its verbal form, to mean "worshipping," in Acts 13.2; in its noun form, to mean a "servant/minister," in Phil. 2.25 and Heb. 1.7; and in a verbal noun form (cf. Phil. 2.31) to mean "service" in broad terms. In Christian history it has come to mean a pattern, program, or prescribed form of congregational worship, and whereas its use would at first sight apply to any such worship event, in some traditions it has been used without qualification almost exclusively to mean a **eucharistic** liturgy. Thus the "Liturgy of St. John Chrysostom" means the eucharistic liturgy, and, where such conventions exist, other liturgical forms have to be distinguished from this core usage by qualifying words, as, for example, "**marriage** liturgy."

In the reformed Church of **England**, in the 16th and 17th centuries the whole usage of the word "liturgy" was in the broader sense, usually referring to the whole **Book of Common Prayer**. This is well illustrated in the opening lines of the preface to the 1662 Book, which begins: "It hath been the wisdom of the Church of England, ever since the first compiling of her Publick Liturgy . . . ." More recently, the ancient usage, by which "liturgy" means "eucharistic liturgy" (unless otherwise specified), has become more frequent in Anglican circles.

LIVINGSTONE, DAVID (1813–1873). David Livingstone was born in **Scotland** and from the age of 20 was sure he was called to the work of a **missionary** doctor. He duly qualified in both medicine and theology, was **ordained** as a **Congregationalist minister** in 1840, and, after some difference of view as to where he should serve, was sent by the London Missionary Society to South Africa. He then spent 32 years mixing in his life a preaching of the **gospel**, a planting of medical missions, an impassioned opposition to the slave trade, and a sheer urge for pioneer exploration (with a view to these other ends)—a combination that took him over all the lands from the Cape to Lake Tanganyika, before he died to the west of Lake Nyasa in what is now **Zambia** at the age of 60. Himself a Congregationalist, his impact on Anglican missions was most directly that the **Universities Mission to Central Africa** (UMCA) was founded in response to his appeal. Less directly, his impact on H. M. Stanley (whose famous "Doctor Livingstone, I presume?" came when he unearthed Livingstone at Ujiji in 1871) had far-reaching results. It led to Stanley's appeal for the **Church Missionary Society** (CMS) to send missionaries to Buganda (in what is now **Uganda**) in the 1870s, to which **Alexander Mackay** responded and from which the conversion of a large proportion of the population stemmed.

LONDON. London was the administrative capital of the Roman colony of Britain, being located at the most convenient river crossing for connecting north and south. As Christianity entered Britain, probably through relatively obscure Christians serving in the Roman army, London through its strategic position may well have been a center for Christian **ministry** and organization. It is known that a **bishop** of London, Restitutus by name, was present at the **Council** of Arles in 314, immediately following the Decree of Constantine. With the end of the Roman occupation 100 years later came an end of any recorded organized British Church in most areas of the country.

The see of London was recreated in 604 in the wake of **Augustine**'s **missionary** activity in Kent, and in time became the second see in the **province** of **Canterbury**. This seniority is sustained to the present time in that the bishop of London has an *ex officio* seat in the House of Lords, is **dean** of the province, and is also (with the two **archbishops**) an *ex officio* member of the monarch's Privy Council. The territory of the **diocese**, since early in the 20th century, has been all London north of the Thames (including the boroughs that were once the county of Middlesex), apart from five boroughs in the east that belong to Chelmsford diocese. South of the river, the whole of the London administrative area is in Southwark diocese, except two eastern boroughs that are in Rochester diocese. The **cathedral** of the London diocese is St. Paul's, the magnificent creation of Sir Christopher Wren built in the aftermath of the great fire of London of 1666.

Bishops of London have held a formative role in the emergence of the **Anglican Communion**. In 1633 the Privy Council ordered that, in all matters of church government overseas, Anglicans "should be under the jurisdiction of the Lord Bishop of London." Thus it was to the bishop of London that candidates for **ordination** came from the colonies in the years before they had their own bishops; likewise, it was to the bishop of London that the American colonists made vain application for him to visit—or to provide a bishop—in the years before the Revolution.

With the creation of new dioceses and then independent provinces around the world, the overseas "jurisdiction" concerned has now virtually ceased. The last stage of this responsibility related to the Anglican chaplaincies in northern **Europe**, where the bishop of London remained the ordinary until 1980; a suffragan see of Fulham, formed in 1926, provided a bishop who in practice exercised the bishop of London's oversight. Then in 1980 the diocese of "**Gibraltar** in Europe" was formed and took the northern Europe chaplaincies into its purview, and the bishopric of Fulham reverted to being an ordinary suffragan bishopric of London. A residual responsibility remains, in that the bishop of London is one of three persons who jointly nominate the bishop of Gibraltar in Europe.

LORD'S DAY. *See* SABBATH.

LORD'S PRAYER. The Lord **Jesus** taught his disciples to pray, giving them words that appear to come in full in Matt. 6.9–13 and in a slightly truncated form in Luke 11.1–4. The prayer appears to have a corporate significance, not only because Jesus appears to address the disciples together, using the plural in addressing them ("when you pray, say . . .") and putting plural pronouns ("we" and "us") into the disciples' prayer, but also because in Matt. 6 it is inserted between passages that use the singular ("when you pray . . . go into your room", and so forth) in evident contrast to them. It is clear it passed into Christian use at a very early stage, quite possibly from the day of **Pentecost** itself. It is found (for individual recitation) in the Didache in the early second century, and again in Hippolytus in the early third. There is little evidence of its use in **liturgy** until rather later; **Augustine** of Hippo refers to it as the devotional approach to receiving **Communion** ("Give us this day the bread of the coming day"—i.e., the **sacrament**); and **Pope** Gregory the Great stated that, as it is the greatest prayer Jesus gave us, it must accompany the greatest prayer we have in liturgy, i.e., the **eucharistic prayer**. It has as a matter of history come after the eucharistic prayer in both Eastern and Western Churches at least since the fifth century. But its use also continued in private devotions, daily offices, and occasional offices, and in the Middle Ages was, in its Latin ("*Pater noster*") form, assumed to be a basic text that **laypeople** could and should know.

At the **Reformation** the Lord's Prayer, now in English, was a core feature of all of **Archbishop Thomas Cranmer**'s new liturgical rites from the 1544 **Litany** onward. In the last stage of his revisions—that is, in the 1552 **Book of Common Prayer**—it came twice in **Morning and Evening Prayer**, twice in the Communion service, once in the litany, once in **baptism** (which itself came within Morning or Evening Prayer), and once each in the **confirmation** (i.e., by being the subject of examination in the **catechism**, which was part of the service), **marriage**, and **funeral** rites. Its text and meaning were one of the three basic items within the catechism that itself formed the first part of the confirmation service.

Its text from 1549 onward was that which has remained traditional in **Protestant** denominations, based more upon the Latin medieval text (e.g., in respect of "trespasses") than upon a close rendering of the Greek of the New Testament. Probably for the same reason it lacked the doxology in the 16th century. When the **King James Version** of the **Bible** was published in 1611, the manuscripts used (actually somewhat untrustworthy ones) brought the doxology to light in

Matt. 6.13—but this reading, the *Textus Receptus*, is almost certainly erroneous. It is also possible that interchange with the Christian East in the 17th century increased awareness of the doxology, and in the 1662 Prayer Book a doxology was added to the first use of the Lord's Prayer in Morning and Evening Prayer and to the post-Communion use in the **eucharist**, though not elsewhere.

While there has at intervals been a wrestling with the theology (and perhaps therefore the accuracy) of "Lead us not into temptation," it is the coming of modern English, addressing God as "you," which has led to a thorough new look at each line, a task done internationally by, first, the **International Consultation on English Texts** (ICET) and, since 1987, the **English Language Liturgy Consultation** (ELLC). This has proved uncontroversial in its retention of "hallowed" and of "daily **bread**" and in the substitution of "sins" (and "sin against") for "trespasses" (and "trespass against"). However, an unresolved conflict lingers on regarding the ninth line, where ICET and ELLC both recommend "Save us from the time of trial" but various **provinces** have retained "Lead us not into temptation."

The "**traditional**" English form (with three minute changes, such as "Our Father, who . . ." rather than "Our Father, which . . .") has run on quite strongly beside the new, not least because in many parts of the world it is the form known to nonchurchgoers. The same problems are not necessarily found in rendering the Lord's Prayer into other **vernacular languages**, in many of which it may never have been deeply entrenched in an antique form.

LORD'S SUPPER. In 1 Cor. 11.20, Paul refers to the malpractices around the Corinthians' following of the dominical command ("Do this in remembrance of me"). He writes, "When you come together, it is not the Lord's supper which you eat." This phrase gave **Thomas Cranmer** the cue, when he was reforming the medieval **mass**, to entitle the **eucharist** "The Lord's Supper." It is found in the title of the service in the 1552 **Book of Common Prayer** and thereafter in the 1559, 1604, **Scottish** 1637, and 1662 Books. The title also comes in the text of the exhortations in the rite and in Article XXVIII of the Thirty-Nine **Articles** (where it is more properly translated as **Supper of the Lord**). It served Cranmer's purposes well, not only by providing a biblical title that enabled him to dispense with "**mass**" but also because in its form and in its biblical setting, it emphasized the sheer eating and drinking which Cranmer believed to be the essence of the rite. *See also* INTINCTION.

LUND PRINCIPLE. The third meeting of Faith and Order of the **World Council of Churches** (WCC) at Lund, Sweden, in 1952 formulated a principle (always called the "Lund Principle") that Christians should only do separately that which in conscience they cannot do together. Anglicans regularly pay lip service to this principle.

LUSITANIAN CHURCH. Following **Vatican I** in 1870, a small portion of the **Roman Catholic** Church in Portugal broke away and in 1880 formed a new **reformed church**, called the Lusitanian Church. It provided **vernacular** forms of worship, drawing heavily upon the Anglican **Books of Common Prayer**. The Church sought the **consecration** of a **bishop** from the Church of **Ireland** and the **Protestant Episcopal Church in the United States of America**, but (unlike what occurred with the **Spanish Reformed Episcopal Church**) no such consecration occurred in those early years, although Irish bishops kept a watching and caring eye upon the Church and performed Episcopal acts for its members. A bishop was finally consecrated in 1958, and a continuity of bishops from within the one **diocese** has been sustained since then. Anglican **provinces** started to enter formal relations of **full Communion** with the Church in the 1960s. In 1980 the diocese requested to be admitted to the **Anglican Communion** and was received as an extraprovincial diocese under the **metropolitical** care of the **archbishop** of **Canterbury**.

The diocese has around a dozen parishes, a little more than 1,000 communicants, and perhaps 5,000 adherents, including some expatriate **Angolans**. It has used Portuguese for its worship from the beginning of its separate life and has developed its own **liturgical** patterns. As Portugal also falls within the territory of the Church of **England**'s diocese of **Gibraltar** in Europe, the Lusitanian diocese has been involved in discussions about the ultimate shape, whether province or not, of the Anglican presence on the Continent.

LUTHERAN CHURCHES. A large proportion of the Churches of the **Reformation** not only followed Martin Luther but also called themselves after his name. They were distinguishable from the **Reformed Churches** because they held to a more objective **doctrine** of a change in the **eucharistic elements** at **consecration**, sometimes called "consubstantiation," and in general they were identified by subscription to the Augsburg Confession of 1530. There were, however, many points of overlap between these two main streams of **Protestantism** at the Reformation; the Anglicans tended more to the reformed position, as is illustrated in Articles XXV–XXIX of the Thirty-Nine **Articles**. A curious result of the Reformation was that Lutherans were found in Germany and Scandinavia, with hardly any at all in the British Isles. Thus, although the Hanoverian dynasty, which began in Britain with King George I in 1714, was Lutheran in its roots, its members inevitably became Anglican by adaptation. German Lutheran **missionaries** were hired by the **Society for Promoting Christian Knowledge** in the 18th century to work in **India** among Indian nationals, but in general the connections were relatively sparse. There was another overlap with German Lutheran missionaries in **East Africa** (where Tanganyika was a German colony until World War I), and Anglicans and Lutherans shared together there in the plans in the 1960s for an East African church unity—which never came to fruition.

In the 19th century, Anglicans evinced a growing interest in the Church of Sweden, because it was the most notable European Church outside of Britain to have undergone a Reformation but to have retained an undoubted continuity of the **historic episcopate** through the Reformation. A desire for closer links was expressed in Resolution 14 of the 1888 **Lambeth Conference**, and this was followed by further resolutions at the 1897 and 1908 Lambeth Conferences. The 1908 resolution led to the **archbishop** of **Canterbury** establishing a "Commission on the Church of **England** and the Church of Sweden," and the 1920 Lambeth Conference recommended a limited inter-Communion and the participation (if invited) of Anglican bishops in the consecration of Swedish **bishops**. Relations were also strengthened through the international and **ecumenical** impact of **Archbishop** Nathan Söderblom (archbishop of Uppsala from 1914; died 1931), and he became a major factor in bringing the Episcopal successions in Norway, Finland, and the Baltic states into the "historic" continuity that the Swedish Church had preserved. To this day the

Church of Denmark, although Episcopal, has resisted any participation by bishops from elsewhere in its consecrations, deliberately for **ecclesiological** reasons, ensuring it did not open itself to any imputation that it found its credentials not in its Lutheran faith but in the historic episcopate.

The particular relations between Anglicans and these Episcopal Lutheran Churches were strengthened in the years after World War II by a series of international Anglican–Lutheran conversations and their respective reports (including the Pullach Report of 1973, the Helsinki Report of 1983, the Cold Ash Report of 1983, and the Niagara Report of 1987). As a result, the 1988 Lambeth Conference recognized a high degree of doctrinal consensus, which was met by a similar affirmation at the Lutheran World Federation assembly in 1990. There arose from this the Anglican–Lutheran International Commission (ALIC), which has largely worked as an umbrella for regional initiatives.

One immediate practical venture was already under way—the eight Lutheran Churches known as the "Nordic and Baltic Churches" (including Iceland) were engaged in conversations with the Anglican Churches of England, **Wales**, **Scotland**, and **Ireland**. These began in 1989 and reached a recommendation of a "Joint Declaration," the "**Porvoo** Common Statement" in 1993. In the following years, all the Churches concerned except the Church of Denmark adopted "Porvoo," and it came into force in 1996 as an agreement for full Communion between the Lutheran and Anglican churches concerned. Anglicans outside Europe have generally viewed themselves as informally involved in the agreement.

In Germany, where the Evangelische Kirche in Deutschland (EKD) is a federal body that includes Lutheran districts, the **Meissen** agreement of 1988 displayed Anglicans expressing as close ties as have been usually deemed possible between the **Anglican Communion** and Churches which, though they have **bishops**, lack the historic episcopate and therefore do not qualify on conventional Anglican terms for full interchangeability of **ministers**.

The Meissen agreement gave birth also to similar conversations in France in 1994–1997. There, the Reuilly Common Statement, agreed between representatives of the Lutheran and Reformed Churches of France and the same four British and Irish Anglican churches and published in 1999 as *Called to Witness and Service*, also stopped short of recommending full Communion. As with Meissen, however, the receiving of the report and the agreeing the declaration in 1999 included a commitment to further wrestling with outstanding theological issues.

In the **United States**, the concordat that was reached between the **Episcopal Church (United States of America)** and the Evangelical Lutheran Church in 2000 includes interchangeability of ministers even without the Lutherans having the historic episcopate and is based upon a "suspension" of the provisions of the **preface** to the **Ordinal**. A similar pattern is followed in the covenant between the Anglican Church of **Canada** and the Evangelical Lutheran Church of Canada, which came into force in July 2001.

During the 1990s an exploration was under way in Africa to provide for a pan-African commission on Anglican–Lutheran relationships, and this led to the formation of the All-Africa Anglican–Lutheran Commission (AAALC), which first met in April 2001.

There has also been an Anglican–Lutheran dialogue in **Australia**, which has led to a report, *Common Ground: Covenanting for Mutual Recognition and Reconciliation* (2001). This report provides for local areas to make progress at different speeds from each other and is in principle a charter for such local developments.

The 1998 Lambeth Conference in its Resolution IV.16 called for the formation of an Anglican–Lutheran International Working Group (ALIWG), and this (with seven members from each Communion) has met annually since 2000 to review the consistency of approach between the various local and regional conversations that are under way. After its meeting in 2002 it presented a report on its work, entitled *Growth in Communion*, to the **Inter-Anglican Standing Commission on Ecumenical Relations** (IASCER).

The documents of the various agreements were drawn together in *Anglican–Lutheran Agreements: Regional and International Agreements, 1972–2004*, published by the **Anglican Consultative Council** and the Lutheran World Federation in December 2004.

LUWUM, JANANI (1922–1977). Janani Luwum came from the Acholi tribe of northern **Uganda** and was trained first as a schoolteacher and then as a lay pastor. He was **ordained** in the Church of

Uganda as **deacon** in 1955 and **presbyter** in 1956. After studies in **England**, he became principal of Buwalasi **Theological College** in 1965 and **provincial** secretary in 1966. Luwum was one of only two African consultants at the **Lambeth Conference** of 1968. In 1969 he became **bishop** of the newly created **diocese** of Northern Uganda, with his seat in Gulu; it was while he was there that in 1971 Idi Amin led the coup that brought him to dictatorial power. Luwum went on in 1974 to become **archbishop** of Uganda, **Rwanda**, **Burundi**, and Boga-Zaire, based in Kampala, Uganda. His time as archbishop coincided with Amin taking an ever tighter and more arbitrary grip upon the nation. In early 1977 the archbishop led the House of Bishops of the Church of Uganda in making a dignified joint protest to Amin against the arrests, imprisonments, and persecutions to which Church members were being subjected in the reign of terror of the time. Following this protest, Luwum was summoned by the police and was imprisoned. He was then executed without trial on 16 February 1977. He has been generally recognized throughout the world since then as a Christian **martyr**. His death day has been listed in many **calendars**, and he is one of the 10 martyrs of the 20th century whose statues stand on the west front of Westminster **Abbey**.

– M –

MACKAY, ALEXANDER MURDOCH (1849–1890). Alexander Mackay was Scottish by birth, but, reading the appeal of H. M. Stanley in the *Edinburgh Review* for **missionaries** for **Uganda**, was led to offer himself to the **Church Missionary Society** (CMS) to join the pioneer missionary party going there in 1876. Mackay gained a favorable hearing from King Mutesa of Buganda, and in various ways obtained a foothold for Christianity in the country. Indeed, he survived both the murder of **James Hannington**, the first **bishop**, in 1885 and also the massacres of 1886, when many of his converts at court were **martyred**. He was, however, expelled from Uganda in 1887, though he continued translation work from the southern end of Lake Victoria, where he died of malaria in 1890. His remains were translated in 1927 to Namirembe Cathedral.

MADAGASCAR. *See* INDIAN OCEAN.

MALINES CONVERSATIONS. Malines, Belgium, was the venue of unofficial conversations between **Roman Catholic** and Church of **England** theologians between 1921 and 1926. They arose from an approach by Lord Halifax to Cardinal Mercier, who was archbishop of Malines and had a strong **ecumenical** interest, and began under a cloak of secrecy. The Church of England's original trio of Armitage Robinson, W. H. Frere, and B. J. Kidd were hardly typical of the whole breadth of Anglicanism, and the **archbishop** of **Canterbury**, **Randall Davidson**, while giving some approval to the venture as exploratory, made it very clear that the three did not "represent" him or the Church of England. **Pope** Pius XI gave some reserved approval also. When the second round of talks showed signs of an Anglican surrender to Rome, in pursuit of the analogy of the relationship to the pope and the Latin Church of the Uniat Churches of the East, Davidson strengthened the team by the addition of **Charles Gore**. The third round of talks in late 1923 then became more important for their precipitation of publicity about the talks than for their content. Davidson recognized the need to communicate with the rest of the **Anglican Communion** and sent a letter to the **primates** at **Christmas** that year, thus making the existence of the "Conversations" public. A fourth round of talks was held in 1925, when Dom Lambert Beauduin's paper "L'Église anglicaine unie non absorbée" took the Uniat concept further and gave it greater shape, but a division over the powers and role of the papal office remained. In 1926 Mercier died, and further talks that year simply addressed the question of what to publish. Publication was delayed until after the December 1927 debate on **Book of Common Prayer** revision in the British Parliament, but the papers were published in January 1928 by Lord Halifax. That same year a new papal encyclical, *Mortalium Animos*, virtually forbade further talks.

MAN. *See* ANTHROPOLOGY; MAN, ISLE OF.

MAN, ISLE OF. The Isle of Man, halfway between **England** and **Ireland**, forms the see of Sodor and Man. While theories abound as to the origins and significance of "Sodor," it is clear that the only territory belonging to the **diocese** is in fact the single Isle of Man. (The inevitable redundancy of the "Sodor" part of the title has enabled the Reverend W. Awdry to utilize the title for his own mythical island where his children's storybook railway runs.) The see is supposed to have been founded by **St. Patrick** in 447 and therefore ranks as the oldest see in the Church of England. However, in the Middle Ages it belonged to first Norway and then **Scotland**, and it was annexed to the **province** of **York** by Act of Parliament only in 1542. Its erstwhile **cathedral** at Peel has been in ruins since the 18th century, and since 1980 the **parish** church of St. German's, Peel, has been established as the diocesan cathedral (though with the bishop himself as **dean** and only a minimal **chapter**). Because the Isle of Man is a self-governing nation within the United Kingdom, not subject for internal purposes to the rule of Westminster, the diocesan bishop is not eligible for membership of the House of Lords, but instead sits *ex officio* in the House of Keys, the parliament of the Isle of Man. Similarly Church legislation that is enacted by the Westminster Parliament does not affect the diocese of Sodor and Man unless and until it is adopted by the House of Keys. The numbers of **clergy** and **laity** are very small compared with the other dioceses of the Church of England, and the representation in the **General Synod** similarly restricted.

MANUAL ACTS. The term "manual acts" refers to actions with the hands—the **ceremonial** lifting or holding the paten and chalice—that are characteristically taken during the **narrative** of institution within the **eucharistic prayer**. The 1549 **Book of Common Prayer** provided, by "**indented rubrics**," for the two actions in succession: the **presbyter** simply took the two vessels in turn into his hands, with his back to the people and without showing the **elements** to the people. The **rubrics** themselves came in tiny print in the margin of the text beside the point in the text to which they applied. In 1552, when there ceased to be any objective **consecration**, there were no manual acts—as indeed there was no rubrical indication that **bread** and wine had even been placed upon the **Communion table**. In the 1637 **Scottish** rite, when a clear doctrine of an objective consecration recurred, the two rubrics of 1549 were restored, and in the second the presbyter was instructed not only to take the cup into his hands but also to lay his hand on every vessel in which there was wine to be consecrated.

The presbyter was now standing at the **north side** or end of the table, so that in principle the manual acts would be visible, but a rubric introducing the "Prayer of Consecration" allowed that "during the time of Consecration" the presbyter might stand "where he may with the more ease and decency use both hands."

At the Church of **England**'s 1661 revision in the **Convocations**, the logic of the Scottish rubrics was worked out more carefully. Now both bread and wine had separate rubrics for two actions each, one to lift the vessel (at "took") and the other to lay his hand upon it (at "this is my body/blood"). This made four rubrics, but in fact there was a fifth, as **Jesus**' words "he brake it" in the narrative were now accompanied by "and here he shall break the bread," which thus came between the "taking" of the paten and the laying of the **presbyter**'s hand upon it. This met the **Puritans**' request at the **Savoy Conference** for an "explicit" **fraction**, and thus passed into historic Anglicanism, though in a place in the rite unique in Christian history.

The relationship of the rubrics ordering manual acts and the concept of consecration via the use of the dominical words in the narrative of institution looks very close indeed. The manual acts were never explicitly ordered for supplementary consecration, but that is a very small exception—and even there, they are probably implicit. In the 20th century, as the idea has grown that consecration is effected by the total thanksgiving in the eucharistic prayer and not by a short formula within it, so the prescription of manual acts has withered away (though they are retained in Order Two of the **Episcopal Church [United States of America]**'s 1979 Book). The fraction has been more and more found as the third of **Gregory Dix**'s "four-action shape" and has thus followed in sequence after the eucharistic prayer; the same logic has led in some places, most notably the Church of England, to locate the "taking" of the paten and cup at a point prior to beginning the eucharistic prayer (though without selling out to the controversial Dix interpretation that the "taking" is fulfilled by an "**offertory**" of bread and wine).

MAR THOMA SYRIAN CHURCH OF MALABAR. The Syrian Orthodox Churches of **South India**, centered in Kerala on the southwestern coast of India, claim to have been founded by St. Thomas in A.D. 52. Certainly Christian remains datable to the second and third centuries are to be found in the area. The churches concerned were until the 15th century loyal to the patriarch of Antioch, but the arrival of the Portuguese brought them into **Communion** with Rome; at the **Synod** of Diamper in 1599 they were virtually Latinized.

The coming of the Dutch in the 17th century changed the political climate and a part of the Church returned to the Antioch patriarchate in 1662–1663. It was this Church, in its heartland of the Malabar coast, which **Claudius Buchanan**, a chaplain of the East India Company in **Calcutta** from 1798 to 1808, visited in 1806, as a result of which he obtained the translation of the **Bible** into Malayalam. His work was followed up by the foundation in 1813, through the initiative of the British resident in Travancore, of a **theological college** in Kottayam. This college, staffed centrally by **Church Missionary Society** missionaries, for 20 years taught ordinands of the Syrian Orthodox Church; and it was the **vernacular** Bible that was central to that work.

In 1836 the Orthodox turned away from the college and used it no longer. But the reading of the Bible led to a **Reformation** within that Church, which happened through Abraham Malpan at parish level in 1840–1845, and a division resulted. There then followed 50 years of dispute about the lawfulness of rival **metropolitans** and the ownership of property. The reformed part largely failed in its attempts to secure rights to property, and thus in legal terms it was that part that left the main body. They formed in the early 1890s a separate Mar Thoma Syrian Church of Malabar, translated the Syriac **liturgy** of St. James into Malayalam, and purged it of some **traditional** features, such as the invocation of the **saints**. In many ways they demonstrated an **evangelical** vigor, living under the **authority** of the scriptures yet within a Syrian cultural tradition and claiming by their very title succession from St. Thomas.

When, soon after their separation, a break occurred in their **Episcopal** succession, they obtained **consecration** in 1893 from the **bishop** of the (one-**diocese**) Malabar Independent Syrian Church, and, when necessary since, they have provided similar consecration of bishops for that Church. In line with the Syrian tradition, bishops have to be **celibate** and are made notional monks (although the Church has no **monastic** communities) some weeks before being **ordained** as bishops. The **metropolitan** resides at Tiruvalla, and its theological college is at the Christian center of Kerala at Kottayam. Fired by the scriptures, the Church has evangelized vigorously and, rooted in its own Malayalam **language** and Syrian liturgical culture, has spread through all the world in the diaspora of the able and energetic South Indian peoples of Kerala. Its great Bible convention, held annually during the dry season on the riverbed at Maramon, has become world famous.

In 1961 the Church of **India**, **Pakistan**, Burma, and Ceylon (CIPBC), then a province of the **Anglican Communion**, and the united Church of **South India** entered into a concordat, including **full Communion**, with the Mar Thoma Church. The question of an actual union with the Church of South India has presented difficulties, partly because the Syrian Christians of the Malabar coast have traditionally held a position in Kerala society comparable to that of Brahmin Hindus, while Western missionaries have found converts among all classes, not least the *dalits* or outcastes. A lesser difficulty has been the Malayalam-based character of the Mar Thoma Church, which has made its leaders wary of becoming just one language group in the multilingual Church of South India. The concordat was sustained when the united Church of **North India** was formed in 1970, and a Joint Council was formed in 1978, so that there are still three parties to the concordat. In its terms, each of the three churches prays for the moderator or metropolitan of the other two, and all participate in the consecration of bishops and many other activities. Individual provinces of the Anglican Communion have made separate decisions about full Communion, as the Church of England did in 1973. Bishops of the Mar Thoma Church have been invited as guests to the **Lambeth Conferences** since 1978. The Mar Thoma Church is thus the only Eastern Church with which Anglicans are in Communion.

MARRIAGE. Marriage (more formally entitled "matrimony") has historically been understood as the pledging of one man and one woman to live together in permanent, bonded, and physically intimate union. Traditionally the taking of public vows and the subsequent sexual union have together constituted the marriage. The couple were always understood as effecting the union themselves by these means, and the role of the **ministers** of the church has been one of administering and witnessing the vows, and also of being master of ceremonies in the **liturgy**. In the pre-**Reformation** church, the vows were made in English (and the bride promised to be "buxom in bed and at board"), which was the only point at which the **vernacular** was used in liturgy—the point being that it was vital that bride and groom should both know exactly what they were taking on and should do so freely and of their own consent. Matrimony was treated as one of the seven **sacraments** according to the scheme of Peter Lombard's *Sententiae* in the 12th century, and this classification itself then became official **doctrine**. The bond, or *vinculum*, created by marriage was viewed as conveying an ontological union, unbreakable except by death (a factor reflected in the classic qualifying clause in the traditional Anglican vows "till death us do part"). Thus it was that King **Henry VIII** sought not a **divorce**, but an annulment.

Whereas many Anglicans have held to the theory of the vinculum, it has never been written into doctrinal statements or **credal** requirements of the Church, so that the theory has been merely compatible with the formularies and disciplines, rather than required by them. Anglicans have generally treated marriages solemnized and registered in civil contexts as having the same binding character as those in Christian contexts, provided that some understanding of marriage as a lifelong mutual commitment has been expressed or represented. In some countries, marriages cannot be solemnized in a church context and require a civil one—though Christian believers may still hold an act of worship in confirmation, thanksgiving, and intercession in relation to the marriage. Whether the couple are joined officially before such a service or at it, Anglicans have held as an ideal, one that often cannot be realized, that the act of worship itself should be a **celebration** of the **eucharist**. Marriage services usually contain statements of the purposes why, in the economy of **God**, marriage was instituted—for mutual love and support, for the joy of physical union, and for the provision of children within the stable context of an enduring family home.

As divorce has come into the secular law of many nations, so has the issue of whether a divorced person may then marry another partner in church, as well as the question of whether the divorced and remarried may be eligible to be **ordained**. In places where the answer to these questions is that, in principle, provision may be made available, there have still often been fairly severe guidelines to be observed, lest the whole of the church's witness to the permanence of marriage and the significance of vows for life be undermined.

Banns of marriage read in advance and further opportunity for objection on the day at the actual rite reflect the church's concern that the two persons should be genuinely free before God to marry each other and should do so with appropriate publicity and not secretly. Impediments to marriage usually include one partner being under age, one being already married, one being of wholly unsound mind, one being forced in some way, the bride being pregnant by another man without the groom's knowledge, both being of the same sex, or the two being related within the "prohibited degrees." **Prayer Books** traditionally contained a "Table of the Prohibited Degrees," and at times this list has been different from that contained in civil law. Marriage to a deceased brother's widow—the very issue that allowed Henry VIII to claim that his marriage to Catherine of Aragon was null—is not now usually ranked as within the prohibited degrees (cf. Luke 20.28–33), but where (as with a father marrying his daughter) the relationship does fall within the prohibitions, then the marriage is void and the joining of the two incestuous.

The Reformers did not classify marriage as a sacrament, for it was a creation ordinance and not ordained by **Jesus Christ** himself in the **Gospel**. Article XXV of the Thirty-Nine **Articles** says it is "a state of life allowed in the Scriptures." Both **bishops** and **Puritans** at the **Savoy Conference** similarly were agreed that it is not a sacrament.

MARTYR. The Greek word "martyr" originally meant simply a "witness" (cf. Acts 1.8), but the meaning began at an early date to move toward its modern meaning (e.g., in Acts 22.20). From early on, Christians treasured the memory of those who died for their faith, and where possible kept the anniversary of the death at or near the place of martyrdom. It is from this practice that fixing the stated days in the **calendar** in commemoration of the one who died that day led to the institution of the "sanctorale" or calendar of fixed dates in memory of the recognized **saints** or outstanding Christians who died on those dates, among whom martyrs had particular reputation.

While the **Anglican Communion** has no machinery for recognizing or "**canonizing**" individuals as saints, it has still been possible to acknowledge the self-sacrifice of those who have died for the faith as martyrs. This began with those burned during the **Reformation** (a contemporary partisan account of whom is in **John Foxe's** *Acts and*

Monuments, commonly known as *Foxe's Book of Martyrs*). In the following century it was conventional Anglican wisdom to refer to the "martyrdom" of King **Charles I**, as is witnessed by a series of church **dedications** to "King Charles the Martyr" and in the title of the special service of commemoration of him on 30 January that was imposed in the Church of **England** from 1665 to 1859.

As Anglicanism has expanded around the world, so local martyrs have been acclaimed and commemorated in many different **provinces**, some of them gaining recognition far beyond their own province. A notable example is **Janani Luwum**, the **archbishop** of **Uganda**, martyred on 16 February 1977. Provincial calendars tend to have a mixture of martyrs ancient and modern, local and distant. *See also* ALBAN, SAINT; HANNINGTON, JAMES; LATIMER, HUGH; MIZEKI, BERNARD; PATTESON, JOHN COLERIDGE; RIDLEY, NICHOLAS.

MARY, MOTHER OF JESUS CHRIST. The Virgin Mary has been a controversial figure in the history of Christian **liturgy** and spirituality. She was honored in the early church for her role in the **Incarnation**, in which her own part was focused in her virginity at the time of the conception of **Jesus Christ**. Her obedience was celebrated and expressed in the song we know as the Magnificat. However, terminology such as "mother of **God**" (*theotokos*) was originally intended to safeguard the deity of her Son, rather than to exalt her own person.

The Middle Ages saw a great growth both in devotion to Mary and in the importance of praying to her—with a consequent development of the "Ave Maria" and of the rosary that stems from it. The actual devotion to her was elaborated into **doctrines**—the exaltation of her status led to the doctrines of both her **immaculate conception** and her bodily **assumption** into **heaven**. It has also been conventional to exalt her virgin status at the time of the **annunciation** and of her conception of Jesus into a much more speculative doctrine of her "perpetual" virginity. These doctrines are discussed below.

The **Reformers** were clear that Mary must not be viewed in any sense at all as mediating. While she survived briefly as one whose prayers and advocacy on our behalf might be sought (she, alone among the **saints**, survived by name in this role in the 1544 English

litany), she was fairly ruthlessly excised in the further stages of compilation of the **Books of Common Prayer** in 1549 and 1552. In line with the relatively light weight of evidence about her in scripture, and the very perils the Reformers believed they saw in the **Roman Catholic Church**'s devotion to her, she now figured in the liturgy only with reference to the Incarnation (as in the Magnificat, at the **Feast** of the Annunciation, and at **Christmas**), and the Ave Maria and Marian feast days were totally eliminated.

In the 19th and 20th centuries two different reactions to Mary have been found concurrently in Anglicanism. On the one hand, the whole return to a cult of the saints by the **Anglo-Catholic** movement has restored her to prominence and has located her more visibly in the **calendar**, even though actual invocation of her and the use of the Ave Maria might still be viewed as partisan and divisive. Shrines and **pilgrimages** in her honor, not least at Walsingham in England, have given added force to this tendency, and feast days of her **conception** (8 December), her birth (8 September), and her death (15 August) have in varying degrees found expression in 20th-century calendars. While the first two dates are speculative (though obviously related to each other), the third may have some claims to credibility—but, where the date is kept simply as "St. Mary's Day," then either it witnesses by silence simply to her death, as all saints' days are assumed to be their death days unless it is otherwise specifically mentioned (as with "The Conversion of St Paul"), or conceivably there is a tacit following of the Roman Catholic doctrine or a variant on it, implied by the resumption of the historic date.

The opposite tendency in Anglicanism arises from the *ex cathedra* Marian decrees of **popes** Pius IX in 1854 and Pius XII in 1950, respectively, that Mary was born from an immaculate conception and that her body was taken up (or experienced an "assumption") into heaven at a point at or just after her death. Both these doctrines appear to arise in a kind of deductive sequence from the given fact that Mary was to bear Christ the sinless Son of God. Therefore, so the deductive argument has gone, she must herself have been without taint of sin in order not to convey that taint to him. Thus, because she had been preserved from sin from her conception, she did not, indeed could not, pass into ordinary bodily corruption through death and must have been taken bodily to heaven at God's good time. Anglicans looking for direct or inferential pointers in the New Testament, let alone the witness of Christian history, have found no reason to accept these latter-day decrees. They have thus viewed the decrees as not only improbable or untrue in themselves but also as self-evidently calling in question any claims that bishops of Rome have power to issue **infallible** decrees.

A subordinate question, though one open to equal division of opinion, is the Roman Catholic insistence that Mary was "ever-Virgin." This doctrine has itself a deductive point of origin, namely, that virginity is a higher state of life than the sexual relationship in **marriage**, and thus, because of her exalted state, Mary must have declined all sexual relationships with Joseph. An inductive process, drawing together both Matt. 1.20 and 1.25 and references to Jesus' brothers and sisters (e.g., in Mark 6.3 and "James, the Lord's brother" in Gal. 1.19), would strongly suggest a normal married life after the birth of Jesus, but those who believe in Mary's perpetual virginity have ways of avoiding the immediate thrust of these references.

The final report of the second **Anglican–Roman Catholic International Commission** (ARCIC-2), entitled *Mary: Grace and Hope in Christ*, having been agreed upon in 2004, was published in May 2005. In exploring possible agreement between the two Communions on their beliefs about Mary, the commission went very far toward accepting the Roman Catholic doctrines. However, the statement appears to reach them by reasoning processes, themselves perhaps open to question, rather than by mere assertion of the authoritative decrees. At the time of going to press, little worldwide reaction had been registered. *See also* AUTHORITY; VATICAN I.

MARY I, QUEEN (1516–1558). Mary was the only child of the union of King **Henry VIII** and his first wife, Catherine of Aragon, to grow to adulthood. At an early age she became the victim of her father's quest for a son and for a younger wife. His insistence that he could not be truly **married** to Catherine because they were within the prohibited degrees of relatedness—she was his brother's widow—entailed that Mary was both illegitimate and the child of incest. She was marginalized in Court until after Catherine's death in January 1536 and was deeply imbued with her mother's dependence upon the **pope** and adherence to the **Roman Catholic** cause. However, she returned to

Henry's favor by a public acknowledgment that his marriage to her mother was void.

Jane Seymour, Henry's third wife, welcomed her, and when a son, Edward, had been born, Henry (despite her acknowledged illegitimacy) named her in his will as second in line to the throne, if Edward were to die childless. Henry VIII died and Edward duly became King **Edward VI** at the age of nine in January 1547, and a hectic six-year period of **Reformation** ensued. During this period, Mary waited in the wings, holding to the "Old Religion." In July 1553 Edward died, and, at a late stage, there was an unsuccessful plot to put Lady Jane Grey on the throne in order not to have Mary.

As queen, Mary became embattled and persecuted her opponents for both their support of the plot and their heretical, that is, **Protestant**, teachings. The **liturgical** reforms of Edward's reign were immediately rescinded, and, while she sought the return of the land to Rome, the position of the Church for over a year had some affinities with how it had been in the last years of her father's reign. Her marriage to Philip of Spain in 1554 confirmed her stance, though it both antagonized her subjects and also failed in its other purposes—to join England to Spain and to provide a Roman Catholic heir to displace her half-sister **Elizabeth**, who in her turn was waiting in the wings, as Mary had during Edward's reign. Mary's persecutions included the burning of the **archbishop** of **Canterbury**, **Thomas Cranmer**, and four other bishops: Robert Ferrar, **John Hooper**, **Nicholas Ridley**, and **Hugh Latimer**. Hundreds of ordinary citizens died also. Cardinal Pole came to England in 1554 as the papal legate to bring the country back to Rome, and this was achieved through the submission of Parliament in November that year and its formal **absolution** from schism. After Cranmer had been burned in 1556, Pole became archbishop of Canterbury.

As the country receded from the loyalty shown at the beginning of her reign and Philip abandoned her, Mary became paranoid and ill. Elizabeth was under grave suspicion and possibly in danger of her life. But Mary died on 17 November 1558, and Pole died in the same night. Elizabeth succeeded, with a country waiting for the new settlement of religion that she was to bring.

MARY II, QUEEN (1662–1694). Mary was the first child and older daughter of King **James II**, by his first wife, Anne Hyde. In her early years, when her father had not yet become a **Roman Catholic**, she was nurtured as a **Protestant**. As King **Charles II** had no legitimate offspring, her father was next in line to the throne, and she herself was therefore viewed in the land as a prospective monarch. This became of great importance when her father became a Roman Catholic in 1670, and from then on attempts of varying credibility were made to exclude him from the succession and have the throne pass to her. However, these came to nothing, and James became king in 1685.

Meanwhile in 1677, she married William, Prince of Orange. She remained the next in line to the throne during her father's reign from 1685 to 1688. However, in 1688, when James' second wife gave birth to a son at the same time that James had run himself into the deepest unpopularity, approaches from the English Parliament to the Netherlands led William to come to England in November to replace James. When James then fled, William was invited by Parliament to become regent, but when he declined, he (as **William III**) and Mary were asked to become joint monarchs. They ruled jointly until she died, herself childless, in 1694. *See also* GLORIOUS REVOLUTION; NONJURORS.

MASS. The "Mass" is a common **Roman Catholic** title for the **eucharist**, probably originating from the "*Ite, missa est*" at the conclusion. The title was excised by the Reformers as suggesting "the sacrifices of the masses" (a quotation from **Article** XXXI of 1571)—in other words, as being of itself an ungodly and misleading term. In the 1549 **Book of Common Prayer**, the title of the **Lord's Supper** had the subtitle "Commonly called the Mass"—but the **Reformation** use of the word "commonly" implied "wrongly but popularly"; furthermore, the subtitle was wholly removed at the next revision and never restored, and thus had no standing as an Anglican title of the Lord's Supper. Until the time of the **Anglo-Catholic** movement in the 19th century, Anglicans general used "Mass" only to indicate the Roman Catholic eucharistic rite, usually with disapprobation. However, the readiness of Anglo-Catholics to use Roman Catholic terminology as their own has brought the term into Anglican use among **parishes** and people who wish to advertise their approximation to Roman Catholic ways.

MATRIMONY. *See* MARRIAGE.

MAUNDY THURSDAY. The designation "Maundy" for the Thursday in **Holy Week** derives from the Latin *mandatum* ("commandment"), reflecting **Jesus**' words about a "new commandment" (John 13.34). The date is obviously also connected with the Lord's institution of Holy **Communion**. In the simplified **calendar** that **Thomas Cranmer** brought into use with the 1549 **Book of Common Prayer**, neither of these specific themes is identified, and the date is merely the "Thursday before Easter," marked solely by the long passion narrative (from Luke 23) that is characteristic of the **Gospel** passages read during Holy Week. The tradition of the "Royal Maundy," which took its origin in the monarch washing the feet of the poor on Maundy Thursday, did persist through the **Reformation**, but the actual ceremony of the **foot washing** had been commuted for a gift of cash long before the Reformation period (and still continues to this day in **En-gland** in the form of the monarch distributing "alms" to needy pensioners).

In the 20th century, **liturgical** revision in the **Anglican Communion** has reverted to a more detailed commemoration of the original Maundy Thursday. **Collects** and readings relating to the institution of the **Lord's Supper** came first, in the early years of the century. But in 1955 the **pope** restored foot washing to the **Roman Catholic** rite for the night and also permitted reception of Communion. Anglicans at their own speed followed suit, and in many places (whether encouraged by the **provincial** liturgy or not) have introduced not only foot washing but also a "stripping of **altars**," a processing with a **reserved consecrated** wafer to an "altar of repose," and a "watch" sustained in silence (or with readings from the accounts of Jesus in the Garden of Gethsemane) until as late as midnight.

A totally separate, but roughly synchronous, development has also sprung from Roman Catholic models. This has been the introduction on the morning of Maundy Thursday of a **cathedral** service for the **clergy** of the **diocese**, over which the diocesan **bishop** presides, for the renewal of **ordination** vows for those in holy **orders**, and the "blessing of the oils." The theory behind the provision of new oils is that **Easter** is the great occasion for **baptisms**, and that is when new oil should be employed—and thus it is prepared before the "triduum" begins, to be available as soon as is needed. Not all Anglicans have welcomed such extra ceremonies or developed such a comprehensive use of oils.

MAURITIUS. *See* INDIAN OCEAN.

MEASURE. A "measure" is a term introduced in the Church of **England** under the Church of England Assembly (Powers) Act 1919. This Act of Parliament provided for parliamentary legislation to be devised, shaped, and approved in the **Church Assembly** (or, from 1970 onward, in the **General Synod**), and then to go to Parliament, where it receives a single debate in both Houses before gaining the royal assent and becoming law. Whether in draft or enacted form, such legislation is always referred to as a "measure," distinguishing it from purely church rules (**canons**) and other Parliamentary legislation (known as a "bill" when in draft and an "act" when enacted). *See also* ENABLING ACT.

MEISSEN. "Meissen" is a form of shorthand for a relationship between the Church of **England** and the main non–**Roman Catholic** Churches of Germany. The relationship took its formal beginning from a meeting at Meissen in Saxony in March 1988 between delegations of the Church of England and of the two federal bodies that then existed in a Germany itself still split between east and west, on two sides of the Iron Curtain. In the west, the body was the Evangelische Kirche in Deutschland (EKD). This was the original body, a federation of **Lutheran** and **Reformed churches**, some of the territories (*Landes*) being Lutheran and some Reformed. The parts in East Germany had been forced under Communism to separate from the west and form their own "federation," and it was that body that sent delegates to join with those of the EKD at the Meissen meeting. The EKD and the Federation became a single restored EKD in 1991 following the political reunification of Germany.

At the Meissen meeting, a "Common Statement," entitled *On the Way to Visible Unity: The Meissen Common Statement*, was agreed upon. This was accepted by the German bodies and the **General Synod** of the Church of England during 1990 and formally signed at the beginning of 1991. The nature of the statement is both to give some measure of mutual recognition (though, because the EKD does not have the "**historic episcopate**," the Church of England has not thus far agreed an interchangeability of **ministries**) and to promote actual sharing of life and worship through such means as "twinning" of English and German cities on the one hand and a series of continuing theological conferences on the other. These conferences began in 1995, and four had been held by 2001. There is a standing Meissen Commission, which monitors progress and reports to the parent Churches.

The term "Meissen" has also become a kind of shorthand for a particular form of mutual sharing, falling short of **full Communion**.

MELANESIA. When **George Augustus Selwyn** was appointed and **consecrated** in **London** in 1841 as the first **bishop** of New Zealand, a clerical error occurred in the charter contained in his letters patent. His sphere of responsibility should have lain between the latitudes of 50° S and 34° S, so as to comprehend New Zealand fairly exactly. The clerical error gave him responsibility as far as 34° N, adding vast stretches of the Pacific to the charter. The islands of Melanesia fell within this area and were relatively close, and Selwyn viewed them from the start as a **missionary** responsibility of New Zealand. The first missionaries were sent in 1856. When New Zealand then became a **province** in 1857, Selwyn had sufficient **authority** to form a **diocese** of Melanesia. He consecrated **John Coleridge Patteson** in Auckland in 1861 and sent him as missionary **bishop** to the islands, where he was assassinated 10 years later in a way that ranks him as a Christian **martyr**. The diocese remained part of the province of New Zealand until 1975, when its own independent provincial structure was created.

In 2000, there were eight dioceses in the province, covering a multitude of islands, a great variety of political structures, and both stable and unstable societies. A feature of the province has been the Melanesian Brotherhood, an order of single men bound under vows for limited periods of years but not for life. This was founded in 1925 by a visionary Melanesian layman, Ini Kopouria, and was a strong (and numerous) spiritual force in the recovery after World War II. The brotherhood then gained world renown when seven brothers were martyred when seeking to mediate between rival forces during political unrest in 2003. *See also* AOTEAROA.

METHODIST CHURCHES. The worldwide family of Methodist Churches takes its origin from the **gospel ministry** of **John and Charles Wesley** and George Whitefield during the **Evangelical Revival** of the 18th century. During the lifetime of the Wesleys, the organization of the "societies" (as they were known) had an element of improvization and sheer pragmatism about them. The societies met separately from the **parish** church congregation, often in homes or chapels. However, John Wesley held that they had not fundamentally separated, and in principle they were supposed to be still somehow within Anglicanism. Thus instances of Methodists continuing to receive **Communion** in their parish churches were recorded until well into the 19th century. But the denomination had by then developed a strong independent life in total constitutional separation from Anglicanism. In the **United States**, Methodism was **Episcopal** in organization, though the Episcopal succession could be traced to no earlier a point than John Wesley's "setting apart" of Thomas Coke, an Anglican **presbyter**, as "superintendent" of the Methodist societies in the United States in 1784. In both countries the societies became an **Evangelical** denominational church, and from both countries the denomination spread across the world, often episcopally structured in accordance with the American pattern. By the early 19th century, British Methodism was divided into different strands, and that factor was inevitably reproduced in their separate overseas **missionary** endeavors.

The rise of **Anglo-Catholicism** distanced Methodism further from Anglicanism in the 19th century. However, in the 20th century various moves toward each other were initiated in different parts of the world. Methodists were involved as early as 1919 in the moves that led to the formation in 1947 of the united Church of **South India**. They also participated in the unions in **North India** and **Pakistan** in 1970 and took part in the less successful negotiations in **Sri Lanka**, **East Africa**, and **Nigeria** in the 1950s and 1960s. In **Canada** in 1925 and in **Australia** in 1977, the Methodist Churches joined with **Presbyterians** and **Congregationalists** to form non-Episcopal united churches. In South Africa, the Methodists and Anglicans were part of a four-cornered agreement in 1996 for interchangeability of ministries.

In 1932 the three major British Methodist Churches united to become a single structure and thereafter showed an interest in uniting with the Church of England. This led after World War II to Anglican–Methodist conversations from 1956 to 1963 and ultimately to a two-stage scheme that was accepted by the Methodist Conference but rejected in both 1969 and 1972 by the Church of England. The Methodists similarly accepted the proposed "covenant" of the years 1978 to 1982, which would have drawn five denominations into a relationship of **full Communion**—but this was also turned down by the

Church of England. A further approach by the Methodist Church in 1994 led to a series of conversations and resulted in a 2001 bilateral "covenant" affirming that both Churches shared the same faith and recognized each other as Churches, but actually requiring no structural or other significant change of either. Both Churches accepted this covenant in 2003 and established a Joint Implementation Commission to work out the implications. The commission has been given five years to complete its work, and in 2005 it produced an interim report, *In the Spirit of the Covenant*, which identified important issues but did not indicate solutions or make specific recommendations.

Methodist Churches in the various countries of the world form a World Methodist Council (WMC). The 1988 **Lambeth Conference** called for the inauguration of a dialogue between the **Anglican Communion** and the WMC. This was established in the following years as the Anglican–Methodist International Commission (AMIC), which produced a 1996 report entitled *Sharing in the Apostolic Communion*. The 1998 Lambeth Conference recommended the formation of a continuing Joint Working Group to sustain a link between the Anglican Communion and the WMC, and the **Inter-Anglican Standing Commission on Ecumenical Relations** (IASCER) considered this in 2001 and agreed to approach the WMC to consider the possible agenda and scope of such a group.

METROPOLITAN. As the early church was organized around cities that acted as centers to **dioceses**, so the chief **bishop** of an area would reside in the metropolis, literally the "mother-city," and become known as the "metropolitan." He would exercise **authority** over the countryside (with oversight of country or **suffragan** bishops). This concept is first expressed in formal terms in the **canons** of the **Council** of Nicea (A.D. 325). As the concept of **provinces** grew, so the sociological relationship of town and country faded from the ecclesiastical understanding. Thus the **archbishop** of **Canterbury** is "metropolitan" of all bishops and dioceses in the South of **England** (i.e., in the province of Canterbury), irrespective of the size or standing of his see city. He is also metropolitan of the scattered extraprovincial dioceses of the **Anglican Communion**. The powers of metropolitans today vary according to the constitution of each Anglican province. *See also* PRIMATE.

MEXICO. Mexico, being from the start of colonization a colony of Spain, was for around three centuries viewed as naturally Spanish-American and **Roman Catholic**. However, following political independence in 1810, some groups of Christians broke away from Rome, and in 1860 such a group (the "Church of Jesus") contacted the **Protestant Episcopal Church in the United States of America** (PECUSA) and asked for support and help. In 1879 Henry Riley was **consecrated** as "**bishop** of the Valley of Mexico," serving there until 1884. Then, after a gap, the **General Convention** of PECUSA of 1904 constituted the **Missionary** District of Mexico and provided a "missionary bishop." This district was divided into three districts in 1972, and they became **dioceses** within **Province** IX in 1980. Further division of dioceses occurred in 1988, and in 1994 these were separated from Province IX to become the Anglican Church of Mexico, a wholly Spanish-speaking province of five dioceses.

MIDDLE EAST. *See* JERUSALEM AND THE MIDDLE EAST.

MINISTER. "Minister" usually translates *diakonos* in the New Testament and in principle should mean "someone who gives service" (e.g., as in Eph. 6.21). However, this broad and informal use was, even in New Testament times, being formalized into denoting the holder of a known and defined office (e.g., Phil. 1.1; 1 Tim. 3.8–10). While historically the **order** of "**deacons**" may have grown from the more formal use, the more general title "minister" has been also passed into use to be a generic term for all who are in any one of the three orders into which people are **ordained**. Thus the classic preface to the **Ordinal**, preceding the rites of 1550, 1552, and 1662, begins with the statement, "[From the apostles' times] there have been these orders of ministers in Christ's church, **bishops**, **priests** and deacons." The word "minister" is often used in the **rubrics** of the **Book of Common Prayer**, usually meaning the "officiant." In non-Episcopal churches, "minister" is the usual word for the one order of ordained persons, and a comparable use was found in the 1604 **canons** of the Church of **England**, where "minister" is almost invariably used in preference to "priest," as in the instruction "none to be made deacon and minister both in one day" (canon 32). The breadth of the word has been expanded in the 20th century to include "lay ministers," that is, people who are of the **laity**, but hold some kind of charter or authorization for tasks they fulfill. Its exact meaning therefore has to be determined by its context. *See also* MINISTRY.

MINISTRY. "Ministry" is the verbal noun from "**minister**," and it has two separate uses. It may be a collective noun for two or more ministers, or it may have a more dynamic sense, denoting the act of ministering, as, for example, one's ministry to or toward some other person (as in the phrase "ministry of word and **sacrament**"). In its role as a collective noun, it usually denotes the **ordained** ministry of the church, though its use can be and is extended beyond that to all those who exercise a ministry (in the second sense of the word explained below). Thus it is perfectly meaningful to refer to "the **lay** ministry" and necessary then to distinguish the "ordained ministry" by the use of the participle "ordained." Its second sense is as an ordinary verbal noun formed from the verb "to minister."

MINSTER. A few **cathedrals** and ancient **parish** churches in **England** are known as "Minsters" (e.g., York Minster, Wimborne Minster). The name has been corrupted from the Latin ***monasterium***, the home (in the Middle Ages) of a community of monks, and (as with "**abbeys**") the building has retained the title long after the monastic community has gone.

MISSIO. MISSIO was the Mission Commission of the **Anglican Communion**, set up by the joint meeting of the ninth **Anglican Consultative Council** (ACC-9) and the **primates** of the Communion at Cape Town in January 1993. It replaced the earlier, more *ad hoc* Mission Issues and Strategy Advisory Group (MISAG), which had been originated (as MISAG I) by ACC-5 in 1981 specifically to oversee the **Partners in Mission** processes and had been reconstituted as MISAG II by ACC-7 with wider terms of reference in 1987. MISSIO at its formation became the first standing commission for the Communion. It was initially chaired by Datuk Yong Ping Chung, the **bishop** of Sabah, and was serviced by Cyril Okorocha, the director for mission and evangelism of the **Anglican Communion Office**.

MISSIO reported at length to the next meeting of the ACC (ACC-10 at Panama City in October 1996), and it was the subject of part of Resolution II.2 at the 1998 **Lambeth Conference**. This came when the post that Okorocha had held had recently been closed, so the resolution asked "that MISSIO be instructed to study further the most efficient and effective ways for the Communion to extend mission and evangelism (e.g., through a mission and evangelism secretary)." MISSIO reported again to ACC-11 in 1999, but Resolution 11 of ACC-11 implemented the recommendation in its report that in effect passed its role on to the new **Inter-Anglican Standing Commission on Mission and Evangelism** (IASCOME).

MISSION. In the New Testament, it was clear that **Jesus** "sent" his disciples into the world, and the Latin verb "to send" (*mittere*, from which "mission" is the verbal noun) is the equivalent of the Greek *apostello*, from which all words of the "apostle" stem derive. Thus the church of **God** was formed by the **Holy Spirit** with God's "mission" task to fulfill. It was thrust out into the world to proclaim the **gospel** in all lands and to make disciples of all nations. Quite apart from the etymology of the word, the concept of "mission" has always been used of an outward thrust in proclamation and service.

However, at the time of the **Reformation**, Christendom prevailed in Europe. There was no "world" outside of the church in a country like **England**. Consequently, the word "mission" does not appear in the **Book of Common Prayer** or the other formularies of the 16th and 17th centuries, and the nearest approach to the concept of "mission" was simply "good works"—as in **Thomas Cranmer**'s **liturgical** text, "that we should do all such good works as thou hast prepared for us to walk in."

The concept of *mission* or *missions* began in the 18th century with a concern for "the heathen," and the word "missionary" had the same connotation. Missions, in this usage, operated at a distance from England and were serviced by **missionary societies** in order that they might evangelize the unbelievers. Though the concept may have been slightly qualified by the rise in the 19th century of "home missions" and by the particular gospel "missions" conducted on both sides of the Atlantic by famous evangelists such as D. L. Moody and R. A. Torrey, the general understanding of missions as being for "heathen lands afar" ran through well into the 20th century. It was the underlying presupposition of the famous interdenominational **Edinburgh Missionary Conference** in 1910, and the overseas field of missionary activity was taken for granted much further into the 20th century in the titles and categorization of "missionary societies."

Later 20th-century reflection not only pinned the task of mission upon the church wherever it resides and functions, but also defined the term "mission" to be a wider concept than "**evangelism**," though containing evangelism within itself. The 1998 **Lambeth Conference** defined "five marks of mission":

(a) to proclaim the Good News of the Kingdom;
(b) to teach, baptize and nurture new believers (incorporating them into the body of Christ);
(c) to respond to human need by loving service;
(d) to seek to transform the unjust structures of society;
(e) to strive to safeguard the integrity of creation and sustain and renew the life of earth. (*The Official Report of the Lambeth Conference 1998*, Section II Report, p. 150)

This fuller understanding of mission roots it in the calling of the whole church, a calling conveyed outwardly in **baptism**, whereby the individual is incorporated **sacramentally** into God's people, his mission on Earth. *See also* MISSIO.

MISSIONARY SOCIETIES. Members of the Church of **England** became first responsive in the 17th century to the need of the **gospel** in newly charted countries in the Americas, in Africa, and in the East (of which there is a hint in the preface to the 1662 **Book of Common Prayer**). No machinery existed for an official creation of branches of the Church of England elsewhere, and energies of individuals with a concern for overseas **mission** moved toward the formation of voluntary societies. An early pointing of the way forward may be found in the establishment by Act of Parliament of the "Society for the Propagation of the Gospel in New England" during the **Commonwealth** period in 1649.

The first two undoubted Anglican societies, both arising from the vision of Thomas Bray, were the **Society for Promoting Christian Knowledge** (SPCK) in 1698 and the **Society for the Propagation of the Gospel** (SPG) in 1701. With the rise in the 18th century of both the **Evangelical Movement** in England and the discovery and annexation by Britain of new lands and peoples across the world's surface, a strong policy was developed, initially among the "**Clapham Sect**," of sending missionaries to bring the gospel to all the world. This led to the formation of the **Church Missionary Society** (CMS) in 1799. Attempts to get the **archbishops** involved merely led to a reply that they would not obstruct or oppose the formation of the society. Other societies followed: the interdenominational British and Foreign Bible Society in 1804, the Church Mission to Jews in 1808, and the **Universities Mission to Central Africa** (UMCA) in 1859. Other missions, with more limited and specific areas of interest, were formed later in the 19th century to work in **Korea**, **India**, **Jerusalem and the Middle East**, **South America**, and elsewhere. To the present time, the descendants of these voluntary societies are the agencies of the Church of England for providing persons and other resources to the Anglican churches overseas; there is no official arm of the **General Synod** or other bodies to do this.

In other **provinces** of the **Anglican Communion**, there has been a tendency to provide overseas missions through a board of General Synod, such as is to be found in the **Episcopal Church (United States of America)** or in the semiofficial **Australian Board of Missions**. Even so, voluntary societies have often continued alongside the official structures, such as in CMS Australia and CMS New Zealand, and a theological debate remains to this day as to whether the banding together of the some, the enthusiasts, to pursue a common missionary purpose is, or is not, to be preferred to the notional involvement of all members through official structures. This was once a debate within the "sending" provinces, but in the second half of the 20th century the developing new provinces of the Communion began to express a mind of their own about the appropriate channels for inter-Anglican sending and receiving of persons and resources.

MIZEKI, BERNARD (c. 1861–1896). Bernard Mizeki was born in Portuguese East Africa (now Mozambique) and migrated to Cape Town at the age of 12, seeking work. There he attended night classes at an Anglican school run by the Society of St. John the Evangelist (the "Cowley Fathers") and became a Christian, being **baptized** on 9 March 1886. He learned at least eight local African **languages** in his years there. In the late 1880s Mizeki accompanied **Bishop** Knight-Bruce, the first bishop of Mashonaland, to a tribal area in what is now **Zimbabwe** and worked as a lay **catechist**. In 1891 he built a mission-complex at Nhowe (near the present-day Marondera) and from there he so ministered the **gospel** that many turned to Christ.

However, he suffered from being portrayed by nationalists as an agent of the colonial power, and during an uprising in 1896, though told he had become a target for violent rebels, he declined to leave and was attacked and speared outside his hut. His newly married wife and a helper found him lying wounded a little way up the hillside and went to get food and blankets for him. On this trip they saw a great light on the hillside, and, when they returned, they found a trail of blood from where they had left him, which went further up the hill until it simply finished near a tree. His body had disappeared and no other trace of it was ever found.

His **martyrdom** has led to his inclusion in the **calendars** of many **provinces** for 18 June, the day of his death. A great commemoration is held annually on the Saturday nearest to 18 June at the shrine built where his hut had stood, and thousands of Anglican worshippers trek from all over Zimbabwe to be present.

MODERNISM. "Modernism" is a 20th-century term for variants on the Christian faith, beginning with a skepticism about the **biblical** accounts and tending toward rationalism, secularism, and humanism. The proponents have usually been more radical in these departures than would be the case with **liberal** theologians, often going to the very edge of theism and even beyond it. In **England** the movement grew in the 1920s, with the foundation of the Modern Churchman's Union, the flourishing of Ripon Hall **Theological College**, and the patronage of E. W. Barnes, **bishop** of Birmingham from 1924 to 1953. Other prominent modernists have included James Pike, bishop of California (1958–1966); Jack Spong, bishop of Newark, New Jersey (1976–1999); Don Cupitt, dean of Emmanuel College, Cambridge (1961–1991); and Richard Holloway, bishop of Edinburgh (1986–2001) and primus of the **Scottish** Episcopal Church (1992–2001).

MOMBASA. Mombasa is a coastal harbor and the major port of the land that is now **Kenya**, and it was a major trading station of the east coast of Africa for centuries before Europeans ever reached it, including being a center of the slave trade with Arabs. This trade was sustained from the 16th century by European entrepreneurs, who famously kept their captives awaiting embarkation in the massive Fort Jesus. Mombasa was the place where Johann Krapf, the first Anglican

missionary in **East Africa**, began his task in 1844, and it was the base of **James Hannington**, when he was **consecrated** in 1884 as the first **bishop** of **Eastern Equatorial Africa**.

When this **diocese** was divided in 1897 and the diocese of **Uganda** was carved from it, the area that is now Kenya along with the northern and central parts of what is now **Tanzania** were renamed the diocese of Mombasa. In 1913 it was the location of the **Kikuyu Controversy**, and its bishop, W. G. Peel, was one of the two Anglican bishops denounced by Bishop **Frank Weston** of **Zanzibar** for participating in the event. The diocese of Central Tanganyika was divided from it in 1927, but it remained the sole diocese for Kenya until the formation of the **province** of East Africa in 1960. Thereafter, as Nairobi became the political center of the independent nation, so, when the province of Kenya was formed in 1970, the archbishopric was located there.

MONASTERY. The etymology of "monastery" derives from the Greek, *mone*, a resting place (cf. John 14.2). But the development of Christian monasticism is usually traced to the late third and early fourth centuries, at a time when persecution of Christians ceased. Indeed, it has been plausibly argued that, in the process of history, monasticism replaced **martyrdom** in modeling extreme self-surrender in the service of Christ and thus exercised the same romantic fascination in the church at large that martyrdom had previously done. The life of such self-surrender took the solitary form of a hermit or the organized life of a "**religious community**." Such communities might be for men or women and were constituted by members binding themselves to each other by vows of poverty, chastity (meaning **celibacy**), and obedience. The obedience involved becoming subject to a community's rules (and to the orders of its superior) and might thus lead to a very tightly controlled life of asceticism, worship, and labor. The term "monk" has usually been confined to men, while "nun" is used for women. However, apart from the presence of **ordained** members of men's communities, the history of the various communities has a parallel character and is treated here together.

At the beginning of the **Reformation** in **England**, King **Henry VIII** saw in the monasteries a likely potential for powerful and organized resistance to his expropriation of the **pope** and his powers. He also saw potential for his own treasury. Between 1536 and 1539 by means of special commissioners, through an Act of Parliament, and by sheer arbitrary pressure, the king closed down all the religious communities and sequestered their assets (this is always known as the "dissolution of the monasteries," though it did of course include the women's communities as well). The assets could hardly have been returned by later generations, and even the fanatically papalist Queen **Mary I** (1553–1558) did not attempt to reverse the effects of the dissolution. Thereafter the lack of monasteries suited the **Protestant** temper of the **Elizabethan** Settlement. Thus it continued for three centuries, though rare experiments, such as **Nicholas Ferrar**'s family community life at Little Gidding in the 17th century, did occur.

The 19th-century revival of monasticism arose from the principles and priorities of the **Anglo-Catholic** movement. **Edward Pusey** administered the first vows to Marion Hughes in 1841, and she founded a convent of nuns in Oxford in 1849. Meanwhile a sisterhood was started in **London** in 1845, and other women's communities followed in quick succession, notably the Community of St. Mary the Virgin at Wantage under the patronage of the vicar, W. J. Butler. Men's communities came a little later, the first being "Father Ignatius's" Benedictine house in Suffolk in 1863. The major initial propagation of the concept of the men's communities came from Richard Meux Benson. He was the moving force behind the founding in 1866 of the Society of St. John the Evangelist (SSJE), in Cowley on the edge of Oxford; its members quickly became known as the "Cowley Fathers." Another of the three cofounders was Charles Grafton, an American, who returned to the **Protestant Episcopal Church in the United States of America** (PECUSA) in 1872 and introduced the Cowley Fathers to the **United States**. Contemplative orders did not begin on either side of the Atlantic until after 1900.

The earlier houses for women were largely involved with working among the poor, but two of the second generation of men's orders—the Community of the Resurrection (CR), which began in Oxford in 1890 and moved to Mirfield in Yorkshire in 1892, and the Society of the Sacred Mission (SSM), which began in London, also in 1890, and moved to Mildenhall in 1897 and on to Kelham in Nottinghamshire in 1903—also provided **theological college** facilities and training. In the case of Mirfield, this was a kind of by-product of the monastic vocation, but in the case of Kelham it represented the main purpose of the community's existence at Kelham itself, and, when, in 1971, it was no longer needed for theological training purposes, it went out of existence there, though the SSM continued work in other places in England and elsewhere in the world. Another religious community that has thrived in Anglicanism is the Society of St. Francis (SSF), though Franciscans have not normally wished to be called "monks."

The monastic communities have had a high **missionary** motivation, and this was exemplified in the founding in England of the Oxford Mission Brotherhood of **Calcutta** in 1879 and the Cambridge Mission to Delhi. But in the 19th century a great variety of such communities existed through the **Anglican Communion**, though they were usually found only where there had been a "high" church background.

Brothers with vows of celibacy for limited periods have also sprung up to meet particular mission needs. Thus the various "bush brotherhoods" in **Australia** usually had a five-year period for individuals to commit themselves, and the **Melanesian** Brotherhood has had a 10-year one. Many communities have also had in fellowship with them people who, while not living with them and not under the same vows, have associated themselves with them as "tertiaries" and endeavored to follow a common rule of life linking them to the particular community.

The first recognition of monastic communities by a **Lambeth Conference** came in 1897. At that conference, a committee expressed thanksgiving for the communities and made recommendations covering vows, the position of ordained monks, Episcopal visitation, and property. Thereafter, the communities were treated as a normal, and beneficial, feature of the Anglican Communion. The first **canon** touching on their relationships with **dioceses** was made in PECUSA in 1913. The 1920 Lambeth Conference gave special attention to women's communities, and the 1930 Lambeth Conference provided a scheme of detailed regulations. An Advisory Council on Religious Communities for the **provinces** of **York** and **Canterbury** arose in the wake of this.

The 1958 Lambeth Conference gave a brief mention in its report, and adopted as Resolution 92 a form of words, that valued the religious communities and hoped that "this form of vocation may find its expression in a wide range of ecclesiastical tradition." It appears that in fact in many provinces in the late 20th century the religious communities were ageing and shrinking, so much so that in the 1998 report the phrase "religious communities" is used to mean the communities formed by the adherents of different religions; the monastic vocation and community life seem not to have been mentioned in the reports since 1958. However, monks and nuns have actually played a valued chaplaincy role in the conferences of 1988 and 1998.

MONASTICISM. *See* MONASTERY; RELIGIOUS COMMUNITIES.

MORAVIAN CHURCH. The original Moravians were a pre-**Reformation Evangelical** body in Bohemia known as the Unitas Fratrum. They were constituted in 1457, broadly following in the steps of John Hus. They continued in Moravia (part of Bohemia) through the Reformation period, but became a **missionary** body with a worldwide vision in the 18th century. Count Nikolaus von Zinzendorf was a key figure in this. Moravians had a vital role in the "heart-warming" of **John Wesley** in 1738.

In the 20th century, the Moravians (not least because they have **bishops** with an arguably respectable succession) appeared to offer real **ecumenical** possibilities to Anglicans. A hope of closer relations with them was expressed at **Lambeth Conferences** between 1878 and 1948, and the hope was briefly reaffirmed at the 1968 conference. Anglicans were involved in conversations with Moravians in **East Africa** in the 1960s, for, perhaps because of their German background, they were a strong Christian presence in **Tanzania**. The relatively small Moravian Church in Great Britain voted in favor of joining the "covenant" proposed between major non–**Roman Catholic** denominations in **England** in 1981–1982, but that was defeated by the Church of England. In 1989 bilateral conversations were opened with the Church of England and these led in 1995 to the "Fetter Lane Agreement," which, though it achieved little except to recommend Local Ecumenical Partnerships where congregations are close to each other, recorded a large measure of **doctrinal** agreement and was accepted by both Churches and by the Church of **Ireland** also. The 1998 Lambeth Conference noted this agreement and commended it to other **provinces**. Its limitations arose not least because to the Moravians the worldwide unity of their Church emerged as of greater significance to them than organic unity in any one country.

In the **United States**, the **Episcopal Church (United States of America)** resolved at its **General Convention** in 1997 to establish a dialogue with the Moravian Church in America. This arose in part from the prior quest for a concordat with the Evangelical **Lutheran Church** of America, which was already in conversation with the Moravians. The dialogue began in 1999 and employed the Fetter Lane Agreement as a starting point. A report in early 2003 recommended to both Churches an "Interim **Eucharistic** Sharing," which did not go to the point of full interchangeability of clergy, but included "joint celebrations of the Eucharist . . . with **ordained ministers** of both churches standing at the **Communion Table** for the Great Thanksgiving." It was accepted by both Churches and was the basis of further progress between Anglicans and Moravians in **Canada** as well.

MORNING (AND EVENING) PRAYER. In the **1549 Book of Common Prayer**, the first comprehensive provision of English-language **liturgy, Thomas Cranmer** produced a new pattern of daily offices. The medieval breviary had a complex structure of daily prayer, involving eight separate offices, and Cranmer reduced these to only two—one for morning and one for evening. They were defended and explained in the **preface**, which in the 1662 Book was reproduced as "Concerning the Service of the Church." Their main features were continuous reading from the Bible on a daily basis, originally for the Old Testament to be read once each year, the New Testament three times, and the Psalter once a month. As daily offices, they have continued through processes of both translation and revision in many **provinces** to be the foundation of the spiritual life of **clergy** and others. In some parts of the world they are said or sung daily as public worship, most notably in **cathedrals**. In the course of history these daily offices also became the main public provision for **Sunday** worship, often enlarged with intercessions, choral items, **hymnody** and preaching, and with a **lectionary** making explicit Sunday provision. Where a weekly main **eucharistic** service has become the heart of a congregation's worship, Morning and Evening Prayer have often been eclipsed; but in less sacramental strands of Anglicanism, or in places where services are inevitably largely **lay**-led, they may still run strongly.

MOTHERS' UNION (MU). The Mothers' Union is an international society of Anglican women. It was founded in **England** in 1876 by Mary Sumner as a **parish** voluntary group in Old Alresford, near Winchester, where her husband was the rector. It remained a parish group only until 1885 when Mary Sumner spoke at a Church Congress in Winchester **diocese**, and the **bishop** decided to make it a diocesan organization with her as president. The first annual report in 1888 showed 88 branches in Winchester diocese and 28 in other dioceses. Fast growth continued, and a national identity was established by the formation in 1896 of a Central Council, with a central constitution—and Sumner as its first central president. Branches had meanwhile been formed since 1886 in various other parts of the **Anglican Communion**, partly through wives of British servicemen abroad and partly through migration of a more permanent sort and the indigenizing of the ideas and principles of the Mothers' Union in new converts and young churches.

An Overseas Committee was formed in 1912 to coordinate relationships, including grants of funds and support of workers alongside overseas **missionary societies**. In 1930, in connection with the **Lambeth Conference**, a first World Wide Conference was held, and in the years since then a series of worldwide presidents has been appointed, specifically to visit diocesan and **provincial** councils of the MU on behalf of the international unity and bonding of the members. However, in the years after 1960, as Anglican provinces around the world have gained autonomy, so their Mothers' Unions have also become autonomous. In many parts of the world, particularly in African provinces, the MU has become an integral feature of official diocesan life, with the bishop's wife as *ex officio* president and with the formation of policy and use of resources relating closely to all other features of diocesan policy.

Whereas for nearly a century membership was confined to women who had been married but once and were living with their husbands or in widowhood, in 1973 the requirements were loosened in various provinces, so that the single and the **divorced** may also belong. There appears to be little or no history of the Mothers' Union in the **United States**.

MOWLL, HOWARD W. K. (1890–1958). Howard Mowll was **ordained** as a **deacon** in **England** in 1913 to join the staff of Wycliffe

College, Toronto; he was then ordained as a **presbyter** in England the following year while still holding the Toronto post. Known as a strong **Evangelical** with a love of **China**, he was **consecrated** as assistant **bishop** of West China in 1922. When Bishop Cassels died in 1925, Mowll succeeded him as diocesan the following year. In 1933 he was elected **archbishop** of **Sydney**, taking up the office in 1934 and continuing there until dying in office in 1958. During these years he entrenched the evangelicalism of the Sydney diocese and became a world leader for Evangelical Anglicans. In 1946 the **Australian** bishops elected him **primate**, a role that gave him further influence across the Commonwealth and internationally.

MUSIC. Christian worship has almost always included the use of music, and its musical needs have elicited down the centuries a great range of creativity and compositions. Music was printed with the first English **litany** in 1544, but the earliest recognized Anglican composer is John Marbeck (or Merbecke), whose *Booke of Common Praier Noted* (1550) set all the singable parts of the 1549 **Book of Common Prayer** to simple chant (partly original, partly adapted from earlier plainsong). In adopting the principle of one note for each syllable and no polyphony, he furthered the whole program of the **Reformation**, revealing a reformed understanding of the importance of conveying the word. This would have been sung by the "clerks," as the 1549 **rubrics** make clear, rather than by the people. With the 1552 Prayer Book, virtually all singing disappeared—largely, it is thought, under the influence of the Swiss Reformers.

Queen **Elizabeth I** gave some encouragement to church musicians. In the Chapel Royal as well as in some of those endowed choral foundations (**cathedrals** and collegiate chapels) that had survived the turmoil of the 1530s and 1540s, there was a flowering of choral music to English texts. Significant composers included Thomas Tallis, William Byrd, and Orlando Gibbons, and many settings of responses and canticles dating from the reigns of Elizabeth and King **James I** remain in the repertoire of Anglican choirs today. The anthem also emerged during this period; "verse anthems" included accompanied solo sections. Cathedrals and some other establishments had organs, although there was increasing opposition from **Puritans**. Despite the rich musical tradition that was developing (though with little impact on **parish** churches) and the staunch defense of music by **Richard Hooker**, the 1604 **canons** give no hint of any use of music in worship at all. With the English Civil War leading to a Puritan victory, organs were banned and often destroyed and all use of music in worship, save possibly the singing of metrical psalms, was discouraged and widely eliminated.

The **Restoration** saw a new interest in music generally, and the 1662 Prayer Book made provision, after the third **collect** at **Morning and Evening Prayer**, for "In quires and places where they sing, here followeth the anthem." What became known as Anglican chant evolved from harmonized psalm tones in the choral foundations as a way of singing prose psalms and canticles, while elsewhere metrical psalms remained popular. Choirs were encouraged, a new phase of organ building was begun, and instrumentalists started to appear in parish churches. On the other hand, much parish life in the 18th century was run in a desultory or dead manner, so that the impact of renewed church music was very patchy, and in large areas nonexistent. It was onto this scene that the **Wesleys** came beginning in 1738, and "**Methodism** was born in song." Except among **Evangelicals**, parish churches took to song more slowly, but **hymnody**, metrical psalms, and even chanting of canticles, responses, and nonmetrical psalms started to find their way into the worship of the Church of **England** in the early 19th century.

In the second half of the 19th century, the **Anglo-Catholic** movement led to vast changes in parish church music in England, and its impact was felt throughout the whole of the world. There was a revival of chant, including plainsong, a vast new provision of hymns, and widespread pressure to provide a pipe organ in every parish church, with a robed choir securely placed in choir stalls in a **Gothic** chancel. Parish churches were being encouraged to become minicathedrals.

By the turn of the 20th century, there were many parishes with a "high mass" as the main service of Sunday morning. Marbeck was revived, and composers began to produce **eucharistic** settings alongside psalm chants and other choral music—whether simply for choirs or with an expectation of congregational singing also. While different hymnbooks were published in many parts of the world and new composers appeared, there appears to have been a period of more than half a century within which a consistent genre of Anglican church music reigned unchallenged—and even **vernacular** hymns in many parts of

Africa and India tended to be either English hymns in translation or locally composed lyrics using English tunes. Without any **missionary society** or other **authoritative** body consciously producing a policy, an English cultural colonialism prevailed across the Earth's surface. Possibly the only variants were the chorus and the mission hymn.

Standards of choral singing and organ playing were raised during the 20th century, partly through the influence of organizations such as the Royal School of Church Music (RSCM, originally founded in 1927 as the School of English Church Music). Official attempts to investigate and improve the contribution of music to Anglican **liturgy** were made, with the **archbishops** of **Canterbury** and **York** appointing a commission that produced the report *Music in Worship* (1922); similar initiatives led to *Music in Church* (1951) and *In Tune with Heaven* (1992). While the tradition of all-male choirs has been maintained in many places, musical opportunities for **women** and girls have also developed. A variety of approaches to singing the psalms has been explored, including responsorial psalmody, and greater **ecumenical** cooperation has been one factor in the expansion of musical styles and repertoire. The organ remains the chief accompanying instrument for many Anglicans, but guitars, keyboards, drums, and various melodic instruments increasingly found a place from the late 1950s, as more popular musical idioms came into use. The **Charismatic Movement** contributed to the development of music groups, with a lay musician often taking an important role in leading the congregation's worship. The liturgical revision that has led to contemporary-**language** texts has not always been matched by the provision of musical settings; the styles of art music prevalent in the late 20th century have not easily lent themselves to congregational singing, and professional musicians have tended to prefer traditional texts.

The music of the **Episcopal Church (United States of America)** has been much influenced by the Church of England, including its choral tradition, but one significant difference is the adoption of some metrical psalms and hymns as an official part of the liturgy. The 1982 edition of *The Hymnal* also includes a substantial liturgical section ("Service Music") along with some songs reflecting the cultural variety of North American society. The hymn-anthem is a widely used form that links choir and congregation.

The Association of Anglican Musicians, founded in 1967, has encouraged composers to write for the Church, and the RSCM has branches in North America and **Canada** as well as in **Europe**, South Africa, **Australia**, and New Zealand. The impact of the simple, repetitive music of the ecumenical Taizé Community has been widespread, and its chants appear in hymnbooks and supplements the world over. A different ethos has sprung from the Charismatic Movement and its songs (often short and repetitive) of renewal, sometimes dubbed "worship songs."

While the influence of European musical styles remains strong throughout the **Anglican Communion**, efforts have been made to explore the use of indigenous music, for example, by using drums as a call to worship in parts of Africa, traditional **dance** rhythms in Latin America, and traditional local instruments in many places. An astonishing array of styles is in use across the world at the start of the 21st century, with technological developments increasing still further the options available to Anglican congregations. The diversity may lead to division or conflict. For some, music remains a separate element "added on" to worship, but recent liturgical revision acknowledges the value of music that is integrated into the liturgy. *See also* EASTER ANTHEMS.

MUTUAL RESPONSIBILITY AND INTERDEPENDENCE IN THE BODY OF CHRIST (MRI). The concept of "mutual responsibility and interdependence" was set out in a document prepared at a meeting of **primates** and **metropolitans** of the **Anglican Communion** in London in 1963 a few days before the opening of the **Anglican Congress** in Toronto that year. It was a call to increase the mutual contributions and sharing between **provinces** so as to benefit a "Directory of Projects" (awaiting funding), and to facilitate this by the appointing of regional officers. The document was duly presented to the congress by some of its signatories, where it encountered a somewhat mixed reaction, there being hesitation as to whether it was forgetting **ecumenical** relationships on the one hand and was insufficiently precise on the other. It was nevertheless viewed as current in the years thereafter, though no worldwide coordinating ever came into existence. The MRI proposal was damned with faint praise at the 1968 **Lambeth Conference**, which also called in its Resolution 67 for a "reappraisal of the policies, methods, and areas of responsibility of the Anglican Communion." It was finally buried by the **Anglican Consultative Council** (ACC) at its second meeting (ACC-2) in 1973, when the concept of **Partners in Mission** was put forward as a better model for interprovincial mutual help and enrichment.

MYANMAR. Myanmar was formerly called Burma and was a British colony until its independence in 1948. It was predominantly Buddhist in its religious stance. From the ministry of occasional chaplains and of **missionaries** sent by the **Society for the Propagation of the Gospel** in the 19th century, an Anglican church was founded, and the **diocese** of Rangoon was formed in 1877. In the 1920s the newly formed **Bible Churchmen's Missionary Society** started missionary work among the animistic hill tribes in the north and west of the country and saw further conversions. In 1930 the diocese became part of a new **province**, the Church of **India**, Burma, and Ceylon (CIBC), which became the Church of India, **Pakistan**, Burma, and Ceylon (CIPBC) when Pakistan was formed as India became independent in 1947. In 1961 Buddhism was declared the state religion of Burma, and visas for expatriate Christian missionaries were no longer issued after 1966. When in 1970 the united churches of **North India** and Pakistan came into existence, the dismantling of CIPBC meant that the province of Myanmar was formed with the creation of new dioceses. The province has labored under great difficulties since the oppressive military regime took power in 1988. In 2004 there were six dioceses.

MYSTERY. In the New Testament, the normal meaning of the Greek word *musterion* is "a plan of **God** not fully disclosed during the Old Testament period but brought to light through the coming of Christ," and it particularly relates to the inclusion of the Gentiles alongside the Jews in the saving purposes of God (see, e.g., Eph. 3.6, 3.9). However, St. Paul goes on in Eph. 5.32 to describe the metaphorical use of **marriage** to depict the relationship between Christ and his church as a great *musterion*. At this point the Greek word *musterion* was translated in the Latin versions (notably St. Jerome's Vulgate) as *sacramentum*. Later theologians in turn used the Greek word as generally interchangeable with the Latin *sacramentum*, and that use has passed deeply into Anglican linguistic currency. **Thomas Cranmer**

retained the concept when, in the post-Communion prayer of the 1552 **Book of Common Prayer**, he wrote, "We, who have duly received these holy mysteries." Although the word does not appear in the Thirty-Nine **Articles**, it has had a regular use in the field of **sacramental** theology since. In the **Roman Catholic Church**, a whole theology of mystery was developed within the **Liturgical Movement**, particularly through Dom Odo Casel at the **monastery** of Maria Laach in the Rhineland, and this usage became a key concept in Anglican–Roman Catholic conversations.

– N –

NARRATIVE. The term "narrative" is used in **liturgical** study to denote the account of our Lord's institution of the **Lord's Supper**. This account, sometimes known by its fuller title of "narrative of institution," has figured in all known Anglican **eucharistic** liturgies, but in somewhat different roles at different times. In the 1549 **Book of Common Prayer**, the marginal **rubrics** (often called "**indented rubrics**") prescribed two **manual acts**, which strongly suggested that the **priest**'s words and actions within the reciting of the narrative provided moments of **consecration** of the **elements** of **bread** and wine. This was clearly not the case in the 1552 Book, where the narrative was simply read for the people to hear, as a warrant text to demonstrate that the **celebration** at which they were present was indeed that which the Lord commanded to his people. The bread and wine did not even have to be within the reach of the priest.

Although the 1559 **Act of Uniformity** revived the 1552 Book, and the eucharistic rite in it remained unaltered, it became standard among Anglicans in Queen **Elizabeth I**'s reign to state that the use of the narrative in the rite demonstrates that there is a concept of objective consecration effected by the use of the dominical words. The 1604 **canons** then required repetition of those words by any officiant adding further bread and wine, though the canons do not use the word "consecration." Indented rubrics and manual acts (and the title "Prayer of Consecration") returned with the 1637 **Scottish** Book, and in 1662 these expanded to five rubrics prescribing five manual acts, including a **fraction**.

As far as the Church of **England** was concerned, the way was now set with very clear moments of consecration matching the normal **Roman Catholic** understanding. Thus there was a framework ready in the 19th century for the advanced **Anglo-Catholics** to impose full Roman **ceremonial** onto the narrative, as it occurred in the 1662 rite. Much of this persists in various parts of the world to the present day, even when the rationale of the rite has changed. However, in 18th-century Scotland, the move toward an Eastern-type **epiclesis** located in the Eastern position after the **anamnesis**, would appear to have called in question the simple view of consecration by the dominical words in the narrative. The 1764 Scottish form of the epiclesis was a very explicit "bless and sanctify . . . these thy gifts and creatures . . . that they may become the body and blood of thy most dearly beloved Son." It would be difficult, using a text of this sort, to assert that the bread and wine had already "become the body and blood" at an earlier point, specifically during the narrative of institution, and that difficulty in turn would make Roman-type ceremonial inappropriate. (The 1764 rite provided for supplementary consecration by the repetition of the whole prayer after the Sanctus as far as this epiclesis—an enormous amount for the officiant to say, but a clear attempt not to determine a "moment" of consecration too closely.) All later rites that have this Eastern position for an epiclesis, from the 1789 use in the **Protestant Episcopal Church in the United States of America** onward, have posed the same problems—as to both the consecratory role (if any) of the narrative and the method to be used for supplementary consecration.

The reformed **tradition** of the Lord's Supper has often included the reading of the narrative as a warrant text before following through with the dominical action. It has then not come in any great thanksgiving, and the thanksgiving has not been adjusted to include it. No consecratory force can then be attributed to the narrative. Some impact of this pattern is found in the eucharistic rites of the united Church of **North India** (CNI), which includes Presbyterian and other **Reformed Churches** in its ancestry. In the CNI rites, reading of the narrative in this "warrant" role is a permitted alternative to providing it within the **eucharistic prayer**. Anglicans in other **provinces** have at intervals expressed an interest in this pattern, but there are no authorized texts following the pattern. Nevertheless, since the 1958 **Lambeth Conference** urged that the whole thanksgiving be viewed as consecratory, some of the past weighting of the dominical words in the narrative has been lightened.

NATAL. *See* COLENSO, JOHN WILLIAM; LAMBETH CONFERENCE; SOUTHERN AFRICA.

NATIONAL ASSEMBLY OF THE CHURCH OF ENGLAND. *See* ENABLING ACT, ESTABLISHMENT.

NAVE. The main body of a church building is called the "nave," a word drawn from the Latin word for a ship (as are "navy" and "naval"). It is usually employed to distinguish the main congregational part of the building (at the "west" end) from the choir or chancel (at the "east" end), from which it may be separated by a screen. *See also* ARCHITECTURE; GOTHIC.

NETWORKS. The **Anglican Consultative Council** (ACC), via its **Anglican Communion Office** (ACO), recognizes and supports a series of networks that draw together Anglicans with common concerns or parallel responsibilities from across the Communion, though with neither commitment of funds nor control of membership or agenda. The networks have usually arisen through a request from the ACC, from a **Primates Meeting**, or from a **Lambeth Conference**. Some began around 1984, but greater development came in the 1990s. In 2005 the following networks were listed as officially recognized by the ACO: the International Anglican Youth Network, the Refugee and Migrants Network, the **International Anglican Family Network** (IAFN), the Colleges and Universities of the Anglican Communion, the Anglican Indigenous People's Network, the **Anglican Urban Network**, the Francophone Network, the Legal Advisers Network, the Network for Interfaith Concerns, the Peace and Justice Network, the Anglican Communion Environmental Network, and the International Anglican Women's Network. The **International Anglican Liturgical Consultation**, while not usually called a "network," shares many common characteristics with the networks.

The 1988 Lambeth Conference, in its Resolution 53, directed the ACC to "explore the establishment of a telecommunication network linked to every Province." The steps the ACC was able to take did not result in such a network, though the ACO has sustained such communications right across the Anglican Communion. However, in 2004 the issue of a network was overtaken by the formation of an **Inter-Anglican Telecommunications Commission**.

NEW GUINEA. *See* PAPUA NEW GUINEA.

NEW ZEALAND. *See* AOTEAROA.

NEWMAN, JOHN HENRY (1801–1890). John Henry Newman was **ordained** as a **deacon** in 1824 and a **presbyter** in 1825. He became vicar of St. Mary the Virgin, the Oxford University church, in 1828, and it was from there that he led the **Oxford Movement** or **Anglo-Catholic** revival. Newman himself always traced the movement's origins to **John Keble**'s Assize Sermon on 14 July 1833, but the wider impact of the movement began with the first publication of ***Tracts for the Times*** in September 1833. These tracts owed much to Newman, and he himself was author of Tract 1 and many subsequent ones, right through to the famous last one, Tract 90 in 1841. The consistent tenor of them was to promote the concept of "**apostolic succession**," in which the allegedly unbroken chain of **ordinations** by **bishops**, from the time of the apostles through the **Reformation** down to the Church of **England** of his own time, was the guarantee of the standing of the Church of England as still the catholic Church of the land.

However, sometime in 1839, according to his own *Apologia pro Vita Sua*, Newman "had seen the shadow of a hand upon the wall." Its meaning, as he understood it, was that the **Roman Catholic Church** would be proved right after all, and from then on he could never be the same again. When in 1841 the Church of England participated in a joint scheme with German **Lutherans** to provide a bishop for **Jerusalem**, to him this was so obviously uncatholic as to disqualify the Church of England's claims. In the same year, Newman published in Tract 90, the last of the *Tracts for the Times*, an exposition of the Thirty-Nine **Articles** such as to make them patient of almost all unreformed doctrine. He viewed this as "proving the cannon," but it proved too much for the "cannon" (i.e., the Church of England) to bear, and the hostility the tract aroused assisted his disenchantment with the *via media* he had previously propounded.

In 1843 Newman withdrew to Littlemore, resigned the incumbency of St. Mary's, retracted all anti-Roman statements he had ever made, ceased taking **Communion**, and gave up any form of **ministry** he might until then have exercised. In October 1845 he was received into the Church of Rome. In due course he led the Oratory in Birmingham and became a cardinal, though he seems to have always been viewed as slightly dangerous by Roman Catholic authorities. His *Apologia*, giving an autobiographical account of much of his time as an Anglican, was published in 1866, as a spirited and detailed reply to a public accusation of deviousness and of economy with the truth. Some commentators have traced the reforming mood of **Vatican II** to the long-term influence of Newman's thought.

NICENE CREED. The **creed** associated with the Councils of Nicea and Constantinople is usually called the Nicene Creed. It was retained at the **Reformation**, not because it stemmed from General **Councils**, nor because it had been universally believed, but (on Reformation grounds) because it "may be proved by most certain warrants of holy Scripture" (**Article** VIII of 1571). Its use has been almost entirely within the **Communion** service. It is bracketed with the **Apostles' Creed** to form the second side of the **Lambeth Quadrilateral**. In recent years international **ecumenical** English-language versions of the creed have been recommended, first by the **International Consultation on English Texts** (ICET) and later by the **English Language Liturgical Consultation** (ELLC). These have been adopted in principle in most English-speaking **provinces**, though there are some difficulties that have led to minor adaptations. The most notable difficulties are finding the best rendering "of the **Holy Spirit** and the Virgin **Mary**"; addressing the phrase "and was made man" in the face of issues of **inclusive language**; and excluding the ***Filioque*** ("and [from] the Son") wording from the line about the procession of the Holy Spirit from the Father.

NIGERIA. Nigeria is the most populous country in sub-Saharan Africa. The first Anglican Christian contact was provided by the **Church Missionary Society** (CMS) missionary Henry Townsend, who arrived with a **Methodist** compatriot and held a **Communion** service on **Christmas** Day 1842. At that stage, freed slaves were being returned from **Sierra Leone**, many of them Christianized, and this led to **Samuel Crowther**'s arrival in the same area in 1843. CMS had a fully settled **mission** by 1857, and a **diocese** of the Niger was created in 1864; Crowther himself was nominated to it and became the first African Christian to be **consecrated** as an Anglican **bishop**.

Nigeria continued as a single Anglican diocese until 1919. Then a diocese of Lagos was formed, and the two Nigerian dioceses were in 1951 grouped with **Sierra Leone**, Gambia and the Rio Pongas, and Accra to become the **province** of **West Africa**. Further division of the Nigerian sees followed almost immediately. Nigeria became an independent nation in 1960, but after a political assassination, it was divided by the Biafran secession in 1967–1970. The Anglican church survived this deep tribal division and has gone on growing. The Nigerian dioceses left the province of West Africa in March 1979 at the formation of the autonomous province of Nigeria.

In 1988 there were 26 dioceses, but in a new venture to mark the "Decade of **Evangelism**," the province created new missionary sees, largely in the relatively unevangelized Islamic northern parts of the country, and sent evangelist bishops to start planting churches there. This led to the division of the province itself into a Church of Nigeria with three provinces in 1997. By 2004 there were 78 dioceses formed into ten provinces.

NIPPON SEI KO KAI. *See* JAPAN.

NONJURORS. "Nonjuror" means literally "nonswearing." At the time of the **Glorious Revolution** in 1689–1690, this title was given to the **clergy** (and in some cases **laity**) who, having already taken an **oath** of loyalty to King **James II** (whether or not they approved of his doings), reckoned themselves unable in conscience to switch their allegiance to **William III** and **Mary II**. The nonjurors included six of the seven **bishops** who had been put on trial by James for seditious libel, notable among them being **William Sancroft**, the **archbishop** of **Canterbury**. All who declined to take the new oath of allegiance were in due course deprived of their livings, and became a semiunderground movement, technically treasonable as praying for James II as king. Some, such as **Thomas Ken**, were content to live out their days quietly, but others, led by George Hickes, determined to continue the movement and began **consecrating** bishops to that end. Hickes himself was the first of these in 1694. In this they were in partnership with the **Scottish** Episcopalians, all of whose bishops had refused the oath and were therefore also semiunderground. The spiritual writer William Law was one of the most notable (and peaceable) of the English nonjurors.

The movement proved to have little internal cohesion, and in 1716 it split into two strands, distinguished from each other by their **liturgical** practices—dubbed the "usagers" and the "non-usagers." The four main "usages" were a departure from the Church of **England's** 1662 **Book of Common Prayer** and a deliberate reversion to "primitive" precedent. They consisted of:

1. the mixed cup (or mandatory addition of water to the wine before consecration)
2. the **epiclesis** (or invocation of the **Holy Spirit** to make the **sacramental** action effective)
3. the **eucharistic** oblation (or **anamnesis** with offering of the **elements** to God)
4. petitions for the faithful **dead**

The nonusagers responded that these practices were not commanded in scripture and that adopting them actually undermined their claim to be the true continuing Church of **England**. The two sides attempted to patch up their disagreement in 1732, but it fell apart, and the whole movement was by then losing impetus and adherents.

The schism ultimately lasted just more than 100 years, during which the two Jacobite rebellions of 1715 and 1745 exposed the nonjurors to further opposition, along with falling self-confidence and a diminishing following. Finally the deaths of Bonnie Prince Charlie ("the Young Pretender") in 1788 and of his younger brother Henry (who was a **Roman Catholic** cardinal) in 1807, neither of whom left a legitimate heir, extinguished all hopes for a return to the Jacobite monarchy. The last bishop of the nonjuring line also died in 1805. The laws against Jacobites had by then been relaxed, as the political threat was over, and the ecclesiastical schism had run out of steam well before those formal last stages.

NORTH INDIA. Northern **India** was the first place in Asia to receive an Anglican **bishop**, when Thomas Middleton was appointed bishop of

Calcutta in 1814, with a jurisdiction that then included not only all of Asia but probably Australasia also. The responsibility for Australasia was made explicit in the mandate to Middleton's successor, Reginald Heber, in 1822. Further Indian dioceses were created in Madras (now Chennai) in 1835 and in Bombay (now Mumbai) in 1837; **Australia**, **New Zealand**, and the Pacific were separated from Calcutta in 1836.

In 1930 the Anglican dioceses in India, Burma, and Ceylon were formed into a self-governing **province**: the Church of India, Burma, and Ceylon (CIBC). Four dioceses in **South India** left this province in 1947 to become part of the united Church of South India, thus leaving the Indian component of what now became the Church of India, **Pakistan**, Burma, and Ceylon (CIPBC) to be labeled "North India."

The Anglican dioceses of North India were in ecumenical conversation before the union in South India was completed, and a negotiating committee drawing together representatives of six different churches was formally constituted in 1951. However, the **Lambeth Conferences** of 1948 and 1958 were so hostile to the way in which South India had integrated the **ordained ministries** into an Episcopal framework—without existing **presbyters** being Episcopally ordained—that North India devised a new (if ambiguous) pattern of inaugurating the union with an Episcopal laying on of hands on all existing presbyters with a carefully devised form of prayer that did not explicitly state that the **ministers** were being ordained. **Baptists**, Brethren, and Disciples of Christ were also involved, bringing together, with careful guidelines, those who **baptize** infants with those who are opposed to baptizing them. A fourth version of the plan was reached in 1965 and adopted by the Churches. Thus the union was finally implemented on 29 November 1970, and the united Church of North India (CNI) came into existence and, like the Church of South India, technically left the **Anglican Communion**.

Very close relationships have continued, beginning with most provinces of the Communion declaring themselves to be in "**full Communion**" with CNI (though with the rider, explicit in some provinces, that the rite of unifying ministries was deemed to have conveyed covert Episcopal **ordination** on those presbyters who had not previously received it). A moderator is appointed for a limited period and acts as **metropolitan**. *The Book of Common Worship* was published in 1995 to mark the 25th anniversary of the uniting of the denominations and to provide a **liturgical** bonding of the Church. There were 26 dioceses in 2004.

Bishops of CNI were guest participants in the Lambeth Conferences of 1978 and 1988, and by a process initiated by the **Anglican Consultative Council** in 1987, between 1987 and 1989 CNI became a full member church of the Anglican Communion (without denying or abandoning its similar relationships to worldwide **Methodism** and other parent bodies). Thus its bishops attended the 1998 Lambeth Conference as members, not guests.

In India itself, a "concordat" binds together the Church of North India, the Church of South India, and the **Mar Thoma Syrian Orthodox Church**. Each prays specifically for the others, shares in the consecration of bishops with the others, and keeps in close friendly relationships.

NORTH SIDE. The fourth **rubric** at the beginning of the **Communion** service in the 1552 **Book of Common Prayer** refers to the **priest** "standing at the North side of the **table**." It appears that at the time the table itself was movable and in many church buildings would have been arranged on an east–west axis, either in the **chancel** or in the **nave** (as the 1552 rubric provided), so that "north side" then represented a position halfway down a long side of an oblong. In the reign of King **Charles I**, however, the action of **Archbishop William Laud** led to Communion tables being generally placed on a north–south axis against the east wall, and "north side"—the text of the rubric being retained and followed literally—now meant the **presbyter** was at one short end of the oblong, sideways to the congregation. In 1662, the 1552 rubric was retained, despite the east wall position of the tables. The revisers were, however, clear that "side" meant the compass point direction from the table and had no implications about the shape or orientation of the table itself.

When **eastward position** reappeared in the Church of **England** in the 1850s, north side started to decline. The Purchas Judgment in 1872 judged eastward position illegal, but the Lincoln Judgment in 1890 accepted it. All around the Anglican world in the late 19th century and until World War II, north side gave way faster and faster to eastward position, which became the dominant and normal Anglican position. North side remained as the use solely of **Evangelicals** in England, though in the Church of **Ireland** a consistent use of north side, as reinforced by the rubrics of the 1878 and 1926 Prayer Books, ran through until the second half of the 20th century. Similarly, other parts of the **Anglican Communion** that had a strongly Evangelical character tended to preserve north side in resistance to the inroads of eastward position.

From the late 1940s on, there was a rise of **westward position**, which marched with the reordering of church building interiors to bring the table nearer to the people and leave space behind it where a **presider** could stand. On the whole, this has carried most of the north side constituency, which had much less reason to resist this than they had had to resist eastward position, and north side has consequently nearly disappeared in most **provinces** where westward has come.

NULLITY. In any rite or relationship conferred once for life, it is necessary to establish the conditions under which it can be attested beyond doubt that the rite has been given or the relationship started. Thus King **Henry VIII**'s famous matrimonial cause was a quest for a nullity (i.e., a declaration that no **marriage** had ever existed) on the grounds that the ceremony he and Catherine had gone through could not have been a marriage, as she was his deceased brother's widow and thus within the "prohibited degrees" that made Henry's relationship to her not marriage but incest.

In the **Roman Catholic** Church today, there is no recognition that an existing marriage can be dissolved by **divorce**; however, an investigation leading (on whatever grounds) to a verdict of nullity leaves both parties technically unmarried and free therefore to marry as if for the first time.

The concept of nullity applies equally to other once-in-a-lifetime rites. Thus it is usual for Anglicans to treat, for example, Mormon **baptism** as null and not Christian baptism at all. Similarly the concept of nullity was famously expressed in the 1896 papal encyclical ***Apostolicae Curae***, which declared Anglican **ordinations** (and thus Anglican **orders**) "absolutely null and utterly void."

NUN. A nun is a female member of a **religious community** under vows. A community of nuns inhabits a nunnery, often called a "convent." The historical place of women's communities is described in the entry for **monasteries** above.

– O –

OATH. To make an oath is to "swear," and there have been two Christian views about the appropriateness of this. **Jesus** taught that we should not swear (Matt. 5.33–37), and in many countries to this day those with a conscience against swearing are allowed to make a solemn affirmation instead. However, St. Paul himself was perfectly ready to support his affirmations with phrases like "As God is my witness." Thus **Article** XXXVII declares that citizens may with good conscience take such oaths.

The issue of an oath took on special significance in Anglican church history in the wake of the **Glorious Revolution** of 1689–1690. The **royal supremacy** and its ecclesiastical undergirding were focused in the oath of allegiance to the monarch taken by the Anglican **clergy**. Thus King **James II**, though himself not only a **Roman Catholic** but also subversive of the Church of **England**, was the one to whom the unbreakable allegiance had been sworn. When he fled the country in 1688, and Parliament in due course offered the crown jointly to William of Orange and his wife Mary, James's **Protestant** daughter, many clergy (from the **archbishop** of **Canterbury** down) felt themselves unable to break their oaths of allegiance to James while he was still alive, and they became "**nonjurors**" (i.e., "nonswearers" from the Latin word for swearing).

The oath of allegiance to the monarch runs on within the life of the Church of England in the 21st century, although because it is not required of non-British clergy, it cannot be interpreted as swearing allegiance to the monarch as supreme governor of the Church of England. It would appear simply to be used as an occasion when British clergy reaffirm their loyalty to the Crown in their role as citizens.

A more general use of the concept of an oath is the widespread use of an oath of **canonical** obedience to the **bishop**, in most **provinces** taken by clergy both at **ordination** and at institution or licensing to a new **ministry**. This views the bishop as the administrator and guardian of **canon law**, but does not bind whoever is taking the oath beyond the limits of canon law.

OFFERTORY. The term "offertory" was received in the reformed rites of the Church of **England** from the medieval **mass**. In the mass, it had been the point of preparation of the **bread** and wine on the **altar** with elaborate **ceremonial**, ready for the **canon** of the mass and the **consecration** of the **elements**. However, in two quick stages, **Thomas Cranmer** changed the content of the word. The first stage came in the 1549 **Book of Common Prayer**, where the "offertorium" was a psalm chanted by the clerks while the people were coming forward to place their alms in the "poor men's box." The second stage in 1552 went further, abolishing the chant and the movement by the people; the "offertory" became simply the title of the collection of money. In both 1549 and 1552 it was completely detached from any idea that the offertory was for preparing either the **table** or the **sacramental** elements—the scripture sentences that were read were exhortations to give money, all mention of preparing the table had disappeared, and the offertory belonged to the ante-Communion and was ordered even for occasions when the service was not proceeding to the **celebration** of the sacrament (which in fact became the regular Sunday practice). In 1662 a **rubric** was added referring to placing the bread and wine on the table immediately after the collection of alms. However, the term "offertory" kept its Cranmerian use and was not related to the bread and wine and was still to be used when there was no Communion.

Throughout the English-speaking world, the "offertory" kept this meaning, and it has been a regular term for a collection of money in many non-Anglican denominations. However, despite the clear Prayer Book use, the **Anglo-Catholic** movement led to a shift to **Roman Catholic** understanding, and since the 19th century the term has regularly referred to the preparation of the bread and wine and has attracted to itself, first, the quotation from 1 Chron. 29 that was introduced into the **Scottish** Episcopal rites in the 18th century to refer to almsgiving and, later, the post–**Vatican II** Roman Catholic "offertory prayers." In the 19th century in England, legal battles were fought over the issue of using credence tables as a place from which, at the "offertory," the elements were to be brought to the main table (or altar) for consecration.

In the 20th century, however, a new emphasis was introduced by the advocacy of **Gregory Dix**; he taught that the bringing up of the elements to the table is the first of the four "instituted" acts commanded of **Jesus**—that is, that this is the "taking" of the bread and wine. This led to a new ceremonial pattern in many places, where the elements were brought up in procession from the back by **laypeople**, to be received by the **president** at the Communion table. Dix called this the "layman's **liturgy**"—a theologically significant and foundational role of the layperson in the celebration of the **eucharist**. This "offertory theology" has been queried as an improper application of the **narrative** of institution (for the preparation of the table would seem to relate more closely to the very preliminary action of the disciples going ahead of Jesus to prepare the upper room), and it was dubbed by **Michael Ramsey** a "shallow and romantic **Pelagianism**." However the popularity of the procession has run on without great respect to such damaging criticism of its underlying theology.

The modern Roman Catholic "offertory prayers," often borrowed by Anglicans, run close to Dix's romanticism and appear to have appealed particularly to the constituency that followed him. The prayers not only refer to the created and manufactured origin of the elements being supplied ("which earth has given and human hands have made") but also treat these still unconsecrated elements as an offering to God. Opponents assert that both these emphases lack scriptural warrant in relation to the eucharistic rite, that the second is simply wrong, and that the style of thanksgiving in the prayers provides an appearance of a short (if unusual) **eucharistic prayer** and is therefore unhelpful.

OLD CATHOLICS. The Old Catholic Churches stem from an extraordinary series of events surrounding the **archbishopric** of Utrecht in the Netherlands in the years from 1723 to 1742. The **diocese** had been founded in 696 by St. Willibrord, and the **dean** and **chapter** of Utrecht **Cathedral** had retained an ancient right, when a vacancy occurred, of choosing the new **bishop** themselves and simply sending notice of his name to the **pope**; this was unlike the normal practice of most **Roman Catholic** sees both in the 18th century and today whereby the pope, after seeking advice—from the papal nuncio, among others—himself nominates the appointee. When the see of Utrecht became vacant in the 1720s, the dean and chapter claimed their ancient right of election and, having chosen Cornelius Steenoven in 1723, notified the pope and sought his **ordination** as bishop. The pope, however, who wished to suppress the see because of its supposed Jansenism, refused to comply.

By providence or odd luck, there was an inactive Roman Catholic bishop living in the Netherlands at the time. Dominique Varlet, assigned as the bishop of Babylon, had earlier conducted **confirmations** in Amsterdam (due to the lack of a Dutch **episcopate**) while en route to his see. On his arrival in Babylon, Varlet had been suspended from his episcopate, in part because of his irregular confirmations in Amsterdam, and he then returned and settled in Amsterdam in 1720. Varlet agreed to **consecrate** Steenoven in 1724 and also went on to consecrate his successors (who were similarly chosen by the dean and chapter and refused by the Pope) until 1742, when Varlet himself died. The **validity** of such single-bishop consecrations was not in doubt either in Utrecht or in Rome and has been recognized ever since.

The diocese of Utrecht went on to revive the defunct see of Haarlem and later added Deventer. Popes regularly excommunicated the new bishops, but the three dioceses continued quietly for 150 years, remaining a small and noncompetitive Dutch peculiarity, though so hampered during the Napoleonic Wars that a point came where two sees were vacant and the bishop of the third, having fallen into an icy canal on a winter night, was rescued by his coachman only just in time to keep the succession alive.

After 1870 and **Vatican I**, the situation changed. Under the leadership of J. J. I. von Dollinger, a professor at Munich who refused to accept the Vatican I decree on papal **infallibility**, thousands of Roman Catholics in Germany, Austria, and Switzerland left the Roman Catholic Church and sought to organize themselves as "Old Catholics" (i.e., Catholics who believed as they reckoned the Catholic Church generally had believed until Vatican I). They held conferences in Bonn in 1871 and 1872 and naturally looked to the archbishop of Utrecht for help, and he visited Germany and performed confirmations. Joseph Reinkens was elected as first German Old Catholic bishop, and, as the archbishop of Utrecht died that same day, Reinkens was then consecrated in 1873 by the bishop of Deventer in Rotterdam. Eduard Hertzog was consecrated for the Swiss Old Catholics in 1876. The different branches of Old Catholics were brought into official relationships with each other by their drafting and acceptance of the Declaration of Utrecht in 1889. There was thus created a **doctrinal** basis for an extended "family" of Old Catholics, which came to include an extensive National Polish Church and branches of the different **language** groups in the **United States**.

The Churches of the **Anglican Communion** took a great interest in the Old Catholic Churches, starting from J. M. Neale's *The History of the So-called Jansenist Church of Holland* in 1858, and this increased after Vatican I. Various degrees of inter-Communion started in a relatively piecemeal way. Kindly reference was made to the Old Catholics at **Lambeth Conferences** from 1888 on. There were misunderstandings, one of which led the Dutch Old Catholics in 1908 to consecrate Arnold Mathew as an Old Catholic bishop for **England**; when he had won over neither Roman Catholics nor Anglicans, he lapsed into the vagaries of an ***episcopus vagans***. But an informal bond was created with the Society of St. Willibrord, which first met in 1909.

In 1925 the Old Catholic Bishops Conference formally recognized Anglican ordinations and paved the way for the 1931 **Bonn Agreement**. Since then, Old Catholic bishops have regularly participated in Anglican ordinations of bishops (even leading some to think Rome ought on its own principles to recognize Anglican orders simply because of the undoubtedly valid succession of the Old Catholic episcopate). They have also been guests at the Lambeth Conferences and participants with Anglicans about closer relationships on the continent of **Europe**.

OLDHAM, JOSEPH HOULDSWORTH (1874–1969). J. H. Oldham was an **Anglican layman** who became a world **missionary** and **ecumenical** leader. He was born in **India** and worked for the Young Men's Christian Association (YMCA) and the Student Christian Movement (SCM) in early life, until in 1908 he was appointed to be organizing secretary to the **Edinburgh Missionary Conference**, held in 1910. He was also secretary to the continuation committee that retained responsibilities from the conference and was the first editor, in 1912, of the *International Review of Missions*. After World

War I Oldham was heavily involved in the reestablishment of German overseas Christian **missions** that had been disrupted or overthrown by the war. His international ecumenical labors ran on, so that he initiated the Oxford Conference on "Life and Work" in 1937 and also arranged the 1938 conference at Utrecht, which set up a provisional committee for a **World Council of Churches** (WCC). Oldham remained in the organizational and secretarial work that went on throughout World War II, in preparation for the actual inauguration of the WCC in 1948.

ORDAIN. To bestow the **authority** of a **ministerial** office through **ordination rites**. *See also* BISHOP; DEACON; ORDERS; ORDINAL; PRESBYTER.

ORDERS. The preface to **Thomas Cranmer**'s **Ordinal**, in both the 1550 and 1552 versions, stated "there have been from the apostles' time these orders in the church:—**bishops**, **priests** and **deacons**." Orders must be distinguished from "appointments," though the word "office" is sometimes used in a way that can be ambiguous. In essence, while a great diversity of theological exposition exists, a mainstream view consistent with Anglican history would be that ordination places the person **ordained** "into" the relevant "order," and that participation in that "order" is fixed and immutable for life, irrespective of what kind of appointment or lack of it the person so "ordained" may hold.

Anglicans (and their **ordination rites**) have generally reflected the divisions of orders shown in the preface to the Ordinal—that there are three orders: bishops, priests (or **presbyters**), and deacons. It is possible, however, that the quotation above from the preface to the Ordinal was not simply expressing a continuity of orders from the early church but was also unobtrusively correcting a medieval distortion (itself traceable to St. Thomas Aquinas and reinforced at the **Council** of **Trent**) that named the three orders as priests, deacons, and subdeacons. While Cranmer's terminology just avoided referring to the "ordination" of bishops (using "**consecration**" throughout), his reference to "these orders," followed by "bishops, priests, and deacons," and the regular reference in the Thirty-Nine **Articles** and elsewhere to the same categories, makes any attempt to show that he thought and drafted in terms of only two orders—presbyters and deacons—somewhat special pleading. In 1662 the returning **Carolines** closed the question completely by using "ordination" (as well as "consecration") in relation to bishops, and that usage has been unobtrusively followed in Anglican ordination rites generally since.

A major theological issue has arisen within the Anglican understanding of orders, as some **provinces** have acted to ordain **women**, first as deacons, then as presbyters, and finally as bishops. A minor theological, but also practical, issue has also arisen as to whether, either in primitive practice or in contemporary pastoral and **missionary** strategies, it is necessary to be ordained to each order in turn before becoming a presbyter or bishop. This debate largely surrounds the issue of a "permanent diaconate." It is conducted on the one side by those who emphasize the unreality of ordaining to a "transitional" diaconate, an unreality which, they urge, detracts from the substantial reality of a genuine calling and ordination for people to be true deacons; on the other side, it is conducted by those who not only value a probationary and preparation time as deacons for those who are to become presbyters but also are ready to urge that the "servant" calling, expressed in ordination to the diaconate, is a vital undergirding for life of the self-understanding and calling of presbyters, and some vital component of that self-understanding will be lacking if they are allowed to short-circuit it by omitting a period as deacons on the way to being presbyters.

ORDINAL. After the Church of **England**'s separation from Rome, the first new **ordination rites** of the reformed Church of England were drafted in English and authorized in 1550 in a separate book and by a separate process from that of the 1549 **Book of Common Prayer**. The collection has traditionally become known as the "Ordinal," so that, for example, the preface to the three rites is known as the "preface to the Ordinal." The Ordinal remained thereafter legally a separate book from the Prayer Book and was not necessarily bound up with it as a single volume—and it was thus possible during Queen **Elizabeth I**'s reign to argue that the 1559 **Act of Uniformity**, which revived the 1552 Prayer Book, had failed to mention the Ordinal (which had been separately mentioned in the 1552 Act), and therefore that ordinations conducted according to it were not lawful (and, the argument continued, bishops **consecrated** by it were unlawful and need not be obeyed). A retrospective **validation** was hastily provided in an Act of Elizabeth in 1566 and in Article XXXVI of the Thirty-Nine **Articles**.

The same distinction remains in the title page of the 1662 Book, which distinguishes the Book of Common Prayer itself from the Ordinal, as did the 1662 Act of Uniformity. The standard printings of the Book from 1662 on included the Ordinal, but with this distinction made in the title page. It is not, however, a distinction that has been universally sustained in other parts of the **Anglican Communion**, and in the Church of England itself the distinction is retained in the Declaration of Assent made by **clergy** on ordination and on taking up office, but is suppressed in the parliamentary Church of England (Worship and Doctrine) Measure 1974 and the **canons** that embody for the Church the provisions of this **measure**.

The preface, which introduces the particular rites, states that "there have been from the apostles' time these orders in the church:—bishops, priests and deacons." It goes on to say that the present rites are provided and are to be exclusively followed, to the end that these particular orders "may be continued and reverently used," though it has to be added that the understanding of the ordained **ministry** contained in the reformed rites was completely remodeled as compared with the unreformed pre-**Reformation** rites.

The unwritten effects of the preface are (1) to eliminate all "minor orders" that had existed during the medieval period; (2) to change the resultant "major" orders from subdeacon, deacon, and priest to deacon, priest, and bishop; and (3) to insist on a continuity of orders so as to preclude anyone objecting that the old Church of England had ceased to exist and that a new brand of clergy had started, and thus to protect the existing officeholders of the time from attack on those grounds. Nevertheless, under that cover of a continuity, a totally new brand of **ministers** did arise, for the actual content of the ordination rites provided now for a ministry of word and **sacrament**, in place of the unbalanced thrust of the unreformed uses.

The preface went on in 1662 with a new phrase to withdraw or withhold recognition from any minister who had not had previous Episcopal ordination. This was reinforced by the 1662 Act of Uniformity, which prescribed penalties for breaches of the tight discipline that resulted. In many **provinces**, the same exclusive necessity of Episcopal ordination has also been entrenched in revisions of the **canons**. It was in pursuit of the same principle that **Samuel Seabury**, in order to be bishop of the Protestant Episcopal Church in Connecticut, sought consecration in 1783 from the **archbishop** of **Canterbury** and finally obtained it in 1784 from the bishops of the Episcopal Church of **Scotland**.

In the second half of the 20th century, Anglican ordinals were widely revised, usually following the pattern of the rites of the Church of **South India**, which was formed in 1947. This Church provided at the outset a common ordinal as one of the necessary bonds of a united church, but then continued work in the 1950s to provide new rites, less tied to the 1662 texts. Space was given to principles of revision of the ordinal in the report of the 1958 **Lambeth Conference**, and the marks of changes in South India are visible in the principles set out in that report.

The trend around the world has been toward using an ordination prayer, as distinct from the injunctions "Receive the Holy Ghost" and "Take thou **authority**," which characterized the 1662 pattern (and arguably left it not well matching the description of ordination as "the laying on hands with prayer"). In addition, at times other secondary ceremonies (such as **vesting**, **anointing**, and so forth) have been added, though the *porrectio* of the New Testament (for deacons) or **Bible** (for **presbyters** and bishops) has been generally left as the main ceremony to follow the laying on of hands with prayer. In the Church of England, however, the option of presenting the Bible just before the dismissal was introduced in 2000. Some principles for revising ordination rites were agreed upon at the sixth **International Anglican Liturgical Consultation** (IALC-6) at Berkeley, California, in 2001, and published in the **Berkeley Statement**, "To Equip the Saints."

ORDINATION OF WOMEN. *See* WOMEN.

ORDINATION RITES. In **Thomas Cranmer**'s processes of revising the inherited Latin rites still in use when King **Henry VIII** died, the reshaping of the ordination rites in the Pontifical came a year after the provision of all the **parish** services that made up the 1549 **Book of**

Common Prayer. The place in the **Communion** service where ordinations were to come was fixed as **deacons** after the Epistle, **priests** (or **presbyters**) after the **Gospel**, and **bishops** after the **creed**. The **litany** and the sermon preceded the beginning of the whole Communion service. The act of ordination was now centrally the laying on of hands by the bishop, assisted by other presbyters in ordaining presbyters, and other bishops in ordaining bishops. The element of prayer was not very clear, and the formula at the laying on of hands was (in the case of presbyters): "Receive the Holy Ghost. Whose sins you forgive, they are forgiven; whose sins you retain, they are retained." These words had been attached to a secondary laying of hands after the Communion in the Sarum rite and were now made central. As Cranmer was simultaneously abolishing auricular confession, it can hardly be that he viewed the great task to which the newly ordained were being commissioned in the rite as the hearing of confessions; it is more likely that he had come to a reformed view of the meaning of **Jesus**' words in John 20.23 and retained the words in the rite on that understanding.

The *porrectio instrumentorum* was altered in two stages for the presbyters. The Sarum use had been for the paten and chalice to be delivered with the instruction: "Receive power to offer sacrifice for the living and the dead." In 1550 the bread and chalice were delivered, but a **Bible** was also handed to the new presbyter, and the words were changed to "Take thou **authority** to preach the word of God and to minister the holy sacraments." So now the newly ordained had symbols of both word and sacrament—but it was the word that was of supreme importance, and this point was reinforced when in 1552 the handing over of the bread and chalice ceased and the Bible alone was given. For a deacon, the gospel book of the Sarum rite became a New Testament in 1550 and remained so. For a bishop, the gospel book placed on the head now became a Bible placed in his hands.

In 1662 little was changed, save that Cosin's translation of *Veni, Creator* (i.e., "Come, Holy Ghost, our souls inspire") was included as a welcome alternative to Cranmer's labored verse, and the words "for the office and work of a priest [*or* bishop] in the Church of God" were inserted after "Receive the Holy Ghost" at the laying on of hands, so that the actual order to which candidates were being ordained was now identified.

There was no provision made in either 1552 or 1662 for subsidiary ceremonies (such as **vesting**), and no provision for what is nowadays called "**concelebration**."

It is ordinations by these rites that were the subject of **Pope** Leo XIII's condemnation in ***Apostolicae Curae***. A small element in the condemnation was the failure in the formula "Receive the Holy Ghost . . ." in 1552 to state explicitly into which order candidates were being ordained, though this had actually been very clear in the context and was made explicit (as shown above) in 1662. A much larger element of the condemnation related less to the ordination rites than to the **eucharistic** ones. The **Roman Catholic** argument went that, as the reformed Prayer Books of King **Edward VI**'s day had excised all reference to the **eucharistic sacrifice**, it was clear that the ordination rites of that period intrinsically lack the "intention" to create priests who would so offer that sacrifice, and thus the succession was broken at the outset in a way that later changes would not correct.

Within Anglicanism, the ordination rites have changed in the second half of the 20th century. *See also* ORDINAL.

ORIENTAL ORTHODOX CHURCHES. The title "Oriental Orthodox" is a convenient term for categorizing various Eastern churches—all of them of ancient if not apostolic origin—that are not in **Communion** with the **Eastern Orthodox** Churches and the ecumenical patriarch. They are sometimes listed as the "non-Chalcedonian" churches, in that they share in common a lack of recognition of the **Council** of **Chalcedon** of 451 and are thus open to the suspicion (which they regularly reject) of being Monophysite. The usual listing of these Churches includes the Coptic Orthodox Church (Egypt), the Syrian Orthodox Church, the Armenian Apostolic Church, the Ethiopian Orthodox Church, and the Malankara Orthodox Syrian Church. A joint Anglican–Oriental Orthodox forum met in 1985–1993, and the **Lambeth Conferences** of 1988 and 1998 recommended that this forum be upgraded into a commission. An exploratory meeting was held in **England** in July 2001, and this led to the first full meeting of the commission in Armenia in November 2002. The initial work of the commission is a joint tackling of questions concerning a common Christology.

ORIGINAL SIN. Original sin, as drawn particularly from St. Paul and taught systematically by **Augustine** of Hippo, was an inherited state of guilt "in Adam," from which **justification** (in which, for these purposes, Augustine included infant **baptism**) delivered its recipients. The Reformers all agreed that the guilt of original sin is forgiven and remitted in justification (which in their theology was signified, but not invariably conveyed, by baptism), but that the corruption of it—the will of the flesh—remains in the justified, and that consequently the life of faith is a continual battle of the flesh against the **spirit**. This is set out briefly in **Thomas Cranmer**'s **liturgical** confessions (e.g., "there is no health in us") and systematically in Articles IX, X, XV, and XVI of the Thirty-Nine **Articles**.

ORNAMENTS RUBRIC. "Ornaments" is a comprehensive term used to cover both the furnishings of church buildings and the **vesture** of **ministers**, and the place of the "ornaments **rubric**" in Anglican history derives from the opening note in the 1559 **Book of Common Prayer**:

> And here is to be noted, that the minister at the time of the **communion**, and at all other times in his ministration, shall use such ornaments in the church as were in use by **authority** of parliament in the second year of the reign of king Edward the VI according to the act of parliament set in the beginning of this book.

Because the 1559 **Act of Uniformity**, to which the rubric refers, ordered the 1552 Book of Common Prayer to be restored with only three specified changes, it appears as though the 1552 rubric about vesture, which was printed there before **Morning Prayer**, should have reappeared in the 1559 Book. This 1552 rubric, which did not use the word "ornaments," prohibited the previous **eucharistic vestments** and ordered "a surplice only." However, although the 1552 rubric was not specified to be changed in the 1559 Act, at another point the Act did order the use of the "ornaments" that were in use by the authority of parliament in the second year of King **Edward VI**, and it has often been thought that the printers (or some authority with direct access to them) concluded that, for consistency, the requirement of the Act should overrule the 1552 rubric and edited the text accordingly. What is certain is that there was virtually no attempt in

Queen **Elizabeth I**'s reign to use or make others use the **traditional** eucharistic vestments, because, irrespective of how the ornaments rubric was understood at the time, enforcing the surplice as a minimum was itself sufficiently difficult. The Act also specified that the ornaments should be retained "until other order be therein taken," but the rubric did not reproduce this important qualifier. "Other order" was taken by various means in Elizabeth's reign, and conclusively in the 1604 **canons**, in each case enforcing the surplice and not mentioning eucharistic vestments.

In 1661, at the **Savoy Conference**, the **Puritans** objected to the implications of the rubric's text in relation to the eucharistic vestments, but the **bishops** replied simply as though the rubric ordered the surplice. In the 1662 Book, the rubric was retained but with slight changes:

> And here it is to be noted, that such Ornaments of the Church, and of the Ministers thereof at all times of their Ministration, shall be retained and be in use, as were in the Church of England by the authority of Parliament, in the Second Year of the Reign of King Edward the Sixth.

Once again, the only actual practice at issue seems to have been the wearing of a surplice, though the text seems clearly to cite the vesture of 1549.

In the middle of the 19th century in **England**, the second generation of the **Anglo-Catholic** movement began to adopt **Roman Catholic** eucharistic vestments, citing the ornaments rubric as not simply allowing but even requiring such usage. This led to cases before the ecclesiastical courts and to contradictory judgments. But the use of full eucharistic vestments spread widely in the Church of England and overseas, and the lesser use of **colored** stoles spread even more widely, until in England the legal dilemma was resolved by the Church of England (Vesture of Ministers) Measure 1964, which, with parliamentary authority, led to a new canon allowing diversity of usage, without officially sanctioning any diversity of **doctrinal** understanding thereby.

Since 1662 there have been no attempts anywhere in the **Anglican Communion** to cover the "ornaments" of ministers by a rubric before Morning Prayer, but rather the issue is resolved in **provincial** canons or is left to custom.

ORTHODOX CHURCHES. After the "Great Schism" in 1054, the Eastern Churches continued to hold sway within their own territories, claiming to be "orthodox" churches of those regions. In the following centuries, they were usually on the defensive in their own localities because of the advance of Islam and the lack of support from the West. The Crusades (1090–1290) were at the very least an embarrassment to the Eastern Christians, and in fact the Crusaders regularly attacked the Orthodox. Constantinople fell to the invading Muslims in 1453, and, although the subsequent flight of scholars to the West quickened the study of the Greek language and texts, it was the weakness and troubles of the Eastern churches that was most obviously seen in the West.

The first substantial contact between the Church of **England** and the Eastern Orthodox churches came in the early 17th century. The patriarch of Constantinople from 1620 was Cyril Lucar, who (whether for theological or, more likely, political reasons) opened up communications with the reformed Churches, not least with the Church of England. As a show of goodwill in 1628, he presented to King **Charles I**, through the chaplain in Constantinople, the "Codex Alexandrinus," one of the leading manuscript texts of the **Bible** surviving from the fifth century of the Christian era. In the following century, there was an abortive correspondence between the **nonjurors** and the ecumenical patriarch, in which the nonjurors sought a concordat (and may have started to think through the implications of Eastern **liturgies**). This was brought to an abrupt end by William Wake, the **archbishop** of **Canterbury** (1716–1737), who complained in 1725 to the patriarch that he was corresponding with a schismatic sect in England.

Another century later, the **Tractarians** showed an interest in the East—as the Orthodox provided a model of patriarchates owing no allegiance to Rome but dependent strongly upon their own **tradition**. The "branch" theory of the church reinforced this interest, and the proposal for a **Jerusalem** archbishopric brought the theory out into the public arena—but controversially so, as the **Anglo-Catholics** insisted that there was already a "bishop of Jerusalem" and that it was therefore schismatic to contemplate creating an Anglican-**Lutheran** bishopric there.

There were resolutions about relationships with the **Eastern Orthodox** at all the early **Lambeth Conferences**, and, following "The

Appeal to All Christian People" issued by the 1920 Conference, the patriarch and Holy Synod of Constantinople made a declaration in 1922 accepting the **validity** of Anglican **orders**. This was followed by other patriarchates, though it is unclear what status such declarations enjoy among the Orthodox, while it is clear that they did not introduce inter-Communion between the Eastern and Anglican churches. The 1930 Lambeth Conference's Resolution 33 thanked the ecumenical patriarch for sending a delegation to the conference to assist the bishops. A Joint Doctrinal Commission was appointed as a result of the resolution, and its fairly thorough report was published in 1932, a careful statement of differences as well as of areas of accord.

After World War II, closer relationships grew between the Orthodox and the churches of the West. After **Archbishop Michael Ramsey** visited the ecumenical patriarch in 1962, the **primates** of the **Anglican Communion** agreed on new talks with the Orthodox, and a Pan-Orthodox Conference at Rhodes in 1964 responded welcoming this. A joint commission was set up in 1966 and produced the Moscow Agreed Statement (1976) and the Athens Report (1978). This latter report considered the **ordination** of **women** as that became a widespread issue in the Anglican Communion, and it made clear the opposition of the Orthodox to such a move. This produced a short halt in the conversations, but they were restarted in 1980, leading to the major **Dublin Agreed Statement** in 1984.

There was another new start made in 1989. A reconstituted commission, entitled the International Commission of the Anglican–Orthodox Theological Dialogue (ICAOTD), met in Finland and drew up a work plan, known from the meeting place as the "New Valamo" scheme. The commission met regularly for "informal talks" during the 1990s and into the 2000s. In these, they were addressing issues related to the **doctrine** of the Church and the **priesthood** of **Jesus Christ**, with a view to publishing further agreed statements around 2005 and certainly prior to the projected 2008 Lambeth Conference. *See also* ORIENTAL ORTHODOX CHURCHES.

OXFORD MOVEMENT. Because the "catholic revival" in the Church of **England** in the 19th century began at Oxford, it is often called the "Oxford Movement." *See also* ANGLO-CATHOLICISM;

KEBLE, JOHN; NEWMAN, JOHN HENRY; PUSEY, EDWARD BOUVERIE; TRACTARIANS.

– P –

PAKISTAN. The nation of Pakistan came into existence with its partition from **India** at the time of independence in 1947, and the (Anglican) Church of India, Burma, and Ceylon (CIBC) then became the Church of India, Pakistan, Burma, and Ceylon (CIPBC), under the existing CIBC constitution without change of **dioceses**. In the 1960s, alongside the plans to form a united Church of **North India**, a similar plan was formed for a united Church of Pakistan. In North India, those planning the union were strongly advised by successive **Lambeth Conferences** in 1948 and 1958 to seek an **Episcopal** laying on of hands on all **presbyters** of the uniting churches at the point of inauguration, in order to avoid the **Anglo-Catholic** opposition that had been registered so forcefully against the Church of **South India** since it had been formed in 1947. The Christians seeking union in Pakistan took the point, and the united church there—drawing together those who had been Anglicans, **Methodists**, **Presbyterians**, and **Lutherans**, along with members of some smaller bodies—came into being on 1 November 1970, four weeks before the formation of the Church of North India. The Church of Pakistan thus became the first union of episcopal and non-Episcopal churches ever to employ this pattern of uniting ministries.

Within a few weeks of the inauguration, there was a political and military debacle that led to the wresting of East Pakistan away from West Pakistan, so that the eastern part was recreated politically as **Bangladesh**, the dioceses there became the Church of Bangladesh, and the Church of Pakistan thereafter belonged only to the western part.

The nation of Pakistan was intended, by the very fact of partition from India, to be an overwhelmingly Islamic state, and Christianity not only has not been strong numerically but also has often labored under considerable adverse political pressure.

In the years 1987–1989 the Church of Pakistan by stages became a full member of the **Anglican Communion** in parallel with the Churches of North India, South India, and Bangladesh. In 2004 it had nine dioceses, one of which included the care of expatriate Pakistani Christians working in the Gulf States.

PAN-ANGLICAN CONGRESS. There was a "Pan-Anglican Congress," initiated by the Central **Board of Missions** of the Church of **England**, held in **London** on 15–24 June 1908, immediately before the **Lambeth Conference** that year. Its themes proved to be wider than the origins would have suggested, and it drew a daily attendance in excess of 17,000 persons. Subsequent congresses, at Minneapolis in 1954 and Toronto in 1963, have been called "**Anglican Congresses**." Initially, another Pan-Anglican Congress was planned to accompany the next Lambeth Conference in 2008, but this plan had to be abandoned.

PAPUA NEW GUINEA. Anglican **missionary** work was begun in Papua New Guinea in the late 1880s, and an agreement about areas of influence was made between the British protectorate government and various **missionary societies** in 1890. This assigned the northeast coastal area of the island to the Anglicans. It came under the auspices of the Australian **Board of Missions**, and there was subsequent growth in the church there, partly through migrants from elsewhere in the Pacific, especially men who had gone to Queensland as indentured laborers and had then been ready to go to Papua on completion of their contracts. This led to the formation in 1898 of a "missionary **diocese**" of the Church of England in Australia, under the oversight of the diocese of Carpentaria and within the **province** of Queensland.

There was great suffering of Christians after the Japanese invasion in 1942, and 12 in particular who died are remembered as **martyrs** among the Anglicans. One, an English **presbyter**, Vivian Redlich, was beheaded on the beach near his mission station at Sangara. In this massacre, Lucian Tapiedi, a Papuan teacher and **evangelist**, was martyred by a local man collaborating with the invaders. He is commemorated not only with a church at Embi built in his memory by the man who killed him and was later converted, but also by his statue being one of the 10 along the west front of Westminster **Abbey** marking Christian martyrs of the 20th century. Another English expatriate missionary, Romney Gill, who insisted on staying at his post, survived in the jungle throughout the occupation without being caught.

The martyrs of Papua New Guinea are commemorated on 2 September in several provinces of the **Anglican Communion**.

Papua New Guinea remained a single diocese, with an expatriate **bishop**, until 1977. An islander became an assistant bishop in 1960, and a **synod** was constituted in 1971. Finally, in 1977 the diocese was divided into five, two of them with Papuan bishops, and a separate province was formed. It has been characteristically of an extreme **Anglo-Catholic** ethos, with exotic **liturgy** and a deep opposition to the **ordination** of **women**. In 2003 it entered as a province into a covenant with the **Roman Catholic** Church of Papua New Guinea.

PARISH. The "parish" is a most characteristic unit of Anglican church life. The word derives etymologically from the Greek *paroikia*, the term for being away from home (as in the use of *paroikoi*—"strangers"—in 1 Pet. 2.11). However, its use at the time of the **Reformation** was to indicate a settled community with territorial boundaries, usually such that the inhabitants could all meet in a single building, the "parish church." The structural separateness of the parish was guaranteed by the appointment of a "rector" (or "ruler"), to whom belonged the "cure of souls," that is, the spiritual responsibility for the people and their spiritual lives. The exclusive rights and duties of the rector in his own parish were a safeguard against schism or competition.

While it is the general pattern of the **Anglican Communion** worldwide that **dioceses** are divided into "parishes," it is clear that the concept of a parish has developed in different ways in different places. In some parts of the Communion, a parish has little territorial significance and is simply the name of single church community. In other places there is a high territorial significance, but (as happens in parts of Africa) the parish may include up to 30 congregations, united simply by having a single **presbyter** who travels vast distances to service the congregations, provide **sacramental ministry**, and hold the dispersed people in a unity. There is a general usage whereby the parish is that subunit of the diocese usually led by a presbyter and has its own church **council** and its own representation on a diocesan **synod**. But in parts of the world (such as the continent of **Europe**) where the bulk of congregations are in fact chaplaincies, the term "parish" would often be confusing or misleading and is avoided. *See also* CURATE.

PARISH COMMUNION. *See* LITURGICAL MOVEMENT.

PARKER, MATTHEW (1504–1575). Matthew Parker was made **deacon** in 1527 and became a fellow of Corpus Christi College, Cambridge. He was chaplain to Anne Boleyn during her years as queen (1533–1536) and was ranked among the moderate reformers. He married during King **Edward VI**'s reign and became **dean** of Lincoln in 1552.

Parker was deprived of his post when Queen **Mary I** inherited the throne in 1553. Mary died in November 1558, and her **archbishop** of **Canterbury**, Cardinal Pole, died in the same night. Thus, when Queen **Elizabeth I** came to the throne, the see of Canterbury was vacant, and in 1559 she chose Parker as her archbishop of Canterbury. His **consecration** is well attested as having been conducted in **Lambeth Palace** Chapel on 17 December 1559, where four bishops surviving from Edward VI's reign conferred the **episcopate** on him. Because the succession of Anglican **orders** is largely traceable to this particular consecration, it has been the subject of close investigation as well as severe misrepresentation. It is one of the significant events of Anglican history portrayed on the ceiling of Lambeth Palace Chapel today.

While Parker's own interests were somewhat academic, he had a major task in leading the Church of **England** into living out the "Elizabethan Settlement." He succeeded in getting the **Book of Common Prayer** and the Thirty-Nine **Articles** largely accepted, while denying the demands of the **Puritans**, not least their opposition to the imposition of the "excepted ceremonies"—chiefly the wearing of the surplice, kneeling for **Communion**, the ring in **marriage**, and the **sign of the cross** in **baptism**.

PAROUSIA. The word *parousia* is in origin the Greek term for **Jesus**' presence, but it is used in the New Testament in the slightly nuanced meaning of Jesus' reappearance at his Second Coming (cf. the **eschatology** of the **Creeds**). It has been simply transliterated to become a slightly technical term in English for the Second Coming. *See also* ADVENT.

PARTNERS IN MISSION. The phrase "Partners in Mission" originated in the second **Anglican Consultative Council** meeting (ACC-2) in

1973. The council's report reproduced a proposal for joint consultations between **provinces** of the **Anglican Communion** that had been drawn up by a meeting of representatives of **missionary** agencies in Connecticut in 1972. It was seen as a development from the principle of **Mutual Responsibility and Interdependence** (MRI), which had been launched at the **Anglican Congress** in Toronto in 1963. The new title—Partners in Mission (PiM)—became the title of the ACC's own report of 1973, and its recommendations set in train the form of a consultative exercise to be used in each province (and, where desired, each **diocese**) of the Communion. The exercise was to be distinguished by the joining together of "internal" and "external" partners, the "external" coming from other provinces of the Communion and from other Christian denominations in the same area as the province or diocese undergoing the exercise. The **secretary-general** was to be responsible for coordinating and rolling forward the program between provinces.

The principle of these consultations was greatly reinforced by the 1978 **Lambeth Conference**, and the actual progress with fulfilling the consultations was intended to be recorded in successive ACC reports from 1981 (ACC-5) onward. The Mission Issues and Strategy Advisory Group (MISAG) formed by a resolution of ACC-5 was supposed to oversee the processes, but the record of actual consultations grew thinner through the 1980s and, when MISAG was reconstituted by ACC-7 in 1987, its terms of reference gave much less space to the PiM processes. Actual consultations continued (e.g., the **Episcopal Church [United States of America]**, which had had a first consultation in 1977, had a second one in 1993), but the ACC reports ceased to mention them, and the 1998 Lambeth Conference, which even had a subsection addressing "How to Support Each Other in Mission" (Section II, subsection 7), showed no evidence of being aware of the PiM process at all. *See also* MISSIO.

PASSOVER. The Jewish **feast** of Passover was the most solemn remembrance in the year, recalling the exodus from Egypt under the blood of the lamb (cf. Exod. 12.21–28). It was kept on 14 Nisan in the Jewish **calendar**, and there is considerable evidence of **Jesus** keeping it as the pilgrim feast it was intended to be (e.g., in Luke 2.41–52; John 2.13, 6.4, 13.1). (The normal reckoning that Jesus had three years of public **ministry** is based simply on the number of separate Passovers that can be discerned in John's **Gospel**.) Jesus' crucifixion occurred at Passover time, and his last supper with his disciples may well have been the Passover meal (seder) itself. In the New Testament, his death is at intervals viewed as the antitype of the slaying of the Passover lamb in Exod. 12 (cf. 1 Cor. 5.7; 1 Pet. 1.19). Theological interpretations of the **eucharist** down through history have differed as to whether the Last Supper was in fact a seder; theologians have also varied in the significance they have given to any connection of that supper with the "blood of the lamb" or the relation of either of them to the death of Jesus. *See also* EASTER.

PATRICK, SAINT (c. 390–460). Patrick is the patron **saint** of **Ireland**, the one to whom is attributed the bringing of the **gospel** there in the fifth century. Born in **England** (or possibly southern **Scotland**), he was captured by Irish pirates as a youth, served as a slave in Ireland for six years, and then escaped and returned to his place of domicile. There he received some basic education, was **ordained**, and around 435 returned to Ireland. He became the first **bishop** in Ireland (though prior claims have been made for the shadowy Palladius, who may have preceded him) and founded the see of **Armagh** sometime between 444 and 450. The main undoubted witness to his life is in his own *Confession*, which is extant, but the legends woven around him run far beyond the evidence. His **feast** day of 17 March is observed in many parts of the **Anglican Communion**.

PATRONAGE. In the Church of **England**, the pattern of appointments of **parish clergy** that the Reformers inherited from the Middle Ages centered on the patronage system. Different parties would possess (as a distinct property) the right of patronage of a particular parish, and that was the right and the duty to provide an incumbent for that parish. The patron might be the local squire, the incumbent of another parish, an Oxford or Cambridge College don, the **cathedral** of the **diocese**, the **bishop**, a liveried company of the City of **London**—or the Crown. As it was a property, patronage could be sold, given away, or bequeathed, so that the range of actual patrons in any century would outstrip attempts to categorize them. In the early 19th century, **Charles Simeon** used inherited assets to purchase rights of patronage and grouped all the parishes concerned under a single agency, Simeon's Trustees.

The sale of patronage rights was stopped in the first decades of the 20th century, but the giving and bequeathing are still allowable processes. The absolute rights of patrons have been greatly curtailed, as both the bishop and parochial representatives now have certain powers to decline a patron's nominee, and provision for reorganization enables a bishop to suspend a patron's rights of presentation, after which he himself may then appoint a "priest-in-charge" on a limited time span. The rights of the Crown in respect of patronage have been exempted from most reforms of the system. In most other **provinces** of the **Anglican Communion**, a single process of appointment is defined in the constitution or the **canons**, giving assigned functions to both bishop and parish, but giving different weighting to those functions in different provinces.

PATRONAL FESTIVAL. The **saint** in whose name a church building is **dedicated** will have his or her "own" day in the Church's **calendar**. In many—but certainly not all—Anglican **parishes** and congregations, that day is a day of particular celebration in the year. It is treated as a festival, even if it falls in a penitential season, and is usually taken to override the **liturgical** provision of a **Sunday**, when it would otherwise have been transferred.

PATTESON, JOHN COLERIDGE (1827–1871). John Patteson was ordained in **England** in 1853 and was brought to **New Zealand** by **Bishop George Selwyn** in 1855 to work as a **missionary** in the **Melanesian** islands, which fell within Selwyn's jurisdiction. Patteson showed great aptitude as sailor, linguist, and **evangelist**, a combination that equipped him comprehensively for that missionary task. In 1861 he was **consecrated** by Selwyn in Auckland **Cathedral** as bishop of Melanesia. Patteson was murdered with two companions on the island of Nukapu on 20 September 1871 for reasons that are not wholly clear, but he thus passed into the Anglican **martyrology** and particularly into the memorials of Melanesia and the "South Seas." His date of 20 September is included in the **calendars** of many **provinces**.

PEACE. The "Peace" is a relatively new feature of Anglican **liturgy**. It stems from the "holy kiss" of the Pauline epistles and the first descriptions of its integration into liturgy in Justin Martyr, Tertullian, and Hippolytus. It had a particular role in the early church in the incorporation of the newly **baptized** into the structure of the church, though it was an integral feature of the **Sunday eucharist** also. By the time of the **Reformation**, it had been reduced to a mere formality in the **sanctuary** between the officiant and his acolytes at the **mass**, and it was eliminated in **Thomas Cranmer**'s liturgical revision (though just possibly leaving a faint footprint in his closing blessing in the eucharist "The peace of God, which passeth all understanding . . ."). Its reappearance in Western liturgy is generally reckoned to stem from the eucharistic liturgy of the Church of **South India** in 1950, and over the following two decades it made inroads into congregational life all over the **Anglican Communion** and quite quickly flowered into a genuine sharing by handshakes, hugs, or a local greeting custom (such as a low bow in **Korea** and rubbing noses in Maori congregations). In general among Anglicans it has assumed the position in liturgical structure that can be read from the accounts in Justin Martyr, that is, a mutual recognition by believers, affirming each other to be in **Jesus Christ**, just before the dominical action of the eucharist begins. The main exception to this would be where there has been a conscious following of modern **Roman Catholic** practice, in which case it comes after the **eucharistic prayer** and follows the **Lord's Prayer** and the **fraction**.

PELAGIUS. Pelagius was the first recorded British heretic, having probably originated in **Wales**. He taught in Rome in the early fifth century, but moved on to Africa and to Palestine when Rome was about to fall to the Goths around 410. His distinctive teaching was that the free will that the human race possesses to choose good and to do it is not illusory but provides a practicable possibility of overcoming evil. It was against Pelagianism that Augustine of Hippo developed his teaching on **original sin** and on grace, particularly to emphasize that human beings cannot save or perfect themselves. The "Pelagians" are specifically indicted in **Article** IX for "vainly" teaching that original sin consists in our merely imitating Adam, not as being caught in an imprisoning entail inherited from Adam without possibility of avoidance. It is a conventional maxim that Pelagianism is the characteristic British **heresy**. *See also* AUGUSTINIANISM.

PENANCE. "Penance" was the normal pre-**Reformation** title for the **sacramental** rite of auricular confession, which was concluded by a formal **priestly absolution** and the imposition of a penitential task upon the penitent. This practice was excluded in the successive revisions of the **Book of Common Prayer** in King **Edward VI**'s reign, and it was named in Article XXV of the Thirty-Nine **Articles** as one of those five "commonly called sacraments" that arose from "the corrupt following of the apostles." There is, however, some evidence of **Laudian bishops** and **clergy** being used as confessors.

Penance was revived by the 19th-century **Anglo-Catholics** and was taught in some Anglican circles on **Roman Catholic** terms as necessary to a true discipleship. After **Vatican II**, the Roman Catholic terminology changed and the "Reconciliation of a Penitent" was preferred. In the **Episcopal Church (United States of America)**, the 1979 Prayer Book has detailed suggestions to make about the tasks to be given by the **presbyter** to the truly penitent; and these very closely correspond to the "penances" awarded in the Roman Catholic Church. In the Church of **England**, **Common Worship** has brought in some pastorally useful **liturgical** resources, but they are not treated as a fully authorized "**alternative service**."

PENTECOST. "Pentecost" is the Greek word for "fifty," and the title is used in the New Testament for the Jewish **pilgrim** feast that comes 50 days after **Passover**. It was originally given by **God** as a celebration of the first fruits of the harvest (cf. Lev. 23.15–21), though there was a rabbinic tradition that the meeting with God at Sinai came 50 days after the initial Passover in Egypt and that the feast of 50 days was to celebrate the giving of the law. In the New Testament, the feast of Pentecost still brings a pilgrim attendance at **Jerusalem**, and it is on that feast day that the **Holy Spirit** descends in power upon the infant church (cf. Acts 2.1–11). While there is no indication in the New Testament that Christians deliberately kept annual festivals, yet the first Christians, themselves Jews, must have been very aware each year of a significance to the anniversary. Certainly St. Paul retained a sense of Pentecost as a major division of the year (cf. Acts 20.16; 1 Cor. 16.8).

The earliest reference in postapostolic authors to a Christian observance of Pentecost for Christian reasons is in Tertullian's references in the *De Baptismo* and the *De Oratione* near the end of the second century. However, Tertullian is actually citing a whole season of Pentecost, that is of all the 50 days that follow the Christian Pasch, the commemoration of the death and **resurrection** of the Lord. It is not until the fifth century that a distinct single 50th day emerges as a Christian festival of the coming of the Spirit. It then becomes a basic component part of the annual **liturgical calendar**, and it is inherited in that way by the Reformers, though **Thomas Cranmer**'s **Books of Common Prayer** refer to it as "Whitsunday." Whitsunday (a title possibly derived from **baptismal** associations and wearing of white vesture for baptisms) remains the main name for it in the 1662 Book, though "Pentecost" is found in the list of **feast** days at the front of the Book. Whereas much of the Western Church counted the following Sundays as those "after Pentecost," the Church of **England** counted them as after **Trinity Sunday**, that is, one week later.

Modern liturgical revision has varied between seeing three focal festivals in the year—**Christmas**, **Easter**, and Pentecost—and seeing only two, in which the Easter season is concluded by the feast of Pentecost, which has no equivalent standing of its own and ushers in no "Pentecost season" following it. In conformity with this latter pattern, the **Common Worship** program in the Church of England has reverted to "Sundays after Trinity Sunday."

PENTECOSTALISM. Pentecostalism on the world scene is a 20th-century phenomenon, with most of its roots in American **Protestantism**. It is highly experiential in its presenting characteristics and has usually been marked by an emphasis on "spiritual gifts"—a category expounded as centrally the gifts of "**tongues**," "**prophecy**," and "interpretation." Tongues in particular was good evidence of "**baptism in the Spirit**."

For the first half of the 20th century these emphases usually meant that the practitioners found the mainstream "historic" churches totally unaccommodating, and both in the **United States** and in Britain, Pentecostalist denominations started to emerge. In **England** they have often been organized as "Elim" or "Assemblies of God." Until the 1950s they seemed to be greatly distanced from the more traditionalist churches. So it was a matter of some comment that Bishop Lesslie Newbigin, in his 1952 lectures published as *The Household* *of God* (1953), discerned three separable strands in world Christianity, namely, the "church of the body" (**Roman Catholicism**), the "church of the word" (Protestantism), and the "church of the Spirit" (Pentecostalism).

The second half of the 20th century saw a vast change for Anglicans touched with these forms of experiential Christianity. From the late 1950s, Pentecostalist phenomena were found within Anglican congregations where these expressions of worship and devotion were encouraged rather than banned, so that the congregations grew *as Anglicans*, instead of seceding, and they in turn passed on their message of the spiritual life to others. In the **Episcopal Church (United States of America)**, the "neo-Pentecostalism," as it began to be called, was found in extreme "high" church congregations. In the Church of England, neo-Pentecostalism grew almost entirely out of **Evangelical** congregations, and this set up questions of the relationships between those who had previously been Evangelicals (and perhaps somewhat cerebral) and the new, Spirit-filled groupings that were becoming typical of the outcome of this movement.

Since it was clear that a substantial strand of Pentecostalist church life was now rooted in the Anglican churches, it has become known more often as the "**Charismatic Movement**," rather than as simply Pentecostalism. It has been characterized by not only baptism in the Spirit and spiritual gifts but also by a "multimember ministry" (affirming and engaging **lay** skills and facilities), a vast new range of **music**, a creation-affirming interest in **sacramental** ways of worship, and a **ceremonial** subculture arising from these concerns that is distinctive of the movement, though some features of it (e.g., popular choruses) have spread into many other parts of the **Anglican Communion**. *See also* TORONTO BLESSING.

PETITIONS FOR THE DEPARTED. The New Testament lacks any petitions on behalf of the **dead** (or "departed"). Such petitions gradually arose in the life of the postapostolic church, mostly in an unselfconscious and artless way. However, the existence of such prayers did over the centuries engender a belief in a **purgatory** and in a specific efficacy of requiem **masses**. The Reformers removed from official **liturgy** all suspicion of praying for the departed and all hints of requiem **celebrations** of the **eucharist**. But the petitions were not condemned (as purgatory was) in the Thirty-Nine **Articles**, so that the elision of such prayers from public worship might be viewed as simply leaving such usage to private practice. Such petitions were, in fact, adopted within the liturgy by the "usagers" among the **nonjurors** of the early 18th century and were strongly revived by the **Anglo-Catholic** movement in the early 19th century. Such prayers have since found a place in many official liturgies. It is usually denied that there is any link between the very natural desire to continue praying for friends when they have died and the offering of mass sacrifice or any belief in purgatory. The 1928 **Book of Common Prayer** of the **Protestant Episcopal Church (United States of America)** prayed for "continual growth" for the departed. **Evangelical** Anglicans in particular have been very suspicious of such prayers.

PHILIPPINE INDEPENDENT CHURCH. The **Philippines** were a Spanish colony, with a dominantly **Roman Catholic** religion, from the first half of the 16th century until the end of the 19th. Those who resisted Spanish rule in the 1890s saw the dominance of a largely Spanish hierarchy in the church as part of the colonial structures they were opposing. Thus when Spanish rule ended in 1898, there was a strong move to form from the Roman Catholic congregations a genuinely Filipino Church, and this was duly constituted in 1902. The **Protestant Episcopal Church in the United States of America** (PECUSA), including **Charles Brent**, the first PECUSA **bishop** in the Philippines, provided moral and practical support from the outset, and in 1948 three bishops of PECUSA gave Episcopal **consecration** to the first bishops of the Philippine Independent Church. This action was commended by the **Lambeth Conferences** of 1948 and 1958, which looked forward to relations of inter-Communion with the Church. The Philippine Independent Church has used the theological training of the Episcopal Church and has remained in friendly relationships with Churches of the **Anglican Communion** ever since. Anglican **provinces** have officially entered into **full Communion** with it since 1961. Bishops of the Church took part in the consultation of a "Wider Episcopal Fellowship" convened by the **archbishop** of **Canterbury** in 1964, and it was invited to send guests as observers to each Lambeth Conference from 1968 on. The Philippine Independent Church has many **dioceses** and roughly 10 times as many adherents as the Anglican province.

PHILIPPINES. The Philippines passed to the political control of the **United States** in 1898 after over 350 years as a Spanish colony, which left it with a pervasive **Roman Catholic** religion and culture. The 1901 **General Convention** of the **Protestant Episcopal Church in the United States of America** (PECUSA) established a "**Missionary** District of the Philippines," and **Charles Brent** was **consecrated** as its first **bishop**. PECUSA began pioneer **evangelism** among indigenous peoples and also set about establishing **parishes** among the Chinese and other expatriate groups. This latter step was congruous with a disenchantment in the islands with Roman Catholicism, as was evidenced by the breaking away of the **Philippine Independent Church**. The first Filipino to be a bishop was consecrated in 1959. The **diocese** had a **suffragan** bishop in the 1960s and divided into three dioceses in 1972. In the 1980s these became four dioceses and in 1990 they became a separate **province**, the Episcopal Church in the Philippines. By 2004 there were six dioceses.

PILGRIMAGE. Pilgrimage was deeply entrenched in Jewish religion at the time of **Jesus Christ** and had roots stretching back before the time of Solomon and the building of the Temple. The Pentateuch itself charters pilgrim feasts, and the psalms include pilgrim songs. The only account we have of the childhood of Jesus is the story of his going to **Jerusalem** on pilgrimage with his parents (Luke 2.22–41). References to **Passover** are foundational to the passion narrative in the **Gospels**, and the day of **Pentecost** (when Jerusalem was crowded with pilgrims) saw the coming of the **Holy Spirit** and the birth of the church in Acts 2. Paul's own visits to Jerusalem in Acts 18 and Acts 21 may suggest a continuing Jewish discipline of pilgrimage in his movements and attitudes.

On the other hand, it is difficult to trace the origins of specifically Christian pilgrimages, and it is at least arguable that the very nature of the Christian faith from its beginning was that there are no "holy places" (Jesus said, "The hour is coming when you will worship the Father neither on this mountain nor in Jerusalem" [John 4.21]). However, even in periods of persecution, it seems that annual gatherings at the tomb of **martyrs** started not only to fix dates for their commemoration but also to attract people from further afield to share in those commemorations. When Christianity was legitimized through the Roman Empire, the Spanish nun Egeria went on a long journey to **Jerusalem** and wrote up the journey, as part tourist, part pilgrim. In Jerusalem itself she recorded an early cult relating to the places associated with Jesus' last week before his passion.

Pilgrimages to places connected with special **saints** and martyrs were a growing phenomenon in the Middle Ages, sometimes associated with doubtful **doctrines**, such as the acquisition of merit by such means. In **England** a typical example was the cult of **Thomas à Becket** at **Canterbury**, and an insight, albeit fictional, into the cross-section of society that went on pilgrimages may be glimpsed from Chaucer's *Canterbury Tales*. When King **Henry VIII** broke up the shrine to Becket and dissolved the **monasteries**, pilgrimages were set aside as a superstitious practice.

The practice has revived in the **Anglican Communion** since the 19th century, often, but not always, through **Anglo-Catholic** forms of devotion and piety—and certainly assisted by easier means of transport. Some revived pilgrimages are to the "Holy Land"; others are to places of martyrs, usually on the anniversary of their death, such as the gathering for the **Mizeki** celebration at Marondera in **Zimbabwe**, or the commemoration of the **Uganda** Martyrs at Namugongo in Uganda. In England there has been a rapid growth in pilgrimages to Walsingham in Norfolk, where a shrine to the Virgin **Mary** has come to evoke devotion rivalling that shown to Becket at Canterbury in the Middle Ages. The shrine at Walsingham, which was destroyed in 1538, was recreated in 1931 by Anglicans. It is sometimes difficult with modern transport to distinguish objectively between pilgrimages and tourism, but the difference is likely to lie in the hazards of the journey, the cost to the pilgrims' life patterns, and the seriousness of devotion that marks the time spent both on the way and at the shrine.

POLYGAMY. The story of the Garden of Eden, the giving of the **Ten Commandments** at Mount Sinai, the consistent witness of the prophets, and the teaching of **Jesus** in the New Testament all present to Christians a stable pattern of sexual union, as being a unique bond between one man and one woman for life, exclusive of all others. Christian **marriage** rites have famously included wording such as is found in the officiating **clergyman**'s question in **Thomas Cranmer**'s 1549 and 1552 **Books of Common Prayer**: "Wilt thou

. . . forsaking all other, keep thee only to her, so long as you both shall live?"

Within historic Christendom, this pattern has been recognized for 1,000 years or more. King **Henry VIII** could have his marriages annulled or terminated by the death of wives, but he could hardly seek **divorce**, and the issue of polygamy never entered the discussion. However, as Christian **missions** in the 19th century brought the **gospel** to many parts of the world where societies had an accepted pattern of polygamy, the issue about the terms on which polygamists could be **baptized** became of acute concern. The issue is still live today, not least because Islam allows men to have up to four wives.

The historic answer has almost universally been that a polygamist must release all but his first wife and live faithfully with her, if he is to be baptized. This discipline, however, ran into serious difficulties from the start, as abandoned wives and their children might have no means of support and be marginalized by their particular society or shunned by their blood relations, without anyone taking responsibility for them. This has appeared as a cruel (and socially destabilizing) outcome of a discipline that was seeking to follow the way of Christ.

The **Lambeth Conference** of 1888 passed the following resolutions, each by a split vote:

> 5.(A) That it is the opinion of this Conference that persons living in polygamy be not admitted to baptism, but that they be accepted as candidates and kept under Christian instruction until such time as they shall be in a position to accept the law of Christ. [83 for, 21 against]
> 5.(B) That the wives of polygamists may, in the opinion of this Conference, be admitted in some cases to baptism, but that it must be left to the local authorities of the Church to decide under what circumstances they may be baptized. [54 for, 34 against]

It has been stated that, within the committee tackling the issue and in the voting in plenary, **Samuel Crowther**, the bishop on the Niger, the sole black African bishop at the conference, was active among the minority. What is certain is that in the following six Lambeth Conferences, although sex and marriage were addressed by both committee reports and plenary resolutions in most of them, polygamy was not even mentioned again until 1958. Then it received some frank discussion in the committee report and was the subject of a fence-sitting resolution (no. 120) that did not visibly touch on the question of the terms for admission to baptism. In 1968 there were merely two lines in Resolution 23, "That this Conference recognizes that polygamy poses one of the sharpest conflicts between faith and particular cultures." That was all.

The first meeting of the **Anglican Consultative Council** (ACC-1) in 1971 handled a request from the South Pacific Anglican Council to provide for polygamists to be baptized under certain conditions, but was unable to come to a mind and asked for more information from **provinces** concerned before the next ACC meeting. ACC-2 in Dublin in 1973 did recommend, under fairly strict conditions, that a polygamist should be baptized "with his believing wives and children." It is unclear, however, how far news of this recommendation was actually publicized in the Communion.

By Lambeth 1988, a settled mind was emerging among the bishops. Over the 100 years since the first resolution on the subject there had been a considerable easing of the position taken by the bishops corporately on **birth control** and on divorce and remarriage, reflecting "Western" concerns. But there had also been an enormous increase in African bishops, who were pressing their own concerns. So the conference adopted unanimously:

> 26. CHURCH AND POLYGAMY
>
> This Conference upholds monogamy as God's plan, and as the ideal relationship of love between husband and wife; nevertheless recommends that a polygamist who responds to the Gospel and wishes to join the Anglican church may be baptized and **confirmed** with his believing wives and children on the following conditions:
>
> 1. that the polygamist shall promise not to marry again as long as any of his wives at the time of his conversion are alive;
> 2. that the receiving of such a polygamist has the consent of the local Anglican community; and
> 3. that such a polygamist shall not be compelled to put away any of his wives on account of the social deprivation they would suffer;
>
> and recommends that Provinces where the churches face problems of polygamy are encouraged to share information of their pastoral approach to Christians who become polygamists so that the most appropriate way of disciplining and pastoring them can be found, and that the ACC be requested to facilitate the sharing of that information.

The 1998 Lambeth Conference did not mention polygamy in either its reports or its resolutions.

POLYNESIA. *See* AOTEAROA.

POPE. From one point of view, the **bishop** of Rome (otherwise known as "il papa" or the pope) provided the defining element in the separation of the Church of **England** (and thus, in the process of history, of the whole of world Anglicanism) from the "Western Church." In 1521 Pope Leo X had lauded and rewarded King **Henry VIII** as *Fidei Defensor* ("**Defender of the Faith**"), but in 1527 Pope Clement VII refused to declare Henry's **marriage** to Catherine of Aragon **null** and void and thus precipitated a political crisis. When Henry, by parliamentary legislation in 1532–1534, separated England and the Church of England root and branch from the **Roman Catholic Church**, it was the powers and roles of the pope that were then terminated or transferred to the Crown. This was the first step in the English **Reformation**—a bold initiative that relocated powers over the beliefs and structures of the Church of England so as to provide a national autonomous authority that enabled, and in the following reign achieved, the far-reaching changes of a **doctrinal** Reformation.

The early years of the English Reformation were marked by an unsurprising hostility to the papacy. The first English-language **liturgical** text, the **Litany** produced by **Thomas Cranmer** in 1544, prayed: "From the tyranny of the Bishop of Rome and all his detestable enormities: Good Lord, deliver us." This text remained in the 1549 and 1552 **Books of Common Prayer**, but was removed when the 1552 Book was revived in 1559.

While much of the doctrinal Reformation was deliberately oriented against the **Council** of **Trent** (1546–1563), the person of the pope in Tudor times represented a political threat to the nation as much as a purveyor of error to the Church. Thus Queen **Mary I**'s marriage to Philip of Spain added fear of annexation to Spain to the existing fears of the restoration of the doctrinal position of the papal system in the Church. Article XXXVII of the Thirty-Nine **Articles** of 1571 contains both the assertion of supreme power resting with the monarch and also the firm exclusion of all foreign powers, with the passing statement: "The Bishop of Rome hath no jurisdiction in this realm of England."

The pope was regularly portrayed in the 16th century as the Antichrist, and suspicion and fear of papal influence greatly affected the life of the Church of England in the 17th century, not least when two Stuart monarchs married Roman Catholics and a third, King **James II**, became a Roman Catholic himself before inheriting the throne, and, by his actions as monarch, provoked the **Glorious Revolution**.

Anglican distancing from the pope has in the succeeding centuries been focused less on temporal power and more on the spiritual claims of the papacy. This suspicion came to a head when, at the General Council held in 1869–1870 known as **Vatican I**, papal **infallibility** was defined. According to the council, the pope could declare matters of faith *ex cathedra* (i.e., when affirming his **authority** in the most solemn way possible) without the backing or confirmation of a General Council or the people of God at large, and such definitions would be irreformable, that is, infallible. The particular instances of the use of this papal spiritual power are confined in Roman Catholic understanding to the two "Marian" decrees, one in 1854 (before Vatican I) on the **Immaculate Conception** of the Virgin **Mary** and the other in 1950 on her bodily **assumption** into **heaven**. By contrast, the condemnation of Anglican **orders** set out in ***Apostolicae Curae*** in 1896 was highly authoritative and claimed to close the question forever, but does not rank as an *ex cathedra* statement.

In the agreements of successive **Anglican–Roman Catholic International Commissions** (i.e., ARCIC-1 and ARCIC-2) there have been three main statements on "Authority in the Church," each of which focuses on the office and powers of a "universal **primate**." The first two such statements ("Authority in the Church I" [1976], which also had an "Elucidation" published later, and "Authority in the Church II" [1981]) registered some disagreements in ARCIC-1 between the two sets of theologians about the office of the pope, though also registering much convergence. "Authority in the Church III" in 1999 (entitled *The Gift of Authority*) was wholly agreed to by ARCIC-2 and involved complete acceptance by the Anglicans as well as by the Roman Catholics of the following points:

1. There ought to be a universal primate in the worldwide church.
2. Such a primate ought to have power to intervene in any **diocese** in the world.

3. Such a primate would be properly (and in the economy of God) located in Rome.
4. Such a primate would speak on behalf of the whole **episcopate**, representing the whole worldwide church.
5. Such a primate would have power, in accordance with his responsibilities, to make "irreformable" definitions of doctrine for the good of the worldwide church.

It is, at the very least, unclear whether such a statement by ARCIC-2 carries the corporate judgment of the **Anglican Communion**. While it appears to expect to incorporate Anglicans into a wholly Roman framework of belief and structure, it has not, at the time of writing, been subject to critical analysis by the **synods** and doctrinal commissions of the 38 provinces of the Communion. Meanwhile it has only the authority of the two teams of theologians who produced it.

PORTUGAL. *See* LUSITANIAN CHURCH.

PORVOO. Porvoo is the location of the **cathedral** in Finland where a service of thanksgiving was held to mark the completion of the agreements between representatives of the Anglican Churches of Britain and **Ireland** and of the **Lutheran** Baltic and Nordic Churches in October 1992. The agreement was published in 1993 as "The Porvoo Common Statement." The term "Porvoo" has passed into common currency to denote the relationship of **Communion** established under those agreements between all the signatory Churches except the Church of Denmark. The Anglican signatories were the Church of **England**, the Church in **Wales**, the Church of Ireland, and the **Scottish** Episcopal Church; the Lutheran ones were the Churches of Finland, Sweden, Norway, Latvia, Lithuania, Estonia, and Iceland. Services to mark the adoption of the Porvoo Declaration were held in different countries in 1996, the first being at Trondheim, Norway, on 1 September 1996. The full interchangeability of **presbyters** between these Anglican and Lutheran Churches has been in operation ever since, and the relationship is sustained by close communication, regular theological dialogue, and a "Porvoo panel" to monitor, guide, and strengthen the sharing.

PRAYER BOOK. *See* BOOK OF COMMON PRAYER.

PREFACE. "Preface" is a technical term, derived from the Latin *praefatio*, used for the first part of the **eucharistic prayer**, following the introductory dialogue. Its original meaning appears to be a "telling out" rather than "telling before [something else]." Thus the **eucharistic** preface is the natural location of a recitation of the "mighty acts" of **God**, as can be seen as far back as the description in Justin Martyr's *First Apology* (c. A.D. 160) and in detail in the prayer in Hippolytus's *Apostolic Tradition* (c. 215) (cf. 1 Pet. 2.10: "to tell out the great deeds of him who has called us out of darkness into his marvellous light"). This principle has been closely observed in almost every 20th-century eucharistic rite in the **Anglican Communion**.

When the wording of a preface varies or is amplified with particular seasons or occasions, the preface is then called a "**proper** preface," that is, a preface "appropriate" to the season. When it does not admit of any variation, it is called a "fixed preface."

PREFACE TO THE BOOK OF COMMON PRAYER. *See* BOOK OF COMMON PRAYER.

PREFACE TO THE ORDINAL. *See* ORDINAL.

PRESBYTER. "Presbyter" is in the first instance a mere transliteration of the Greek word *presbuteros*, the meaning of which is regularly "older in years." In the New Testament, there are "**elders**" of the Jewish synagogues and of the ruling **Council**, the Sanhedrin (e.g., in Acts 4.5, 4.8, 4.23, 5.21, etc.), and they are almost certainly the precedent for the *presbuteroi* of the Christian churches (e.g., in Acts 20.17; Titus 1.5). There has been great debate among scholars as to the qualifications for being appointed as a presbyter and also as to the distinction, if any, between *episkopoi* (**bishops**) and *presbuteroi*. As to the former, it is likely to have been seniority within the life of the church (as distinct from the age since birth) that qualified them; as to the latter, it looks as though the same people were indeed described by both titles (cf. Acts 20.17 and 20.28; Titus 1.5 and 1.7), though the titles were possibly distinguished by an emphasis in one case upon function and another upon standing and respect. A similar interchangeability of terms can be discerned in the letter of Clement of Rome to the Corinthians and in the Didache, just before and probably just after the end of the first century A.D. Thereafter, however, the "threefold" **orders**, in which bishop and presbyter are distinct from each other, emerges strongly, beginning with Ignatius of Antioch (c. 110).

The Greek and Latin of the "presbyter" stem remain the words for the second order of the **ordained ministry** from the time of Ignatius to the present day. However, the more regular English usage has been to call **ministers** in the second order "**priests**," and this has caused linguistic and **doctrinal** confusion. Despite this, the origins of the word have been well known, and the use of the term "presbyter" has continued, at least in a secondary role, since the **Reformation**. Its Latin form has continued in the text of the Thirty-Nine **Articles** and in the **rubrics** in Latin forms of the **Book of Common Prayer**. "Presbyter" is the term regularly employed since the 17th century in the **Scottish** Episcopal Church; it is used at intervals informally across the **Anglican Communion** (and **John Henry Newman**'s Tract 1 of ***Tracts for the Times*** began, "I am one of yourselves—a presbyter"); it is the alternative title given in the **ordination rites** in the Church of **England**; and it was agreed as the only title of the second order of ordained ministers at the formation of the united churches of **South India**, **North India**, **Pakistan**, and **Bangladesh**.

In theory, each **language** group ought to use for this second order the term by which they translate *presbuteros* when it occurs in the New Testament. But the Church of England failed to do this in the formative period of the English **Bible** (keeping "priest" as the primary word for the second order of ministers in the Prayer Book rubrics, yet translating *presbuteros* as "elder" in the English Bible), and so no good model was set for other language groups, and the nuance or shades of meaning in the terms used for the second order of ministry may vary from one **province** to another and one language to another. "Presbyter" is preferred throughout this dictionary.

PRESBYTERIAN. *See* REFORMED CHURCHES.

PRESIDENT. "President" is a verbal noun meaning "the one who presides," a word that has come into Anglican **rubrics** in some **provinces** since the early 1970s. It corresponds to the phrase *ho prohestos* in

Justin Martyr's account of the **eucharist** in the middle of the second century. By describing the officiant at **liturgy** with a word signifying function rather than **order**, it conveys a more dynamic concept of the role being fulfilled, without prejudice to the question of order. Equally, by avoiding the word "celebrant," it has enabled the concept that the whole congregation **celebrates** the eucharist to gain ground. Its use has thus also enabled "**lay presidency**" to be considered without any ambiguity of meaning. On the other hand, it has had to replace an old-fashioned **Anglo-Catholic** concept of a **bishop** or eminent **presbyter** "presiding" by being present in a seat of honor at the eucharist, but without any function, while the rite is performed as the effective officiant by another **ordained** "celebrant." In some parts of the **Anglican Communion**, the alternative word "**presider**" is used.

PRESIDER. "Presider" has exactly the same function as "**president**," but is a word preferred in countries or **provinces**, such as the **United States**, where "president" has very strong secular or civic significance, and it has been thought there might be risk of confusion.

PRIEST. In the New Testament, the Greek word that is usually translated into English as "priest" is the word *hiereus*. The use of it and of its cognates in the New Testament is threefold: It is used, first, of Old Testament (levitical) priests (e.g., Luke 1.5; Heb. 7.5); second, of **Jesus Christ** as "priest after the order of Melchisedek" (e.g., Heb. 7.17); and third, derivatively, of all believers as together holding a "priesthood" (1 Pet. 2.5, 2.9; cf. Rev 1.6, 5.10). However, the English word "priest" is itself etymologically a corruption of the Greek word *presbuteros*, which in the New Testament is translated as "**elder**." The distinction is clear in Greek—the "elders" are a category of Christian leaders, while the three uses of "priest" shown above do not include that category, for the *hiereus* terms "priest" and "priesthood" are applied only to the whole church. Despite this consistent New Testament usage, from the second century onward, the *hiereus* terminology began to be applied to the **ordained ministers**—initially only to **bishops**, but later to **presbyters** also. The growth in church history of this misapplication of the New Testament usage matched a comparable growth in the understanding of the **eucharist** as a distinct ritual offering of a sacrifice to God. Thus, by the time of the **Reformation**, the distinctive function of the "priest" was expressed in the bishop's words at the handing over of the paten and chalice to the new priest at his ordination: "Receive **authority** to offer sacrifice for the living and the dead."

In the Reformation formularies, all suggestion that the eucharist is in itself a sacrifice was eliminated, and the presbyterate was recreated as primarily a **ministry** of the word, to which the ministry of the **sacraments** was joined derivatively. In the Latin texts, the term *presbyterus* was used for the second **order** of the ministry, except that in **Article** XXXI, the Roman **doctrine** was reported as "in which it was commonly said that the priest [*sacerdotem*] did offer sacrifice," and the title of Article XXXII was "Concerning the **marriage** of priests [*sacerdotum*]," a heading that covered bishops, presbyters, and **deacons** and was clearly not meant simply for the second order of the threefold order.

Although the Latin texts safeguarded the distinctions of the Greek New Testament, the **rubrics** of **Thomas Cranmer**'s English **Books of Common Prayer** invariably said "priest" where "presbyter" might have been more exact. English translations of the **Bible** translated *presbuteros* as "elder" (except the **Roman Catholic** Douay New Testament of 1582, which, for its own purposes, used "priest" instead). Thus it was difficult to see the connection between the "priest" of popular speech and liturgical rubrics, and the "elder" of the New Testament language.

In later Anglican history, the **Anglo-Catholic** movement of the 19th century tended to delight in the language of priesthood for the second order of the ordained ministry, and this has affected Anglicanism worldwide. Every **language** group has reached its own decisions, depending upon the words available from New Testament translation, the **provincial** understanding of the presbyterate, the degree to which the muddle in English has affected the assumptions of the drafters, and the implicit doctrine of the eucharist to which the role of the presbyter has to relate.

PRIMATE. "Primate" is a title regularly used for the leading **bishop** of a **province**, usually, but not always, an **archbishop** or **metropolitan**. However, in some contexts, the primate is a bishop who has **authority** over more than one province in a particular church with two or more provinces. A historical conflict led in **England** to the paradoxical result that the archbishop of **Canterbury** has the title of "primate of all England" and the archbishop of **York** the title of "primate of England." This oddity is exactly mirrored in the Church of **Ireland**, where the archbishop of **Armagh** is primate of all Ireland and the archbishop of **Dublin** is the primate of Ireland. Elsewhere in the **Anglican Communion**, the title has been used strictly to denominate the leading bishop of a "particular or national church," so that even Churches which have several provinces and a similar number of archbishops, such as the Anglican Church in **Australia** or the Anglican Church in **Canada**, have only the one presiding bishop or archbishop who (whatever his local title) can be treated for inter-Anglican purposes as the primate. In Canada and the **United States**, the primate has a separated nondiocesan role, without the territorial responsibilities that come with the diocesan jurisdiction of a bishop or archbishop. *See also* PRIMATES' MEETINGS.

PRIMATES' MEETINGS. Meetings of the **primates** of the churches of the **Anglican Communion** were the subject of a hope expressed in a section report of the 1978 **Lambeth Conference**, to which the then **archbishop** of **Canterbury**, **Donald Coggan**, responded positively in his address on "**Authority** in the Anglican Communion," saying that he thought such meetings (for which there was occasional precedent) "should be held perhaps as frequently as once every two years" and going on to express a hope that "that body . . . should be in the closest and most intimate contact with the **Anglican Consultative Council** [ACC]."

Coggan himself then convened the first meeting, at Ely in 1979. This was followed in Archbishop **Robert Runcie**'s time by meetings in Washington, D.C., in 1981; Limuru, **Kenya**, in 1983; Toronto in 1986; and Cyprus in 1989. The first meeting of **George Carey**'s archiepiscopate was held in Newcastle, County Down, Northern **Ireland**, in 1991. In 1993 he convened a Primates Meeting in Cape Town, South Africa, to coincide with a meeting of the ACC. A further separate meeting was held in **Jerusalem** in 1997.

At the 1998 Lambeth Conference, there was a request that each national Church appoint its primate as its Episcopal member of the ACC. If that had been implemented, it would have largely integrated the two bodies; however, few provinces have made that change, and there is apparent difficulty, in that representation of a province on the ACC is supposed to be for a limited period only. Separate meetings of the primates continue and are now planned on an annual basis. Meetings have been held in **Brazil** in 2000; in Kanuga, North Carolina, in 2001; in Canterbury in May 2002; in southern Brazil, the first meeting convened by **Rowan Williams**, in May 2003; and, in an emergency way, in **London** in October 2003.

Much of the agenda has been devoted to exploring ways of sustaining and strengthening the bonds of the Communion. The October 2003 meeting arose from the imminent **consecration** of a practicing **homosexual** as bishop of New Hampshire in the **Episcopal Church (United States of America)**. It led to the appointment by the archbishop of Canterbury of the **Lambeth Commission**, which in turn led to the Primates Meeting at Dromantine, near Belfast, Northern Ireland, in 2005—a meeting at which the Anglican Churches in the **United States** and **Canada** were asked to withdraw from the ACC (of which the next meeting was due in June of that year). Thus the Primates Meetings have not only come to be viewed as one of the instruments of unity within the Anglican Communion but also have begun to practice a major corporate oversight of the Communion and to initiate and direct policies that bear upon its unity. At ACC-13 in June 2005, the members voted to make the primates additional *ex officio* members of ACC, thus leaving existing bishop representatives in place and exempting primates from the time limit.

PROPER PREFACE. *See* PREFACE.

PROPERS. The adjective "proper" means in ecclesiastical usage "appropriate to the season" (e.g., as in "proper **preface**"). Thus the set of "propers" of any Sunday, **feast**, or season is the set of variable features of the **liturgy** that together belong to that occasion.

PROPHECY. The Old Testament prophets are largely listed by name and are recognized as able to speak God's word, including words of judgment, with particular knowledge or foreknowledge. Their listing is usually concluded with John the Baptist. But in the New Testament, there are both named prophets, quite apart from the 12 apostles (e.g., Agabus in Acts 11.28 and 21.10–11), and an apparently widespread practice of "prophesying" (cf. Rom. 12.6; 1 Cor. 12.28–29, 13.2, 13.9, 14. *passim*; 1 Thess. 5.20; 1 Tim. 4.14). There have been different views in history as to the nature of prophecy in the New Testament and as to its **authority** in relation to the present day. Thus the **Puritan** dissidents in Queen **Elizabeth I**'s reign described their meetings for preaching and mutual encouragement as "prophesyings" (a move that **Archbishop John Whitgift** worked to abolish). Others have viewed confrontation with the powers of the day (e.g., **William Wilberforce** attacking slavery) as the exercise of a prophetic role. But in the **Charismatic Movement** beginning around 1960 arose a practice of individuals addressing assemblies with the grammatical style of "Thus says the Lord"—a style that enables the speaker to go on to offer comfort, encouragement, or even accusation and judgment, in the first person singular ("I, the Lord, will have mercy," etc.). This has been claimed as the "gift" of prophecy. There is no current single **hermeneutical** resolution.

PROTESTANT EPISCOPAL CHURCH IN THE UNITED STATES OF AMERICA (PECUSA). The first **General Convention** of Episcopalians in the **United States** after independence was held in 1785 and adopted the title Protestant Episcopal Church in the United States of America. Hence the title, or its initials (PECUSA), are necessarily in use in all accounts of history. In the 20th century, however, large numbers of Anglicans came to disavow the term "**Protestant**," and steps were taken to play down its significance in the Church's name. In 1967, the official title was not abolished, but was largely superseded by a declaration that the title "**Episcopal Church (United States of America)**" (ECUSA) would suffice for most purposes. The change was made substantive at the General Convention of 1979.

PROTESTANTISM. The word "Protestant" arises from a gathering of **Lutherans** at the Diet of Speyer in 1529. Under pressure from opponents, they issued a "Protestatio," but the character of this suggests it would be better translated as an "attestation" of their faith, rather than as a protest against some stance or tendency of others. Because it was an early Lutheran use, it was sometimes used at this early stage of the

Reformation to distinguish Lutherans from **Reformed Church** Christians. However, by the end of the 16th century, the adjective and the adjectival noun "Protestant" had passed into widespread use as a cover term for any persons or groups opposed to **Roman Catholicism** in the 16th-century divide. The Reformation itself has often been known since then as the "Protestant Reformation," and thus any church involved **doctrinally** in the Reformation has qualified to be called "Protestant."

On the whole, in **England** it was a title accepted by both sides in the **Elizabethan** and Stuart divide between churchmen and **Puritans**, though the latter may have used it more vigorously. Its primary reference lay in being distanced from the Roman Catholic Church. This usage passed into legislation when King **James II** had vacated the throne in 1688, and it became necessary, when Parliament was offering the throne to William of Orange and Princess Mary jointly, to ensure that the succession did not revert to Roman Catholics. Thus the Bill of Rights in 1689 states that "King James II . . . . did endeavour to subvert and extirpate the Protestant religion, and the laws and liberties of this kingdom"—and a further reference to "this Protestant kingdom" also clearly refers to the Church of England. Similarly the Act of Settlement in 1700 regularly insists (in the dynastic succession of monarchs) on their belonging to "the Protestant line"—that is, that they are "Church of England" and not Roman Catholic.

Monarchs at their **coronation** have since then been asked by the **archbishop** of **Canterbury**: "Will you to the utmost of your power maintain in the United Kingdom the Protestant Reformed Religion established by law?" When the first **General Convention** of Episcopalians in the **United States** met in 1785, the title they deliberately chose for their church was the **Protestant Episcopal Church in the United States of America** (PECUSA).

A different approach to the terminology arose through the impact of the **Anglo-Catholic** movement in the 19th century. The original **Tractarians** rejected the term "Protestant," reckoning it had to be seen as opposed to "catholic"—and "catholic" is what they were. It is what they asserted the Church of England to be, pointing out that "catholic" occurs in the 16th-century formularies in the **creeds**, but "Protestant" does not. They regretted the Reformation and minimized its impact on the Church of England. The Anglo-Catholics had no wish to be bracketed with Lutherans or reformed Christians. They slowly affected the terminology of the whole **Anglican Communion**, so that Anglicans generally started to view themselves as a distinct grouping, separate from Rome in some respects, but also distanced from Protestantism. It is this sense that Anglicans do not properly view themselves as "Protestant" that led to the first word being made optional for PECUSA by resolution of the General Convention in 1967, and since then it has been legally possible to identify the Church by the title the "Episcopal Church"—though to those outside of the United States it is helpful to add the location in brackets: "**Episcopal Church (United States of America)**."

PROVINCE. A cluster of **dioceses** with an organic (usually constitutional) relationship forms a province. The minimum is typically four dioceses to constitute a province, thereby conforming visibly to the requirement that, when there is a vacancy in a **bishop**'s post, there will still be three bishops available to **consecrate** a new bishop for the vacancy. This entails some provincial endorsement of the diocesan appointment, and in most provinces of the **Anglican Communion** there are earlier constitutional provisions to ensure strong provincial support of the person nominated to be a bishop, whether diocesan bishop or **suffragan**.

Most of the autonomous churches of the Anglican Communion each comprise a single province. However, the Church of **England** itself has had two provinces for more than 1,000 years, and that characteristic is paralleled in the Anglican churches in five other countries: **Australia**, **Canada**, **Ireland**, **Nigeria**, and the **United States**. Where there are more than one provinces in a church, the individual provinces usually have a low-key or almost invisible role, and central **authority** is held by the **General Synod** and its House of Bishops, or their equivalents.

The **metropolitan** of a province is usually described as the "**archbishop**." However, in the **Episcopal Church (United States of America)**, there is no metropolitan of each province and the provincial presidency is held by an elected person who need not be a bishop. *See also* PRIMATE.

PROVINCIAL EPISCOPAL VISITOR (PEV). "PEVs" or (as they are sometimes called) "flying **bishops**" are a special provision of the Church of **England** in the wake of the **ordination** of **women** as **presbyters**. The legal background to this, contained in a parliamentary **measure**, is the provision that allows **parishes** to vote not to have women as **presidents** of the **eucharist** and/or not to have women as incumbents of the parish. Under a further provision of 1993 by the **General Synod** (the Episcopal Ministry Act of Synod), parishes that have passed both these resolutions may also petition their **diocesan** bishop for "extended Episcopal care." This is done in order that a diocesan bishop whose own ministrations are unwelcome to a parish because of his participation in the ordination of women, may ask a specific other bishop to provide **sacramental** "care" to any parish requesting the provision. The extended care may then be provided from within the diocese or by agreement from a neighboring diocese, or, in default of such arrangements, by the diocesan bishop commissioning a provincial Episcopal visitor. The PEVs, who by definition are themselves totally opposed to the ordination of women, are at the time of writing two suffragan bishops of the diocese of **Canterbury** and one of the diocese of **York**, who are then available via the respective **archbishops** of the two provinces to exercise such "extended Episcopal care" when diocesan bishops in the respective provinces have need of such Episcopal assistance. There is a simpler but similar provision in the Church in **Wales**, but not elsewhere in the **Anglican Communion**.

PROVOOST, SAMUEL (1742–1815). Samuel Provoost was born in New York City and studied for a time at Cambridge. He was **ordained** as a **deacon** and **presbyter** in 1766. His main appointment was to be rector of **Trinity Church, Wall Street,** in New York for 16 years. After the formation of the **Protestant Episcopal Church in the United States of America** (PECUSA) through the **General Convention** of 1785, he was elected the first **bishop** of New York. By that point, the British Parliament had changed the law to allow the **archbishop** of **Canterbury** to **consecrate** bishops for foreign territories, so Provoost traveled to **London** with **William White**, elected to be bishop of Pennsylvania, and on 4 February 1787 the two of them became the first Anglican bishops consecrated in **England** for overseas territories. Provoost took part in the General Convention of 1789 in the seminal House of Bishops, and in 1792 shared with White, **Samuel Seabury**, and James Madison (who had been consecrated in England in 1790 as bishop of Virginia) in the consecration of Thomas Claggett for Maryland, the first consecration of a bishop on American soil. When Provoost sought to retire in 1801, the House of Bishops provided him instead with an assistant bishop.

PROVOST. "Provost" is a term sometimes used to denote a head of house in higher education in different parts of the world. It passed from this use to become available in **England** when new **dioceses** were being formed in the 19th century and were gaining diocesan **cathedrals** in new places. In some cases, **parish** churches became cathedrals without ceasing to be parish churches, and the term "provost" was adopted for the chief **presbyter** of the parish church cathedral. For virtually all cathedral purposes, the provost was the equivalent of a **dean**, and in England, legislation was introduced early in the 21st century to enable provosts to change their title to "dean." In some other parts of the **Anglican Communion**, cathedrals founded in the 19th and 20th centuries are led by provosts, and again there is virtually no substantial difference of function as between the roles of provost and dean.

PULPIT. A pulpit is the distinctive church furniture designated as the chief place for preaching. Traditionally it was raised well above the floor of the building and was reached by steps. In some **cathedrals**, there have been two separate pulpits, one in the choir and one in the **nave**, and sometimes these have been placed by a pillar not at the most easterly point of choir or nave, but one or two pillars further west. The classical form of it was the "triple-decker," sometimes, in classical buildings, placed centrally in a square, galleried, one-room chamber. In this form, the pulpit for preaching was the "top deck," sometimes canopied by a sounding board, all designed for maximum "auditory" effect, especially enabling the gallery to hear what was said. Since the 19th century, however, pulpits have more usually been placed to one side, so as to leave the **Communion table** visually central. The grandeur of design of pulpits slowly faded in the 20th century, so that now churches affected by the **Liturgical Movement** are not infrequently equipped with ambos, quite near to floor level, where both the reading of scripture and the preaching of sermons is done from the same **lectern** or ambo as each other, or from two equally balanced ones.

PURGATORY. The concept of a place for the **dead** of waiting for the judgment, a place of purgation in the meantime, was greatly developed in the West during the Middle Ages. While the origins of the **doctrine** probably lay in the practice of praying on behalf of the dead, the systematization provided an understanding of the projected length (in earthly years and days) of each person's anticipated stay in purgatory. This in turn enabled ecclesiastical authorities to offer as indulgences the remission of all or part of that length of stay in return for prayers or works of merit, or possibly the intervention of the **saints**, or even for cash. The Reformers were entirely convinced from the New Testament that no intermediate place of this sort existed and that pressure to shorten people's time in it was corrupting. Their central persuasion was that the New Testament doctrine of **justification** guarantees that the justified sinner would not need any further purgation after death in relation to his or her sins. They stated in Article XXII of the Thirty-Nine **Articles** that "the Romish doctrine concerning Purgatory . . . is a fond thing vainly invented" and "repugnant to the Word of God." They matched this with an elimination from the **Book of Common Prayer** of all **petitions for the departed**. The rejection of purgatory did not necessarily of itself entail that all private petition for the departed was necessarily labeled heretical; but the reformers were clearly conscious of where it might lead if practiced in the public arena.

PURITANS. The English **Reformation**, even in its genesis, produced two different kinds of **Protestant** churchpeople. The leaders set their own pace for reform, a fast pace but one that others were not to "run afore" (as it appeared in the royal proclamation preceding the 1548 *Order of the* ***Communion***). To many, however, this meant compromising in ways they did not believe the scriptures permitted, and they pressed and worked for instant radical reform. In King **Edward VI**'s reign, two instances of such pressure gained renown: The first came when **John Hooper**, nominated in 1551 to become **bishop** of Gloucester, declined to wear the Episcopal vesture or invoke "**all saints** and the holy Evangelist" in aid in an **oath** of repudiating the **pope** and acknowledging the king as the head on Earth of the Church of **England**. The second was when John Knox preached an inflammatory sermon before the king in September 1552 inveighing against the requirement in the forthcoming 1552 **Book of Common Prayer** that communicants should be kneeling (*see also* **Black Rubric**). These instances are generally viewed as the first public outcropping of a much wider semi-underground unease with the discerned inadequate speed and style of the Reformation.

During the reign of Queen **Mary I**, many of the Puritans were in exile on the Continent, where they were often able on the local scene to move further along the reformed path than had been envisaged in Edward's reign. Richard Cox and others wrote to John Calvin from Frankfurt in 1555, "We gave up private **baptisms**, **confirmation** of children, **saints**' days, kneeling at the holy communion, surplices . . . not as being impure and papistical, which certain of our brethren often charged them with being." Thus there was a party that said much in the **Book of Common Prayer** was "papistical," and others who would go with them in such abolition, without making the same judgment.

When Queen **Elizabeth I** succeeded in 1558, her policy of restoring the 1552 position was immediately tested by the strong Puritan element in the restored Protestant **clergy**. A classic case was the proposal in the Lower House of **Canterbury Convocation** in 1562 that saints' days, the **sign of the cross** in baptism, and the necessity of kneeling to receive Communion should be abolished, and the proposal was lost by one vote. The foundational principle that the Puritans were asserting was that nothing should be required in worship that was not required in the scriptures, and the requirement of wearing a surplice figured heavily and consistently in the application of this principle. The response of the queen and bishops was to add to Article XX in the slight revision of the Thirty-Nine **Articles** in 1563 the telling opening sentence: "The Church hath power to decree Rites or **Ceremonies**, and **authority** in controversies of faith"—and the role of the scriptures (which ran on from Article XXI of 1553) was that "it is not lawful for the Church to ordain anything that is contrary to God's word written." An enormous gulf was opening between those who wanted specific **biblical** warrant for every **rubrical** requirement and those who conceived of considerable middle ground, not specifically identified in scripture, where "the Church hath power."

After 1563 the Puritan program was pursued much more heavily in Parliament, and, when the queen made her displeasure at such bills known, it took the more radical form of a semiunderground pamphlet, *An Admonition to the Parliament* (1572). This was answered by **John Whitgift** in *An Answer to a Certain Libel entitled An Admonition to Parliament* (1573), but that only led to *A Second Admonition to Parliament*, and a further reply by Whitgift and the battle was joined. By the 1580s it had led on from the ceremonies to the forms of government, focusing opposition also on the role and powers of Elizabethan bishops. The use of authority against the Puritans by Whitgift was now reinforced by the Anglican theology of **Richard Hooker** and the growing influence of the claims for **episcopacy** of Richard Bancroft (1544–1610), who succeeded Whitgift as **archbishop** of Canterbury at the very beginning of King **James I**'s reign in 1604.

In 1603, when James inherited the throne of England, he was met in his way south by Puritans bearing the "Millenary Petition," a document signed by 1,000 citizens asking for the reform of some of the more disliked ceremonies. James responded by summoning the **Hampton Court Conference** and presiding at it himself. However, the concessions allowed as an outcome of the conference were few, and the tendency in the reigns of both James and his son, **Charles I**, was consistently to bring more and more pressure upon the Puritans to conform to a totally inflexible **liturgical** regime. The emergence of Archbishop **William Laud** was both an outcome of royal policy and a powerful reinforcement of it. This resulted in the English Civil War, the defeat of the royalists, and the execution of both the archbishop and monarch.

In the process at least two streams were appearing within Puritanism, one usually labeled "**Presbyterian**" and the other "Independent." They were distinguished not only by their ideals of church government: the former were ready for a liturgy (though with options and high flexibility), while the latter opposed any "praying upon the Book." Both were tolerated during the **Commonwealth** period, and the **Westminster Directory** was an uneasy compromise between them.

At the **Restoration**, when revision of the Prayer Book was in view, the so-called Presbyterians (though Richard Baxter insisted they were moderate Episcopalians) were invited to the **Savoy Conference**, which the Independents by definition could not be. When the Great Ejectment came in 1662, most of the Puritans left the Church of En-gland and became nonconformist. However, in various ways, from the time of the **Evangelical Revival** onward, both in England and in other parts of the **Anglican Communion**, a strand of Puritan theology and outlook has been visible within Anglican evangelicalism. *See also* PROPHECY.

PUSEY, EDWARD BOUVERIE (1800–1882). Edward Pusey graduated in 1822 and in 1824 became a fellow of Oriel College, Oxford, and thus a colleague of **John Henry Newman**. He was **ordained** as a **deacon** and **presbyter** in 1828 and immediately became Regius Professor of Hebrew and canon of Christ Church, Oxford, positions he held until his death. He was one of the original **Tractarians**, closely engaged with Newman and **John Keble**, and an author of various works of the ***Tracts for the Times***. He was one of the few married men in the group, but his wife died in 1839, and he was deeply saddened. His sermon on the **eucharist** was condemned as **heretical** by the Convocation of the university in 1843. Of the three most notable founders of the **Anglo-Catholic** movement, he alone remained at Oxford, becoming the senior figure of the movement. He was instrumental in the formation of the first Anglican sisterhood, the Sisterhood of the Holy Cross, in 1845. He saw out his days in constant controversy, fighting against incipient **liberalism** as well as **evangelicalism**. His name lives on in the Anglo-Catholic study and research center in Oxford, Pusey House, founded in his memory. He is remembered in various Anglican **calendars** on 16 September, the date of his death.

PYX. A pyx is a container for **consecrated** wafers. One of the ways of reserving the **elements** before the **Reformation** was in a hanging pyx, suspended by a chain from a ceiling or a bracket. A pyx was also used to carry the consecrated wafer to the sick. All such uses of a pyx disappeared at the Reformation, when first in 1549 permanent **reservation** ceased, and then in 1552 there remained no objective consecration, the **bread** was leavened, and, if any remained after the service, it could be taken home for use as ordinary bread. As reservation has reappeared in the **Anglican Communion**, so the use of a pyx has sometimes been resumed.

– R –

RAMSEY, ARTHUR MICHAEL (1904–1988). Michael Ramsey was **ordained** as a **deacon** in 1928 and **presbyter** a year later. He wrote *The Gospel and the Catholic Church* when on the staff of Lincoln **Theological College** in 1936. Then in 1940 he became **canon**–professor of theology at Durham, and in 1950 Regius Professor of Theology at Cambridge. In 1952 Ramsey became **bishop** of Durham, in 1956 **archbishop** of **York**, and in 1961 archbishop of **Canterbury**. His time at **Lambeth Palace** was marked in the Church of **England** by many years (1963–1972) of wrestling with an Anglican–**Methodist** unity scheme that, because of its proposed way of uniting Episcopal and non-Episcopal **ministries**, was not actually viable. This was also the period of the first provision for trying out revised **liturgical** texts without recourse to Parliament, the period when **synodical** government was introduced in the Church of England, the period of the publication of John Robinson's *Honest to God* (1963), and the period of **Vatican II** (1962–1965), which led, in 1967, to the preliminary and, in 1969, the substantial **Anglican–Roman Catholic International Commission** (ARCIC). In the **Anglican Communion** at large Ramsey presided over the 1968 **Lambeth Conference**, and, arising from that, he oversaw the formation of the **Anglican Consultative Council** in 1971. Ramsey retired as archbishop in 1974, modeling in his own practice the requirement that was shortly to come into force in England that officeholders should retire at 70, though, like all retired archbishops, he became a life peer in the House of Lords. There were suggestions after his death that he should be commemorated in the **calendar** of the Church of England, but prevailing counsels opined that this should await a point 50 years from his death.

READER. While the Anglican **Reformation** delivered a change of **doctrine**, it retained, by the very methods of its implementation, a deep-seated clericalism. In particular, **laypeople** had virtually no responsibility in leading worship, though **parish** clerks might respond to **clergy** versicles and take other secondary roles in the service. Captains of ships at sea had some responsibility for leading prayers (and forms for this were provided in the 1662 **Book of Common Prayer**, possibly drawing on the provision of the **Westminster Directory**). In the 18th century, **Methodism** was distinguished by its use of lay preachers and class leaders—but, almost by definition, there were no parallel or comparable pastoral or **liturgical** lay **ministries** in the Church of **England**. There was an informal arrangement of lay readers in the American colonies, some, no doubt, being men who would have been **ordained** had it not been for the necessary sea voyage to **London**. It is claimed that the greater use of "**minister**" in place of "**priest**" in the **rubrics** of the 1789 Book of Common Prayer of the **Protestant Episcopal Church in the United States of America** (PECUSA) reflected the shortage of ordained men to lead **Morning and Evening Prayer**, with a consequent regular use of these lay readers. In later years a category of "lay preachers" developed in the **United States**.

In the 19th century there was a development of **catechists** and recognized lay pastors in pioneer situations opened up by Anglican **missionaries** around the world. A typical phenomenon was the medical missionary, who, though lay, became pastor, leader, and **Bible** teacher to a congregation. Another was the indigenous Christian who was judged not yet ready for **ordination** but was trained and given responsibility for one or more congregations.

In the Church of England, when the **Convocation** of **Canterbury** was revived in 1852, an early action was a report in 1859 that recommended "an extension of the diaconate." This was transmuted by stages until the **archbishops** of both Canterbury and **York** agreed to a form of "reader's license" in 1866. This permitted the recipient only to read the scriptures in a specified parish, but it led in the 1880s to the concept of preaching readers, at least some of whom had a **diocesan** rather than a parochial license. National rules were first agreed upon in 1905, and in the revision of **canon law** in the 1960s the position, qualifications, licensing, and powers of readers were canonically defined, and **women** were admitted to the office for the first time.

RECEPTION. The **Roman Catholic Church** has used for some centuries the concept of "reception," which is the process whereby a **doctrine** or belief, centrally formed and defined, is then "received" by the local churches throughout the world. It is, strictly speaking, only affirmed in retrospect to refer to a doctrine, of which it is known that it won the adherence of the faithful universally. It obviously cannot be said of a belief that was rejected by the faithful (such as Arianism, as defined at the **Council** of Ariminum in 359). The careful use of the term "reception" is of relevance in Anglicanism, where there has often been a tendency to invoke the concept of reception at the outset of a change in view or even a doctrinal shift. Thus the proponents of, for example, the **ordination** of **women**, have been keen to say that the concept was around, but was "in the process of reception." However, this use of the term "reception" somewhat prejudges the outcome of the process, and would be clearer if "reception" were applied only with hindsight, and prospectively the process were called "testing" or "trial" or "probation."

RECEPTIONISM. The reformed **doctrine** of the **eucharist**, such as was embraced by **Archbishop Thomas Cranmer**, does not attempt to assert any defined or localized presence of **Jesus Christ** in, with, or "under" the forms of **bread** and wine. Instead, there is asserted a dynamic in the action of eating the bread and drinking the wine whereby the power of Jesus Christ is conveyed to the faithful recipients.

The doctrine became explicit over the two stages of Cranmer's **Books of Common Prayer** in 1549 and 1552. In the "consecratory **epiclesis**" (before the **narrative**) in the two stages, the wording moved forward as follows:

1549: "By Thy word and **Holy Spirit** vouchsafe to bless and sanctify these thy creatures of bread and wine, that they may be unto us the body and blood of thy dear Son."

1552: "Hear us, most merciful Father, and grant that we, receiving these thy creatures of bread and wine, according to thy Son our Saviour Jesus Christ's holy institution, in remembrance of his death and passion, may be partakers of his most blessed body and blood."

The doctrine is also the most natural reading of Articles XXV, XXVIII, and XXIX of the Thirty-Nine **Articles**. Article XXIX, in its title, "Of the Wicked which eat not the body of Christ in the **Lord's Supper**," allows virtually no other understanding of the eucharist. The issue as to how to state what the "wicked" receive may appear a bizarre approach to doctrine, but in fact it provides the test case. If the benefits of Christ are "there" (i.e., in the eating and drinking) for the faithful recipient, what can be asserted to be "there" for the unfaithful or hypocritical?

However much the 16th century formularies point to some pattern of receptionism as the doctrine most in accord with those formularies, it is clear that a proportion of the whole **Anglican Communion** is more inclined to believe in some objective (and even localized) "real presence." *See also* ANGLO-CATHOLICISM; BLACK RUBRIC; CONSECRATION; RESERVATION.

REFORMATION. The vast religious movement for change that ran across **Europe** in the 16th century is commonly called the "Reformation" or, sometimes, the "**Protestant** Reformation." The vigor of the movement came from an encounter with the written scriptures as the living word of **God**, bringing a knowledge of **Jesus Christ** direct into people's lives, without the mediation of **priest** or church structures. It particularly called into serious question the **Roman Catholic Church**'s inherited **traditions** and ways of operating, and, when the structures appeared impervious to the kinds of change desired, that led in turn to the separation of great numbers from their affiliation to Rome.

The role of the **Bible** in the movement is fundamental. Printing came to Europe in the mid-15th century, and William Caxton set up the first printing press in **England** in 1477. Initially, the use of printing for religious purposes was directed to printing copies of the missal and the breviary, the standard books used in the church, previously available only in manuscript. However, Erasmus's edition of the Greek New Testament came in 1516, and this released considerable scholarship and investigation of its meaning. In 1517 Martin Luther nailed his 95 "theses" to the church door in Wittenburg, and, as he pursued the implications for the reform of the faith and life of the church of his newfound **justification**, he moved not only to question Rome but also to translate the Bible into the **vernacular**. His German New Testament was first published in 1522, and printed copies ran through the land.

In England, where King **Henry VIII** was being lauded by the **pope** as "**Defender of the Faith**" in 1521 for his attack on Luther, **William Tyndale** was conceiving a plan like Luther's for getting printed copies of an English-language Bible (initially of the New Testament) into the hands of not only the **clergy** but also **laypeople**. However, as he had to function in the face of both strictures and attacks from the church authorities, notably the **bishop** of **London**, his New Testaments were printed on the Continent and from 1525 shipped clandestinely into London, where they were greatly welcomed. Thus a Reformation time bomb was being laid, and it was printing—the new information technology of the period—that was the clue to its success.

While the clarity, **authority**, and widespread availability of the Bible were establishing themselves, the actual **doctrines** contained in the Bible were also emerging to challenge the Roman Catholic system of faith as taught in medieval times. Central to these biblical doctrines was justification through faith, and closely allied to its prominence were a radically restated doctrine of the **sacraments** and a series of other implications, such as the abolition of **purgatory** and an end of seeking the intercession, let alone the intervention of the **saints**. Doctrines of the **ordained ministry** varied among the Reformed Churches, partly through accidents of history. Thus, in places where the Reformation was led by fervent laypeople against the church authorities, some measure of Presbyterianism or Independency was likely to appear in the resultant church polity, whereas when the Reformation was led doctrinally by the bishops, as happened in the Church of England, it was unnecessary to overthrow the Episcopal church structure.

It has to be acknowledged, however, that a "top-down" Reformation had severe limitations. Although in a reformed context there was supposed to be liberty for individuals to read the Bible freely and reach their own conclusions, in fact the official interpretation tended to hold the field and **dissent** was dangerous. The type of Christianity followed by the citizens of a state was to be settled by the civic authorities, and the maxim "*Cuius Regio eius Religio*" gave expression to that principle.

REFORMED CHURCHES. While all churches deeply affected by the **Protestant Reformation**, or even arising from it, may properly be called "reformed," as a matter of historical nomenclature the term "Reformed Churches" has tended to attach to those Churches that derive from the Swiss Reformation, owe their theological roots to Calvinism, and have a **Presbyterian** polity. The Church of **Scotland** has historically been the church of this family closest to the Church of **England**. After the Reformation, it developed a Presbyterian polity and yet was listed on a par with the Churches of England and **Ireland** in **canon** 55 of 1604. Meanwhile, however, in 1603 the union of the Crowns whereby King James VI of Scotland became also King **James I** of England had been effected. James I, having rejected **Puritan** overtures in the Millenary Petition in 1603 and in the **Hampton Court** Conference of 1604, intended to export **episcopacy** to Scotland. The Church of Scotland duly became Episcopal in 1610. It expelled its **bishops** in 1637, got them back again in 1661, but finally lost them in 1689, when they all refused to swear an **oath** of allegiance to King **William III** and Queen **Mary II** and became **nonjurors**. Since then, the Church of Scotland has been Presbyterian.

The Church of England had conversations with the Church of Scotland (with the minority churches, the Episcopal Church of Scotland and the Presbyterian Church of England, also participating) in the years leading up to 1957, when their report, *Relations between Anglican and Presbyterian Churches*, was published. The report recommended a pattern of "bishops-in-presbytery," which gained mild approbation from the 1958 **Lambeth Conference** but was roundly condemned in the Scottish press and made little progress in Scotland.

Other places where reformed churches were in purposeful dialogue with Anglicans included **South India**, where the Presbyterians and **Congregationalists** had united in 1908 and the resultant South India United Church had then become one of the three uniting churches in the formation of the Church of South India in 1947. There was similar reformed participation in the united churches of **Pakistan** (1970), **North India** (1970), and **Bangladesh** (1971), and Presbyterians have also taken an integral part in rounds of negotiation toward union in **Sri Lanka**. A precedent was created in the Church of the Province of **Southern Africa** in 1996 when a covenant was implemented between the Anglican province and three non-Episcopal churches (of which the Presbyterians were one) providing for an interchangeability of **presbyters** between the four denominations.

A set of world conversations was established between the **Anglican Communion** and the World Reformed Alliance in 1979, leading to a report, *God's Reign and Our Unity*, in 1984. In England, the Presbyterian and Congregationalist Churches had united in 1972 to become the United Reformed Church (URC), and that Church declared itself "uniting" with a view to further unions in the future. When in 1978–1982 a project was formed to bring together all the main non–Roman Catholic Churches in England in a "covenant" (which would have involved the adoption of the **historic episcopate** by each covenanting church), the URC voted in favor (though without unanimity), but the defeat of the proposal by the Church of England **General Synod** (largely on the grounds of involving a recognition of the **ordination** of **women** in the non-Episcopal churches) meant that the covenant could not be implemented. The URC has united with other smaller bodies over the years, and, when Anglican–Methodist formal conversations were being held in England in 1998–2001, informal trilateral conversations involving the URC were held simultaneously as well. These addressed issues of concern to the URC, such as "eldership," which might not have been raised in the main bilateral conversations, but hardly impacted the **synodical** handling of the report of the formal bilateral conversations.

REFORMED EPISCOPAL CHURCH (REC). The Church normally known as the "Reformed Episcopal Church" began in New York in 1873; its derivative with the same name in **England** is described in this dictionary in the entry on the **Free Church of England**.

On 2 December 1873, **George David Cummins**, after resigning as assistant **bishop** of Kentucky on 14 November, convened a gathering of **Evangelicals** who at that time were finding themselves under great pressure from the growing **Anglo-Catholicism** in the **Protestant Episcopal Church in the United States of America** (PECUSA). The gathering formed the Reformed Episcopal Church, with Cummins as its bishop and Edward Cheney elected to be its "**missionary** bishop." Cummins **consecrated** Cheney in Chicago a few days later, and the structure of an Episcopal church started to emerge.

The Reformed Episcopal Church provided Episcopal consecration for bishops of the Free Church of England in 1878, and shortly after began a branch of its own in England. It has also had a branch in **Canada**. It has often been divided over the issue of whether to attempt to look and sound approximately like PECUSA or simply to become another evangelical body under no such constraint. The first conversations with representatives of PECUSA, with a view to some kind of rapprochement, were held in 1938; at that point, the REC's **orders** were recognized (which they had not been for the previous 50 years) and a "uniat relationship" was offered. But the REC at large was not prepared to acknowledge PECUSA as a "true Church," and the prospect was aborted from the REC side. A renewed attempt was made in 1988, but without any positive advance in relationships emerging. In the 1990s, the REC's communicant membership numbered around 6,000.

RELIGIOUS COMMUNITIES. The institutions known as "religious communities" when King **Henry VIII** was breaking the links with the **Roman Catholic Church** were the **monasteries** and nunneries or convents of the various orders of monks and nuns. While it is arguable that, on the strictest definition, the term "religious communities" may have a slightly wider reference than "monastery" or "nunnery" (and covers men's, women's, and even mixed communities with a single term), for the historical purposes of this dictionary they are covered by the entry on "monasteries."

RESERVATION. The term "reservation" refers to keeping back **consecrated eucharistic elements** at the end of a service and "reserving" them, by careful identification and usually under lock and key, for future use. There was a long-standing pre-**Reformation** Western practice of reserving consecrated wafers ceremonially, in a **tabernacle**, **aumbry**, or hanging **pyx**, so that **parish** churches would always have a reserved stock thus stored—though a reserved wafer might also be put on view by "exposition" for a special purpose and might also appear in outdoor procession in a monstrance on the **feast** of Corpus Christi and other occasions.

At the Reformation in the Church of **England**, the reserved wafer survived the 1547 royal *Injunctions*, but was clearly not intended to be found in use under the 1549 **Book of Common Prayer** provisions. In that Book, the **Communion** of the Sick allowed **bread** and wine to be set aside at the end of a church **celebration** in order that they should be taken to sick persons, provided that they were to receive Communion that same day. On other days there would need to be a full separate celebration in the sickroom, a clear indication that permanent reservation had ceased.

In 1552 there ceased to be any objective consecration of the elements at all, so that, as its **rubric** says, "if any of the bread or wine remain the **curate** shall have it to his own use." In line with this, the Communion of the Sick provided only for a separate celebration at the bedside, and the "same-day" usage of elements from a service in church, which had been permitted in 1549, now ceased. In any case, the change from wafers to "bread . . . such as is usual to be eaten . . . but the best and purest wheat bread" would have rendered permanent reservation impossible. **Article** XXIX of 1553 (Article XXVIII of 1571) stated, "The **Sacrament** of the **Lord's Supper** was not commanded by Christ's ordinance to be kept, carried about, lifted up, nor worshipped."

With the return to the concept of an objective "consecration" prior to distribution in 1662, a new rubrical direction was needed. The final rubric now read, "If any remain of that which was consecrated, it shall not be carried out of the Church, but the **Priest** . . . shall, immediately after the Blessing, reverently eat and drink the same." All consecrated elements would thus be consumed "immediately" after the service, so none could be reserved; only unconsecrated elements could now be taken home by the curate.

There are some records of the Jacobite **Scottish** Episcopalians in the 18th century, who did not view themselves as bound by the English Prayer Book, carrying consecrated wafers with them when under harassment by the authorities, in order that they might communicate their scattered flocks in their own homes with a minimum of risk. The practice probably never ceased among Scottish Episcopalians, but that does not appear to have been the point of origin of the practice as it developed elsewhere. For that, the emergent **Anglo-Catholic** movement in England in the 19th century seems to have been both the incentive and the validation.

This Anglo-Catholic revival led in its second generation to imitation of the ritual of the Roman rite, and this led by stages, with the reintroduction of wafers to be the element of bread, to reservation of consecrated wafers. Where the zealots of the movement planted Anglican churches in other parts of the world, reservation was a natural concomitant of their sacramental outlook—and, when **ordained** ministers were few and far between in widely scattered communities and there was no contrary pressure from **authority**, the practice of reservation for later use flourished. The practice has regularly meant the reservation of bread, specifically wafers, only.

In England, however, between 1890 and 1914 the **bishops** fought to restrict the practice, attempting to limit reservation to places where the likely need to communicate the sick existed, and to limit the method of reservation to the use of unobtrusive aumbries in locked chapels. A middle line doctrinally was taken by Bishop **Charles Gore**, who stated that the presence of Christ in or with the consecrated elements in the **liturgy** was not to be extrapolated into assertions about the same elements reserved outside of the liturgy. Bolder spirits, especially in **dioceses** with indulgent bishops, went much further and not only reserved elements at high **altars** but also used the (post Counter-Reformation) liturgical devotion "**Benediction** with the Blessed Sacrament" to (and with) the reserved wafer, as well as all the pre-Reformation extraliturgical uses. The genuine needs of the sick were alleged, but they tended to appear as a mere excuse to the opponents of reservation.

Reservation became the key stumbling block in the attempt to provide a revised Prayer Book in England in 1927–1928. The text that was passed by the **Church Assembly** allowed bishops to issue licenses to reserve, when they were satisfied in any particular parish that there was a need on behalf of the sick. This, however, was too restrictive for Anglo-Catholics—and too Romanizing for **Protestants**. Ultimately, the practice of reservation became the whipping boy in the debates in the House of Commons under the banner of "no popery," and these led to two successive defeats of the Book. Some of this polarization was also experienced elsewhere in the **Anglican Communion**, most notably in the Church of England in **Australia**.

In more recent days, a milder temper has not only seen the catholic wing of Anglicanism less embattled on behalf of a practice that has clearly diminished in its profile in the **Roman Catholic Church** since **Vatican II** but has also seen the **Evangelical** wing become more open to the possibility of "extended Communion" by which the elements are taken from a celebration of the eucharist to the sick or shut-in. However, the position has been affected by the Vatican's response in 1991 to the statement on the Eucharist from the first **Anglican–Roman Catholic International Commission** (ARCIC-1), dating from 1971, and its "Elucidation" from 1979; the **pope** required assurances not only that Anglicans believed the bread to be the body of Christ, nor only that Anglicans would therefore reserve consecrated wafers, but also that all Anglicans worldwide would pay outward reverence to consecrated wafers being reserved. ARCIC-2, in replying to this in ***Clarifications*** (1994), went a long way toward meeting the pope's requirement, asserting that the 1662 Book of Common Prayer itself taught principles that justify such reverence, but the principle is tortuously difficult to assert from the rubrics in that Book, as the actual rubrics (quoted above) require the consumption of all consecrated remains. Yet the authors of *Clarifications* asserted it, though to have met the pope by stating that the whole Anglican world agreed with them would have gone beyond all credibility.

A different use of reservation has become far more visible in the Communion in the second half of the 20th century. This provides for consecrated wafers to be used later on, on the same premises where they were originally consecrated. This pattern of giving Communion can be conducted by a **deacon** or authorized layperson, which may be pastorally helpful when no ordained **presbyter** is available. Various provinces allow such uses. A particular further pattern is provided in many places for elements consecrated on **Maundy Thursday** evening to be retained for distribution on **Good Friday** morning.

The uses of reservation in the Communion may thus be graded from the "lowest" to the "highest" in an ascending scale:

1. Reservation does not exist.
2. No permanent reservation exists, but consecrated bread and wine are taken from corporate celebrations to sick and shut-in people (and this can be done in both kinds, and with the use, where that is the local use, of leavened bread).
3. Permanent reservation exists and is used for taking the consecrated elements to the sick and shut-in, even on days with no main celebration.

4. Permanent reservation exists and is used on occasion not only for the sick but also to provide for the distribution of communion at a main congregational service for which no presbyter is available.

These first four categories can be sustained without any prominence being given to any place of reservation. The next three usually have a prominent place of reservation.

5. Permanent reservation exists, and, quite apart from distribution, the aumbry, pyx, or tabernacle is a focus for outward reverence and devotion.
6. Permanent reservation exists, and, quite apart from distribution and outward reverence, the reserved consecrated wafer is at intervals exposed in a monstrance to heighten the devotion.
7. Permanent reservation exists, and, quite apart from distribution, outward reverence, and exposition, the reserved consecrated wafer is also used for the rite of "Benediction with the Blessed Sacrament," and for processions with accompanying **ceremonial**.

The different practices reflect different stances, and the stances are in many cases held with considerable firmness and are not treated as matters of indifference.

RESTORATION. When King **Charles I** was beheaded on 30 January 1649, by all royalist principles he was succeeded as monarch immediately and automatically by his son, King **Charles II**. But *de facto* power belonged to the parliamentary authority, marshalled by Oliver Cromwell, which had defeated the king and acknowledged no occupant of the throne. The period from 1649 to 1660 is known as the **Commonwealth** period. After the death of Cromwell in 1658, however, the Parliamentarians lost confidence in themselves and negotiated with Charles (who was in exile in Breda in the Netherlands) for his return. On 4 April 1660 Charles made the Declaration of Breda, promising to allow freedom of conscience, and on this basis he was officially invited back. He reached London on 29 May 1660, and this arrival is known as the "Restoration." Charles naturally did not view this as ascending the throne *de novo*, but duly dated his reign from the execution of his father.

With the restoration of the monarchy, the full structure of the Church of **England** was restored also. The surviving **bishops** returned to their sees, new bishops were nominated and **consecrated**, **chapters** retook possession of the **cathedrals**, and the king announced, in the Worcester House Declaration on 25 October 1660, that he would summon a conference between **Puritans** and churchmen to consider changes to the **Book of Common Prayer**. The **Savoy Conference** of March–July 1661 saw the bishops give short shrift to the Puritan "exceptions" and proposals, and in December 1661 the **Convocation** made only very small changes to the existing 1604 Prayer Book. This was then **annexed** to the 1662 **Act of Uniformity**, which came into force on 24 August 1662. The Act not only enforced the Book of Common Prayer as the "uniform" use across the land but also required all **clergy** to renounce the "Solemn League and Covenant," which had bonded the opposition to Charles I, and to be **Episcopally ordained**, or to lose their office. Those who did not conform to the Church of England were subject to highly restrictive laws (the "Clarendon Code"), and no provision was made to accommodate or tolerate them.

Finally, the Restoration was marked by the provision by royal warrant of an annual service to be held on 29 May to give thanks for the return of the king and monarchy. This was printed at the back of copies of the Book of Common Prayer (accompanied by new services for "King Charles the **Martyr**" on 30 January, and thanksgiving for deliverance from the popish plot on 5 November) until all were deleted by royal warrant in 1859.

RESURRECTION. The belief in the bodily resurrection of **Jesus Christ**, the Son of **God**, from the dead is central to the Christian faith. It is commemorated every Sunday, affirmed in every **credal** confession, celebrated at the **Easter** season, and underlined in **funeral** services. Some free-thinking Anglican teachers have in effect denied the **doctrine**, of which the most famous in recent years was David Jenkins, bishop of Durham from 1984 to 1994.

RETREAT. Retreats are the organizing of formal devotions for **clergy** and **laity** by their silent or nearly silent withdrawal from usual work or **ministry**. While their background is the 40 days of **Jesus** in the wilderness, reinforced by the ideals of both the eremitic and the **monastic** ascetic traditions, the latter-day patterns appear to spring from a Counter-Reformation **Roman Catholic** usage. Specially designated "retreat houses" are traceable in Roman Catholic circles to the 17th century, and the concept of retreat "conductors" emerged at the same time. Retreats were then a practice that the 19th-century **Anglo-Catholics** adopted from Roman Catholic usage, and a practice that spread widely in the **Anglican Communion**. They are now to be found among all sorts of Anglicans. They are recommended as part of their life-patterns for Christian leaders and are almost universal as a provision made by the **bishop** for candidates for **ordination**, to give them space for reflection and meditation in preparation for their ordination.

REYNOLDS, EDWARD (1599–1676). Edward Reynolds was a **Puritan** who was **ordained** before the English Civil War, but was then a member of the Westminster Assembly and held ecclesiastical office during the **Commonwealth**. At the **Restoration** Reynolds accepted the **bishopric** of Norwich from King **Charles II** in January 1661 before the **Savoy Conference** was convened, and therefore long before he knew the outcome of the struggle about the order and worship of the Church of **England**. He was encouraged to accept this by his Puritan colleagues **Richard Baxter** and Edward Calamy, though they themselves were refusing such appointments. Reynolds thus appeared as a bishop among the Puritan divines at the Savoy Conference, and he duly conformed when the 1662 **Act of Uniformity** was implemented. Reynolds is regularly credited with having done the original drafting of the General Thanksgiving in the 1662 **Book of Common Prayer**, and he may well have originated the Prayer for All Sorts and Conditions of Men also.

RIDLEY, NICHOLAS (c. 1500–1555). Nicholas Ridley was **ordained** in the 1520s, met with others studying the **Bible** at Cambridge, and became master of Pembroke Hall, Cambridge, in 1530. From 1537 he was chaplain to **Archbishop Thomas Cranmer** and is credited in this role with a profound theological influence on Cranmer, particularly in relation to questions about the **eucharist**. Ridley drew Cranmer's attention to the work of Ratram, a ninth-century theologian of Corbie in France, who had written of a "spiritual" presence of Christ in a work that had been opposed and overridden when first composed but had been printed on behalf of reformed views in 1531. Ridley's role was attested by the accusation at his trial: "**Latimer** leaneth unto Cranmer, Cranmer unto Ridley, and Ridley unto the singularity of his own wit." He was made **bishop** of Rochester in 1547 and bishop of **London** when the reactionary Edward Bonner was deprived in 1550. There he was active in entrenching the **Reformation** as swiftly and thoroughly as possible. Ridley was party to the plot to put Lady Jane Grey on the throne when King **Edward VI** died in 1553, and thus incurred Queen **Mary I**'s wrath. He was arrested for both treason and **heresy** within days of Mary's succession, was kept in prison (with various interrogations and disputations) for more than two years, and was finally burned at the stake at Oxford with Hugh Latimer on 16 October 1555. Ridley is commemorated with Latimer on 16 October in various **calendars**, and the nearest Sunday to that day has in **Evangelical** circles at times been kept as "Reformation Sunday."

RITUAL. A rite is simply an "order," in principle a word used in a neutral factual sense. However, the derivative noun and adjective "ritual" have at times acquired a negative overtone of fussiness, of overdoing the **ceremonial** in a rite, and of an emphasis on the externals of a rite without regard to its essential meaning. Thus, when the second generation of **Anglo-Catholics** in the Church of **England** in the 19th century began to increase and exaggerate the ceremonial attaching to the rites in the 1662 **Book of Common Prayer**, they became known as "ritualists" and their legal conflicts as "ritual cases." These pejorative uses of the word have slightly damaged its neutral application.

ROMAN CATHOLIC CHURCH. The Roman Catholic Church was, at the time of the **Reformation**, both the historical point of origin of a separate Church of **England** and also itself an obvious cause of that separation. Once it was in its separate identity, the Church of England inevitably experienced Rome as hostile; and the reign of Queen **Mary I** (1553–1558), who effected a return of the nation to the Roman Catholic obedience, confirmed this view. The original Forty-Two **Articles** of Religion of 1553 defended the Church of England against that hostility and asserted reformed **doctrine** to replace the Roman Catholic system.

However, when Queen **Elizabeth I** succeeded and largely restored the Church of England's position as it had been in 1553, she did not at that point bring back the Articles, and she even deleted the petition against the **pope** in the restored **litany**. The pope, for his part, did not forbid loyal Roman Catholics to attend the services in their **parish** churches. But all was changed in 1570, as the pope issued a bull that stated that Elizabeth had no right to the throne and stating that whoever killed her would do God service. Then every Roman Catholic became at one blow a traitor (and those who were arrested were tried for treason, not **heresy**), and the animosity mounted.

Elizabeth let the Thirty-Nine Articles go through in 1571, and these came very close to denying that the Church of Rome was a Christian church at all. The division was total. Roman Catholics started to become the "English **martyrs**," and fear of a Roman Catholic succeeding to the throne led to the arrest of Mary, Queen of Scots, on English territory in 1569 and ultimately (when her actual compliance in a plot was discovered) to her execution in 1587. Both the Spanish Armada in 1588 and the Gunpowder Plot in 1605 reinforced the fear and suspicion. These were hardly reduced later in the 17th century when first King **Charles I** and then King **Charles II** had Roman Catholic wives, and, in the latter reign, the heir to the throne, Charles's brother James, became a Roman Catholic himself.

All this, as well as the massacres of **Protestants** in France in 1685 following the revocation of the Edict of Nantes, lay behind the later attempts to stop King **James II** succeeding or to overthrow him once in power. Once he had inherited in 1685, his promotion of Roman Catholicism within the life of the nation of whose Church of England he was legally the supreme governor provoked a strong reaction. This led to the trial of seven bishops, including the **archbishop** of **Canterbury**, **William Sancroft**, for seditious libel, and their acquittal sounded such an alarm for James that he fled the country. James II was replaced by William of Orange who, with James's Protestant daughter Mary as his wife, reigned jointly with her as King **William III** and Queen **Mary II**. The Bill of Rights in 1689 and the Act of Settlement in 1700 protected the throne (and thus the Church) from falling into Roman Catholic hands again.

In the 18th and 19th centuries, there were occasional outbursts of hostility to Roman Catholics in England. These included the reaction to the Jacobite rebellions of 1715 and 1745 and the Gordon Riots of 1770, as well as some flurries associated with Catholic Emancipation in the 1820s (which arose in part from the union with **Ireland** in 1801). But in general Roman Catholics became viewed as a tiny minority who were now a threat to neither Church nor state.

It became different when **John Henry Newman** became a Roman Catholic in 1845, and the **Anglo-Catholic** movement seemed to be trying to move the Church of England to be nearer to Rome. Pope Pius IX's declaration in 1854 that the **Immaculate Conception** of the Virgin **Mary** was *de fide* and his authoritative promulgation of the *Syllabus of Errors* in 1864 did not help. Roman Catholicism was important politically because of the Irish representation in Parliament, and it was a major factor in the **disestablishment** of the Church of **Ireland** in 1870. But **Vatican I**'s decree on the **infallibility** of the pope in 1870 further greatly divided Rome from Anglicanism, and this was reinforced in 1896 by Pope Leo XIII's encyclical ***Apostolicae Curae***, which condemned Anglican **orders** as invalid, deliberately distancing Rome from any imitations of true **ordination** that there might be.

In the first half of the 20th century, the nearest the two Communions came to official relationships with each other was in the **Malines Conversations** in 1921–1927. These were ended by the death of Cardinal Mercier, but were then in effect condemned by Pope Pius XI's encyclical *Mortalium Animos* in January 1928. The distancing was further confirmed by the papal *ex cathedra* decree in 1950 enforcing the belief in the bodily **assumption** of **Mary** as *de fide*.

A great change happened with the succession of Pope John XXIII in 1958. He summoned a General **Council**, **Vatican II**, which met from 1962 to 1965 and had an overtly **ecumenical** stance. The pope was himself visited in a brief personal way before the Council by the then archbishop of Canterbury, **Geoffrey Fisher**, in the last month's before Fisher's own retirement. In March 1966, soon after the close of the Council, Fisher's successor, Michael Ramsey, made an official visit to John XXIII's successor, Pope Paul VI. From this emerged a whole pattern of conversations, first in a preliminary way, but from 1969 onward in the fully fledged **Anglican–Roman Catholic International Commission** (ARCIC).

In 1982 Pope John Paul II, who since his election in 1978 had already been traveling the world and meeting Anglicans in many places, paid a visit to Britain, the first by a pope since before the Reformation. In the course of this visit, he met with Church of England leaders (including the whole **General Synod**) in Canterbury **Cathedral**. Alongside the official conversations, the pope has also issued a variety of statements that indicated changing views by the authorities in Rome of the **Anglican Communion**. It has to be acknowledged, however, that to Anglicans, along with encouraging moves, there have also been more daunting ones, not least in the encyclical *Dominus Jesus*, and in three publications of ARCIC-2: ***Clarifications***, *The Gift of* ***Authority***, and *Mary: Grace and Hope in Christ*.

ROME, ANGLICAN CENTRE IN. Immediately following the end of **Vatican II**, the **archbishop** of **Canterbury**, **Michael Ramsey**, made an official visit to the **pope** in March 1966. Arising from the welcome he received, a project was initiated the following month with support from the **primates** around the **Anglican Communion**, to found an Anglican center in Rome. The premises provides library and study facilities, particularly with a view to enhancing Anglican and **Roman Catholic** mutual understanding and dialogue, both in Rome itself and around the world. The centre has a resident director (usually an Anglican **bishop** who has retired or accepted this appointment after working as a bishop), runs courses and seminars, and publishes a quarterly magazine, *Centro*.

ROYAL SUPREMACY. King **Henry VIII** in 1532–1534 took the Church of **England** away from the previous papal supremacy and annexed it instead to a royal supremacy. This has remained the formal position of the Church of England to the 21st century, although since the **Glorious Revolution** of 1689, the membership of the Church of England has been ever more obviously a sectional interest within the nation of England. Because the exercise of the supremacy is effected through the "monarch in Parliament," that is, via the laws of the land, the practical description of the relationship is usually that it is an "**establishment**." In all other parts of the **Anglican Communion**, whether or not **dioceses** are in places where the English monarch is or once was head of state, all vestiges of such a relationship with the Crown have ceased; Barbados, in the **province** of the **West Indies**, was the last to break the links, in 1961.

RUBRICS. Instructions and directives in the text of worship books are generally known as "rubrics," the etymology of which (derived from the Latin for "red") indicates that, in the days of manuscript texts, such directions were frequently written in a shade of red. When printing came, **liturgical** books were regularly printed in one color only, and the genre of text was often distinguished by the typeface rather than the color; nevertheless the title "rubric" remained. In modern texts, two-color printing is regularly found. Rubrics that were in earlier centuries often restrictive are in modern rites usually enabling and facilitatory, and they are often read in the light of the "General Notes," which precede and govern the whole rite or, in some cases, cover all the services contained in one book. *See also* BLACK RUBRIC.

RUNCIE, ROBERT ALEXANDER KENNEDY (1921–2000). Robert Runcie, the 102nd **archbishop** of **Canterbury**, served as a tank commander during World War II and was awarded the Military Cross. He was **ordained** as a **deacon** in 1950 and a **presbyter** in 1951 and joined the staff of Westcott House, Cambridge, in 1953. He went on to become principal of Cuddesdon **Theological College**, **Oxford**, in 1961. Runcie was **consecrated** as **bishop** of St. Albans in 1970, then declined the offer of the archbishopric of **York** in 1975. However, he accepted Canterbury in 1979 and served in that office until January 1991. His archiepiscopate was marked by an ever-growing pattern of world travel, by the visit of **Pope** John Paul II to Britain in 1982, by Runcie's distancing of himself from Margaret Thatcher's Tory government (not least through his contribution to the service to commemorate the end of the Falklands conflict in 1982, and through the publication of *Faith in the City* in 1985), and by his very vigorous support for Archbishop **Desmond Tutu** as he strove against the apartheid regime of South Africa. Runcie convened the 1988 **Lambeth Conference** and wrestled with the worldwide tensions in the **Anglican Communion** caused by the ordination of **women**, first as **presbyters** and later as bishops.

RWANDA. The territory of Ruanda-Urundi was assigned by the Berlin Conference of 1884 to Germany as part of German East Africa. After World War I, it was transferred in 1919 to become a trusteeship territory of Belgium and thus became a Francophone society. In that same year, "CMS Ruanda" (which in recent times has become "Mid-Africa Ministry [CMS]") was formed as an offshoot from the **Church Missionary Society** in **London**, and its first Anglican missionaries reached the country in 1922. The first **baptisms** occurred in 1926 and the first **ordination** of a Ruandan in 1933, when the **mission** stations were still in the **diocese** of **Uganda**. In 1936 the **East Africa** Revival began in Ruanda-Urundi, spreading in time to other countries.

After World War II, the **United Nations** directed that the territory should move toward self-government. This led, through a revolution in 1959, to the declaration of the Republic of Rwanda (whose name thereafter was usually spelled that way) in 1961; **Burundi** broke away from the republic in 1962. The Anglican church in the country became part of the new **province** of Uganda, Rwanda, and Burundi in 1961. An English expatriate in 1964 became the first **bishop** of Ruanda-Urundi (covering both republics), in preparation for the creation of two separate sees in 1965, one of which was the diocese of Rwanda.

Through the next 30 years, Rwanda was rarely without violence and civil war, particularly through the effects of worse strife and cruelty in intertribal conflict in Burundi, but also through revolution in Rwanda itself and arbitrary rule in Uganda. A new province of Rwanda, Burundi, and Boga-Zaire was produced through separation from Uganda in 1980. The diocese of Rwanda divided into Kigali, Butare, and Shyira, and a new diocese of Byumba was formed in 1991 in preparation for the creation of a separate province of Rwanda in 1992. Further division of dioceses occurred during the first 10 years of the province, despite desperate lawlessness and suffering in the country, particularly in the genocide of 1994. There were nine dioceses in 2004.

– S –

SABBATH. The original Sabbath of the Old Testament was the seventh day, marked as a day of rest from the account of creation onward (cf.

Gen. 2.2–3). It was reinforced by the practical lesson of the manna (Exod. 16) and the detailed provision of the fourth of the **Ten Commandments** (Exod. 20.8–11). It became a mark of the legalism of the Pharisees that **Jesus** in his time both infringed and denounced (cf. Mark 2.23–28, etc.). The Christian church from the apostles' time forward used the first day of the week as the day of meeting for worship, no doubt initially to enable Jewish believers to fulfill the requirements of the Sabbath, including synagogue worship, but also symbolically to commemorate the Lord's **resurrection** on the first day of the week.

The status of Sunday, even when dubbed the "Lord's Day," has never been closely defined, so that it has always run the opposite dangers of being observed legalistically, on the one hand, or casually or minimally, on the other. At an ideological level, Christians have differed as to whether the Sabbath has actually been transferred to Sunday (thus bringing the requirements of the Fourth Commandment to bear upon the day, even if not legalistically) or whether the concept of "rest" has been fulfilled in the whole relationship to **God** of his people (cf. Col. 2.16; Heb. 4.9, *sabbatismos*), thus leaving the duty and privilege of corporate worship without any actual divine sanction as to regularity and timescale. The **Puritans** at the **Savoy Conference** in 1661 pressed for the use of the **King James Version** of the Ten Commandments on the grounds that it used "Sabbath day" in the Fourth Commandment, whereas other versions (including that in the 1604 **Book of Common Prayer**) had said "seventh day," and this desire expressed their understanding of Sunday as being Sabbath (and the text was then altered to meet the request). At a practical level Christians have continued to organize their **calendars** and **lectionaries** on the basis of Sunday as the first day of a seven-day week, and Anglican provision of these has identified all Sundays as **feast** or festival days, usually in the 20th and 21st centuries with a cycle of readings different from that of the dependent weekdays.

SACRAMENT. The term "sacrament" translates no one particular word in the New Testament. It derives from *sacramentum*, a Latin word for an "**oath**," a word first found in a Christian context in Pliny's account of Christians in Bithynia around 112, where he states that the Christians bound themselves to their way of life with an oath.

The concept of a category of Christian "sacrament" as an outward sign of an inward grace only emerged slowly in the patristic era, and the systematization of the concept is usually attributed to the 12th-century Peter Lombard in his *Sententiae*. He provided a scheme of seven sacraments—**baptism**, **confirmation**, **eucharist**, **penance**, extreme **unction**, **orders**, and **matrimony**—and this enumeration became standard in the medieval church. A comparable pattern is also found in the **Eastern Orthodox** Churches.

At the **Reformation** a sacrament was more tightly defined as "an outward and visible sign of an inward and spiritual grace given unto us, ordained by Christ himself" (according to the **catechism**, where this section was first included in the 1604 **Book of Common Prayer**), and this definition, requiring an identifiable **biblical** command by **Jesus**, reduced the category of sacraments to simply two, namely, baptism and eucharist; the others were relegated to the status of "those five commonly [i.e., mistakenly] called sacraments" (**Article** XXV) which, the Article asserted, either had arisen through the "corrupt following of the apostles" or were "states of life allowed in the Scriptures." While these latter five still occur in one shape or another in Anglican life (not necessarily comparable to their position in **Roman Catholicism**), it has generally proved safer to call them by names other than "sacraments."

The catechism quoted from the Prayer Book identifies "two only as generally necessary for salvation." Similarly, references in the **ordinals** to the newly **ordained** being a "**minister** of the sacraments" and the mention in Article XIX of the visible church of Christ being where "the sacraments be duly ministered according to Christ's ordinance" must refer solely to these two sacraments. It was agreed on both sides of the **Savoy Conference** that it was inappropriate to call confirmation and matrimony "sacraments."

The phrase "an outward and visible sign of an inward and spiritual grace" does not of itself determine by what means the outward conveys the inward. That is the subject of Article XXV, which itself corresponds to the language of **Thomas Cranmer**'s 1552 eucharistic rite, "Grant that we, receiving . . . , may be partakers of . . ." It is reinforced by Article XXIX, added in 1571. But Anglicans have expressed a variety of understandings of how sacramental grace is conveyed to recipients.

SAEPIUS OFFICIO. In 1896 **Pope** Leo XIII issued the encyclical ***Apostolicae Curae***, in which he condemned Anglican **orders** on the grounds that, after 1559, Anglicans in their **ordinations** had lacked a true intention of ordaining **valid priests**, partly through defects in the **ordinals** themselves but more through the defects in Anglican **doctrine** and **liturgy** of Holy **Communion**. In 1897 the two English **archbishops**, Frederick Temple and William MacLagan, responded with a long statement, entitled *Saepius Officio* from its opening words in the Latin version. This asserted bluntly that Anglican orders suffer from no defects, and certainly not from lack of intention, and ought to be recognized by the pope on Rome's own terms. It strongly made the point that, if the pope's principles were applied to the Roman Catholic ordination rites and their early church precedents and antecedents, those same principles would **nullify** and disqualify those rites just as effectively as they did the Anglican ones. The statement did, however, answer more defensively the pope's point about **eucharistic sacrifice**, claiming that the **Book of Common Prayer** of 1662 taught a doctrine that did meet his requirements, although it is arguable that the text of the Communion rite in 1662 hardly warrants such an interpretation. There is a popular story that, when Leo XIII read the text of it—a text apparently drafted by John Wordsworth, **bishop** of Salisbury—he said that he wished he himself had people available who could write such elegant Latin. *See also* ANGLICAN–ROMAN CATHOLIC INTERNATIONAL COMMISSION.

SAINT. The Greek adjective for "holy" (*hagios*) is often used as a noun in the New Testament and is translated into English as "saint," a noun. Thus in the English-language New Testament, the Christian believers are frequently called "the saints who are in [a particular city]," and "saints" is a much more common word for believers than is "Christians." In those contexts, the term is always inclusive of all the believers and has little implication about any varying gradations in their personal qualities of life (see, e.g., Rom. 1.7, 16.15; 1 Cor. 6.1, 7.14, 16.1). However, in postapostolic years, as the adjective "holy" tended to be attached to particularly outstanding individual Christians, whether apostles or **martyrs**, so the concept of "saints" came to belong almost exclusively to this elité group. Usually such commemorations of "saints" occurred initially in places where they had lived or died, but the *cultus* in course of time tended to spread beyond purely local use, and, as the Western Church became more centralized, so some control over the cultus arose. The first recorded process of "**canonization**," that is, of recognition of a dead Christian as being a "saint," came in 993, but a large body of generally acknowledged "saints" had been in existence long before that. The process itself, once begun, was located by **authority** in Rome and began to accumulate its own criteria for recognition of saints (which has led to the careful weighing of evidence employed in the **Roman Catholic** Church today).

At the **Reformation** the Church of **England** inherited and retained the concept of "saints" in three ways: first, church **dedications** to the saints remained intact; second, a small number of "red-letter" saints, all of them found in the scriptures, retained both a **feast** day and "**proper**" **liturgical** provision in the **calendar**; and, third, lesser, or "black-letter," saints, having been dropped from the calendar in **Thomas Cranmer**'s time, returned to it in Queen **Elizabeth I**'s reign, although they still had no other provision made for them and some were eliminated altogether—for instance, **Thomas à Becket** had all remembrance abolished by King **Henry VIII**. Despite the retention of many saints, however, the Reformers held that the invocation of saints not only was unbiblical and superstitious but also undermined the doctrine of **justification** through faith. A residual provision of three petitions of this sort was found in the 1544 **Litany**, but this survival was removed from the 1549 text; a grateful memory of the saints was retained in the **canon** of the 1549 **eucharistic** rite, but was eliminated in 1552. The invocation of saints was condemned in Article XXII of the Thirty-Nine **Articles** in 1571.

Although the Elizabethan calendar restored a listing of various postbiblical saints, the latest to appear in the list was St. Richard of Chichester, who had died in 1253. No process continued by which the Church of England could investigate the lives and deaths of notable Christians and pronounce them "saints," and, as the eliminations cited above demonstrate, the Roman Catholic process had now no standing in Anglican circles. When a liturgical commemoration of King **Charles I** was instituted after the **Restoration** in 1660, he was described as "King Charles the Martyr" (a term used of him also in a few church dedications), but still no official categorization of him as "saint" emerged.

With the expansion of the Anglican churches through the **missionary** movement of the 19th century and the witness of the church in the 20th, many pioneers and converts have died for their faith in Christ and become the subject of local commemoration as martyrs. This has led to serious reflection on whether there should be a process of recognition, and a major report, *The Commemoration of Saints and Heroes of the Faith in the Anglican Communion*, was commissioned for the 1958 **Lambeth Conference**. The Cape Town Joint Meeting of the **Anglican Consultative Council** (ACC) and the **primates** in January 1993 agreed on a long statement of principles under "Calendar Revision" (*A Transforming Vision*, pp. 148–52), including guidelines for a process to be followed in each **province** in listing notable Christians in their calendars; nevertheless, the statement disavows any intention of creating a canonization process.

SANCROFT, WILLIAM (1617–1693). Sancroft was a **Laudian** churchman who was **ordained** before the Civil War in Britain. He was a fellow of Emmanuel College, Cambridge, until he was deprived of his fellowship by the **Puritans** in 1651. After the **Restoration** Sancroft became chaplain to John Cosin, the **bishop** of Durham, and in that capacity he was present at the **Savoy Conference** in 1661. He edited Cosin's desired alterations to the **Book of Common Prayer** and made them available at the revision of the Book in the **Convocations** in November and December 1661, where he acted as secretary to the revisers. Sancroft became master of Emmanuel College in 1662 and was briefly **dean** of **York** before becoming dean of St. Paul's **Cathedral**, **London**, in December 1664. He was thus responsible after the great fire of 1666 for working with Sir Christopher Wren, the architect, in the rebuilding of the cathedral. In 1678 Sancroft became **archbishop** of **Canterbury**, the last person (bar Tillotson in 1691) not already a bishop so to succeed.

Sancroft organized the **coronation** of King **James II** in 1685, striking out the **Communion** because the king was a **Roman Catholic**. He then was the leader of the seven bishops put on trial for seditious libel by James in 1688, and on acquittal he led them through the streets of London before a cheering crowd. Nevertheless, Sancroft would not swear an **oath** of allegiance to King **William III** and Queen **Mary II** while James was still alive, and, with others who refused to swear and were known as **nonjurors**, he was absent from the House of Lords when, in early 1689, by a majority of three the throne was declared "vacant." Sancroft issued a commission to Henry Compton, the bishop of London, to officiate at the coronation of William and Mary. Because of his refusal to swear the oath, he was suspended from and eventually, by Act of Parliament on 1 February 1690, deprived of his archbishopric. He then declined to leave **Lambeth Palace** until legal judgment was obtained against him on 23 June 1690. In enforced retirement, he delegated his **metropolitical** authority to Lloyd, the deprived bishop of Norwich, and it was Lloyd who took steps to secure the nonjuring Episcopal succession.

SANCTUARY. The area surrounding a **Communion table** (or "**altar**") has often been described as the "sanctuary," and its bounds are regularly marked either by a step down from a raised east end of the church or from a platform or dais, or by the provision of Communion rails, or both. However, the **Books of Common Prayer** of 1552 and 1662 have **rubrics** which imply that the table itself, being a table, is movable and thus might not occupy a single identifiable space. So, although the term "sanctuary" is in popular use and various **Roman Catholic** instructions are at intervals followed in Anglicanism, generally the concept is insufficiently precise to allow the writing of rubrics that mention the "sanctuary," and **liturgical** texts around the **Anglican Communion** have generally avoided any such mention. In many church buildings, let alone in more informal contexts for Christian worship, there is no such identifiable area.

"Sanctuary" is also the traditional name for the supposed provision that accused or hunted persons may find refuge within a church building and there be safe from arrest or harassment (cf. the "cities of refuge" in the Old Testament, Josh. 20). It is not clear that this has any standing in either **provincial canons** or, more crucially, in statute law in countries where Anglicans live and worship. Nevertheless it has been used on occasion in relation to the potential deportation of refugees or asylum-seekers, sometimes with beneficial publicity.

SANDERSON, ROBERT (1587–1663). Sanderson was a moderate **Laudian** divine, who in 1641 sat on the House of Lords Committee that attempted to find a unitive way through the parties polarized over **liturgy** and **ceremonial**. He was appointed Regius Professor of Divinity at Oxford in 1642, but was deprived during the Civil War and imprisoned for a period. In 1660 at the **Restoration**, he was made **bishop** of Lincoln, in which capacity he took a vigorous part in the **Savoy Conference** in 1661. His fame rests particularly upon his being credited with having drafted the **preface** to the 1662 **Book of Common Prayer**.

SAVOY CONFERENCE. After the **Restoration**, King **Charles II** undertook, through his Worcester House Declaration of 25 October 1660, to convene a conference of divines to consider the **liturgy** of the Church of **England**. This duly took place at the Savoy chapel in the Strand from 15 April to 24 July 1661. Twelve **bishops** met with 12 **Puritans** (one of whom, **Edward Reynolds**, had already accepted the bishopric of Norwich), with a further nine on each side as assessors. The Puritans were in essence appointed as moderate **Presbyterians**, as the true Independents could not contemplate a book of liturgies in any form (John Bunyan, for instance, later went to jail for preaching against the set liturgy). On the other hand, the 12 Puritan representatives themselves rejected the term "Presbyterians" and insisted they were moderate Episcopalians. The leading participants were, on the bishops' side, Gilbert Sheldon of **London** and John Cosin of Durham, and, on the Presbyterians' side, Richard Baxter of Kidderminster.

The procedure followed, which was unwelcome to most of the Presbyterians, was that the bishops in effect put on the table the 1604 **Book of Common Prayer**, which had been proscribed by Parliament in 1645, and asked their opponents where, if anywhere, they had problems with it. Since the Presbyterians at the 1604 **Hampton Court Conference** had been wrong-footed by having relatively few small criticisms to bring against the Book, this time their successors determined to list everything that might ever have been viewed as difficult. These amounted to 19 "General Exceptions" and more than 80 "Particular" ones. The answer of the bishops, given in writing to each point made, left the Presbyterians with little hope of much change; for their part, the Presbyterians had asked Baxter to produce his own entirely new liturgy, but this too had little impact.

The Conference duly dispersed, and in due course the **Convocations** and Parliament provided the 1662 Book of Common Prayer with hardly any changes of substance in the rites. Perhaps the most notable positive outcome of the "exceptions" was the incorporation of the text of the **King James Version** of 1611 for the printed Epistles and **Gospels**, perhaps giving birth to that **Bible**'s self-description as "Appointed to be read in Churches."

SCOTLAND. Scotland has a famous early history of the planting of Christianity by Ninian in central and southern Scotland in the fifth century and by **Columba** at Iona in 563–597. It was from Iona that the Celtic missionaries, notably **Aidan**, first came to Northumbria in the seventh century. Scotland itself was Christianized over the subsequent centuries and duly passed under the religious authority of Rome. The Middle Ages provided a continuous saga of wars with **England**, usually of a fiercely defensive sort, to retain the independent identity of Scotland as a nation.

As a separate nation, Scotland had a **Reformation** distinct from England's, and its more radical form and nature led in Queen **Elizabeth I**'s reign to a **Presbyterian** polity. When King James VI of Scotland became King **James I** of England in 1603, uniting the thrones, he took steps to provide **bishops** for Scotland, and the first of these were **consecrated** in England in 1610. The Church of Scotland continued its life largely uninterrupted, though it came under considerable pressure from the king and his advisers to become more **liturgical**. In time this pressure prompted the bishops to provide a complete **Book of Common Prayer**, authorized by royal warrant in 1637. The Book was slightly altered from the Church of England's Book, but, paradoxically, partially in an unreformed direction, that of the 1549 **eucharistic** rite (though in some respects—for example, in the use of "**presbyter**" for "**priest**"—it was more reformed). There was instant resistance to it in Scotland, and it caused such unrest as to be a contributory cause of the Civil War in the 1640s, when the bishops were run out of their sees and the church reverted to Presbyterianism. Scottish divines took part in the Westminster assembly in 1643–1645, at which the Westminster Confession was adopted as a

doctrinal formula of the Church, and the ***Directory for the Public Worship*** was advertised for the "three kingdoms," of which Scotland was one.

In 1661, following the **Restoration**, bishops were again consecrated for Scotland and exercised an arbitrary rule over an often-resistant church. There appears to have been no attempt to impose a liturgical pattern upon the church, and the bishops had a hard time retaining any control at all. They were resisted in particular by the "covenanters," against whom they responded with harsh punishments and persecution.

In 1689, after the **Glorious Revolution**, no Scottish bishop would swear allegiance to King **William III** and Queen **Mary II**, so the bishops lost their positions, and the national church reverted to Presbyterianism. The bishops were left with small, semiunderground Jacobite congregations, parallel to those of the **nonjurors** in England. However, a number of separate Episcopalian congregations were prepared to pay allegiance to the new line of monarchs, and these became the "qualified congregations"—Episcopalians without a bishop, though in some cases in touch with English bishops. After the 1715 rising of the Old Pretender (**James II**'s son), the bishops were for a time sufficiently harassed to cease any attempt at diocesan jurisdiction, becoming a single "college" of bishops. The 1745 rising of Bonnie Prince Charlie made the harassment worse, but, as Jacobite hopes thereafter faded, the bishops were less and less marginalized, and, after the death of the prince, who died without heir in 1788, they took **oaths** of loyalty to King George III, and the Episcopal Church of Scotland began a properly above-ground existence.

The underground years were, however, productive of two linked matters that have given the Church a noted place in the wider history of the **Anglican Communion**.

First, from 1716 the bishops were in close touch with the English nonjurors and with the liturgical changes desired by the "usagers" and incorporated in the nonjuring liturgy of 1718. From 1722 on, the Scottish bishops engaged in their own liturgical experimentation, a task that was made all the easier because congregations were sparse and few. They went through a series of revisions of the **eucharistic** text, beginning not with that in the English 1662 Book of Common Prayer but with the earlier abortive 1637 Scottish rite. The successive drafts became known from their style of publication as "wee bookies." From the 1740s, these revisions came under the influence of Bishop Thomas Rattray's conclusion that the "Liturgy of St. James" is the original rite of **Jerusalem** and thus apostolic in its provenance (a conclusion he reinforced by an appeal to the "Clementine Liturgy" in the eighth book of the *Apostolic Constitutions* as also attesting to apostolic use). Consequently, in the **eucharistic prayer** or **canon**, the revisers moved the epiclesis from its 1549/1637 position before the **narrative** of institution to a fully Eastern position after the **anamnesis**. The text of this **epiclesis** also became strongly "realist," and at the same time an oblation of the **elements** was introduced into the anamnesis. Finally, the intercessions were moved from the Cranmerian place in the ante-Communion, coming instead at the end of the canon. The last revision of 1764 became then the definitive text, the ancestor of Scottish rites that have been revised in 1912, 1929, 1966, and 1970, before coming into a somewhat different era of modern English in 1982.

Second, a relationship with the **Protestant Episcopal Church in the United States of America** (PECUSA) emerged. There is evidence of the Scottish **Communion** rite crossing the Atlantic before the American Revolutionary War, but the significant change came when, after independence, the clergy of Connecticut elected **Samuel Seabury** to be their bishop. Seabury came to London in 1783, but when the **archbishop** of **Canterbury** for legal reasons was unable to consecrate him, he finally went to the Scottish bishops (who owed no allegiance then to King George III, and so would not ask a loyalty oath from anyone being consecrated), and he was consecrated in Aberdeen by three Scottish bishops on 14 November 1784. Seabury entered into a concordat with the Scottish bishops, and, although the emergent American Episcopal Church was considerably "lower" in churchmanship than the Scottish Episcopalians, many features of the Scottish 1764 rite, particularly the shape of the Prayer of Consecration, with **anamnesis** (and oblation) and epiclesis, though modified in many particulars, were to be found in the American Book of Common Prayer approved in 1789 at the second **General Convention** of PECUSA.

After the death of Bonnie Prince Charlie in 1788, the life of the Scottish Episcopal Church changed. The penal laws were revoked in

1792, provided that the congregations would pray for the Hanoverian monarchs by name. The Church became a fully public institution, and a Convocation at Laurencekirk in 1804 saw the official adoption of the Thirty-Nine **Articles** of Religion and paved the way for a healthy reunion with the "qualified congregations." The Church held its first **synod** in 1811, and for much of the 19th century it seemed set on an assimilation in style and liturgy to the Church of England. This was reversed through a gentle reassertion of their Scottishness, which led to the Prayer Book of 1912 mentioned above.

The Church is a minority Church in a country where most Christians have traditionally been Presbyterian or **Roman Catholic**, and since the late 19th century it has been keen to maintain its native Scottishness and avoid charges of being the "English Church." It has for many years had seven dioceses, and the office of "primus" (i.e., the **metropolitan** or **primate**) is not restricted to any one diocese. It has no state connection but is an entirely voluntary society. It changed its title in 1979 from the Episcopal Church of Scotland to the Scottish Episcopal Church (SEC). It has not had sufficient numbers in training for **ordination** to sustain its own **theological college** (Coates Hall, which was founded in 1810, was closed in the early 1990s), so for residential training, ordinands have to go to England or elsewhere. While its mainstream history has suggested a uniform (though often mild) **Anglo-Catholicism** (apart from two famous **Evangelical** congregations in Glasgow and Edinburgh), recent decades have seen a new concern for **ecumenism** and the beginning of a **liberal** theology in its ranks. This liberal tendency was powerfully illustrated and reinforced through the role and profile of Richard Holloway, bishop of Edinburgh (1986–2000) and primus of the SEC (1992–2000). The Church shares in the **Porvoo Declaration** of unity with the **Lutheran Churches** of the Baltic and Nordic nations. In 2003 it became the first Anglican Church in Britain and **Ireland** to approve the principle of the **ordination** of **women** to the **episcopate**.

SEABURY, SAMUEL (1729–1796). Samuel Seabury was born in Connecticut, went to **Scotland** to study medicine, and was then **ordained** in **England**. He returned to America, where he was first a **missionary** of the **Society for the Propagation of the Gospel** (SPG) in New Brunswick and then rector of two **parishes** in the colony of

New York. Seabury was a strong royalist and acted as chaplain to British troops during the War of Independence. Nevertheless, he remained in Connecticut after the British recognition of independence and was there elected as **bishop** by the 12 **clergy** of that state who met on 25 March 1783. Seabury then went to **London** to seek **consecration** by the **archbishop** of **Canterbury**, but this proved to be legally impossible, as, apart from other questions, the archbishop was required to exact an **oath** of loyal allegiance to King George III. After a year's delay, Seabury was finally consecrated in Aberdeen, **Scotland**, on 14 November 1784 by three bishops of the Scottish Episcopal Church (who themselves, being **nonjurors**, acknowledged no allegiance to George III and sought no loyal oaths).

Seabury returned to find himself at the center of controversy. On the one hand, he held the loyalty of the Connecticut clergy and was able to ordain men and provide for the pastoral care of parishes, without recourse to England. On the other hand, he had no part in the separate plans of churchmen from seven other states to stage a **General Convention**, which met in September 1785 and, in effect, created the **Protestant Episcopal Church in the United States of America** (PECUSA). The Episcopalians of Connecticut were invited by the planners to send representatives, but declined, both because they feared too strong a **lay** voice in church government and because it appeared inevitable that Seabury, though the only bishop present, would not be president or otherwise leader of the Convention, but possibly be little more than a guest.

At the next General Convention, in 1789, a small Connecticut delegation included Seabury, which enabled a House of Bishops (consisting of Seabury, **William White** of Pennsylvania, and **Samuel Provoost** of New York) to be formed, and the Convention ruled that the senior bishop by consecration, that is, Seabury, should preside. Resolutions were also passed looking toward further consecrations being conducted in the **United States** by the three bishops, though as it turned out, one more, James Madison of Virginia, was consecrated in London in 1790 before Seabury shared with bishops of the English line in consecrating Thomas Claggett for Maryland in 1792.

Seabury had a higher view of **episcopacy** than most Americans of the time and revealed this not only in his concern for the powers and responsibilities of the clergy in the General Convention but also in, for instance, the occasional wearing of a miter. From 1790 until his death, he was also bishop of Rhode Island, while he remained rector of St. James, New London, Connecticut. His name is enshrined in many ways in the life of the Episcopal Church, and his consecration is commemorated in the **calendar** of the 1979 the Church's **Book of Common Prayer** on 14 November.

SECRETARY-GENERAL. Following the 1958 **Lambeth Conference**, an **executive officer of the Anglican Communion** was appointed for the first time. Then, when the **Anglican Consultative Council** (ACC) was formed in 1971, the office of executive officer was changed into that of secretary-general of the ACC. The initial secretary-general was the existing executive officer, **Bishop** John Howe of the **Scottish** Episcopal Church. He was succeeded at the end of 1982 by **Canon** Sam Van Culin from the **Episcopal Church (United States of America)** (ECUSA), and he in turn was succeeded in 1994 by Canon John Peterson, also from ECUSA though serving in **Jerusalem** at the time of his appointment. Canon Peterson's period expired at the end of 2004, and Canon Kenneth Kearon from the Church of **Ireland** became the ACC secretary-general on 1 January 2005.

SELWYN, GEORGE AUGUSTUS (1809–1878). George Selwyn was **ordained** in 1833 and **consecrated** in 1841 at the age of 32 to be the first **bishop** of **New Zealand**. He stayed in office there for 26 years, at every point pioneering and laying down church principles for the future. He was constantly active, establishing church buildings all around the country, building St. John's **Theological College** in Auckland, separating the Anglican church from all state connection to **England**, forming a **province** in 1857, calling a **General Synod** in 1859, and creating new sees. In 1861 he consecrated **John Coleridge Patteson**, who was later **martyred**, as the first bishop of **Melanesia**. In 1867 Selwyn attended the first **Lambeth Conference** and then became bishop of Lichfield in 1868. He proved in England as strong a supporter of **establishment** as in New Zealand he had been an opponent. His name lives on in Selwyn College, Cambridge.

SIERRA LEONE. The **West African** coast was chosen by the British government in 1787 as a place for settling freed slaves (mostly Christianized and **baptized**), and thus Freetown, the port and capital of the territory, came into existence. The settling of the ex-slaves increased after the Westminster Parliament banned the slave trade in 1807 and started to capture slave ships of other nations (though these freed slaves would rarely be Christian). Because of this growth, the territory as a whole became the colony of Sierra Leone in 1808, the first British colony in Africa. The Christian church flourished there (it is where **Samuel Crowther** was educated and where he taught at Fourah Bay College). Fourah Bay College, founded in 1827, became a great resource for the Christian church.

Beginning in 1804 the **Church Missionary Society** (CMS) sent its first **missionaries**—German **Lutherans**—to Sierra Leone, though these men mostly then settled and worked (and died) upcountry in Rio Pongas. In 1816 the focus became Freetown, and over the next four decades, despite the appallingly short life-expectancy for Europeans in such a disease-ridden area, Anglican initiatives planted missionaries in each village in its neighborhood. The first **bishop** was Owen Vidal, **consecrated** in 1852; as the first Anglican bishop in West Africa, he initially had as his **diocese** the whole of West Africa (except Liberia, which had its own bishop and looked toward the **United States**, from where the country had been founded), along with the North Africa coast and the Canary Islands.

In the second half of the 19th century, the Anglican Church in Sierra Leone gradually assumed responsibility for its own propagation and growth, and CMS finally ceased from primary missionary work in 1907. By 1951 there were five dioceses in West Africa to be formed into a separate **province**. This was, inevitably, very strongly Nigerian, until the formation of a new province of Nigeria in 1979 left a different kind of province of West Africa. In Sierra Leone the diocese of Bo was formed in 1981 and the parent diocese of Sierra Leone became the diocese of Freetown.

SIGN OF THE CROSS. The sign of the **cross** was made with the right hand at many points in the medieval **mass**, and in other rites as well. In the 1549 **Book of Common Prayer**, this was reduced to a total of five occasions, two of them in the **consecratory epiclesis** in the **eucharistic canon**. A note at the back of the 1549 Book entitled "Of Ceremonies," carrying the subtitle (still there in 1662 in the title to the same material, though since 1552 to be found at the front of the Book) "Why some be abolished and some retained," makes it clear that where medieval **ceremonial** had disappeared from the **rubrics**, it was generally to be viewed as "abolished." However, "Certain Notes" at the end of the section added, "As touching, kneeling, crossing, holding up of hands, and other gestures; they may be used or left as every man's devotion serveth, without blame," which presumably gave liberty to the worshipper to use the sign of the cross or not, while the officiant's use of it was clearly circumscribed by the rubrical injunctions.

In 1552 the five prescribed uses were further reduced to just one—and that one in effect a new one: the marking of the newly **baptized** infant straight after the baptism with the sign of the cross "in token that *he* shall not be ashamed to confess the faith of Christ crucified." When the 1552 Book was revived in 1559, this single instance of a mandatory sign of the cross became one of the four central **Puritan** objections to the ceremonies set out in the Book. The official response to these objections usually took the form of the assertion in **Article** XX that "the church hath power to decree rites or ceremonies"—with the added twist in Queen **Elizabeth I**'s reign that, although a particular ceremony is a small thing (and admittedly not of biblical commandment), because the church has the **authority** to order it and has so ordered, disobedience in a small thing becomes itself a large thing.

After the **Hampton Court Conference**, where the Puritans again set out their objections, the new code of **canons** in 1604 contained in canon 30 a long explanation of the status and significance of the single use of the sign of the cross in the Prayer Book, justifying the requirement based not on any suggestion that **God** himself had commanded it but only on the need for good order and edifying ceremonies in the Church. Then, at the **Savoy Conference** in 1661, when the Puritans made the same "exceptions" (as they were now called) yet again, the **Convocations** declined to make the use of the sign of the cross after baptism optional, but instead inserted at the end of the service for the public baptism of infants a rubrical reference to canon 30 for the benefit of any who had doubts. This hardly answered the thrust of the exception, however, and the continued imposition of the "airy sign" of the cross (as the Puritans called it) contributed to the subsequent departure from the **parishes** of the Church of **England** of more than 1,000 Puritan **ministers**.

When the first Prayer Book of the **Protestant Episcopal Church in the United States of America** was authorized in 1789, the use of the sign of the cross in baptism was made optional, presumably because there were "tender consciences" among the **clergy** or congregations. However, at the next revision in 1892, the signing was made mandatory again.

In the 20th century most hints of scruple about the sign of the cross disappeared among Anglicans, and actual crosses (and sometimes crucifixes) became more common. Devout worshippers in a more catholic tradition learned to cross themselves both during **liturgy** and in private devotions, and formal blessings and **absolutions** were frequently done with the tracing of the form of a cross in the air. In baptism, **godparents** or sponsors also sign candidates in some **provinces**, and services for the renewal of baptismal vows (whether in **confirmation** or in another way) started to suggest, if not require, that **anointing** with oil and/or signing with baptismal water should be done in the form of a cross. Signing other people in the context of liturgy, known as "consignation," is found not only in baptism, but also in confirmation, in **healing**, and in a variety of other rites.

SIMEON, CHARLES (1759–1836). Charles Simeon was **ordained** a **deacon** in 1782 as a fellow of King's College, Cambridge, and underwent an **Evangelical** conversion through embracing the meaning of the **Lord's Supper** (which, as a fellow of the college, he had a statutory duty to attend). He was ordained **presbyter** the following year and became vicar of Holy Trinity Church, Cambridge, a post he then held until his death, 53 years later. For years he battled with the opposition to his **ministry** of his inherited congregation, but his **Bible** preaching, Christ-centered ministry, and personal holiness in time gave him enormous influence. Simeon was a founder-member of the **Church Missionary Society** (CMS) in 1799 and was instrumental in the call of many to be ordained and in the dispatch of many to serve in overseas **missionary** contexts. He invested a personal inheritance in the purchase of advowsons (i.e., the "right" of **patronage**, which is the presenting of an incumbent to a **parish**), and these were placed in the care of the patronage board of Simeon's Trustees, which still exercises considerable patronage in the incumbencies of the Church of **England** to this day.

SINGING. *See* HYMNODY; MUSIC.

SOCIETY FOR PROMOTING CHRISTIAN KNOWLEDGE (SPCK). In 1698 Thomas Bray, a learned **clergyman**, together with four **lay** Anglicans, formed a voluntary society "for promoting Christian knowledge." Other religious societies existed at the time, though usually on a local basis. The SPCK had the makings in its founders of a nationwide scope for the tasks it set itself—largely to provide Christian literature and, by means of grants and other support, to facilitate the education of children in the Christian way. Bray's own interest in overseas **mission** (to which his founding of the **Society for the Propagation of the Gospel** [SPG] in 1701 bears further witness) led to support for the church in the "colonies and plantations" being included among the original objects of the SPCK, and in the 18th century this was implemented in the regular dispatch of books and other literature to the American colonies. The society took on the support of Danish **Lutheran missionaries** in **India** in 1728 and continued it until passing on responsibility to the SPG in 1825. It also began in 1757 a pattern of book grants for ordinands that has run to the present day.

In the 19th century, the SPCK began to open its own bookshops in England. It began its own publishing arm and developed its own Foreign Translation Committee. It also provided sea chaplains for emigrants from Britain to the new lands that were being colonized.

In the 20th century, there was a major expansion of the bookshops in England and of the publishing for worldwide purposes. An Indian branch, the Indian Society for Promoting Christian Knowledge (ISPCK), was established with its autonomous life in 1958. A parallel organization of the Church of **Ireland**, the Association for Promoting Christian Knowledge (APCK), founded in 1792, became part of the SPCK worldwide in 1996.

SOCIETY FOR THE PROPAGATION OF THE GOSPEL (SPG). Thomas Bray, the founder in 1698 of the **Society for Promoting Christian Knowledge** (SPCK), went on in 1701 to found a true **missionary society**, the Society for the Propagation of the Gospel. Its charter commissioned it to provide Christian ministry for British people overseas and also to bring the Christian **gospel** to non-Christian inhabitants of British territories. The first of these roles was exemplified by the provision of chaplains in the North American colonies in the 18th century (a total of 310 were sent, including **John Wesley**, **Samuel Seabury**, and **Charles Inglis**). The second of the roles led to concerns for the gospel in **India** (though these were largely taken over in the early years by the SPCK) and to great efforts in the Americas to get access for the gospel to slaves on the plantations; the origin of the **episcopate** in the **West Indies** bears witness to the society's concern in this area. In the 19th century, the SPG was operating all over the world—in **South Africa**, Madagascar, India, **Ceylon**, **China**, **Korea**, and **Japan**, to mention but a few.

These inherited concerns were continued in the 20th century, with a slow move toward the facilitation and equipping of an indigenous leadership, a strategy greatly strengthened by the advocacy of one of the SPG's most notable missionaries, **Roland Allen**. The SPG was always scrupulously Anglican in the sense of seeking to put all church life under the **authority** of a **bishop** and taking considerable trouble to raise funds to create and sustain overseas bishoprics for this purpose. Its **Anglo-Catholicism** meant, however, that in the years preceding and following the formation of the Church of **South India** (CSI) in 1947, it opposed the union in principle. Because the SPG declined to sustain payments to missionaries or institutions that were becoming part of CSI, there was a break in Dornakal **diocese**, where the **archdeaconry** of Nandyal insisted for some years on remaining an Anglican enclave.

In the early 1960s, for reasons of convenience of administration in England, the SPG talked through a union with the **Universities Mission to Central Africa** (UMCA), and this union was effected in 1965 and gave birth to a new society, the **United Society for the Propagation of the Gospel** (USPG).

SODOR AND MAN. *See* MAN, ISLE OF.

SONGS. *See* HYMNODY; MUSIC.

SOUTH AFRICA. *See* SOUTHERN AFRICA.

SOUTH AMERICA. *See* BRAZIL; SOUTH AMERICAN MISSIONARY SOCIETY; SOUTHERN CONE OF SOUTH AMERICA.

SOUTH AMERICAN MISSIONARY SOCIETY (SAMS). South America was from the times of first European exploration a largely **Roman Catholic** preserve—at least among Europeans, who took possession of vast territories, the Portuguese in what is now **Brazil**, and the Spanish in most of the rest of the continent. The main languages of each country still reflect that colonization process, even though independence of the colonial powers came in the 19th century.

The English took possession of the **Falkland Islands** in 1832, and the islands gave their name to the **diocese** when it was founded in 1869, with a view to taking care of chaplaincies. Meanwhile a vision of a genuine evangelizing of indigenous peoples had been conceived by **Allen Gardiner**. He founded the Patagonia Mission, and, when he died in 1851, left a written note urging that the **mission**'s name be changed to the South American **Missionary Society**, as the scope of the task ahead of the society was so much greater than the title "Patagonia" indicated. This change was made, and South America at large has been the purview of this **Evangelical** society, with virtually no other Anglican missionaries working on the whole continent (save American Episcopalians in Brazil) for more than a century and a half since.

In the first 100 years, reaching out to the indigenous people (along with provision of chaplains for English-speaking expatriates) was kept as a very strict priority. This involved the society in the translation of the scriptures into local **languages**, in solidarity with the marginalized (particularly in the changes for nomadic peoples to become settled agricultural communities), and in the facilitating of many socioeconomic projects.

The society, functioning on a small financial and human base, was greatly weakened by World War II. However, partly through pressure in the 1950s from the American Episcopalians, the 1958 **Lambeth Conference** came to recognize that the continent as a whole should be viewed as open to Anglican proclamation of the **gospel**. This change of perception was matched by a change of personnel, when Harry Sutton became general secretary of SAMS in 1960. A new generation of British and other missionaries was soon being sent to strategic places; a new readiness to **minister** in urban areas and among **Pentecostalists** and lapsed **Roman Catholics** was experienced; and, within very few years, new **dioceses** were being created and the SAMS expatriates were being nominated as **bishops** of them. A feature of this was that the standard SAMS stipend continued, without any increase that might suggest that bishops are a class apart.

As the dioceses grew from one in 1960 to seven in 2004, so the society developed programs of theological training "by extension" and sought to move the leadership on from the expatriate dominance to being truly South American. The process has been slow, but the desired goal of the society—that it should become a resource and support for a Church with a vibrant life of its own, rather than the society itself being largely in charge—has been to a considerable degree achieved. The **province** of the **Southern Cone of South America** was formed in 1983 and marks the coming of age of Anglicanism in the six main countries included. Other Anglican societies have come to assist in South America, and, through common languages, SAMS itself has taken on responsibilities in **Spain** and **Portugal**.

SOUTHEAST ASIA, COUNCIL OF CHURCHES OF. Prior to 1960, a Council of Churches of Southeast Asia was formed, providing a consultative organ initially for the **dioceses** of Rangoon (at that time a member diocese of the Church of **India**, **Pakistan**, Burma, and Ceylon), **Hong Kong** and Macao (previously part of the Church in **China**), Borneo, **Korea**, and Singapore (each of these three then being extraprovincial dioceses of the **Canterbury** jurisdiction), along with the **Philippines** and Taiwan, two dioceses of the **Protestant Episcopal Church in the United States of America**'s jurisdiction). This council roughly covered the area of the Chinese dispersion, without attempting to include dioceses within Communist China, and thus had a common general concern. It had certain grant funds to handle, and the representatives met annually, but it had no **provincial** or constitutional role.

Borneo divided in 1962 into the dioceses of Jesselton (renamed Sabah in 1964) and Kuching, and West Malaysia was formed from Singapore in 1970. The council did have a place within the **Anglican Consultative Council** (ACC) when the ACC was formed in February 1971. At its own meeting in April 1971, the Southeast Asian council took the first steps toward changing its name to the Council of Churches of East Asia, and this came to pass after ACC-2 in 1973.

As particular dioceses became separate autonomous provinces, its role became of less importance. Finally, when most of the last separate dioceses had become the new province of **Southeast Asia** in 1995, at the next meeting of the **Anglican Consultative Council** (ACC-10 in Panama City in 1996), the new province was received into membership of the ACC and the previous council ceased its membership. The council remains in existence for consultative purposes and, for those purposes, now also includes Nippon Sei Ko Kai (**Japan**), the Anglican Church of **Australia**, and the **Philippine Independent Church**.

SOUTHEAST ASIA, PROVINCE OF. From before 1960, there existed a lightweight Council of Churches of **Southeast Asia** (renamed "Council of Churches of East Asia" in 1973). By 1995 separate **provinces** had been formed in **Myanmar**, the **Philippines**, and **Korea**; Taiwan remained a **diocese** of the **Episcopal Church (United States of America)**, while the diocese of **Hong Kong** and Macao was preparing for a new future after the British yielded sovereignty of Hong Kong to **China** in 1997 (and in fact became a new province in 1998). A more manageable grouping, genuinely of Southeast Asia, was emerging from the four remaining dioceses—Kuching, Sabah, and West Malaysia in the nation of Malaysia, and Singapore. These became a new province in 1995. The diocese of Singapore also takes responsibility for chaplaincies in Laos, Thailand, and Cambodia and has begun some **missionary** work in those countries also.

SOUTH INDIA, THE CHURCH OF. South **India** was always a strong part of the Anglican **missionary** and other growth in India, and it proved to be the place where the first union of an Episcopal (i.e., Anglican) church with non-Episcopal ones ever occurred. A key to the church union that came about in the 20th century lay in 19th-century agreements of **missionary societies** of different denominations in Britain that they would largely work in different areas of India, and thus (except perhaps in large cities) would in no sense be in competition with each other. This "comity" pattern of working gave a framework within which a thrust toward uniting with each other on an Indian basis was both natural and possible.

From 1919 onward, largely through the initiative and efforts of Indian Christians, official conversations were conducted between the main non–**Roman Catholic** denominations in South India with a eye toward the formation of a united church. The four Anglican **dioceses** involved included three with a strong **Church Missionary Society** (CMS) background; this meant that they were **Evangelical** in **doctrine** and outlook and would, in principle, be more easily able to unite with their non-Episcopal partners, the **Methodist Church** of South India and the South India United Church (the latter itself the outcome a union in 1908 of **Congregationalists** and **Presbyterians**). In all three bodies, there were existing organizational reasons for confining the quest to South India. A moving spirit in the first two decades of discussions and negotiations was **Bishop Azariah** of Dornakal, the first Indian national to become an Anglican bishop and a keen **ecumenist**. Despite occasional hesitations in one quarter or another, the general outline of the scheme remained relatively constant—that all concerned would be within an Episcopal church; some of the initial bishops would be drawn from the existing Anglican episcopate, while others would be **presbyters** in the other two churches who would be **consecrated** directly to the **episcopate** at inauguration. Other presbyters from each of the three churches would be accepted as presbyters of the new Church of South India (CSI) without any further **ordination** or supposed enhancement of ordination.

The plan was opposed with enormous energy by the **Anglo-Catholic** movement in **England** because of the lack of insistence on Episcopal ordination for all presbyters, and much of this opposition was expressed and channeled through the **Society for the Propagation of the Gospel** (SPG), which withdrew its financial and other support. However, in the crucial vote in the **synod** of the (Anglican) **Church of India**, Burma, and Ceylon (CIBC) in 1945, the House of Bishops, by a vote of 6-4 in favor, settled the synodical agreement to let the four bishops and their dioceses go to join the projected united church. After that, the actual arrangements proceeded unhindered toward the inauguration of the united church at Madras (now Chennai) on 27 September 1947. The 14 initial dioceses included one, Jaffna, in Ceylon (now **Sri Lanka**), which was included because of the large Tamil-speaking population that had migrated from South India to the north of the island.

The main synodical proceedings of the CSI have usually been conducted in English, but there are four recognized Indian **languages** that have official standing: Tamil, Telegu, Malayalam, and Canarese (or Kannarese). The church does not have an **archbishop** or **metropolitan**, but instead a moderator, elected from among the bishops for a stated term only.

It was generally agreed that the new united church had totally severed itself from Anglican structures and was no longer a member of the **Anglican Communion**. Indeed, the issue appeared to be how antipathetic toward its formation other Anglicans could be; the SPG ended grants in all parts of South India where Anglicans joined the CSI, and this monetary sanction had its own impact upon the **archdeaconry** of Nandyal in the (previous) diocese of Dornakal, where around 20 presbyters and over half the **laity** refused to join CSI and became "**continuing Anglicans**." The **Lambeth Conference** of 1948 gave only the most grudging and minimal recognition to CSI and virtually instructed other places not to imitate CSI's misdeeds. This was strongly repeated in the report of the 1958 Lambeth Conference also.

The first synod of CSI in 1948 appointed a **Liturgy** Committee to bring proposals for a South India liturgy to the next synod in 1950. This committee recommended a **eucharistic** liturgy that not only broke new ground at the time, as the first rite consciously regarding **Gregory Dix**'s book *The Shape of the Liturgy* (1945) in its compilation, but also had a substantial effect later on Anglican liturgy. This effect was mediated through worldwide interest and through the presence at the 1958 Lambeth Conference of Leslie Brown, by then bishop of **Uganda** but previously secretary of that CSI Liturgy Committee (1948–1952). In 1957, CSI also pioneered a revision of the **Ordinal**. Its *Book of Common Worship* (1963) included the definitive forms of ordination, incorporating the act of laying on of hands within the ordination prayers, almost certainly through the influence of Edward Ratcliff, and this principle has also been since widely adopted in the **Anglican Communion**.

Among the initial understandings that led the uniting churches to pledge themselves to each other was the agreement that, 30 years after inauguration, the rules for the **ordained ministry** would be revisited. In the interim period, it was not really expected that

provinces of the Anglican Communion would grant full Communion to CSI as not all its **ministers** would be Episcopally ordained (and the 1948 and 1958 Lambeth Conferences made this point very strongly). The situation became less clear in the 1970s, as there arose a tendency for Anglican provinces to say they were in **full Communion** with CSI, even though they had not altered their rules about invariable Episcopal ordination and no changes in the CSI's rules were made when the 30-year period elapsed. But in the meantime, the presbyters of non-Episcopal churches who were in their posts at the time of Indian independence in 1947 had been dying out, and (with the occasional exception of an imported Methodist or Presbyterian minister) all presbyters of CSI were now episcopally ordained, making "full Communion" no longer just a courteous fiction but a description of the reality.

The CSI is a party to the concordat with the Church of **North India** and the **Mar Thoma Syrian Church of Malabar**, and a Joint Council was formed in 1978. Under its terms, each of the three churches prays for the moderator or metropolitan of the other two, and all participate in the consecration of bishops of the other churches and many other activities. Although the CSI and the Mar Thoma churches overlap in their territory, particularly in Kerala, there have been many reasons why a further union has not occurred there. CSI has also at times been in conversation with **Lutheran Churches** in South India, but without any structural result.

In 1978 and 1988, bishops of CSI were invited as guests to the Lambeth Conferences. Before the 1988 conference, the **Anglican Consultative Council** (ACC) had already invited the participation of all "churches in full Communion," and at the request of the ACC the Conference passed Resolution 12 asking that bishops of the united churches with which the Anglican Communion was in full Communion be invited to the Lambeth Conferences as members and their **primates** to the Primates Meetings. Thus in 1990, CSI joined the Anglican Communion and was recognized as a constituent member of the ACC, and its bishops were invited to the 1998 Lambeth Conference as members. There were great celebrations in 1997 at the golden jubilee of the Church, not least for the last surviving bishop from its inauguration, Lesslie Newbigin, originally a Presbyterian, who had served two separate periods as a bishop of the CSI and had become both an apologist for CSI and a world-famous apologist for the Christian faith.

SOUTHERN AFRICA. Anglican chaplaincies arose in South Africa in the 18th and 19th centuries to serve English immigrants, particularly in the Cape Colony and Natal. When the first **bishop** of **Calcutta** was appointed in 1814, South Africa may well have been viewed as within his undefined jurisdiction, even though it was not mentioned in his charter, and at intervals in the 1820s and 1830s bishops of Calcutta exercised an Episcopal **ministry** when their ships stopped in South Africa on the way to or from **India**.

The first bishop specifically appointed for South Africa was Robert Gray, **consecrated** in Westminster **Abbey** on the basis of royal letters patent in April 1847. He was followed in 1853 by bishops for Natal and Grahamstown, and Gray himself, having resigned his comprehensive role as bishop of the whole of South Africa, then by new letters patent became bishop of Cape Town and **metropolitan**. It was in Cape Town that the first consecration of a bishop for **Central Africa** took place—that of Charles MacKenzie, consecrated by Gray and his fellow bishops in 1861 to be bishop of the Zambezi. He went north to the Zambezi River and died there.

As diocesan and metropolitan, Gray asserted powers that, under British law and with the limitations of the letters patent under which he had become metropolitan, he did not possess. Thus, attempting to administer discipline in 1860–1865, he saw first an incumbent (William Long, of Mowbray, Cape Town) and then a bishop (**William Colenso**, of Natal) appeal successfully to the Privy Council in London against his judgments and sentences of deprivation. The latter case led indirectly to the first **Lambeth Conference** in 1867. At that conference, Gray received enough encouragement to act on his already existent intention to treat Colenso as deprived and to consecrate another bishop in his place. He failed to get letters patent for such a consecration, but nevertheless in 1869 consecrated W. K. Macrorie as bishop of Maritzburg, with a mandate to raise money and provide for all the Anglican churchpeople of Natal who could be helped away from Colenso's Episcopal jurisdiction.

These difficulties and setbacks led Gray to summon in 1870 a **synod** at which a voluntary constitution was adopted, and (as was ruled in a later court judgment) the Church of the **Province** of South Africa (CPSA) thus "separated root and branch" from the Church of **England**; it has been wholly independent of the Church of England since then. When, after the Boer War, the British colonies were joined politically with the Afrikaaner territories to become the Union of South Africa (1910), the province found itself the Anglican church of a great nation.

Meanwhile, Colenso (who had not been summoned) and various other **clergy** and lay representatives had been absent from that synod in 1870, so that, alongside the Church led by Gray, a proportion of those who claimed to be Anglicans in South Africa disclaimed membership in the CPSA and reckoned themselves still to be members of the **established** Church of England. They viewed Gray and the CPSA as having voluntarily departed from the legal position of the Church of England and affirmed that they themselves continued as the "Church of England in South Africa" (CESA). Unaffiliated **parishes** outside Natal gained no encouragement from Colenso and remained simply individual parishes until 1938, when they themselves formed themselves into a voluntary body by contractual association. In 1955, after various attempts to obtain Episcopal leadership, they called a retired Anglican bishop from elsewhere, G. F. B. Morris, to join them; he consecrated other bishops beginning in 1959, and the line continues.

CESA has never been granted a place at the Lambeth Conference or in the **Anglican Consultative Council**, though discussions by joint committees and working parties with CPSA have had intermittent existence since World War II. One or two attempts have been made to list the bishops of CESA as ***episcopi vagantes***, but, as they have been leading and nurturing very genuine congregations, such listing has been seen as inappropriate. Equally, in 1984 a brief attempt at closer relations with the **Anglican Communion** took the form of the archbishop of **Sydney** consecrating a bishop for CESA with an officially appointed representative of CPSA sharing in the laying on of hands. This did not, however, lead on to the expected closer relations.

CPSA grew from the days of Gray and acquired a strong provincial structure, coming to cover seven nations, a vast plurality of **languages**, and enormous distances. It was characteristically **Anglo-**

Catholic, partly because of the polarization produced by CESA. The province produced its own experimental **eucharistic** rite (on the lines of 1549) in 1924, made it definitive in 1929, and incorporated it into a full CPSA **Book of Common Prayer** in 1954.

While the province was originally formed from a core of English missionaries and chaplains and had many marks of, at best, paternalism toward the native peoples of its territories, it developed into a fully multiethnic church, and in the years of the worst apartheid made a bold witness against the ideology and practical politics of the dominant white forces in the republic. In 1983–1984 it changed its name from South Africa to Southern Africa to recognize its multinational composition. In 1986 it gained its first black archbishop of Cape Town, **Desmond Tutu**, who received a Nobel Peace Prize and became a world Christian figure. The witness of the Anglican province (along with that of many other Christians) had an impact that helped lead toward the end of apartheid and the transition to a full democracy.

The 1970s and 1980s also saw a **charismatic** renewal arising within the province's ranks, such as to give different dimensions to the inherited catholicism and provide a new style of Anglicanism. In 1989 a new Prayer Book was authorized, notable particularly for its immediate publication in six languages simultaneously, to which others were soon added. In 1996 the province became the first Anglican church since the 17th century to enter into a concordat with non-Episcopal churches such as to warrant an interchangeability of presbyteral ministries. *See also* ANGOLA; HUDDLESTON, ERNEST URBAN TREVOR; ZIMBABWE.

SOUTHERN CONE OF SOUTH AMERICA. The planting of Anglicanism in South America (apart from **Brazil**, which had a somewhat separate history) had two almost independent lines of development. The first came through the English-speaking Anglican chaplaincies, usually associated with British embassies or business interests, which were created from the early 19th century onward in the newly independent republics of South America. The second came from **missionary** endeavors to bring the **gospel** to the indigenous populations. These latter efforts began with the formation in **England** in 1844, through the efforts of **Allen Gardiner**, of the "Patagonia Mission." After his death in 1851 at Tierra del Fuego, others were inspired to follow, and the society took on a continentwide brief as the **South American Missionary Society** (SAMS).

After the British occupation of the **Falkland Islands** in 1832, a **cathedral** was built in the capital, Stanley, and the first **bishop** of the Falkland Islands was **consecrated** in 1869. The title of "Falkland Islands" was chosen because it was the sole British territory that might provide a credible title (the only British territory in mainland South America, British Guiana, clearly belonged with the **West Indies**). The first bishop, Waite Hocking Stirling, served his 31 years (1869–1900) based in Buenos Aires, Argentina; and, for nearly 100 years from his consecration, the chief responsibility of the bishop was viewed as relating to the various chaplaincies for expatriates, with a lesser role in relation to congregations arising from the SAMS missionary work.

There was disapproval from many parts of the **Anglican Communion**, directed against efforts at **evangelizing** in what was described as a "**Roman Catholic** continent." Thus in 1910 the **Edinburgh Missionary Conference** treated South America as a settled Roman Catholic sphere and off-limits for strategies of non-Roman evangelism. Curiously, the same year saw the division of the **diocese**, whereby the "Falklands Islands" jurisdiction retained the west coast republics (which became the diocese of the "West Coast of South America with the Falkland Islands"), and the eastern ones became "Argentina and Eastern South America." Brazil had meanwhile become a part of the **Protestant Episcopal Church in the United States of America** (PECUSA), with its first bishop consecrated in 1900.

The two dioceses were reunited in 1934 as "Argentina and Eastern South America with the Falkland Islands" and remained so until 1963. However, partly through American influence, the committee on "missionary appeal and strategy" at the 1958 **Lambeth Conference** gave ungrudging approval to the principle of Anglican missionary work throughout the whole continent, and this was followed up by a vigorous new regime in SAMS from 1960. There was also further involvement by the Church Missionary Society of **Australia** and by the Anglican Church of **Canada**. There arose considerable growth not only in the SAMS' traditional missions to the indigenous people but in the beginning of new Spanish-speaking **parishes** among the city populations.

New dioceses were created: Chile, Bolivia, and Peru (separating again from Argentina) in 1963; Northern Argentina (formed from Argentina and Eastern South America) in 1969, Peru and Bolivia (hiving off from Chile) in 1973, Paraguay (splitting from Northern Argentina) in 1973, Uruguay in 1988, and Bolivia (separating from Peru) in 1995. The dioceses were initially bonded by the formation in 1973 of a quasi-provincial Anglican Council of South America ("CASA" from its Spanish form), and in 1977 the Falkland Islands (which did not now appear in any diocesan title) was returned to the direct oversight of the **archbishop** of **Canterbury**.

The wholly autonomous **province** of the Southern Cone of South America was formed in 1983. Spanish provides a common **language** (though there are many **vernacular** tongues among the indigenous people), and there has been a slow indigenization of the leadership. The **primacy** belongs to no one diocese but is conferred through election by the triennial Provincial **Synod** for a limited term only. Because of the vast distances to be covered within the dioceses, there has been a serious concern for a **lay presidency** of the **eucharist** (though in split voting, it has not yet been approved at the provincial synod). Also, because there has been a necessary distancing of Anglicanism from Roman Catholicism, a strong affinity has often been sensed with the vigorous **Pentecostalism** that is the dominant non–Roman Catholic Christianity in most South American countries.

SPAIN. *See* SPANISH REFORMED EPISCOPAL CHURCH.

SPANISH REFORMED EPISCOPAL CHURCH. In 1868 some Spanish **priests** left the **Roman Catholic Church** and formed the Episcopal Church in Spain. They were joined by other **clergy** and **laity** after **Vatican I** and, led by a priest, Juan Cabrera, formed a **synod** in 1880 and looked for support to the Church of **England** and the Church of **Ireland**, as well as to the American bishop of the Valley of Mexico (because he and his **diocese** were Spanish speaking). They elected Cabrera as the first **bishop** at that synod, though they had difficulty getting him **consecrated**. The Church published its own Spanish-**language liturgy** in 1883 and put it into definitive form in 1889, citing both Mozarabic and Anglican sources.

With encouragement from both the 1888 **Lambeth Conference** and the **General Synod** of the Church of Ireland of April 1894, in September 1894 **Archbishop** Lord Plunket of **Dublin**, with two other Irish bishops, consecrated Cabrera as bishop of the tiny church. When Cabrera died in 1916, however, no successor was consecrated for another 40 years, and Church of Ireland bishops occasionally visited to administer **confirmation** and to ordain **deacons** and **presbyters**.

During the years of Francisco Franco's rule in Spain (1939–1976), the tight concordat between the Fascist regime and the Roman Catholic hierarchy provided a very difficult context for non-Roman Churches to survive. In 1958 the archbishop of Dublin and two bishops of the **Protestant Episcopal Church in the United States of America** consecrated the next bishop for the Spanish church, and the continuity of the succession has been sustained by similar procedures ever since.

In 1980 the church asked to join the **Anglican Communion**, roughly in step with its sister-church, the **Lusitanian Church** in Portugal, and it was officially admitted on 2 November 1980. By this step the archbishop of **Canterbury** became constitutionally the **metropolitan** to the single, extraprovincial **diocese**. Further modernization of its liturgical forms has followed. Its adherents were probably fewer than 1,000 in the second half of the 20th century, but near the end of the century and into the 21st the Church has benefited from the immigration into Spain of Spanish-speaking **Protestant** Christians from other parts of the world such as Central and South America, such as to take its numbers well into four figures. In 2003 there were 22 congregations, with 20 licensed presbyters. Its territory is within the bounds of the Church of England's diocese of "**Gibraltar** in Europe," and close relationships are maintained between them.

SPRINKLING. Sprinkling water on a candidate for **baptism** has been widely, though somewhat irregularly, practiced in Anglicanism through neglect or ignorance of the standard **rubrical** requirement of dipping or pouring. It is generally allowed that, if water has touched the candidate's skin, then a sufficient outward sign has occurred for the baptism to be **valid**, even if irregular. However, in clinical baptisms, as in the case of infants in intensive care in an incubator, it may be necessary to confine the mode of baptism to sprinkling or even smearing. Sprinkling is also used—entirely appropriately—as a *reminder* of baptism, particularly on **Easter** Eve and on other occasions of the renewal of baptismal vows (and it may be dubbed "asperges"). Sprinkling is then done by hand, by use of a sprig with leaves, or with an aspergillium. *See also* SUBMERSION.

SRI LANKA. Sri Lanka is the modern name for Ceylon. The island was first colonized in the 16th century by the Portuguese, who brought **Roman Catholic missionaries**. The Portuguese were dispossessed by the Dutch in 1658, and they introduced **Protestant** missionaries. The British then drove out the Dutch in 1796 and turned the island into a Crown Colony in 1802. Various British **missionary societies** started work in the colony, including two Anglican societies, the **Church Missionary Society** in 1818 and the **Society for the Propagation of the Gospel** in 1840. The first **bishop** of Colombo was **consecrated** in 1845.

The Ceylonese **diocese** was brought into the constitution of the **province** formed in 1930 to be the Church of **India**, Burma, and Ceylon (CIBC). Because of the vast distances on the one hand and the different political and religious contexts on the other, considerable independence remained. The diocese of Colombo produced its own **eucharistic** rite in 1933. In the years after World War II, when in 1947 the Church of **South India** was formed (which included the diocese of Jaffna on the island of Ceylon) and in 1948 the island gained political independence, great efforts were made to bring about Church union in Ceylon. A proposed scheme for union between the Anglicans and non-Episcopal churches was agreed upon by a negotiating committee and went through three successive drafts between 1949 and 1955. It was further amended in 1964, but was never sufficiently accepted by the Churches. It interestingly gave birth to the title "Church of Lanka."

As it turned out, in 1970 the Church of India, **Pakistan**, Burma and Ceylon (CIPBC) dissolved itself as a province, when united churches were formed in **North India** and Pakistan and a separate province was formed for Burma. The two Sri Lankan Anglican dioceses, Colombo and Kurunagala, were left as extraprovincial entities, under the **metropolitan** care of the archbishop of Canterbury. This is still the position today.

Meanwhile in 1972 Sri Lanka recognized a status for Buddhism as the state religion.

SUBMERSION. The first option for the mode of **baptism** in Anglican **initiation rubrics** and practice has usually been "dipping." In the 16th century, when no provision was made for baptizing adults, dipping the infant was only to be reduced to "pouring" if the **godparents** certified that the child was weak and could not well withstand being dipped. In the 17th century, when provision was made for those "of riper years," no such certification was mentioned, with dipping and pouring being made equal options, and those alternatives have generally been found in Anglicanism since. In many parts of the world, pioneer **missionary evangelism** has been marked by baptism in rivers, lakes, or the sea.

In the **Baptist**, Independent, and **Pentecostalist** traditions, the mode of baptism has to be submersion (often through an over-rigorous and exclusive identification of the symbolism of baptism with union with **Jesus Christ** in his death and **resurrection**, as in Rom. 6.1–4, an identification that is thought to require a dramatization for its credibility if not its **validity**). However, their usual terminology has been to call this "total immersion," or sometimes simply "immersion." In the light of this usage, Anglicans are not always consistent in their terminology, but the practice of dipping a candidate underwater is better termed "submersion," while having a candidate stand or kneel in water as water is poured over him or her is better termed "immersion." In Anglican practice, it is usual to pour or dip three times at the naming of the three Persons of the **Trinity**, but rubrics have usually allowed a single administration, if preferred.

In the 20th century, new church buildings and old ones being reordered have sometimes been equipped with a baptismal tank, thus making explicit the first option in the rubrics. This equipment is sometimes called a "**baptistery**," but that is a confusing use of a term that has traditionally meant a room in a church building specifically set aside for baptisms.

SUDAN. After the defeat of the Mahdi at the battle of Omdurman in 1898, the Sudan became an Anglo-Egyptian condominium. The northern part of the country was primarily Islamic, but the Nubian southern tribes were much more open to the Christian **gospel**, and the **Church Missionary Society** sent Llewellyn Gwynne to the Sudan as its first **missionary** there. He ultimately reached the south in 1905, and then in 1908 was consecrated as **suffragan bishop** of Khartoum, where he was formally part of the **Jerusalem** bishopric. He became first bishop of the **diocese** of Egypt and the Sudan when it was formed in 1920.

The first Sudanese to be **ordained** were made **deacons** in 1941, and a separate diocese of Sudan was formed in 1945. It became part of the "Jerusalem **Archbishopric**" in 1957, but was detached from it in 1974, as both Sudan and the archbishopric faced reorganization. In Sudan, four dioceses were created from the one, and it became a separate **province** in 1976. Since then, despite enormous political division in the country with an endemic state of civil war, further division of dioceses has ensued, until in 2004 there were 24 dioceses. These are mainly in the south, where Christianity has taken a firm root, but has been deeply threatened by the anti-Christian harshness of the Khartoum regime. An agreement between the Khartoum government and the rebel armies of the south in January 2005 gave some hope of a more peaceful future.

SUFFRAGAN. Suffragan **bishop** is the term used for an assistant bishop in a diocese that has officially provided for such an appointment in its structures. *See also* AREA BISHOP; COADJUTOR BISHOP.

SUNDAY. *See* SABBATH.

SUPPER OF THE LORD. This is a variant form of the title "The **Lord's Supper**," words which were drawn from 1 Cor. 11.20 and were used as the first and main title of the **Communion** service in the 1552 **Book of Common Prayer** and retained in the 1559, 1604, 1662, and other Prayer Books of the **Anglican Communion** until the early 20th century. The translation is, however, put in this exact form, "The Supper of the Lord," in Articles XXV and XXVIII of the Thirty-Nine **Articles**. These alternative titles were clearly favored by the Reformers on scriptural grounds.

SYDNEY. Richard Johnson, nominated by **William Wilberforce**, sailed as chaplain with the first convict fleet to New South Wales in

1788. His assistant, Samuel Marsden, recommended by **Charles Simeon**, joined him in 1794 and later succeeded him when Johnson himself returned to **England** in poor health. **Australia** was named as part of the jurisdiction of the **bishop** of **Calcutta** in the letters patent by which the second bishop of Calcutta, Reginald Heber, was appointed in 1824. The first bishop of Australia, William Broughton, was **consecrated** in 1836 and became bishop of Sydney in 1847 when **dioceses** were created for other parts of Australia.

A particular feature of Sydney's history was a bequest of Thomas Moore. Moore was a layman, a ship's carpenter, who went ashore in the infant colony of New South Wales in 1796, married, and settled there. Moore was a devout Anglican, and when he died in 1840, he left his estate to the Australian branch of the Church of England specifically to found a college, to be known as Moore's College. Bishop Broughton did not act on this, but the second bishop of Sydney, Frederick Barker, quickly founded Moore College after his arrival in 1855. In 1889 the college moved to its present site of Newtown in Sydney, and it has remained a very strong center of **Evangelical** Anglicanism since that day, closely managed under the aegis of Sydney diocese and served by fine scholars. Three of the four **archbishops** of Sydney since 1963 have previously been principals or vice-principals of Moore College.

The evangelicalism of the whole diocese was greatly reinforced by **Howard Mowll**, archbishop (1932–1958) and **primate** (1946–1958) of what was then still the Church of England in Australia. This had considerable effect in other parts of the world, not least through the **Church Missionary Society** of Australia. Sydney also became a friendly support for the Church of England in **South Africa** (CESA). Then, in the second half of the 20th century, the resources of the diocese within the city of Sydney (where roughly one-third of all Australians live) grew, and, because of its strong evangelicalism, set up a tension with other parts of the Anglican Church in Australia. This led the **General Synod** to allow separate developments in different dioceses, so that by 2004 **women** could not be ordained or licensed as **presbyters** in Sydney, but could in most other dioceses; the new *An Australian Prayer Book* (1995) was not authorized for use in Sydney; in the late 1990s the diocesan **synod** was constantly on the brink of authorizing **lay presidency** of the **eucharist**; and at the 1998 **Lambeth**

Conference and in the years following, Sydney diocese threw tremendous weight internationally against any move toward the approval of **homosexual** relationships. The evangelicalism of the diocese was evident within the city through a strong and purposeful **evangelism**.

SYNOD. The etymological origin of "synod" is *syn-odos*, a "road together" or "route together," but since classical times, the word has had the derived meaning of a "meeting" or "assembly" (a hint of its original meaning is to be found in the kindred *synodia* in Luke 2.44). The Church had "synods" from an early date, usually through the **bishops** of a region meeting together. The Anglican **Reformers** were largely opposed to such gatherings, partly because of their own excessive deference to monarchs and their actual dependence upon "top-down" methods of church government. Thus Article XXI of the Thirty-Nine **Articles** says, "General councils may not be gathered together without the commandment and will of princes." There was mention of "the sacred Synod of this nation" in the 1604 **canons** (nos. 139–41), but this almost certainly meant Parliament, and the Church of **En-gland**'s structural relationship to the state prevented any true ecclesiastical governing body from coming into being until the second half of the 20th century.

In other parts of the **Anglican Communion**, such bodies were constituted much earlier; the **General Convention** of the **Protestant Episcopal Church in the United States of America** (PECUSA) held in 1785 was the first such representative body and opened the way for others. The Episcopal Church of **Scotland** held its first synod in 1811. Churches in British colonies, in various ways still tied to the British constitution, evolved more uncertainly, but a pioneer in this field was Bishop **George Selwyn**, the first bishop of New Zealand (1841–1868), who created a **clergy** synod that met at Waimate in 1844 and then at St. John's College, Auckland, in 1847 (and was charged with illegality by critics in England). Selwyn then laid plans to include the **laity** also, and this policy was entrenched in a constitution for a **province** drawn up by a representative conference in 1857. His **diocese** was divided with the formation of Christchurch (1856) and Nelson and Wellington (1858), and he then summoned a General Synod for the province in 1859. At that synod, Selwyn and his fellow bishops **consecrated** the bishop for the new diocese of Waiapu. His provincial synod constitution paved the way for other provinces, providing for three houses of bishops, clergy, and laity, each with representation from the constituent dioceses.

The province of **Canada** (which, despite its title, consisted of only some of the eastern dioceses of what in 1867 became the Dominion of Canada) was formed with a provincial synod on similar lines in 1861. It was followed by Robert Gray's formation of the province of South Africa in 1870, and then by the voluntary bonding into a General Synod of representatives of the Church of **Ireland** in 1871 in the wake of that Church's disestablishment.

It has become normal since then in each autonomous Anglican church for a province to be formed at the outset with a constitution providing for self-government by General Synod. However, the relative powers of the three houses of synod may vary from one province to another; for example, the General Convention of PECUSA—begun in 1785, and continuing under the renamed **Episcopal Church (United States of America)**—has a unusual pattern of only two houses, as, in a different way, does the General Synod of the Church of Ireland. The powers of a General Synod in relation to diocesan synods may also vary from one Church to another. The underlying principle generally followed by Anglicans is that the three "estates" of bishops, clergy, and laity should form separate electoral constituencies and be separately represented in the General Synod or its equivalent. In many provinces, they may also vote separately for designated purposes, and weighty matters may in such cases be decided only by the concurrence of all three houses.

– T –

TABERNACLE. In the developed **sacramental** practices of the medieval **Roman Catholic Church**, **consecrated** wafer-breads were retained after the **mass** for permanent **reservation**, under conditions providing for both great security (for fear of sacrilegious treatment of the reserved **elements**) and great visibility of the container of the elements (in order to provide for devotions directed toward the reserved elements). The tabernacle, a locked receptacle placed on the back of the **altar** itself or fixed into the east wall above the altar, became by the 16th century the most popular place of reservation. The **Reformation** led to the total removal of tabernacles, as exhibiting a sacramental theology now discarded as superstitious. The **Anglo-Catholic** movement of the 19th century led to a new wave of the provision of tabernacles, and they are now to be found in many parts of the **Anglican Communion** where reservation has again come into use. *See also* AUMBRY; BENEDICTION; PYX.

TABLE, HOLY. At the **Reformation**, the **altars** of the pre-Reformation church were replaced both in substance and in title. The substantial change came through the order-in-council of 1550 requiring the removal of the stone altars from the east walls of church buildings and their replacement with (movable) wooden tables. The change of title came in two stages: In 1549 the word "altar" was retained in the **rubrics** of the **Book of Common Prayer** at some points, although there was now alternating with it the term "God's board"; in 1552 it became, quite simply, "the table" (or "the holy table"). Behind the changes lay the conviction that the Lord had instituted a **feast** rather than a sacrifice, that the **liturgical** text was to give expression to that fact, and that a table was therefore more appropriate than an altar. The table might well be placed at right angles to the position of the old altar and might rest out of **Communion** time at a different place from where it was used for Communion—and the rubric of 1552, still conserved in the 1662 Book, provides for the Communion service to be held either in the **nave** or in the **chancel** "where **Morning and Evening Prayer** are appointed to be said," which itself suggests that the place might be changed.

In the 17th century, **Archbishop William Laud** required tables to be placed back against the east wall, fenced in with rails, supposedly so that they would not be profaned. This position remained in the normal ordering of the interiors of Anglican buildings well into the 20th century (despite the freedom apparently given in the 1662 rubric quoted above). Furthermore, the **Anglo-Catholic** movement of the 19th century **canonized Gothic** Revival **architecture**, with its pattern of nave and chancel and with the table (often now redubbed "altar") not only against the east wall but once again made of stone, reached by a stepped ascent, and surrounded by reredos, riddel curtains, and other **Roman Catholic** features. **Eastward position** for the officiant became very widespread.

Under the influence of the **Liturgical Movement** beginning in the 1930s, tables in many buildings have been brought forward to be near the congregation and to provide for the **westward**-facing position of the **president**. This has accompanied a change of emphasis back toward the concept of a shared meal rather than a ritual sacrifice. The term "altar" has nevertheless often persisted, and its translated equivalent has become the rubrical word for the holy table in many other languages used in Anglican liturgy. *See also* SANCTUARY.

TANZANIA. The **Universities Mission to Central Africa** (UMCA) began its **missionary** work on behalf of the land that is now Tanzania, when it nominated Charles MacKenzie to be the first **bishop** on the Zambezi and arranged for him to be **consecrated** in Cape Town on 1 January 1861. However, his death from disease in January 1862 soon after reaching the Zambezi entailed a new appointment. In 1863 William Tozer was consecrated as MacKenzie's successor and within a short time of his arrival moved the **diocesan** base to the island of **Zanzibar**, which was recognized as such by UMCA in 1865 and established by the purchase of the erstwhile slave market as the site for the **cathedral** in 1873. From here missionary expeditions were made to mainland Tanganyika, which in 1885 became German **East Africa**. Zanzibar itself became a British protectorate in 1890. Islam has always had a strong footing in the country.

The **Church Missionary Society** (CMS), and particularly CMS **Australia**, followed in the northern parts of Tanganyika from 1878. The churches they planted remained part of **Mombasa** diocese, until CMS Australia funded a bishopric and the diocese of Central Tanganyika was formed in 1927. Meanwhile Zanzibar was made famous by **Frank Weston**, who was bishop of the island from 1908 until his death in 1924. Tanganyika itself was the scene of warfare and considerable hardship during World War I, as the Germans there were defeated. After the war it became a British protectorate under a League of Nations mandate, and this was renewed by the **United Nations** after World War II, with an expectation of independence, which came in 1961.

When independence was drawing near, Zanzibar was to be joined to Tanganyika in one nation of Tanzania, and dioceses were multiplied. The various dioceses were joined with the **Kenyan** dioceses to be incorporated in 1960 into a new **province** of **East Africa**. Further growth and the formation of new dioceses followed, and in 1970 a separate province of Tanzania was formed with nine initial dioceses. A feature of the province has been the uniting of the (previously somewhat polarized) **Evangelical** and **Anglo-Catholic** dioceses, and the creation in 1973 of a single Tanzanian **liturgy**, drafted and published in Swahili, as an expression and undergirding of that unity. In 1995 the two **theological colleges** merged into a single provincial college in Kongwa. In 2004, there were 19 dioceses.

TEMPLE, WILLIAM (1880–1944). William Temple was the son of Frederick Temple, who was the **bishop** of Exeter (1869–1886), bishop of **London** (1886–1896), and **archbishop** of **Canterbury** (1896–1903). After graduating from Balliol College, Oxford, William Temple became a fellow of Queen's College. There, while seeking **ordination**, he himself delayed it, as he was unsure of the **resurrection** of **Jesus Christ**. He resolved this issue and was then **ordained** in 1908 on his fellowship.

Temple was an usher at the **Edinburgh Missionary Conference** of 1910 and immediately after became headmaster of Repton School. In 1914 he became rector of St. James, Piccadilly, and it was in that capacity that he headed the Life and Liberty Movement from 1917. He also became a notable author. In 1919 Temple became a canon of Westminster **Abbey** and in 1921 bishop of Manchester. From an early age he was a member of the British Labour Party and was deeply involved in all issues of the social outworking of the Christian faith. Thus he was a founder of the international **ecumenical** Life and Work Movement in 1927. But he was also for most of its 15 years chairman of the Commission on **Doctrine** in the Church of England (it began in 1923 and reported in 1938).

When **Cosmo Lang** moved from **York** to Canterbury in 1928, Temple succeeded him in 1929 as archbishop of York. In that period he chaired the Edinburgh Conference on Faith and Order in 1937 and went on to become chairman of the "provisional committee" of the **World Council of Churches** from 1938 to 1942. Then, when Lang retired from Canterbury in 1942, Temple succeeded him in Canterbury also. His period of office there was cut short by ill health, and he died on 26 October 1944.

Temple is perhaps best known today not for his political and economic concerns, which were weighty and far-reaching, but for his *Readings in St. John's Gospel*, first published (in two series) in 1939 and 1940, which has remained in print more or less continuously since. A few church buildings have been **dedicated** in his memory in England, and his name is entered in various **calendars** for commemoration on 6 November, though this was not the date of his death.

TEN COMMANDMENTS. The Ten Commandments (or Decalogue) take a major place in the Pentateuch (Exod. 20.1–17 and Deut. 5.6–21) and are liberally quoted by **Jesus Christ** and his apostles in the New Testament (e.g., Matt. 5.27–37; Mark 10.19; Rom. 13.9–19). The Reformers gave them a central place in the **liturgy** and life of the Church of **England**. They formed a guide to life within the **catechism** from the 1549 **Book of Common Prayer** onward; they became both a measure of sin past and an aspiration for future conduct in the **Communion** service (with an expanded form of the Kyries as the congregational response to them) from 1552; and in Queen **Elizabeth I**'s reign, they were ordered to be displayed on the east walls of churches. In some parts of the **Anglican Communion**, they retain a comparable role to the present day. However, without their importance ever being explicitly denied, they slipped away from that central place in most **provinces** of the Communion.

The Lord's "Summary of the Law," drawn from Matt. 22.37–40 and Mark 12.28–31, became over a period of time a favorite substitute for the Ten Commandments in the Communion service. This began as an actual substitution for the commandments in the **nonjurors**' liturgy of 1718 and was incorporated as an addition to the commandments in the 1789 rite of the **Protestant Episcopal Church in the United States of America**, where it then became an alternative to the commandments in the 1892 revision. More recently, both the Decalogue and that summary have been omitted or relegated as an option to an appendix. Similarly, catechisms have fallen into disuse, at least in Western nations, and east walls now display great varieties of style, but very rarely the commandments. Those who have been keenest on the place of the Ten Commandments in **eucharistic** liturgy have been the **Evangelicals** who have used the rite least.

A liturgical variant on the Mosaic commandments has been provided in modern revisions in the Church of England, where, from "Series 3" in 1973 onward, there has been an optional alternative text that (using the Sermon on the Mount as a model) gave a New Testament text to expound each Old Testament one.

In the **Roman Catholic** Church, the numeration of the Commandments was settled differently at the Counter-**Reformation**. The first two are run together (thus perhaps diminishing or obscuring slightly the prohibition of graven images), and the last one is split into two separate prohibitions of coveting; the result is that the numbering of all the others differs from that in the non-Roman Churches.

THEOLOGICAL COLLEGES. Theological colleges are in principle institutions within which candidates are prepared for **ordination**. They did not exist for the Church of **England** at the time of the **Reformation**, for the ancient universities of Oxford and Cambridge were viewed as the normative route to **orders**. This assumption continued in the Church of England long after the planting of Anglicanism in other parts of the world had disclosed a great need for proper residential training and formation on a **provincial** or national basis. Thus Codrington College was founded in Barbados through a bequest of Christopher Codrington in 1710 and after considerable delays was opened in the 1740s.

Coates Hall in Edinburgh was founded for the Episcopal Church of **Scotland** in 1810, and the General Theological Seminary, New York, followed as the first seminary of the **Protestant Episcopal Church in the United States of America** in 1817. Fourah Bay College, in Freetown, **Sierra Leone**, came in 1827. St. John's College, Auckland, **New Zealand**, was founded in 1843. A short-lived St. James College was formed in **Sydney** in 1845; it was succeeded by Moore College in 1856.

In England itself, the first college was almost certainly that at St. Bees in Cumberland in 1816, although it closed in 1895. Chichester Theological College was founded in 1839; Wells in 1840; St. Aidan's, Birkenhead, in 1847; Cuddesdon in 1854; and St. John's Hall, Highbury (nowadays St. John's College, Nottingham) in 1863.

Further colleges followed in England, until by 1969 there were 18 such residential colleges recognized by the House of Bishops as offering appropriate theological training for ordination purposes. With occasional exceptions, they were privately owned foundations, administered by trustees, and often propounding a particular form of churchmanship. In the second half of the 20th century, the colleges had to adjust to training married students, training women candidates, and teaching to degree and higher-degree standards. Part-time training developed swiftly in the last quarter of the century, and some unions and closures of residential colleges also occurred, bringing the total recognized by the House of Bishops down to 11 in 2004.

In the 20th century, colleges, often modeled on English or American patterns, were inaugurated in many of the new **provinces** of the **Anglican Communion**. Typical examples are St. John's, Bangalore, in **South India**; St. Paul's, Limuru, **Kenya**; and Bishop Tucker Theological College (now a Christian University) at Mukono, **Uganda**. Some of these were **ecumenical** in character.

THIRTY-NINE ARTICLES. *See* ARTICLES OF RELIGION.

TONGUES. The Greek word *glossai* is regularly translated in the **King James Version** of the **Bible** as "tongues," though it is equally appropriate to render it as "**languages**"—indeed, the two English words are often interchangeable in their use. However, in the occurrences of the word in 1 Cor. 12 and 14, the King James Version translators added the gratuitous (and thus italicized in their Version) adjective "*unknown* tongues." This terminology provided a point of reference when, at the outbreak of **Pentecostalism** in the first decade of the 20th century, the Christians moved by the **Holy Spirit** began to break out in "tongues" that were unknown to themselves and to most people present, though there might be one person present who could "interpret" and would do so.

There has followed through the 20th century a tendency in Pentecostal and **charismatic** circles to value the "gift" of tongues as *the* clinching evidence in any believer of the **baptism** and empowering of the Holy Spirit. This in turn has meant that, even if the New Testament passages do imply there is a gift of unknown tongues that the Holy Spirit bestows on some believers, the practice has gone well beyond that. Pentecostalism has been marked by an insistence that somehow this one gift is almost indispensable for first-class Christians with the truest Christian experience. In point of fact, the "gift of languages" in the New Testament may not imply any such phenomenon at all, but a facility with known languages. That would not preclude or invalidate the use of unknown tongues, but it would locate them in a category of acknowledged Christian experience rather than one of obeying a scriptural command.

TORONTO BLESSING. A phenomenon known as being "slain in the Spirit" was well known in Anglican (and other) **charismatic** circles in the 1980s and even before. Individuals touched by a deep and striking encounter with God would faint gently to the ground, rest peacefully there, and after a short space apparently revive equally gently and without disturbance. However, in the early 1990s worldwide fame attached to accounts of large-scale occurrences of the phenomena at the Airport Church at Toronto (broadly in the **Pentecostalist** strand of churches), and such phenomena became known as the "Toronto Blessing." Many from all around the world—not least from Anglican churches—traveled to Toronto to witness and experience the "Blessing" and to seek to introduce it into their own parts of the world. It has been by no means uncontroversial, not least because of the temptations toward manipulation. It is to be distinguished from the **Toronto Statement**.

TORONTO STATEMENT. The Fourth **International Anglican Liturgical Consultation** (IALC-4) was held in Toronto in 1991 and produced a widely publicized **doctrinal** and pastoral statement on Christian **Initiation**, "Walk in Newness of Life." This statement strongly commended infant **baptism**, while deprecating its indiscriminate practice; it insisted that baptism is complete **sacramental** initiation, and it accordingly commended admission to **Communion** from baptism onward, a reform of **confirmation**, and the provision of an adult **catechumenate**. These policies implied a reform of much received and existing Anglican practice, but many **provinces** have implemented them in whole or part, while others have conscientiously wrestled with them. The Toronto Statement is to be distinguished from the "**Toronto Blessing**" and also from the joint Anglican and **Roman Catholic** statement of 2000, issued from a joint conference of bishops at Mississauga (part of Toronto), which is best called the "Mississauga Statement" *See also* INTERNATIONAL ANGLICAN–ROMAN CATHOLIC COMMISSION FOR UNITY AND MISSION.

TRACTARIANS. Followers of the **Anglo-Catholic movement**, because of their involvement with the ***Tracts for the Times*** or their embracing of them, were from an early point known as "Tractarians." The title is still sometimes used to betoken those who today stand near in spirit and outlook to the original writers and lovers of the *Tracts*.

TRACTS FOR THE TIMES. Following **John Keble**'s Assize Sermon on 14 July 1833, a small number of like-minded younger **clergy** set in motion the **Anglo-Catholic** movement—sometimes, from their provenance, known as the "**Oxford Movement**"—and did so most effectively through the launching in September 1833 of a set of *Tracts for the Times*. The series ran in an intermittent way until 1841. The thrust of the tracts was to promote the "**apostolic succession**," the **Episcopal** succession that, it was argued, gave an unbroken passing on of apostolic **authority** from the apostles themselves. This succession had been preserved in the Church of **England** through the **Reformation** and was the key, the tracts proclaimed, to the authority of the Anglican **episcopate** and the **validity** of the **ordained ministry**, and thus of the **sacraments**, derived from that episcopate. Whereas the early tracts were light (if pungent) pamphlets, some of the later ones were massive theological treatises, all concerned to establish and promote the "catholic" credentials of the Church of England. The series came to an end with Tract 90, written in 1841 by **John Henry Newman**, in which he argued, with what was viewed at the time as Jesuitical hairsplitting, for the full compatibility of **Roman Catholic doctrines** with the Thirty-Nine **Articles**. The tract incurred the wrath of the University of Oxford, which condemned it at a Hebdomadal Board (a meeting of the heads of houses) a month after publication. Many **bishops** also attacked it, and these reactions both helped move Newman toward Rome and also spelled the end of the *Tracts for the Times*. *See also* TRACTARIANS.

TRADITION. As a verbal noun, "tradition" in its origins simply means the process of handing on a message or a possession. More usually in historical theology, it has come to mean the *content* of what is handed on. **Jesus Christ** referred to the Pharisees setting aside the commands of **God** in favor of the "traditions of human beings" (Mark 7.8). However, he was thereby attributing the origin of such traditions to human invention, as opposed to God's revelation. In this, he set up a sharper contrast than would apply in many other contexts. The stories of Jesus himself were from the start "handed on" by those who had known him in the flesh and who, far from inventing the stories, were doing their utmost to conserve them. This more positive understanding of "handing on" is enshrined in Paul's testimony that he was teaching that which he, who had not known Jesus in the flesh, had received from others (cf. 1 Cor. 11.17, 15.3–4)—and wanted to be handed on again (2 Tim. 2.2).

As the New Testament books came to be written and to be recognized by the Church as "scripture," in the way in which the Old Testament was already received and recognized as "the scriptures," so a normative form was given to "the tradition"; thereafter anything taught orally or in secondary written sources was in principle open to the appeal to scripture. Thus, in the early centuries of the Church's life, the truths of the **gospel** were handed on orally in **catechetical** and **liturgical** forms, and to that extent were "traditions." But, as Irenaeus (c. 130–c. 200) makes clear in a famous passage, the teaching and beliefs of the church were not handed on orally to become autonomous and beyond appeal. On the contrary, they were always to be checked and adjusted by appeal to the written scriptures themselves. "Tradition" was found in its highest form in the ecumenical **creeds** and in liturgical forms such as the **Lord's Prayer**, which carried from generation to generation summaries or extracts of scriptural truth.

Nevertheless, in the Dark Ages and Middle Ages, the teachings of the Western Church moved slowly away from the plain sense of scripture, and the findings of **Councils** and the entrenched conventions of church life took on a momentum (and thus an autonomy) that tended to distance the beliefs and practice of the church from those of the apostolic age. Thus when Martin Luther challenged on scriptural grounds the propriety of indulgences, the **pope** defended them;

they were by then part of the "tradition," and in principle self-authenticating as such. A similar illustration is provided by the withdrawal of the cup from the **laity** at the **eucharist**; this withdrawal was practiced from the 13th century onward on the **authority** of the church, but was questioned at the **Reformation** on the authority of scripture. Here a clear choice of authority was involved, and the Anglican Reformers, like those on the Continent, restored the cup to the laity at the outset of their movement for reform. The principle that scripture must judge and reform tradition was thus built into the very foundations of an Anglicanism separate from the **Roman Catholic Church**. It was expressed clearly in Article VIII of the Thirty-Nine **Articles** in relation to the creeds, for these formulations were now to be accepted not because they were more than 1,000 years old, nor because they sprang from the findings of Councils, nor because they were received as tradition, but because "they may be proved by most certain warrants of holy scripture."

A very high authority is still rightly accorded to tradition. The church still learns the faith by the telling from one generation to another; by liturgy (including songs and **hymns**); by teaching programs and courses; by books, websites, and other writings; and by word of mouth in families and elsewhere. The tradition broadly encompasses and conveys the faith revealed in scripture, but is always subject to restating and reformulating in the light of scripture.

A latter-day convention of speech which states that Anglican faith draws jointly and equally upon scripture, tradition, and reason has no basis in official formularies, does less than justice to the supreme authority of scripture, and does not in itself indicate which of its three "sources" is to prevail when (as at the Reformation, as shown above) any two of them clash with each other.

TRENT, COUNCIL OF. As the **Reformation** spread across the face of Europe after 1521, the **Roman Catholic Church** detected a need for a General **Council** that would deal **authoritatively** with the errors that were flourishing. The Council was finally summoned to Trent, in the Dolomites in what is now northern Italy, and opened in the year 1546. There were three separate groups of sessions—1546–1547, 1551–1552, and 1562–1563. Their relevance to Anglicanism is that the Forty-Two **Articles** of 1553 were drawn up with the decrees of the first two conciliar sessions in view, specifically in order to distance the reformed Church of **England** from contemporary Roman Catholicism. Similarly the third group of sessions of the Council probably had the text of the Articles in view in some of its anathemas. There was considerable tightening of the internal life of the Roman Catholic Church brought about through the Council, including the first authoritative standardization of the Latin **liturgy** (which was accordingly known as the "Tridentine" rite). Trent represents the heart of the Counter-Reformation. As there was no further Roman Catholic Council until **Vatican I**, for more than 300 years all definitions of distinctive Anglican **doctrine** and identity were made in light of the decrees of Trent.

TRINITY. Belief in God as Trinity is the most basic defining feature of Christianity. The early **Councils**, often dealing with subtle heresies, adopted formulae which stated that there is but one God, but that the "Persons" of the Father, the Son, and the Holy Spirit are each fully God, so that there are three Persons in the one God. The **Anglican Communion** has always enthusiastically proclaimed belief in the Holy Trinity. This has been exemplified not only in its adherence to the **credal** affirmations of the first four centuries but also in its readiness for Trinitarian **liturgical** formulations (e.g., in the **baptismal** formula, the opening dialogue in the **litany** of the 1662 **Book of Common Prayer**, doxologies, longer endings of **collects**, and the blessing), in its church **dedications**, and in its retention of **Trinity Sunday**. Those who deny any part of the **doctrine** of the Trinity are usually viewed as putting themselves outside the sphere of Christianity. However, the masculine language involved in "Father" and "Son" (and in any pronouns referring to them) has led **feminists** to seek alternative nomenclature using more **inclusive language** for the three Persons of the Trinity. It is not clear that such alternatives suffice to sustain the classic doctrine.

TRINITY CHURCH, WALL STREET. The original Trinity Church was built on land purchased in Manhattan in 1696 and was opened for worship in 1698. The church received a charter and land grant from King **William III** in 1697. In 1705 its lands were increased by a grant from Queen Anne and the governor of the colony to 215 acres.

Three successive church buildings have stood on the original site in what is now Wall Street (and thus the center of the American financial industry). But the fame of Trinity Church arises from the uniquely large historic endowment that its valuable lands have given it. This was formalized as the "Grants Board" in 1971 and enables it now to administer large-scale charitable trust funds for disposal for Anglican projects and purposes throughout the world, often as channeled through the requests or recommendations of the **archbishop** of **Canterbury**. Trinity Church also gained some wide publicity as being only a stone's throw from the "Twin Towers" of the World Trade Center; **Rowan Williams**, then archbishop of **Wales**, was visiting the church at the very time the towers were destroyed by terrorists on 11 September 2001.

TRINITY SUNDAY. Trinity Sunday, the first Sunday after the **Feast** of **Pentecost**, was kept in the Middle Ages as a feature of the Church year in **England**, and the provision of **lectionary** and other **propers** in the period following was based on a scheme of "Sundays after Trinity." The Sunday itself was kept as a single "stand-alone" date, without eve or octave, and at the **Reformation** it passed unchanged into the Tudor and Stuart **Books of Common Prayer** in that form and consequently entered into Anglican **calendars** around the world. It was inherited by the Reformers as one of the "four seasons" for **ordinations**, so that the Wednesday, Friday, and Saturday prior to it were **ember** days, and they are listed explicitly as **fast** days for praying for the ordinations in the 1662 Book of Common Prayer. In the second half of the 20th century, the international and interdenominational pressure from the "Revised Common Lectionary" led to a tendency to date the relevant Sundays from Pentecost, rather than Trinity, but this became of less consequence as the modern **Roman Catholic** principle of "Sundays of the year" related the propers of each Sunday to the date in the civil calendar, rather than to the number of Sundays that had elapsed from a date of Pentecost, which itself derived from a movable **Easter**.

TUTU, DESMOND MPILO (1931–). Desmond Tutu was born of African parents in western Transvaal and was brought up in the pre-Nationalist context of apartheid. When he was around 10 years of age, he was amazed to see a white man (**Trevor Huddleston**) raise his hat to Tutu's mother, a gesture he had never seen from a white man before. In his teens, when living at the Community of the Resurrection hostel in Sophiatown, he spent nearly two years in the hospital with tuberculosis, and there Huddleston and his Christian impact helped shape Tutu's life.

Tutu trained as a teacher, but decided to leave schoolteaching in the wake of the Bantu Education Act, which came into force in March 1955. Instead he trained for **ordination**, and he was accordingly **ordained** as a **deacon** by Ambrose Reeves in the Johannesburg **diocese** in 1960. That was the year of the Sharpeville Riot, and Reeves was deported in 1961 before Tutu was ordained as a **presbyter**. In 1962 Tutu went to **England**, where he earned a first degree in theology and also a master's degree before returning in 1966 to teach in the segregated African seminary of Alice and to be Anglican chaplain to Fort Hare, one of the only three universities allowed to receive black Africans. His four years there, with much conflict and suffering, helped form in him a defiance of apartheid and a commitment to a just solution.

In 1970, Tutu then went to lecture in Lesotho, and from there in 1972 he went to become associate director of the Theological Fund, working in **London**. Then, with his contract for five years not half completed, he was called in 1974 to be **dean** of Johannesburg. As the first black dean of the **cathedral**, he elected to live in the black township of Soweto. This period saw his total engagement against apartheid, with his theology and all his powers united in that struggle. It was the time when children were shot when protesting in Soweto.

In 1976, Desmond Tutu was **consecrated bishop** of Lesotho, but in March 1978 he returned to Johannesburg as general secretary of the South African Council of Churches (SACC). There he became a world figure, a reputation enhanced when the South African government withdrew his passport and crowned in October 1984 by the award of the Nobel Peace Prize. His role became prophetic not simply because of the position he held but particularly through his own combination of committed discipleship, clear thought, and brilliant communication, sparkling with pointed humor.

In 1984 also he was elected bishop of Johannesburg and then in 1986 **archbishop** of Cape Town. Here he called for trade sanctions against the apartheid government, while pleading with the desperately disadvantaged black population to work peacefully for the political transition that was bound to come. In the late 1980s he claimed that his political orientation was all the stronger because all political opponents of apartheid had been locked up, and the task fell to the Christian leaders to sustain the protest. When democracy finally came and a free election was held in 1994, Tutu made it clear he not only had no political role to play but that he also wished his **clergy** generally to keep clear of such involvement. He reached retirement in 1996, but the Nelson Mandela government immediately called upon him to chair the "Truth and Reconciliation Commission," the means whereby the hatreds and cruelties of the past were to be named, admitted, forgiven, and left behind.

TYNDALE, WILLIAM (1494–1536). William Tyndale graduated at Magdalen Hall, Oxford, in 1512, continued his studies, and was **ordained** as a **deacon** and **presbyter** at unknown dates in the late 1510s. The publication of Erasmus's Greek text of the New Testament in 1516 appears to have affected him deeply, and around 1520 he became clear that his life's work was to lie in the translation of the **Bible** into English and the distribution of it as widely as possible. He came to **London** in 1522, and in 1523 sought the patronage of Cuthbert Tunstall, the bishop of London. When he failed in this and recognized the difficulties and dangers of publishing the New Testament in London, he left for the Continent. His first attempts at getting his translation published were in Cologne, but there in 1525 the printing was interrupted at an early stage and Tyndale had to flee. In Worms in early 1526 he achieved the publication of his first edition of the full New Testament in English, the foundation text for all succeeding versions until the 20th century and one very strongly present in the New Testament of the "Authorized Version" (the **King James Version**) of 1608. Copies of the New Testament quickly reached England (for which they were intended) and both brought about conversions and stoked up persecution.

From 1528 on, Tyndale worked from Antwerp. He engaged in written controversy with the authorities in **England** and worked at the Hebrew of the Old Testament until he published the Pentateuch in English in 1530. A revised New Testament followed in 1534. By this time, Tyndale's publications (New Testament, Pentateuch, and controversial letters and essays) probably constituted the most widespread and thoroughgoing force for **Reformation** principles in King **Henry VIII**'s England. But in 1535 he was arrested and in the following year tried for **heresy** through the intervention of **Roman Catholic** authorities on the Continent. Tyndale was condemned to be burned at the stake (actually being strangled first), and he is reported to have died saying, "Lord, open the king of England's eyes." While the actual date of his death is uncertain, Anglican **calendars** have usually commemorated him on 6 October.

– U –

UGANDA. Missionary work by Anglicans in the territory that is now Uganda was begun in 1876 by a pioneer team sent out by the **Church Missionary Society** (CMS) in London, among whom **Alexander Mackay** has remained famous. As there seemed to be a favorable hearing from the Baganda people and especially their chief Mutesa, further missionaries were sent, and steps were taken to establish a **diocese** of **Eastern Equatorial Africa**, based in **Mombasa**. There was a strong reaction by Mutesa around the end of 1879, however, and when he died in 1884, his successor, Mwanga, was a pagan. Soon after, **James Hannington**, having been consecrated in 1884 as the first **bishop** of the new diocese, arrived in **East Africa**. Marching up from the coast, he was put to death with his company on Mwanga's orders on 29 October 1885. When young Christian page boys of Mwanga's court (both **Roman Catholic** and Anglican) subsequently both showed maturity in the Christian faith and declined to participate in **homosexual** orgies at his command, he burned many alive, most notably on 3 June 1886. These are commemorated, as the Ugandan Martyrs, at the place of their martyrdom, Namugongo.

Within a short time, there came what is known as "a Christian revolution," a widespread turn to Christianity before the coming of colonialism. In 1890 a victory in battle brought Christians into power and also established **Protestantism** (in the Ugandan context, Anglicanism), as the dominant force. European missionaries were welcomed, and a strong Anglican Church grew from those beginnings, so much so that it called itself without qualification the Church of Uganda.

A separate diocese of Uganda was formed in 1897, and a central **cathedral** for the diocese was built on Namirembe Hill on the outskirts of Kampala. It was the second bishop, J. J. Willis (1908–1937), who was involved in the **Kikuyu Controversy** (1913–1915), which touched the whole **Anglican Communion**. A diocese of Upper Nile, covering the northern parts of Uganda, was separated from the parent diocese in 1926. During the interwar years, the Ugandan Church was deeply influenced by the East African Revival. In 1961, more dioceses were formed, as the Church of Uganda became the **province** of Uganda, **Rwanda**, and **Burundi**, with Leslie Brown, who had been bishop of Uganda since 1952, as its first **archbishop**. Independence for the nation came in 1962, and Brown was then succeeded in 1965 by the first Ugandan archbishop, Erica Sabiti. The province was enlarged in the 1970s by the creation of dioceses in Boga-Zaire, and was then reduced as Burundi, Rwanda, and Zaire became a separate province in 1980.

The Church of Uganda went through harrowing times during the dictatorship of Idi Amin between 1971 and 1979. **Janani Luwum**, who succeeded Sabiti as archbishop in 1974, led protests from the House of Bishops against the arbitrary cruelties, injustices, and torture of the Amin regime. This led to his assassination by Amin on 16 February 1977 and his recognition as a **martyr** by the entire Christian world. His statue stands among those of the 10 Christian martyrs of the 20th century chosen to adorn the west front of Westminster **Abbey**. Some bishops went into exile in the last days of Amin, and they returned after the **Tanzanian** army had "liberated" Uganda from the tyrant in 1979.

The Anglican Church in Uganda claims about one-third of the population as its adherents (another one-third or more being Roman Catholic). It is divided into 29 dioceses, with its provincial administration (which includes provision for medical and famine relief) on Namirembe Hill, and its theological training and resources in Bishop Tucker **Theological College**, now a Christian university, at Mukono.

The **calendars** of many Anglican provinces include Janani Luwum on 16 February (17 February through error in the Church of **England**), the Martyrs of Uganda on 3 June, and James Hannington on 29 October.

UNCTION. *See* ANOINTING.

UNIFORMITY. The **liturgical Reformation** in **England** was enforced by **Acts of Uniformity** in 1549, 1552, and 1559. The uniformity intended by these Acts was to be virtually exhaustive, in order that no liberty should remain for unreformed **clergy** to continue uses that had been superseded and thus abolished. The uniformity, being implemented by printed books, also now meant that the whole realm was to have a single use, and the preface to the 1549 **Book of Common Prayer** drew attention to the diversity of uses there had been in previous times.

The 1549 and 1552 Acts each had the text of their respective Book of Common Prayer **annexed** to the Act, but in 1559 the Act merely stated that the 1552 Book (with minor identified changes) was to be restored. The small changes in the Prayer Book in 1604 were authorized by royal warrant without any Act of Parliament.

After the Restoration in 1660, the previously existing Book of Common Prayer of 1604 was revised in **Convocation** in December 1661 and was then enforced by a new 1662 Act of Uniformity. The uniformity required by it removed all liberty in leading worship from the **Puritans** and enforced upon them the **ceremonies** to which they conscientiously objected. It also required invariable Episcopal **ordination** for those holding office in the Church of England and presiding at **Communion**, and such clergy also had to renounce the Solemn League and Covenant by which those who had held office in the **Commonwealth** period had been bound. The Act was a major cause of the departure from office of between 1,000 and 2,000 ministers before it came into force on 24 August 1662.

Since 1662 all legislative moves in respect of liturgical uniformity in England have been toward a relaxing of its rigors. The term "uniformity" has rarely appeared in other parts of the **Anglican Communion**.

UNITED CHURCH OF ENGLAND AND IRELAND. At the **Reformation**, the historic church in **Ireland** was reformed by force of Parliament, just as the Church of **England** was, but the two Churches were viewed as belonging to two separate nations, indeed, as being two Churches. However, when the union of the two nations occurred on 1 January 1801, the two Churches became the "United Church of England and Ireland," a title found in the **Books of Common Prayer** published between 1801 and 1870.

One of the most notable features of the Westminster Parliament's control of the United Church was the legislation of 1833 providing for the union of sees in Ireland. It was this that led to **John Keble**'s Assize Sermon of 14 July 1833—which in turn led to the ***Tracts for the Times***, the **Anglo-Catholic** movement, and vast changes in the Church of England. The uniting of sees was arguably a desirable reform in itself, as, throughout all Ireland outside the six counties in Ulster, the Church of Ireland was in a tiny minority alongside the **Roman Catholic Church**. The Roman Catholic Church claimed the allegiance of well over 90 percent of the population in the other 26 counties, and the polarization from **Protestantism** was assisted by a political confrontation also. Correspondingly the structure of the Church of Ireland in those 26 counties looked top-heavy with **bishops** and **dioceses** and needed reform. But the 1833 protest lay against the peremptory unilateral action by the Westminster Parliament, a body that, with the coming of the Roman Catholic franchise, was itself no longer a visibly Anglican source of **authority**.

Even with the restructuring, in the following years the continued **establishment** of the United Church was felt as a provocation by the Roman Catholic population of Ireland. Thus in 1868 a general election (of the whole United Kingdom) was fought on the one electoral issue: whether the Church of Ireland should be separated and disestablished. The answer was yes, and the united church ceased to be on 31 December 1870; the two Anglican churches separated from each other, one still established, the other now disestablished.

UNITED NATIONS (UN). Through the granting of a special privilege by the United Nations in 1990, the **Anglican Communion** was enabled to send an official observer to the United Nations. Funding was arranged starting in 1991, and the **Anglican Consultative Council** (ACC) appointed Sir Paul Reeves, who had been **archbishop** (1980–1985) and then governor-general of **New Zealand** (1985–1990), as the first observer. Reeves held the post in 1991–1993. From 1994 to 1999, the position was held by **Bishop** James Ottley, previously bishop of Panama in the **Episcopal Church (United States of America)**. There were then two one-year interim appointments of Bishop Paul Moore (1999–2000) and Bishop Herbert Donovan (2000–2001). In 2002 a substantive appointment was again made, and **Archdeacon** Taimalelagi Fagamalama Tuatagaloa-Matalavea of Samoa became the observer.

UNITED SOCIETY FOR THE PROPAGATION OF THE GOSPEL (USPG). In 1965 the **Society for the Propagation of the Gospel**, an Anglican **missionary society** in **England**, united with the **Universities Mission to Central Africa** (UMCA), to form the United Society for the Propagation of the Gospel. The smaller Cambridge Mission to Delhi also joined USPG in 1968. The resultant society has since then shared with the **Church Missionary Society** (CMS) the leadership in overseas missionary societies of the Church of England. There was a general understanding that the USPG represented **Anglo-Catholic** parishes and generally serviced Anglo-Catholic **dioceses** abroad, while CMS was correspondingly **Evangelical**. However, USPG moved into the CMS headquarters building in 1988, and until 2004 the **Anglican Consultative Council** (ACC) located the **Anglican Communion Office** there also, so that a fruitful juxtaposition of agencies was achieved, not least through a shared library, chapel, and other facilities. The societies have also worked together in providing joint resources for the **Anglican Communion** through their respective residential colleges at Selly Oak in Birmingham, and in helping fund **Partners in Mission** and similar consultations in various parts of the world.

UNITED STATES. It is thought that the first Anglican **Communion** service in the territory that is now the United States was celebrated on the West Coast by Sir Francis Drake's chaplain during his circumnavigation of the globe in 1577–1580. Anglicans settled on the East Coast from early in the 17th century. In 1633 a jurisdiction over British chaplaincies outside of **England** was conferred on the **bishop** of **London** by parliamentary statute. While this primarily affected **European** congregations, its terms were so drawn as to include the American colonies as well. Thus, until the American Revolution, the Anglican congregations in the various American colonies were technically under the Episcopal care of the bishop of London, and anyone wishing to be **ordained** crossed the Atlantic to London for that purpose. No bishop of London ever visited the colonies and so there were no **confirmations** there (curiously, two **nonjuring** bishops were **consecrated** for America in 1722, but they were apparently not welcomed).

When independence came, there was a move in some states to follow through the logic of having no bishop and so to become overtly **Presbyterian**. However, in Connecticut the Episcopalian **clergy** met and elected **Samuel Seabury** as their bishop, and he came to London in 1783 to seek consecration. After a 12-month delay, he was finally consecrated in Aberdeen, **Scotland**, on 14 November 1784 by Scottish Episcopalian bishops; he returned to America to a far from unanimously favorable reception. The British Parliament soon after changed the law to provide for the consecration of bishops for overseas territories without requiring them to take an **oath** to the monarch, and the next two American bishops (**William White** of Pennsylvania and **Samuel Provoost** of New York) were consecrated in London in 1787.

The first **General Convention** was held in 1785 and constituted the **Protestant Episcopal Church in the United States of America** (PECUSA). Seabury and the Anglicans of Connecticut were notably absent from this Convention, objecting to powers being given to the **laity**—and the convention thus lacked a House of Bishops. However, after the consecration of White and Provoost, a reconciliation was effected. There was then a full participation by the whole of the Episcopal Church in the determinative Convention of 1789, which adopted new **canons** and a marginally revised **Book of Common Prayer**, in which the **eucharistic** rite sprang in large part from the 1764 Scottish **liturgy**, and the state prayers were rewritten for the republic.

The General Convention has usually met at three-year intervals since. It is distinguished from others in the **Anglican Communion** by a unique voting system in which the House of Deputies (four clergy and four **laypeople** from each **diocese**) may vote by dioceses, the eight deputies of each diocese voting among themselves on a diocesan basis and then registering the overall majority as the mind of the diocese. In the House of Bishops, all retired bishops as well as **suffragans** and **coadjutors** have a seat. Overseas and **missionary** dioceses are fully part of the single church, and French and Spanish are, jointly with English, official **languages** of the Church. During the U.S. Civil War (1861–1865), the dioceses in the Southern states seceded and formed the Protestant Episcopal Church in the Confederate States of America, but reunited with the continuing PECUSA when the war was over.

The dioceses are grouped regionally into **provinces**, but for most purposes dioceses are independent and nearly autonomous, and the General Convention provides the main supradiocesan authority. The presiding bishop is the bishop of no diocese, and although treated as the **primate** for international purposes, does not have the title of "**archbishop**," "**metropolitan**," or "primate." The title "**Protestant**" in the official name of the church was dropped from use in 1967, when the General Convention adopted a preamble to its constitution stating that it "is otherwise known as The Episcopal Church (which name is hereby recognized as also designating the Church)." Thus the initials ECUSA (**Episcopal Church [United States of America]**) replaced PECUSA from that date (within this dictionary, the titles are used in relation to the dating to which they refer, whether before or after 1967). ECUSA became the substantive title of the Church in 1979.

Historically, all overseas missionary dioceses founded from PECUSA were initially constituent dioceses of PECUSA, but steps have been taken to enable such dioceses to form independent provinces, as has happened, for example, in **Brazil** in 1965, the **Philippines** in 1990, **Mexico** in 1995, and the **Central Region of America** in 1998.

ECUSA provided the first **woman** bishop in the Anglican Communion when Barbara Harris became coadjutor bishop of Massachusetts in February 1989. It has been the subject of various minor secessions in the years since women were first ordained to the **presbyterate** in January 1977. Churchpeople declaring themselves "traditionalists" have labeled the leadership of the Church as "**liberal**" and as ready to compromise on the teachings of scripture, **tradition**, and morality, and these groups have at times left ECUSA and provided patterns of "**continuing Anglicanism**."

Since 1999 there has also been an unauthorized move by Anglican archbishops elsewhere in the Communion to consecrate bishops for an alternative oversight in America, to which "traditionalist" parishes are then encouraged to affiliate. The election of an openly practicing **homosexual** divorced man, Gene Robinson, as bishop of New Hampshire in 2003 increased the pressure for such moves; however, the opposition now was not simply at the fringes. The House of Bishops at the General Convention of 2003 ratified the choice of Robinson 62–45, and an outcry from around the world led to the archbishop of **Canterbury**, **Rowan Williams**, convening an emergency meeting of the primates of the Communion in October 2003. A statement by the primates (which included as a signatory Frank Griswold, the presiding bishop of ECUSA) foresaw deep distress in the Anglican Communion if the consecration went ahead on 2 November. When it did so, the archbishop of Canterbury appointed the **Lambeth Commission**, to consider how the Communion could sustain unity in the face of such divisive actions. The commission reported in October 2004 in the **Windsor Report**.

A further meeting of the primates in February 2005 called upon ECUSA to refrain from sending representatives to the **Anglican Consultative Council** (ACC) until the Lambeth Conference in 2008. The ECUSA House of Bishops responded by stating that they would consecrate no person at all to be a bishop until summer 2006. When ACC-13 met in Nottingham in June 2005, ECUSA members attended to make a short presentation of their position, but took no other part in the agenda. *See also* CUMMINS, GEORGE DAVID; *EPISCOPUS VAGANS*; REFORMED EPISCOPAL CHURCH.

UNITY. *See* ECUMENISM.

UNIVERSITIES MISSION TO CENTRAL AFRICA (UMCA). UMCA was an English overseas **missionary society** formed in response to the appeal of David Livingstone in the Senate House at Cambridge in 1857. It was strongly **Anglo-Catholic**, and, after an abortive start when Charles Mackenzie was consecrated as a **missionary** bishop of the Zambezi in Cape Town in 1861 but died soon after in Nyasaland (now Malawi), the base of the mission and title of the see were transferred in 1863 to **Zanzibar**. Further **dioceses** serviced by UMCA were formed in Nyasaland in 1892, Northern Rhodesia (now Zambia) in 1910, Masasi in 1926, and South West

Tanganyika in 1952. The **cathedral** in Zanzibar was built on the site of the previous slave market, and its name became known worldwide through **Frank Weston**, bishop of Zanzibar from 1908 to 1924. A **province** was formed in **Central Africa** in 1955, including Nyasaland and Northern Rhodesia. Similarly a province of **East Africa** was formed in 1960, uniting the UMCA-related Tanganyikan and Zanzibar dioceses with the more **Evangelical** dioceses of Central Tanganyika and **Mombasa**. As these changes happened in Central Africa, UMCA decided to seek a continuing role within a larger missionary society and world context and therefore united with the **Society for the Propagation of the Gospel** (SPG) in 1965, to form the **United Society for the Propagation of the Gospel** (USPG).

USAGERS. *See* NONJURORS.

– V –

VALIDITY. Any rite or ordinance that is to be administered once for a lifetime and is to be viewed thereafter as having continued force necessitates a concept of validity. **Baptism** is the most obvious and widespread example of such a rite. Because it is of great importance, and because a person once baptized remains a baptized person thereafter, the issue as to whether or not a baptism has been administered at some point earlier in life is an important question, and it raises issues about the necessary components of the event for it to be a "true" (or "valid") baptism. This accounts for the questions raised in the 16th- and 17th-century **Books of Common Prayer** when a child baptized privately (being in danger of **death**) was then later brought to church. It is also of relevance when someone baptized as an infant later seeks "believer's baptism"—because those who reject infant baptism are not saying that someone can be baptized twice (there is no such thing as "rebaptism") but rather that infant baptism is not valid and is not therefore baptism at all.

Similar lines of argument attach to issues of **ordination**. Anglicans have essentially said to non-Episcopalians that ordination is valid only when performed by a **bishop**—and more specifically by a bishop in the historic line of succession. Meanwhile, **Roman Catholics** have stated about Anglicans, in the 1896 encyclical ***Apostolicae Curae***, that Anglican orders are invalid on the grounds of a lack of the right "intention"; thus Anglican **clergy** joining the Church of Rome, if they are to **minister** as **priests**, are ordained *ab initio*, with virtually no recognition of their previous ordination.

Similar conditions might arguably attach to the covenant of matrimony, which involves vows of lifelong fidelity. The Roman Catholic Church has always acted on the basis that only death can end the bond (or *vinculum*) of a valid **marriage**, but it has also taught that, if two partners in what has been treated as a marriage decide to separate, an inquiry can be held as to whether the conditions for a valid marriage existed at the point of the original ceremony, and, if any such condition was not fulfilled, then a decree of "**nullity**" can be obtained and the two persons are not married at all. This is, of course, what King **Henry VIII** was seeking. Other Churches have tended to act on a different supposition—that, although the vows of marriage are to live together "till death us do part," the bond established is not absolutely unbreakable, and in certain circumstances it is truer to say that the couple genuinely were married and now are not. The marriage has died. Anglicans have been divided on this issue.

Issues relating to the validity of **eucharistic celebrations** are somewhat different, as there is no suggestion that there is a run-on implication from any one eucharist of the past into the future; the eucharist is not in the category of rites that are given once for life. Thus discussions of eucharistic validity are usually about the advice or guidance to be given as to the standing of a potential **president** of the eucharist, and thus as to the propriety of joining in a particular future celebration, without comparable concern as to whether anyone's past practice had such far-reaching present or future implications.

VATICAN I. The First Vatican **Council** was convened by **Pope** Pius IX in Rome in late 1869 specifically for the purpose of defining and promulgating the **infallibility** of the pope, when speaking *ex cathedra*, without any necessary participation by a General Council or the prior consent of the faithful **laity**. While the definition was made under extreme political pressure (as the Papal States were alienated by Garibaldi) and the Council broke up quickly after defining the infallibility (and arguably never addressed the complete agenda attaching to the definition), it formed the basis for the retrospective **validation** by a Council of Pius IX's own *ex cathedra* decree of 1854 affirming the **Immaculate Conception** of the Virgin **Mary** as *de fide.*

The definition of papal infallibility polarized Anglicans further from **Roman Catholics**, and, although the **bishops** at the Council had only two voting against the definition (on the stated grounds that it was "inopportune" rather than untrue), there were both abstaining and absentee bishops. The definition provoked a schism within Roman Catholicism. The major impact occurred in Germany and Switzerland, and it arose from the opposition of J. J. I. von Dollinger, a theologian of Tübingen, who led up to half a million Roman Catholics into a new extension of the **Old Catholics** of Utrecht, Deventer, and Haarlem in Holland. Small separations occurred also in Spain and Portugal and led to the formation of the **Spanish Reformed Episcopal Church** and the **Lusitanian Church**, respectively, in the two countries. These two Churches are now extraprovincial **dioceses** of the **Anglican Communion**.

One further papal *ex cathedra* decree has followed, when Pius XII in 1950 declared infallibly the bodily **assumption** of the Virgin Mary into **heaven**. This decree, alongside the Immaculate Conception decree, provides the test case as to whether the pope can speak infallibly, and that question in turn underlies the **Anglican–Roman Catholic International Commission** (ARCIC) statements on **Authority** in the Church. Despite this, both Marian decrees were ignored in the 1999 joint statement, *The Gift of Authority,* which attributes at least a theoretical infallibility to the papal office, without discussing those Marian decrees. Instead ARCIC-2 discussed Mary in its final agreed statement, *Mary: Grace and Hope in Christ* (2005).

VATICAN II. Pope John XXIII, who was pope from 1958 to 1963, announced in 1959 that he was convening a General **Council**. Its outcome was to be not **doctrinal**, but pastoral—its task to be *aggiornamento*, its outlook to be **ecumenical**. The Council met through the four autumns of 1962–1965, though John XXIII died before the second session began. Both the Council's style and its actual published documents changed the face of the Church of Rome—not least toward the Anglican churches. Its own task was to renew the face the **Roman Catholic** Church presented to the world, not only to enrich the quality of faith and practice of the Church of Rome itself but also, in so doing, to narrow the ground of difference from other Churches and make the Roman Church more ecumenically credible. Its main internal changes came with fully **vernacular** (and revised) **liturgical** norms, an encouragement of the use of the scriptures (and a succession of new translations), a new affirmation of the abilities and gifts of **laypeople**, and a new openness to other Christian denominations. In relation to Anglicans, Vatican II led to setting up an international dialogue on a semipermanent basis, and this in turn resulted in the creation of the **Anglican–Roman Catholic International Commission** (ARCIC), which first met in 1969. It also brought the Roman Catholic Church into open participation in ecumenical agencies and councils in every part of the world, though not into membership of the **World Council of Churches**.

VERNACULAR LITURGY. It was a foundation principle of the English **Reformation** that the **Bible** and the **Prayer Book** should be available to the people in their vernacular **language**. After a period of struggle (marked by the **martyrdom** of **William Tyndale**), King **Henry VIII** ordered in 1537 that the Bible be set up in churches in English, and the people taught from it in their own language. The beginning of the **liturgical** change came with the 1544 **Litany** in English, and it was followed by *The Order of the Communion* in March 1548 and the complete new **Book of Common Prayer** in the English language in June 1549. The process was completed with the publishing of **ordination rites** in 1550. The new liturgy was reinforced in the 1552 Prayer Book and entrenched as a matter of **doctrine** in the Forty-Two **Articles** of 1553 and the Thirty-Nine Articles of 1571.

The principle was reversed in Queen **Mary I**'s reign (1553–1558) when the Latin rites were restored. While Article XXIV said that worshippers should not be addressed in languages they did not understand, little effort was made in the 16th and 17th centuries to provide the Book of Common Prayer in Cornish, **Welsh**, or **Irish**, though the 1662 **Act of Uniformity** did require a translation into Welsh. The principle was, however, very fully observed in the permission for the ancient universities to continue using Latin; and Latin translations of the 1559 and 1662 Books were made, specifically to be the "vernacular" in such learned circles. A French version of the

1604 Book was used in the Channel Islands from 1616, and the 1662 Book was similarly translated in 1667. In **Canada**, the French version was available in Quebec province from the 18th century, and in the **United States**, successive versions of the Book of Common Prayer since 1789 have been translated into both French and Spanish for U.S. congregations, and through their availability those translations have also been used in Francophone Africa and in Latin America, respectively.

With the **missionary** expansion of the **Anglican Communion**, the principle of teaching and worshipping in the vernacular was the major concession usually made to African, Asian, or other indigenous cultures. This course was prompted by the provision of vernacular Bibles by the British and Foreign Bible Society (BFBS) and was in line with Article XXIV and the perceived needs of pioneer **evangelism**. However, other forms of **inculturation**—for example, in **music**, art, **architecture**, or **ceremonial**—were usually very slow to march with the use of the vernacular language. This became of greater concern in the latter part of the 20th century.

VESTING. A vesting of the candidate during the **ordination rites** was used only for **bishops** in the 1552 and 1662 **Ordinals**, and there it was ordered that the candidate, already wearing a rochet, after the formal interrogation "shall . . . put on the rest of the episcopal habit," that is, the black chimere. However, the return of **eucharistic vestments** in the 19th century has led in some **provinces** to a vesting of **deacons** and **priests** (or **presbyters**) with stoles, across one shoulder for deacons and around the neck for presbyters. This is usually done after the act of ordination and the giving of the **Bible**. In some provinces, there is also a vesting in the chasuble. The comparable vesting for a new bishop at that point in the rite would be the receiving of a miter, pectoral **cross**, or ring (or any combination of them), and such "vestings" do occur in a small number of provinces.

VESTMENTS. It has been characteristic of Anglicans to robe the officiants at **liturgical** services. At the **Reformation**, the existing **eucharistic** vestments, while retained as an option in 1549, were in 1552 set aside, and the surplice, previously used in "choir offices" only, was then ordered for all **Book of Common Prayer** services (and a **bishop** was to wear a rochet). This was reinforced during her reign by Queen **Elizabeth I**'s *Injunctions* of 1559 and by **Archbishop Matthew Parker**'s "Advertisements" of 1566, though the surface meaning of the "**Ornaments Rubric**" printed at the beginning of **Morning Prayer** in the 1559 Prayer Book might have suggested otherwise. However, the issue in Elizabeth's reign, and through until 1662, was not how to restrain Romanizers from wearing full eucharistic vestments, but how to get **Puritans** to wear even a surplice. The 1604 **canons** provide for the surplice with hood, or "decent Tippet of black" (canon 58), except that in **cathedrals** and collegiate churches the officiant at Holy **Communion** was to wear also a cope "the **Gospeller** and Epistler agreeably" (canon 24). Apart from this mention of a cope, no distinction is drawn between any of the Prayer Book services.

The Puritans made a last attempt to have the surplice made optional at the **Savoy Conference** in 1661, and, with their submission or exclusion the following year, that controversy was then finished in the Church of **England**. However, the "Ornaments Rubric" before Morning Prayer in the 1662 Book followed the 1559 rubric fairly closely and again made reference to what was in use "by the **authority** of Parliament in the second year of King **Edward VI**." The reply of the bishops to the Puritans' "exceptions" at the Savoy Conference suggests that they read this historical reference as enforcing the surplice (which, arguably, was not its true meaning at all). At any rate, the standard use of surplice, hood, and tippet (scarf) was universal for almost 200 years after 1662, and thus spread throughout the world wherever Anglicanism was to be found. The cassock, whether worn by **clergy** beneath the surplice or independently of it, was never a strictly liturgical vestment, but an all-purpose clergy garment.

With the rise of **Anglo-Catholicism** in the 19th century, the issue of eucharistic vestments arose at an early stage. In England, the first recorded revival of such uses dates from around 1851. The **Roman Catholic** eucharistic vestments have traditionally been:

- alb (the white "foundation garment")
- stole (a strip of colored material worn as a scarf around the neck)
- amice (a collar, formed by folding back a hood)
- maniple (a strip of material hanging from the left wrist)

- chasuble (a poncho-type of outer garment, dropped over the head and often carrying designs)

Apart from the alb (which is always white), the other four vestments would be in matching **colors**, varying with the liturgical seasons and corresponding to other use of changing seasonal colors within the church building. Other assistants at a **celebration**, **lay** or **ordained**, would sometimes wear a dalmatic or tunicle, also in matching colors. Colored stoles, sometimes worn over a surplice, sometimes with an alb, were adopted in many parts of the Communion, far beyond those parts where the full set of eucharistic vestments was worn.

The unauthorized adoption of Roman Catholic vestments caused much conflict in the Church of England in the second half of the 19th century. In an **established** church, this conflict reached as far as Parliament, and the major outcome was the Royal Commission on Ecclesiastical Discipline (1904–1906). This commission reported with a recommendation that the **Convocations** draft a revision of the Ornaments Rubric to make some provision for the use of the eucharistic vestments. This recommendation led by a devious path to the abortive 1927–1928 attempts to get a complete new Prayer Book authorized by Parliament, but never produced a credible revised Ornaments Rubric. In 1965 a new canon (B8) was authorized, allowing the officiant at Holy Communion to wear either a surplice or alb with scarf or stole and, if the stole is used, then "other customary vestments" may be added; the canon also stated that the Church of England does not attach any **doctrinal** difference to the permitted diversity of vesture. Meanwhile, the use of the Roman Catholic vestments, whether allowed by the canons of individual **provinces** or not, has spread far and wide within the **Anglican Communion**, including many parts that would never have described themselves as Anglo-Catholic.

Since **Vatican II**, the maniple, and to a lesser extent the amice, have been regularly omitted in Roman Catholic usage. Anglican practice has tended to follow these changes.

The vesture of bishops, while mentioned in the 1552 ornaments rubric, has not recurred in the canons of the Church of England. From the Reformation on, the anticipated wear was rochet (the equivalent of the surplice) and chimere with scarf and sleeve-bands. The black chimere (in which bishops are initially **consecrated** in many provinces) over the rochet has been popularly known as "magpie." The red chimere (which with the rochet are known as "Convocation robes") probably derives from the doctoral gown, as bishops in England were until 1960 awarded a "Lambeth D.D." by the archbishop of **Canterbury** the day after consecration. A pectoral **cross** is conventional among bishops also. Miters reappeared toward the end of the 19th century and spread rapidly; they are worn with cope or eucharistic vestments; the first archbishop of Canterbury to wear one since the Reformation was **Cosmo Lang** in 1929. There is a wide variety of usage as to when a bishop wears or doffs the miter during liturgy, though the purist answer has always been that the miter is doffed for prayer (even for prayers accompanying the laying on of hands in **ordination**). Provinces vary as to whether miters are in regular usage at all. But it is more universal for bishops to wear a pectoral cross, and they usually carry a pastoral staff when involved in liturgy within their own dioceses.

In some parts of the Anglican Communion, there is very little use of liturgical vesture; in others, local forms are used (as, for instance, the use of a chief's cloak among indigenous **Canadians** and of indigenous ponchos in Peru). In some provinces there is distinctive vesture for lay **readers**. In formal rites, not only assisting ministers but also acolytes and servers may be robed, and the use of special choir robes is very widespread.

VIRGIN MARY. *See* MARY, MOTHER OF JESUS CHRIST.

VIRGINIA REPORT. Resolution 18 of the 1988 **Lambeth Conference** called for "further exploration of the meaning and nature of **Communion**," being pressed in that direction both by issues about the unity of Anglicanism and by stresses within that unity occasioned by the **ordination** of **women** as **presbyters** and the likely ordination of them as **bishops**. The **archbishop** of **Canterbury** convened a consultation at Virginia Theological Seminary in December 1991 to begin the exploration. This group produced an initial report entitled *Belonging Together*, which was circulated around the **Anglican Communion** for the next two years. Robin Eames, the archbishop of **Armagh** and chairman of the **Eames Commission**, chaired this and subsequent meetings, not least because the work of the Eames Commission was being enlarged within the consultation's task.

The group met again, now as the **Inter-Anglican Theological and Doctrinal Commission**, at Virginia Theological Seminary in December 1994 and January 1996 to consider the responses and produce a final report. This, *The Virginia Report*, was published as part of *Being Anglican in the Third Millennium*, the report of the 10th **Anglican Consultative Council** meeting (ACC-10), held in Panama City in October 1996. *The Virginia Report* contained an exploration in depth both of primacy and oversight and of the nature of Communion, and it was a major feature of the agenda of Section III of the 1998 **Lambeth Conference**. Resolution III.8 of that conference welcomed the report and stated that more work needed to be done both "with respect to the report's discussion of reason in relation to the primacy of Holy Scripture" and in the study of "whether effective communication at all levels, does not require appropriate instruments, with due safeguards, not only for legislation, but also for oversight." *The Virginia Report* itself was reproduced within the published report of the 1998 Lambeth Conference.

– W –

WAFERS. *See* BREAD.

WALES. The historic **dioceses** in Wales (St. Asaph, Bangor, St. David's, and Llandaff) date from Celtic times, with names of **bishops** first recorded in the sixth century, prior to the foundation of **Canterbury**. These dioceses were fully part of the **province** of Canterbury within the Church of **England** at the **Reformation**, and the Principality of Wales was fully part of King **Henry VIII**'s kingdom. Therefore, Henry's Acts of Parliament separating the Church of England from Rome, as well as the later Acts of King **Edward VI** and Queen **Elizabeth I** that put through the Reformation, affected Wales just as they did England. However in 1662 the **Act of Uniformity** required translations of the annexed **Book of Common Prayer** into the Welsh **language** within a stated length of time (interestingly, the Act named the bishop of Hereford as responsible with the four Welsh bishops for securing the translation).

For various reasons, the 18th-century **Evangelical Revival** led Welsh Evangelicals into almost total secession, resulting in a corresponding strengthening of the free church chapels, and in the 19th century this section of the population began to call for the disestablishment of the Anglican dioceses in Wales, as being unrepresentative of Christianity in Wales yet elevated by the **establishment** into a falsely privileged position. This political thrust reached its desired end in 1912, when the Welsh Church Act began its journey through the Lords and Commons. Its implementation was delayed by the outbreak of World War I, but it was revived and, with small amendments, enacted in 1919. Under its terms, the following year the four dioceses in Wales were released from the province of Canterbury by vote in **Convocation** and were thus canonically separated from the Church of England.

As had happened with the Church of **Ireland** in 1871, the four dioceses then became a voluntary body, forming themselves into a new province with its own constitution and making its own **canons**, thereby creating a new diocese of Monmouth (soon to be followed by Swansea and Brecon). The role of the **parish** church in relation to the rights of parishioners to **marry** in it remained protected by law, and parishes on the border of England could choose to belong to the established Church of England still and be transferred to the relevant English diocese. There was some degree of disendowment, but less than had been threatened before World War I.

The Church in Wales (as its title became, in deference to the sensitivities of the chapels) has a **metropolitan**, known as the **archbishop** of Wales, who is elected by the House of Bishops from among the bishops of any diocese in Wales. The Church has become distinguished for its vigorous bilingual policy, giving scope to the use of the Welsh **language** in every part of its life, not least in its **liturgical** revision. It has its own centers of theology, and despite the hostility that led to its disestablishment, it has strong **ecumenical** relationships with other churches in Wales. It shares with the other Anglican Churches of Britain and Ireland in the **Porvoo Declaration** relationship of Communion with the Nordic and Baltic **Lutheran Churches**. In 2002 the then archbishop of Wales, **Rowan Williams**, became the first bishop from outside the Church of England to be nominated as archbishop of **Canterbury** since the Reformation.

WARDENS. The provision of two **lay** officers, known as wardens or churchwardens, in each **parish** is part of the historic character of the Church of **England**. The pattern has spread around the **Anglican Communion**. They are traditionally chosen by the incumbent and the people, sometimes with the "fallback" provision that, if they cannot agree, the incumbent will choose one, and the people the other. Until the coming of official church councils (mostly in the 20th century), the wardens were usually the only responsible lay officers of a parish. **Traditionally** churchwardens carried staffs (or "wands") on formal occasions as symbols of their office and preceded the **bishop** in procession when he or she was visiting the parish. *See also* LAITY.

WATERLOO DECLARATION. The Anglican Church in **Canada** engaged in conversations with the Evangelical **Lutheran Church** in Canada beginning in 1983. From this emerged two stages of the Canadian Lutheran–Anglican Dialogue (CLAD), which led in 1989 to an "interim **eucharistic** sharing" between the two churches. This experience led to further convergence, and an agreement in 1995 to work for **full Communion** by 2001. A joint working group in June 1997 produced at Waterloo, Ontario, "The Waterloo Declaration" as a draft basis and definition of this full Communion. In its text, there was drafted a recognition by each that the other holds the apostolic faith, an affirmation of **episcopacy** in each church, an actual declaration of full Communion, and a series of future commitments of joint growth. The declaration was circulated to both churches in a resource book, *Called to Full Communion*, and became, as intended, the basis of the actual decisions undertaken by both churches in 2001 to enter full Communion.

WESLEY, JOHN (1703–1791), AND CHARLES (1707–1788). Born into a **clergy** family at Epworth, the Wesley brothers were both **ordained** as Anglican clergy in the 1720s. John became a fellow of Lincoln College, Oxford, and there helped found the Holy Club, a band of friends who, in somewhat dissolute times, bound themselves by a rigorous rule of life. Charles also belonged to the Holy Club. One of the derisory titles given them by their mockers was the "**Methodists**," a title that came into its own later.

John Wesley crossed to the Georgia colony in 1735 as a "**missionary**" with the **Society for the Propagation of the Gospel** (SPG), though in fact he was simply a chaplain rather clumsily pastoring a congregation in a colony. On shipboard, frightened in a storm, he was deeply impressed by the calm faith of some **Moravians** there with him. On his return from the chaplaincy in 1738, with a deep sense of need, he sought out the Moravians in **London**, until on 24 May 1738 at a Moravian meeting he felt his heart "strangely warmed" and was assured of being **justified** through faith. Soon he was preaching conversion up and down the land, often in the open air, and for 10 years his brother, who had undergone a similar experience three days before him, followed the same path.

The brothers' itinerancy and open-air preaching took them into and across the **parishes** of the settled Anglican clergy and led to a polarization from them. New converts acknowledged no duties to their parish churches (and were often turned away or cold-shouldered by them), and they found their home in the revivalist atmosphere of the "societies" of "the people called Methodists." While John Wesley believed that the "societies" were in some sense within the life of the Church of **England**, the reality was that his own organization, with **lay** preachers and a breaking of each local gathering into "classes" with class leaders, quickly became self-sufficient (except only for the provision of the **sacrament**) and established its own chapels as meeting places. The contribution of Charles Wesley was largely that of a prolific and inspired hymnwriter, and his **hymns** were sung with a fervor uncharacteristic of Anglicans, but highly enriching to the spiritual lives of the Methodist people.

Although John Wesley came to believe that in scripture there is no difference between an **elder** or **presbyter** and a **bishop**, he stayed his hand from acting on this until a late stage. Then in 1784 he "set aside" by the laying on of hands Thomas Coke, a man already a presbyter in Anglican **orders**, as "superintendent" of the Methodist societies in the **United States**, and Coke on arrival called himself "bishop." American Methodists have been "episcopal" ever since. John Wesley went on to ordain **ministers**, first of all for Methodists in **Scotland**, and finally three for ministry in England; and this formally completed the separation from the Church of England. After his death, the lay preachers were commissioned to act as ministers and administer the sacraments.

The Wesleys are remembered by Anglicans for their labors in the **gospel**, their contribution to the **Evangelical Revival** of the 18th century on both sides of the Atlantic, their developing of lay **ministry**, and their writings in both prose and hymnody. They are commemorated together on 24 May in the modern **calendars** of the Church of England and in the Anglican Church in **Australia**, and on 3 March (the day following John Wesley's death) in the **Episcopal Church (United States of America).**

WEST AFRICA. The first Anglican **missionary** to West Africa was the Reverend Thomas Thompson, sent by the **Society for the Propagation of the Gospel** to the Gold Coast (now Ghana) in 1752. Over the next 100 years various societies and individuals engaged in scattered missionary efforts around the West African coast, the earliest settled pattern emerging in **Sierra Leone**, where there was the rehabilitation of released slaves. **Dioceses** followed over the next 100 years: Sierra Leone in 1852, the Niger (subsequently Equatorial West Africa) in 1864, Accra in 1909, Lagos in 1919, and Gambia and the Rio Pongas in 1935. These five dioceses were formed into the **province** of West Africa in 1951, and it was within that framework that Africans were appointed and **consecrated** as diocesan **bishops**, slightly ahead of the independence gained by the colonies from their colonial powers. Five new dioceses were created in **Nigeria** in the 1950s. The constitution of the province was finally adopted in 1963; under its terms, the **archbishop** of West Africa may be the bishop of any of the constituent dioceses and is chosen by his fellow bishops.

In 1977 the diocese of Liberia, constitutionally (because of its history) part of the **Episcopal Church (United States of America)**, entered an agreed association with the province. The Nigerian dioceses left the province in 1979 to develop a new province on their own. The province of West Africa then retained the four dioceses of Gambia and Guinea, Sierra Leone, and Accra and Kumasi in Ghana. In 1981, Sierra Leone was divided into Freetown and Bo, and four new dioceses were formed in Ghana. In March 1982 Liberia's status was upgraded into full membership, and in 1985 Gambia and Guinea became two separate dioceses. Cameroon also became a missionary diocese.

WEST INDIES. Anglicanism in the West Indies derives from English settlers who colonized some islands and drove the Spanish out of others in the 16th and 17th centuries. They remained "Church of **England**," and in the British colonies of the Caribbean, the Church was "**established**" from the earliest coming of chaplains in the 17th century. Some **evangelism** among slaves occurred (the reference in the **preface** to the 1662 **Book of Common Prayer** to "natives in our plantations" may be germane), though there was a widespread hostility of planters to any education or instruction of slaves that might create in them discontent with their lot. Anglican **clergy** provided chaplaincies for settlers from the 17th century, and a lead was given by the **Society for the Propagation of the Gospel** (SPG), which owned estates in Barbados bequeathed by Thomas Codrington, where provision of a chaplain was made for education and religious instruction of the slaves. Codrington College was founded between 1714 and 1742 and, as a **theological college**, provided training for ordinands almost 100 years earlier than any comparable institution elsewhere in the Anglican world. However, as with the American colonies, the only Episcopal oversight came from the **bishop** of **London**, and men had to travel to England to be **ordained**.

Through pressure from the SPG on the British Parliament, the first bishops were **consecrated** for Jamaica and Barbados in 1824. The point of the pressure was to provide objective, weighty, and concerned authorities to press locally for education and limited freedoms for the slaves' benefit, which, although largely granted by that date in Westminster, were not easily realized in the face of the planters and slaveholders in the islands. Parliament funded the bishoprics and confirmed the established status of the Church of England in the colonies. Later bishoprics were formed for the South American mainland colony of Guiana (nowadays spelled "Guyana") in 1842; Trinidad in 1872; the Windward Islands in 1878; and British Honduras, now Belize, on the Central American mainland in 1883. The **province** was formed in 1883, though initially the only provincial organ of unity and administration was an "Episcopal **synod**"—a meeting simply of the diocesan bishops. Two further **dioceses** have been formed since then. The link with the Crown and the British Parliament was broken step by step, island by island, until the Anglican Church in Barbados, the last church outside of the Church of England to have remained legally established, was disestablished in 1961.

WESTMINSTER DIRECTORY. *See DIRECTORY FOR THE PUBLIC WORSHIP OF GOD IN THE THREE KINGDOMS*.

WESTON, FRANK (1871–1924). Born into an **Evangelical** family, Frank Weston embraced in his teens an obdurate and extreme **Anglo-Catholicism**, which became the key to his whole life thereafter. He was **ordained** as a **deacon** in 1895 and a **presbyter** in 1896 and did two **curacies** in England before going to **Zanzibar** in 1898 through the agency of the **Universities Mission to Central Africa**. He was **consecrated** as **bishop** of Zanzibar in 1908 and added to a distinguished **missionary** record a highly controversial one on behalf of a rigorous Anglo-Catholicism. In 1913 he denounced the bishops of **Mombasa** and **Uganda** for sharing in Communion at **Kikuyu** with **Presbyterians** and **Methodists**, and delated them to the **archbishop** of **Canterbury** for **heresy**, though the coming of World War I prevented a wholesale schism over the issue. At the 1920 **Lambeth Conference**, Weston helped draft and pilot the famous "Appeal to All Christian People." He also took a very prominent part in the 1923 Anglo-Catholic Congress.

WESTWARD POSITION. There is reason to think that in the first millennium of the church in Western Europe, the **president** of the **eucharist** regularly faced across the eucharistic **table** toward the ecclesiastical west. Somewhere between the 10th and 12th centuries, a change occurred in which the table itself was moved to be fixed against the east wall, and the president stood before it, facing east, with his back to the people. (This change was possibly precipitated by the coming of **tabernacles** for **reservation**, which were ideally both to occupy a central position and also to be fixed to the east wall without the president turning his back to them.) The resultant "**eastward position**" was retained in the 1549 **Book of Common Prayer**, where the **rubric** spoke of "the **priest** standing humbly afore the **altar**."

However, the stone altars were broken up by order-in-council in 1550, and in 1552 the second Book of Common Prayer ordered the priest to stand "at the **North side** of the table." The table itself was to be movable and could stand in the **nave** or **chancel** at **Communion** time. It may frequently have been placed at right angles to the previous position against the east wall, and the new position meant that a president at north side would be facing across the table in a central position.

Westward position, while absolutely normal in **Presbyterian** and other **Reformed** uses, was, with one possible exception, virtually unknown in Anglicanism until the late 1940s. The exception was the academic advocacy of such a change by an **Evangelical** layman in the Church of **England**, Albert Mitchell, between the world wars. The actual practice is thought to have started around 1947 at the Queen's College, Birmingham (where the chapel was built with this practice in view), and in **South India** (where Leslie Brown claimed to have introduced it in 1946, upon hearing of the unhappiness of a Hindu convert at the visual effects of eastward position). Westward position then got a favorable commendation in the **liturgy** of the Church of South India in 1950.

The impact of the **parish** Communion movement in England, the **United States**, and other "western" parts of the **Anglican Communion** led to widespread reordering of the interiors of church buildings, which frequently led to Communion tables being brought forward to a point where the president naturally faced the people across it. Such changes had made limited progress when, following **Vatican II**, they became widely adopted in Roman Catholic practice, and this gave new impetus to its use in Anglicanism. It is now, almost certainly, the most widespread use in the whole Anglican Communion. It has implications both for the **ornaments** that may have traditionally been placed upon the table and also for the liturgical actions of the president where the previous **ceremonial** (such as elevation) arose from the practice of facing east.

WHITBY, SYNOD OF. The **Synod** of Whitby was held in 664 and is represented by **Bede** as the crucial point of decision bringing the Church throughout **England** within the influence of the Church of Rome. King Oswy of Northumbria summoned the synod, as he realized his own Celtic mode of Christianity (stemming from **Aidan** and his successor Finan and their ministry in the northeast) differed in what seemed important respects (e.g., the date of **Easter**) from the Roman practices that had originated in **Augustine**'s **mission** in Kent. Bede calls it both a "synod" and a "**council**," but his account makes it appear nearer to a simple ordered public dispute. It was held at Whitby because of the fame of Hilda, then prioress there, and because Agilbert, the **bishop** of the West Saxons, was visiting King Oswy's son Alfred, who sympathized with Agilbert's pro-Roman position. At the synod, Bishop Colman, who had succeeded Finan as bishop of Lindisfarne, presented the Celtic case; the youthful Wilfrid, then abbot of Ripon but soon to become bishop of **York**, presented the Roman case on behalf of Agilbert. The issues included forms of tonsure and other matters of "discipline," as well as the date of Easter, but Bede records only the controversy about Easter. All issues were settled simultaneously through Wilfrid's advocacy of a single principle of **authority**—that Rome spoke with the authority of Peter, who is "guardian of the gates of **heaven**," and **Columba** could not match that. Colman accepted this principle, and Oswy ruled in favor of Roman ways; all present concurred, thus setting the general direction of the Church of England for centuries to come.

WHITE, WILLIAM (1748–1836). William White was born and raised in Philadelphia and went to **London** to be **ordained** as a **deacon** in 1770 and a **presbyter** in 1772. After the American Declaration of Independence in 1776, White acted as a chaplain to the Continental Congresses and then to the U.S. Senate until 1801. In 1782 he published a famous book, *The Case of the Episcopal Churches Considered*, in which he made proposals for meeting the emergency caused by the obvious severance from the Church of **England** ensuing upon the unilateral declaration of political independence from the Westminster Parliament. In the book, White proposed that the **parishes** be viewed as separate voluntary autonomous bodies, which should then gravitate toward federating with each other in state conventions. He envisaged a temporary breach in Episcopal ordination, which would be covered by presbyteral ordination during the emergency. More far-reaching was his recommendation that state conventions should include **lay** representation; this happened in practice at the first **General Convention** in 1785, and the **Protestant Episcopal Church in**

the United States of America thus became the first Anglican **province** in the world to seat **laypersons** in this **synodical** role.

It became clear through Westminster legislation passed in 1786, after the agonies of **Samuel Seabury**'s search for Episcopal **consecration**, that Americans could now be consecrated as **bishops** by the **archbishop** of **Canterbury** without taking any **oath** of allegiance to the monarch. White then shared with **Samuel Provoost** in being the first recipients of such orders, White as bishop of Pennsylvania, Provoost as bishop of New York. They were both consecrated on 4 February 1787 in **Lambeth Palace** chapel. White became presiding bishop of PECUSA for a short time in 1789, and then, after Seabury's death in 1795, he regained this office, retaining both it and his bishopric in Pennsylvania until his death 40 years later.

WHITGIFT, JOHN (1532–1604). Born in the year King **Henry VIII** began the break from Rome, John Whitgift lived through all the changes of the **Reformation**, **ministered** throughout Queen **Elizabeth I's** reign, and finally, as **archbishop** of **Canterbury** from 1583, steered the Church of **England** into the period of the Stuarts. He appears during his undergraduate years at Cambridge to have been of a reformed conviction (partly through the tutelage of John Bradford, who was **martyred** under Queen **Mary I**), yet he continued his studies without rocking boats and became a tutor in Peterhouse during Mary's reign.

Whitgift was **ordained** as a **deacon** and **presbyter** in 1560, continuing in his fellowship. In 1563 he was appointed Lady Margaret's Professor of Divinity, and in 1567 he became Regius Professor and master of Trinity College, where his stern rule presaged his later archiepiscopal style. Controversy with the **Puritans** started in 1569–1570 when Thomas Cartwright, the new Lady Margaret's Professor, attacked the existing ecclesiastical order. Whitgift's response was the provision of a new set of university statutes, the effects of which were to curb the independence of the Puritans within the university. The next four years saw the controversy break into print, in which Whitgift's *An Answer to a certain Libel entitled An Admonition to the Parliament* (1573) and his further *Defense of the Answer* (1574) were the trenchant defense of the Elizabethan Settlement against Cartwright's attacks. The queen appointed him **bishop** of

Worcester in 1577 and in 1583 archbishop of Canterbury. While his **doctrine** of salvation was essentially Calvinist (as the so-called **Lambeth Articles** that he issued in 1595 demonstrated), his defense of the Church of England in its Episcopal structure and national comprehensiveness and **uniformity** was strongly anti-Puritan. Similarly, his respect for the early **Fathers** was alien to the Puritan spirit, and his recourse to discipline strict and vigilant. Whitgift survived just far enough into the reign of King **James I** to appear in a token way at the **Hampton Court Conference**.

WILBERFORCE, WILLIAM (1759–1833). Wilberforce was a wealthy **lay** Anglican who by deploying his wealth was elected to the House of Commons to represent Hull at the age of 21. He was converted in the mid-1780s, became a convinced **Evangelical**, and was guided by John Newton, an ex–slave trader who had since his conversion been writing against slavery. By 1789 Wilberforce had begun to take up in Parliament a sustained attack on slavery, and one of the last of **John Wesley**'s letters is an encouragement to Wilberforce to persevere. In 1794 he carried the House of Commons for a complete abolition of slavery, but was blocked by the House of Lords. In 1797 Wilberforce moved to South **London** and joined the **Clapham Sect**. In the same year, he published his *Practical View of the Prevailing System of Professed Christians in the Higher and Middle Classes of this country contrasted with real Christianity*, an indictment of the love of luxury and the moral laxity of his own social contemporaries; the publication went through 50 printings in 50 years. Wilberforce was closely engaged with the formation of the **Church Missionary Society** (1799) and of the British and Foreign Bible Society (1804) and the creation of a **bishopric** and scope for **missionaries** in **India** (1812–1814). But the major labor of his life was the continuing assault on slavery, successfully leading to the abolition of the slave trade in 1807 and (after he left the Commons in 1825) the Emancipation Act (1833), news of which reached him shortly before he died. His third son, Samuel, became bishop of Oxford, though two other sons, after **ordination** in the Church of **England**, joined the **Roman Catholic Church**.

WILLIAM III, KING (1650–1702). William was brought up as Prince of Orange, a district of the Netherlands or Holland. He was a Calvinist, and he married Mary, the older daughter of James, the Duke of York and brother of King **Charles II**. Mary had herself been brought up in her early years as a **Protestant**, though her father became a **Roman Catholic** in 1670. As it became clear that Charles II would have no lawful heir, many hopes were affixed to William and Mary, in fear of James's Roman Catholicism. When in 1685 James inherited as **James II** and showed all the intransigence of a convert in his Roman Catholicism, these hopes grew. In 1688, when James's second wife gave birth to a son (who would therefore become his heir) at the very time when the seven **bishops** were on trial for seditious libel for resisting him, a widespread popular antagonism to James arose. Overtures to William thereupon increased, and he landed in the West Country on 5 November 1688 and marched on **London**. James fled London. Then negotiations began with Parliament. The hope of their leaders was that William would become the "regent," operating on behalf of an absentee monarch. William, however, was unwilling to take on such an ambiguous and unsatisfactory role—he would be king or nothing. Thus it was that Parliament voted in early 1689 to declare the throne vacant through James's departure, and, having so voted, then viewed itself as able to offer the crown to William and Mary jointly. This was, however, a highly controversial decision, and many members—even those bishops put on trial by James—took the view that an **oath** to a monarch is binding for his lifetime and that Parliament was engaging in actions tantamount to treason in declaring the throne vacant. This minority, in defeat, formed the "**nonjuring**" succession.

William III and **Mary II** were duly crowned by the bishop of London, the country breathed again, and the transition became known as the **Glorious Revolution**. During the joint monarchs' reign, the Bill of Rights was passed in Parliament, new bishops were appointed, and "King Billy" duly brought **Ireland** to heel in 1690. Mary died childless in 1694, and thereafter William III ruled alone. As the prospects of a succession of Protestant Stuart monarchs faded, so steps were taken in the Act of Settlement (1700) to secure the future of the throne, lest it fall again into Roman Catholic hands. Meanwhile the annual service for thanksgiving for deliverance from the Gunpowder Plot on 5 November had the landing of the Prince of Orange on the same day of the year added to it for redoubled thanksgiving.

WILLIAMS, ROWAN DOUGLAS (1950–). Rowan Williams, who is Welsh by birth, was trained at the College of the Resurrection at Mirfield and was **ordained** in 1977 directly onto the staff of Westcott House, Cambridge. In 1980 he left Westcott House and became until 1986 a lecturer in theology in the University of Cambridge, being also dean of Clare College from 1984 to 1986. Williams was widely recognized for his scholarship, attested by a continuous flow of theological and spiritual publications; he published *The Wound of Knowledge* when he was 29. In 1986, at the age of 36, he was appointed Lady Margaret's Professor of Divinity in the University of Oxford and **canon** residentiary of Christ Church, Oxford.

In 1992 Williams was **consecrated** in St. Asaph **Cathedral** as **bishop** of Monmouth of the Church in **Wales**. He held this see for 10 years, becoming in 1999 **archbishop** of Wales also. There he learned Welsh, as part of his commitment to the **province** and the principality. Williams's theological prowess and his lecturing and writing made him a world figure long before he became a bishop, and he enhanced this reputation during his years in Wales. He was visiting **Trinity Church**, **Wall Street**, on 11 September 2001, in close proximity to the collapse of the Twin Towers of the World Trade Center, and he reflected on this experience in his small book *Writing in the Dust: Reflections on 11th September and Its Aftermath* (2002).

In 2002 Williams was nominated by the queen to become archbishop of **Canterbury**; he was confirmed in that office in December 2002 and enthroned in February 2003 as 104th archbishop of Canterbury. He was the first bishop to have been the **primate** of another church of the **Anglican Communion** before being nominated as archbishop of Canterbury.

Williams's first few months at Canterbury were marked by worldwide disputes over the blessing of same-sex unions and the ordaining of practicing **homosexuals**, and the disputes were brought to a head by the election of an openly practicing homosexual to be bishop of New Hampshire in the **Episcopal Church (United States of America)**. After this election was confirmed by the two Houses of the **General Convention** in August 2003, Archbishop Williams summoned an emergency **Primates Meeting** for mid-October that year. Following a request made at that meeting, he then set up the **Lambeth Commission** under Archbishop Robin Eames to tackle, within the space of 12 months, issues of how the Anglican Communion can remain a single **Communion** under such divisive pressure. The Lambeth Commission duly reported with the **Windsor Report**. One of its recommendations related specifically to the archbishop of Canterbury, namely, that he should have a "Council of Advice." Williams accepted this recommendation, and such a council was appointed and first met in 2005.

WINDSOR REPORT. The **Lambeth Commission** was appointed by **Archbishop Rowan Williams** in October 2003 after an emergency meeting of the **primates** of the **Anglican Communion**. It deliberated for a year and its findings were then published by the **Anglican Communion Office** on 18 October 2004 as *The Windsor Report 2004*. The commission had been created to address the situation in the Communion following the **consecration** of a practicing **homosexual** as bishop of New Hampshire. Its task was not directly to reach a judgment on homosexual relationships but to seek ways in which the Communion, riven through the impact of this consecration and of the promoting of the blessing of same-sex unions in New Westminster in **Canada**, could sustain its unity and avoid schismatic moves. In the report, the commission addresses precisely these strains upon the unity of the Communion, but in passing inevitably accepts a *prima facie* judgment that no sufficient reason for dislodging the **biblical** and **traditional** sexual morality has been adduced.

The Windsor Report is a tightly argued thesis, with a full documentation in appendixes. It argues that the Communion must theologically function by an element of interdependence and not by an unaccountable or arbitrary use of the constitutional autonomy of separate **provinces**. It recommends that the **Episcopal Church (United States of America)** (ECUSA) and the Canadian **diocese** of New Westminster should "express regret" over their breaching the "bonds of affection" in the Communion, and it also calls upon ECUSA to set out scriptural and **doctrinal** reasons why a person in the position of the bishop of New Hampshire should be entrusted with leadership in the Church. It opposes the irregular exercise of **episcopacy** from outside the **United States** that has followed upon the dismay and distrust of many members of the Communion arising from the stance of the leadership of ECUSA; for there has been a growing phenomenon of bishops crossing diocesan boundaries (sometimes even in other continents) to offer pastoral care and support to parishes and individuals who believe themselves to have been abandoned by the leaders of their own dioceses or provinces in the United States.

The report finally addresses the Anglican church's "Instruments of Unity," which have traditionally been fourfold: the archbishop of Canterbury, the **Lambeth Conferences**, the **Anglican Consultative Council**, and the **Primates Meetings**. It recommends various ways of strengthening these "instruments" and proposes to add to them a Council of Advice for the archbishop of Canterbury. It furthermore recommends the adoption by all constituent bodies of the Communion of a substantial mutual "covenant." A draft text of this covenant is included in the report. According to the commission's proposal, it would bind the covenanting parties to procedures of consultation before making partisan decisions.

WOMEN, ORDINATION OF. At the **Reformation**, there was no change made to extend **ordination** beyond the exclusively male **clergy** of the pre-Reformation Church. Indeed, John Knox, the radical **Scottish** Reformer, provoked the hostility of Queen **Elizabeth I**, as, just before her accession, he had published his "First Blast of the Trumpet against the Monstrous Regiment [i.e. regimen or rule] of Women"—a cry against women having any ruling force, whether in church or in society. On the whole, Anglicans settled for women monarchs, while not anticipating that women would ever be **ordained**. The ancient lay office of **warden** or churchwarden was reserved for men only; when lay **readers** were first licensed in the 19th century, they were entirely male; and when **laypeople** took part in Church government, beginning with the **General Convention** of the **Protestant Episcopal Church in the United States of America** in 1785, those laypeople were also entirely male.

In the 19th century, women generally held an inferior position in society in most parts of the **Anglican Communion**, and this was reflected within the life of the Christian churches, not least in Anglicanism. Women had to find public **ministry** either by belonging to a **religious community** or by taking office in the **Mothers' Union** (where the ministry would be entirely to women), or, in a few cases, by becoming a recognized "**parish** worker" or possibly a **deaconess**.

Nevertheless, overseas **missionary societies** in Britain were sometimes ready to send women into administrative or leadership roles in Asia and Africa, positions that were still technically lay but involved ecclesiastical responsibilities well beyond those open to women in Britain itself.

The generally inferior position women held in Western church life was slowly improved into the 20th century, roughly in line with the emergence of more roles and opportunities for women in Western society itself. It was against that changing background that the issue of women's **ordination** arose within the 20th century, and there were some non-Episcopal churches in various countries that did ordain women in the first half of the century. In Anglicanism the first such ordination occurred when R. O. Hall, the **bishop** of **Hong Kong**, during the Japanese occupation on 25 January 1944 ordained Florence Li Tim Oi, who was already a **deacon**, as a **presbyter** to provide ministerial and **sacramental** care for congregations that would otherwise be deprived. It was made very clear at the time that this was an emergency provision, and after World War II she voluntarily ceased exercising a presbyteral ministry so as to avoid division.

The Church in **China** then brought before the 1948 **Lambeth Conference** a proposal from the **diocese** of South China that for an experimental period deaconesses might be ordained as presbyters. This was rejected in Resolution 113 of that conference. Nevertheless, it was in the diocese of Hong Kong, after it had been separated from the mainland Chinese dioceses as a consequence of the Communist takeover in 1949–1950, that the next ordination of women as deacons was recorded. It was also the diocese of Hong Kong that asked the first meeting of the **Anglican Consultative Council** (ACC) in 1971 for its goodwill toward the ordaining of women deacons to the presbyterate and, when the ACC had given approval (by 24 votes to 22), officially ordained the first two women as presbyters at **Advent** 1971. Florence Li Tim Oi, who was living in Communist China and was suffering under the Cultural Revolution, resumed her own presbyteral ministry as well, once corporate church life emerged from the political chaos and churches were reopened in 1979.

After that, other **provinces** followed suit—usually ordaining women as deacons first. In the **Episcopal Church (United States of America)** (ECUSA) there were irregular ordinations of women as presbyters in 1974, rites conducted by retired bishops without **canonical** sanction. Soon after, the fully canonical ordinations followed in **Canada** (1976), ECUSA (1977), and **New Zealand** (1978). The path was rarely easy, as "traditionalists," seeing grave ecclesial principles at stake, usually fought against such a decision. **Anglo-Catholics** have regularly, though not unanimously, opposed such ordinations as being neither **biblical** nor part of the historic **traditions** of the church (Eastern or Western), while some **Evangelicals**, such as the leaders of **Sydney** diocese in **Australia**, have opposed the ordinations on the grounds that they would confer on women teaching roles and "headship" which are unbiblical. Australia has therefore seen a very untidy entry into women's ordination, with considerable liberty for different dioceses to adopt different practices—an outcome precipitated in part by the unilateral decision in 1992 of Peter Carnley, the **archbishop** of Perth (and later **primate** of Australia), to ordain women as presbyters before there was canonical sanction.

Much Anglo-Catholic opposition has asserted that, even by undergoing ordination rites, women in fact are not thereby ordained, as they are not in the economy of God appropriate candidates. There have also been claims from the same quarters that, even if in theory the ordination of women were possible, no province of the Anglican Communion has **authority** to so alter the inherited pattern of **orders** without something like a papal decree or a General **Council** to warrant it. Evangelical opponents have been more inclined to say women *should* not be ordained rather than that they *cannot* be.

Despite these conflicts, by 2000 more than half the provinces of the Anglican Communion were ready to ordain women as presbyters. In some of these provinces, internal strains were experienced as some parishes distanced themselves from women presbyters and even declined the ministry of bishops who were prepared to ordain women. In the Church of **England**, where the ordination of women as presbyters began in 1994, special provision was made in advance by the Episcopal Ministry Act of **Synod** (1993) for parishes opposed. Under this Act, "extended Episcopal care" was provided for parishes that passed resolutions both distancing themselves from the ministry of ordained women and asking the diocesan bishop to implement this "care" for them—an arrangement in which the diocesan afforded a special role of "care" to another bishop who was similarly distanced from the ordination of women. Sometimes such a bishop would be from within the diocese, sometimes from a neighboring diocese, and sometimes he would be a **provincial episcopal visitor**—and special **suffragan** bishoprics belonging to the **metropolitan** dioceses of **Canterbury** and **York** were created in 1994 to provide bishops to whom diocesans in both southern and northern provinces could give this commission, when formally requested to do so by parishes. These suffragans, in their role of giving "care" to widely scattered parishes across many dioceses, were at an early stage dubbed "Flying Bishops," and the title has stuck. A bishop with somewhat similar functions was provided in the Church in **Wales** in 1997, but other provinces have not taken this step.

Overlapping with the wake of such ordinations came the issue of the ordination of women as bishops. In some provinces, the change in rules to allow women to be admitted to the presbyterate also opened the door for them at the same time to the **episcopate**. In others, as in the Church of England, a wholly separate subsequent decision has been needed. In 1988 the Lambeth Conference, recognizing from the progress of Episcopal elections in ECUSA that the first appointment of a woman as a bishop might soon occur, asked the archbishop of Canterbury to set up a commission to consider the implications of such a step for **Communion** among the provinces. This task was remitted to the archbishop of **Armagh**, Robin Eames, and his commission has been known as "the **Eames Commission**."

The first woman bishop in the Anglican Communion was Barbara Harris, consecrated as assistant bishop in the diocese of Massachusetts in ECUSA in 1989. The first woman diocesan bishop was Penelope Jamieson, consecrated as bishop of Dunedin in the province of **Aotearoa**, New Zealand, and Polynesia in 1990. At the 1998 Lambeth Conference there were 11 women bishops present (out of a total of more than 700) from ECUSA, Aotearoa, and Canada.

Because some provinces do not recognize the Episcopal acts of the women bishops of other provinces, presbyters ordained by women bishops may still find their orders disallowed when wishing to visit other parts of the Communion, and to that extent the **full Communion** between Anglican provinces has been impaired. In Australia the **General Synod** in 2004 declined to open the way to women bishops.

In the Church of England, the General Synod decided in 2000 to establish a commission to review the theological and other implications of ordaining women bishops. The resultant Rochester Commission, with a membership that included opponents of women's ordination, reported in October 2004 with a substantial treatment of both theology and the range of possible ways forward if the Church of England wished to proceed. This report was twice debated in the General Synod in 2005, and, with a minority in opposition, the Synod voted to begin the process of removing the legal obstacles in 2006.

WORLD COUNCIL OF CHURCHES (WCC). The roots of a world council of churches are generally reckoned to lie in the **Edinburgh Missionary Conference** of 1910. After World War I, there was a run-on from the conference in three different strands, Faith and Order, Life and Work, and the International Missionary Conference. Arising from Faith and Order and from Life and Work, when both held conferences in 1937, the idea of an overarching World Council of Churches, initiated by a merging of these two movements, took shape quite quickly. A conference was held at Utrecht in 1938 under the chairmanship of **William Temple** to take the idea forward; a constitution was drawn up there, and an interim organization (entitling itself the "World Council of Churches in Process of Formation") was established. The office was moved to Geneva for the period of World War II.

Further progress was inhibited by World War II, until plans could be laid for the first official assembly, which was convened in Amsterdam in 1948. Because Temple had died, the next **archbishop** of **Canterbury**, **Geoffrey Fisher**, opened the conference, and the bishop of Chichester, George Bell, became the secretary of the Central and Executive Committees. A secretariat was established in Geneva.

The Anglican **provinces** generally have been full members of the WCC, joining with virtually all the non-Roman denominations that have any claim to a substantial presence in one or more countries, and have been ready to agree to the declaration that is the basis of membership. In 1948 this read as it was drafted in 1938, simply: "The World Council of Churches is a fellowship of churches which accept the Lord Jesus Christ as God and Saviour." In 1961 the declaration was expanded, adding: ". . . according to the scriptures and therefore seek to fulfill together their common calling to the glory of the one **God**, Father, Son and **Holy Spirit**."

Assemblies have been held since 1948 in Evanston, Illinois (1954); New Delhi (1961); Uppsala, Sweden (1968); Nairobi (1975); Vancouver (1983); Canberra (1991); and Harare, **Zimbabwe** (1998). At the New Delhi assembly, the International Missionary Council (IMC), the third strand of ecumenical cooperation that had arisen from the 1910 Edinburgh Missionary Conference, was merged with the WCC. The **Roman Catholic Church** has never been a member church, but it does belong to the Faith and Order Commission, which works under the umbrella of the WCC. The assembly at each of its meetings elects a Central Committee, which discharges its functions between the plenary assemblies and oversees and directs the work of the secretariat. *See also* BRENT, CHARLES HENRY; LIMA; LUND PRINCIPLE; OLDHAM, JOSEPH HOULDSWORTH.

WYCLIFFE, JOHN (c. 1330–1384). John Wycliffe is usually hailed as a reformer before the **Reformation**, sometimes as the "morning star" of the Reformation. He was **ordained** in early life, lived most of his adulthood in Oxford, and taught philosophy and theology. His independent judgment led him to diverge from the schools of the time, and he denounced transubstantiation on philosophical grounds, while feeling his way toward asserting the sole **authority** of the **Bible** in matters theological and ecclesiastical—an assertion that implied (and Wycliffe spelled it out) that the authority of the **pope** was ill founded. Wycliffe initiated translations of the Bible into English around 1380, although most of the actual work is usually attributed to his followers. Nevertheless, the manuscript "Wycliffe Bibles" were the first **vernacular** Bibles in English and provided much of the head of steam for his followers, known as "Lollards." Wycliffe's last years were spent as rector of Lutterworth, where he is especially commemorated, but they were marked by the condemnation of his teachings (though not as directly attributed to him) by **Archbishop** Courtenay in 1382. He died in relative obscurity on 31 December 1384, the date on which he is commemorated in various Anglican **calendars**. After his death, the connection of his teachings with his person led to retrospective condemnation. In **England**, the vigor of the Lollards led to thorough repression. However, Czech scholars took up his work, which influenced John Hus and provoked both the decree *De Heretico Comburendo* in 1401 and the wholesale condemnation of Lollard and Hussite teachings at the **Council** of Constance in 1415.

– Y –

YORK. Paulinus was a **missionary** to Kent sent by Gregory in 601 to assist **Augustine**. When the king of Northumbria married the Kent princess Ethelburga in 625, Paulinus was **consecrated** to go as missionary **bishop** to York. He established a mission there, administered the first **baptisms** in 627, and founded a **cathedral** on the site of the old Roman administrative headquarters building for the north of **England**. The present medieval York **Minster** stands on the same site. From 734, the bishops of York claimed **metropolitical** status as **archbishops** of the north of England, and in the ninth century they contested the **primacy** of all England with the archbishops of **Canterbury**—a contest resolved when it was agreed that the archbishops of Canterbury would hold the title "primate of all England" and that of archbishops of York the title "primate of England." Both York's distance from London and the superior authority of the Canterbury archbishopric have led to a relatively small distinctive role for archbishops of York, save in respect of their own province. Since 1927 this has had 14 **dioceses** (including the diminutive but ancient Sodor and **Man**), compared to the present 30 in the southern province. The archbishop of York is a joint president of the **General Synod** along with the archbishop of Canterbury and has certain powers in the whole Church of England during a vacancy in the archbishopric of Canterbury.

YORK STATEMENT. The third **International Anglican Liturgical Consultation** (IALC-3) was held at the College of St. Mark and St. John, **York**, in August 1989. Thirty participants from 15 provinces of the **Anglican Communion** agreed upon a statement, entitled "Down-to-Earth Worship," but more commonly known as the "York Statement." Its thrust was to call for the **inculturation** of Anglican worship in the vastly different local cultures in which Anglicans were to be found throughout the world. It drew for this purpose upon a section report and two resolutions of the 1988 **Lambeth Conference**. The York Statement was compiled and adopted against a background of a very strong but arguably dated Anglo-Saxon **liturgical** culture, which, it was urged, had so dominated the worship of the Anglican Communion as to press hard upon Anglicans in countries or places of a very different culture. The theme did not recur directly at later IALCs, though the issue of adapting the **elements** of wheat **bread** and grape wine for cultures where the Western norms were absurdly untypical kept recurring but was not definitively addressed—and was omitted from the 1998 Lambeth Conference report when the whole draft statement on liturgy was quashed at the behest of another section.

– Z –

ZAIRE. *See* CONGO.

ZAMBIA. The British colony of Northern Rhodesia involved very few chaplaincies and **missionaries** in the 19th century, although it was viewed as being within the sphere of influence of the **Universities Mission to Central Africa** (UMCA). The formation of a **diocese** was proposed by **Randall Davidson**, the **archbishop** of **Canterbury**, at a celebration in **London** in 1907 to mark the 50th anniversary of UMCA. The diocese was formed in 1910, and John Edward Hine, who had been bishop of **Zanzibar** but had resigned in ill health, was now recovered sufficiently to become bishop of the new diocese. Some time around the early 1920s the diocese provided its own **eucharistic liturgy**, which, like the Zanzibar liturgy, owed a debt to **Roman Catholic** sources. As with Nyasaland (now Malawi), the grouping with UMCA dioceses in Tanganyika and Zanzibar was altered when the **province** of **Central Africa** was created in 1955, matching the creation by the British authorities the previous year of the (short-lived) Central Africa Federation. The province, including what are now Botswana and **Zimbabwe**, tended to look south for support, and soon after its creation it adopted the **South African** 1954 **Prayer Book** for its own use. Northern Rhodesia became independent as Zambia in 1963, and over the following years, the diocese was divided until in 2004 there were four Zambian dioceses.

ZANZIBAR. The island of Zanzibar was a separate British protectorate until joined with mainland Tanganyika to become the independent nation of **Tanzania** in 1963. After the formation of a **diocese** of the Zambezi in 1861, and the death of its first **bishop**, Charles Mackenzie in 1862, the base of Anglican **missionary** work in the region was transferred in 1863 to Zanzibar. Zanzibar was a single Anglican diocese, springing from **Universities Mission to Central Africa** (UMCA) **missionary** work, with its **cathedral** in the old slave market of the island. It was famous for one of its **bishops**, **Frank Weston** (1908–1924). When the **province** of **East Africa** was formed in 1960, Zanzibar was incorporated into it, and thus took its place in the province of Tanzania when that in turn was formed in 1970.

ZIMBABWE. The first **bishop** of Mashonaland, G. W. H. Knight-Bruce, was appointed in 1891, as the British colony of Rhodesia was opened up through the ambition of Cecil Rhodes. Converts were made among the Mashona people and **mission** stations were established, even while tribal and anti-European conflicts continued. It was in the midst of this turmoil that the Mozambican **lay evangelist Bernard Mizeki** was assassinated in 1896, and he has been recognized as a **martyr** ever since. The original **diocese** included the Bechuanaland Protectorate and was part of the **province** of **South Africa**.

In 1953 the Matabeleland diocese, including the western part of what was then Southern Rhodesia along with Bechuanaland, was carved from the Mashonaland diocese, and in 1955 both dioceses became part of the new province of **Central Africa**, which also included both Northern Rhodesia (now **Zambia**) and Nyasaland (now Malawi). Shortly after that, Bechuanaland became a separate diocese (now Botswana). In 1980, when Rhodesia became Zimbabwe upon its independence, two new dioceses were formed, so that there were the dioceses of Matabeleland in the west, Harare in the north, Central Zimbabwe (previously Lundi) in the south, and Manicaland in the east. A further diocese of Masvingo was formed in the south in 2002. These dioceses belong to the province of Central Africa, but are joined to each other by a somewhat uncertain Anglican Council of Zimbabwe. At the time of writing, political and economic troubles of the nation are inhibiting a divided Anglican church, and further steps in development, such as becoming a separate Anglican province, are currently hard to envisage.

Appendix A: Bishops and Archbishops of Canterbury

597	Augustine
604	Laurentius
619	Mellitus
624	Justus
627	Honorius
655	Deusdedit
668	Theodorus
693	Berhtwald
731	Tatwine
735	Nothelm
740	Cuthbert
761	Bregowine
765	Jaenberht
793	Æthelheard
805	Wulfred
832	Feologild
833	Ceolnoth
870	Æthelred
890	Plegmund
914	Æthelhelm
923	Wufhelm
942	Oda
959	Ælfsige
959	Byrhthelm
960	Dunstan
c. 988	Athelgar
990	Sigeric Serio
995	Ælfric
1005	Ælfheah

1013	Lyfing [Ælfstan]
1020	Æthelnoth
1038	Eadsige
1051	Robert of Jumièges
1052	Stigand
1070	Lanfranc
1093	Anselm
1114	Ralph d'Escures
1123	William de Corbeil
1139	Theobald of Bec
1162	Thomas Becket
1174	Richard (of Dover)
1184	Baldwin
1193	Hubert Walter
1207	Stephen Langton
1229	Richard le Grant
1234	Edmund Rich
1245	Boniface of Savoy
1273	Robert Kilwardby
1279	John Pecham
1294	Robert Winchelsey
1313	Walter Reynolds
1328	Simon Mepham
1333	John Stratford
1349	Thomas Bradwardine
1349	Simon Islip
1366	Simon Langham
1368	William Whittlesey
1375	Simon Sudbury
1381	William Courtenay
1396	Thomas Arundel
1398	Roger Walden
1414	Henry Chichele
1443	John Stafford
1452	John Kempe
1454	Thomas Bourgchier
1486	John Morton
1501	Henry Deane

1503	William Warham
1533	Thomas Cranmer
1556	Reginald Pole
1559	Matthew Parker
1576	Edmund Grindal
1583	John Whitgift
1604	Richard Bancroft
1611	George Abbott
1633	William Laud
1660	William Juxon
1663	Gilbert Sheldon
1678	William Sancroft
1691	John Tillotson
1695	Thomas Tenison
1716	William Wake
1737	John Potter
1747	Thomas Herring
1757	Matthew Hutton
1758	Thomas Secker
1768	Frederick Cornwallis
1783	John Moore
1805	Charles Manners Sutton
1828	William Howley
1848	John Bird Sumner
1862	Charles Thomas Longley
1868	Archibald Campbell Tait
1883	Edward White Benson
1896	Frederick Temple
1903	Randall Thomas Davidson
1928	Cosmo Gordon Lang
1942	William Temple
1945	Geoffrey Francis Fisher
1961	Arthur Michael Ramsey
1974	Frederick Donald Coggan
1980	Robert Alexander Kennedy Runcie
1991	George Leonard Carey
2002	Rowan Douglas Williams

Appendix B: The Thirty-Nine Articles of Religion

I. OF FAITH IN THE HOLY TRINITY

There is but one living and true God, everlasting, without body, parts, or passions; of infinite power, wisdom, and goodness; the Maker and Preserver of all things both visible and invisible. And in unity of this Godhead there be three Persons, of one substance, power and eternity; the Father, the Son, and the Holy Ghost.

II. OF THE WORD OR SON OF GOD, WHICH WAS MADE VERY MAN

The Son, which is the Word of the Father, begotten from everlasting of the Father, the very and eternal God, and of one substance with the Father, took Man's nature in the womb of the blessed Virgin, of her substance: so that two whole and perfect Natures, that is to say, the Godhead and Manhood, were joined together in one Person, never to be divided, whereof is one Christ, very God, and very Man; who truly suffered, was crucified, dead and buried, to reconcile his Father to us, and to be a sacrifice, not only for original guilt, but also for all actual sins of men.

III. OF THE GOING DOWN OF CHRIST INTO HELL

As Christ died for us, and was buried, so also is it to be believed, that he went down into Hell.

IV. OF THE RESURRECTION OF CHRIST

Christ did truly rise again from death, and took again his body, with flesh, bones, and all things appertaining to the perfection of Man's nature; wherewith he ascended into Heaven and there sitteth, until he return to judge all Men at the last day.

V. OF THE HOLY GHOST

The Holy Ghost, proceeding from the Father and the Son, is of one substance, majesty and glory, with the Father and the Son, very and eternal God.

VI. OF THE SUFFICIENCY OF THE HOLY SCRIPTURES FOR SALVATION

Holy Scripture containeth all things necessary to salvation: so that whatsoever is not read therein, nor may be proved thereby, is not to be required of any man, that it should be believed as an article of the Faith, or be thought requisite or necessary to salvation. In the name of the holy Scripture we do understand those Canonical Books of the Old and New Testament, of whose authority there was never any doubt in the Church.

Of the Names and Numbers of the Canonical Books

Genesis
Exodus
Leviticus
Numbers
Deuteronomy
Joshua
Judges
Ruth
The First Book of Samuel

The Second Book of Samuel
The First Book of Kings
The Second Book of Kings
The First Book of Chronicles
The Second Book of Chronicles
The First Book of Esdras
The Second Book of Esdras
The Book of Esther
The Book of Job
The Psalms
The Proverbs
Ecclesiastes or Preacher
Cantica, or Songs of Solomon
Four Prophets the greater
Twelve Prophets the less

And the other Books (as *Hierome* saith) the Church doth read for example of life and instruction of manners; but yet it doth not apply them to establish any doctrine; such are these following:

The Third Book of Esdras
The Fourth Book of Esdras
The Book of Tobias
The Book of Judith
The rest of the Book of Esther
The Book of Wisdom
Jesus the Son of Sirach
Baruch the Prophet
The Song of the Three Children
The Story of Susanna
Of Bel and the Dragon
The Prayer of Manasses
The First Book of Maccabees
The Second Book of Maccabees

All the Books of the New Testament, as they are commonly received, we do receive, and account them Canonical.

VII. OF THE OLD TESTAMENT

The Old Testament is not contrary to the New: for both in the Old and New Testament everlasting life is offered to Mankind by Christ, who is the only Mediator between God and Man, being both God and Man. Wherefore they are not to be heard, which feign that the old Fathers did only look for transitory promises. Although the Law given from God by Moses, as touching Ceremonies and Rites, do not bind Christian men, nor the Civil precepts thereof ought of necessity to be received in any commonwealth; yet notwithstanding, no Christian man whatsoever is free from the obedience of the Commandments which are called Moral.

VIII. OF THE THREE CREEDS

The Three Creeds, *Nicene* Creed, *Athanasius's* Creed, and that which is commonly called the *Apostles*' Creed, ought thoroughly to be received and believed: for they may be proved by most certain warrants of holy Scripture.

IX. OF ORIGINAL OR BIRTH-SIN

Original Sin standeth not in the following of *Adam*, (as the *Pelagians* do vainly talk;) but it is the fault or corruption of every man, that naturally is ingendered of the offspring of *Adam*; whereby man is very far gone from original righteousness, and is of his own nature inclined to evil, so that the flesh lusteth always contrary to the spirit; and therefore in every person born into this world, it deserveth God's wrath and damnation. And this infection of nature doth remain, yea in them that are regenerated; whereby the lust of the flesh called in the Greek, *Phronema sarkos* [printed in Greek letters], which some do expound the wisdom, some sensuality, some the affection, some the desire, of the flesh, is not subject to the Law of God. And although there is no condemnation for them that believe and are baptized, yet the Apostle doth confess, that concupiscence and lust hath of itself the nature of sin.

X. OF FREE-WILL

The condition of Man after the fall of *Adam* is such, that he cannot turn and prepare himself, by his own natural strength and good works, to faith, and calling upon God: Wherefore we have no power to do good works pleasant and acceptable to God, without the grace of God in Christ preventing us, that we may have a good will, and working with us, when we have that good will.

XI. OF THE JUSTIFICATION OF MAN

We are accounted righteous before God, only for the merit of our Lord and Saviour Jesus Christ by Faith, and not for our own works or deservings: Wherefore, that we are justified by Faith only is a most wholesome Doctrine, and very full of comfort, as more largely is expressed in the Homily of Justification.

XII. OF GOOD WORKS

Albeit that Good Works, which are the fruits of Faith, and follow after Justification, cannot put away our sins and endure the severity of God's Judgment; yet are they pleasing and acceptable to God in Christ, and do spring out necessarily of a true and lively Faith; insomuch that by them a lively Faith may be as evidently known as a tree discerned by the fruit.

XIII. OF WORKS BEFORE JUSTIFICATION

Works done before the grace of Christ, and the Inspiration of his Spirit, are not pleasant to God, forasmuch as they spring not of faith in Jesus Christ, nor do they make men meet to deserve grace, or (as the School-authors say) deserve grace of congruity: yea rather, for that they are not done as God hath willed and commanded them to be done, we doubt not but they have the nature of sin.

XIV. OF WORKS OF SUPEREROGATION

Voluntary Works besides, over and above, God's Commandments, which they call Works of Supererogation, cannot be taught without arrogance and impiety: for by them men do declare, that they do not only render unto God as much as they are bound to do, but that they do more for his sake, than of bounden duty is required: whereas Christ saith plainly, When ye have done all that are commanded to you, say, We are unprofitable servants.

XV. OF CHRIST ALONE WITHOUT SIN

Christ in the truth of our nature was made like unto us in all things, sin only except, from which he was clearly void, both in his flesh, and in his spirit. He came to be the Lamb without spot, who, by sacrifice of himself once made, should take away the sins of the world, and sin, as Saint *John* saith, was not in him. But all we rest, although baptized, and born again in Christ, yet offend in many things; and if we say we have no sin, we deceive ourselves, and the truth is not in us.

XVI. OF SIN AFTER BAPTISM

Not every deadly sin willingly committed after Baptism is sin against the Holy Ghost and unpardonable. Wherefore the grant of repentance is not to be denied to such as fall into sin after Baptism. After we have received the Holy Ghost, we may depart from grace given, and fall into sin, and by the grace of God we may arise again, and amend our lives. And therefore they are to be condemned, which say, they can no more sin as long as they live here, or deny the place of forgiveness to such as truly repent.

XVII. OF PREDESTINATION AND ELECTION

Predestination to Life is the everlasting purpose of God, whereby (before the foundations of the world were laid) he hath constantly decreed by his counsel secret to us, to deliver from curse and damnation those whom he hath chosen in Christ out of mankind, and to bring them by Christ to everlasting salvation, as vessels made to honour. Wherefore, they which be endued with so excellent a benefit of God be called according to God's purpose by his Spirit working in due season: they through Grace obey the calling: they be justified freely: they be made sons of God by adoption: they be made like the image of his only-begotten Son Jesus Christ: they walk religiously in good works, and, at length, by God's mercy, they attain to everlasting felicity.

As the godly consideration of Predestination, and our Election in Christ, is full of sweet, pleasant, and unspeakable comfort to godly persons, and such as feel in themselves the working of the Spirit of Christ, mortifying the works of the flesh, and their earthly members, and drawing up their mind to high and heavenly things, as well because it doth greatly establish and confirm their faith of eternal Salvation to be enjoyed through Christ, as because it doth fervently kindle their love towards God: So, for curious and carnal persons, lacking the Spirit of Christ, to have continually before their eyes the sentence of God's Predestination, is a most dangerous downfall, whereby the Devil doth thrust them either into desperation, or into wretchlessness of most unclean living, no less perilous than desperation.

Furthermore, we must receive God's promises in such wise, as they be generally set forth to us in holy Scripture: and, in our doings, that Will of God is to be followed, which we have expressly declared unto us in the Word of God.

XVIII. OF OBTAINING ETERNAL SALVATION ONLY BY THE NAME OF CHRIST

They also are to be had accursed that presume to say, That every man shall be saved by the Law or Sect which he professeth, so that he be diligent to frame his life according to that Law, and the light of Nature. For holy Scripture doth set out unto us only the Name of Jesus Christ, whereby men must be saved.

XIX. OF THE CHURCH

The visible Church of Christ is a congregation of faithful men, in the which the pure Word of God is preached, and the Sacraments be duly ministered according to Christ's ordinance in all those things that of necessity are requisite to the same.

As the Church of *Jerusalem*, *Alexandria*, and *Antioch*, have erred; so also the Church of *Rome* hath erred, not only in their living and manner of Ceremonies, but also in matters of Faith.

XX. OF THE AUTHORITY OF THE CHURCH

The Church hath power to decree Rites or Ceremonies, and authority in Controversies of Faith: And yet it is not lawful for the Church to ordain any thing that is contrary to God's Word written, neither may it so expound one place of Scripture, that it be repugnant to another. Wherefore, although the Church be a witness and a keeper of holy Writ, yet, as it ought not to decree any thing against the same, so besides the same ought it not to enforce any thing to be believed for necessity of Salvation.

XXI. OF THE AUTHORITY OF GENERAL COUNCILS

General Councils may not be gathered together without the commandment and will of Princes. And when they be gathered together, (forasmuch as they be an assembly of men, whereof all be not governed with the Spirit and Word of God,) they may err, and sometimes have erred, even in things pertaining unto God. Wherefore things ordained by them as necessary to salvation have neither strength nor authority, unless it may be declared that they be taken out of holy Scripture.

XXII. OF PURGATORY

The Romish Doctrine concerning Purgatory, Pardons, Worshipping and Adoration, as well of Images as of Reliques, and also invocation of Saints, is a fond thing, vainly invented, and grounded upon no warranty of Scripture, but rather repugnant to the Word of God.

XXIII. OF MINISTERING IN THE CONGREGATION

It is not lawful for any man to take upon him the office of publick preaching, or ministering the Sacraments in the Congregation, before he be lawfully called, and sent to execute the same. And those we ought to judge lawfully called and sent, which be chosen and called to this work by men who have publick authority given unto them in the Congregation, to call and send Ministers into the Lord's vineyard.

XXIV. OF SPEAKING IN THE CONGREGATION IN SUCH A TONGUE AS THE PEOPLE UNDERSTANDETH

It is a thing plainly repugnant to the Word of God, and the custom of the Primitive Church, to have publick Prayer in the Church, or to minister the Sacraments in a tongue not understanded of the people.

XXV. OF THE SACRAMENTS

Sacraments ordained of Christ be not only badges or tokens of Christian men's profession, but rather they be certain sure witnesses, and effectual signs of grace, and God's good will towards us, by the which he doth work invisibly in us, and doth not only quicken, but also strengthen and confirm our Faith in him.

There are two Sacraments ordained of Christ our Lord in the Gospel, that is to say, Baptism, and the Supper of the Lord.

Those five commonly called Sacraments, that is to say, Confirmation, Penance, Orders, Matrimony and extreme Unction, are not to be counted for Sacraments of the Gospel, being such as have grown partly of the corrupt following of the Apostles, partly are states of life allowed in the Scriptures; but yet have not like nature of Sacraments with Baptism, and the Lord's Supper, for that they have not any visible sign or ceremony ordained of God.

The Sacraments were not ordained of Christ to be gazed upon, or to be carried about, but that we should duly use them. And in such only as worthily receive the same they have a wholesome effect or operation: but they that receive them unworthily purchase to themselves damnation, as Saint *Paul* saith.

XXVI. OF THE UNWORTHINESS OF THE MINISTERS, WHICH HINDERS NOT THE EFFECT OF THE SACRAMENT

Although in the visible Church the evil be ever mingled with the good, and sometimes the evil have chief authority in the Ministration of the Word and Sacraments, yet, forasmuch as they do not the same in their own name, but in Christ's, and do minister by his commission and authority, we may use their Ministry, both in hearing the Word of God and in receiving of the Sacraments. Neither is the effect of Christ's ordinance taken away by their wickedness, nor the grace of God's gifts diminished from such as by faith and rightly do receive the Sacraments ministered unto them; which be effectual, because of Christ's institution and promise, although they be ministered by evil men.

Nevertheless, it appertaineth to the discipline of the Church, that inquiry be made of evil Ministers, and that they be accused by those that have knowledge of their offences; and finally being found guilty, by just judgement be deposed.

XXVII. OF BAPTISM

Baptism is not only a sign of profession, and mark of difference, whereby Christian men are discerned from others that be not christened, but it is also a sign of Regeneration or new Birth, whereby, as by an instrument, they that receive Baptism rightly are grafted into the Church; the promises of forgiveness of sin, and of our adoption to be the sons of God by the Holy Ghost, are visibly signed and sealed; Faith is confirmed, and Grace increased by virtue of prayer unto God. The Baptism of young Children is in any wise to be retained in the Church, as most agreeable with the institution of Christ.

XXVIII. OF THE LORD'S SUPPER

The Supper of the Lord is not only a sign of the love that Christians ought to have among themselves one to another; but rather is a Sacrament of our Redemption by Christ's death: insomuch that to such as rightly, worthily, and with faith, receive the same, the Bread which we break is a partaking of the Body of Christ; and likewise the Cup of Blessing is a partaking of the Blood of Christ.

Transubstantiation (or the change of the substance of Bread and Wine) in the Supper of the Lord, cannot be proved by holy writ; but is repugnant to the plain words of Scripture, overthroweth the nature of a Sacrament, and hath given occasion to many superstitions.

The Body of Christ is given, taken, and eaten, in the Supper, only after an heavenly and spiritual manner. And the mean whereby the Body of Christ is received and eaten in the Supper is Faith.

The Sacrament of the Lord's Supper was not by Christ's ordinance reserved, carried about, lifted up, or worshipped.

XXIX. OF THE WICKED WHICH EAT NOT THE BODY OF CHRIST IN THE USE OF THE LORD'S SUPPER

The Wicked, and such as be void of a lively faith, although they do carnally and visibly press with their teeth (as Saint *Augustine* saith) the Sacrament of the Body and Blood of Christ, yet in no wise are they partakers of Christ: but rather, to their condemnation, do eat and drink the sign or Sacrament of so great a thing.

XXX. OF BOTH KINDS

The Cup of the Lord is not to be denied to the Lay-people: for both the parts of the Lord's Sacrament, by Christ's ordinance and commandment, ought to be ministered to all Christian men alike.

XXXI. OF THE ONE OBLATION OF CHRIST FINISHED UPON THE CROSS

The Offering of Christ once made is that perfect redemption, propitiation, and satisfaction, for all the sins of the whole world, both original and actual; and there is none other satisfaction for sin, but that alone. Wherefore the sacrifices of the Masses, in the which it was commonly said, that the Priest did offer Christ for the quick and the dead, to have remission of pain or guilt, were blasphemous fables, and dangerous deceits.

XXXII. OF THE MARRIAGE OF PRIESTS

Bishops, Priests, and Deacons, are not commanded by God's Law, either to vow the estate of single life, or to abstain from marriage: therefore it is lawful for them, as for all other Christian men, to marry at their own discretion, as they shall judge the same to serve better for godliness.

XXXIII. OF EXCOMMUNICATE PERSONS, HOW THEY ARE TO BE AVOIDED

That person which by open denunciation of the Church is rightly cut off from the unity of the Church, and excommunicated, ought to be taken of the whole multitude of the faithful, as an Heathen and Publican, until he be openly reconciled by penance, and received into the Church by a Judge that hath authority thereunto.

XXXIV. OF THE TRADITIONS OF THE CHURCH

It is not necessary that Traditions and Ceremonies be in all places one, and utterly like; for at all times they have been divers, and may be changed according to the diversities of countries, times, and men's manners, so that nothing be ordained against God's Word. Whosoever through his private judgement, willingly and purposely, doth openly break the traditions and ceremonies of the Church which be not repugnant to the Word of God, and be ordained and approved by common authority, ought to be rebuked openly, (that others may fear to do the like,) as he that offendeth against the common order of the Church, and hurteth the authority of the Magistrate, and woundeth the consciences of the weak brethren.

Every particular or national Church hath authority to ordain, change, and abolish, ceremonies or rites of the Church ordained only by man's authority, so that all things be done to edifying.

XXXV. OF THE HOMILIES

The Second Book of Homilies, the several titles whereof we have joined under this Article, doth contain a godly and wholesome Doctrine and necessary for these times, as doth the former Book of Homilies, which were set forth in the time of *Edward* the Sixth; and therefore we judge them to be read in Churches by the Ministers, diligently and distinctly, that they may be understanded of the people.

Of the Names of the Homilies

1. Of the right Use of the Church
2. Against peril of Idolatry
3. Of repairing and keeping clean of Churches
4. Of Good Works: first of Fasting
5. Against Gluttony and Drunkenness
6. Against Excess of Apparel
7. Of Prayer
8. Of the Place and Time of Prayer
9. That Common Prayers and Sacraments ought to be ministered in a known tongue
10. Of the reverend estimation of God's Word
11. Of Alms-doing
12. Of the Nativity of Christ
13. Of the Passion of Christ
14. Of the Resurrection of Christ
15. Of the worthy receiving of the Sacrament of the Body and Blood of Christ
16. Of the Gifts of the Holy Ghost
17. For the Rogation-Days
18. Of the State of Matrimony
19. Of Repentance

20. Against Idleness
21. Against Rebellion

XXXVI. OF CONSECRATION OF BISHOPS AND MINISTERS

The Book of Consecration of Archbishops and Bishops, and Ordering of Priests and Deacons, lately set forth in the time of *Edward* the Sixth, and confirmed at the same time by the authority of Parliament, doth contain all things necessary to such Consecration and Ordering: neither hath it any thing that of itself is superstitious and ungodly. And therefore whoever are consecrated or ordered according to the Rites of that Book, since the second year of the forenamed King *Edward* unto this time, or hereafter shall be consecrated, or ordered according to the same Rites; we decree all such to be rightly, orderly, and lawfully consecrated and ordered.

XXXVII. OF THE CIVIL MAGISTRATES

The King's Majesty hath the chief power in this Realm of England, and other his Dominions, unto whom the chief Government of all Estates of this Realm, whether they be Ecclesiastical or Civil, in all causes doth appertain, and is not, nor ought to be, subject to any foreign Jurisdiction.

Where we attribute to the King's Majesty the chief government, by which Titles we understand the minds of some slanderous folks to be offended; we give not to our Princes the ministering either of God's Word, or of the Sacraments, the which thing the Injunctions also lately set forth by *Elizabeth* our Queen do most plainly testify; but that only prerogative, which we see to have been given always to all godly Princes in holy Scriptures by God himself: that is, that they should rule all estates and degrees committed to their charge by God, whether they be Ecclesiastical or Temporal, and restrain with the civil sword the stubborn and evildoers.

The Bishop of *Rome* hath no jurisdiction in this Realm of *England*.

The Laws of the Realm may punish Christian men with death, for heinous and grievous offences.

It is lawful for Christian men, at the commandment of the Magistrate, and to wear weapons, and to serve in the wars.

XXXVIII. OF CHRISTIAN MEN'S GOODS, WHICH ARE NOT COMMON

The Riches and Goods of Christians are not common, as touching the right, title, and possession of the same, as certain Anabaptists do falsely boast. Notwithstanding, every man ought, of such things as he possesseth, liberally to give alms to the poor, according to his ability.

XXXIX. OF A CHRISTIAN MAN'S OATH

As we confess that vain and rash Swearing is forbidden Christian men by our Lord Jesus Christ, and *James* his Apostle, so we judge, that Christian Religion doth not prohibit, but that a man may swear when the Magistrate requireth, in a cause of faith and charity, so it be done according to the Prophet's teaching, in justice, judgement, and truth.

Bibliography

INTRODUCTION

Anglicanism is a worldwide Christian denomination that has operated in print in the English language for more than four and a half centuries. It has a correspondingly enormous literature. As the history of the Church of England itself lies at the root and the heart of the worldwide development, so a general history of that Church is a key to an initial understanding of the whole Communion. A one-volume history, such as John R. H. Moorman's *A History of the Church of England* (1953), not only covers the ground of this dictionary but also provides a comprehensive background of the period from the first century to the 16th. It was matched for many years by a kind of predecessor of this volume, *A Dictionary of English Church History*, edited by S. L. Ollard, Gordon Crosse, and Maurice F. Bond (1912; 3rd ed., 1948). It remains valuable, but more than half a century has passed since it was last updated.

The relationship between the history of Anglicanism in its originating country and the growth from it of a worldwide Communion is told in succinct form in Stephen Neill's *Anglicanism* (1958). In this, and in his revised edition in 1977, a man with unrivaled experience and knowledge of the Communion not only gave an overview of its growth but also appended his own comprehensive bibliography, with a careful evaluation of the authors and books concerned. His presentation of history is well matched and undergirded by sample key documents in G. R. Evans and J. Robert Wright (eds.), *The Anglican Tradition: A Handbook of Sources* (1991), as this gives more than 600 extracts, one-fifth from before the Reformation, and over half covering worldwide developments since 1784.

Other outline histories, with an emphasis on the creation of dioceses and provinces, are to be found in H. C. G. Herklots, *Frontiers of the*

Church: The Making of the Anglican Communion (1961); J. W. C. Wand, *Anglicanism in History and Today* (1961); and a book published more recently but still taking the story only to 1960, William M. Jacob's *The Making of the Anglican Church Worldwide* (1997). A very thorough work that comes nearer to the present time is William Sachs's *The Transformation of Anglicanism: From State Church to Global Communion* (1993). A pocket overview is given in James Rosenthal's *The Essential Guide to the Anglican Communion* (1998). *The Oxford Dictionary of the Christian Church* (3rd ed., 1999) gives generous space to Anglican history and persons, and in the United States, there is a first-rate resource available in the reference work specifically compiled for the Episcopal Church by Don S. Armentrout and Robert Boak Slocum, *An Episcopal Dictionary of the Church: A User-Friendly Reference for Episcopalians* (1999); both of these dictionaries contain valuable bibliographies themselves, the former attached to each entry where it comes in the dictionary, the latter grouped in an appendix. In various countries, a dictionary of national biography provides a close look at hundreds of leading citizens of the various centuries, including church leaders. Britain and the United States have a much higher output of serious books on Anglicanism and Anglican topics than the rest of the world, and there has been a tendency for British and American books to dominate the academic scene in most parts of the Communion.

Foundation features of Anglicanism in the 16th century were the Thirty-Nine Articles of Religion and the Book of Common Prayer in its 1552/1559 form. Alongside and interlocked with them were the institutions of a threefold ordained ministry (and the ordinal by which the ministers were ordained), a governmental role for bishops, and a unique church–state relationship. The actual text of the Articles (to be found in appendix B in this volume) and the overall character of the Book of Common Prayer are central to the history of Anglicanism. In the 20th century, useful and scholarly books on the Articles have included E. J. Bicknell, *A Theological Introduction to the Thirty-Nine Articles* (1925), and W. H. Griffith Thomas, *The Principles of Theology: An Introduction to the Thirty-Nine Articles* (1930)—Bicknell from an Anglo-Catholic standpoint, Thomas from an evangelical one. The more recent report of the Church of England's Doctrine Commission, *Subscription and Assent to the Thirty-Nine Articles* (1969), sets the issue of the status of the Articles in close relation to the study of their meaning. For the

Book of Common Prayer, there are enormous resources available, but no single-volume scholarly and readable overview to match Geoffrey Cuming's *History of Anglican Liturgy* (2nd ed., 1981). A large part of the bibliography below records the primary sources and secondary literature in this enormous field.

While the Lambeth Conferences that began in 1867 have no formal or constitutional position in the Communion's structures, they provide a record every 10 years of the leading issues of the Communion and the way bishops are addressing them. Their reports, listed below, are indispensable for pan-Anglican issues. Since 1971 they have been supplemented by the work of the Anglican Consultative Council, and there are 13 meetings of the Council recorded since then; their reports are listed below also. Through the role of the archbishops of Canterbury and other initiatives, there have been significant international conversations with other world denominations; the work of the Anglican–Roman Catholic International Commissions (ARCIC-1 and ARCIC-2) has been prominent among such ecumenical conversations, and their reports, beginning from the agreed statement on the Eucharist in 1971 and running through to ARCIC-2's *The Gift of Authority* in 1999 and *Mary: Grace and Hope in Christ* in 2005, deserve close attention. In the ecumenical field, the uniting of Anglican dioceses with non-Episcopal churches in 1947 to form the Church of South India is a unique field of historical study in its own right, and Bengt Sundkler's detailed account in *Church of South India: The Movement towards Union, 1900–1947* demonstrates both the complexity and frustrations of such ecumenical planning, as well as recording the overcoming of difficulties. It was in the ecumenical field that the "Lambeth Quadrilateral" was first deployed in 1888, and its origins, text, and impact are usefully surveyed in J. Robert Wright's compilation, *Quadrilateral at One Hundred* (1988).

In the biographical section below, the archbishops of Canterbury from Thomas Cranmer to Rowan Williams are inevitably key players, and the careful biographies of them (arranged here in chronological order) often provide the best-documented historical records available. In the 20th century, there is little doubt that the biographies of Randall Davidson by George Bell and of Michael Ramsey by Owen Chadwick hold pride of place. But there are other kinds of biographies, providing a many-faceted view of world Anglicanism—whether the pioneer church builder in New Zealand, George Augustus Selwyn (*Churchman*

Militant); the African lay evangelist martyr, Bernard Mizeki (*Mashonaland Martyr*); or the prophetic Desmond Tutu (*Tutu, Voice of the Voiceless*).

Each province or church of the Anglican Communion has its own provincial office and usually has archives and records—or access to them in university, theological college, or civic libraries. Many of them have websites, and if they do not, they have a webpage at the Anglican Communion Office's website. These means should enable inquirers to gain access to such records. In England itself, Lambeth Palace Library has unique archives, and the Anglican Communion Office has an overview of the Communion as it is today. Other historic records are to be found in the ancient universities, in cathedral libraries or archives, in missionary society records, at the Lambeth Palace library, and at the Church of England Record Centre, 15 Galleywall Road, South Bermondsey, London SE16 3PB (e-mail: archivist@c-of-e.org.uk).

Under each heading in this bibliography, a rough chronological order has been observed, either of the authors or of the historical themes or periods being listed. Inspection will quickly show the basis in each section. Biographies are also listed chronologically, and where the name does not appear in the title or as the author, it is shown in brackets after the title.

Note that in many cases the publishers listed have addresses in countries other than those shown. In other cases, books were published by two or more publishers at one time. In each case, only one publisher is listed here, with only one place of publication noted.

The following acronyms are used for frequently cited publishers in the bibliographical list:

ABC	Anglican Book Centre
ACC	Anglican Consultative Council
APCK	Association for Promoting Christian Knowledge
CHP	Church House Publishing
CIO	Church Information Office
CUP	Cambridge University Press
DLT	Darton, Longman & Todd
IERE	Iglesia Española Reformada Episcopal
ISPCK	Indian Society for Promoting Christian Knowledge
IVP	Inter-Varsity Press

LWF	Lutheran World Federation
OUP	Oxford University Press
SCM	Student Christian Movement
SPCK	Society for Promoting Christian Knowledge
SPG	Society for the Propagation of the Gospel
WCC	World Council of Churches'

CONTENTS

I. General Reference Works 517
II. Official Church Documents 517
A. Reports of the Anglican Congresses 517
1. Minneapolis, 1954 517
2. Toronto, 1963 518
B. Reports of the Lambeth Conferences 518
1. 1867, 1878, and 1888 518
2. 1897 518
3. 1908 518
4. 1920 518
5. 1930 518
6. 1948 519
7. 1958 519
8. 1968 519
9. 1978 519
10. 1988 519
11. 1998 519
12. Ancillary Books and Documents 519
C. Reports of the Anglican Consultative Council (ACC) 520
1. ACC-1:. Limuru, Kenya, 1971 520
2. ACC-2:. Dublin, 1973 520
3. ACC-3:. Trinidad, 1976 520
4. ACC-4:. London, Ontario, 1979 520
5. ACC-5:. Newcastle upon Tyne, 1981 520
6. ACC-6:. Badagry, Lagos, Nigeria, 1984 520
7. ACC-7:. Singapore, 1987 521
8. ACC-8:. Cardiff, 1990 521
9. ACC-9:. Cape Town, 1993 521

10. ACC-X:. Panama City, Panama, 1996 521
11. ACC-XI:. Dundee, Scotland, 1999 521
12. ACC-XII:. Hong Kong, 2002 521
III. The Anglican Communion: General Works 521
IV. General Histories 522
A. From Early Times to the 20th Century 522
B. Reformation in Britain 523
C. Canon Law and Convocations of the Church of England 523
D. The 17th Century in Britain 523
E. The Formation of a Worldwide Communion 523
F. The 18th–20th Centuries in England 524
G. Ireland 524
H. Scotland 524
I. Wales 524
J. North America 524
1. Canada 524
2. United States of America 524
K. Central and South America 525
L. Africa 525
1. Southern Africa 525
2. Uganda 525
M. Asia 525
N. Australasia 526
O. Spain and Portugal 526
P. Religious Communities 526
V. Biographies 526
A. Archbishops of Canterbury 526
1. Thomas Cranmer, 1533–1556 527
2. Matthew Parker, 1560–1575 527
3. John Whitgift, 1583–1604 527
4. George Abbot, 1611–1633 527
5. Thomas Tenison, 1695–1716 527
6. William Wake, 1716–1737 527
7. Archibald Campbell Tait, 1868–1882 527
8. Edward White Benson, 1883–1896 527
9. Frederick Temple, 1896–1903 527
10. Randall Davidson, 1903–1928 528

11. Cosmo Gordon Lang, 1928–1942 528
12. William Temple, 1942–1944 528
13. Geoffrey Fisher, 1945–1961 528
14. Arthur Michael Ramsey, 1961–1974 528
15. Frederick Donald Coggan, 1974–1980 528
16. Robert Alexander Kennedy Runcie, 1980–1991 528
17. George Leonard Carey, 1991–2002 528
18. Rowan Douglas Williams, 2002– 528

B. Other Church of England 528
C. Ireland 529
D. North America 530
E. East Africa 530
F. Central Africa 530
G. South Africa 530
H. China 530
I. India 530
J. Australia 531
K. New Zealand 531

VI. The Anglican Communion in an Ecumenical Context 531

A. General Works 531
B. Anglican–Roman Catholic Reports and Commentaries 531
1. Reports 531
2. Commentaries 532
C. Anglican–Lutheran Reports 532
D. Anglican–Methodist Reports 532
E. Anglican–Moravian Reports 532
F. Anglican–Reformed Reports 532
G. Old Catholic Churches 532
H. Reformed Episcopal Church 533
I. Free Church of England 533

VII. Doctrinal Foundations 533

A. Official 16th-Century Texts 533
B. Thirty-Nine Articles 533
C. Classic Writings 534
D. Modern Surveys 534
E. Reports 535

VIII. Liturgical Texts 535
A. Church of England 535
B. Church of Scotland—Scottish Episcopal Church 536
C. Church of Ireland 536
D. Protestant Episcopal Church of the United States of America 536
E. The Anglican Church of Canada 537
F. The Church of the Province of South Africa 537
G. The Anglican Church in Australia 537
H. The Church of Aotearoa, New Zealand, and Polynesia 537
I. The Anglican Church in Nigeria 537
J. The Anglican Church of Kenya 537
K. The Church of South India 537
L. The Church of North India 538
M. Resources for the Texts 538
N. General Histories and Commentaries on the Church of England Prayer Books 538
O. Music and Hymnody 539
P. Architecture 539
Q. Pan-Anglican Collections 540
1. Eucharist 540
2. Baptism and Confirmation 540
3. Ordination 540
4. Publications of the International Anglican Liturgical Consultations (IALC) 540
R. Ceremonial 541
IX. Specific Doctrines 541
A. Scriptural Authority 541
B. The Church 541
C. Church and State: Establishment and Disestablishment in England 542
D. The Sacraments 543
E. Baptism and Confirmation 543
F. The Eucharist 543
G. Orders 544
H. Presidency of the Eucharist 544
I. Ordination of Women 544

J. Validity of Anglican Orders 545
K. *Episcopi Vagantes* 545
X. Strands of Anglicanism 545
A. Anglo-Catholicism 545
B. Evangelicalism 546
C. Anglo-Catholics and Evangelicals Together 546
D. Charismatic Movement 546
XI. Spirituality 547
XII. Periodicals 547
XIII. Websites 547
A. Anglican Communion 547
B. Individual Churches or Provinces 547
XIV. Addresses of Provinces or Churches of the Anglican Communion 548
A. Anglican Communion 548
B. Individual Churches or Provinces 549

I. GENERAL REFERENCE WORKS

Armentrout, Don S., and Robert Boak Slocum, eds. *An Episcopal Dictionary of the Church: A User-Friendly Reference for Episcopalians*. New York: Church Publishing, 1999.

Cross, F. L., and E. A. Livingstone, eds. *Oxford Dictionary of the Christian Church*. 3rd ed. Oxford: OUP, 1997.

Latourette, Kenneth Scott. *A History of the Expansion of Christianity*. 7 vols. London: Eyre & Spottiswoode, 1937–1945.

Neill, Stephen, Gerald H. Anderson, and John Goodwin, eds. *Concise Dictionary of the Christian World Mission*. London: Lutterworth Press, 1970.

Ollard, S. L., Gordon Crosse, and Maurice F. Bond, eds. *A Dictionary of English Church History*. London: Mowbray, 1912; 3rd ed., 1948.

II. OFFICIAL CHURCH DOCUMENTS

A. Reports of the Anglican Congresses

1. Minneapolis, 1954

Dawley, Powell Mills, ed. *Anglican Congress, 1954: Report of Proceedings—August 4–13, Minneapolis, Minnesota*. Greenwich, Conn.: Seabury Press, 1954.

2. Toronto, 1963

Fairweather, E. R., ed. *Anglican Congress, 1963: Report of Proceedings—August 13–23, Toronto, Canada.* Toronto: Published by the Editorial Committee and distributed by Anglican Book Centre, 1963.

B. Reports of the Lambeth Conferences

1. 1867, 1878, and 1888

The Very Rev. the Dean of Windsor [Randall T. Davidson], ed. *The Lambeth Conferences of 1867, 1878, and 1888: With the Official Reports and Resolutions, together with the Sermons preached at the Conferences*. New and rev. ed. London: SPCK, 1896.

Conference of Bishops of the Anglican Communion, Holden at Lambeth Palace, in July 1888: Encyclical Letter from the Bishops with the Resolutions and Reports. London: SPCK, 1888.

2. 1897

Conference of Bishops of the Anglican Communion, Holden at Lambeth Palace, in July 1897: Encyclical Letter from the Bishops with the Resolutions and Reports. London: SPCK, 1897.

Davidson, Randall T., ed. *The Lambeth Conference of 1897: With the Official Reports and Resolutions, together with Sermons preached at the Conference—Being a Supplementary Volume to "The Lambeth Conferences of 1867, 1878, and 1888."* London: SPCK, 1907.

3. 1908

Report of the Lambeth Conference, 1908. London: SPCK, 1908.

4. 1920

Davidson, Randall T., ed. *The Six Lambeth Conferences*. London: SPCK, 1929.

The Lambeth Conference, 1920: Encyclical Letter from the Bishops with Resolutions and Reports. London: SPCK, 1920.

5. 1930

The Lambeth Conference, 1930: Encyclical Letter from the Bishops with Resolutions and Reports. London: SPCK, 1930.

Lambeth Conferences, 1867–1930: The Reports of the 1920 and 1930 Conferences, with Selected Resolutions from the Conferences of 1867, 1878, 1888, 1897 and 1908. London: SPCK, 1948.

6. 1948

The Lambeth Conference, 1948: Encyclical Letter from the Bishops Together with the Resolutions and Reports. London: SPCK, 1948.

7. 1958

The Lambeth Conference, 1958: Encyclical Letter from the Bishops Together with the Resolutions and Reports. London: SPCK, 1958.

8. 1968

The Lambeth Conference, 1968: Resolutions and Reports. London: SPCK, 1968.

9. 1978

The Report of the Lambeth Conference, 1978. London: CIO, 1978.

10. 1988

The Truth Shall Make You Free: The Lambeth Conference, 1988; The Reports, Resolutions and Pastoral Letters from the Bishops. London: CHP for the ACC, 1988.

11. 1998

The Official Report of the Lambeth Conference, 1998. Harrisburg, Pa.: Morehouse for the Anglican Communion, 1999.

12. Ancillary Books and Documents

Bayne, Stephen, ed. *An Anglican Turning Point: Documents and Interpretations.* Austin, Texas: Church Historical Society, 1964.

Lambeth Conference 1968 Preparatory Information. London: SPCK, 1968.

Archbishop of Canterbury, ed. *Lambeth Essays on Faith.* London: SPCK, 1969.

——. *Lambeth Essays on Ministry.* London: SPCK, 1969.

——. *Lambeth Essays on Unity.* London: SPCK, 1969.

Stephenson, Alan M. G. *Anglicanism and the Lambeth Conferences 1867–1968.* London: SPCK, 1978.

The Lambeth Conference 1978 Preparatory Articles: Today's Church and Today's World, with a Special Focus on the Ministry of Bishops. London: CIO, 1978.

The Lambeth Conference 1978 Preparatory Information: Statistics, Documentation, Addresses, Maps. London: CIO, 1978.

Samuel, Vinay, and Christopher Sugden. *Lambeth: A View from the Two Thirds World*. London: SPCK, 1988.

C. Reports of the Anglican Consultative Council (ACC)

Note: The numbering of these meetings moved from Arabic to Roman numerals after no. 9, the titles given to reports had no consistency, and the "compilers" are shown below where their names are on the outside cover of the report. The report of ACC-XIII (held in Nottingham, England, in 2005) was not available at the time of going to press.

1. ACC-1:. Limuru, Kenya, 1971

The Time Is Now. London: SPCK, 1971.

2. ACC-2:. Dublin, 1973

Partners in Mission. London: SPCK, 1973.

3. ACC-3:. Trinidad, 1976

ACC-3 Trinidad. N.p., n.d.

4. ACC-4:. London, Ontario, 1979

ACC-4 Anglican Consultative Council. N.p., n.d.

5. ACC-5:. Newcastle upon Tyne, 1981

ACC-5 Anglican Consultative Council. London: ACC, 1981.

6. ACC-6:. Badagry, Lagos, Nigeria, 1984

Bonds of Affection. London: ACC, 1985.

7. ACC-7:. Singapore, 1987

Many Gifts, One Spirit. London: CHP for ACC, 1987.

8. ACC-8:. Cardiff, 1990

Mission in a Broken World. London: CHP for ACC, 1990.

9. ACC-9:. Cape Town, 1993

A Transforming Vision, Cape Town, 1993. London: CHP for the Anglican Communion Office, 1993.

10. ACC-X:. Panama City, Panama, 1996

Being Anglican in the Third Millennium—Includes the Virginia Report and the Dublin Liturgical Report. Harrisburg, Pa.: Morehouse for the Anglican Communion Office, 1997.

11. ACC-XI:. Dundee, Scotland, 1999

Rosenthal, James M., and Margaret Rodgers, compilers. *The Communion We Share*. Harrisburg, Pa.: Morehouse for the Anglican Communion Office, 2000.

12. ACC-XII:. Hong Kong, 2002

Rosenthal, James M., compiler. *For the Life of the World*. Harrisburg, Pa.: Morehouse, 2003.

III. THE ANGLICAN COMMUNION: GENERAL WORKS

Church Assembly Overseas Council. *The Moving Spirit: A Survey of the Life and Work of the Churches of the Anglican Communion*. London: CIO, 1957.

Eaton, Peter, ed. *The Trial of Faith: Theology and the Church Today*. Worthing, England: Churchman Publishing, 1988.

Evans, Gillian R., and J. Robert Wright, eds. *The Anglican Tradition: A Handbook of Sources*. London: SPCK, 1991.

Gomez, Drexel W., and Maurice W. Sinclair, eds. *To Mend the Net: Anglican Faith and Order for Renewed Mission*. Carollton, Tex.: Ekklesia Society, 2001.

Herklots, H. C. K. *Frontiers of the Church: The Making of the Anglican Communion*. London: Ernest Benn, 1961.

Jacob, William M. *The Making of the Anglican Church Worldwide*. London: SPCK, 1997.

Johnson, Howard A. *Global Odyssey: Visiting the Anglican Churches*. London: Geoffrey Bles, 1963.

Neill, Stephen. *Anglicanism.* Harmondsworth, England: Penguin, 1958; 2nd ed., London: Mowbray, 1977.

Platten, Stephen. *Augustine's Legacy: Authority and Leadership in the Anglican Communion*. London: DLT, 1997.

Rosenthal, James M., compiler. *The Essential Guide to the Anglican Communion.* Harrisburg, Pa.: Morehouse, 1998.

Sachs, William L. *The Transformation of Anglicanism: From State Church to Global Community*. Cambridge: CUP, 1993.

Sansbury, C. Kenneth. *Truth, Unity and Concord: Anglican Faith in an Ecumenical Setting*. London: Mowbray, 1967.

Sykes, Stephen W. *The Integrity of Anglicanism.* London: Mowbray, 1978.

———. *Unashamed Anglicanism*. London: DLT, 1995.

———, ed. *Authority in the Anglican Communion: Essays Presented to John Howe.* Toronto: Anglican Book Centre, 1987.

Sykes, Stephen W., and John E. Booty, eds. *The Study of Anglicanism*. London: SPCK, 1988.

Turner, Philip, and Frank Sugeno, eds. *Crossroads Are for Meeting: Essays on the Mission and Common Life of the Church in a Global Society*. Sewanee, Tenn.: SPCK (USA), 1986.

Wand, J. W. C. *Anglicanism in History and Today*. London: Weidenfeld & Nicholson, 1961.

Wingate, Andrew, Kevin Ward, Carrie Pemberton, and Wilson Sitshebo, eds. *Anglicanism: A Global Communion.* London: Mowbray, 2001.

Wolf, William J., ed. *The Spirit of Anglicanism: Hooker, Maurice, Temple.* Wilton, Conn.: Morehouse-Barlow, 1979.

Wright, J. Robert, ed. *Quadrilateral at One Hundred: Essays on the Centenary of the Chicago-Lambeth Quadrilateral, 1886/88–1986/88.* Cincinnati: Forward Movement, 1988.

IV. GENERAL HISTORIES

A. From Early Times to the 20th Century

Moorman, J. R. H. *A History of the Church of England.* London: A. & C. Black, 1953. There have been frequent reprintings.

B. Reformation in Britain

Dickens, A. G. *The English Reformation*. New York: Schocken Books, 1964.

Duffy, Eamon. *The Stripping of the Altars: Traditional Religion in England, 1400–1580*. New Haven, Conn.: Yale University Press, 1992.

George, Charles H., and Katherine George. *The Protestant Mind of the English Reformation.* Princeton, N.J.: Princeton University Press, 1961.

McCulloch, Diarmaid. *Reformation: Europe's House Divided, 1490–1700*. London: Allen Lane, 2003.

Powicke, F. M. *The Reformation in England.* London: OUP, 1941.

Ryrie, Alec. *The Gospel and Henry VIII: Evangelicals in the Early English Reformation.* Cambridge: CUP, 2003.

C. Canon Law and Convocations of the Church of England

Bray, Gerald, ed. *The Anglican Canons, 1529–1947*. Woodbridge, Suffolk: Boydell Press for the Church of England Record Society, 1998.

Cardwell, Edward, ed. *Synodalia: A Collection of Articles of Religion, Canons, and Proceedings of Convocations in the Province of Canterbury, from the Year 1547 to the Year 1717*. 2 vols. Oxford: OUP, 1842.

D. The 17th Century in Britain

Bosher, R. S. *The Making of the Reformation Settlement: The Influence of the Laudians, 1649–1662.* London: Dacre, 1961.

E. The Formation of a Worldwide Communion

Allen, Roland. *Missionary Methods: St. Paul's or Ours?* 2nd ed. Grand Rapids, Mich.: Eerdmans, 1962.

Blood, A. G. *The History of the Universities Mission to Central Africa*. 3 vols. London: UMCA, 1955–1962.

Cnattingius, Hans. *Bishops and Societies: A Study of Anglican Colonial and Missionary Expansion, 1698–1850*. London: SPCK for the Church Historical Society, 1952.

MISSIO. *Anglicans in Mission: A Transforming Journey; Report of MISSIO, the Mission Commission of the Anglican Communion, to the Anglican Consultative Council, Meeting in Edinburgh, Soctland, September 1999*. London: SPCK, 1999.

Neill, Stephen C. *A History of Christian Missions.* Harmondsworth, England: Penguin, 1964.

Stock, Eugene. *The History of the Church Missionary Society*. 4 vols. London: Church Missionary Society, 1899–1916.

Thompson, H. P. *Into All Lands* [a history of the SPG]. London: SPG, 1951.

Wheeler, Andrew, ed. *Voices from Africa: Transforming Vision in a Context of Marginalization: An Anthology.* London: Church House, 2002.

F. The 18th–20th Centuries in England

Brilioth, Y. *Anglican Revival.* London: Longmans, 1925.

Chadwick, Owen. *The Victorian Church*. 3rd ed. London: SCM, 1971.

——, ed. *The Mind of the Oxford Movement*. London: A. & C. Black, 1960.

Hastings, Adrian. *A History of English Christianity, 1920–2000*. London: SCM, 2001.

Lloyd, Roger. *The Church of England, 1900–1965.* London: SCM, 1966.

Ollard, S. L. *A Short History of the Oxford Movement*. London: Mowbray, 1915.

Wand, J. W. C. *The High Church Schism* [Nonjurors]. London: Faith Press, 1951.

G. Ireland

Acheson, Alan. *A History of the Church of Ireland, 1691–2001*. 2nd ed. Dublin: Columba Press, 2002.

Phillips, Walter Alison, ed. *History of the Church of Ireland from the Earliest Times to the Present Day*. London: OUP, 1933.

H. Scotland

Goldie, Frederick. *A Short History of the Episcopal Church in Scotland*. Edinburgh: St. Andrew Press, 1976.

I. Wales

Harris, Christopher, and Richard Startup. *The Church in Wales: The Sociology of a Traditional Institution*. Cardiff: University of Wales Press, 1999.

K. North America

1. Canada

Carrington, Philip. *The Anglican Church in Canada*. Toronto: Collins, 1963.

2. United States of America

Albright, Raymond W. *A History of the Protestant Episcopal Church*. New York: Macmillan, 1964.

Herklots, H. C. G. *The Church of England and the American Episcopal Church: From the First Voyages of Discovery to the First Lambeth Conference.* London: Mowbray, 1966.
Mills, Frederick V. *Bishops by Ballot: An Eighteenth-Century Ecclesiastical Revolution.* New York: OUP, 1978.
Prichard, Robert W. *A History of the Episcopal Church.* 2nd ed. Harrisburg, Pa.: Morehouse, 1999.
Woolverton, John Frederick. *Colonial Anglicanism in North America*. Detroit: Wayne University Press, 1984.

K. Central and South America

Every, Edward. *Anglican Church in Latin America*. 2 vols. London: SPCK, 1915.
Milmine, Douglas. *The History of Anglicanism in Latin America*. Tunbridge Wells, England: South American Missionary Society, 1994.

L. Africa

Sundkler, Bengt, and Christopher Steed. *A History of the Church in Africa*. Cambridge: CUP, 2000.

1. Southern Africa

Hinchliff, Peter. *The Anglican Church in South Africa*. London: DLT, 1963.
Huddleston, Trevor. *Naught for Your Comfort*. London: Collins, 1956.

2. Uganda

Taylor, John V. *The Growth of the Church in Buganda: An Attempt at Understanding*. London: SCM, 1958.

M. Asia

George, K. M. *Church of South India: Life in Union, 1947–1997*. Delhi: ISPCK, 1997.
Gibbs, M. E. *The Anglican Church in India, 1600–1970*. Delhi: ISPCK, 1972.
Mar Thoma, Alexander. *The Mar Thoma Church: Heritage and Mission*. Tiruvalla, Kerala, India: Mar Thoma Church, 1985.
Marshall, W. J. *A United Church: Faith and Order in the North India/Pakistan Unity Plan, a Theological Assessment*. Delhi: ISPCK, 1987.

Sundkler, Bengt. *The Church of South India: The Movement towards Union, 1900–1947*. London: Lutterworth, 1954.

N. Australasia

Breward, Ian. *A History of the Church in Australasia*. Oxford, England: Clarendon Press, 2002.
Davis, Brian. *The Way Ahead: Anglican Change and Prospect in New Zealand*. Christchurch, New Zealand: Caxton Press, 1995.
Kaye, Bruce, ed. *Anglicanism in Australia: A History*. Melbourne, Australia: Melbourne University Press, 2002.

O. Spain and Portugal

Lozano, Carlos Lopez. *Precedentes de la Iglesia Española Reformada Episcopal*. Madrid: IERE, 1991.
Noyes, H. E. *Church Reform in Spain and Portugal*. London: Cassell & Co., 1897.
Taibo, Ramon. *Cien Annos de Testimonio, 1880–1980: Datas para la historia de la Iglesia Española Reformada Episcopal*. Madrid: IERE, 1980.

P. Religious Communities

Allchin, A. M. *The Silent Rebellion: Anglican Religious Communities, 1845–1900*. London: SCM, 1958.
Anglican Religious Communities Year Book. Norwich, England: Canterbury Press, annual.
Anson, Peter F. *The Call of the Cloister: Religious Communities and Kindred Bodies in the Anglican Communion*. London: SPCK, 1964.
Mumm, Susan. *Stolen Daughters, Virgin Mothers: Anglican Sisterhoods in Victorian Britain*. Leicester, England: Leicester University Press, 1999.
Williams, Barrie. *The Franciscan Revival in the Anglican Communion*. London: DLT, 1982.

V. BIOGRAPHIES

A. Archbishops of Canterbury

Carpenter, Edward. *Cantuar: The Archbishops in Their Office*. London: Cassell, 1971; 3rd ed. with a new introduction and additional chapters by Adrian Hastings, London: Mowbray, 1997.

1. Thomas Cranmer, 1533–1556

MacCulloch, Diarmaid. *Thomas Cranmer*. New Haven, Conn.: Yale University Press, 1996.

2. Matthew Parker, 1560–1575

Brook, V. J. K. *Life of Archbishop Parker*. Oxford: OUP, 1962.

3. John Whitgift, 1583–1604

Brook, V. J. K. *Whitgift and the English Church.* London: English Universities Press, 1957.

4. George Abbot, 1611–1633

Welsby, Paul. A. *George Abbot: The Unwanted Archbishop, 1562–1633*. London: SPCK, 1962.

5. Thomas Tenison, 1695–1716

Carpenter, Edward. *Thomas Tenison, Archbishop of Canterbury: His Life and Times*. London: SPCK, 1948.

6. William Wake, 1716–1737

Sykes, Norman. *William Wake, Archbishop of Canterbury, 1657–1737*. Cambridge: CUP, 1957.

7. Archibald Campbell Tait, 1868–1882

Davidson, Randall T., and William Benham. *Life of Archibald Campbell Tait, Archbishop of Canterbury*. 2 vols. London: Macmillan, 1891.

8. Edward White Benson, 1883–1896

Benson, Arthur Christopher. *The Life of Edward White Benson, Sometime Archbishop of Canterbury*. 2 vols. London: Macmillan, 1899.

9. Frederick Temple, 1896–1903

Hinchliff, Peter. *Frederick Temple.* Oxford: Clarendon Press, 1997.

10. Randall Davidson, 1903–1928

Bell, George K. A. *Randall Davidson, Archbishop of Canterbury.* Oxford: OUP, 1952.

11. Cosmo Gordon Lang, 1928–1942

Lockhart, J. G. *Cosmo Gordon Lang.* London: Hodder & Stoughton, 1949.

12. William Temple, 1942–1944

Iremonger, F. A. *William Temple, Archbishop of Canterbury: His Life and Letters*. Oxford: OUP, 1948.

13. Geoffrey Fisher, 1945–1961

Carpenter, Edward. *Archbishop Fisher: His Life and Times*. Norwich, England: Canterbury Press, 1991.

14. Arthur Michael Ramsey, 1961–1974

Chadwick, Owen. *Michael Ramsey: A Life*. Oxford: Clarendon Press, 1990.

15. Frederick Donald Coggan, 1974–1980

Pawley, Margaret. *Donald Coggan, Servant of Christ*. London: SPCK, 1987.

16. Robert Alexander Kennedy Runcie, 1980–1991

Hastings, Adrian. *Robert Runcie.* London: Mowbray, 1991.

17. George Leonard Carey, 1991–2002

Carey, George L. *Know the Truth: A Memoir.* London: HarperCollins, 2004.

18. Rowan Douglas Williams, 2002–

Shortt, Rupert. *Rowan Williams: An Introduction*. London: DLT, 2003.

B. Other Church of England

Daniell, David. *William Tyndale: A Biography.* New Haven, Conn.: Yale University Press, 1994.

Ridley, Jasper Godwin. *Henry VIII*. London: Constable, 1984.

——. *Nicholas Ridley: A Biography.* London: Longmans, 1957.

MacCulloch, Diarmaid. *Tudor Church Militant: Edward VI and the Protestant Reformation*. London: Allen Lane, 1999.

Welsby, Paul A. *Lancelot Andrewes, 1555–1626.* London: SPCK, 1958.

Maycock, A. L. *Nicholas Ferrar of Little Gidding.* London: SPCK, 1938. Reprint, Grand Rapids, Mich.: Eerdmans, 1980.

Nuttall, Geoffrey F. *Richard Baxter.* London: Nelson, 1965.

Carpenter, Edward. *The Protestant Bishop: Being the Life of Henry Compton, 1632–1713, Bishop of London.* London: Longmans, Green, 1956.

Wesley, John. *The Journal of John Wesley*. 1909–1916, Everyman Library (but also edited and reprinted in many forms).

Moule, H. C. G. *Charles Simeon*. London: Methuen, 1892.

Newman, John Henry. *Apologia pro Vita Sua, Being a History of His Religious Opinions*. London: Longmans, Green, 1864. Reprinted in many editions since.

Battiscombe, Georgina. *John Keble: A Study in Limitations*. London: Constable, 1963.

Liddon, Henry P. *Life of Edward Bouverie Pusey, D.D.* 4 vols. London: Longmans, Green, 1894.

Prestige, G. L. *The Life of Charles Gore, a Great Englishman*. London: William Heinemann, 1935.

Henson, Herbert Hensley. *Retrospect of an Unimportant Life*. Oxford: OUP, 1942.

Jasper, Ronald C. D. *George Bell, Bishop of Chichester.* Oxford: OUP, 1967.

De-la-Noy, Michael. *Mervyn Stockwood: A Lonely Life*. London: Mowbray, 1996.

James, Eric. *A Life of John A. T. Robinson, Scholar, Pastor, Prophet*. London: Collins, 1987.

Montefiore, Hugh W. *Oh God! What Next?* London: Hodder & Stoughton, 1994.

Peart-Binns, John. *Living with Paradox: John Habgood, Archbishop of York*. London: DLT, 1987.

Dudley-Smith, Timothy. *John Stott: A Global Ministry*. Leicester, England: IVP, 2001.

——. *John Stott: The Making of a Leader.* Leicester: IVP, 1999.

Marshall, Rob. *Hope the Archbishop: A Portrait.* London: Continuum, 2004.

C. Ireland

McCreary, Alf. *Nobody's Fool: The Life of Archbishop Robin Eames.* London: Hodder & Stoughton, 2004.

D. North America

Fleming, Archibald Lang. *Archibald the Arctic.* New York: Appleton-Century-Crofts, 1956.

E. East Africa

Dawson, E. C. *James Hannington, First Bishop of Eastern Equatorial Africa.* London: Seeley & Co., 1890.

Luck, Anne. *African Saint: The Story of Apolo Kivebulaya.* London: SCM, 1963.

Smith, H. Maynard. *Frank, Bishop of Zanzibar: Life of Frank Weston, D.D., 1871–1924*. London: SPCK, 1926.

Ford, Margaret. *Janani: The Making of a Martyr*. London: Marshall, Morgan & Scott, 1978.

F. Central Africa

Chadwick, Owen. *MacKenzie's Grave*. London: Hodder & Stoughton, 1959.

Farrant, J. C. *Mashonaland Martyr: Bernard Mizeki and the Pioneer Church*. Cape Town, South Africa: OUP, 1966.

G. South Africa

Gray, Charles, ed. *Life of Robert Gray, Bishop of Cape Town and Metropolitan of Africa*. 2 vols. London: Rivington's, 1876.

Hinchliff, Peter. *John William Colenso.* London: Nelson, 1964.

McGrandle, Piers. *Trevor Huddleston, Turbulent Priest.* London: Continuum, 2004.

Du Boulay, Shirley. *Tutu: Voice of the Voiceless.* London: Hodder & Stoughton, 1988.

H. China

Broomhall, Marshall. *W. W. Cassels: First Bishop in Western China.* London: China Inland Mission, 1926.

Allen, Hubert J. B. *Roland Allen: Pioneer, Priest and Prophet*. Cincinnati, Ohio: Forward Movement, 1995.

I. India

Jackson, E. M., ed. *God's Apprentice: The Autobiography of Bishop Stephen Neill.* London: Hodder & Stoughton, 1991.

Brown, Leslie. *Three Worlds: One Word*. London: Rex Collings, 1981.
Newbigin, J. E. Lesslie. *Unfinished Agenda: An Updated Autobiography*. Edinburgh: St. Andrew Press, 1993.

J. Australia

Loane, Marcus L. *Archbishop Mowll: The Biography of Howard West Kilvinton Mowll, Archbishop of Sydney and Primate of Australia*. London: Hodder & Stoughton, 1960.

K. New Zealand

Evans, John H. *Churchman Militant: George Augustus Selwyn, Bishop of New Zealand and Lichfield*. London: Allen & Unwin, 1964.

VI. THE ANGLICAN COMMUNION IN AN ECUMENICAL CONTEXT

A. General Works

Bell, George K. A., ed. *Documents on Christian Unity*. 4 vols. (*1920–1924*, *1924–1930*, *1930–1948*, and *1948–1957*). Oxford: OUP, 1924, 1930, 1948, 1958.
Faith and Order. *Baptism, Eucharist, and Ministry*. Geneva: WCC, 1982.
Hanson, Anthony Tyrell. *Beyond Anglicanism*. London: DLT, 1965.
Hastings, Adrian. *Oliver Tomkins: The Ecumenical Enterprise*. London: SPCK, 2001.
Lossky, Nicholas, Jose Miguel Bonino, John Pobee, Tom F. Stransky, Geoffrey Wainwright, and Pauline Webb, eds. *Dictionary of the Ecumenical Movement*. 2nd ed. Geneva: WCC, 2002.
Rouse, R., and Stephen. C. Neill, eds. *A History of the Ecumenical Movement, 1517–1948*. London: SPCK, 1954.

B. Anglican–Roman Catholic Reports and Commentaries

1. Reports

Anglican–Roman Catholic International Commission (ARCIC-1). *The Final Report*. London: SPCK, 1982.
Anglican–Roman Catholic International Commission (ARCIC-2). *Salvation and the Church*. London: SPCK, 1987.

——. *Church as Communion*. London: SPCK, 1991.
——. *Clarifications*. London: SPCK, 1994.
——. *Life in Christ: Morals, Communion and the Church*. London: SPCK, 1994.
——. *The Gift of Authority*. London: SPCK, 1999.
——. *Mary: Grace and Hope in Christ*. Harrisburg, Pa.: Morehouse, 2005.

2. Commentaries

Purdy, William. *The Search for Unity: Relations between the Anglican and Roman Catholic Churches from the 1950s to the 1970s*. London: Geoffrey Chapman, 1996.

C. Anglican–Lutheran Reports

Osterlin, Lars. *Churches of Northern Europe in Profile: A Thousand Years of Anglo-Nordic Relations*. London: Canterbury Press, 1996.

D. Anglican–Methodist Reports

Sharing in the Apostolic Communion: The Report of the International Commission to the World Methodist Council and the Lambeth Conference. Lake Junaluska, N.C.: World Methodist Council, 1996.

E. Anglican–Moravian Reports

Anglican–Moravian Conversations: The Fetter Lane Common Statement with Essays in Moravian and Anglican History. London: CHP, 1996.

F. Anglican–Reformed Reports

Relations between Anglican and Presbyterian Churches: A Joint Report. London: SPCK, 1958.
God's Reign and Our Unity: The Report of the Anglican–Reformed International Commission, 1984. London: SPCK, 1984.
Called to Witness and Service: The Reuilly Common Statement with Essays on Church, Eucharist and Ministry. London: CHP, 1999.

G. Old Catholic Churches

Moss, C. B. *The Old Catholic Movement: Its Origins and History.* London: SPCK, 1964.

H. Reformed Episcopal Church

Guelzo, Allen C. *For the Union of Evangelical Christendom: The Irony of the Reformed Episcopalians*. Philadelphia: Pennsylvania State University, 1994.

I. Free Church of England

Fenwick, John R. K. *The Free Church of England: Introduction to an Anglican Tradition.* London: T. & T. Clark, 2004.

VII. DOCTRINAL FOUNDATIONS

A. Official 16th-Century Texts

A Necessary Doctrine and Erudition for Any Christian Man ["The King's Book"]. Modern ed. with an introduction by T. A. Lacey. London: SPCK for Church Historical Society, 1932.

Certain Sermons or Homilies: Appointed to be read in Churches in the time of Queen Elizabeth of Famous Memory. London: SPCK, 1864. Reprinted with a foreword by David Samuel, Lewes: Focus Ministries Trust, 1986.

B. Thirty-Nine Articles

Hardwick, Charles. *A History of the Articles of Religion: to which is added a Series of Documents, from A.D. 1536 to A.D. 1615; together with Illustrations from Contemporary Sources*. Cambridge, England: Deighton Bell & Co., 1859.

Rogers, Thomas. *The Catholic Doctrine of the Church of England: An exposition of the Thirty-Nine Articles*. First published in two parts in 1579 and 1585; the definitive edition under the present title first published in 1607. Published in a new edition by J. J. S. Perowne for the Parker Society, Cambridge, 1854.

Burnet, Gilbert. *An Exposition of the Thirty-Nine Articles*. N.p., c. 1690.

Beveridge, William. *Ecclesia Anglicana Ecclesia Catholica; or, the Doctrine of the Church of England consonant to Scripture, Reason, and Fathers: a Discourse upon the Thirty-Nine Articles*. 2 vols. Oxford: OUP, 1840.

Newman, John Henry. *Remarks on Certain Passages in the Thirty-Nine Articles. Tracts for the Times* no. 90. London: Rivingtons, 1841.

Browne, E. Harold. *An Exposition of the Thirty-Nine Articles: Historical and Doctrinal.* 12th ed. London: Longmans, Green, 1882.

Litton, E. A. *Introduction to Dogmatic Theology.* In two parts, 1882 and 1892. Reprinted with an introduction by Philip E. Hughes, London: James Clarke, 1960.

Boultbee, T. P. *An Exposition of the Thirty-Nine Articles forming an Introduction to the Theology of the Church of England.* London: Longmans, Green, c. 1890.

Gibson, E. C. S. *The Thirty-Nine Articles of the Church of England explained with an Introduction.* London: Methuen, 1898.

Bicknell, E. J. *A Theological Introduction to the Thirty-Nine Articles.* London: Longmans, Green, 1925.

Griffith Thomas, W. H. *The Principles of Theology: An Introduction to the Thirty-Nine Articles.* London: Church Book Room Press, 1930.

Ross, Kenneth. *The Thirty-Nine Articles.* London: Mowbray, 1957.

Turner, H. E. W., ed. *The Articles of the Church of England.* London: Mowbray, 1964.

Subscription and Assent to the Thirty-Nine Articles: A Report of the Archbishops' Commission on Christian Doctrine. London: SPCK, 1968.

C. Classic Writings

Note: The collected works of most of the Anglican Reformers were published by CUP in the *Parker Society Volumes* in the 1840s and 1850s. The collected works of many of the 17th-century authors are published in the *Library of Anglo-Catholic Theology*, Oxford: Parker, 1840s.

Foxe, John. *Acts and Monuments of matters happening in the Church.* 1563.

Jewel, John. *Apologia pro Ecclesia Anglicana.* Modern ed., edited by John E. Booty, *An Apology of the Church of England*, New York: Church Publishing, 2001.

Hooker, Richard. *Of the Laws of Ecclesiastical Polity* (8 vols.). Vols. 1–4 published in 1594, vol. 5 in 1597, and vols. 6–8 posthumously between 1648 and 1662; vols 1–8 together in 1662, and also in E. B. Pusey, ed. *The Works of that Learned and Judicious Divine Mr. Richard Hooker* (2 vols). Oxford; OUP, 1836.

D. Modern Surveys

Davies, Horton. *Worship and Theology in England.* 5 vols. (*1535–1600*, *1600–1690*, *1690–1850*, *1850–1900*, and *1900–1965*). Princeton, N.J.: Princeton University Press, 1961–1975.

McGrath, Alistair, ed. *SPCK Handbook of Anglican Theologians.* London: SPCK, 1998.

Ramsey, A. Michael. *From Gore to Temple: The Development of Anglican Theology between* Lux Mundi *and the Second World War.* London: Longmans, 1960.

E. Reports

Doctrine in the Church of England: The Report of the Commission on Christian Doctrine Appointed by the Archbishops of Canterbury and York in 1922. London: SPCK, 1938. Reprinted with an introduction by G. W. H. Lampe, London: SPCK, 1982.

Inter-Anglican Theological and Doctrinal Commission. *For the Sake of the Kingdom: God's Church and the New Creation*. London: CHP for the ACC, 1986.

VIII. LITURGICAL TEXTS

A. Church of England

1544 Litany, Reprinted as an appendix in William Keatinge Clay (ed), *Private Prayers put Forth by Authority During the Reign of Queen Elizabeth*. Cambridge: Parker Society, 1851.

Order of the Communion. 1548. Reprinted in Colin O. Buchanan, ed., *Eucharistic Liturgies of Edward VI*, Grove Liturgical Study no. 34 (Nottingham: Grove Books, 1983). The royal proclamation preceding it is in G. A. Mitchell, *Landmarks in Liturgy* (London: D. L. Todd, 1961), and in Colin O. Buchanan, ed., *Background Documents to Liturgical Revision, 1547–1549*, Grove Liturgical Study no. 35 (Nottingham: Grove Books, 1983).

Book of Common Prayer. 1549. This and the following two texts are most conveniently found in E. C. S. Gibson, ed., *First and Second Prayer-Books of Edward VI* (London: Dent Everyman Edition, 1910; frequently reprinted since).

Ordinal. 1550. Reprinted in Gibson, *First and Second Prayer-Books of Edward VI*.

Book of Common Prayer and Ordinal. 1552. Reprinted in Gibson, *First and Second Prayer-Books of Edward VI*.

Communion services. 1549 and 1552. Reprinted (with 1548 *Order of the Communion*) in Buchanan, *Eucharistic Liturgies of Edward VI*.

Book of Common Prayer. 1559. Reprinted in W. K. Clay, ed., *Liturgies and Occasional Forms of Prayer set forth in the Reign of Queen Elizabeth* (Cambridge: Parker Society, 1847).

A Directory for the Public Worship of God in the Three Kingdoms. 1645. Edited with an introduction by Ian Breward in *The Westminster Directory*, Grove Liturgical Study no. 21 (Nottingham: Grove Books, 1981).

Book of Common Prayer. 1662. Many editions are available from OUP, CUP, and Eyre & Spottiswoode.

"Deposited Book." 1928. Many editions are available.

Alternative Service Book 1980. London: Hodder & Stoughton, 1980. Additional editions are available from OUP and CUP.

Common Worship: Initiation Services. London. CHP, 1998.

Common Worship: Services and Prayers of the Church of England. London: CHP, 2000.

Common Worship: Pastoral Services. London: CHP, 2000.

B. Church of Scotland—Scottish Episcopal Church

Sprott, George, ed. *Scottish Liturgies of the Reign of James VI*. Edinburgh: Edmonston and Douglas, 1871.

Book of Common Prayer. Edinburgh: Robert Young, 1637.

Donaldson, Gordon. *The Making of the Scottish Prayer Book of 1637*. Edinburgh: Edinburgh University Press, 1954.

The Communion Office. Edinburgh: Drummond, 1764.

The Book of Common Prayer . . . and the Scottish Liturgy and the Permissible Additions to and Deviations from the Service Books of the Scottish Church as Canonically Sanctioned. Edinburgh: CUP, 1912.

The Scottish Book of Common Prayer. Edinburgh: CUP, 1929.

Dowden, John. *The Scottish Communion Office of 1764*. 2nd ed. Oxford: OUP, 1922.

C. Church of Ireland

Book of Common Prayer. Dublin: APCK, 1878.

Book of Common Prayer. 1926.

Alternative Prayer Book 1984. London: Collins Liturgical, 1984.

Book of Common Prayer. Dublin: Columbia, 2004.

Miller, Harold C. *The Desire of Our Soul: A User's Guide to the Book of Common Prayer.* Dublin: Columba, 2004.

Kennedy, Michael, Richard Clarke, Edgar Turner, and Brian Mayne. *The Prayer Books of the Church of Ireland 1551–2004*. Dublin: Columba, 2004.

D. Protestant Episcopal Church in the United States of America

Book of Common Prayer. 1789. Philadelphia: Hall & Sellers, 1790.

Hatchett, Marion. *The Making of the First American Book of Common Prayer.* New York: Seabury, 1982.

Book of Common Prayer. New York: Bible and Common Prayer Book Society, 1892.

Book of Common Prayer. New York: Church Pension Fund, 1928.

Shepherd, Massey H., Jr. *The Oxford American Prayer Book Commentary*. New York: OUP, 1950.

Standing Liturgical Commission. *Prayer Book Studies*. New York: Church Pension Fund, 1950– . From 1950 onward, liturgical revision in the United States has been explored and encouraged by this long series of publications.

Book of Common Prayer. New York: Church Hymnal Corporation and Seabury, 1979.

E. The Anglican Church of Canada

The Book of Common Prayer: Canada. Toronto: General Board of Religious Education, Toronto, 1922.

The Book of Common Prayer: Canada. Toronto: Anglican Book Centre, 1962.

The Book of Alternative Services. Toronto: Anglican Book Centre, 1985.

F. The Church of the Province of South Africa

A Book of Common Prayer. London: OUP, 1954.

An Anglican Prayer Book 1989. London: Collins, 1989.

G. The Anglican Church of Australia

An Australian Prayer Book. Sydney, Australia: The Church of England of Australia, 1978.

A Prayer Book for Australia. Alexandria, NSW, Australia: E.J. Dwyer, 1995.

H. The Church of Aotearoa, New Zealand, and Polynesia

A New Zealand Prayer Book. Auckland, New Zealand: Collins, 1989.

I. The Anglican Church in Nigeria

The Book of Common Prayer . . . According to the Use of the Church of Nigeria (Anglican Communion). Lagos: CSS Press, 1996.

J. The Anglican Church of Kenya

Our Modern Services: Anglican Church of Kenya. Nairobi, Kenya: Uzima Press, 2002.

K. The Church of South India

The Book of Common Worship. 1963.

L. The Church of North India

The Book of Worship. Delhi, India: ISPCK, 1995.

M. Resources for the Texts

Cardwell, Edward, ed. *A History of Conferences and other proceedings connected with the revision of the Book of Common Prayer; From the year 1558 to the year 1690*. 2nd ed. Oxford, OUP, 1841. The 3rd edition (1849) was reprinted by photoreproduction, Ridgewood, N.J.: Gregg Press, 1966.

Buchanan, Colin O., ed. *Background Documents to Liturgical Revision, 1547–1549*. Grove Liturgical Study no. 35. Nottingham: Grove Books, 1983.

Whitaker, Charles E. ed. *Martin Bucer and the Book of Common Prayer*. Great Wakering, England: Alcuin/Mayhew-McCrimmon, 1974.

Leaver, Robin A., ed. *The Liturgy of the Frankfurt Exiles, 1555*. Grove Liturgical Study no. 38. Nottingham: Grove Books, 1984.

Buchanan, Colin O., ed. *The Savoy Conference Revisited*. Alcuin/GROW Joint Liturgical Study no. 54. Cambridge: Grove Books, 2002.

Cuming, Geoffrey J., ed. *The Durham Book: Being the First Draft of the Revision of the Book of Common Prayer in 1661*. Oxford: OUP, 1961.

Gould, G., ed. *Documents Relating to the Settlement of the Church of England by Act of Uniformity 1662*. London: W. Kent & Co., 1862.

Fawcett, Timothy J., ed. *The Liturgy of Comprehension, 1689: An Abortive Attempt to Revise the Book of Common Prayer*. Great Wakering, England: Alcuin/Mayhew-McCrimmon, 1973.

Smith, James David. *The Eucharistic Doctrine of the Later Non-Jurors: A Revisionist View of the Eighteenth-Century Usages Controversy*. Alcuin/GROW Joint Liturgical Study no. 46. Cambridge: Grove Books, 2000.

N. General Histories and Commentaries on the Church of England Prayer Books

Wheatly, Charles. *A Rational Illustration of the Book of Common Prayer*. London: N.p., 1715. There have been frequent reprintings.

Peaston, A. Elliott. *The Prayer Book Reform Movement in the XVIIIth Century*. Oxford: Blackwell, 1940.

Jasper, Ronald C. D. *Prayer Book Revision in England, 1800–1900*. London: SPCK, 1954.

Blunt, J. H. *The Annotated Book of Common Prayer*. London: Rivingtons, 1866.

Tomlinson, J. T. *The Prayer Book, Articles and Homilies: Some forgotten Facts in their History which may decide their Interpretation*. London: Church Association, 1897.

Procter, Francis, and Walter H. Frere. *A New History of the Book of Common Prayer with a Rationale of Its Offices* [a revised version of the original book by F. Procter]. London: MacMillan, 1901.

Harford, George, and Morley Stevenson, eds. *The Prayer Book Dictionary.* London: Waverley Book Co., c. 1912.

Brightman, F. E. *The English Rite: Being a Synopsis of the Sources and Revisions of the Book of Common Prayer*. 2 vols. London: Rivingtons, 1915.

Lowther Clarke, W. K., and Charles Harris, eds. *Liturgy and Worship: A Companion to the Prayer Books of the Anglican Communion.* London: SPCK, 1932.

Cuming, Geoffrey J. *A History of Anglican Liturgy.* 2nd ed. London: Macmillan, 1982.

Jasper, Ronald C. D. *The Development of the Anglican Liturgy, 1662–1980.* London: SPCK, 1989.

The Alternative Service Book 1980: A Commentary by the Liturgical Commission. London: CIO, 1980.

Buchanan, Colin O., and B. Trevor Lloyd, eds. *Anglican Worship Today: Collins' Illustrated Guide to the Alternative Service Book 1980*. London: Collins Liturgical Publications, 1980.

Buchanan, Colin O. *Latest Liturgical Revision in the Church of England, 1978–1984.* Grove Liturgical Study no. 39. Nottingham: Grove Books, 1984.

Bradshaw, Paul, ed. *Companion to Common Worship*. Vols. 1 and 2. London: Alcuin/SPCK, 2001 and 2005.

Earey, Mark, and Gilly Myers, eds. *Common Worship Today: An Illustrated Guide to Common Worship.* London: HarperCollins, 2001.

Hebblethwaite, David. *Liturgical Revision in the Church of England, 1984–2004: The Working of the Liturgical Commission.* Alcuin/GROW Joint Liturgical Study no. 57. Cambridge: Grove Books, 2004.

O. Music and Hymnody

Three Churches of the Anglican Communion are known to have an officially authorized hymnbook: the Church of Ireland, the Episcopal Church (United States of America), and the Anglican Church of Kenya. However, the general run of church music and hymnody, while often drawing greatly upon Anglican imagination or creativity, overspills all denominational boundaries and is a subject sufficient for a dictionary in itself.

P. Architecture

Addleshaw, George W. O., and Frederick Etchells. *The Architectural Setting of Anglican Worship*. London: Faber & Faber, 1948.

Hammond, Peter. *Liturgy and Architecture.* London: Barrie & Rockliff, 1960.
Giles, Richard. *Repitching the Tent.* 3rd ed. Collegeville, Minn.: Liturgical Press, 2004.

Q. Pan-Anglican Collections

1. Eucharist

L'Estrange, Hamon. *Alliance of Divine Offices.* 1659. The 3rd ed. is reprinted in the 19th-century *Library of Anglo-Catholic Theology.*
Grisbrooke, W. Jardine, ed. *Anglican Liturgies of the Seventeenth and Eighteenth Centuries.* London: Alcuin/SPCK, 1958.
Arnold, J. H., ed. *Anglican Liturgies.* London: OUP for Alcuin, 1939.
Wigan, Bernard J., ed. *The Liturgy in English.* London: OUP, 1962.
Buchanan, Colin O., ed. *Modern Anglican Liturgies, 1958–1968.* London: OUP, 1968.
——. *Further Anglican Liturgies, 1968–1975.* Nottingham: Grove Books, 1975.
——. *Latest Anglican Liturgies, 1976–1984.* London: Alcuin/SPCK, 1985.

2. Baptism and Confirmation

Jagger, Peter E., ed. *Christian Initiation, 1552–1969.* London: Alcuin/SPCK, 1970.

3. Ordination

Buchanan, Colin O., ed. *Modern Anglican Ordination Rites.* Alcuin/GROW Joint Liturgical Study no. 3. Nottingham: Grove Books, 1987.

4. Publications of the International Anglican Liturgical Consultations (IALC)

International Anglican Liturgical Consultation (IALC-1). *Children and Communion* [The Boston Statement]. Nottingham: Grove Books, 1985.
Buchanan, Colin O., ed. *Nurturing Children in Communion.* Grove Liturgical Study no. 44. Nottingham: Grove, 1985.
Meyers, Ruth A., ed. *Children at the Table.* New York: Church Hymnal Corporation, 1995.
Talley, Thomas, ed. *A Kingdom of Priests: Liturgical Formation of the Laity* [IALC-2, 1987]. Alcuin/GROW Joint Liturgical Study no. 5. Nottingham: Grove Books, 1988.

Holeton, David, ed. *Liturgical Inculturation in the Anglican Communion* [IALC-3, 1989]. Alcuin/GROW Joint Liturgical Study no. 15. Nottingham: Grove Books, 1990.

International Anglican Liturgical Consultation (IALC-4). "Walk in Newness of Life" [The Toronto Statement]. In *Christian Initiation in the Anglican Communion*, edited by David Holeton. Grove Worship Series no. 118. Nottingham: Grove Books, 1991.

Holeton, David, ed. *Growing in Newness of Life.* Toronto: Anglican Book Centre, 1993.

International Anglican Liturgical Consultation (IALC-5 [1995]). "The Renewal of the Anglican Eucharist" [The Dublin Statement]. In *Renewing the Anglican Eucharist*, edited by David Holeton. Grove Worship Series. Cambridge: Grove Books, 1991.

Holeton, David, ed. *Thanks and Praise*. Toronto: Anglican Book Centre, 1998.

International Anglican Liturgical Consultation (IALC-6 [2001]). "To Equip the Saints" [The Berkeley Statement]. In *Anglican Ordination Rites*, edited by Paul Gibson. Grove Worship Series no. 168. Cambridge: Grove Books, 2002.

R. Ceremonial

Yates, Nigel. *Anglican Ritualism in Victorian Britain, 1830–1910*. Oxford: OUP, 1999.

Report of the Royal Commission on Ecclesiastical Discipline. London: HMSO, 1906.

IX. SPECIFIC DOCTRINES

A. Scriptural Authority

Stott, John R. W., et al. *The Anglican Communion and Scripture*. Oxford: Regnum and EFAC, 1996.

B. The Church

Avis, Paul. *Anglicanism and the Christian Church.* Edinburgh: T. & T. Clark, 1989.

———. *The Anglican Understanding of the Church*. London: SPCK, 2000.

Bradshaw, Tim. *The Olive Branch: An Evangelical Anglican Doctrine of the Church.* Carlisle: Paternoster Press, 1992.

Buchanan, Colin O. *Is the Church of England Biblical? An Anglican Ecclesiology*. London: DLT, 1998.

Mascall, Eric R. *Corpus Christi: Essays on the Church and the Eucharist*. London: Longmans, Green, 1953.

Ramsey, A. Michael. *The Gospel and the Catholic Church.* London: Longmans, Green, 1936.

Thornton, Lionel S. *Common Life in the Body of Christ*. London: Dacre Press, 1942.

C. Church and State: Establishment and Disestablishment in England

Selborne Commission. *Report of the Archbishops' Committee on Church and State*. London: SPCK, 1916.

Henson, H. Hensley. *Disestablishment.* London: Macmillan, 1929.

Cecil Commission. *Report of the Archbishops' Commission on Church and State*. London: Press and Publications Board, 1935.

Moberley Commission. *Church and State: Being the Report of a Commission Appointed by the Church Assembly in June 1949*. London: Church Information Board of the Church Assembly, 1952.

Kemp, Eric W. *Counsel and Consent: Aspects of the Government of the Church as Exemplified in the History of English Provincial Synods.* London: SPCK, 1961.

Howick Commission. *Crown Appointments and the Church*. London: CIO, 1964.

Hinchliff, Peter B. *The One-Sided Reciprocity: A Study in the Modification of the Establishment*. London: DLT, 1966.

Nicholls, David. *Church and State in Britain since 1820.* London: Routledge & Kegan Paul, 1967.

Chadwick Commission. *Church and State, 1970*. London: CIO, 1970.

Cornwell, Peter. *Faith and the Future: Church and Nation*. Oxford: Blackwell, 1983.

Reeves, Donald, ed. *The Church and the State*. London: Hodder & Stoughton, 1984.

Hastings, Adrian. *Church and State: The English Experience.* Exeter, England: University of Exeter Press, 1991.

Palmer, Bernard. *High and Mitred: Prime Ministers as Bishop-Makers, 1837–1977.* London: SPCK, 1992.

Buchanan, Colin O. *Cut the Connection: The Church of England and Disestablishment.* London: DLT, 1994.

Moses, John. *A Broad and Living Way: Church and State, a Continuing Establishment*. London: Canterbury Press, 1995.

Avis, Paul. *Church, State and Establishment.* London: SPCK, 2001.

Hobson, Theo. *Against Establishment: An Anglican Polemic*. London: DLT, 2003.

D. The Sacraments

Quick, Oliver C. *The Christian Sacraments*. London: Nisbet, 1927.

E. Baptism and Confirmation

Goode, William. *The Doctrine of the Church of England as to the Effects of Baptism in the Case of Infants*. 2nd ed. London: Hatchard, 1850.
Nias, J. C. S. *Gorham and the Bishop of Exeter*. London: SPCK, 1951.
Buchanan, Colin. *Anglican Confirmation*. Grove Liturgical Study no. 48. Nottingham: Grove Books, 1986.
Holeton, David, ed. *Christian Initiation in the Anglican Communion*. Grove Worship Series no. 118. Nottingham: Grove Books, 1991.
——. *Growing in Newness of Life: Christian Initiation in Anglicanism Today*. Toronto: Anglican Book Centre, 1993.
Buchanan, Colin. *Infant Baptism and the Gospel.* London: DLT, 1993.

F. The Eucharist

Brooks, Peter N. *Thomas Cranmer's Doctrine of the Eucharist*. 2nd ed. Basingstoke, England: Macmillan, 1992.
Clements, R. E., et al. *Eucharistic Theology Then and Now*. SPCK Theological Collection no. 9. London: SPCK, 1968.
Cocksworth, Christopher J. *Evangelical Eucharistic Theology in the Church of England.* Cambridge: CUP, 1993.
Doctrine Commission of Church of England. *Thinking about the Eucharist: Essays by Members of the Archbishops' Commission on Christian Doctrine.* London: SCM, 1972.
Dugmore, C. W. *Eucharistic Doctrine in the Church of England from Hooker to Waterland.* London: SPCK, 1942.
Gore, Charles. *The Body of Christ: An Enquiry into the Institution and Doctrine of Holy Communion.* London: John Murray, 1907.
Hicks, F. C. Nugent. *The Fullness of Sacrifice: An Essay in Reconciliation.* London: Macmillan, 1930.
House of Bishops. *The Eucharist: Sacrament of Unity*. Occasional paper. London: CHP, 2001.
MacDonald, A. J., ed. *The Evangelical Doctrine of Holy Communion*. Cambridge: Heffer, 1930.
McAdoo, H. R., and Kenneth W. Stevenson. *The Mystery of the Eucharist in the Anglican Tradition*. Norwich, England: Canterbury Press, 1995.
Pusey, Edward B. *The Real Presence of the Body and Blood of our Lord Jesus Christ: The Doctrine of the English Church with a Vindication of the*

Reception by the Wicked and of the Adoration of our Lord Jesus Christ truly present. Oxford: James Parker, 1869

G. Orders

Working Party of House of Bishops. *Deacons in the Ministry of the Church.* Report to the House of Bishops. London: CHP, 1988.

For Such a Time as This: A Renewed Diaconate in the Church of England. Report to the General Synod. London: CHP, 2001.

Board for Mission and Unity. *The Priesthood of the Ordained Ministry.* London: CHP, 1986.

Harvey, Anthony E. *Priest or President?* London: SPCK, 1975.

Moberly, R. C. *Ministerial Priesthood: Chapters (preliminary to a Study of the Ordinal) on the Rationale of Ministry and the Meaning of Christian Priesthood.* London: John Murray, 1897.

Sykes, Norman J. *Old Priest, New Presbyter.* Cambridge: CUP, 1957.

Carey, Kenneth M., ed. *The Historic Episcopate in the Fullness of the Church.* London: Dacre Press, 1954.

Gore, Charles. *The Ministry of the Christian Church.* 3rd ed. London: Longmans, Green, 1893.

Halliburton, John. *The Authority of a Bishop.* London: SPCK, 1987.

House of Bishops. *Apostolicity and Succession.* London: General Synod of the Church of England, 1994.

Kirk, Kenneth E., ed. *The Apostolic Ministry: Essays on the History and the Doctrine of Episcopacy.* London: Hodder & Stoughton, 1946.

Episcopal Ministry. Report of the Archbishops' Group on the Episcopate. London: CHP, 1990.

H. Presidency of the Eucharist

House of Bishops. *Eucharistic Presidency.* London: CHP, 1996.

Lloyd, B. Trevor, ed. *Lay Presidency of the Eucharist.* Grove Liturgical Study no. 9. Nottingham: Grove Books, 1977.

I. Ordination of Women

Avis, Paul. *Anglican Orders and the Priesting of Women.* London: DLT, 1999.

Bennett, Joyce. *Hasten Slowly: The First Legal Ordination of Women Priests.* Chichester, England: Little London Associates, 1991.

Eames Commission. *Women in the Anglican Episcopate: Theology, Guidelines and Practice.* Toronto: Anglican Book Centre for the ACC, 1998.

House of Bishops. *The Ordination of Women to the Priesthood: A Report by the House of Bishops*. London: General Synod of the Church of England, 1988.

———. *The Ordination of Women to the Priesthood: A Second Report by the House of Bishops*. London: General Synod of the C/E, 1987.

House of Bishops Working Party. *Suffragan Bishops*. London: CHP, 2002.

Rochester Working Party. *Women Bishops in the Church of England? A Report of the House of Bishops' Working Party on Women in the Episcopate*. London: CHP, 2004.

J. Validity of Anglican Orders

Leo XIII. *Apostolicae Curae*. 1896. Reprinted in Church Historical Society, *Anglican Orders (Latin)* (London: SPCK, 1932).

Archbishops of Canterbury and York. *Saepius Officio*. 1897. Reprinted in Church Historical Society, *Anglican Orders (Latin)* (London: SPCK, 1932).

Lowndes, A. *Vindication of Anglican Orders*. New York: James Pott, 1898.

Lacey, T. A. *A Roman Diary and Other Documents Relating to the Papal Inquiry into English Ordinations, 1896*. London: Longmans, Green, 1910.

Dix, Gregory. *The Question of Anglican Orders*. London: Dacre Press, 1944.

Hughes, John Jay. *Absolutely Null and Utterly Void: An Account of the Papal Condemnation of Anglican Orders, 1896*. London: Sheed & Ward, 1968.

———. *Stewards of the Lord: A Reappraisal of Anglican Orders.* London: Sheed & Ward, 1970.

Franklin, R. William, ed. *Anglican Orders: Essays on the Centenary of* Apostolicae Curae*, 1896–1996: With an English Translation of the Document and the Anglican Response*. London: Mowbray, 1996.

K. *Episcopi Vagantes*

Brandreth, Henry R. T. *Episcopi Vagantes and the Anglican Church*. London: SPCK, 1947.

Anson, Peter F. *Bishops at Large.* London: Faber & Faber, 1964.

X. STRANDS OF ANGLICANISM

A. Anglo-Catholicism

Tracts for the Times. 90 tracts. London: Rivingtons, 1833–1841.

Reports of the Anglo-Catholic Congresses. Several. Various publishers, 1920–1933.

Selwyn, E. G., ed. *Essays Catholic and Critical*. London: SPCK, 1929.

Catholic Renewal in the Church of England. *Loughborough Conference Report.* London: CLA, 1979.

Sutcliffe, Tom, ed. *Tracts for Our Times, 1833–1983.* London: St. Mary's, Bourne Street, 1983.

Penhale, Francis. *The Anglican Church Today: Catholics in Crisis.* London: Mowbray, 1986.

Pickering, W. S. F. *Anglo-Catholicism: A Study in Religious Ambiguity*. London: Routledge, 1989.

B. Evangelicalism

Balleine, G. R. *A History of the Evangelical Party in the Church of England*. London: Longmans, Green, 1908.

Hylson-Smith, Kenneth. *Evangelicals in the Church of England, 1734–1984.* Edinburgh: T. & T. Clark, 1988.

Saward, Michael A. *The Anglican Church Today: Evangelicals on the Move.* London: Mowbray, 1987.

France, R. T., and A. E. McGrath, eds. *Evangelical Anglicans: Their Role and Influence in the Church Today*. London: SPCK, 1993.

C. Anglo-Catholics and Evangelicals Together

Browning, Wilfred R. F., ed. *The Anglican Synthesis: Essays by Catholics and Evangelicals.* Derby, England: Peter Smith, 1964.

Buchanan, Colin, E. L. Mascall, J. I. Packer, and the Bishop of Willesden. *Growing into Union: Proposals for Forming a United Church in England.* London: SPCK, 1970.

Baxter, Christina, ed. *Stepping Stones*. London: Hodder & Stoughton, 1987.

D. Charismatic Movement

Harper, Michael J. *As at the Beginning: The Twentieth Century Pentecostal Revival*. London: Hodder Stoughton, 1965.

Bennett, Dennis J. *Nine O'Clock in the Morning*. Plainfield, N.J.: Logos International, 1970.

Church of England. *The Charismatic Movement in the Church of England.* London: CHP, 1981.

Craston, Colin, ed. *Open to the Spirit: Anglicans and the Experience of Renewal.* London: Inter-Anglican Publishing Network for ACC, 1987.

Smail, Tom, Andrew Walker, and Nigel Wright. *Charismatic Renewal: The Search for a Theology*. London: SPCK, 1993.

XI. SPIRITUALITY

More, Paul Elmer, and Frank Leslie Cross, eds. *Anglicanism: The Thought and Practice of the Church of England, Illustrated from the Religious Literature of the Seventeenth Century*. London: SPCK, 1935.
Williams, Rowan D. *The Wound of Knowledge*. London: Darton, Longman & Todd, 1979.
Rowell, Geoffrey, ed. *The English Religious Tradition and the Genius of Anglicanism*. Wantage, England: Ikon, 1992.
Rowell, Geoffrey, Kenneth Stevenson, and Rowan Williams, compilers. *Love's Redeeming Work: The Anglican Quest for Holiness*. Oxford: OUP, 2001.

XII. PERIODICALS

Theology. A monthly Anglican journal of theology published by the SPCK, London.
Anglican Theological Review. An American Anglican quarterly published in Evanston, Ill., since around 1919.
Church Quarterly Review. A quarterly Anglican journal published in England until 1967.
Journal of Anglican Studies. A twice-yearly Anglican journal published since 2004 for the Anglican Church of Australia by SAGE Publications, London.
Anglican World. A monthly glossy tabloid publshed by the Anglican Communion Office since 1993.
Churchman. Published quarterly by the Church Society in England.
Anvil. Published three times a year by open evangelicals in England.

XIII. WEBSITES

A. Anglican Communion

anglicancommunion.org (this website has pages for many of the churches shown below at http://www.anglicancommunion.org/tour/index.cfm)

B. Individual Churches or Provinces

Aotearoa, New Zealand, and Polynesia anglican.org.nz
Australia anglican.org.au
Bangladesh [see anglicancommunion.org]
Brazil ieab.org.br

Burundi [see anglicancommunion.org]
Canada recwcan.ca
Central Africa [see anglicancommunion.org]
Central Region of America iarca.org
Congo [see anglicancommunion.org]
England cofe.anglican.org
Hong Kong 1.hkskh.org
Indian Ocean [see anglicancommunion.org]
Ireland ireland.anglican.org
Japan nskk.org
Jerusalem and the Middle East jerusalem.anglican.org
Kenya ackenya.org
Korea anck.skh.or.kr
Melanesia melanesia.anglican.org
Mexico [see anglicancommunion.org]
Myanmar [see anglicancommunion.org]
Nigeria nigeria.anglican.org
North India cnisynod.org
Pakistan [see anglicancommunion.org]
Papua New Guinea [see anglicancommunion.org]
Philippines philippines.ang.org
Rwanda [see anglicancommunion.org]
Scotland scotland.anglican.org
South India csisynod.org
Southeast Asia [see anglicancommunion.org]
Southern Africa cpsa.org.za
Southern Cone of South America anglicanos.net
Sudan [see anglicancommunion.org]
Tanzania anglican.or.tz
Uganda [see anglicancommunion.org]
United States episcopalchurch.org
Wales churchinwales.org
West Africa [see anglicancommunion.org]
West Indies thebahamas.net/cpwi

XIV. ADDRESSES OF PROVINCES OR CHURCHES OF THE ANGLICAN COMMUNION

A. Anglican Communion

The Anglican Communion Office, St. Andrew's House, 2 Tavistock Road, Westbourne Park, London W11 1BA United Kingdom

B. Individual Churches or Provinces

Aotearoa, New Zealand, and Polynesia: P.O. Box 885, Hastings, New Zealand
Australia: Box Q190, Queen Victoria Building P.O., Sydney, NSW 1230, Australia
Bangladesh: St. Thomas' Church, 54 Johnson Road, Dhaka 1100, Bangladesh
Brazil: P.O. Box 11.510, Teresepolis, CEP, 90841–970, Porto Alegre, RS, Brasil
Burundi: B.P. 2098, Bujumbura, Burundi
Canada: 80 Hayden Street, Toronto, Ont. M4Y 3G2, Canada
Central Africa: Private Bag 1, Chilema, Malawi
Central Region of America: Apt 10520–1000, San Jose, Costa Rica
Congo: B.P. 134, Cyangugu, Rwanda
England: Church House, Great Smith Street, London SW1P 3NZ United Kingdom
Hong Kong: 1 Lower Albert Road, Hong Kong, People's Republic of China
Indian Ocean: Eveche Anglican, Ambohimanoro, 101 Antananarivo, Madagascar
Ireland: C/I House, Church Avenue, Rathmines, Dublin 6, Eire
Japan: NSKK, 65–3 Yaraicho, Shinjuku-ku, Tokyo 162–0805, Japan
Jerusalem and the Middle East: P.O. Box 22075, Nicosia 1517, Cyprus
Kenya: P.O. Box 40502, 00100 Nairobi, Kenya
Korea: #3 Chong-dong, Ching-ku, Seoul 100–120, Korea
Melanesia: Provincial HQ, P.O. Box 19, Honiara, Solomon Islands
Mexico: Calle La Otra Banda #40, Col. San Angel, Delegación Alvaro Obregon, 01000, Mexico
Myanmar: P.O. Box 1412, 140 Pyidaungsu Yeiktha Road, Dagon, Yangon, Myanmar
Nigeria: Episcopal House, P.O. Box 212, AD CP, Abuja, Nigeria
North India: CNI Bhavan, 16 Pandit Pant Marg, New Delhi 110–001, India
Pakistan: St. John's Cathedral, 1 Sir Syed Road, Peshawar, Pakistan
Papua New Guinea: P.O. Box 673, Mae, Morobe Province, Papua New Guinea
Philippines: P.O. Box 10321, Broadway Centrum, 1112 Quezon City, Philippines
Rwanda: B.P. 2487, Kigali, Rwanda
Scotland: 21 Grosvenor Crescent, Edinburgh EH12 5EE, Scotland
South India: 5 Whites Road, Royapettah, Chennai 600 014, India
Southeast Asia: P.O. Box 347 93 704 Kuching, Sarawak, Malaysia
Southern Africa: P.O. Box 53014, Kenilworth 7745, South Africa
Southern Cone of South America: (executive secretary) Casilla de Correo 187, CP4400, Salta, Argentina
Sudan: P.O. Box 604, Khartoum, Sudan
Tanzania: P.O. Box 899, Dodoma, Tanzania
Uganda: P.O. Box 14123, Kampala, Uganda
United States: 815 Second Avenue, New York, NY 10017, USA
Wales: 39 Cathedral Road, Cardiff CF11 9XF, South Wales
West Africa: P.O. Box Lt 226, Accra, Ghana
West Indies: Bamford House, Society Hill, St. John, Barbados, West Indies

About the Author

Colin Buchanan, born in 1934, graduated from Oxford in classics in 1959, was trained at Tyndale Hall Theological College in Bristol from 1959 to 1961, and was then ordained deacon for a curacy in the Anglican diocese of Chester. He was on the staff of the London College of Divinity from 1964, largely teaching liturgy for ordination purposes. He helped the college move to Nottingham in 1970 to become St. John's College. He served there for a further 15 years, the last six of them as principal. He then became bishop of Aston in Birmingham diocese from 1985. In 1989 he resigned and became an assistant bishop in Rochester diocese, serving from 1991 to 1996 as the vicar of St. Mark's, Gillingham, in that diocese and for one year as the diocese's ecumenical officer. In 1993 he was awarded a Lambeth Doctorate of Divinity. In December 1996 he became bishop of Woolwich, an area bishop within the diocese of Southwark, and ministered there until he retired in July 2004. He retired to Leeds, where he continues ministering as an assistant bishop in Bradford diocese.

During his 43 years in active ministry, Buchanan served in six dioceses, two in the province of York and four in the province of Canterbury. He was a member of the Church of England's Liturgical Commission from 1964 to 1986, of its Doctrinal Commission from 1986 to 1991, of its Council for Christian Unity from 1991 to 2001, and of its Committee for Minority Ethnic Anglican Concerns from 1991 to 2001. He represented the Church of England on the Assembly of the British Council of Churches from 1971 to 1981 and on the Forum of the Council of Churches of Britain and Ireland from 1990 to 1996. He was also a member of the Urban Bishops' Panel of the Church of England from 1997 to 2004. He was a founder-member of General Synod in 1970, serving as a clergy representative of Southwell diocese until 1985. In 1990 he was elected by the suffragan bishops of Canterbury Province to be one of their six representatives in the House of Bishops (and thus on General Synod) and was reelected for further five-year terms in 1995 and 2000. During his period in the House of Bishops, he voted for the ordination of women to the presbyterate in 1992 and for the Episcopal Ministry Act of Synod in 1993.

Buchanan has been ready to be known as an evangelical Anglican and had a creative part in each of the four National Evangelical Anglican Congresses in 1967, 1977, 1988, and 2003. He was also a participant in the two Anglo-Catholic conferences at Loughborough in 1978 and 1983. He drafted the report *The Charismatic Movement in the Church of England* in 1981.

As a bishop, Buchanan took part in the Lambeth Conferences of 1988 and 1998. During the former, he acted as secretary of the group that produced an extensive statement on liturgy in the "Mission and Ministry" section, and in the latter he was responsible for organizing the texts and liturgical programs for all the worship of the conference.

Buchanan was a founder-member of the International Anglican Liturgical Consultation in 1985 and is one of the only two persons to have attended all meetings of the Consultation. He has also been a member of the two CAPA consultations on liturgy in 1993 and 1996. In England he was a founder-member of the (voluntary) Group for Renewal of Worship (GROW) in 1961, chairing it from 1970 until 2003. GROW has been responsible for Grove Worship Booklets, Grove Liturgical Studies, and (jointly with the Alcuin Club) the Alcuin/GROW Joint Liturgical Studies. GROW was also one of the cosponsors of Praxis in 1990, and Buchanan has served on the Council of Praxis since it began. From 1975 to 2003 he was the editor of the monthly Church of England journal of liturgy, *News of Liturgy*.

Around the Anglican Communion, Colin Buchanan has ministered in various ways in 15 different provinces. He was a participant, as one of two persons from the Church of England, in the "Seabury Bi-Centenary Symposium" in Hartford, Connecticut, in 1984, celebrating 200 years from the consecration of Samuel Seabury as bishop. For many years he contributed a regular column from England to *Church Scene*, the weekly tabloid newspaper of the Anglican Church in Australia. His 21 years on the staff of what was for a long time the largest theological college in the Church of England meant that his former students are now to be found all around the Communion, many of them as bishops; one such was Janani Luwum, who became archbishop of Uganda and was martyred by Idi Amin in 1977.

His own publications include three edited collections of eucharistic liturgies of the Anglican Communion: *Modern Anglican Liturgies, 1958–1968* (1968), *Further Anglican Liturgies, 1968–1975* (1975), and *Latest Anglican Liturgies, 1976–1984* (1985). He was one of the three editors of *Anglican Worship Today: Collins Illustrated Guide to the Alternative Service Book 1980* (1980) and one of two consultant editors for its successor, *Common Worship Today* (2001); in both books he was also a major contributor to the contents. His other studies in the history of liturgy include *What Did Cranmer Think He Was Doing?* (1976, now in its fourth printing), *The End of the Offertory: An Anglican Study* (1978), *Eucharistic Liturgies of Edward VI* (1983), *Background Documents to Liturgical Revision, 1547–1549* (1983), *Essays in Eucharistic Sacrifice* (edited, 1984), *Anglican Confirmation* (1986), *Modern Anglican Ordination Liturgies* (1987), *The Bishop in Liturgy* (edited, 1988), *The Lord's Prayer in the Church of England* (1994), and *The Savoy Conference Revisited* (2002).

Outside the strictly liturgical field, Colin Buchanan has also been the author of *Growing into Union: Proposals for Forming a United Church in England* (jointly with three others, 1970), *Infant Baptism and the Gospel* (1993), *Cut the Connexion: The Church of England and Disestablishment* (1994), and his major work, *Is the Church of England Biblical?* (1998). A smaller controversial work is his *Is Papal Authority a Gift to Us?* (2003).

He has contributed to various other works of reference, including *Coena Domini I* and *Coena Domini II*, *Handbuch der Liturgik*, *The New SCM Dictionary of Liturgy and Worship*, the World Council of Churches' *Dictionary of the Ecumenical Movement*, the IVP *New Dictionary of Theology*, and the Lion *Handbook of Church History*. He was a consultant on Prayer Book history for the third edition of the *Oxford Dictionary of the Christian Church* and is a consultant editor for the forthcoming *Oxford Guide to the Book of Common Prayer*. He was also consulted for assistance in translation in the preparation of *The New Jerusalem Bible*.

In his capacity as bishop of Woolwich, Colin Buchanan has written *Mission in South East London* (2002) and *Follow-up in 2003 of Mission in South East London* (2003), both published by the Southwark diocese. He has also contributed to many other symposia and journals, usually on Anglican matters, including disestablishment. He is president of Baptismal Integrity (previously the Movement for the Reform of Infant Baptism), and from July 2005 honorary president of the Electoral Reform Society.